T0235119

Oracle SQL Tuning with Oracle SQLTXPLAIN

Oracle Database 12c Edition

Second Edition

Stelios Charalambides

⟨**IOUG**⟩
Independent oracle users group

Apress®

Oracle SQL Tuning with Oracle SQLTXPLAIN: Oracle Database 12c Edition

Stelios Charalambides
New Hampton, New Hampshire, USA

ISBN-13 (pbk): 978-1-4842-2435-9   ISBN-13 (electronic): 978-1-4842-2436-6
DOI 10.1007/978-1-4842-2436-6

Library of Congress Control Number: 2017938282

Copyright © 2017 by Stelios Charalambides

This work is subject to copyright. All rights are reserved by the Publisher, whether the whole or part of the material is concerned, specifically the rights of translation, reprinting, reuse of illustrations, recitation, broadcasting, reproduction on microfilms or in any other physical way, and transmission or information storage and retrieval, electronic adaptation, computer software, or by similar or dissimilar methodology now known or hereafter developed.

Trademarked names, logos, and images may appear in this book. Rather than use a trademark symbol with every occurrence of a trademarked name, logo, or image we use the names, logos, and images only in an editorial fashion and to the benefit of the trademark owner, with no intention of infringement of the trademark.

The use in this publication of trade names, trademarks, service marks, and similar terms, even if they are not identified as such, is not to be taken as an expression of opinion as to whether or not they are subject to proprietary rights.

While the advice and information in this book are believed to be true and accurate at the date of publication, neither the authors nor the editors nor the publisher can accept any legal responsibility for any errors or omissions that may be made. The publisher makes no warranty, express or implied, with respect to the material contained herein.

Managing Director: Welmoed Spahr
Editorial Director: Todd Green
Acquisitions Editor: Jonathan Gennick
Development Editor: Laura Berendson
Technical Reviewers: Ignatius Fernandez and Arup Nanda
Coordinating Editor: Jill Balzano
Copy Editor: Karen Jameson
Compositor: SPi Global
Indexer: SPi Global
Artist: SPi Global

Distributed to the book trade worldwide by Springer Science+Business Media New York, 233 Spring Street, 6th Floor, New York, NY 10013. Phone 1-800-SPRINGER, fax (201) 348-4505, e-mail orders-ny@springer-sbm.com, or visit www.springeronline.com. Apress Media, LLC is a California LLC and the sole member (owner) is Springer Science + Business Media Finance Inc (SSBM Finance Inc). SSBM Finance Inc is a **Delaware** corporation.

For information on translations, please e-mail rights@apress.com, or visit http://www.apress.com/rights-permissions.

Apress titles may be purchased in bulk for academic, corporate, or promotional use. eBook versions and licenses are also available for most titles. For more information, reference our Print and eBook Bulk Sales web page at http://www.apress.com/bulk-sales.

Any source code or other supplementary material referenced by the author in this book is available to readers on GitHub via the book's product page, located at www.apress.com/9781484224359. For more detailed information, please visit http://www.apress.com/source-code.

Printed on acid-free paper

I dedicate this book to my beautiful family, who put up with my strange working hours and endless nights seemingly strapped to a laptop writing obscure text for what seems forever. As always, Lesley is still my core and without her I would achieve nothing; thank you for helping me achieve this.

About IOUG Press

*IOUG Press is a joint effort by the **Independent Oracle Users Group (the IOUG)** and **Apress** to deliver some of the highest-quality content possible on Oracle Database and related topics. The IOUG is the world's leading, independent organization for professional users of Oracle products. Apress is a leading, independent technical publisher known for developing high-quality, no-fluff content for serious technology professionals. The IOUG and Apress have joined forces in IOUG Press to provide the best content and publishing opportunities to working professionals who use Oracle products.*

Our shared goals include:

- Developing content with excellence
- Helping working professionals to succeed
- Providing authoring and reviewing opportunities
- Networking and raising the profiles of authors and readers

To learn more about Apress, visit our website at **www.apress.com**. Follow the link for IOUG Press to see the great content that is now available on a wide range of topics that matter to those in Oracle's technology sphere.

Visit **www.ioug.org** to learn more about the Independent Oracle Users Group and its mission. Consider joining if you haven't already. Review the many benefits at www.ioug.org/join. Become a member. Get involved with peers. Boost your career.

www.ioug.org/join

Apress®

Contents at a Glance

Contents

About the Author

Stelios Charalambides has more than 20 years experience working with Oracle databases, having started working on Oracle 5! He is OCP certified from 7 to 11g and is an Exadata Certified Implementation Specialist and has worked as a senior Consultant DBA on both sides of the Atlantic, dealing with all aspects of system design, implementation, and post-production support, solving practical problems in a wide variety of environments. He has worked as an Oracle Support Engineer for Exadata, Supercluter, and ODA and is currently working with the Performance team, developing time-critical solutions for tier one customers with high-profile performance problems.

About the Technical Reviewers

Iggy Fernandez has been working in the IT industry for almost three decades including almost two decades of experience as an Oracle Database administrator supporting databases big and small, for companies big and small, including a stint as the manager of the Oracle Database administration team of a large service provider. His favorite part of Oracle Database administration is database tuning and SQL tuning because they can often be puzzles that require creative solutions. He edits the *NoCOUG Journal* (https://nocoug.wordpress.com/nocoug-journal-archive/), organizes the NoCOUG SQL Challenges, speaks at Oracle user group conferences, and blogs at https://iggyfernandez.wordpress.com/ and http://www.toadworld.com/members/iggy_5f00_fernandez/blogs/default.aspx. He is @OraTweets on Twitter.

Arup Nanda has been an Oracle Database administrator (DBA) since 1993, dealing with everything from modeling to security, and has a lot of gray hairs to prove it. He has coauthored five books, written 500+ published articles, presented 300+ sessions, delivered training sessions in 22 countries, and actively blogs at arup.blogspot.com. He is an Oracle ACE director, a member of Oak Table Network, an editor for *SELECT Journal* (the IOUG publication), and a member of the board for Exadata SIG. Oracle awarded him the DBA of the Year in 2003 and Architect of the Year in 2012. He lives in Danbury, CT, with his wife Anu and son Anish.

Acknowledgments

First and foremost of course is Carlos Sierra, who wrote the SQLT product and who inspired me to write this book in the first place. His enthusiasm and patience and willingness to listen allowed me to enter the world of Oracle SQL tuning with SQLT. Without his help this book would never have come into existence. I hope that this second edition of the book meets his expectations and I also hope I haven't made any errors in my description of his baby. If I have I apologize and of course the error was all mine. Abel Macias deserves a special mention for keeping me on the right track, when I could not see the obvious path. His clarity of thought is inspiring; I learned a lot from him and hope to use that knowledge to help others see the path of righteous tuning.

I feel I must also thank many members of my first family within Oracle (The Oracle Performance Group), Chris Crocker, and Cathy Scully who had the good sense to hire a Brit; and Mike Matagranno, whose persistence in getting me to move to Oracle was truly astounding. I hope none of you have regretted that decision. Special mention must go to Mauro Pagano, whose special knowledge and endless enthusiasm convinced me that I had something to say that was useful about SQLT.

Special thanks go to Mike Gervais, who was my manager at Oracle and whose kindness and fairness got me through the first few months at Oracle. Alan Bashy, Nick Meola, and Peter Gadah get a special mention for being awesome and showing me that no matter how much you think you know about tuning, there's always more to learn. Many other managers and colleagues have all supported me in many ways. I have been very lucky to come across an endless number of knowledgeable and enthusiastic colleagues and all-round nice people.

On the book side Jonathan Gennick was the one who made the final decision to publish this book. He showed faith when others were doubtful. Chris Nelson deserves a mention: his Herculean efforts have immeasurably improved the first edition of this book and created something useful from my poor illiterate scratchings (don't change that) and allowed me to produce what I hope will be a useful book for years to come. Chris shouted at me during the marathon that is writing a book and kept me going by telling me the finishing line was just around the corner. For your patience and hard work I sincerely thank you. Arup Nanda and Iggy Fernandez are especially to be thanked for making many useful suggestions for improvement in the book text.

Introduction

What a journey you have ahead of you! If you are new to SQLT or have only recently heard something about it you will be amazed and forever smitten with that brilliant tool called SQLT. If you've struggled for years to get a grip on tuning, endlessly collecting facts and techniques in the hope that it could all make sense one day, then the time is at hand. SQLT will make sense of that complex skill called Oracle SQL tuning.

No matter how complex your system and no matter how many layers of technology are between you and your data, getting your query to run efficiently is where the rubber meets the road. Whether you are a junior DBA, just starting your career in the exciting Oracle world or an old hand who's seen it all before, I sincerely hope that this book will show you something that will be useful in your day-to-day work. From developers to DBAs you will find that SQLT will enhance your ability to fix tuning problems and give you an effective check list to use against new code and old code.

This book is not entirely about 'raw' SQL tuning, it's about how to use SQLT in conjunction with other techniques to do Oracle SQL tuning. There are more than enough books about tuning using scripts, looking at v$ and x$ views, and using obscure hidden parameters to get the optimizer to jump through hoops. I will carefully stay away from complex concepts that add nothing to a busy DBA's life. I have used a JIT (Just In Time) methodology for concepts that are related to SQLT by avoiding complex subjects unless they are needed to understand the use of the SQLT tool. I've used practical examples wherever possible to show the SQLT tool in action or to explain a concept.

I hope you'll be as excited and rewarded as I have been in writing this book.

Second Edition

This second edition is an exciting expansion of the first book. First I've tried to use 12c examples wherever possible, and second I have added several completely new chapters to cover the 12c optimizer comprehensively. For example, Adaptive plans and Adaptive Statistics as well as Directives; all these new features have their own chapters. I've also made the book broader by including chapters on SQL Monitor and parallel processing as both of these have been significantly enhanced in 12c, while keeping the emphasis on using the simplest and most effective tool to understand what is happening with your SQL. I hope these new chapters help you to tune your SQL with confidence.

CHAPTER 1

■ ■ ■

Introduction

Welcome to the world of fast Oracle SQL tuning with SQLT. Never heard of SQLT? You're not alone. I'd never heard of it before I joined ORACLE, and I had been a DBA for more years than I care to mention. That's why I'm writing this book. SQLT is a fantastic tool because it helps you diagnose tuning problems quickly. What do I mean by that? I mean that in half a day, maximum, you can go from a 'slow' SQL to having an understanding of why the SQL is malfunctioning, and finally, to knowing how to fix the SQL. This of course assumes that your SQL can run faster. Some SQLs are just doing their best with the data and what you are asking them to do. It's not miraculous, but it's pretty close.

Will SQLT fix your SQL? No. Fixing the SQL takes longer. Some tables are so large that it can take days to gather statistics. It may take a long time to set up the test environment and roll the fix to production. You may find that you need to make design changes that affect other application SQLs. The important point is that in half a day working with SQLT, you will have an explanation. You'll know what needs to be done (if anything) to improve the SQL, and if not you'll be able to explain why it can't go any faster. That may sound like a losing scenario, but when you know something can't be improved, you can move on to other tasks.

You need to know about SQLT because it will make your life easier. But let me back up a little and tell you more about what SQLT is, how it came into existence, why you probably haven't heard of it, and why you should use it for your Oracle SQL tuning.

What Is SQLT?

SQLT is a set of packages and scripts that produces HTML-formatted reports, some SQL scripts, and some text files. The entire collection of information is packaged in a zip file and often sent to Oracle Support, but you can look at these files yourself. There are just over a dozen packages and procedures (called "methods") in SQLT. These packages and procedures collect different information based on your circumstances. We'll talk about the packages suitable for a number of situations later.

What's the Story of SQLT?

They say that necessity is the mother of invention, and that was certainly the case with SQLT. Oracle support engineers handle a huge number of tuning problems on a daily basis; problem is, the old methods of linear analysis are just too slow. You need to see the big picture fast so you can zoom in on the detail and tell the customer what's wrong. As a result, Carlos Sierra, a support engineer at the time (NEW CARLOS ROLE) created SQLT. The routines evolved over many visits to customer sites to a point where they can gather *all* the information required quickly and effectively. He then provided easy-to-use procedures for reporting on those problems.

© Stelios Charalambides 2017

S. Charalambides, *Oracle SQL Tuning with Oracle SQLTXPLAIN*, DOI 10.1007/978-1-4842-2436-6_1

The Oracle SQLTXPLAIN tool (that this book is about) was always an unsupported product until recently. Any fixes to the free tool were done by Oracle on a best efforts basis. Now you can log a bug against this useful tool in case there are problems.

Why Haven't You Heard of SQLT?

If it's so useful, why haven't you heard about SQLT? Oracle has tried to publicize SQLT to the DBA community, but still I get support calls and talk to DBAs who have never heard of SQLT—or if they have, they've never used it. This amazing tool is free to supported customers, so there's no cost involved. DBAs need to look at problematic SQL often, and SQLT is hands down the fastest way to fix a problem. The learning curve is nowhere near as high as the alternatives: interpreting raw 10046 trace files or 10053 trace files. Looking through tables of statistics to find the needle in the haystack, guessing about what might fix the problem and trying it out? No thanks. SQLT is like a cruise missile that travels across the world right to its target. Over the past few years SQLT has certainly gained some prominence (I hope partially due to the first edition of this book), but still there are too many sites that do not use it on a regular basis, and that, in my opinion is a lost opportunity.

Perhaps DBAs are too busy to learn a tool, which is not even mentioned in the release notes for Oracle. It's not in the documentation set, and even though it is officially part of the product now, it's just a tool that happens to be better than any other tool out there. Let me repeat. It's free.

It's also possible that some DBAs are so busy focusing on the obscure minutiae of tuning that they forget the real world of fixing SQL. Why talk about a package that's easy to use when you could be talking about esoteric hidden parameters for situations you'll never come across? SQLT is a very practical tool. It even collects other tuning information, such as AWRs and SQLMonitor reports if it can. So SQLT saves you even more time.

Whatever the reason, if you haven't used SQLT before, my mission in this book is to get you up and running as fast and with as little effort from you as possible. I promise you that installing and using SQLT is easy. Just a few simple concepts, and you'll be ready to go in 30 minutes.

How Did I Learn about SQLT?

Like the rest of the DBA world (I've been a DBA for many years), I hadn't heard of SQLT until I joined Oracle. It was a revelation to me. Here was this tool that's existed for years, which was exactly what I needed many times in the past, although I'd never used it. Of course I had read many books on tuning in years past: for example, Cary Millsaps's classic *Optimizing Oracle Performance*, and of course *Cost-Based Oracle Fundamentals* by Jonathan Lewis.

The training course (which was two weeks in total) was so intense that it was described by at least two engineers as trying to drink water from a fire hydrant. Fear not! This book will make the job of learning to use SQLT much easier.

Now that I've used SQLT extensively in day-to-day tuning problems, I can't imagine managing without it. I want you to have the same ability. It won't take long. Stick with me until the end of the book, understand the examples, and then try and relate them to your own situation. You'll need a few basic concepts (which I'll cover later), and then you'll be ready to tackle your own tuning problems. Remember to use SQLT regularly even when you don't have a problem; this way you can learn to move around the main HTML file quickly to find what you need. Locate the useful extra files that SQLT collects for you, including AWRs, special Exadata Cell configuration information, and many other goodies. Run a SQLT report against SQL that isn't a problem. You'll learn a lot. Stick with me on this amazing journey.

Getting Started with SQLT

Getting started with SQLT couldn't be easier. I've broken the process down into three easy steps.

1. Downloading SQLT

2. Installing SQLT

3. Running your first SQLT report

SQLT will work on many different platforms. Many of my examples will be based on Linux, but Windows or Unix is just as easy to use, and there are almost no differences in the use of SQLT between the platforms. If there are, I'll make a note in the text.

How Do You Get a Copy of SQLT?

How do you download SQLT? It's simple and easy. I just did it to time myself. It took two minutes. Here are the steps to get the SQLT packages ready to go on your target machine:

1. Find a web browser and log in to My Oracle Support (http://support.oracle.com)

2. Go to the knowledge section and type "SQLT" in the search box. Note 215187.1 entitled "SQLT (SQLTXPLAIN) – Tool that helps to diagnose a SQL statement performing poorly [ID 215187.1]" should be near the top of the list.

3. Scroll to the bottom of the note and choose the version of SQLT suitable for your environment. There are currently versions suitable from 9.2 to 12c.

4. Download the zip file.

5. Unzip the zip file. The current version is 12.1.160429 (from April 29, 2016).

You now have the SQLT programs available to you for installation onto any suitable database. You can download the zip file to a PC and then copy it to a server if needed.

How Do You Install SQLT?

So without further ado, let's install SQLT so we can do some tuning:

1. Download the SQLT zip file appropriate for your environment (see steps above).

2. Unzip the zip file to a suitable location.

3. Navigate to your "install" directory under the unzipped area (in my case it is /home/oracle/sqlt/install, but your locations will be different).

4. Connect as sys, for example, `sqlplus / as sysdba`.

5. Make sure your database is running.

6. Run the `sqcreate.sql` script.

7. Select the default for the first option. (We'll cover more details of the installation in Appendix A.)

8. Enter and confirm the password for SQLTXPLAIN.

9. Assuming you know which Tablespaces you want to use to keep the SQLT objects and procedures, select the default "NO" again to avoid listing all the Tablespaces.

10. Select the tablespace where the SQLTXPLAIN will keep its packages and data (in my case, USERS).

11. Select the temporary tablespace for the SQLTXPLAIN user (in my case, TEMP).

12. Then enter the username of the user in the database who will use SQLT packages to fix tuning problems. Typically this is the schema that runs the problematic SQL (in my case this is STELIOS).

13. Then enter "T", "D," or "N." This reflects your license level for the tuning and diagnostics packs. Most sites have both so you would enter "T" (this is also the default). My test system is on my private server (an evaluation platform with no production capability) so I would also enter "T." If you have the diagnostics pack, only enter "D"; and if you do not have these licenses, enter "N".

The last message you see is "SQCREATE completed. Installation completed successfully." Make sure you have granted sys the appropriate privilege on SQLTXADMIN (This is for 12c databases only).

```
SQL> grant inherit privileges on user sys to sqltxadmin;
```

Running Your First SQLT Report

Now that SQLT is installed, it is ready to be used. Remember that installing the package is done as sys and that running the reports is done as the target user. Please also bear in mind that although I have used many examples from standard schemas available from the Oracle installation files, your platform and exact version of Oracle may well be different, so please don't expect your results to be exactly the same as mine. However, your results will be similar to mine, and the results you see in your environment should still make sense.

1. Now exit SQL and change your directory to /home/oracle/sqlt/run. From here log in to SQLPLUS as the target user.

2. Then enter the following SQL (this is going to be the statement we will tune):

```
SQL> select count(*) from dba_objects;
```

3. Then get the SQL_ID value from the following SQL:

```
SQL> select sql_id from v$sqlarea where sql_text like 'select count(*)
from dba_objects%';
```

In my case the SQL_ID was g4pkmrqrgxg3b.

4. Now we execute our first SQLT tool sqltxtract from the target schema (in this case STELIOS) with the following command:

```
SQL> @sqltxtract g4pkmrqrgxg3b
```

5.   Enter the password for SQLTXPLAIN (which you entered during the installation). The last message you will see if all goes well is "SQLTXTRACT completed".

6.   Now create a zip directory under the run directory and copy the zip file created into the zip directory. Unzip it.

7.   Finally from your favorite browser navigate to and open the file named sqlt_ s<nnnnn>_main.html. The symbols "nnnnn" represent numbers created to make all SQLT reports unique on your machine. In my case the file is called sqlt_ s89906_main.html

Congratulations! You have your first SQLT XTRACT report to look at.

When to Use SQLTXTRACT and When to Use SQLTXECUTE

SQLT XTRACT is the easiest report to create because it does not require the execution of the SQL at the time of the report generation. The report can be collected after the statement has been executed. SQLTXECUTE, on the other hand, executes the SQL statement and thus has better runtime information and access to the actual rows returned. This happens when statistics_level=all or " _rowsource_execution_ statistics=true". This means it can assess the accuracy of the estimated cardinality of the steps in the execution plan (see "Cardinality and Selectivity" later in this chapter). SQLTXECUTE will get you more information, but it is not always possible to use this method, perhaps because you are in a production environment or perhaps the SQL statement is currently taking three days to run, which is why you are investigating this in the first place. Another reason for not running SQLTXECUTE for some SQL statements is if they are DML (insert, update, delete, or merge), they will change data. We will look at both SQLTXECUTE and SQLTXTRACT report (and other SQLT options also). For now we will concentrate on one simple SQLTXTRACT report on a very simple SQL statement. So let's dive in.

Your First SQLT Report

Before we get too carried away with all the details of using the SQLT main report, just look at Figure 1-1. It's the beginning of a whole new SQLT tuning world. Are you excited? You should be. This header page is just the beginning. From here we will look at some basic navigation, just so you get an idea of what is available and how SQLT works, in terms of its navigation. Then we'll look at what SQLT is actually reporting about the SQL.

<u>215187.1</u> SQLT XTRACT 12.1.160429 Report: sqlt_s46414_main.html

Review log and fix following errors:
sqlt$a: *** i:compute_estim_size_if_rebuilt: ORA-01031: insufficient privileges

Global

- Observations
- SQL Text
- SQL Identification
- Environment
- CBO Environment
- Fix Control
- CBO System Statistics
- DBMS_STATS Setup
- Initialization Parameters
- NLS Parameters
- I/O Calibration
- Tool Configuration Parameters

Cursor Sharing and Binds

- Cursor Sharing
- Adaptive Cursor Sharing
- Peeked Binds
- Captured Binds

SQL Tuning Advisor

- STA Report
- STA Script

Plans

- Summary
- Performance Statistics
- Performance History (delta)
- Performance History (total)
- Execution Plans

Plan Control

- Stored Outlines
- SQL Patches
- SQL Profiles
- SQL Plan Baselines
- SQL Plan Directives

SQL Execution

- Active Session History
- AWR Active Session History
- SQL Statistics
- SQL Detail ACTIVE Report
- Monitor Statistics
- Monitor ACTIVE Report
- Monitor HTML Report
- Monitor TEXT Report
- Segment Statistics
- Session Statistics
- Session Events
- Parallel Processing

Tables

- Tables
- Statistics
- Statistics Extensions
- Statistics Versions
- Modifications
- Properties
- Physical Properties
- Constraints
- Columns
- Indexed Columns
- Histograms
- Partitions
- Indexes

Objects

- Objects
- Dependencies
- Fixed Objects
- Fixed Object Columns
- Nested Tables
- Policies
- Audit Policies
- Tablespaces
- Metadata

Figure 1-1. *The top part of the SQLT report shows the links to many areas*

Some Simple Navigation

Let's start with the basics. Each hyperlinked section has a Go to Top hyperlink to get you back to the top. There's a lot of information in the various sections, and you can get lost. Other related hyperlinks will be grouped together above the Go to Top hyperlink. For example, if I clicked on Indexes (the last link under the Tables heading), I would see the page shown in Figure 1-2.

Indexes

#	Table Name	Owner	Count[1]	Num Rows[2]	Sample Size[2]	Blocks[2]	Last Analyzed[2]	Indexes
1	LINK$	SYS		0	0	0	07-JUL-14	1
2	OBJ$	SYS	92190	19416	19416	300	07-JUL-14	5
3	SUM$	SYS	2	0	0	0	07-JUL-14	3
4	USER$	SYS		63	63	3	07-JUL-14	2
5	USER_EDITIONING$	SYS	2	2	2	1	07-JUL-14	1

(1) SELECT COUNT(*) performed in Table as per tool parameter "count_star_threshold" with current value of 10000.
(2) CBO Statistics.
Go to Indexed Columns
Go to Tables
Go to Top

SYS.LINK$ - Indexes

#	In Plan	Index Name	Owner	Index Type	Uniqueness	Col ID	Column Name	Column Name[1]	Num Rows[2]	Sample Size[2]	Last Analyzed[2]
1	TRUE	I_LINK1	SYS	NORMAL	NONUNIQUE	1	OWNER#	OWNER#	0	0	07-JUL-14
						2	NAME	NAME			

(1) Column names including system-generated names.
(2) CBO Statistics.
Go to Indexes
Go to Tables
Go to Top

SYS.LINK$ - Index Statistics

Figure 1-2. *The Indexes section of the report*

Before we get lost in the SQLT report, let's again look at the header page (Figure 1-1). The main sections cover all sorts of aspects of the system.

- CBO environment
- Cursor sharing
- Adaptive cursor sharing
- SQL Tuning Advisor (STA) report
- Execution plan(s) (there will be more than one plan if the plan changed)
- SQL*Profiles
- Outlines
- Execution statistics
- Table metadata
- Index metadata
- Column definitions
- Foreign keys

Take a minute and browse through the report.

Did you notice the hyperlinks on some of the data within the tables? SQLT collected all the information it could find and cross-referenced it all.

So, for example, continuing as before from the main report at the top (Figure 1-1):

1. Click on Indexes, the last heading under Tables.

2. Under the Indexes column of the Indexes heading, the numbers are hyperlinked (see Figure 1-2). I clicked on 2 of the USERS$ record.

   Now you can see the details of the columns in that table (see Figure 1-3). As an example here we see that the Index I_USER2 was used in the execution of my query (the In Plan column value is set to TRUE).

SYS.USER$ - Indexes

#	In Plan	Index Name	Owner	Index Type	Uniqueness	Col ID	Column Name	Column Name[1]	Num Rows[2]	Sample Size[2]	Last Analyzed[2]	Index Stats	Index Prop	Index Phys Prop	Index Cols	Index Meta
1	TRUE	I_USER2	SYS	NORMAL	UNIQUE	1	USER#	USER#	63	63	07-JUL-14	Stats	Prop	Phys	Cols	Meta
						3	TYPE#	TYPE#								
						20	SPARE1	SPARE1								
						21	SPARE2	SPARE2								
2	FALSE	I_USER1	SYS	NORMAL	UNIQUE	2	NAME	NAME	63	63	07-JUL-14	Stats	Prop	Phys	Cols	Meta

(1) Column names including system-generated names.
(2) CBO Statistics.
Go to Indexes
Go to Tables
Go to Top

SYS.USER$ - Index Statistics

#	In Plan	Index Name	Owner	Index Type	Part	Temp	Num Rows[1]	Sample Size[1]	Perc	Last Analyzed[1]	Distinct Keys[1]	Blevel[1]	Segment Extents	Segment Blocks	Total Segment Blocks[2]	DBMS_SPACE Allocated Blocks[3]	Leaf Blocks[1]	Leaf Estimat Target Size[4]
1	TRUE	I_USER2	SYS	NORMAL	NO	N	63	63	100.0	2014-07-07/05:56:06	63	0	1	8	8		1	
2	FALSE	I_USER1	SYS	NORMAL	NO	N	63	63	100.0	2014-07-07/05:56:06	63	0	1	8	8		1	

(1) CBO Statistics.
(2) It considers the blocks from all partitions (if the index is partitioned).
(3) This is the estimated size of the index if it were rebuilt, as computed by DBMS_SPACE.CREATE_INDEX_COST.
(4) Estimated leaf blocks with a 90% index efficiency. Only evaluated for non-partitioned normal indexes with more than 10000 leaf blocks.
(5) BEST:less than 18. GOOD:between 18 and 33. POOR:between 33 and 48. WORST:greater than 48.
(6) It assumes default CBO environment, including optimizer_index_cost_adj=100 and optimizer_index_caching=0 among others.
(7) Index Selectivity where Full Index Scan Cost meets Full Table Scan Cost. A value of 0.02 means that if selecting 2% of the rows or less, an index scan is cheaper than a FTS.
(8) Index Size if it were to be rebuilt, the estimation comes from EXPLAIN PLAN FOR of the CREATE INDEX command so it's dependent on good statistics.
Go to Index Statistics Versions
Go to Indexes
Go to Tables
Go to Top

Figure 1-3. *An Index's detailed information about statistics*

3. Now, in the Index Meta column (far right in Figure 1-3), click on the Meta hyperlink for the I_USER2 index to display the index metadata shown in Figure 1-4.

SYS.I_USER2 - Index Metadata

```
CREATE UNIQUE INDEX "SYS"."I_USER2" ON "SYS"."USER$" ("USER#", "TYPE#", "SPARE1", "SPARE2")
PCTFREE 10 INITRANS 2 MAXTRANS 255
STORAGE(INITIAL 65536 NEXT 1048576 MINEXTENTS 1 MAXEXTENTS 2147483645
PCTINCREASE 0 FREELISTS 1 FREELIST GROUPS 1
BUFFER_POOL DEFAULT FLASH_CACHE DEFAULT CELL_FLASH_CACHE DEFAULT)
TABLESPACE "SYSTEM"
```

SYS.I_USER_EDITIONING - Index Metadata

```
CREATE INDEX "SYS"."I_USER_EDITIONING" ON "SYS"."USER_EDITIONING$" ("USER#")
PCTFREE 10 INITRANS 2 MAXTRANS 255
STORAGE(INITIAL 65536 NEXT 1048576 MINEXTENTS 1 MAXEXTENTS 2147483645
PCTINCREASE 0 FREELISTS 1 FREELIST GROUPS 1
BUFFER_POOL DEFAULT FLASH_CACHE DEFAULT CELL_FLASH_CACHE DEFAULT)
TABLESPACE "SYSTEM"
```

SYS.SYS_IL0000001147C00030$$ - Index Metadata

```
CREATE UNIQUE INDEX "SYS"."SYS_IL0000001147C00030$$" ON "SYS"."SUM$" (
PCTFREE 10 INITRANS 2 MAXTRANS 255
STORAGE(INITIAL 65536 NEXT 1048576 MINEXTENTS 1 MAXEXTENTS 2147483645
PCTINCREASE 0 FREELISTS 1 FREELIST GROUPS 1
BUFFER_POOL DEFAULT FLASH_CACHE DEFAULT CELL_FLASH_CACHE DEFAULT)
TABLESPACE "SYSTEM"
PARALLEL (DEGREE 0 INSTANCES 0)
```

SYS.SYS_IL0000001147C00031$$ - Index Metadata

```
CREATE UNIQUE INDEX "SYS"."SYS_IL0000001147C00031$$" ON "SYS"."SUM$" (
PCTFREE 10 INITRANS 2 MAXTRANS 255
STORAGE(INITIAL 65536 NEXT 1048576 MINEXTENTS 1 MAXEXTENTS 2147483645
PCTINCREASE 0 FREELISTS 1 FREELIST GROUPS 1
BUFFER_POOL DEFAULT FLASH_CACHE DEFAULT CELL_FLASH_CACHE DEFAULT)
TABLESPACE "SYSTEM"
PARALLEL (DEGREE 0 INSTANCES 0)
```

Go to Metadata
Go to Top

Synonym - Metadata

- DBA_OBJECTS

Go to Metadata
Go to Top

PUBLIC.DBA_OBJECTS - Synonym Metadata

```
CREATE OR REPLACE NONEDITIONABLE PUBLIC SYNONYM "DBA_OBJECTS" FOR "SYS"."DBA_OBJECTS"
```

Go to Metadata
Go to Top

Figure 1-4. *Metadata about an index can be seen from the "Meta" hyperlink*

Here we see the statement we would need to create this index. Do you have a script to do that? Well SQLT can get it better and faster. So now that you've seen a SQLT report, how do you approach a problem? You've opened the report, and you have one second to decide. Where do you go?

Well, that all depends.

How to Approach a SQLT Report

As with any methodology, different approaches are considered for different circumstances. In the next chapter we look at AWR how that helps us decide if we should be tuning SQL or the system. After all there's no point in trying to tune a SQL if your system is not able to run it properly. Once you've decided there is something wrong with your SQL, you could use a SQLT report. Once you have the SQLT report, you are presented with a header page, which can take you to many different places (no one reads a SQLT report from start to finish in order). So where do you go from the main page?

If you're absolutely convinced that the execution plan is wrong, you might go straight to "Execution Plans" and look at the history of the execution plans. We'll deal with looking at those in detail later.

Suppose you think there is a general slowdown on the system. Then you might want to look at the "Observations" section of the report.

Maybe something happened to your statistics, so you'll certainly need to look at the "Statistics" section of the report under "Tables."

All of the sections I've mentioned above are sections you will probably refer to for every problem. The idea is to build up a picture of your SQL statement, understand the statistics related to the query, understand the cost-based optimizer (CBO) environment, and try and get into its "head." Why did it do what it did? Why does it not relate to what you think it ought to do? The SQLT report is the explanation from the optimizer telling you why it decided to do what it did. Barring the odd bug, the CBO usually has a good reason for doing what it did. Your job is to set up the environment so that the CBO agrees with your worldview and run the SQL faster!

Cardinality and Selectivity

My objective throughout this book, apart from making you a super SQL tuner, is to avoid as much jargon as possible and explain tuning concepts as simply as possible. After all we're DBAs, not astrophysicists or rocket scientists.

So before explaining some of these terms, it is important to understand why these concepts are key to the CBO operation and to your understanding of the SQL running on your system. Let's first look at cardinality. It is defined as the number of rows expected to be returned for a particular column if a predicate selects it. If there are no statistics for the table, then the number is pretty much based on heuristics about the number of rows, the minimum and maximum values, and the number of nulls. If you collect statistics then these statistics help to inform the guess, but it's still a guess. If you look at every single row of a table (collecting 100 percent statistics), it might still be a guess because the data might have changed, or the data may be skewed (we'll cover skewness later). That dry definition doesn't really relate to real life, so let's look at an example. Click on the "Execution Plans" hyperlink at the top of the SQLT report to display an execution plan like the one shown in Figure 1-5.

Execution Plan phv:1203538133 [B]
[W] sqlt_phv:47043 sqlt_phv2:24547 source:GV$SQL_PLAN inst:1 child:1(00000000D21DBF88) ‹

SQL Text: [.]

```
select count(*) from dba_objects
```

SQL: [±]

ID	Exec Ord	Operation	Go To	More	Cost[2]	Estim Card	Work Area
0	19	SELECT STATEMENT			1199	1	
1	18	SORT AGGREGATE		[+]	1199	1	
2	17	. VIEW DBA_OBJECTS			1199	409749	
3	16	.. UNION-ALL			401		
4	11	... FILTER		[+]	401		
5	5	.... HASH JOIN		[+]	395	411335	[+]
6	1	....+ INDEX FULL SCAN I_USER2	[+]	[+]	1	132	
7	4	....+ HASH JOIN		[+]	393	196319	[+]
8	2	....+. INDEX FULL SCAN I_USER2	[+]	[+]	1	132	
9	3	....+. TABLE ACCESS FULL OBJ$	[+]	[+]	392	93698	
10	6	.... TABLE ACCESS FULL USER_EDITIONING$	[+]	[+]	2	1	
11	9	.... NESTED LOOPS SEMI			2	1	
12	7	....+ INDEX SKIP SCAN I_USER2	[+]	[+]	1	1	
13	8	....+ INDEX RANGE SCAN I_OBJ4	[+]	[+]	1	1	
14	10	.... TABLE ACCESS FULL USER_EDITIONING$	[+]	[+]	2	1	
15	15	... NESTED LOOPS			0	1	
16	12	.... INDEX FULL SCAN I_LINK1	[+]	[+]	0	1	
17	14	.... TABLE ACCESS CLUSTER USER$		[+]	0	1	
18	13	....+ INDEX UNIQUE SCAN I_USER#	[+]	[+]	0	1	

Performance statistics are only available when parameter "statistics_level" was set to "ALL" at hard-parse time, or SQL contains "gather_plan_statistics" I
(1) If estim_card * starts < output_rows then under-estimate. If estim_card * starts > output_rows then over-estimate. Color highlights when exceeding * 10›
(2) Largest contributors for cumulative-statistics columns are shown in red.

Other XML (id=1) [±]
Outline Data (id-1): [±]

Figure 1-5. *An execution plan in the "Execution Plan" section*

In the "Execution Plan" section, you'll see the "Estim Card" column. In my example, look at the TABLE ACCESS FULL OBJ$ step. Under the "Estim Card" column the value is 93,698. Remember cardinality is the number of rows returned from a step in an execution plan. The CBO (based on the table's statistics) will have an estimate for the cardinality. The "Estim Card" column then shows what the CBO expected to get from the step in the query. The 93,698 shows that the CBO *expected* to get 93,698 records from this step, but in fact got 92,681. So how good was the CBO's estimate for the cardinality (the number of rows returned for a step in an execution plan)? In our simple example we can do a very simple direct comparison by executing the query shown below.

```
SQL> select count(*) from dba_objects;
  COUNT(*)
----------
    92,681
SQL>
```

So cardinality is the actual number of rows that will be returned, but of course the optimizer can't know the answers in advance. It has to guess. This guess can be good or bad, based on statistics and skewness. Of course, histograms can help here.

For an example of selectivity, let's look at the page (see Figure 1-6) we get by selecting Columns from the Tables options on the main page (refer to Figure 1-1).

Table Columns

#	Table Name	Owner	Count[1]	Num Rows[2]	Sample Size[2]	Blocks[2]	Last Analyzed[2]	Column Stats	Column Usage	Column Prop	Hgrm	Single Table SQL Plan Directives
1	LINK$	SYS		0	0	0	07-JUL-14	11	2	Prop		
2	OBJ$	SYS	92190	19416	19416	300	07-JUL-14	25	14	Prop	8	5
3	SUM$	SYS	2	0	0	0	07-JUL-14	40	4	Prop		
4	USER$	SYS		63	63	3	07-JUL-14	30	11	Prop	6	2
5	USER_EDITIONING$	SYS	2	2	2	1	07-JUL-14	2	2	Prop	1	

(1) SELECT COUNT(*) performed in Table as per tool parameter "count_star_threshold" with current value of 10000.
(2) CBO Statistics.
Go to Tables
Go to Top

SYS.LINK$ - Table Column

- Column Statistics
- Column Usage
- Column Properties
- Histograms

Go to Table Columns
Go to Tables
Go to Top

Figure 1-6. *The "Table Column" section of the SQLT report*

Look at the "SYS.OBJ$ - Table Column" section. From the "Table Columns" page, if we click on the "25" under the "Column Stats" column, we will see the column statistics for the SYS.OBJ$. Figure 1-7 shows a subset of the page from the "High Value" column to the "Equality Predicate Cardinality" column. Look at the "Equality Predicate Selectivity" and "Equality Predicate Cardinality" columns (the last two columns). Look at the values in the first row for OBJ$.

High Value[2]	Last Analyzed	Avg Col Len	Density	Num Buckets	Histogram	Fluctuating Endpoint Count[3]	Popular Values	Global Stats	User Stats	Equality Predicate Selectivity	Equality Predicate Cardinality
"50"	2014-07-07/05:55:43	3	2.575196e-05	9	FREQUENCY	FALSE	0	YES	NO	0.111111	2158
"115"	2014-07-07/05:55:43	4	2.575196e-05	44	FREQUENCY	FALSE	0	YES	NO	0.022727	442
"50"	2014-07-07/05:55:43	3	2.575196e-05	9	FREQUENCY	FALSE	0	YES	NO	0.111111	2158
"19646"	2014-07-07/05:55:43	2	2.440215e-04	1	NONE	FALSE		YES	NO	0.000052	2
"old_values49_T"	2014-07-07/05:55:43	20	6.900000e-05	254	HYBRID	FALSE	0	YES	NO	0.000069	2
	2014-07-07/05:55:43	0	0.000000e+00	0	NONE	FALSE		YES	NO		
"7405568"	2014-07-07/05:55:43	6	2.575196e-05	17	FREQUENCY	FALSE	0	YES	NO	0.058824	1143
"6"	2014-07-07/05:55:43	3	5.000000e-01	1	NONE	FALSE		YES	NO	0.500000	9708
"65535"	2014-07-07/05:55:43	5	9.090909e-02	1	NONE	FALSE		YES	NO	0.090909	1766

Figure 1-7. *Selectivity is found in the "Equality Predicate Selectivity" column*

Selectivity is 0.111111, and cardinality is 2158.

This translates to "I expect to get 2158 row back for this equality predicate, which is equivalent to a 0.111111 chance (1 is certainty 0 is impossible) or in percentage terms I'll get 11.11 percent of the entire table if I get the matching rows back."

Notice that as the cardinality increases the selectivity also increases. The selectivity only varies between 0 and 1 (or if you prefer 0 percent and 100 percent), and cardinality *should* only vary between 0 and the total number of rows in the table (excluding nulls). I say *should* because these values are based on statistics. What would happen if you gathered statistics on a partition (say it had 10 million rows) and then you truncate that partition, but don't tell the optimizer (i.e., you don't gather new statistics, or clear the old ones). If you ask the CBO to develop an execution plan in this case it might expect to get 10 million rows from a predicate against that partition. It might "think" that a full table scan would be a good plan. It might try to do the wrong thing because it had poor information.

To summarize, cardinality is the count of expected rows, and selectivity is the same thing but on a 0-1 scale. So why is all this important to the CBO and to the development of good execution plans? The short answer is that the CBO is working hard for you to develop the quickest and simplest way to get your results. If the CBO has some idea about how many rows will be returned for steps in the execution plan, then it can try variations in the execution plan and choose the plan with the least work and the fastest results. This leads into the concept of "cost," which we will cover in the next section.

What Is Cost?

Now that we have cardinality for an object we can work with other information derived from the system to calculate a cost for any operation. Other information from the system includes the following:

- Speed of the disks
- Speed of the CPU
- Number of CPUs
- Database block size

These metrics can be easily extracted from the system and are shown in the SQLT report also (under the "Environment" section). The amount of I/O and CPU resource used on the system for any particular step can now be calculated and thus used to derive a definite cost. This is the key concept for all tuning. The optimizer is always trying to reduce the cost for an operation (even when the lowest cost, which after all is only an estimate, is not a guarantee of the best plan). I won't go into details about how these costs are calculated because the exact values are not important. All you need to know is this: higher is worse, and worse can be based on higher cardinality (possibly based on out-of-date statistics), and if your disk I/O speeds are wrong (perhaps optimistically low) then full table scans might be favored when indexes are available. Cost can also be directly translated into elapsed time (on a quiet system), but that probably isn't what you need most of the time because you're almost always trying to get an execution time to be reduced, that is, lower cost. As we'll see in the next section, you can get that information from SQLT. SQLT will also produce a 10053 trace file in some cases, so you can look at the details of how the cost calculations are made.

Reading the Execution Plan Section

We saw the execution plan section previously. It looks interesting, and it has a wobbly left edge and lots of hyperlinks. What does it all mean? This is a fairly simple execution plan, as it doesn't go on for pages and pages (like SIEBEL or PeopleSoft execution plans). There are of course many different ways of getting an execution plan, which don't involve SQLT, but I prefer SQLT's presentation (see Figure 1-5) because it easily identifies the execution order (and much else besides).

There are a number of simple steps to reading an execution plan. I'm sure there's more than one way of reading an execution plan, but this is the way I approach the problem. Bear in mind in these examples that if you are familiar with the pieces of SQL being examined, you may go directly to the section you think is wrong; but in general if you are seeing the execution plan for the first time, you will start by looking at a few key costs.

> Philosophically speaking 'cost' is always an estimate. The optimizer derives a cost, but it is always an estimate for a 'true' cost, which can never be determined. So for the sake of brevity always assume that when I refer to cost, I am talking about the optimizer's estimated cost.

The first and most important cost is the overall cost of the entire query. This is always shown as "ID 0" and is always the first row in the execution plan. In our example shown in Figure 1-5, this is a cost of 1199. So to get the cost for the entire query, just look at the first row. This is also the last step to be executed ("Exec Ord" is 19). The execution order is not top to bottom.

> The Oracle engine will carry out the steps in the order shown by the value in the "Exec Ord" column.

So if we followed the execution through, the Oracle engine would do the execution in this order:

1. INDEX FULL SCAN I_USER2

2. INDEX FULL SCAN I_USER2

3. TABLE ACCESS FULL OBJ$

4. HASH JOIN

5. HASH JOIN

6. TABLE ACCESS FULL USER_EDITIONING$

7. INDEX SKIP SCAN I_USER2

8. INDEX RANGE SCAN I_OBJ4

9. NESTED LOOP SEMI

10. TABLE ACCESS FULL USER_EDITIONING$

11. FILTER

12. INDEX FULL SCAN I_LINK1

13. INDEX UNIQUE SCAN I_USERS#

14. TABLE ACCESS CLUSTER USER$

15. NESTED LOOPS

16. UNION-ALL

17. VIEW DBA_OBJECTS

18. SORT AGGREGATE

19. SELECT STATEMENT

However, nobody ever represents the plan of a SQL statement like this. What is important to realize is that the wobbly left edge gives information about how the steps are carried out. The less-indented operations indicate parent (also called outer) operations that are being carried out in child (also called inner) (more indented) operations. So for example steps 2, 3, and 4 would be read as "An index full scan is carried out using I_USERS2, then a full table scan of OBJ$ and the results of these are HASH JOINED to produce a result set." Each operation produces results for a less-indented section until the final result is presented to the SELECT (ID=0).

> The "Operation" column is also marked with "+" and "-" to indicate sections of equal indentation. This is helpful in lining up operations to see which result sets an operation is working on.

So, for example, it is important to realize that the HASH JOIN at step 5 is using results from steps 1, 4, 2, and 3. We'll see more complex examples of these later. It is also important to realize that the costs shown are aggregate costs for each operation as well. So the cost shown on the first line is the cost for the entire operation, and we can also see that most of the cost of the entire operation came from step 2. (SQLT helpfully shows the highest cost operation in red). So let's look at step 1 (as shown in Figure 1-5) in more detail. In our simple case this is

```
"INDEX FULL SCAN I_USER2"
```

Let's translate the full line into English: "First get me a full index scan of index I_USERS2. I estimate 132 rows will be returned which, based on your current system statistics (Single block read time and multi-block read times and CPU speed), will be a cost of 1."

The second and third steps are another INDEX FULL SCAN and a TABLE ACCESS FULL of OBJ$. This third step has a cost of 392. The total cost of the entire SQL statement is 1199 (top row). Now place your cursor over the word "TABLE" on step 3 (see Figure 1-8).

```
select count(*) from dba_objects
```

SQL: [±]

ID	Exec Ord	Operation	Go To	More	Cost[2]	Estim Card	Work Area
0	19	SELECT STATEMENT			1199	1	
1	18	SORT AGGREGATE		[±]	1199	1	
2	17	. VIEW DBA_OBJECTS			1199	409749	
3	16	.. UNION-ALL			401		
4	11	... FILTER		[±]	401		
5	5	.... HASH JOIN		[±]	395	411335	[±]
6	1	....+ INDEX FULL SCAN I_USER2	[±]	[±]	1	132	
7	4	....+ HASH JOIN		[±]	393	196319	[±]
8	2	....+. INDEX FULL SCAN I_USER2	[±]	[±]	1	132	
9	3	....+. TABLE ACCESS FULL OBJ$	[±]	[±]	392	93698	
10	6	.... TABLE A	Object#: 18		2	1	
11	9	.... NESTED	Owner: SYS QBlock: SEL$1FF6F973		2	1	
12	7	....+ INDEX	Alias: O@SEL$4		1	1	
13	8	....+ INDEX	**Current Table Statistics:**		1	1	
14	10	.... TABLE A	Analyzed: 07-JUL-14 05:55:44 TblRows: 19416		2	1	
15	15	... NESTED L	Blocks: 300		0	1	
16	12	.... INDEX F	Sample: 19416		0	1	
17	14	.... TABLE A	**Statistics for Plan:**		0	1	
18	13	....+ INDEX	Same as Current		0	1	

Performance statistics are only available when parameter "statistics_level" was set to "ALL" at hard-parse time, or SQL contains "(*
*(1) If estim_card * starts < output_rows then under-estimate. If estim_card * starts > output_rows then over-estimate. Color highligh*
(2) Largest contributors for cumulative-statistics columns are shown in red.

Other XML (id=1): [±]
Outline Data (id=1): [±]
Leading (id=1): [±]
<u>Go to Tables</u>
<u>Go to Indexes</u>
<u>Go to Top</u>

Figure 1-8. *More details can be obtained by 'hovering' over links*

Notice how information is displayed about the object.

    Object#: 18

    Owner: SYS

    Qblock: SEL$1FF6F973

Alias: O@SEL$4

Current Table Statistics:

Analyzed: 08-JUN-14 05:55:44

TblRows: 19416

Blocks: 300

Sample 19416

Just by hovering your mouse over the object, you get its owner, the query block name, when it was last analyzed, and how big the object is.

Now let's look at the "Go To" column. Notice the "+" under that column? Click on the one for step 3, and you'll get a result like the one in Figure 1-9.

SQL Text: [.]

```
select count(*) from dba_objects
```

SQL: [+]

ID	Exec Ord	Operation	Go To	More	Cost^2	Estim Card	Work Area
0	19	SELECT STATEMENT			1199	1	
1	18	SORT AGGREGATE		[+]	1199	1	
2	17	. VIEW DBA_OBJECTS			1199	409749	
3	16	.. UNION-ALL			401		
4	11	... FILTER		[+]	401		
5	5	.... HASH JOIN		[+]	395	411335	[+]
6	1	....+ INDEX FULL SCAN I USER2	[+]	[+]	1	132	
7	4	....+ HASH JOIN		[+]	393	196319	[+]
8	2	....+. INDEX FULL SCAN I USER2	[+]	[+]	1	132	
9	3	....+. TABLE ACCESS FULL OBJ$	[-]	[+]	392	93698	

Table Columns
Col Statistics
Stats Versions
Column Usage
Col Properties
Histograms
Table
Constraints
Indexed Cols
Indexes
Partitions
Metadata

ID	Exec Ord	Operation	Go To	More	Cost^2	Estim Card	Work Area
10	6	.... TABLE ACCESS FULL USER EDITIONING$	[+]	[+]	2	1	
11	9	.... NESTED LOOPS SEMI			2	1	
12	7	....+ INDEX SKIP SCAN I USER2	[+]	[+]	1	1	
13	8	....+ INDEX RANGE SCAN I OBJ4	[+]	[+]	1	1	
14	10	.... TABLE ACCESS FULL USER EDITIONING$	[+]	[+]	2	1	
15	15	... NESTED LOOPS			0	1	
16	12	.... INDEX FULL SCAN I LINK1	[+]	[+]	0	1	
17	14	.... TABLE ACCESS CLUSTER USER$		[+]	0	1	
18	13	....+ INDEX UNIQUE SCAN I_USER#	[+]	[+]	0	1	

Figure 1-9. *More hyperlinks can be revealed by expanding sections on the execution plan*

So right from the execution plan you can go to the "Col Statistics" or the "Histograms" or many other things. You decide where you want to go next, based on what you've understood so far and on what you think is wrong with your execution plan. Now close that expanded area and click on the "+" under the "More" column for step 3 (see Figure 1-10).

SQL Text: [...]

```
select count(*) from dba_objects
```

SQL: [±]

ID	Exec Ord	Operation	Go To	More	Cost[2]	Estim Card	Work Area
0	19	SELECT STATEMENT			1199	1	
1	18	SORT AGGREGATE		[±]	1199	1	
2	17	. VIEW DBA_OBJECTS			1199	409749	
3	16	.. UNION-ALL			401		
4	11	... FILTER		[±]	401		
5	5	.... HASH JOIN		[±]	395	411335	[±]
6	1	....+ INDEX FULL SCAN I_USER2	[±]	[±]	1	132	
7	4	....+ HASH JOIN		[±]	393	196319	[±]
8	2	....+. INDEX FULL SCAN I_USER2	[±]	[±]	1	132	
9	3	....+. TABLE ACCESS FULL OBJ$	[±]	[...]	392	93698	

Filter Predicates
(O.TYPE#<>10 AND O.NAME<>'_NEXT_OBJECT' AND
O.NAME<>'_default_auditing_options_' AND O.LINKNAME IS NULL AND
BITAND(O.FLAGS,
128)=0)

Projection
O.OBJ#, O.OWNER#, O.TYPE#, O.FLAGS, O.SPARE3

ID	Exec Ord	Operation	Go To	More	Cost[2]	Estim Card	Work Area
10	6	.... TABLE ACCESS FULL USER_EDITIONING$	[±]	[±]	2	1	
11	9	.... NESTED LOOPS SEMI			2	1	
12	7	....+ INDEX SKIP SCAN I_USER2	[±]	[±]	1	1	
13	8	....+ INDEX RANGE SCAN I_OBJ4	[±]	[±]	1	1	
14	10	.... TABLE ACCESS FULL USER_EDITIONING$	[±]	[±]	2	1	
15	15	... NESTED LOOPS			0	1	
16	12	.... INDEX FULL SCAN I_LINK1	[±]	[±]	0	1	
17	14	.... TABLE ACCESS CLUSTER USER$		[±]	0	1	
18	13	....+ INDEX UNIQUE SCAN I_USER#	[±]	[±]	0	1	

Performance statistics are only available when parameter 'statistics_level' was set to "ALL" at hardparse time, or SQL contains 'gather_plan_statistics' hint.
(1) If estim_card * starts < output_rows then under-estimate, if estim_card * starts > output_rows then over-estimate. Color highlights when exceeding * 10x, ** 100x and *** 1000x over/under-estimates.
(2) Largest contributors for cumulative-statistics columns are shown in red.

Other XML (id=1): [±]
Outline Data (id=1): [±]
Loading (id=1): [±]
Go to Tables
Go to Indexes
Go to Top

Figure 1-10. *Here we see an expansion under the "More" heading*

Now we see the filter predicates and the projections.

> **Filter predicates** describe operations where some rows from a source are rejected for not matching a criterion or are filtered, for example "Name Like 'ABC%'".
> **Projections** refer to a sub-set of a set of data and **Access Predicates** refer to a clause in a query where a column is referred to that has an index on it (for example "Age=50").

These can help you understand which line in the execution plan the optimizer is considering predicates for and which values are in play for filters.

Just above the first execution plan is a section called "Execution Plans." This lists all the different execution plans the Oracle engine has seen for this SQL. Because execution plans can be stored in multiple places in the system, you could well have multiple entries in the "Execution Plans" section of the report. Its source will be noted (under the "Source" column). Here is a list of sources I've come across:

- GV$SQL_PLAN

- GV$SQLAREA_PLAN_HASH

- PLAN_TABLE

- DBA_SQLTUNE_PLANS

- DBA_HIST_SQL_PLAN

SQLT will look for plans in as many places as possible so that it can give you a full range of options. When SQLT gathers this information, it will look at the actual elapsed time associated with each of these plans and label them with "W" in red (worst) (worst Elapsed Time) and "B" in green (best) (best Elapsed Time). In my simple test case, the "Best" and "Worst" are the same, as there is only one execution plan in play. However you'll notice there are two records: one came from mining the memory GV$SQL_PLAN, and one came from the PLAN_TABLE (i.e., an EXPLAIN PLAN). You could also have one from DBA_SQLTUNE_PLANS, (SQL Tuning Analyzer).

When you have many records here, perhaps a long history, you can go back and see which plans were best and try to see why they changed. Noting the timing of a change can sometimes be crucial, as it can help you zoom in on the change that made things worse.

Before we launch into even more detailed use of the "Execution Plans" section, we'll need more complex examples.

Join Methods

This book is focused on very practical tuning with SQLT. I try to avoid unnecessary concepts and tuning minutiae. For this reason I will not cover every join method available or every DBA table that might have some interesting information about performance or every hint. These are well documented in multiple sources, not least of which is the Oracle Performance guide (which I recommend you read). However, we need to cover some basic concepts to ensure we get the maximum benefit from using SQLT. So, for example, here are some simple joins. As its name implies, a join is a way of "joining" two data sets together: one might contain a person's name and age and another table might contain the person's name and income level. In which case you could "join" these tables to get the names of people of a particular age and income level. As the name of the operation implies, there must be something to join the two data sets together: in our case, it's the person's name. So what are some simple joins? (i.e., ones we'll see in out SQLT reports).

> HASH JOINS (HJ) – The *smaller* table is hashed and placed into memory. The *larger* table is then scanned for rows that match the hash value in memory. If the larger and smaller tables are the wrong way around this is inefficient. If the tables are not large, this is inefficient. If the smaller table does not fit in memory, then this is more than inefficient: it's really bad!

> NESTED LOOP (NL) – Nested Loop joins are better if the tables are smaller. Notice how in the execution plan examples above there is a HASH JOIN and a NESTED LOOP. Why was each chosen for the task? The details of each join method and its associated cost can be determined from the 10053 trace file. It is a common practice to promote the indexes and NL by adjusting the optimizer parameters Optimizer_index_cost_adj and optimizer_index_caching parameters. This is not generally a winning strategy. These parameters should be set to the defaults of 100 and 0. Work on getting the object and system statistics right first.

> CARTESIAN JOINS – Usually bad. Every row of the first table is used as a key to access every row of the second table. If you have a very few number of rows in the joining tables this join is OK. In most production environments, if you see this occurring then something is wrong, usually statistics.

> SORT MERGE JOINS (SMJ) – Generally joined in memory if memory allows. If the cardinality is high then you would expect to see SMJs and HJs.

Summary

In this chapter we covered the basics of using SQLTXTRACT. This is a simple method of SQLT that does not execute the SQL statement in question. It extracts the information required from all possible sources and presents this in a report.

In this chapter we looked at a simple download and install of SQLT. You've seen that installing SQLT on a local database can take very little time, and its use is very simple. The report produced was easy to unzip and can be used to investigate the SQL performance. In this first example we briefly mentioned cardinality and selectivity and how these affect the cost-based optimizer's plans. Now let's look at the bigger picture and what SQLT can do for you.

CHAPTER 2

■ ■ ■

AWR: Your Guide on What to Do Next

Why Use AWR?

In the dim and distant past there used to be a utility called Statspack. More people now use AWR than Statspack, but Statspack is still useful for those sites where there is no Enterprise edition and for which there is no Diagnostic pack. It also works the same as it did back in 7.3.4. Statspack was replaced long ago by the more sophisticated tool AWR (Automatic Workload Repository). Has AWR now been replaced by SQLT? No. They are different blades on the same Utility toolkit that you always carry with you as a DBA. One for tuning SQL and one for tuning the system. Let me explain what I mean by that last statement.

One of the biggest challenges in tuning is keeping to a structured methodology. Too many tuning problems are beguiling. They draw you in with the assumption that there is something wrong with the SQL you are currently working on. You naturally start to try and tune that SQL, but the Oracle-recommended strategy with tuning problems is to step back first and look at the big picture. As with any complex problem, there is sometimes something in the environment that might have a material influence on the tuning problem in question. In the performance group at Oracle we use the same methodology. Always figure out if the problem with the SQL is because of the environment before trying to fix the SQL. This makes sense, because if the problem is environmental (by which I mean, things like too little memory, insufficient CPU resource, slow disks, other competing SQLs etc.), then no amount of tuning will fix the 'problem'. Tuning a system is like the tired cliché I used at my job interview before I joined the Performance Team. "Tuning is like peeling an onion, one layer after another to be peeled back, and each one of them making you cry." So before we work on tuning an individual SQL I thought it would be important to you as a tuner to realize that looking at the overall system performance is the first step before trying to tune an individual SQL.

The Golden Rules of Tuning

- Get the AWR and review that first

I forgot there is only one Golden Rule of Tuning.

How and When Are AWR Snapshots Collected?

AWR snapshots are by default collected on a regular basis, usually every hour and by default kept for 8 days (on 12c). You can even select to collect a snapshot manually.

```
SQL> exec dbms_workload_repository.create_snapshot();

PL/SQL procedure successfully completed.
```

© Stelios Charalambides 2017
S. Charalambides, *Oracle SQL Tuning with Oracle SQLTXPLAIN*, DOI 10.1007/978-1-4842-2436-6_2

The data is kept in the AWR repository, which is in SYSAUX. You can change both the INTERVAL and the RETENTION (the period of time that the snapshots are kept). If you increase the number of snapshots that you keep you should take into account how much space this will take up and the maintenance overhead. The repository can become very big, so if you do make changes make sure you have the space for them. If you want to disable them completely you can set the snapshot interval to 0. You can also collect Snapshots manually. Here are some typical DBMS_WORKLOAD_REPOSITORY calls and what they mean.

```
SQL> column snap_interval format a20
SQL> column retention format a20
SQL> select snap_interval, retention, topnsql from dba_hist_wr_control;

SQL> SNAP_INTERVAL          RETENTION              TOPNSQL
-------------------- -------------------- -------------
+00000 01:00:00.0    +00008 00:00:00.0        DEFAULT
```

So in this case We collect snapshots every hour, keep them for 8 days and collect detailed information on the DEFAULT number of Top SQLs, which in this case is 30. If you think this value is too low you can increase it, in this case to 60.

```
SQL> exec dbms_workload_repository.modify_snapshot_settings(retention=>11520, interval=>60,
topnsql=>60);

PL/SQL procedure successfully completed.
```

The RETENTION value and the INTERVAL value are both in minutes.

```
SQL> select snap_interval, retention, topnsql from dba_hist_wr_control;

SNAP_INTERVAL          RETENTION            TOPNSQL
-------------------- -------------------- ----------
+00000 01:00:00.0    +00008 00:00:00.0            60
```

So now instead of collecting the default value of Top SQLs (30) we are collecting 60. We could also specify the value of TOPNSQL as a string, in this way.

```
SQL> exec dbms_workload_repository.modify_snapshot_settings(retention=>11520, interval=>60,
topnsql=>'MAXIMUM');

PL/SQL procedure successfully completed.

SQL> select snap_interval, retention, topnsql from dba_hist_wr_control;

SNAP_INTERVAL          RETENTION            TOPNSQL
-------------------- -------------------- ----------
+00000 01:00:00.0    +00008 00:00:00.0    MAXIMUM
```

This is a little bit extreme because this means it will collect ALL SQLs.
We could also do this.

```
SQL> exec dbms_workload_repository.modify_snapshot_settings(retention=>11520, interval=>60,
topnsql=>'30');
```

```
PL/SQL procedure successfully completed.

SQL> select snap_interval, retention, topnsql from dba_hist_wr_control;

SNAP_INTERVAL           RETENTION              TOPNSQL
--------------------    --------------------   ----------
+00000 01:00:00.0       +00008 00:00:00.0            30
```

You could ask so why have '30' if DEFAULT is the same. The answer is that DEFAULT is 30 if the Statistics_level value is TYPICAL but if it is ALL then the value used is 100.

Finally I set it back to the default values.

```
SQL> exec dbms_workload_repository.modify_snapshot_settings(retention=>11520, interval=>60,
topnsql=>'DEFAULT');

PL/SQL procedure successfully completed.

SQL> select snap_interval, retention, topnsql from dba_hist_wr_control;

SNAP_INTERVAL           RETENTION              TOPNSQL
--------------------    --------------------   ----------
+00000 01:00:00.0       +00008 00:00:00.0      DEFAULT
```

You might be tempted when seeing these options to set the RETENTION period to MAX_RETENTION (100 Years) and the INTERVAL to the lowest value (10 minutes) and the TOPNSQL to MAXIMUM to collect everything. If you did you might well regret this choice in 90 days. On an active system the repository will be huge and the maintenance on it will probably time-out in the maintenance window overnight. You can manually purge snapshots with dbms_workload_repository.drop_snapshot_range, or you can manually remove the ASH data for some snapshots (which is the bulk of the data volume) with dbms_workload_repository.purge_sql_details.

If you want to increase your monitoring, do this is small steps, be very patient, and monitor the size of the repository. You can do so with awrinfo.sql, which can be found in $ORACLE_HOME/rdbms/admin. It takes no parameters

```
SQL> @awrinfo.sql
```

and produces by default a text file with information about the AWR repository. I can't reproduce the whole output here but this section tells you how much space AWR is taking up.

```
***********************************************************
(1b) SYSAUX occupants space usage (v$sysaux_occupants)
***********************************************************
|
| Occupant Name          Schema Name            Space Usage
| --------------------    --------------------   -----------------
| SDO                     MDSYS                       77.8 MB
| XDB                     XDB                         68.8 MB
| SM/AWR                  SYS                         53.8 MB<<<
| SM/OTHER                SYS                         50.9 MB
| AO                      SYS                         38.8 MB
```

```
| XSOQHIST                  SYS                          38.8 MB
| ORDIM/ORDDATA             ORDDATA                      16.1 MB
| LOGMNR                    SYSTEM                       13.9 MB
| SM/OPTSTAT                SYS                           9.6 MB
| SM/ADVISOR                SYS                           8.4 MB
| WM                        WMSYS                         7.2 MB
| TEXT                      CTXSYS                        3.7 MB
| SQL_MANAGEMENT_BASE       SYS                           2.4 MB
| PL/SCOPE                  SYS                           1.6 MB
| AUDSYS                    AUDSYS                        1.5 MB
| LOGSTDBY                  SYSTEM                        1.5 MB
```

So if it's too burdensome to collect everything all the time, but we want the right information when we need it (perhaps a few days later), how much should you collect? The answer is it depends. All systems are different. If you monitor your system frequently you may notice performance problems soon after they occur, so you may not need a long RETENTION period. If you have lots of space and spare capacity to deal with the maintenance, you could reduce the value of INTERVAL, and if you want to look at more than the DEFAULT 30 SQLs you could increase this number. If your problems are likely to be at a very granular level (i.e., short-running SQLs), you may want to try and reduce the snapshot interval to catch those SQLs.

Generally speaking, I would say to collect the MINIMUM you need to solve and understand any problems you have. Don't overcollect. If it turns out you've undercollected then you can always make a small increase to collect what you need.

This step is very important, because with insufficient collection, you are left in the dark when you try and look back at problems that have already passed.

What Kind of Report Should I Collect?

Now that you've told Oracle what to collect, and how often to aggregate the data and how long to keep it, what choices are there for how you look at the data?

Here are the names of the files to use.

```
awrrpt.sql – General Report
awrrpti.sql – General Report for an Instance
awrsqrpt.sql – General Report for a SQL ID
awrsqrpi.sql – General Report for a SQL ID on an Instance
awrddrpt.sql – Difference Report
awrddrpi.sql – Difference Report on a specific Instance
```

If you don't really know what kind of report you want but you know you will want to look at something in the future, you can even export the repository information with awrextr.sql and then use awrload.sql on a target test system to load that data so that you can explore it without being worried about losing the data. We could spend a long time on AWR (a whole book perhaps), but in this chapter I want to review how you use AWR in conjunction with SQLT. I'm also not going to review Difference Reports or Global Reports or RAC specific reports. Not because they are not useful, but because I find the Instance reports often have better granular detail.

The designers of SQLT realized that you should look at the AWR report around the time of the problem (see Golden Rule 001 above) and so they automatically collect AWR reports for you. See Figure 2-1 below.

Name ▲	Size	Type	Date Modified
sqlt_s78831_10053_explain.trc	2,836 KB	TRC File	1/6/2016 2:18 PM
sqlt_s78831_10053_i1_c19_extract.trc	1,613 KB	TRC File	1/6/2016 2:18 PM
sqlt_s78831_addmrpt_0007.zip	3 KB	Compressed (zippe…	1/6/2016 4:32 PM
sqlt_s78831_ashrpt_0007.zip	35 KB	Compressed (zippe…	1/6/2016 4:36 PM
sqlt_s78831_awrrpt_0007.zip	523 KB	Compressed (zippe…	1/6/2016 4:32 PM
sqlt_s78831_cell_state.zip	452 KB	Compressed (zippe…	1/6/2016 4:37 PM
sqlt_s78831_driver.zip	9 KB	Compressed (zippe…	1/6/2016 4:37 PM
sqlt_s78831_lite.html	2,485 KB	Firefox HTML Docu…	1/6/2016 2:18 PM
sqlt_s78831_log.zip	2,006 KB	Compressed (zippe…	1/6/2016 4:37 PM
sqlt_s78831_main.html	30,881 KB	Firefox HTML Docu…	1/6/2016 2:18 PM
sqlt_s78831_opatch.zip	2,594 KB	Compressed (zippe…	1/6/2016 4:37 PM
sqlt_s78831_readme.html	117 KB	Firefox HTML Docu…	1/6/2016 2:18 PM
sqlt_s78831_sql_monitor_active.html	16 KB	Firefox HTML Docu…	1/6/2016 2:18 PM
sqlt_s78831_sql_monitor_active_0013.zip	148 KB	Compressed (zippe…	1/6/2016 2:17 PM
sqlt_s78831_sqldx.zip	2,338 KB	Compressed (zippe…	1/6/2016 4:38 PM
sqlt_s78831_sta_report_awr.txt	57 KB	Text Document	1/6/2016 2:18 PM
sqlt_s78831_sta_report_mem.txt	57 KB	Text Document	1/6/2016 2:18 PM
sqlt_s78831_sta_script_awr.sql	2 KB	SQL File	1/6/2016 2:18 PM
sqlt_s78831_sta_script_mem.sql	2 KB	SQL File	1/6/2016 2:18 PM
sqlt_s78831_tc.zip	6,933 KB	Compressed (zippe…	1/6/2016 4:37 PM
sqlt_s78831_tc_script.sql	5 KB	SQL File	1/6/2016 4:37 PM
sqlt_s78831_tc_sql.sql	4 KB	SQL File	1/6/2016 4:37 PM
sqlt_s78831_tcb.zip	1,090 KB	Compressed (zippe…	1/6/2016 4:36 PM
sqlt_s78831_tcx.zip	882 KB	Compressed (zippe…	1/6/2016 4:37 PM
sqlt_s78831_trc.zip	912 KB	Compressed (zippe…	1/6/2016 4:37 PM
sqlt_s78831_xpand.sql	3 KB	SQL File	1/6/2016 4:36 PM
sqlt_s78831_xtract_74y5y1q3qhuch.zip	20,756 KB	Compressed (zippe…	1/14/2016 4:42 PM

Figure 2-1. *Default Files Collected by SQLT. AWR Zip file is identified*

Let me also digress briefly to mention the other interesting files we see there and what they are for:

- sqlt_s78831_10053_explain.trc – 10053 trace file from Explain Plan

- sqlt_s78831_10053_i1_c19_extract.trc – 10053 collected with DBMS_SQLDIAG.DUMP_TRACE

- sqlt_s78831_addm_0007.zip – A zip file containing an ADDM reports.

- sqlt_s78831_ashrpt.zip – An ASH report for the SQL being investigated.

- sqlt_78831_cell_state.zip – An Exadata Cell Server state file. For non-Exadata platforms this will be empty.

- sqlt_s78831_lite.html – A cut-down version of the main report.

- sqlt_s78831_log.zip – A log file of the installation. Useful for debugging installation problems.

- sqlt_s78831_main.html – The main report.

- sqlt_s78831_opatch.zip – A log file of patch installations.

- sqlt_s78831_sql_monitor_active.sql – The active SQL monitor report.

- sqlt_s78831_sta_awr.txt – An SQL Tuning Analyzer report.

The Main AWR Report

So finally let's look at an AWR report and try and understand the important things to look for when analyzing one of these reports. Before you analyze, you need to understand what you are dealing with, for example, version, RAC or non-RAC amount of memory and a few other basic facts. This is all in the header section.

The Header

In Figure 2-2 above we see the name of the Database, the instance, the version, whether this is RAC or non-RAC where the database is hosted, the amount of physical RAM on the system, and the time period of the snapshot. This might seem like relatively unimportant information, but making sure you are looking at the right report is pretty important. The version of course makes a huge difference, including what the AWR report looks like. The most important thing to look for is the time start and time end of the report. If it's too long you may not be able to see the signal of whatever you are looking for. If too short you may have missed it. Once you know where you are and when you are, you can look at how busy the system is in the Report Summary Section.

WORKLOAD REPOSITORY report for

DB Name	DB Id	Instance	Inst num	Startup Time	Release	RAC
DB001	803458230	DB0011	1	14-Jan-16 00:01	12.1.0.2.0	YES

Host Name	Platform	CPUs	Cores	Sockets	Memory (GB)
HOST001.doma.com	Linux x86 64-bit	24	12	2	94.16

	Snap Id	Snap Time	Sessions	Cursors/Session	Instances
Begin Snap:	13667	03-Feb-16 06:15:21	107	2.2	2
End Snap:	13668	03-Feb-16 06:30:22	108	2.2	2
Elapsed:		15.02 (mins)			
DB Time:		0.05 (mins)			

Figure 2-2. *Header of a typical AWR report*

Report Summary

Here in Figure 2-3 you are looking for Transactions per second. Is it busy? This system doesn't look busy. 0.1 transactions per second translates to an average of 1 transaction per 10 seconds. While this may not mean the system is not busy (there could be one massive transaction eating up resources), we don't see any evidence here of a busy system. Redo is very small also. Then we come to the Instance Efficiency Percentage section of the report.

Report Summary

Load Profile

	Per Second	Per Transaction	Per Exec	Per Call
DB Time(s):	0.0	0.0	0.00	0.00
DB CPU(s):	0.0	0.0	0.00	0.00
Background CPU(s):	0.0	0.2	0.01	0.00
Redo size (bytes):	66,523.8	491,535.6		
Logical read (blocks):	971.7	7,180.0		
Block changes:	479.7	3,544.1		
Physical read (blocks):	13.7	101.0		
Physical write (blocks):	8.4	62.2		
Read IO requests:	4.9	36.0		
Write IO requests:	3.5	26.0		
Read IO (MB):	0.1	0.8		
Write IO (MB):	0.1	0.5		
IM scan rows:	0.0	0.0		
Session Logical Read IM:				
Global Cache blocks received:	1.0	7.0		
Global Cache blocks served:	32.2	237.5		
User calls:	4.7	34.9		
Parses (SQL):	2.9	21.6		
Hard parses (SQL):	0.1	.5		
SQL Work Area (MB):	0.3	1.9		
Logons:	0.4	3.1		
Executes (SQL):	4.9	36.3		
Rollbacks:	0.0	0.0		
Transactions:	0.1			

Figure 2-3. The Report Summary Section of the AWR report

Instance Efficiency

This section of the report shown in Figure 2-4 is the section indicating how efficiently everything is working. Yes, we know how much Redo was generated and how many transactions are being completed, but are we doing it without wasting resources? Look at the Buffer Hit%; is it near a 100% - if it is, probably the Buffer access for queries is not a problem. Is Execute to Parse near 100% - if not then there might be some Shared Pool problems or some Parsing problem. In the example we have 40% Execute to Parse; this is a sign of an application that could be using too many literals in SQLs that don't run for very long or a Shared Pool that might be undersized, or some other Shared Pool problem like fragmentation. How about these numbers?

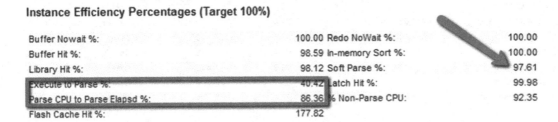

Instance Efficiency Percentages (Target 100%)

Buffer Nowait %:	100.00	Redo NoWait %:	100.00
Buffer Hit %:	98.59	In-memory Sort %:	100.00
Library Hit %:	98.12	Soft Parse %:	97.61
Execute to Parse %:	40.42	Latch Hit %:	99.98
Parse CPU to Parse Elapsd %:	86.36	% Non-Parse CPU:	92.35
Flash Cache Hit %:	177.82		

Figure 2-4. Instance Efficiency section of AWR

In Figure 2-5 we see another AWR report, and again we see the "Instance Efficiency" section. The "Parse CPU to Parse Elapsed %" metric is far worse at 3.22% instead of 86.36%. This second report is indicative of something much worse going on in the Shared Pool. Perhaps a higher rate of Parsing, perhaps a complex SQL that is popular on the system is taking a long time to parse. These kinds of metrics are not directly indicative of problems, but they point to something that *might* be a problem. You should be on the lookout for SQL that is filled with literals or some application firing system generated SQL at a high rate. These are warning signs, and this gives you a clue for what to look for next in the most important section, the Top 10 waits (or the top 5 waits from 11g).

Instance Efficiency Percentages (Target 100%)

Buffer Nowait %:	100.00	Redo NoWait %:	100.00
Buffer Hit %:	99.97	In-memory Sort %:	99.77
Library Hit %:	98.56	Soft Parse %:	99.25
Execute to Parse %:	53.88	Latch Hit %:	99.86
Parse CPU to Parse Elapsd %:	3.22	% Non-Parse CPU:	98.28

Figure 2-5. *Another Instance Efficiency section*

Top 10 Waits

Most DBAs, when they look at the Top 10 waits, know from experience when they are looking at a 'bad' AWR. This is because they look at the report and see some wait that they don't normally see. Instinctively they know that some waits are wasteful waits, while others are expected of 'good' waits. For example, in the following section, would you say there was a problem? Which wait would you go after?

Let's look at Figure 2-6 and the top 3 waits in this section (the other waits are less than 1% so they probably can be ignored). CPU is 64% – is this good? Parsing is a high CPU activity, especially Hard Parsing, so if we see low ratios as we did in the previous section we probably should expect high CPU usage anyway. Should the fact that we see high CPU usage cause us to start tuning? That probably depends on if CPU is a valuable resource. If this system had 98% spare CPU then I would say if you want to tune this system, look at ways to improve the parsing overhead, either by reducing the number of individual SQLs or by reducing the number of literals; or if neither of those can be done then leave the CPU to do its job.

Top 10 Foreground Events by Total Wait Time

Event	Waits	Total Wait Time (sec)	Avg(ms)	% DB time	Wait Class
DB CPU		36.1K		64.6	
library cache lock	2,807	9366.7	3337	16.8	Concurrency
cursor: pin S wait on X	3,943	9315.7	2363	16.7	Concurrency
direct path read temp	53,403	380.1	7	.7	User I/O
gc current block 2-way	1,461,058	132.4	0	.2	Cluster
PX Deq: reap credit	6,093,147	69.5	0	.1	Other
direct path write temp	11,584	60.4	5	.1	User I/O
DFS lock handle	84	39.9	475	.1	Other
cell single block physical read	93,731	33.1	0	.1	User I/O
gc cr multi block request	23,542	23.4	1	.0	Cluster

Figure 2-6. *Top 10 Waits. Which wait do we chase?*

Then we come to the wait class "Concurrency." In this report it totals 33.5% between "library cache lock" and "cursor: pin S wait on X." These types of waits are normal and are happening all the time on any Oracle system, but 33.5% is probably too high. If these were less than 10% and the system was otherwise efficient you could probably ignore these. Don't forget than in 12c; we now have 10 waits to look at compared to the 5 waits we had before, so more of the responsibility for determining which waits are important falls on us as DBAs. Choose wisely if you value your time. Before you rush in to 'fix' the Concurrency problem, take a quick look at the Average Wait column (in milliseconds) – 3337ms and 2363ms. These waits are over 1 second, 3 seconds, and 2 seconds (to the nearest second). A "Library cache lock" of 3 seconds is way too long. This is something that needs to be fixed, especially since there are 2,807 of them. Sometimes you will see a long wait and the count is 1 or 2, in which case you might conclude that it was one off and can also be ignored. For the Top 10 list (Figure 2-6), we would now concentrate on "library cache lock" waits and find out where they are coming from. I'm trying to explain the methodology here of dealing with an AWR, not necessarily in how to solve every combination of waits that you might see in an AWR Top 10 section. So let's move on to another example where the system is in much worse shape.

The Top 10 waits seen in Figure 2-7 show a system that does not have any useful waits until we get to "db file sequential read" at 6.8%. This indicates a badly tuned system. In this example we would concentrate on "enq: HW – contention." Fix that problem and the other problems will also most likely disappear. The methodology however is to fix the biggest problem and then see where you are.

Top 10 Foreground Events by Total Wait Time

Event	Waits	Total Wait Time (sec)	Wait Avg(ms)	% DB time	Wait Class
enq: HW - contention	169,568	382.6K	2256	49.	Configuration
buffer busy waits	1,959,428	161.2K	82	20.	Concurrency
enq: TX - index contention	2,156,478	91.3K	42	11.	Concurrency
flashback buf free by RVWR	93,542	64.9K	694	8.	Configuration
db file sequential read	1,038,389	52.9K	51	6.8	User I/O
db file scattered read	247,476	13.4K	54	1.7	User I/O
latch: ges resource hash list	2,185,134	9398.4	4	1.2	Other
log file sync	1,678,443	5414.4	3	.7	Commit
DB CPU		3506		.5	
enq: FB - contention	4,176	1024.4	245	.1	Other

Figure 2-7. Top 10 Waits for a badly tuned system

Quite often it is hard to figure out with 'good' waits if they are really good. Especially when it comes to I/O, because I/O systems vary widely. A 'good' I/O on one system could be a 'bad' I/O on another. For Exadata, for example, on a well-tuned system you should expect single block reads to be in the 1-2 ms range. 3 ms might be a busy system, while 5 ms would indicate overloading. Overloading of course doesn't mean the system is tuned badly; it could mean that the load is too high. Even Exadata systems can be overloaded by bad SQL, although they can do a pretty amazing job at shifting I/O.

In the example system below (Figure 2-8), we see 2 ms for "cell single block physical read." Probably OK and barring other evidence this would not be the primary area of interest on this system.

Top 5 Timed Foreground Events

Event	Waits	Time(s)	Avg wait (ms)	% DP ne	Wait Class
DB CPU		1,084		33.20	
cell single block physical read	323,120	539	2	16.50	User I/O
latch: parallel query alloc buffer	59,348	256	4	7.83	Other
enq: TX - row lock contention	64	235	3677	7.20	Application
gc cr multi block request	1,108,068	231	0	7.08	Cluster

Host CPU (CPUs: 24 Cores: 12 Sockets: 2)

Load Average Begin	Load Average End	%User	%System	%WIO	%Idle
1.21	1.69	6.8	2.8	0.0	90.1

Figure 2-8. Top 5 waits on an Exadata system

I can't go into all the variations on possible top waits; there are too many types, but suffice to say you can look all of them up on Metalink. With the information on what the waits are for you can build up a picture of your system and what is normal. Once you've scanned up to the Top waits section you get to what I call the "How's the Computer Doing" section.

All computers from a humble PC up to and including a Massive Exadata system deal in three main resources: CPU, I/O, and Memory. If a bottleneck develops it is usually first in one of these. I say first because most systems if they hit one of these bottlenecks usually compensate by using another one until, if you keep pushing, all three are overwhelmed.

For example, a system that runs out of Memory may try to swap or page the data to disk, which uses I/O resource and as this activity is very CPU intensive (system CPU), which results in CPU being loaded also. Quite often the challenge in tuning is figuring out which resource ran out first and started the whole chain of events that led to a slow system. If you understand how the different resources affect each other, than you can determine a rationale that makes sense, which often leads to the right culprit.

Resources

CPU, I/O, and Memory are shown in the next few sections, in that order. See Figure 2-9 where we highlight these important resources.

If CPU is high in the Top waits yet you have 99% idle CPU, what does this mean? It means your CPU is not overloaded, so you have more if needed and the system is dealing with the Workload with CPU, which is a good situation to be in. It means if you want to improve the system, your options are to improve the system resources by improving the clock speed or adding more CPUs (if you have many processes). It means that if you want the Elapsed Time for an SQL to improve you need to look at the SQL itself, which would of course need you to get a SQLTXPLAIN for it.

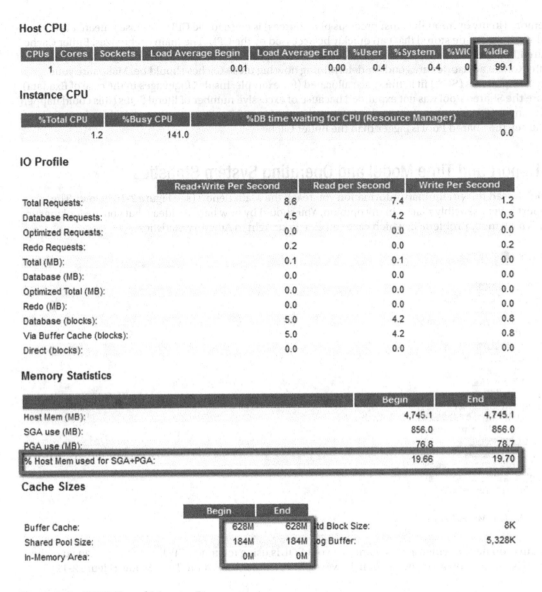

Host CPU

CPUs	Cores	Sockets	Load Average Begin	Load Average End	%User	%System	%WIO	%Idle
1			0.01	0.00	0.4	0.4	0	99.1

Instance CPU

%Total CPU	%Busy CPU	%DB time waiting for CPU (Resource Manager)
1.2	141.0	0.0

IO Profile

	Read+Write Per Second	Read per Second	Write Per Second
Total Requests:	8.6	7.4	1.2
Database Requests:	4.5	4.2	0.3
Optimized Requests:	0.0	0.0	0.0
Redo Requests:	0.2	0.0	0.2
Total (MB):	0.1	0.1	0.0
Database (MB):	0.0	0.0	0.0
Optimized Total (MB):	0.0	0.0	0.0
Redo (MB):	0.0	0.0	0.0
Database (blocks):	5.0	4.2	0.8
Via Buffer Cache (blocks):	5.0	4.2	0.8
Direct (blocks):	0.0	0.0	0.0

Memory Statistics

	Begin	End
Host Mem (MB):	4,745.1	4,745.1
SGA use (MB):	856.0	856.0
PGA use (MB):	76.8	78.7
% Host Mem used for SGA+PGA:	19.66	19.70

Cache Sizes

	Begin	End		
Buffer Cache:	628M	628M	td Block Size:	8K
Shared Pool Size:	184M	184M	og Buffer:	5,328K
In-Memory Area:	0M	0M		

Figure 2-9. CPU I/O and Memory Resources

We saw that you can quickly assess I/O loading by the Average Wait time for I/O (and for this you need to know some of your system metrics). If the metrics are high (or the queues on your disks are consistently above 1-2) then you need to address this resource. As I mentioned above, CPU, I/O, and Memory are somewhat interchangeable in terms of covering for each other. So, for example, if you determine that your I/O is overloaded (not due to some poorly performing SQL), then you might be able to help by increasing memory resources. A common example of this is PGA. Some SQL that needs lots of sorting space may find itself writing to disk and reading from disk, which is slow compared to memory, so in this case the solution would be to increase pga_aggregate_target. Memory has compensated for I/O's limitation.

Memory (in my opinion the most precious of resources) is close to the CPU. By close I mean it is the place where data can be stored that can quickly be accessed by the CPU. The main cache sizes, Buffer Cache and Shared Pool Cache, also give you a good idea of how big your system is and if memory is under pressure. The Buffer Cache advisories are good for determining how big these Caches should be. Make sure your Memory components (SGA) fit in the space allocated (for example, inside HugePages in the case of Exadata). Make sure the Shared Pool has not expanded because of excessive number of literal SQLs (this could happen if constant new SQLs are seen that need to be stored in the Shared Pool). A sign that something is amiss is when you see the Shared Pool is bigger than the Buffer Cache.

Main Report and Time Model and Operating System Statistics

Once you've read this preliminary information you reach the Main Report (see Figure 2-10 below). The Main report is very sensibly placed in my opinion. You should by now have an idea what you are looking for. Maybe it's a Memory problem, in which case you can go straight to Advisory Statistics.

Main Report

- Report Summary
- Wait Events Statistics
- SQL Statistics
- Instance Activity Statistics
- IO Stats
- Buffer Pool Statistics
- Advisory Statistics
- Wait Statistics
- Undo Statistics
- Latch Statistics
- Segment Statistics
- Dictionary Cache Statistics
- Library Cache Statistics
- Memory Statistics
- Streams Statistics
- Resource Limit Statistics
- Shared Server Statistics
- init.ora Parameters

Figure 2-10. The Main Report

Perhaps you have decided at this point that your SQL is using too much CPU, so then you can go to the SQL statistics. Before you go to this section, however, have a quick look at the Time Model (Figure 2-11).

Time Model Statistics

- Total time in database user-calls (DB Time): 4595.3s
- Statistics including the word "background" measure background
- Ordered by % or DB time desc, Statistic name

Statistic Name	Time (s)	% of DB Time
sql execute elapsed time	4,214.71	91.72
DB CPU	2,215.54	48.21
PL/SQL execution elapsed time	1,848.51	40.23
parse time elapsed	228.80	4.98

Figure 2-11. Time Model Statistics

In the above example SQL execution is taking 91% of the resources. This is what you want. A high percentage of resources are being used by actual work. If this was low, say 70%, you might wonder where is 30% of my system going? In this example we also see that most SQL is probably coming from PL/SQL procedures, which is not unusual. The system is also not overloaded with excessive parsing (5% is quite acceptable).

Now look at this system in Figure 2-12. IDLE_TIME is very low, only 5,433 seconds out of 34,741,105 seconds. Is CPU a problem? Well, it's a symptom of something else. Remember we said resources try to compensate for each other. In this case CPU is trying to compensate for Paging. If you see VM_OUT_BYTES with a non-zero value it means the system is spending time (CPU resource in the form of SYS_TIME) trying to get things on and off disk to make up for the Memory problem. In a case like this you should fix the memory problem first and then see if you still have a CPU problem.

Operating System Statistics

- *TIME statistic values are diffed. All others display actua:
- ordered by statistic type (CPU Use, Virtual Memory, Har

Statistic	Value	End Value
BUSY_TIME	34,741,105	
IDLE_TIME	5,433	
IOWAIT_TIME	2	
NICE_TIME	54,030	
SYS_TIME	2,122,158	
USER_TIME	31,969,661	
LOAD	72	151
VM_IN_BYTES	7,471,104	
VM_OUT_BYTES	1,081,344	
PHYSICAL_MEMORY_BYTES	270,577,192,960	
NUM_CPUS	24	
NUM_CPU_CORES	12	
NUM_CPU_SOCKETS	2	

Figure 2-12. *Operating System Statistics*

If I were writing an entire book on AWR then I could spend more time covering all the different scenarios (if you feel you need an AWR book then please contact Apress and let them know), but this is a book on SQLT so let's skip to the SQL section of the report skimming past all the other sections in the AWR report.

SQL Statistics

One of the biggest skills in collecting a SQLT report is to know which SQL to investigate (Figure 2-13). Often as a DBA of a system you will have a good idea of what to look at, but that doesn't mean you should skip the AWR report. The AWR report should be used to confirm your suspicions and be used to identify in what way the SQL is bad. The first question you should ask is, "What metric should I judge the SQL by?" After all, there are so many.

SQL Statistics

- SQL ordered by Elapsed Time
- SQL ordered by CPU Time
- SQL ordered by User I/O Wait Time
- SQL ordered by Gets
- SQL ordered by Reads
- SQL ordered by Physical Reads (UnOptimized)
- SQL ordered by Executions
- SQL ordered by Parse Calls
- SQL ordered by Sharable Memory
- SQL ordered by Version Count
- SQL ordered by Cluster Wait Time
- Complete List of SQL Text

Figure 2-13. *The SQL Statistics header page*

If in doubt you should work with Elapsed Time, as this is the metric that users go by. But as you've reviewed the AWR you should already know which resource is most under pressure. If your CPU is overloaded (low idle time), then you might want to look at the "SQL order by CPU Time." If parsing is a problem, you might want to look at "SQL order by Parse Calls,"

Look at the section of the AWR report in Figure 2-14. Notice how the top SQL by Elapsed Time is 87% of all Elapsed Time. (Forget for the moment that the Percentages do not add up to 100; this often happens when a system is loaded). Notice also the number of executions is 0. A zero in this column means that the SQL is still running, that is, it has not completed one execution yet. It means that this one SQL is dominating the system and is still running at the end of the AWR snapshot. It means that if you could eliminate or tune this SQL you would hugely reduce the resource usage on the system. This is the time to call on SQLT.

SQL ordered by Elapsed Time

- Resources reported for PL/SQL code includes the resources used by
- % Total DB Time is the Elapsed Time of the SQL statement divided into
- %Total - Elapsed Time as a percentage of Total DB time
- %CPU - CPU Time as a percentage of Elapsed Time
- %IO - User I/O Time as a percentage of Elapsed Time
- Captured SQL account for 113.8% of Total DB Time (s): 116,746
- Captured PL/SQL account for 88.0% of Total DB Time (s): 116,746

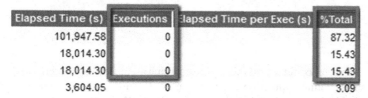

Elapsed Time (s)	Executions	Elapsed Time per Exec (s)	%Total
101,947.58	0		87.32
18,014.30	0		15.43
18,014.30	0		15.43
3,604.05	0		3.09

Figure 2-14. *SQL Order by Elapsed Time*

We've now covered the general disposition of the system CPU-wise, I/O-wise, and Memory-wise. We know how to look for problem SQLs as a final check on the system. I would always recommend you look at the parameter section to make sure you haven't forgotten some hidden parameter or left some strange configuration on your system.

I would always recommend checking on hidden parameters, even if they are historic to make sure they still make sense. Old hidden parameters may have crept in during migrations without making any sense on the current version of Oracle. Always know why you have hidden parameters set and if you don't know why, find out. I don't recommend removing them until you know why they were set. Then you can make a sensible decision based on the current requirements.

34

Summary

In this chapter we covered the absolute basics of reading an AWR. This is because any tuning session should begin with AWR. Without this you do not have the proper context for dealing with a badly tuned system. You should know how individual SQLs fit in the overall scheme of things. You should know if it is the top SQL or some new SQL that you just want to tune because it is still in development. You could find that tuning the system is more effective than tuning a SQL. Make sure you know which resources, CPU, I/O, and Memory are most likely to be overloaded first, and remember that resources can compensate for each other.

In the next chapter we look at SQLs in more detail and talk about the optimizer's abilities and how it can be misled by bad Statistics.

■ ■ ■

## CHAPTER 3

The Cost-Based Optimizer Environment

After reviewing the AWR report and homing in on the SQL you want to work on (bear in mind there could be more than one), you now approach the tricky problem of dealing with an individual SQL.

Every SQL needs individual attention. Approach it with skepticism and caution and watch out for hidden complications and unexpected traps. Be like the alien who came to earth to try his hand at driving. He'd read all about it and knew the physics involved in the engine. It sounded like fun. He sat down in the driver's seat and turned the ignition; the engine ticked over nicely, and the electrics were on. He put his seatbelt on and tentatively pressed the accelerator pedal. Nothing happened. Ah! Maybe the handbrake was on. He released the handbrake and pressed the accelerator again. Nothing happened. Later, standing back from the car and wondering why he couldn't get it to go anywhere, he wondered why the roof was in contact with the road.

My rather strange analogy is trying to help point out that before you can tune something, you need to know what it should look like in broad terms. Is 200ms reasonable for a single block read time? Should system statistics be collected over a period of 1 minute? Should we be using hash joins for large table joins? There are 1,001 things that to the practiced eye look wrong, but to the optimizer it's just the truth.

Just like the alien, the Cost-Based Optimizer (CBO) is working out how to get the best performance from your system. It knows some basic rules and guestimates (heuristics) but doesn't know about your particular system or data. You have to tell it about what you have. You have to tell the alien that the black round rubbery things need to be in contact with the road. If you 'lie' to the optimizer, then it could get the execution plan wrong, and by wrong I mean the plan will perform badly. There are rare cases where heuristics are used inappropriately or there are bugs in the code that lead the CBO to take shortcuts (Query transformations) that are inappropriate and give the wrong results. Apart from these, the optimizer generally delivers poor performance because it has poor information to start with. Give it good information, and you'll generally get good performance.

So how do you tell if the "environment" is right for your system? In this chapter we'll look at a number of aspects of this environment. We'll start with (often neglected) system statistics and then look at the database parameters that affect the CBO. We'll briefly look at histograms (these are covered in more detail in Chapter 5). Finally, we'll look at both overestimates and underestimates (one of SQLT's best features is highlighting these), and then we'll dive into a real-life example, where you can play detective and look at examples to hone your tuning skills (no peeking at the answer). Without further ado, let's start with system statistics.

System Statistics

System statistics are an often-neglected part of the cost-based optimizer environment. If no system statistics have been collected for a system, then the SQLT section "Current System Statistics" will show nothing for a number of important parameters for the system. An example is shown in Figure 3-1. It will guess these values. But why should you care if these values are not supplied to the optimizer? Without these values

© Stelios Charalambides 2017

S. Charalambides, *Oracle SQL Tuning with Oracle SQLTXPLAIN*, DOI 10.1007/978-1-4842-2436-6_3

the optimizer will apply its best guess for scaling the timings of a number of crucial operations. This will result in inappropriate indexes being used when a full table scan would do or vice versa. These settings are so important that in some dynamic environments where the workload is changing, for example, from the daytime OLTP to a nighttime DW (Data Warehouse) environment, that different sets of system statistics should be loaded. In this section we'll look at why these settings affect the optimizer, how and when they should be collected, and what to look for in an SQLT report.

Let's remind ourselves what the first part of the HTML report looks like (see Figure 3-1). Remember this is one huge HTML page with many sections.

215187.1 SQLT XTRACT 12.1.160429 Report: sqlt_s46414_main.html

Global

- Observations
- SQL Text
- SQL Identification
- Environment
- CBO Environment
- Fix Control
- CBO System Statistics
- DBMS_STATS Setup
- Initialization Parameters
- NLS Parameters
- I/O Calibration
- Tool Configuration Parameters

Cursor Sharing and Binds

- Cursor Sharing
- Adaptive Cursor Sharing
- Peeked Binds
- Captured Binds

SQL Tuning Advisor

- STA Report
- STA Script

Plans

- Summary
- Performance Statistics
- Performance History (delta)
- Performance History (total)
- Execution Plans

Plan Control

- Stored Outlines
- SQL Patches
- SQL Profiles
- SQL Plan Baselines
- SQL Plan Directives

SQL Execution

- Active Session History
- AWR Active Session History
- SQL Statistics
- SQL Detail ACTIVE Report
- Monitor Statistics
- Monitor ACTIVE Report
- Monitor HTML Report
- Monitor TEXT Report
- Segment Statistics
- Session Statistics
- Session Events
- Parallel Processing

Tables

- Tables
- Statistics
- Statistics Extensions
- Statistics Versions
- Modifications
- Properties
- Physical Properties
- Constraints
- Columns
- Indexed Columns
- Histograms
- Partitions
- Indexes

Objects

- Objects
- Dependencies
- Fixed Objects
- Fixed Object Columns
- Nested Tables
- Policies
- Audit Policies
- Tablespaces
- Metadata

Figure 3-1. *The top section of the SQLT report*

From the main screen, in the Global section, select "CBO System Statistics." This brings you to the section where you will see a heading "CBO System Statistics" (See Figure 3-2).

CBO System Statistics

- **Info System Statistics**
- Current System Statistics
- **Basis and Synthesized Values**
- **System Statistics History**

Figure 3-2. *The "CBO System Statistics" section*

Now click on "Info System Statistics." Figure 3-3 shows three interesting sections.

Info System Statistics

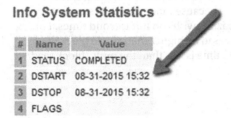

#	Name	Value
1	STATUS	COMPLETED
2	DSTART	08-31-2015 15:32
3	DSTOP	08-31-2015 15:32
4	FLAGS	

Current System Statistics

#	Name	Value
1	CPUSPEEDNW	2759
2	IOSEEKTIM	9
3	IOTFRSPEED	4096
4	CPUSPEED	
5	MBRC	
6	SREADTIM	
7	MREADTIM	
8	MAXTHR	
9	SLAVETHR	

Basis and Synthesized Values

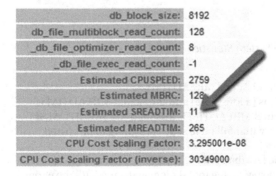

db_block_size:	8192
db_file_multiblock_read_count:	128
_db_file_optimizer_read_count:	8
_db_file_exec_read_count:	-1
Estimated CPUSPEED:	2759
Estimated MBRC:	128
Estimated SREADTIM:	11
Estimated MREADTIM:	265
CPU Cost Scaling Factor:	3.295001e-08
CPU Cost Scaling Factor (inverse):	30349000

Figure 3-3. *The "Info System Statistics" section*

The "Info System Statistics" section shows many pieces of important information about your environment. This screenshot also shows the "Current System Statistics" and the "Basis and Synthesized Values" section. Notice when the System Statistics collection was started. It was begun on August 31, 2015 (quite a while ago). Has the workload changed much since then? Has any new piece of equipment been added? New SAN drives? Faster disks? All of these could affect the performance characteristics of the system. You could even have a system that needs a different set of system statistics for different times of the day. Also notice how there is a blank section for "Current System Statistics." We'll see how to fix that later in this section in a worked example.

Notice anything else strange about the system statistics? The start and end times are identical. The start and end time **should** be scheduled to collect information about the system characteristics at the *start* and *end* times of the representative workload. These values mean that they were set at database creation time and never changed. Look at the "Basis and Synthesized Values" sections shown at the bottom of Figure 3-3.

The estimated SREADTIM (single block read time in ms.) and MREADTIM (multi-block read time in ms) are 11ms and 265ms. Are these good values? It can be hard to tell because modern SAN systems can deliver blistering I/O read rates. Exadata systems are even more amazing, with sub millisecond times. For traditional non-SAN systems you would expect multi-block read times to be higher than single block read times and the normally around 9ms and 22ms. The single block read time is less than the multi-block read time (you would expect that, right?).

Now look in Figure 3-4 at a screenshot from a different system.

Basis and Synthesized Values

db_block_size:	8192
db_file_multiblock_read_count:	16
Estimated CPUSPEED:	189.009678206414
Estimated MBRC:	16
Estimated SREADTIM:	12
Estimated MREADTIM:	42
CPU Cost Scaling Factor:	4.408945e-07
CPU Cost Scaling Factor (inverse):	2268116
Actual SREADTIM:	6.809
Actual MREADTIM:	3.563

Figure 3-4. Basis and synthesized values section under Info System Statistics

Notice anything unusual about the Actual SREADTIM and Actual MREADTIM?

Apart from the fact that the Actual SREADTIM is 6.809ms (a low value) and the Actual MREADTIM is 3.563ms (also a low value). The problem here is that the Actual MREADTIM is less than the SREADTIM. If you see values like these, you should be alert to the possibility that full table scans are going to be costed lower than operations that require single block reads.

What does it mean to the optimizer for MREADTIM to be less than SREADTIM? This is about equivalent to you telling the optimizer that it's OK to drive the car upside down with the roof sliding on the road. It's the wrong way around. If the optimizer takes the values in Figure 3-4 as the truth, it will favor steps that involve multi-block reads. For example, the optimizer will favor full table scans. That could be very bad for your runtime execution. If on the other hand you have a fast SAN system, you may well have a low Actual MREADTIM.

The foregoing is just one example how a bad number can lead the optimizer astray. In this specific case you would be better off having no actual values and relying on the optimizer's guesses, which are shown as the estimated SREADTIM and MREADTIM values. Those guesses would be better than the actual values.

How do you correct a situation like I've just described? It's much easier than you would think. The steps to fix this kind of problem are shown in the list below:

1. Choose a time period that is representative of your workload. For example, you could have a daytime workload called WORKLOAD.

2. Create a table to contain the statistics information. In the example below we have called the table SYSTEM_STATISTICS.

3. Collect the statistics by running the GATHER_SYSTEM_STATS procedure during the chosen time period.

4. Import those statistics using DBMS_STATS.IMPORT_SYSTEM_STATS.

Let's look at the steps for collecting the system statistics for a 2-hour interval in more detail. In the first step we create a table to hold the values we will collect. In the second step we call the routine DBMS_STATS.GATHER_SYSTEM_STATS, with an INTERVAL parameter of 120 minutes. Bear in mind that the interval parameter should be chosen to reflect the period of your representative workload.

```
exec DBMS_STATS.CREATE_STAT_TABLE ('SYS','SYSTEM_STATISTICS');
BEGIN
    DBMS_STATS.GATHER_SYSTEM_STATS ('interval',interval => 120, stattab => 'SYSTEM_
STATISTICS', statid => 'WORKLOAD');
END;
/
execute DBMS_STATS.IMPORT_SYSTEM_STATS(stattab => 'SYSTEM_STATISTICS', statid => 'WORKLOAD',
statown => 'SYS');
```

Once you have done this you can view the values from the SQLT report or from a SELECT statement.

```
SQL> column sname format a20
SQL> column pval2 format a20
SQL> column pname format a20
SQL> set pagesize 100
SQL> select * from sys.aux_stats$;
```

SNAME	PNAME	PVAL1	PVAL2
SYSSTATS_INFO	STATUS		COMPLETED
SYSSTATS_INFO	DSTART		06-20-2016 10:24
SYSSTATS_INFO	DSTOP		06-20-2016 10:44
SYSSTATS_INFO	FLAGS	0	
SYSSTATS_MAIN	CPUSPEEDNW	972.327	
SYSSTATS_MAIN	IOSEEKTIM	10	
SYSSTATS_MAIN	IOTFRSPEED	4096	
SYSSTATS_MAIN	SREADTIM	8.185	
SYSSTATS_MAIN	MREADTIM	55.901	
SYSSTATS_MAIN	CPUSPEED	972	
SYSSTATS_MAIN	MBRC		
SYSSTATS_MAIN	MAXTHR		
SYSSTATS_MAIN	SLAVETHR		

```
13 rows selected.
```

If you get adept at doing this you can even set up different statistics tables for different workloads and import them and delete the old statistics when not needed. To delete the existing statistics you would use

```
SQL> execute DBMS_STATS.DELETE_SYSTEM_STATS;
```

One word of caution, however, with setting and deleting system stats. This kind of operation will influence the behavior of the CBO for every SQL on the system. It follows therefore that any changes to these parameters should be made carefully and tested thoroughly on a suitable test environment. In special cases such as Exadata or Oracle Database Appliance, specific settings are defined as the best practice, such as IOTRFSPEED on Exadata. These should be followed, but even in these cases you may need to collect system statistics. Cases where cell servers are sharing databases can result in non-default appropriate values for system settings. In such cases the only way to determine the correct values is to collect appropriate system statistics during a representative system load.

Cost-Based Optimizer Parameters

Another input into the CBO's decision-making process (for developing your execution plan) would be the CBO parameters. These parameters control various aspects of the cost-based optimizer's behavior. For example, optimizer_dynamic_sampling controls the level of dynamic sampling to be done for SQL execution. Wouldn't it be nice to have a quick look at every system and see the list of parameters that have been changed from the defaults? Well with SQLT that list is right there under "CBO Environment."

Figure 3-5 is an example where almost nothing has been changed. It's simple to tell this because there are only 3 rows in this section of the SQLT HTML report. The value of optimizer_secure_view_merging have been changed from the default. You can tell this because under the "Is Default" column it says "FALSE." What about "optimizer_secure_merging"; this is a non-default setting. Might be worth investigating the reason for this. If you see hundreds of entries here then you should look at the entries carefully and assess if any of the parameters that have been changed are causing you a problem. This example represents a DBA who likes to leave things alone.

CBO Environment

Non-Default or Modified CBO Parameters

[.]
Non-default or modified CBO initialization parameters in effect for the session where SQLT XECUTE was executed. Includes all instances.

#	Is Default[1]	Is Modified[2]	Name	Inst ID	Value	Display Value	Modified on	Is Adjusted	Is Deprecated	Is Basic	Is Session Modifiable	Is System Modifiable
1	FALSE	FALSE	optimizer_secure_view_merging	2	"FALSE"			FALSE	FALSE	FALSE	FALSE	IMMEDIATE
3	FALSE	FALSE	pga_aggregate_target	2	"8589934592"	"8G"		FALSE	FALSE	TRUE	FALSE	IMMEDIATE
4	TRUE	MODIFIED	statistics_level	2	"TYPICAL"			FALSE	FALSE	FALSE	TRUE	IMMEDIATE

(1) TRUE: Parameter value was specified in the parameter file.
(2) FALSE: Parameter has not been modified after instance startup. MODIFIED: Parameter has been modified with ALTER SESSION. SYSTEM_MOD: Parameter has been modified with ALTER SYSTEM.
Go to Top

Figure 3-5. *The CBO environment section. Only 3 records indicates a system very close to the default settings*

Figure 3-6 shows the right-hand section of this same section where we even see the Descriptions of the parameters, in case you've forgotten what they mean.

Is System Modifiable	Is Instance Modifiable	Type	Description
IMMEDIATE	TRUE	1	optimizer secure view merging and predicate pushdown/movearound
IMMEDIATE	TRUE	6	Target size for the aggregate PGA memory consumed by the instance
IMMEDIATE	TRUE	2	statistics level

***Figure 3-6.** The CBO environment parameter descriptions*

Figure 3-7 shows an example where more than just 2 parameters have been changed from their default setting. Now instead of 3 rows of the previous example we have 9 non-default parameters. Each one of these parameters needs to be justified.

CBO Environment

Non-Default or Modified CBO Parameters

[.]
Non-default or modified CBO initialization parameters in effect for the session where SQLT XECUTE was executed. Includes all instances.

#	Is Default[1]	Is Modified[2]	Name	Inst ID	Value	Display Value	Is Adjusted	Is Deprecated	Is Basic	Is Session Modifiable
1	FALSE	FALSE	_b_tree_bitmap_plans	1	"FALSE"		FALSE	FALSE	FALSE	TRUE
2	FALSE	FALSE	_fast_full_scan_enabled	1	"FALSE"		FALSE	FALSE	FALSE	TRUE
3	FALSE	FALSE	_like_with_bind_as_equality	1	"TRUE"		FALSE	FALSE	FALSE	TRUE
4	FALSE	FALSE	_sort_elimination_cost_ratio	1	"5"		FALSE	FALSE	FALSE	TRUE
5	FALSE	FALSE	cursor_sharing	1	"EXACT"		FALSE	FALSE	FALSE	TRUE
6	FALSE	FALSE	optimizer_secure_view_merging	1	"FALSE"		FALSE	FALSE	FALSE	FALSE
7	FALSE	FALSE	pga_aggregate_target	1	"1073741824"	"1G"	FALSE	FALSE	TRUE	FALSE
8	FALSE	FALSE	workarea_size_policy	1	"AUTO"		FALSE	FALSE	FALSE	TRUE
9	TRUE	MODIFIED	statistics_level	1	"TYPICAL"		FALSE	FALSE	FALSE	TRUE

(1) FALSE: Parameter value was specified in the parameter file.
(2) FALSE: Parameter has not been modified after instance startup. MODIFIED: Parameter has been modified with ALTER SESSION. SYSTEM_MOD: Parameter has been modifi
Go to Top

Default Unmodifed CBO Parameters

[+]

***Figure 3-7.** The CBO environment with many non-standard parameter settings*

We also have 4 hidden parameters set (they are preceded by underscores). In this example each of the hidden parameters should be carefully researched to see if it can be explained. If you have kept careful records or commented on your changes you may know why _b_tree_bitmap_plans has been set to FALSE. Often, however, parameters like these can stay set in a system for years with no explanation
The following are common explanations:

- Somebody changed it a while ago, we don't know why, and he/she has left now.

- We don't want to change it in case it breaks something.

This section is useful and can often give you a clue as to what has been changed in the past (perhaps you're new to the current site). Take special note of hidden parameters. Oracle support will take a good look at these and decide if their reason for being still holds true. It is generally true that hidden parameters are not likely doing you any favors, especially if you don't know what they're for. Naturally, you can't just remove them from a production system. You have to build and execute key SQL statements on a test system and then remove those parameters on that test system to see what happens to the overall optimizer cost.

Hints

Continuing our review of the Optimizer environment, we now come to another influence on the CBO behavior and the plans produced. The humble hint. Hints were created to give the DBA some control over what choices the optimizer is allowed to make. A common hint is USE_NL. In the example below I have created two tables called test and test2, each with identical 2 rows created from dba_objects. If I let the optimizer choose a plan it will use a HASH JOIN.

```
SQL> create table test1 as select * from dba_tables;
SQL> create table test2 as select * from dba_tables;

SQL> select count(*) from    test1 t1, test2 t2
where t1.object_id=t2.oject_id;
COUNT(*)
----------
    92697

SQL> set autotrace traceonly explain;
SQL> /
Execution Plan
Plan hash value: 2688559368
-------------------------------------------------------------------------------------
| Id | Operation           | Name  | Rows  | Bytes | TempSpc | Cost (%CPU)| Time     |
-------------------------------------------------------------------------------------
|  0 | SELECT STATEMENT    |       |     1 |    10 |         | 1016   (1)| 00:00:01 |
|  1 |  SORT AGGREGATE     |       |     1 |    10 |         |           |          |
|* 2 |   HASH JOIN         |       | 92697 |  905K |   1544K | 1016   (1)| 00:00:01 |
|  3 |    TABLE ACCESS FULL | TEST2 | 92698 |  452K |         |  433   (1)| 00:00:01 |
|  4 |    TABLE ACCESS FULL | TEST1 | 92697 |  452K |         |  433   (1)| 00:00:01 |
-------------------------------------------------------------------------------------

Predicate Information (identified by operation id):
---------------------------------------------------

   2 - access("T1"."OBJECT_ID"="T2"."OBJECT_ID")

SQL> list
  1* select count(*) from    test1 t1, test2 t2 where t1.object_id=t2.oject_id;
```

The command list above shows the previous DML (Data Manipulation Language). I then amended the SQL to contain a single hint. The syntax for all hints begins with /*+ and ends with */. In the case of USE_NL the portion inside the bracket can take multiple entries representing tables (either a table name, as in our case, or an alias if used). Here is the modified query.

```
SQL> select /*+ USE_NL(T1 T2) */ count(*) from test t1, test2 t2 where t1.object_id=t2.
object_id;

Execution Plan
----------------------------------------------------------------
Plan hash value: 1459699139
----------------------------------------------------------------
```

Id	Operation	Name	Rows	Bytes	Cost (%CPU)	Time
0	SELECT STATEMENT		1	10	39M (1)	00:26:02
1	SORT AGGREGATE		1	10		
2	NESTED LOOPS		92697	905K	39M (1)	00:26:02
3	TABLE ACCESS FULL	TEST1	92697	452K	433 (1)	00:00:01
* 4	TABLE ACCESS FULL	TEST2	1	5	431 (1)	00:00:01

Predicate Information (identified by operation id):

```
   4 - filter("T1"."OBJECT_ID"="T2"."OBJECT_ID")
```

Notice how in the second execution plan a NESTED LOOP was used.

What we're saying to the optimizer is this: "we know you're not as clever as we are, so ignore the rules and just do what we think at this point."

Sometimes using hints is right, but sometimes it's wrong (for example in the example above we went from a cost of 1016 to 39Million). This is not to say that the cost calculations that the optimizer makes are always right. They are not. The reason I mention the optimizer environment is that the optimizer is working with this environment, ignorant of your data. It only has the statistics and other environmental factors to work with. As such, poor statistics or limitations in older versions of Oracle (254 buckets in HEIGHT BALANCED histograms in 11g comes to mind) can cause plans to be unpredictable. In such cases, hints might be enough to point the optimizer in the right direction. Know your data!

Occasionally hints are inherited from old code, and it is a brave developer who removes them in the hope that performance will improve. Hints are also a form of data input to the CBOs process of developing an execution plan. Hints are often needed because the other information fed to the optimizer is wrong. So, for example, if the object statistics are wrong you may *need* to give the optimizer a hint because its statistics are wrong.

Is this the correct way to use a hint? No. The problem with using a hint like this is that it may have been right when it was applied, but it could be wrong later, and in fact it probably is. If you want to tune code, first remove the hints, let the optimizer run free, while feeling the blades of data between its toes, free of encumbrances. Make sure it has good recent, statistics, and see what it comes up with.

You can always get the SQL text that you are evaluating by clicking on the "SQL Text" link from the top section of the SQLT report, so you can check for hints.

But it is important to realize that the hint (in this case, "USE_NL(T1 T2)") must be valid. If the Hint usenot is valid or the hint syntax is not valid, no error is generated and the optimizer carries on as if there was no hint. Look at what happens.

```
SQL> select /*+ MY_HINT(T1 T2) / count(*) from test1 t1, test2 t2 where t1.object_id=t2.
object_id;

Execution Plan
-----------------------------------------------------------
Plan hash value: 2688559368
```

Id	Operation	Name	Rows	Bytes	TempSpc	Cost (%CPU)	Time
0	SELECT STATEMENT		1	10		1016 (1)	00:00:01
1	SORT AGGREGATE		1	10			00:00:01
* 2	HASH JOIN		92697	905K	1544K	1016 (1)	00:00:01
3	TABLE ACCESS FULL	TEST2	92698	452K		433 (1)	00:00:01

```
|   4 |   TABLE ACCESS FULL  | TEST1    |  92697|   452K|       |   433  (1)| 00:00:01
------------------------------------------------------------------------------------

Predicate Information (identified by operation id):
---------------------------------------------------

   1 - access("T1"."OBJECT_ID"="T2"."OBJECT_ID")
```

The optimizer saw my hint, didn't recognize it as a valid hint, ignored it and did its own thing, which in this case was to go back to the hash join.

History of Changes

Often when investigating a performance problem, it is crucial to get an idea when SQL performance changed. Vague reports like "it was fine yesterday" are not precise enough, although they may help you by directing your analysis to a particular time period in your SQLT report. Every change in the optimizer environment (parameter changes) is timestamped. Every time an execution changes a new execution plan is created that is also timestamped, every time an SQL statement is executed its metrics are gathered and stored in the AWR. This is the same source of data that the automatic facilities in Oracle use to suggest improvements in your SQL. SQLT uses these sources to build a history of the executions of your chosen SQL ID. This mine of information is only one click away from the top of the SQLT report. Click on the "Performance History" link under the "Plans" heading from the top of the SQLT HTML report. Depending on how many executions of your SQL there are in the system, you may see something like the screenshot in Figure 3-8 There are other columns in the full HTML report but we'll limit our discussion to the "Opt Env Hash Value" for now.

Plan Performance History

List restricted up to 1000 rows as per tool parameter "r_rows_table_l".
SQL: [+]

#	Inst ID	Begin Time	End Time	Plan Hash Value	Opt Env Hash Value
1	1	2012-02-22/03:00:30	2012-02-22/04:00:56	3817381141	2904154100
2	1	2012-02-22/02:00:36	2012-02-22/03:00:30	350656730	3945002051
3	1	2012-02-21/02:00:01	2012-02-21/03:00:25	350656730	3945002051
4	1	2012-02-19/03:00:13	2012-02-19/04:00:23	350656730	3945002051
5	1	2012-02-19/00:00:49	2012-02-19/01:00:30	350656730	3945002051
6	1	2012-02-18/23:00:34	2012-02-19/00:00:49	350656730	3945002051
7	1	2012-02-17/05:00:07	2012-02-17/06:00:32	3817381141	2904154100
8	1	2012-02-17/04:00:15	2012-02-17/05:00:07	350656730	3945002051
9	1	2012-02-17/03:00:06	2012-02-17/04:00:15	350656730	3945002051
10	1	2012-02-17/02:00:50	2012-02-17/03:00:06	350656730	3945002051
11	1	2012-02-16/03:00:27	2012-02-16/04:00:02	3817381141	2904154100

Figure 3-8. *The optimizer Env Hash Value changed on the February 22 from 3945002051 to 2904154100. This means something in the CBO enviroment changed on that date*

Look at the "Opt Env Hash Value" for the statement history in Figure 3-8. For the one SQL statement that we are analyzing with its list of "Begin Time" and "End Times" we see other changes taking place. For example, the plan hash value changed (for the same SQL statement) and so did the "Opt Env Hash Value." Its value is 2904154100 until February 17, 2012. Then it changes to 3945002051 then back to 2904154100 and then back to 3945002051 (on February 18) and finally back to 2904154100. Something about the optimizer's environment changed on those dates. Did the change improve the situation or make it worse? Notice that every time the optimizer hash value changes, the hash value of the plan changes also. Somebody or something is changing the optimizer's environment and affecting the execution plan.

Column Statistics

One of the example SQLT reports (the first one we looked at) had the following line in the observation (see Figure 3-9 below):

20	TABLE	SYS.USER$	Table CBO statistics are 693 days old: 2014-07-07/05:56:06	[+]
21	TABLE	SYS.USER_EDITIONINGS	Table CBO statistics are 693 days old: 2014-07-07/05:56:06	[+]
22	TABLE	SYS.USER_EDITIONINGS	Table contains 1 column(s) referenced in predicates where the number of buckets is 1 for a "FREQUENCY" histogram.	[+]

Figure 3-9. One of the observations

If I expand the link on the plus at the end of the line we see the following as shown in Figure 3-10. follow the link "table statistics" and we see the following (Figure 3-11).

| 20 | TABLE | SYS.USER$ | Table CBO statistics are 693 days old: 2014-07-07/05:56:06 | [-] Consider gathering fresh table statistics. Old statistics could contain low/high values for which a predicate may be out of range, producing then a poor plan. Suggested sample size: DBMS_STATS.AUTO_SAMPLE_SIZE (default). |

Figure 3-10. Expanding an Observation

Table Statistics

#	Table Name	Owner	Part	Temp	Count[1]	Num Rows[2]	Sample Size[2]	Perc	Last Analyzed[2]
1	LINK$	SYS	NO	N		0	0		2014-07-07/05:55:39
2	OBJ$	SYS	NO	N	92190	19416	19416	100.0	2014-07-07/05:55:44
3	SUM$	SYS	NO	N	2	0	0		2014-07-07/05:56:03
4	USER$	SYS	NO	N		63	63	100.0	2014-07-07/05:56:06
5	USER_EDITIONING$	SYS	NO	N	2	2	2	100.0	2014-07-07/05:56:06

Figure 3-11. Following the Observation Link leads to the evidence

If we decide to check on USER$ some more we could follow the "Tables" link from the main page and check on the columns of the USER$ table by clicking on the "30" under "Table Cols" (see Figure 3-12).

Tables

#	Table Name	Owner	Count[1]	Num Rows[2]	Sample Size[2]	Blocks[2]	Last Analyzed[2]	Table Stats	Table Modif	Table Prop	Table Phys Prop	Table Cons	Table Cols
1	LINK$	SYS		0	0	0	07-JUL-14	Stats		Prop	Phys	3	11
2	OBJ$	SYS	92190	19416	19416	300	07-JUL-14	Stats	Modif	Prop	Phys	9	25
3	SUM$	SYS	2	0	0	0	07-JUL-14	Stats	Modif	Prop	Phys	7	40
4	USER$	SYS		63	63	3	07-JUL-14	Stats	Modif	Prop	Phys	10	30
5	USER_EDITIONING$	SYS	2	2	2	1	07-JUL-14	Stats		Prop	Phys	2	2

***Figure 3-12.** Following the Columns description from the Tables section*

From the column statistics section we can see the low and high values (this screenshot only shows the low values). On the right side of the report you can also see what kind of histogram you have (See Figure 3-13).

SYS.USER$ - Column Statistics

#	In Pred	In Index	In Proj	Col ID	Column Name	Data Default	Not Null with Default Value	Num Rows	Num Nulls	Sample Size	Perc	Num Distinct	Fluctuating NDV[1]	Low Value[2]
1	[+]	[+]	TRUE	1	USER#			63	0	63	100.0	63	FALSE	"0"
2	[+]	[+]	TRUE	3	TYPE#			63	0	63	100.0	2	FALSE	"0"
3	[+]	[+]	TRUE	20	SPARE1			63	0	63	100.0	3	FALSE	"0"
4	[+]	[+]	TRUE	21	SPARE2			63	63		100.0	0	FALSE	
5	[+]	[+]	FALSE	2	NAME			63	0	63	100.0	63	FALSE	"ADM_PARALLEL_EXECUTE_TASK"
6	[+]	FALSE	TRUE	22	SPARE3			63	63		100.0	0	FALSE	
7	FALSE	FALSE	FALSE	4	PASSWORD			63	47	16	100.0	16	FALSE	" "
8	FALSE	FALSE	FALSE	5	DATATS#			63	0	63	100.0	3	FALSE	"0"
9	FALSE	FALSE	FALSE	6	TEMPTS#			63	0	63	100.0	2	FALSE	"0"
10	FALSE	FALSE	FALSE	7	CTIME			63	0	63	100.0	26	FALSE	" 2014/07/07 05:39:13"
11	FALSE	FALSE	FALSE	8	PTIME			63	47	16	100.0	10	FALSE	" 2014/07/07 05:39:13"
12	FALSE	FALSE	FALSE	9	EXPTIME			63	50	13	100.0	10	FALSE	" 2014/07/07 05:39:13"
13	FALSE	FALSE	FALSE	10	LTIME			63	49	14	100.0	10	FALSE	" 2014/07/07 05:39:13"

***Figure 3-13.** Column statistics*

It is possible that the number of buckets does not match the number of distinct values (perhaps old statistics). In 12c where there is a large number of distinct values (> 255) you may see something like this (See Figure 3-14).

Num Distinct	Fluctuating NDV[1]	Low Value[2]	High Value[2]	Last Analyzed	Avg Col Len	Density	Num Buckets	Histogram
9	FALSE	"0"	"50"	2014-07-07 05:55:43	3	2.575196e-05	9	FREQUENCY
44	FALSE	"0"	"115"	2014-07-07 05:55:43	4	2.575196e-05	44	FREQUENCY
9	FALSE	"0"	"50"	2014-07-07 05:55:43	3	2.575196e-05	9	FREQUENCY
4098	FALSE	"2"	"19646"	2014-07-07 05:55:43	2	2.440215e-04	1	NONE
14550	FALSE	"ABSPATH"	"old_values49_T"	2014-07-07 05:55:43	20	6.900000e-05	254	HYBRID

***Figure 3-14.** Hybrid histogram*

In cases where the number of distinct values does not match the number of buckets in a histogram we get behavior caused by the optimizer guessing values between buckets.

Imagine this situation.

Between "STELIOS" and "STEVEN" (adjacent buckets) there is a new user "STEPHAN," who happens to be the biggest owner of objects in OBJ$. Let's say the values are

> STELIOS – 100 objects

> STEVEN – 110 objects

The optimizer now guesses the cardinality of STEPHAN as 105, when in fact STEPHAN has 500 objects. The result is that the CBO's guess for cardinality will be a long way out. We would see this in the execution plan (as an underestimate, if we ran a SQLT XECUTE) and we would drill into the OWNER# column and see that the column statistics were wrong.

To fix this we would gather statistics for SYS.OBJ$.

Out-of-Range Values

The situation the CBO is left with when it has to guess the cardinality between two values is bad enough but is not as bad as the situation when the value in a predicate is out of range: either larger than the largest value seen by the statistics or smaller than the smallest value seen by the statistics. In these cases the optimizer assumes that the estimated value for the out-of-range value tails off toward zero. If the value is well above the highest value, the optimizer may estimate a very low cardinality, say 1. A cardinality of 1 might persuade the optimizer to try a Cartesian join, which would result in very poor performance if the actual cardinality was 10,000. The method of solving such a problem would be the same.

1. Get the execution plan with XECUTE.

2. Look at the execution plan in the Execution Plan section and look at the predicates under "more" as described earlier.

3. Look at the statistics for the columns in the predicates and see if there is something wrong. Examples of signs of trouble would be:

   a. A missing bucket (as described in the previous section)

   b. No histograms but highly skewed data

Out-of-range values can be particularly troublesome when data is being inserted at the higher or lower ends of the current data set. In any case by studying the histograms that appear in SQLT you have a good chance of understanding your data and how it changes with time. This is invaluable information for designing a strategy to tune your SQL or collecting good statistics.

Overestimates and Underestimates

Now let's look at a sample of a piece of SQL having so many joins that the number of operations is up to 96. See Figure 3-15, which shows a small portion of the resulting execution plan.

SQL: [+]

ID	Exec Ord	Operation	Go To	More	Cost²	Estim Card	Last Starts	Last Output Rows	Last Over/Under Estimate¹
0	96	SELECT STATEMENT			444				
1	95	NESTED LOOPS		[+]	446		1	680	
2	93	. NESTED LOOPS		[+]	444	1	1	680	** 680x under
3	91	.. NESTED LOOPS		[+]	442	1	1	680	** 680x under
4	88	... NESTED LOOPS		[+]	440	1	1	680	** 680x under
5	85	.... NESTED LOOPS		[+]	439	1	1	1291	*** 1291x under
6	82	....+ NESTED LOOPS		[+]	438	1	1	1291	*** 1291x under
7	79	....+. NESTED LOOPS		[+]	437	1	1	1291	*** 1291x under
8	76	....+.. VIEW VW_NSO_1		[+]	435	5	1	1319	** 264x under
9	75	....+... HASH UNIQUE		[+]	435	1	1	1319	*** 1319x under
10	74	....+.... VIEW VIEW1		[+]	435	5	1	1319	** 264x under
11	73	....+....+ SORT UNIQUE		[+]	435	5	1	1319	** 264x under
12	72	....+....+. UNION-ALL		[+]	432		1	11985	
13	11	....+....+.. NESTED LOOPS		[+]	268	1	1	0	
14	9	....+....+... HASH JOIN		[+]	266	1	1	0	
15	7	....+....+.... NESTED LOOPS		[+]	265	12	1	0	
16	5	....+....+....+ NESTED LOOPS		[+]	160	52	1	948	* 18x under
17	3	....+....+....+. NESTED LOOPS		[+]	56	52	1	948	* 18x under
18	1	....+....+....+.. INDEX RANGE SCAN UNIQUE1	[+]	[+]	3	52	1	948	* 18x under
19	2	....+....+....+.. INDEX RANGE SCAN FLAT_U1	[+]	[+]	2	1	948	948	1x
20	4	....+....+....+. INDEX RANGE SCAN GROUPS_NUM1	[+]	[+]	2	1	948	948	1x
21	6	....+....+....+ INDEX RANGE SCAN BSIGN_N100	[+]	[+]	2	1	948	0	
22	8	....+....+.... INDEX RANGE SCAN SECURITY200	[+]	[+]	1	1	0	0	
23	10	....+....+... INDEX RANGE SCAN GROUPS_NUM1	[+]	[+]	2	1	0	0	
24	14	....+....+.. NESTED LOOPS		[+]	3	1	1	1	1x

Figure 3-15. *A small part of the execution plan, with 96 steps shown*

How do we handle an execution plan that has 96 steps, or more? Do we hand that plan over to development and tell them to tune it? With SQLT you don't need to do this.

Let's look at this page in more detail, by zooming in on the top right-hand portion and look at the over and under estimates part of the screen (see Figure 3-16).

Estim Card	Last Starts	Last Output Rows	Last Over/Under Estimate¹
	1	680	
1	1	680	** 680x under
1	1	680	** 680x under
1	1	680	** 680x under
1	1	1291	*** 1291x under
1	1	1291	*** 1291x under
1	1	1291	*** 1291x under
5	1	1319	** 264x under

Figure 3-16. *The top right-hand portion of the section showing the execution plan's over- and underestimates*

We know that Figure 3-16 is a SQLT XECUTE report (we know this because we have over- and underestimate values in the report). But what are these over- and underestimates? The numbers in the "Last Over/Under Estimate" column represent by how many factors the actual number of rows expected by the optimizer for that operation is wrong. The rows returned are also dependent on the rows returned from the previous operation. So, for example, if we followed the operation count step by step from "Exec Ord" 1 we would have these steps (See Figure 3-15):

1. INDEX RANGE SCAN actually returned 948 rows

2. INDEX RANGE SCAN actually returned 948 rows

3. The result of step 1 and 2 was fed into a NESTED LOOP that actually returned 948 rows

4. INDEX RANGE SCAN actually returned 948 rows

5. NESTED LOOP (of the previous step with result of step 3)

32	18	....+....+.... INDEX RANGE SCAN MODAL150	[±]	[±]	2	5	0		0	
33	20	....+....+... INDEX RANGE SCAN OBJ200	[±]	[±]	2	11	0		0	
34	33	....+....+.. NESTED LOOPS		[±]	120	1	1		11984	*** 11984x under
35	31	....+....+... NESTED LOOPS		[±]	118	1	1		275	** 275x under
36	29	....+....+... HASH JOIN		[±]	116	1	1		14	* 14x under
37	26	....+....+...+ HASH JOIN		[±]	113	67	1		51	1x
38	24	....+....+...+. HASH JOIN		[±]	20	67	1		51	1x
39	22	....+....+...+.. INDEX RANGE SCAN UNIQUE1	[±]	[±]	3	52	1		948	* 18x under
40	23	....+....+...+.. INDEX FAST FULL SCAN COMMON_SECURITY	[±]	[±]	17	432	1		1334	3x under
41	25	....+....+...+. INDEX FAST FULL SCAN M2000	[±]	[±]	90	127807	1		127604	1x
42	28	....+....+...+ TABLE ACCESS BY INDEX ROWID CMN_SEC_RIGHT	[±]	[±]	2	1	1		11	* 11x under
43	27	....+....+...+. INDEX RANGE SCAN CMN_SEC_RIGHT_IE01	[±]	[±]	1	1	1		11	* 11x under

Figure 3-17. More Steps in the plan

And so on. The best way to approach this kind of problem is to read the steps in the execution plan, understand them, look at the over- and underestimates and from there determine where to focus your attention. Once you have located the biggest under- or overestimates (and some plans sufficiently big for this takes time), then work backward in the plan steps to the earliest plan step that caused that over- or underestimate.

Now look at Figure 3-17. Step ID 34 (which is the third line in Figure 3-17 and the 33rdstep in the execution plan. Remember the execution order is shown by the numbers immediately to the left of the operation names, e.g., INDEX RANGE SCAN) shows an under estimate of 11,984. This NESTED LOOP Is a result of the sections below it. We can drill into why the estimates are as they are by clicking on the "+" in the "More" column. From the "More" column we can look at the access predicates and see why the estimated cardinality and the actual rows returned diverged.

So for large statements like this, we work on each access predicate, each under- and overestimate, working from the biggest estimation error to the smallest until we know the reason for each. Remember to work backward from the point of the over- or underestimate to the line in the plan where the problem originated. In some cases, the cause will be stale statistics. In other cases, it will be skewed data. With SQLT, looking at a 200-line execution plan is no longer a thing to be feared. If you address each error as far as the optimizer is concerned (it expected 10 rows and got 1000), you can, step by step, fix the execution plan. You don't need hints to twist the CBO into the shape you *guess* might be right. You just need to make sure it has good statistics for system performance, single and multi-block read times, CPU speed, and object statistics. Once you have all the right statistics in place, the optimizer will generate a good plan. If the execution plan is sometimes right and sometimes wrong, then you could be dealing with skewed data, in which case you'll need to consider the use of histograms. We discuss skewness as a special topic in much more detail in Chapter 4.

The Case of the Mysterious Change

Now that you've learned a little bit about SQLT and how to use it, we can look at an example without any prior knowledge of what the problem might be. Here is the scenario:

A developer comes to you and says his SQL was fine up until 3 p.m. the previous day. It was doing hash joins as he wanted and expected, so he went to lunch. When he came back the plan had changed completely. All sorts of weird bit map indexes are being used. His data hasn't changed, and he hasn't collected any new statistics. What happened? He ends by saying, "Honest, I didn't change anything,"

Once you've confirmed that the data has not changed, and no one has added any new indexes (or dropped any), you ask for a SQLT XECUTE report (as the SQL is fairly short running and this is a development system).

Once you have that you look at the execution plans. The plan in Figure 3-18 happens to be the one you view first.

SQL: [±]

ID	Exec Ord	Operation	Go To	More	Cost[2]	Estim Card	LAST Starts	LAST Output Rows
0	14	SELECT STATEMENT			78	5557		
1	13	HASH JOIN		[+]	78	5557	1	1127
2	3	. TABLE ACCESS BY INDEX ROWID PRODUCTS	[+]	[+]	1	72	1	72
3	2	.. BITMAP CONVERSION TO ROWIDS		[+]			1	72
4	1	... BITMAP INDEX FULL SCAN PRODUCTS_PROD_STATUS_BIX	[+]	[+]			1	1
5	12	. NESTED LOOPS		[+]	152		1	1127
6	10	.. NESTED LOOPS		[+]	76	5557	1	1127
7	6	... TABLE ACCESS BY INDEX ROWID CUSTOMERS	[+]	[+]	26	43	1	62
8	5	.... BITMAP CONVERSION TO ROWIDS		[+]			1	55500
9	4	....+ BITMAP INDEX FULL SCAN CUSTOMERS_GENDER_BIX	[+]	[+]			1	5
10	9	... PARTITION RANGE ALL		[+]			62	1127
11	8	.... BITMAP CONVERSION TO ROWIDS		[+]			1736	1127
12	7	....+ BITMAP INDEX SINGLE VALUE SALES_CUST_BIX	[+]	[+]			1736	46
13	11	.. TABLE ACCESS BY LOCAL INDEX ROWID SALES	[+]	[+]	76	130	1127	1127

Performance statistics is only available when parameter "statistics_level" was set to "ALL" at hard-parse time, or SQL contains "gather_plan_statistics" hint.
*(1) If estim_card * starts < output_rows then under-estimate. If estim_card * starts > output_rows then over-estimate. Color highlights when exceeding " 10x, "*
(2) Largest contributors for cumulative-statistics columns are shown in red.
Other XML (id=1): [±]
Outline Data (id=1): [±]
Leading (id=1): [±]
Go to Tables
Go to Indexes
Go to Top

Figure 3-18. *Execution plan being investigated*

Looking at the plan, you can confirm what the developer said about a "weird" execution plan with strange bit map indexes. In fact though, there is nothing strange about this plan. It's just that the first step is:

... BITMAP INDEX FULL SCAN **PRODUCTS_PROD_STATUS_BIX**

This step was not in the developer's original plan. Hence the reason the developer perceives it as strange. For the one SQL statement the developer was working with we suspect that there are at least 2 execution plans (there can be dozens of execution plans for the one SQL statement, and SQLT captures them all).

Further down in the list of execution plans, we see that there are indeed plans using hash joins and full table scans. See Figure 3-19, which shows a different execution plan for the same SQL that the developer is working with. In this execution plan, which returns the same rows as the previous execution plan, the overall cost is 908.

SQL: [±]

ID	Exec Ord	Operation	Go To	More	Cost[2]	Estim Card	PStart	PStop	Work Area
0	7	SELECT STATEMENT			908	5557			
1	6	HASH JOIN		[+]	908	5557			[+]
2	1	. TABLE ACCESS FULL PRODUCTS	[+]	[+]	3	72			
3	5	. HASH JOIN		[+]	904	5557			[+]
4	2	.. TABLE ACCESS FULL CUSTOMERS	[+]	[+]	405	43			
5	4	.. PARTITION RANGE ALL		[+]	494	918843	1	28	
6	3	... TABLE ACCESS FULL SALES	[+]	[+]	494	918843	1	28	

Performance statistics is only available when parameter "statistics_level" was set to "ALL" at hard-parse time, or SQL contains "gather_plan_sta
*(1) If estim_card * starts < output_rows then under-estimate. If estim_card * starts > output_rows then over-estimate. Color highlights when excee*
(2) Largest contributors for cumulative-statistics columns are shown in red.
Other XML (id=1): [±]
Outline Data (id=1): [±]
Leading (id=1): [±]
Go to Tables
Go to Indexes
Go to Top

Figure 3-19. *An execution planan showing a hash join*

So far we know there was a plan involving a hash join and bitmap indexes and that earlier there were plans with full table scans. If we look at the times of the statistics collection we see that indeed the statistics were gathered before the execution of these queries. This is a good thing, as statistics should be collected before the execution of a query! Let me make that crystal clear, in case you decide this means collecting statistics before every execution of a query is a good idea. Collect relevant, meaningful statistics before every query once, or until there is a significant change in the data that will influence the optimizer. So for example if one table never changes, fix the statistics for that table (although you should review your assumption on a regular basis). If the data changes every time it is loaded, then you should collect statistics after loading. The important thing is that the statistics must accurately represent the data. This is the assumption implicit in the CBO. Some sites take the view that if it ain't broke don't fix it and leave the statistics unchanged unless a query regresses. This policy will seem like a good idea, until the day multiple queries regress and you find all your statistics are out of date. Then where do you start?

■ **Note**   As an aside, the ability of SQLT to present all relevant information quickly and easily is its greatest strength. It takes the guesswork out of detective work. Without SQLT, you would probably have to dig out a query to show you the time that the statistics were collected. With SQLT, the time of the collection of the statistics is right there in the report. You can check it while still thinking about the question!

So what happened in our case? The statistics are unchanged since they were collected before the query and the SQL text didn't change. It's possible that an index was added sometime over lunchtime. You can check that by looking at the objects section of the report, as shown in Figure 3-20.

Objects

Restricted list of objects related to the SQL being analyzed. Partitions and Subpartitions are excluded.
Further restricted up to 1000 rows as per tool parameter "r_rows_table_l".
SQL: [+]

#	Object Type	Object Name	Object Owner	Object ID	Data Object ID	Created	Last DDL Time
1	INDEX	CUSTOMERS_GENDER_BIX	SH	74363	73904	2011-10-11/20:27:00	2011-10-11/20:27:00
2	INDEX	CUSTOMERS_MARITAL_BIX	SH	74364	73905	2011-10-11/20:27:00	2011-10-11/20:27:00
3	INDEX	CUSTOMERS_PK	SH	74152	73681	2011-10-11/20:26:54	2011-10-11/20:26:54
4	INDEX	CUSTOMERS_YOB_BIX	SH	74365	73906	2011-10-11/20:27:00	2011-10-11/20:27:00
5	INDEX	PRODUCTS_PK	SH	74144	73682	2011-10-11/20:26:52	2011-10-11/20:26:52
6	INDEX	PRODUCTS_PROD_CAT_IX	SH	74146	73903	2011-10-11/20:26:52	2011-10-11/20:26:52
7	INDEX	PRODUCTS_PROD_STATUS_BIX	SH	74362	73901	2011-10-11/20:27:00	2011-10-11/20:27:00
8	INDEX	PRODUCTS_PROD_SUBCAT_IX	SH	74145	73902	2011-10-11/20:26:52	2011-10-11/20:26:52
9	INDEX	SALES_CHANNEL_BIX	SH	74246		2011-10-11/20:26:58	2011-10-11/20:26:58
10	INDEX	SALES_CUST_BIX	SH	74188		2011-10-11/20:26:57	2011-10-11/20:26:57
11	INDEX	SALES_PROD_BIX	SH	74159		2011-10-11/20:26:57	2011-10-11/20:26:57
12	INDEX	SALES_PROMO_BIX	SH	74275		2011-10-11/20:26:59	2011-10-11/20:26:59
13	INDEX	SALES_TIME_BIX	SH	74217		2011-10-11/20:26:58	2011-10-11/20:26:58
14	TABLE	CUSTOMERS	SH	74151	73676	2011-10-11/20:26:54	2011-10-11/20:28:04
15	TABLE	PRODUCTS	SH	74143	73673	2011-10-11/20:26:52	2011-10-11/20:28:04
16	TABLE	SALES	SH	74083		2011-10-11/20:26:43	2011-10-11/20:28:04

Go to Top

Figure 3-20. *Object information and creation times*

The objects section in Figure 3-20 will confirm the creation date of the index PRODUCTION_PROD_
STATUS_BIX. As you can see, the index used in the BITMAP INDEX FULL SCAN was created long ago. So
where are we now?

Let's review the facts:

- No new indexes have been added.

- The plan has changed — it uses more indexes.

- The statistics haven't changed.

Now you need to consider what else can change an execution plan. Here are some possibilities:

- System statistics. We check those, and they seem OK. Knowing what normal looks
  like helps here.

- Hints. We look to be sure. There are no hints in the SQL text.

- CBO parameters. We look and see the values in Figure 3-21.

CBO Environment

Non-Default or Modified CBO Parameters

[-]
Non-default or modified CBO initialization parameters in effect for the session where S(

#	Is Default[1]	Is Modified[2]	Name	Inst ID	Value	Display Value
1	FALSE	MODIFIED	statistics_level	1	"TYPICAL"	
2	TRUE	MODIFIED	_parallel_syspls_obey_force	1	"TRUE"	
3	TRUE	MODIFIED	optimizer_index_cost_adj	1	"1"	

(1) FALSE: Parameter value was specified in the parameter file.
(2) FALSE: Parameter has not been modified after instance startup. MODIFIED: Parameter has been r
Go to Top

Figure 3-21. *The CBO environment section*

Figure 3-21 shows statistics_level, *_parallel_*syspls_obey_force, and optimizer_index_cost_adj. This is in the section "Non-Default CBO Parameters," so you know they are not normal values. As optimizer_index_cost_adj is a parameter for adjusting the cost used by the optimizer for indexes this may have something to do with our change in execution plan. Then notice that the "Observations" section (see Figure 3-22) highlights that there are non-standard parameters.

Observations

List of concerns identified by the health-check module. Please review. Some may require further attention.

#	Type	Name	Observation
1	CBO PARAMETER	NON-DEFAULT	There is one CBO initialization parameter with a non-default value.
2	CBO PARAMETER	MODIFIED	There are 3 CBO initialization parameters with a modified value.

Figure 3-22. *The "Observation" section of the HTML report shows non-default and modified parameters, in this case 3 modified parameters*

If you look up optimizer_index_cost_adj, you will see that its default is 100 not 1. So now you have a working theory: The problem could lie with that parameter.

Now you can go to the users terminal, run his query, set the session value for optimizer_index_cost_adj to 100, re-run the query and see the different execution plan. We see the results below.

```
Execution Plan
-------------------------------------------------------------
Plan hash value: 725901306
----------------------------------------------------------------------------------
| Id | Operation              | Name      | Rows  | Bytes | Cost (%CPU)| Time     ||
----------------------------------------------------------------------------------
|  0 | SELECT STATEMENT       |           | 5557  | 303K|  908    (3)| 00:00:11 ||
|* 1 |  HASH JOIN             |           | 5557  | 303K|  908    (3)| 00:00:11 ||
|  2 |   TABLE ACCESS FULL    | PRODUCTS  |   72  | 2160 |    3    (0)| 00:00:01 ||
|* 3 |   HASH JOIN            |           | 5557  | 141K|  904    (3)| 00:00:11 ||
|* 4 |    TABLE ACCESS FULL   | CUSTOMERS |   43  | 516  |  405    (1)| 00:00:05 ||
|  5 |    PARTITION RANGE ALL|           | 918K|  12M|  494    (3)| 00:00:06 ||
|  6 |     TABLE ACCESS FULL  | SALES     | 918K|  12M|  494    (3)| 00:00:06 ||
----------------------------------------------------------------------------------
Predicate Information (identified by operation id):
-------------------------------------------------
   1 - access("S"."PROD_ID"="P"."PROD_ID")
   3 - access("C"."CUST_ID"="S"."CUST_ID")
   4 - filter("C"."CUST_FIRST_NAME"='Theodorick')
SQL> alter session set optimizer_index_cost_adj=1;
Session altered.
SQL> @q2
Execution Plan
Plan hash value: 665279032
-------------------------------------------------------------------------------------
| Id | Operation                       | Name                     |Rows |Bytes|Cost(%CPU)|
| 0  | SELECT STATEMENT                |                          | 5557| 303K|  78   (7)|
|* 1 |  HASH JOIN                      |                          | 5557| 303K|  78   (7)|
| 2  |   TABLE ACCESS BY INDEX ROWID   | PRODUCTS                 |   72|2160 |   1   (0)|
| 3  |    BITMAP CONVERSION TO ROWIDS  |                          |     |     |          |
| 4  |     BITMAP INDEX FULL SCAN      | PRODUCTS_PROD_STATUS_BIX |     |     |          |
| 5  |   NESTED LOOPS                  |                          |     |     |          |
| 6  |    NESTED LOOPS                 |                          | 5557| 141K|  76   (6)|
|* 7 |     TABLE ACCESS BY INDEX ROWID | CUSTOMERS                |   43| 516 |  26   (4)|
| 8  |      BITMAP CONVERSION TO ROWIDS|                          |     |     |          |
| 9  |       BITMAP INDEX FULL SCAN    | CUSTOMERS_GENDER_BIX     |     |     |          |
| 10 |     PARTITION RANGE ALL         |                          |     |     |          |
| 11 |      BITMAP CONVERSION TO ROWIDS|                          |     |     |          |
|*12 |       BITMAP INDEX SINGLE VALUE | SALES_CUST_BIX           |     |     |          |
| 13 | TABLE ACCESS BY LOCAL INDEX ROWID| SALES                   | 130|1820 |  76   (6)|
Predicate Information (identified by operation id):
   1 - access("S"."PROD_ID"="P"."PROD_ID")
   7 - filter("C"."CUST_FIRST_NAME"='Theodorick')
  12 - access("C"."CUST_ID"="S"."CUST_ID")
```

Now we have a cause and a fix, which can be applied to just the one session or to the entire system.

The next step of course is to find out why optimizer_index_cost_adj was set, but that's a different story, involving the junior DBA (or at least hopefully not you!) who set the parameter at what he thought was session level but turned out to be system level.

Summary

In the chapter we learned about the inputs to the cost-based optimizer's algorithm and how these inputs affect the optimizer. For the optimizer to work effectively and efficiently, these inputs need to be considered and set up in a way that reflects the usage of your environment and business requirements. SQLTXPLAIN helps with all of the environmental considerations by collecting information and displaying it in a way that is easy to understand. SQLTXPLAIN also helpfully highlights those elements that are out of the ordinary so that you can consider them more critically and decide if those elements are needed and are what you intended. In the next chapter we consider one of the most important aspects of the CBO environment, the object statistics. These take the most time to collect by far and are very frequently the cause of performance problems. We'll look at the effect of lack of statistics, poor timing of statistics, and other elements of this important maintenance job.

CHAPTER 4

■ ■ ■

How Object Statistics Can Make Your Execution Plan Wrong

In this chapter we'll discuss what is considered a very important subject if you are tuning SQL. Collecting good statistics! They know that under most circumstances, DBAs who are under pressure to get their work done as quickly as possible, in the tiny maintenance windows they are allowed, will opt for the easiest and simplest way forward. If there is a check box that says "click me, all your statistics worries will be over," they'll click it and move on to the next problem. In Oracle 12c there is even more automated collection of statistics and even more options for column types. (We cover some options in Chapter 6).

The automated procedure has, of course, improved over the years, and the latest algorithms for automatically collecting statistics on objects (and on columns especially) are very sophisticated. However, this does not mean you can ignore them. You need to pay attention to what's being collected and make sure it's appropriate for your data structures and queries. In this chapter we'll cover how partitions affect your plans. We'll also look at how to deal with sampling errors and how to lock statistics and when this should be done. If this sounds boring, then that's where SQLT steps in and makes the whole process simpler and quicker. Let's start with object statistics.

What Are Statistics?

When SQL performs badly, poor-quality statistics are the most common cause. Poor-quality statistics cover a wide range of possible deficiencies:

- Inadequate sample sizes.

- Infrequently collected samples.

- No samples on some objects.

- Collecting histograms when not needed.

- Not collecting histograms when needed.

- Collecting statistics at the wrong time.

- Collecting very small sample sizes on histograms.

- Not using more advanced options like extended statistics to set up correlation between related columns.

- Relying on auto sample collections and not checking what has been collected.

© Stelios Charalambides 2017
S. Charalambides, *Oracle SQL Tuning with Oracle SQLTXPLAIN*, DOI 10.1007/978-1-4842-2436-6_4

It is crucial to realize that the mission statement of the cost-based optimizer (CBO) is to develop an execution plan that runs fast and to develop it quickly. Let's break that down a little:

- "Develop quickly." The optimizer has very little time to parse or to get the statistics for the object, or to try quite a few variations in join methods, not to mention to check for SQL optimizations and develop what it considers a good plan. It can't spend a long time doing this; otherwise, working out the plan could take longer than doing the work.

- "Runs fast." Here, the key idea is that "wall clock time" is what's important. The CBO is not trying to minimize I/Os or CPU cycles, it's just trying to reduce the elapsed time. If you have multiple CPUs, and the CBO can use them effectively, it will choose a parallel execution plan.

Chapter 1 discussed cardinality, which is the number of rows that satisfy a predicate. This means that the cost of any operation is made up of three operation classes:

- Cost of single-block reads

- Cost of multi-block reads

- Cost of the CPU used to do everything

When you see a cost of 1,000, what does that actually mean? An operation in the execution plan with a cost of 1,000 means that the time taken will be *approximately* the cost of doing 1,000 single-block reads.

The translation of estimated cost to estimated elapsed time is more sophisticated in later versions of Oracle (11gR2 onward) and involves I/O calibration. The result is that E-Time may not exactly be the product of cost and sreadtim, but this doesn't really matter since we work with cost, not e-time, since this is what the optimizer does. Think of it this way: cost is an estimate calculated by the optimizer, then e-time is even more of an estimate.

So in the case of a plan with a cost of 1,000 the time taken will be the time taken to do 1,000 single-block I/Os on the machine on which the plan was developed. In this case 1,000 x 12 ms, which gives 12 seconds. This takes into account that machines can take a different amount of time to do the same SQL (different machine characteristics).

So what steps does the CBO take to determine the best execution plan? In very broad terms the query is transformed (put in form which will better allow the optimizer algorithms to take advantage of improvements in performance), and then plans are generated by looking at the size of the tables and deciding which table will be the inner and which will be the outer table in joins. Different join orders are tried and different access methods are tried. By "tried" I mean that the optimizer will go through a limited number of steps (its aim is to develop a plan quickly, remember) to calculate a cost for each of them and by a process of elimination get to the best plan. Sometimes the options the optimizer tries are not a complete list of plans, and this means it could miss the best plan. This is the estimation phase of the operation. If the operation being evaluated is a full table scan, this will be estimated based on the number of rows, the average length of the rows, the speed of the disk subsystem, and so on.

Now that we know what the optimizer is doing to try and get you the right plan, we can look at what can go wrong when the object statistics are misleading.

Object Statistics

The main components comprising object statistics are tables and indexes. To simplify the discussion, we will mainly look at table statistics, but the same principles will apply to all objects. In the estimation phase of the hard parsing mentioned above, where size of tables is estimated and joins are chosen, the number of rows in the table is crucial. A simple example would be a choice between a nested loop or a hash join. If the number of rows is wrong, then the join method may be wrong. Other ways in which statistics can be wrong is by being out of date. Let's look at the example in Figure 4-1. In this example we see "Table Statistics" for TABLE_A, a non-partitioned table with a row count of 92,190, which was 100 percent analyzed.

Table Statistics

#	Table Name	Owner	Part	Temp	Count[1]	Num Rows[2]	Sample Size[2]	Perc	Last Analyzed[2]
1	LINK$	SYS	NO	N		0	0		2014-07-07/05:55:39
2	OBJ$	SYS	NO	N	92190	19416	19416	100.0	2014-07-07/05:55:44

Figure 4-1. In the "Table Statistics" section you can see the number of rows in a table, the sample size, and the percentage of the total data set that this sample represents

Object statistics are a vital input to the CBO, but even these can lead the optimizer astray when the statistics are out of date. The CBO also uses past execution history to determine if it needs better sampling or makes use of bind peeking to determine which of many potential execution plans to use. Many people rely on setting everything on AUTO but this is not a panacea. Even this can go wrong if you don't understand what it is doing for you.

Just to clarify, in the very simplest terms, why does the optimizer get it wrong when the statistics are out of date? After all once you've collected all that statistical information about your tables, why collect it again? Let's do a thought experiment just like Einstein sitting in the trolley bus in Vienna.

Imagine you've been told there are few rows in a partition (<1,000 rows) that match your predicate. You're probably going to do a index scan and not use the full table scan, but if your statistics are out of date and you've had a massive data load (say 2.5 million rows) since the last time they ran and all of them match your predicate, then your plan is going to be suboptimal. That's tuning-speak for "regressed," which is also tuning-speak for "too slow for your manager." This underlines the importance of collecting statistics at the right time: after the data loads, not before.

So far we've mentioned table statistics and how these statistics need to be of the right quality and of a timely nature. As data sets grew larger and larger over the years, so too did tables grow larger. Some individual tables became very large (terabytes in size). This made handling these tables more difficult, purely because operations on these tables took longer. Oracle Corporation saw this trend early on and introduced table partitioning. These mini tables split a large table into smaller pieces partitioned by different keys. A common key is a date. So one partition of a table might cover 2012. This limited the size of these partitions and allowed operations to be carried out on individual partitions. This was a great innovation (that has a license cost associated with it) that simplified many day-to-day tasks for the DBA and allowed some great optimizer opportunities for SQL improvement. For example, if a partition is partitioned by date and you use a date in your predicate you might be able to use partition pruning , which only looks at the matching partitions. With this feature come great opportunities for improvement in response times but also a greater possibility you'll get it wrong. Just like tables, partitions need to have good statistics gathered for them to work effectively.

Partitions

Partitions are a great way to deal with large data sets, especially ones that are growing constantly. Use a range partition, or even better, an interval partition. These tools allow "old" data and "new" data to be separated and treated differently, perhaps archiving old data or compressing it. Whatever the reason, many institutions use partitioning to organize their data. Especially with partitions based on date, it is common to have a new partition created that has zero or very few rows just after it is created (see Figure 4-2 for an example of this situation). The new partition MAIN_TABLE_201202 has zero rows (it's only just been created), but the other partitions have millions.

List is restricted up to 1000 rows as per tool parameter "r_rows_table_l".
SQL: [+]

#	Part Pos	Partition Name	Composite	Sub Part Count	Num Rows[1]	Sample Size[1]	Perc
1	5	MAIN_TABLE_201202	NO	0	0		
2	4	MAIN_TABLE_201201	NO	0	21538894	21538894	100.0
3	3	MAIN_TABLE_201112	NO	0	20191792	20191792	100.0
4	2	MAIN_TABLE_201111	NO	0	18245699	18245699	100.0
5	1	MAIN_TABLE_201110	NO	0	19329406	19329406	100.0

(1) CBO Statistics.

Figure 4-2. *A newly created partition will have different characteristics than an old partition. In this case, the number of partitions in MAIN_TABLE_201202 is zero*

For the recently finished partition, any new data added will not result in a huge change in the actual data versus the statistics, but for the newly created partition the optimizer currently thinks there are zero rows in this partition. How will this affect the execution plan if there are now 10,000 rows just a few hours after the statistics were collected? This kind of "initialization" of partitions can have a huge impact on execution plans, the kind of impact that comes and goes with the time of the month. Bad on the first of the month, then gradually better.

These types of situations require careful timing of statistics, collections, and good samples. During the time just after the creation of a new partition, there may be periods of time when a higher sample collection percentage of a partition is beneficial in order to collect any unusually skewed data in that time partition. Just being aware of what is (or could) be happening, is half the battle. If more statistics collections are not an option soon after the load, then you may have to resort to SQL Profiles or even hints.

Stale Statistics

From the point of view of SQLT if more than 10 percent of the data in a table has changed then the statistics are marked with a "YES" in the "Stale Stats" column. In the example below (Figure 4-3) you can see an index with stale statistics.

Avg Leaf Blocks per Key[1]	Avg Data Blocks per Key[1]	Clustering Factor[1]	Global Stats[1]	User Stats[1]	Stat Type Locked	Stale Stats	Avg Cached Blocks
1	1	5	YES	NO		YES	

Figure 4-3. An index row is shown with "Stale Stats" as "YES" in this example, indicating stale statistics for this index

What should you do with this information? That depends. Sometimes stale statistics are not a problem; it may be that even though the table has changed by more than 10 percent, the data could still be the same statistically. Ten percent is a pretty arbitrary number, and in some situations you may decide that it's too low or too high. If so, you can always change it

```
SQL> exec dbms_stats.set_table_prefs(null,'USER2','STALE_PERCENT',5)
```

Having said that, what should you do if you see "YES" in the Stale Stats column for a particular table or index? The simple answer is (once again), "It depends." It's like a murder mystery. If you already suspect that the butler did it, and then you see he has a gun in his pocket, that might be a good lead.

The point here is that the column would be a clue that something was wrong, and that it might be materially important in your current investigation. For example, suppose you have a table with an interval partition created and loaded with data every day. Its statistics are going to be STALE unless you run statistics collection every day after you load data in a new partition. The key is to realize that statistics collection is a tool provided by Oracle that you can use in many different ways. That control must be informed by your knowledge of the architecture, the data model, and the queries you expect on your database.

Sampling Size

This is one of the most hotly argued points of statistics collection. Many sites depend on the DBMS_STATS. AUTO_SAMPLE_SIZE, and this is a good choice for some if not most situations, but it's not perfect. It's just a good starting point. If you have no problems with your queries, and your statistics run in a reasonable time, then leave the defaults and go do something more useful.

If you struggle to collect the level of statistics you need to get your online day working efficiently, you may want to look closely at the statistics you are gathering. If 100 percent is not possible, then work out how much time you do have, and try to aim for that percentage. Look at what you are collecting and see if all of it is needed. If you are gathering schema stats, then ask yourself: Are all the tables in the schema being used? Are you collecting statistics on columns with no skewness? In such situations you are wasting resources collecting information that will make no difference to the optimizer. It stands to reason that changing statistics collection sample sizes should be done carefully and in small steps, with enough time between changes to evaluate the effect. This is what test systems are for.

You can see what you have set up on the system by clicking on the "DBMS_STATS" setup hyperlink from the SQLT report (Figure 4-4).

DBMS_STATS Setup

- DBMS_STATS System Preferences
- DBMS_STATS Table Preferences
- Auto Task "auto optimizer stats collection"
- Statistics for SYS Tables
- Statistics for Fixed Objects
- DBMS_STATS Operations History

Go to Top

DBMS_STATS System Preferences

Approximate NDV:	"null"
Auto Stats Target:	AUTO
Cascade:	DBMS_STATS.AUTO_CASCADE
Concurrent:	"null"
Degree:	NULL
Estimate Percent:	DBMS_STATS.AUTO_SAMPLE_SIZE
Granularity:	AUTO
Incremental Internal Control:	"null"
Incremental:	FALSE
Method Opt:	FOR ALL COLUMNS SIZE AUTO
No Invalidate:	DBMS_STATS.AUTO_INVALIDATE
Publish:	TRUE
Stale Percent:	10
Stats Retention:	"null"

Figure 4-4. *It's always good to check what DBMS_STATS preferences you have. In this example, everything is set to the defaults*

Here you can see the DBMS_STATS preferences. Everything is set to AUTO. The "Estimate Percent" is set to the default DBMS_STATS.AUTO_SAMPLE_SIZE; "Cascade" is set to DBMS_STATS.AUTO_CASCADE; and "Method Opt" is set to FOR ALL COLUMNS SIZE AUTO.

Do any of these settings cause problems? Generally not. Sometimes, however, the sample sizes can be very small. This is a deliberate attempt by the algorithm designers to reduce the amount of time spent gathering statistics on these columns. If too many samples are similar, then the algorithm will decide that there is no point in looking any further and will finish collecting for the column. If from the top of the SQLT report we click on "columns," we are able to see the "Table Columns" area of the report. From here, if we click on "Column Stats" for one of the columns we can see column statistics. Of special interest are the sample sizes and the percentage that these represent (about halfway across the report). See Figure 4-5 for an example of this area (I've only shown columns 8 to 12 of the report) Notice that some sample sizes are extremely small.

Num Rows	Num Nulls	Sample Size	Perc	Num Distinct
1960484	0	6230	0.3	1960484
1960484	0	6230	0.3	11
1960484	225148	1735336	100.0	1411500
1960484	0	6230	0.3	1584
1960484	118405	375575	20.4	332886
1960484	0	6230	0.3	3123
1960484	0	6230	0.3	3121

Figure 4-5. *In this section of the "Column Statistics" example (found by clicking on the "Columns" hyperlink from the top of the report) the auto sampling size has collected very small sample sizes of 0.3 percent*

So how do we get such small sample sizes? Imagine organizing your socks. You're a real fan of socks, so you have ten drawers full of socks. You want to know how many types of socks you have. You look in the first drawer and pick a pair of socks at random. Black. The second pair is also black, and the third. Do you keep going? Or do you now assume all the socks are black? You see the problem. The algorithm is trying to be efficient and will sample randomly, but if it is unlucky it may get too many similar samples and give up. What if there are millions of socks and they are all black except one pair (gold with silver stripes). You probably will not find that pair in your random sample. But suppose further that you love those gold-and-silvery striped socks and you want to wear them every day. In this case you will always do a full table scan of your sock drawer (as you think most socks are black and you think that all colored socks you look for will have the same distribution). This sounds counterintuitive, but you need to see that the optimizer has no idea about your actual data distribution in that column, it only has a sample (and a very small one). It then applies the rules it has worked out for that drawer for all sock searches. In fact your sock color distribution is highly skewed, and the one rare sock pair is the one you want to query all the time. Data is exactly the same. Random samples may not pick up the rare skewed values and if these are popular in queries, you may need to adjust your column sample size. In 11g the sample sizes were very small (often a few percent of all of the rows) but in 12c all rows are sampled.

How to Gather Statistics

SQLT can help you come up with a methodology to use when creating a plan for gathering statistics. For preproduction environments with a realistic workload, you'll find it sensible to run a SQLT report on key SQL statements (the ones performing badly) and look at the overall performance. Don't rely on the overall runtime alone to decide if your workload is going to be OK. Choose the top SQLs, as identified by AWR or SQL Tuning Advisor. You can even pick them off Enterprise Manager (see Figure 4-6).

Top SQL

Select	Activity (%)	SQL ID	SQL Type
☐	6.67	d972cwyzqpk6a	SELECT
☐	6.67	5r2nw00888cpc	SELECT
☐	4.44	fndjrj10u6q7d	SELECT
☐	2.22	7kqy5g7jg9578	SELECT
☐	2.22	a7c82d9hfgy28	INSERT
☐	2.22	at02ugrkdshca	SELECT
☐	2.22	1170gkqwym6n4	SELECT
☐	2.22	61sqzmg58ghqm	SELECT
☐	2.22	463gmquwstd4	SELECT
☐	2.22	502bbjd9s5mxj	INSERT

Actions Schedule SQL Tuning Advisor ☑ (Go)

Total Sample Count: 45

Figure 4-6. *You can even select the Top SQL to investigate from OEM*

Then run a SQLT XTRACT report and look at the statistics for these SQLs. Remember, you've picked the heavy hitters on the system so you need to tune these SQLs' statistics gathering to improve their performance (if possible) while having no adverse effect on other queries. If you can see sample sizes less than 100%, *which are adversely affecting performance,* then you have a candidate for statistics collection amendments.

In 12c you can set preferences for statistics gathering at many granular levels; at the database level (dbms_stats.set_database_prefs) the schema level (dbms_stats.set_schema_prefs), or the table level (dbms_stats.set_table_prefs). Don't just increase the percentage blindly because performance is bad. Look at the SQL that performs badly and tune those SQL statements. Turning up all statistics to 100 percent will just eat up resources and in some cases will not collect enough statistics on columns. This is why it is important to look at what is actually happening.

Saving and Restoring and Locking Statistics

Saving and restoring statistics can be extremely useful. In an earlier example, you saw that collecting statistics at the wrong time could break your execution plan. If you collected statistics when a table was empty you need to make another statistics collection when the table has a representative data set in it. On the other hand, if you collect statistics when the data in the table are representative, you can save that collection and later restore it for that table. This should allow you to represent the newly loaded table correctly, while collecting statistics at a convenient time. See Figure 4-7 below.

You can also lock statistics from a convenient time.

```
begin
dbms_stats.lock_table_stats(ownname=> 'STELIOS', tabname=> 'TEST2' );
end;
```

Figure 4-7. *If your table statistics are very volatile, you may be better off locking them*

Here is an example sequence to collect statistics on an object and save them to a table called MYSTATS2.

```
SQL> create table test2 as select object_id from dba_objects;

Table created.

SQL> exec dbms_stats.gather_table_stats('STELIOS','TEST2');

PL/SQL procedure successfully completed.

SQL> exec dbms_stats.create_stat_table('STELIOS','MYSTATS2');

PL/SQL procedure successfully completed.

SQL> delete from test2;

92686 rows deleted.

SQL> commit;

Commit complete.

SQL> select count(*) from test2;

  COUNT(*)
----------
         0

SQL> exec dbms_stats.import_table_stats('STELIOS','TEST2',null,'MYSTATS2');

PL/SQL procedure successfully completed.

SQL>
```

These simple steps are all that is required to save statistics for later use. This is what SQLT does for you when you collect information about an SQL statement. The statistics for the objects are collected together and placed into the ZIP file so you can build test cases where a query will work as if it were on production but requires no data. We'll look at creating a test case in Chapter 18. It is one of the most useful tools you get with SQLT.

The Case of the Midnight Truncate

Time to look at the second case in our detective series. You're new onsite and see a query with lots of hints. When you ask about it and why it has so many hints, you're told that the execution plan is wrong if the hints are removed. You also notice that Cartesian joins have been disabled with _optimizer_cartesian_ enabled=FALSE (see Figure 4-8).

CBO Environment

Non-Default or Modified CBO Parameters

[.]
Non-default or modified CBO initialization parameters in effect for the session where S

#	Is Default[1]	Is Modified[2]	Name	Inst ID	Value	Display Value
1	FALSE	FALSE	_optimizer_cartesian_enabled	4	"FALSE"	

(1) FALSE: Parameter value was specified in the parameter file.

(2) FALSE: Parameter has not been modified after instance startup. MODIFIED: Parameter has been

Go to Top

Figure 4-8. *The CBO Environment section can often reveal "odd" parameter settings*

Now I'm not suggesting that you leap into every situation and remove hints without thinking, but SQLs with hints are sometimes a sign of something else that is going wrong. Usually the culprit is Moriarty, I mean statistics, of course! Don't be prejudiced; always go with the evidence, so the first thing to do is collect some. In a duplicate environment you run the query without hints.

First look at the execution plan, specifically the one in memory (see Figure 4-9).

SQL Text: [+]
SQL: [+]

ID	Exec Ord	Operation	Go To	More	Peek Bind	Capt Bind	Cost[2]	Estim Card	LAST Starts	LAST Output Rows	OBSY Over/Under Estimate[1]	PStart	PStop
0	15	INSERT STATEMENT					3		1	1			
1	14	LOAD AS SELECT	[+]				3		1	1			
2	13	. HASH GROUP BY	[+]				3	1	521158	1	*** 521158x under		
3	12	.. FILTER	[+]	[+]	[+]		4		1	6959622			
4	11	... NESTED LOOPS	[+]				4		1	6959622			
5	9	.... NESTED LOOPS	[+]				2		1	6959622	*** 6959622x under		
6	8	....+ NESTED LOOPS	[+]				0		1	6959622	*** 6959622x under		
7	2	....+. PARTITION RANGE ITERATOR	[+]				0		1	1361000	*** 1361000x under	KEY	KEY
8	1	....+.. INDEX RANGE SCAN INDEX1	[+]	[+]	[+]	[+]	0		1	1361000	*** 1361000x under	KEY	KEY
9	5	....+. PARTITION RANGE AND	[+]				0	1	1361000	6959622		KEY(AP)	KEY(AP)
10	4	....+.. INLIST ITERATOR	[+]				0		1361000	6959622			
11	3	....+... INDEX RANGE SCAN INDEX2	[+]	[+]	[+]	[+]	0	8	8166000	6959622	1x	KEY(AP)	KEY(AP)
12	8	....+ PARTITION RANGE AND	[+]				1	1	6964549	6959622	1x	KEY(AP)	KEY(AP)
13	7	....+. INDEX UNIQUE SCAN INDEX3	[+]	[+]	[+]	[+]	1	1	6964549	6959622	1x	KEY(AP)	KEY(AP)
14	10	.... TABLE ACCESS BY LOCAL INDEX ROWID TAB1	[+]	[+]			2	1	6991373	6959622	1x	1	1

Figure 4-9. *This execution plan has a glaring problem (highlighted in red no less)*

Luckily SQLT has done all the work for you. Following a SQLT XECUTE you saw that in the current execution plan, on Execution Step 1, the INDEX RANGE SCAN, the optimizer expected a cardinality of 1. (To see this look at the Exec Ord column, go down until you find "1." This is the first line to be executed.)

Then read across until you get to the Estim Card column. Here you'll see a value of "1". But as this was a SQLT XECUTE the SQL was executed, and the actual number of rows returned was greater than a million. The 1 row was expected, but there were actually 1 million rows. This is a big clue that something is wrong. The question at this point is, "Why does the optimizer think the cardinality is going to be 1"?

Look at the Cost column. You will see that the cost is expected to be 0. The optimizer thinks there is no cost in retrieving this data.

To continue following the evidence-based trail you have to know the situation with the index statistics.

Take a look at the index. You can expand the button in the Go To column to display more links (see Figure 4-10).

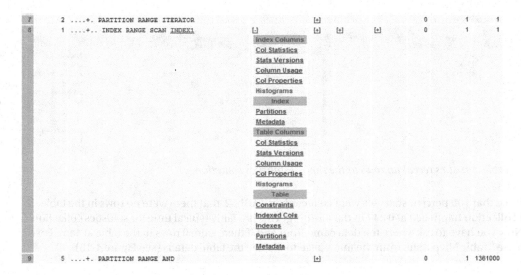

Figure 4-10. *An expansion under the "more" column in an execution plan can show more links to other information*

Then click on Col Statistics under either the "Index Columns" or "Table Columns" heading to display the Column Statistics (see Figure 4-11).

SCHEMA1.INDEX1 - Column Statistics

Index type:IOT - TOP PART rows:0 smpl:0 Ms:0 #lb:0 #dk:0 cluf:0 anlz:2012-06-19/04:47:47

#	Col Pos	In Pred	In Proj	Col ID	Column Name	Data Default	Not Null with Default Value	Descend	Num Rows	Num Nulls	Sample Size	Perc
1	1	[+]	TRUE	9	COL1			ASC	0	0		100.0
2	2	[+]	TRUE	10	COL2			ASC	0	0		100.0
3	3	[+]	TRUE	1	COL3			ASC	0	0		100.0
4	4	[+]	TRUE	2	COL4			ASC	0	0		100.0
5	5	[+]	TRUE	3	COL5			ASC	0	0		100.0
6	6	[+]	TRUE	4	COL6			ASC	0	0		100.0

Figure 4-11. *Column statistics reveal no rows*

Here you can see an interesting situation. The number of rows is 0 for all the columns. This means the table was empty when the statistics were collected. So, when were the statistics collected on the parent table? For that you need the parent table name. Click the back button to get to the execution plan again, and this time click on Col Statistics under the Table Columns section to display the table statistics (see Figure 4-12).

SCHEMA1.TABLE2 - Column Statistics

#	In Pred	In Index	In Proj	Col ID	Column Name	Data Default	Not Null with Default Value	Num Rows	Num Nulls	Sample Size	Perc	Num Distinct	Mutating NDV[1]	Low Value[2]	High Value[2]	Last Analyzed
1	[±]	[±]	TRUE	1	COL3			0	0		100.0	0	TRUE			2012-06-19 04:47:47
2	[±]	[±]	TRUE	2	COL4			0	0		100.0	0	TRUE			2012-06-19 04:47:47
3	[±]	[±]	TRUE	3	COL5			0	0		100.0	0	TRUE			2012-06-19 04:47:47
4	[±]	[±]	TRUE	4	COL6			0	0		100.0	0	TRUE			2012-06-19 04:47:47
5	[±]	[±]	TRUE	9	COL1			0	0		100.0	0	TRUE			2012-06-19 04:47:47
6	[±]	[±]	TRUE	10	COL2			0	0		100.0	0	TRUE			2012-06-19 04:47:47
7	FALSE	FALSE	TRUE	7	COL7			0	0		100.0	0	TRUE			2012-06-19 04:47:47
8	FALSE	FALSE	TRUE	8	COL8			0	0		100.0	0	TRUE			2012-06-19 04:47:47
9	FALSE	FALSE	FALSE	5	COL9			0	0		100.0	0	TRUE			2012-06-19 04:47:47
10	FALSE	FALSE	FALSE	6	COL10			0	0		100.0	0	TRUE			2012-06-19 04:47:47

Figure 4-12. Table statistics reveal no rows at the time of statistics collection

You will see that 100 percent statistics were collected on TABLE2, that there were no rows in the table, and that the collection happened at 04:47 in the morning. This is a fairly typical time for statistics collection to happen. Now you have to ask where the data came from and if there were 0 rows in the table at 4am. For this, click on the "Table" hyperlink from the main page to display the table details (see Figure 4-13).

Tables

#	Table Name	Owner	Count[1]	Num Rows[2]	Sample Size[2]	Blocks[2]	Last Analyzed[2]	Table Stats	Table Stats Versn	Table Modif	Table Prop
1	TABL1	SCHEMA1	6633980	6634683	6634683	177202	19-JUN-12	Stats	11		Prop
2	TABLE3	SCHEMA1	10000000	0	0		19-JUN-12	Stats	11	Modif	Prop
3	TABLE2	SCHEMA1	10000000	0	0		19-JUN-12	Stats	11	Modif	Prop
4	TABLE4	SCHEMA1	0	0	0		19-JUN-12	Stats	9	Modif	Prop

Figure 4-13. The table details section shows where we can go for modification information

This shows a new column of interest, the "Table Modif" column. Click on the "Modif" hyperlink for TABLE2 to see the modification history (see Figure 4-14).

Table Modifications

#	Table Name	Owner	Num Rows	Inserts	Updates	Deletes	Total	Perc	Stale Stats	Timestamp
1	TABL1	SCHEMA1	6634683						NO	
2	TABLE3	SCHEMA1	0	109716077	72880	0	109788957		YES	2012-06-22/16:26:12
3	TABLE2	SCHEMA1	0	21595050	0	0	21595050		YES	2012-06-22/16:09:13
4	TABLE4	SCHEMA1	0	8401095	0	8401095	16802190		YES	2012-06-22/17:30:40

Go to Tables
Go to Top

Figure 4-14. The table modifications section shows rows being inserted, deleted, and updated

---

■ **Note** I know what you're thinking. SQLT is the utility that just keeps on giving. I know all this information is in the database and can be obtained with suitable queries, but SQLT has done that for you already. You don't have to go back to the database to find it. SQLT collected it, just in case.

Now you can see the modifications to the tables, with timestamps. Read across the row for the TABLE2 entry. There were zero rows in the table, then roughly 2 million rows were inserted, there were no updates and no deletes, which resulted in roughly 2 million rows in the table. The statistics became stale because of this (more than a 10 percent change), and this happened at 4:09 pm.

The steps are now clear. The table was empty. Statistics were collected. Two million rows were added, the query was run, the optimizer estimated a cardinality of 1 (remember it rounds up to 1 if the value would be 0), and hence calculated that NESTED LOOPS (or even worse CARTESIAN JOINS) would be fine and got it completely wrong.

Now that you know what happened, you can fix the problem (if it seems appropriate), in a few different ways:

- You could collect statistics at a different time.

- You could export and import statistics as appropriate.

- You could freeze the statistics for when the table is populated.

There are probably even more ways to do this. The solution is not the issue here. The point is that once you know what happened you can design a solution that suits your circumstances. You can also see why in this case the _optimizer_cartesian_enabled=FALSE was needed. It was a possibility that the optimizer may have chosen a Cartesian join because one of the key steps would have a cardinality of 1 (one of the few cases where a CARTESIAN JOIN makes sense). You can test your theory very simply. With TABLE2 fully loaded, collect statistics. Then retry the query, or even better, just check what the execution plan would be.

The optimizer had bad statistics and "decided" to do something that didn't seem to make sense. SQLT collects enough information to let you see why the optimizer did what it did, and then you can set up statistics collection so that the optimizer doesn't get it wrong. The optimizer is your friend, an awesome piece of code that is nearly always right, as long as it gets the information it needs.

Summary

In this chapter we saw clearly from practical examples that statistics make a real difference and that just leaving everything on automatic pilot is not always the best strategy. You need to pay attention to what statistics you are collecting, the quality of those statistics, and how often you are collecting them. Take special care with column histograms. SQLT helps you to do this quickly and efficiently and gives you more information than a pile of scripts ever could. We touched on skewness in this chapter; but in the next chapter we'll dive right into the detail and look at what skewness is and how it affects your execution plan.

CHAPTER 5

■ ■ ■

How Skewness Can Make Your Execution Times Variable

Skewness is one of those topics that for some reason is often ignored, or misunderstood. Skewness is an important part of data handling for the cost-based optimizer. It makes a difference as to what the optimizer decides to do. It is so important that Oracle created new features such as Adaptive Cursor Sharing just to handle the consequences of skewness. Skewness and the types of skewness are so important that in 12c there are more types of histograms to take account of the different ways in which data can be skewed. So understanding skewness is pretty important.

Skewness

In this section we are going to look at what skewness is, how it comes about, and how it affects your execution plan. If you handle skewness every day, you're likely to know immediately what kind of situations are likely to produce skewed data. Sometimes skewed data can arise unexpectedly as well. We'll also look at how to detect skewness, both from SQL and from SQLT.

What Is Skewness?

In the simplest terms possible, a table is a representation of data and skewness is a property of a data set that results in an unexpectedly large or unexpectedly low number of matches for a particular column predicate.

A predicate in a query is the value used in the 'where' clause. In the example below the predicate might be 'where spend>10.00'. This is a column predicate because the rows returned from the column 'spend' are predicated on matching 'greater than $10'.

For example, if we plotted the amount in dollars spent at a hardware store for June, July, and August we might find that the amount spent varied by only 10 percent. The variability per week would be very low. If we now extend our timeline to include Thanksgiving and Christmas, we would find that the amount spent peaks around those dates, so the amount could be twice or three times the "normal," June–August amount. If we only had June–August to predict the future, we might expect a much lower level of spending. This unexpectedly large spending around Thanksgiving and Christmas would give a skewed data set. If we now instead plotted the amount each person spent per visit, in groupings of $10 we would find another distribution. A few people spend in the $0–$10 range, perhaps more in the $10.01 to $20 range. The trend

© Stelios Charalambides 2017
S. Charalambides, *Oracle SQL Tuning with Oracle SQLTXPLAIN*, DOI 10.1007/978-1-4842-2436-6_5

would continue up to some peak and then fall off. Most people would spend in some specific range, and then we would have the "high rollers," who spend $1,000 or more. The graph of the amount spent vs. the number of people who spent in this range will be skewed. If everybody came to the mall and spent exactly the same amount, then everybody would fall into the same range. All the other ranges would have a value of zero. This would be highly skewed data.

This highlights a crucial point for which DBAs and developers should constantly be on the alert. Do you really truly understand your data. Sometimes it can be hard because the columns are not named in a way that is obvious. This is where database designers, developers, and DBAs must work together to get good structures, relevant indexes, and primary and foreign keys. Do not assume that just because everything is set to automatic all sampling will be sufficient. It is wise to check. In Figure 5-1 we see the information about what statistics were collected for each of the columns in the table TABLE1.

SCHEMA.TABLE1 - Table Column

- Column Statistics
- Column Statistics Versions
- Column Usage
- Column Properties
- Histograms

Go to Table Columns
Go to Tables
Go to Top

SCHEMA.TABLE1 - Column Statistics

#	In Pred	In Index	In Proj	Col ID	Column Name	Data Default	Not Null with Default Value	Num Rows	Num Nulls	Sample Size	Perc	Num Distinct
1	[+]	FALSE	FALSE	1	COLUMN_1			3387323	0	1016197	30.0	3387323
2	FALSE	[+]	FALSE	16	COLUMN_2			3387323	0	1016207	30.0	19533
3	FALSE	[+]	FALSE	19	COLUMN_3			3387323	0	1015832	30.0	3
4	FALSE	FALSE	TRUE	93	COLUMN_4			3387323	3387323		100.0	0
5	FALSE	FALSE	FALSE	2	COLUMN_5			3387323	0	1016197	30.0	3569
6	FALSE	FALSE	FALSE	3	COLUMN_6			3387323	0	1016197	30.0	72
7	FALSE	FALSE	FALSE	4	COLUMN_7			3387323	2996190	117340	30.0	70
8	FALSE	FALSE	FALSE	5	COLUMN_8			3387323	86	1016171	30.0	72
9	FALSE	FALSE	FALSE	6	COLUMN_9			3387323	0	1016197	30.0	3031
10	FALSE	FALSE	FALSE	7	COLUMN_10			3387323	0	1016197	30.0	71
11	FALSE	FALSE	FALSE	8	COLUMN_11			3387323	2996190	117340	30.0	70

Figure 5-1. *Table column statistics showing the sample size and number of distinct values*

In the figure for the SQLT report collected, we see, under the "Table Column" section, for the particular table TABLE1, that a number of columns have had column statistics collected. Look at the highlighted section for COLUMN_4. It had 100 percent statistics collected. COLUMN_1 had 30.0 percent collected. Why is there a difference between COLUMN_1 and COLUMN_? This is because the automatic sampling algorithm, chose only 5,791 rows for its COL4 sample size. Let me explain what the optimizer does when it samples these columns.

In 11g you could get very small samples from some columns, sometimes resulting in poor execution plans. In 12c the sampling algorithm has improved, but you still need to look at the column sampling percentages to see what was collected.

In this case, for table TABLE1, for **each** column COLUMN_1, COLUMN_2, COLUMN_3, COLUMN_4, etc., the statistics-gathering algorithm is sampling the values from the table with at least 30% sampling rate. The sample size is shown in the "Sample Size" column. So if COLUMN_1 was the amount spent (in our skewness explanation above), then the statistics sampling algorithm would sample the columns and find there was some skewed distribution of data. If COLUMN_6 was the store name it would sample the data and find there were a certain number of distinct values (72 in this case). In each case, however, there are 3,387,323 rows of data. If your data is highly skewed and there is only one value in the entire column population of, say, "Sally's Hardware" inserted in COLUMN_4, then by random sampling the statistics collection algorithm might miss this value even at 30%. Suppose further that despite the fact that the "Sally's Hardware" value is very rare, it is the value used in the predicate used for this query. In Oracle 10g, you might well end up with a suboptimal plan depending on the first value used for the predicate. In 11g you would have Adaptive Cursor Sharing to help you and in Oracle 12c you have Adaptive Plans and Adaptive Statistics all designed to help you with this kind of situation. If on the other hand, however, you knew that your data was highly skewed in this way, and you saw that your auto sample size was tiny, you might very well decide that choosing a larger sample size might be a good idea.

How to Tell If Data Is Skewed

Skewness is so important that as a DBA or developer you should be on the alert for columns that might contain skewed data. When data sets are as large as they are today, it is very difficult to immediately tell if a data set is skewed. SQLTXPLAIN makes the job much easier for you by showing the statistics for the histograms, if there are any. So how do you find out if data is skewed? There's more than one way of seeing the collected data, but all methods rely on sampling. The simplest way to sample is with a query (as shown below). In this simple example we create a test table test3 with a CTAS (Create Table As Select) statement from a known (at least to me) skewed data set. The object_type column of the dba_objects view. The dba_objects view lists attributes of the objects in the database, including the object type. There are many different object types: for example, table (this is a very common object type) and dimension (this is a very rare object type). Once we've created a test table called test3, which will contain 73,583 rows, we can sample the number of each type of object: this will give us an idea of the data set's skewness.

```
SQL> Set Pagesize 100
SQL> create table test3 as select * from dba_objects;
Table created.
SQL> select object_type, count(object_type)
  from test3 group by object_type order by count(object_type);

OBJECT_TYPE              COUNT(OBJECT_TYPE)
----------------------- -------------------
EDITION                                   1
RULE                                      1
DESTINATION                               2
JAVA SOURCE                               2
MATERIALIZED VIEW                         2
SCHEDULE                                  4
SCHEDULER GROUP                           4
DIMENSION                                 5
INDEXTYPE                                 7
UNIFIED AUDIT POLICY                      8
WINDOW                                    9
CLUSTER                                  10
PROGRAM                                  10
CONTEXT                                  10
RESOURCE PLAN                            11
LOB PARTITION                            13
JOB CLASS                                14
```

```
EVALUATION CONTEXT                     15
UNDEFINED                              17
CONSUMER GROUP                         18
RULE SET                               21
DIRECTORY                              22
JOB                                    23
QUEUE                                  30
TABLE SUBPARTITION                     32
XML SCHEMA                             45
OPERATOR                               54
PROCEDURE                             205
LIBRARY                               228
TYPE BODY                             232
SEQUENCE                              274
JAVA DATA                             310
TABLE PARTITION                       333
FUNCTION                              348
INDEX PARTITION                       384
TRIGGER                               599
LOB                                  1012
JAVA RESOURCE                        1014
PACKAGE BODY                         1262
PACKAGE                              1323
TYPE                                 2583
TABLE                                2688
INDEX                                4690
VIEW                                 6637
JAVA CLASS                          30816
SYNONYM                             37366

46 rows selected.
```

The example above shows the object type in the database vs. the number of those object types. Here the "bucket" is the object_type value ("bucket" has come to mean the range of values covered in a data set). So, for example, the object type of SYNONYM (bottom line in the example) has 37,366 values. Sometimes buckets are days of the week such as Saturday or Sunday, sometimes primary colors such as red or blue, and sometimes buckets are ranges such as "dates in 2016." In each case these are the values you plot on your X-axis if you were plotting a graph. From here on in, we will use the term "bucket" to represent the range of values in question.

Once you have issued the query you will see information that will help you decide how skewed the data is. Please note, however, that almost all data is skewed to some extent. The data will be skewed even in our example in the previous section regarding the spending of money in a superstore. The question you need to answer is this: is it skewed enough to cause a problem with my queries? A 10 percent variability doesn't usually cause a problem, but if you have one bucket with 90 percent of the samples, then the data is highly skewed. So decisions on skewness are somewhat subjective. In the example query above if I am querying my table test3 and my predicate value is SYNONYM, then I am likely to get many more rows returned than if I issued my query against the value "RESOURCE PLAN." See the example code below. If we sample our test table for the rare value we only get 11 values.

```
SQL> select count(*) from test3 where object_type='SYNONYM';

  COUNT(*)
----------
```

```
        37366

SQL> select count(*) from test3 where object_type='RESOURCE PLAN';

  COUNT(*)
----------
        11
```

Do we care about this skewness, and is this data skewed a lot? Technically speaking even the slightest deviation from the "norm" can be classed as skewness, but the term has come to mean an amount of skewness that makes my execution plan change from one plan to another to take account of the peeked bind variables for a predicate. This kind of plan is called unstable because different peeked bind variables require different plans for the best execution time. From a more objective point of view, however, if you see as in the example above that some predicates return more than 10 times the values of other predicates, then this is very skewed. If you see a ratio of the most common to the least common value of 1.5 or higher, you can start to consider skewness as a factor.

SQLT makes the job of collecting queries like this much easier. It shows the distribution of data for a column histogram. First from the top of the report, (see Figure 5-2) we can click on "Tables," "Columns," or we could click on "Histograms." In this example we'll click on "Tables" since that's the route you'll most likely follow in an investigation.

215187.1 SQLT XTRACT 12.1.14 Report: sqlt_s90918_main.html

Global

- Observations
- SQL Text
- SQL Identification
- Environment
- CBO Environment
- Fix Control
- CBO System Statistics
- DBMS_STATS Setup
- Initialization Parameters
- NLS Parameters
- I/O Calibration
- Tool Configuration Parameters

Cursor Sharing and Binds

- Cursor Sharing
- Adaptive Cursor Sharing
- Peeked Binds
- Captured Binds

SQL Tuning Advisor

- STA Report
- STA Script

Plans

- Summary
- Performance Statistics
- Performance History (delta)
- Performance History (total)
- Execution Plans

Plan Control

- Stored Outlines
- SQL Patches
- SQL Profiles
- SQL Plan Baselines
- SQL Plan Directives

SQL Execution

- Active Session History
- AWR Active Session History
- SQL Statistics
- SQL Detail ACTIVE Report
- Monitor Statistics
- Monitor ACTIVE Report
- Monitor HTML Report
- Monitor TEXT Report
- Segment Statistics
- Session Statistics
- Session Events
- Parallel Processing

Tables

- Tables
- Statistics
- Statistics Extensions
- Statistics Versions
- Modifications
- Properties
- Physical Properties
- Constraints
- Columns
- Indexed Columns
- Histograms
- EBS Histograms
- Partitions
- Indexes

Objects

- Objects
- Dependencies
- Fixed Objects
- Fixed Object Columns
- Nested Tables
- Policies
- Audit Policies
- Tablespaces
- Metadata

Figure 5-2. *The top of the SQLXECUTE report*

The "Tables" page shows us the screen in Figure 5-3.

Tables

#	Table Name	Owner	Count[1]	Num Rows[2]	Sample Size[2]	Blocks[2]	Last Analyzed[2]	Table Stats	Table Stats Versn	Table Stats Exten	Table Modif	Table Prop	Table Phys Prop	Table Cons	Table Cols	Idxed Cols	Table Hgrm
1	DUAL	SYS	1	1	1	1	17-DEC-15	Stats	2			Prop	Phys		1		
2	TABLE1	SCHEMA1	40900000	40183609	40183609	741302	25-NOV-15	Stats	1		Modif	Prop	Phys	14	20	5	5
3	TABLE2	SCHEMA1	222000000	214529155	214529155	2304460	10-DEC-15	Stats	2	1	Modif	Prop	Phys	10	11	8	4
4	TABLE3	SCHEMA1	8658000	8565536	8565536	63338	17-NOV-15	Stats	1		Modif	Prop	Phys	9	6	3	
5	TABLE4	SCHEMA1	194000000	191925995	191925995	1894220	10-DEC-15	Stats	2		Modif	Prop	Phys	12	11	5	3

(1) SELECT COUNT(*) performed in Table as per tool parameter "count_star_threshold" with current value of 10000.
(2) CBO Statistics.
Go to Indexed Columns
Go to Indexes
Go to Top

Figure 5-3. *The tables section of the report*

From Figure 5-3, which shows only the left-hand side of the screen, we can now click on the hyperlinks under the "Table Cols" heading. The number under this column shows the number of columns and is the hyperlink for any individual table to see the column details. In this case we are looking at TABLE1 so we click on the corresponding link. This gets us to the screen shown in Figure 5-4 (which is the right-hand side of the screen), where I have highlighted the "FREQUENCY" hyperlink with a box, which takes us to the histogram for COL2 of TABLE1. I've also pointed out the two new types of histogram introduced in 12c, the HYBRID and TOP_FREQUENCY histograms.

Avg Col Len	Density	Num Buckets	Histogram	Fluctuating Endpoint Count[3]	Popular Values	Global Stats	User Stats	Equality Predicate Selectivity	Equality Predicate Cardinality
11	2.741305e-08	1	NONE	FALSE		YES	NO	0.000000	2
7	2.488577e-08	1	NONE	FALSE		YES	NO	0.000000	1
3	1.244288e-08	29	FREQUENCY	FALSE	0	YES	NO	0.034483	1385642
7	2.554841e-08	1	NONE	FALSE		YES	NO	0.000000	2
3	1.244288e-08	10	FREQUENCY	FALSE	0	YES	NO	0.100000	4018361
2	5.000000e-01	1	NONE	FALSE		YES	NO	0.000414	16635
8	0.000000e+00	254	HYBRID	FALSE	0	YES	NO	0.000000	3
8	5.409719e-08	1	NONE	FALSE		YES	NO	0.000000	3
3	3.333333e-01	1	NONE	FALSE		YES	NO	0.333333	13394537
3	2.500000e-01	1	NONE	FALSE		YES	NO	0.250000	10045903
4	1.244288e-08	32	FREQUENCY	FALSE	0	YES	NO	0.031250	1255738
15	1.244288e-08	254	TOP-FREQUENCY	FALSE	0	YES	NO	0.003623	145593

Figure 5-4. *The hyperlink for the histogram for TABLE2*

We arrived at the screen shown in Figure 5-5, by clicking on the "FREQUENCY" histogram for column COL3. The four types of histograms, "FREQUENCY," "HEIGHT BALANCED," HYBRID, and TOP_FREQUENCY will be discussed in a later section, but suffice to say that they are both ways of representing bucket frequencies.

SCHEMA1.TABLE1.COL2 - Histogram

"Frequency" histogram with 41 buckets. Number of rows in this table is 5144909. Number of nulls in this column is 0 and its sample size was 5791.
SQL: [±]

#	Endpoint Number	Endpoint Value[1]	Endpoint Actual Value[1]	Estimated Endpoint Value[1]	Estimated Cardinality	Estimated Selectivity
1	1847	1 —		"1"	1959902	0.318943
2	3569	2 —		"2"	1827261	0.297358
3	4458	3 —		"3"	943342	0.153514
4	4949	4 —		"4"	521014	0.084787
5	5205	5 —		"5"	271649	0.044207
6	5408	6 —		"6"	215409	0.035054
7	5512	7 —		"7"	110357	0.017959
8	5580	8 —		"8"	72157	0.011742
9	5630	9 —		"9"	53056	0.008634
10	5660	10 —		"10"	31834	0.005180
11	5683	11 —		"11"	24406	0.003972
12	5698	12 —		"12"	15917	0.002590
13	5711	13 —		"13"	13795	0.002245
14	5723	14 —		"14"	12734	0.002072
15	5734	15 —		"15"	11672	0.001899
16	5742	16 —		"16"	8489	0.001381
17	5746	17 —		"17"	4245	0.000691

Figure 5-5. A sample histogram from SQLT

This figure shows us that for a value of "1" the estimated cardinality is approximately 1.9 million, while the value for "17" is approximately 4,000. Is this data skewed? It sure is. I've also pointed out the Estimated Selectivity values for these two endpoints (or buckets). Approximately 0.31 is nearly a third of all values. The other endpoint has an Estimated Selectivity of 0.000691 (that's 6/10ths of 1 percent). In Figure 5-5 the estimated cardinality popularity has been ordered, but this is not always the case. Look at Figure 5-6 from our example TEST3 table.

STELIOS.TEST3.OBJECT_TYPE - Histogram

"Frequency" histogram with 33 buckets. Number of rows in this table is 73583 Number of nulls in this column is 0 and its sample size was 5502.
SQL: [±]

#	Endpoint Number	Endpoint Value[1]	Endpoint Actual Value[1]	Estimated Endpoint Value[1]	Estimated Cardinality	Estimated Selectivity
1	1	34949240546757700000000000000000000	"CONSUMER GROUP"	"CONSUMER GROUP"	13	0.000182
2	2	35456292429910400000000000000000000	"DIMENSION"	"DIMENSION"	13	0.000182
3	4	35456332042662300000000000000000000	"DIRECTORY"	"DIRECTORY"	27	0.000364
4	22	36519098554781600000000000000000000	"FUNCTION"	"FUNCTION"	241	0.003272
5	335	38062510759802900000000000000000000	"INDEX"	"INDEX"	4186	0.056888
6	375	38062510759818200000000000000000000	"INDEX PARTITION"	"INDEX PARTITION"	535	0.007270
7	2101	38555515793332000000000000000000000	"JAVA CLASS"	"JAVA CLASS"	23083	0.313704
8	2124	38555515793324000000000000000000000	"JAVA DATA"	"JAVA DATA"	308	0.004180
9	2190	38555515793339100000000000000000000	"JAVA RESOURCE"	"JAVA RESOURCE"	883	0.011996
10	2191	38583750694899200000000000000000000	"JOB"	"JOB"	13	0.000182
11	2192	38583751693387000000000000000000000	"JOB CLASS"	"JOB CLASS"	13	0.000182
12	2207	39610043166517900000000000000000000	"LIBRARY"	"LIBRARY"	201	0.002726
13	2276	39622210066606100000000000000000000	"LOB"	"LOB"	923	0.012541
14	2279	41181953679250600000000000000000000	"OPERATOR"	"OPERATOR"	40	0.000545
15	2392	41670743688420500000000000000000000	"PACKAGE"	"PACKAGE"	1511	0.020538
16	2501	41670743688420500000000000000000000	"PACKAGE BODY"	"PACKAGE BODY"	1458	0.019811
17	2514	41705318611435800000000000000000000	"PROCEDURE"	"PROCEDURE"	174	0.002363
18	2516	42230554349048700000000000000000000	"QUEUE"	"QUEUE"	27	0.000364
19	2517	42717442915245900000000000000000000	"RESOURCE PLAN"	"RESOURCE PLAN"	13	0.000182
20	2518	42749838991098300000000000000000000	"RULE"	"RULE"	13	0.000182
21	2519	42749838995006200000000000000000000	"RULE SET"	"RULE SET"	13	0.000182
22	2520	43232528656661200000000000000000000	"SCHEDULER GROUP"	"SCHEDULER GROUP"	13	0.000182
23	2537	43236656939221800000000000000000000	"SEQUENCE"	"SEQUENCE"	227	0.003090
24	4575	43277197805382500000000000000000000	"SYNONYM"	"SYNONYM"	27256	0.370411
25	4822	43747654540416600000000000000000000	"TABLE"	"TABLE"	3303	0.044893
26	4841	43747654540431800000000000000000000	"TABLE PARTITION"	"TABLE PARTITION"	254	0.003453
27	4892	43782189941988500000000000000000000	"TRIGGER"	"TRIGGER"	682	0.009269
28	5093	43796443017911700000000000000000000	"TYPE"	"TYPE"	2688	0.036532
29	5109	43796443021811600000000000000000000	"TYPE BODY"	"TYPE BODY"	214	0.002908
30	5110	44293266987903300000000000000000000	"UNDEFINED"	"UNDEFINED"	13	0.000182

#	Endpoint Number	Endpoint Value[1]	Endpoint Actual Value[1]	Estimated Endpoint Value[1]	Estimated Cardinality	Estimated Selectivity
31	5498	44802363940347100000000000000000000	"VIEW"	"VIEW"	5189	0.070520
32	5500	45321664353116900000000000000000000	"WINDOW"	"WINDOW"	27	0.000364
33	5502	45848990043507600000000000000000000	"XML SCHEMA"	"XML SCHEMA"	27	0.000364

(1) The display of values in this column is controlled by tool parameter "s_mask_for_values". Its current value is "CLEAR".
Remarks for this "Frequency" histogram:
a) Estimated cardinality for values not present in histogram is 1/2 the cardinality of the smallest bucket (after fix 5483301).
b) Smallest bucket shows an estimated cardinality of 13 rows, thus for equality predicates on values not in this histogram an estimated cardinality of 7 rows would be considered.

Figure 5-6. *Another example histogram table for our TEST3 example. SYNONYMs are popular*

In this example histogram, we see the basic facts shown on the column display: the number of buckets (33), the number of rows in the table, the number of nulls, and the sample size. In this case the sample size is extremely small.

This data looks highly skewed. For the "Endpoint Actual Value" of "DIMENSION" the estimated selectivity is 0.00182. For SYNONYM the Estimated Selectivity is 0.370411. This means that since there were 0 null values more than a third of the table will be returned if a predicate against object_type uses the value "SYNONYM." If the predicate used the value "JAVA RESOURCE" then the selectivity is only 0.011996 or a cardinality of 883, compared to the value of 27,256 values for "SYNONYM." Even with this highly skewed data, you could ask yourself: "Is this skewness relevant for my query?" If the column object_type is not involved in your query, then the skewness does not matter to you.

How Skewness Affects the Execution Plan

Now that we know what skewness is and how statistics are shown in a SQLT report for a particular SQL statement, we should look at how skewness can cause problems with an execution plan.

Suppose we wanted to know the sum of all the financial transactions we had carried out in the previous month with each financial institution we had done business with. We might well have the name of the institution in the description field, possibly a company_ID to represent the company and a field to represent the amount of the financial transaction. We would probably have lots of other fields as well of course, but these are the ones we would be interested in with regard to skewness. We could query this table to find the sum of all the records where the company_ID matched the company for which we were currently looking. If we chose a company we had not done much business with we might only get a few records. The optimizer might well be expecting only one record for some companies, and so might choose to do a Cartesian join. If the company was a big bank, however, we might expect thousands (perhaps millions) of transactions. In this case a hash join might be a better choice. The "good" plan for these two extreme cases is very different.

If the Cartesian join is used with the big bank records, there would be a disastrous drop in performance as Oracle tried to do a Cartesian join on thousands of records. Even Exadata can't cope with errors like this. So depending on the predicate value (peaked bind variable or literal), we could well need different execution plans. To fix these kinds of problems, we need to consider what the options are: removing the histogram, improving the histogram, using Adaptive Cursor Sharing, adding a Profile, changing the query; there are other options also. There is no hard and fast rule here for what to do in these circumstances. SQLT will show what is happening and how skewness is affecting the execution plan; then you, in conjunction with the developers, can decide which is the best strategy for your situation: which indexes to add or remove and which histograms are helpful to collect.

Histograms

Fear not! Histograms are not as confusing as they first appear. The confusing and sometimes contradictory terminology used by different documents does not help, but histograms are really easy to explain and their use just as easy to understand. So let me start by defining a bucket. A bucket is a range of values for a particular column. So, for example, if we had a column called TRUE_OR_FALSE and it could only have two values (TRUE or FALSE), then we could have up to two buckets: each bucket would have a value counting the number of values that were TRUE and the number that were FALSE. A histogram is a data representation that describes the relative population of different ranges of data value.

Here is a list of TRUE and FALSE values listed from our imaginary table

TRUE

FALSE

FALSE

TRUE

FALSE

FALSE

FALSE

TRUE

The histogram would represent these values for this FREQUENCY histogram like this

Bucket 1: TRUE: 3

Bucket 2: FALSE: 5

Histogram Types

To understand the histogram types in 12c you need to understand how the types of histograms have evolved over time to take account of data distributions and more sophisticated ways of dealing with skewness. You might imagine that to begin with all distributions could be dealt with using FREQUENCY histograms. After all, histograms are just a representation of the number of values of a particular type. When the number of types exceeded 254 Oracle can use a HEIGHT BALANCED histogram. This is a type where all the possible values have to be squashed into the limited 254 buckets. As I'm sure you can imagine a HEIGHT BALANCED histogram might end up being used when many rare low selectivity values 'fill up' the buckets to the detriment of more popular values, which might well be well represented by a FREQUENCY histogram. The TOP-FREQUENCY histogram deals with this case by consigning all unpopular values to a low frequency and dealing with the popular values with a FREQUENCY type representation. Finally the HYBRID histogram is both a FREQUENCY histogram and a HEIGHT BALANCED histogram combined, hence the name. Suffice to say that all the histogram types work by allowing the optimizer to check a selectivity by looking up the value in the histogram.

Rather than give a long-winded description of the types of histogram I'm going to show below an example of the data distribution for each type so that you can understand what the histograms mean.

Frequency Histogram

The most basic type of histogram and the easiest to understand, a frequency histogram is a histogram with a discrete number of buckets where a count is kept for individual values.

Distribution: All numbers from 1 to 5 once.

```
Endpoint . Cardinality
1:                      1
2:                      1
3:                      1
4:                      1
5:                      1
```

Distribution: All numbers from 1 to 5 with 5 being three times as popular

```
Endpoint . Cardinality
1:                      1
2:                      1
3:                      1
4:                      1
5:                      3
```

Height Balanced Histogram

A HEIGHT BALANCED histogram is a histogram with 254 buckets that is used to contain ALL the possible values of the column data even though there are MORE than 254 discrete values. To do this, unlike the FREQUENCY histogram, the HEIGHT BALANCED histogram bucket can contain a range of values. This is OK as long as the distribution of data is smooth, but this is not always the case. Suppose you had a table called CAR_POPULARITY and a column called CAR_MAKE. You might have a histogram on the column CAR_MAKE (since there are more than 254 makes of car. So for example 'Ford', would be more popular than 'Ferrari'.

Because we are limited by the number of buckets we might end up putting 'Ford' and 'Ferrari' in the same bucket. This would mean we would end up not representing 'Ford' correctly or 'Ferrari' correctly. This could give us problems when we try and work out the best plan when we search for MAKE='Ferrari' or MAKE='Ford'. This is a situation where a popular value is next to a rare value.

This type of histogram is generally not found in 12c by default. You have to explicitly sample the table. By default in 12c a Full Sample is collected of the table and a HYBRID or TOP_FREQUENCY histogram is created.

Distribution: 508 values (2x254), each number represented once (even distribution)

```
Endpoint . Cardinality
2:              2
4:              2
6:              2
...
252             2
254             2
```

This would be a case where the HEIGHT BALANCED HISTOGRAM was an accurate representation of the data

Distribution: 517 values, each number represented once but "5" being 10 times more popular

```
Endpoint . Cardinality
2:              2
4:              2
6:              5
...
252             2
254             2
```

This is a case where all values are represented accurately except "5" and "6". "5" is under represented by a factor of 2 (it should be 10) and "6" is overrepresented by a factor of 5 (it should be 1). In this case buckets are being shared between two values. In cases where there are many more values buckets could be shared by more than two values, leading to a greater chance of values being overestimated or underestimated. The new histograms in 12c deal with these kinds of distributions in a better way.

Top-Frequency Histogram

Distribution: Even numbers up to 6 (2, 4, and 6 – Not including 0) are present 10 times while all other numbers up to 512 are only seen once (incuding odd numbers 1, 3, and 5).

```
Endpoint . Cardinality
1:              1
2:              10
3:              1
4:              10
5:              1
6:              10
7-512:          1
```

This is the kind of distribution that cannot be represented by a FREQUENCY histogram (too many buckets) and would not be well represented by a HEIGHT BALANCED histogram (adjacent values have widely different cardinalities), but is an accurate representation of this particulare distribution.

Hybrid Histogram

HYBRID histograms assume there is a FREQUENCY histogram section to the data and a HEIGHT BALANCED section to the data.

Distribution: 10 Values from each of the numbers from 1-5 and all other values from 6 to 500 only seen once. Think of this as a TOP-FREQUENCY histogram where the rare values get their own HEIGHT_BALANCED histogram.

```
Endpoint . Cardinality
1:                 10
2:                 10
3:                 10
4:                 10
5:                 10
7:                  1
9:                  1
...
500                 1
```

What Histogram Is Best for You?

Now that you understand what types of histograms there are in 12c you might begin to wonder if the histograms chosen for your columns are the right ones. After all 254 is a very small number when compared to almost any range of possible values of anything! "Colors of paint," "Names of Banks," or "Zip Codes." If the number of distinct values (shown as NDV in many SQLT reports) is greater than 254 and the statistics-gathering process detects this, then you will have to somehow squeeze the data distribution into fewer buckets than there are distinct values. In 12c the number of histograms now available is an improvement on previous choices but there is still the possibility that the cardinality choices generated from these histograms may not be ideal. If this happens, you are exposing the optimizer to the risk of incomplete information that may adversely affect your execution plan.

What happens if we artificially squeeze the number of buckets down to 10?

```
SQL>exec dbms_stats.set_table_prefs(
  ownname=>'STELIOS',
  tabname=>'TEST3',
  pname=>'method_opt',
  pvalue=>'for all columns size 10');

PL/SQL procedure successfully completed.
```

This is the histogram we get (see Figure 5-7).

STELIOS.TEST3.OBJECT_TYPE - Histogram

"Top-Frequency" histogram with 10 buckets. Number of rows in this table is 92709. Number of nulls in this column is 0 and its sample size was 92709.
SQL: [±]

#	Endpoint Number	Endpoint Value[1]	Endpoint Actual Value[1]	Estimated Endpoint Value[1]	Estimated Cardinality	Estimated Selectivity
1	1	349432112834658000000000000000000000000	"CLUSTER"	"CLUSTER"	1	0.000011
2	4691	380625107598029000000000000000000000000	"INDEX"	"INDEX"	4690	0.053680
3	35507	385555157933320000000000000000000000000	"JAVA CLASS"	"JAVA CLASS"	30816	0.352707
4	36830	416707436884205000000000000000000000000	"PACKAGE"	"PACKAGE"	1323	0.015142
5	38092	416707436884205000000000000000000000000	"PACKAGE BODY"	"PACKAGE BODY"	1262	0.014444
6	75458	432771978053825000000000000000000000000	"SYNONYM"	"SYNONYM"	37366	0.427675
7	78146	437476545404166000000000000000000000000	"TABLE"	"TABLE"	2688	0.030766
8	80732	437964430179117000000000000000000000000	"TYPE"	"TYPE"	2586	0.029598
9	87369	448023639403471000000000000000000000000	"VIEW"	"VIEW"	6637	0.075964
10	87370	458489900435076000000000000000000000000	"XML SCHEMA"	"XML SCHEMA"	1	0.000011

(1) The display of values in this column is controlled by tool parameter "s_mask_for_values". Its current value is "CLEAR". Go to Table Columns

Figure 5-7. *A height-balanced histogram with 10 buckets*

In the TOP-FREQUENCY histogram, the endpoint values are shown. For example "CLUSTER" is the first endpoint. There are no other types before CLUSTER so in this case the cardinality of 1 represents "CLUSTER" only. The second endpoint is INDEX and includes everything after CLUSTER and up to INDEX, so

```
CONSUMER_GROUP
CONTEXT
DESTINATION
DIMENSION
DIRECTORY
EDITION
EVALUATION CONTEXT
FUNCTION
INDEX
```

are all included in this second bucket.

As you can see, with only 10 buckets the estimate of the distribution of data for object type (which in fact has 46 distinct types) is poor. With a histogram of this poor quality we might well end up with some poor plans. It is therefore important that we know when to have histograms and when they are a hindrance.

When to Use Histograms

If you use the default values for optimizer statistics collection then you will most likely have some histograms on columns that you aren't aware of. If you have a query with poor performance, or one you want to tune, you may want to examine what has been collected to make sure it makes sense. There are a few guidelines to consider when deciding if you want a histogram on a column or not. Histograms were designed to take care of skewed data, so if your data is not very skewed then it follows that histograms are not useful. An example might be a date-stamp against a table record. If the database activity happens every day and we have 100 transactions every day each with a timestamp, a histogram on the date column is not going to help. In FREQUENCY histograms this would be equivalent to the height of all buckets being the same. If there is no skewness then histograms do not help us. It just means we spend time overnight gathering statistics that we don't need.

If on the other hand you have a system that allocates a 'special' date such as 1st of January 1970, perhaps representing the date when there is no date data, you might have some popular values for dates. In fact this case might be suitable for a TOP-FREQUENCY histogram. As I've mentioned before the auto sample size is very clever about when to quit sampling if the data is hardly skewed, so you probably will not lose much time in this way.

If you have very skewed data, then histograms may be very important for you; but if you do have them, you should check with SQLT that the histograms are appropriate and correct. In Figure 5-8, we see the column statistics for TABLE4.

Perc	Num Distinct	Fluctuating NDV[1]	Low Value[2]	High Value[2]	Last Analyzed	Avg Col Len	Density	Num Buckets	Histogram
0.0	36515840	FALSE	" 2014/04/01 00:00:02"	" 2015/12/10 14:05:45"	2015-12-10/22:02:48	11	0.000000e+00	254	HYBRID
100.0	40419328	FALSE	"225153386"	"265386022"	2015-12-10/22:02:48	7	2.474064e-08	1	NONE
100.0	191135744	FALSE	"417183422"	"611022054"	2015-12-10/22:02:48	7	5.231884e-09	1	NONE
100.0	10	FALSE	"1"	"13"	2015-12-10/22:02:48	3	2.605171e-09	10	FREQUENCY
0.0	26540032	FALSE	" 2014/04/01 00:00:02"	" 2015/12/10 14:05:53"	2015-12-10/22:02:48	8	0.000000e+00	254	HYBRID
100.0	33	FALSE	"1"	"13174"	2015-12-10/22:02:48	4	3.030303e-02	1	NONE

Figure 5-8. *A section from some column statistics*

Notice how the histograms with a sample size of 0.0 percent are both for date columns. If you know by examining these columns that the date columns are not skewed then you can set preferences on these columns and remove the histograms. Although these histograms do no harm on this type of column they are just a waste of time to collect, so why collect them!

How to Add and Remove Histograms

If you want to remove a column's histogram you can simply use the dbms_stats procedure as shown in the example below.

```
SQL> exec dbms_stats.delete_column_stats(
  ownname=>'STELIOS',
  tabname=>'TEST3',
  colname=>'OBJECT_TYPE');
PL/SQL procedure successfully completed.
```

However, this does not remove the statistics permanently. The next time the statistics job comes across the table, it may decide that the same column needs column statistics again. You would remove statistics from a column on a one-time basis if you were testing the execution of a query. Removing the column statistics might then allow you to re-parse a statement and see if the execution plan is materially affected by the change. If you wanted to remove the column statistics collection forever then you could set the table preferences, as in the example below, by setting the method_opt value to "FOR ALL COLUMNS SIZE 1," which means no column histograms.

```
SQL> exec dbms_stats.set_table_prefs(
  ownname=>'STELIOS',
  tabname=>'TEST3',
  pname=>'method_opt',
  pvalue=>'FOR ALL COLUMNS SIZE 1');

PL/SQL procedure successfully completed.
```

If the table has other columns for which you need statistics, you may decide that you want to set the preferences so that only one column in particular is ignored for column statistics. This is the command example show in the following example.

```
SQL> exec dbms_stats.set_table_prefs(
  ownname=>'STELIOS',
  tabname=>'TEST3',
  pname=>'method_opt',
  pvalue=>'FOR COLUMNS OBJECT_TYPE SIZE 1');

PL/SQL procedure successfully completed.
```

If on the other hand you want to add column statistics you can gather them manually with a dbms_stats.get_column_stats command.

Bind Variables

Bind variables are one of those mysteries that a new Oracle DBA might not immediately be aware of. Developers, on the other hand, will use bind variables all the time and be comfortable with the definitions and the meanings. If you are familiar with the concept of a variable and its value, then there is nothing more to understand from a bind variable. It's just Oracle's version of a variable. A variable (and bind variable) is just a symbolic name for a value that can change depending on the needs of the code. Bind peeking and bind capture, however, are ideas that are more specific to Oracle and are techniques allowing the optimizer to make better decisions when skewness is present. Bind variables, skewness, and bind peeking all work with CURSOR_SHARING to improve the CBO plan. We cover all these concepts and how they work for you, in the following sections.

What Are Bind Variables?

Now that we have entered the world of histograms and have looked at skewness, we see that the value used as the value for the predicate could have a material effect on the number of rows returned. In the example below we see that depending on whether we select "EDITION" or "TABLE," we get a different count.

```
SQL> select count(*) from test3 where object_type='EDITION';
  COUNT(*)
----------
         1
SQL> select count(*) from test3 where object_type='TABLE';
  COUNT(*)
----------
      2688
```

If we wanted to avoid literal values in our SQL, which would all be parsed separately (and would have an adverse effect on performance), we might have introduced bind variables. Bind variables are a way to pass parameters to routines by setting the values of the parameters. Below I show a simple procedure to count the number of different object types in TEST3, using a bind variable called b1.

```
SQL> set serveroutput on;
SQL> create or replace procedure object_count(b1 in char)
  2  as
  3    object_count number;
  4    begin
  5    select count(*) into object_count from test3 where object_type=b1;
  6    dbms_output.put_line(b1||' = '||object_count);
  7    end;
  8  /
```

```
Procedure created.
```

If we ran this procedure a few times we could see that different values are being passed in and being used.

```
SQL> exec object_count('EDITION');
EDITION = 1

PL/SQL procedure successfully completed.

SQL> exec object_count('TABLE');
TABLE = 2688

PL/SQL procedure successfully completed.
```

In the example above, b1 is taking the value "EDITION" and then the value "TABLE." The text in the procedure that actually does the work is a simple select statement. Its predicate is object_type=b1. The text of the query did not change as far as the optimizer is concerned.

What Are Bind Peeking and Bind Capture?

By using bind variables we are hiding the actual value of the bind variable from the optimizer. We did this for a good reason. We want to avoid excessive parsing of every SQL with a different predicate value. That's a good strategy when the data is not skewed and your execution plan is not likely to change depending on the value passed in as the bind variable. With skewed data, the optimizer could benefit from knowing the value of the bind variable being passed to the SQL. This process is called "bind peeking" and is done during hard parsing. Bind capture, on the other hand, is a snapshot of the value of actual bind variables being used during execution of the SQL. The values used for the bind, in this case b1, are collected and available to SQLT. In the example below (Figure 5-9) we see the header section in the SQLT report where you hyperlink to the bind section.

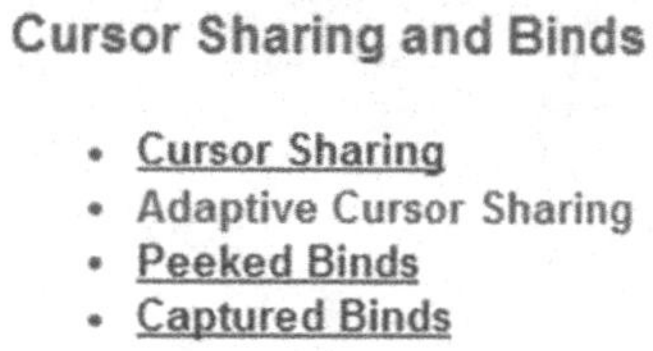

Cursor Sharing and Binds

- Cursor Sharing
- Adaptive Cursor Sharing
- Peeked Binds
- Captured Binds

Figure 5-9. *Where do you find your binds?*

In cases where skewness is important and you suspect that the values of the binds are sending the optimizer down the wrong path, you may want to look at the section "Captured Binds." In conjunction with the captured binds and the timestamps (and any reports of poor performance) you can track down why a particular statement decided to do the wrong thing.

Cursor_Sharing and Its Values

The CURSOR_SHARING parameter was introduced by Oracle to address the issues caused by code, which did not use bind variables as described above. When bind variables are not used, the SQL text has to be parsed by the optimizer. This is a costly operation, and it's probably a waste of time if the only thing that's changed is the value of a literal.

CURSOR_SHARING has two supported values: EXACT, FORCE, (SIMILAR is deprecated). EXACT is the default and tells the optimizer to consider each SQL text as it comes across it. If your application is well written and uses binds and literals as seems most efficient, then leaving EXACT alone is the best choice.

CURSOR_SHARING set to FORCE tells the optimizer to use binds for all the predicates (and it will make its own names). This is a value you would use if you had a badly written application and you wanted to take advantage of the performance gains from using bind variables, without modifying your application to use bind variables.

CURSOR_SHARING set to SIMILAR is deprecated as of 11g and should not be used, but it's probably worth mentioning that it was an "intelligent" version of CURSOR_SHARING=FORCE. It created system-defined bind variables in most cases unless the bind variable affected the optimization in some way. It was not a complete solution, and the introduction of Adaptive Cursor Sharing is a big improvement on CURSOR_SHARING=SIMILAR. The value of the parameter CURSOR_SHARING is important to note so that you understand if the bind variables are in play. You will also see in the SQL text section of the SQL report that if literals have been replaced by bind variables they will have system-defined names.

The Case of the Variable Execution Time

Sometimes it is better to have a slightly longer stable execution time than a slightly faster unstable plan. Unstable execution times (where the execution time can vary widely) cause problems with scheduling of batch jobs. In the example case here, the execution times have never been stable. You're in a preproduction environment and you want to get some information on what can be done to improve the stability of the execution time. You have a luxury in that you have a test environment with representative queries and data. So after the test you look at the AWR reports and decide that one particular query needs attention, because sometimes it takes a long time. We get the SQL_ID and generate the SQLT. We want to know what's happening with the execution plans, so we look in the "Execution Plans" section as shown in Figure 5-10.

Execution Plans

List ordered by phv and source.

#	Plan Hash Value	SQLT Plan Hash Value[1]	SQLT Plan Hash Value2[1]	Source	Optimizer	Optimizer Cost	Estimated Cardinality E-Rows
1	120554201	61390	99667	GV$SQL_PLAN	ALL_ROWS	7842	1
2	120554201	61390	61390	DBA_HIST_SQL_PLAN	ALL_ROWS	8270	1
3	131373180	64036	64036	DBA_HIST_SQL_PLAN	ALL_ROWS	1375	1
4	1614338826	64983	64983	DBA_HIST_SQL_PLAN	ALL_ROWS	2150	1
5	1668747783	76929	76929	DBA_HIST_SQL_PLAN	ALL_ROWS	2505	1
6	2119495741 [W]	45009	99974	GV$SQL_PLAN	ALL_ROWS	5716	1
7	2119495741 [W]	45009	45009	DBA_HIST_SQL_PLAN	ALL_ROWS	1602	1
8	2400898817	65212	66561	GV$SQL_PLAN	ALL_ROWS	471	1
9	2400898817	65212	65212	DBA_HIST_SQL_PLAN	ALL_ROWS	114	1
10	2940811422	96795	34746	GV$SQL_PLAN	ALL_ROWS	639	1
11	2940811422	96795	96795	DBA_HIST_SQL_PLAN	ALL_ROWS	752	1
12	3804161108	55912	50329	GV$SQL_PLAN	ALL_ROWS	7075	1
13	3804161108	55912	55912	DBA_HIST_SQL_PLAN	ALL_ROWS	1996	1
14	89845702 [B]	49559	49559	DBA_HIST_SQL_PLAN	ALL_ROWS	994	1
15	97911461	40164	40164	DBA_HIST_SQL_PLAN	ALL_ROWS	8083	1
16	997939244	53015	53015	DBA_HIST_SQL_PLAN	ALL_ROWS	2650	1

(1) SQLT PHV considers id, parent_id, operation, options, index_columns and object_name. SQLT PHV2 includes also access and filter predicat
(2) Display of child plans is restricted up to 10 per phv as per tool parameter "r_rows_table_xs".

Figure 5-10. Shows many different execution plans

In the "Execution Plans" section we see that there are many different execution plans. Why would we have so many different execution plans? Let's look at the worst execution plan first, as shown in Figure 5-11 (the left side of the screen) and Figure 5-12 (on the right side). We see many Nested Loop steps in Figure 5-11 and many underestimates in Figure 5-12.

SQL: [±]

ID	Exec Ord	Operation	Go To	More	Cost²
0	23	SELECT STATEMENT			5716
1	22	SORT AGGREGATE		[+]	5716
2	21	. VIEW VIEW1			5716
3	20	.. FILTER		[+]	5716
4	19	... HASH GROUP BY		[+]	5716
5	18	.... NESTED LOOPS		[+]	7871
6	16	.... NESTED LOOPS		[+]	5715
7	13	.... NESTED LOOPS		[+]	3559
8	9	.... NESTED LOOPS		[+]	1404
9	7	.... NESTED LOOPS		[+]	1404
10	4	.... NESTED LOOPS		[+]	1368
11	1	....+....+ TABLE ACCESS FULL TABLE1	[+]	[+]	1362
12	3	....+....+ TABLE ACCESS BY INDEX ROWID INDEX1	[+]	[+]	1
13	2	....+....+. INDEX UNIQUE SCAN PK_INDEX1	[+]	[+]	0
14	6	....+.... TABLE ACCESS BY INDEX ROWID TABLE1	[+]	[+]	6

Figure 5-11. *The worst execution plan as selected by clicking on the "W" from the list of execution plans in Figure 5-10*

Cost²	Estim Card	Last Starts	Last Output Rows	Last Over/Under Estimate[1]
5716	1	1	1	1x
5716	1	1	1	1x
5716	1	1	3	3x under
5716		1	3	
5716	1	1	6	6x under
7871		1	26	
5715	1	1	165633	*** 165633x under
3559	1	1	31	* 31x under
1404	1	1	2058237	*** 2058237x under
1404	1	1	2058237	*** 2058237x under
1368	6	1	25382	*** 4230x under
1362	6	1	25382	*** 4230x under
1	1	25382	25382	1x
0	1	25382	25382	1x
6	1	25382	2058237	* 81x under

Figure 5-12. *The numbers highlighted with *** show very big underestimates by the optimizer*

Since we have actual rows returned, we can look at the over- and underestimates. We have quite a few of them, so something is not right. Possibly more than one thing is not right. Since the first step, Line 11, is already "wrong," by a factor of 4,230.

This is where your investigation would start, by looking at the predicates which give rise to the Cardinality Estimates on those lines. Check the histograms against what you expect. For more complex predicates the same methodology applies, you just might have to combine predicates to determine the estimated selectivity. For example 'Ferrari' AND 'red' or SUBSTR(CAR_MAKE,0,1)='F'. These kinds of functions can obscure the intended histogram bucket (by making it unclear which bucket we will hit). This means the optimizer can't use the histogram which could cause cardinality misestimates and bad plans. So use complex predicates with care. Extended statistics can help with this (more about this in the next chapter).

Once you have decided you need a histogram, do you have the right histogram? Do you have special values requiring TOP_FREQUENCY or HYBRID histograms? SQLT has the details for you to investigate.

Summary

Skewness is one of the most difficult concepts to understand and one of the most troublesome to deal with in SQL. Many attempts have been made through iterations of the Oracle software to deal with the problem. SQLTXPLAIN is there with the information to get your plan stable and the right statistics collected. In the next chapter we will look at query transformation that the optimizer does during parsing to get your execution plan to execute quickly.

CHAPTER 6

■ ■ ■

Collecting Good Oracle 12c Statistics

I probably do go on and on about statistics, how it is crucial to collect good statistics, how statistics are to blame for all the tuning ills in the world, and how all tuning problems would be fixed if we just had good statistics. But what exactly are good statistics and why can't we rely on the default mechanisms and auto-collection mechanism to do the job for us? The answer is that you probably can, most of the time! But when the automation is not ideal then you have to know what is happening, what good practices are, and how to get the show back on the road.

It's like flying a, airplane on auto-pilot. Sure you can learn to turn it on when you take off, twiddle a couple of buttons, and then let it take you wherever it takes you, land using the ILS, use auto-throttle and auto-braking and then stand by the airplane door while the passengers disembark and you take all the credit. The passengers wouldn't be too pleased to learn, however, if they found out you didn't know what to do if the auto-pilot failed, or if you didn't know what the auto-pilot was doing in every phase of the flight. While this may not be a perfect analogy, the lesson is you should at least know what the automated procedures are doing for you and know what corrective measures to take if things start to go wrong.

What Does the Auto Stats Job Do For you?

The automatic jobs (which run from 10 p.m. until 2 a.m. at night by default) is a good first step in managing statistics on your system, but you should be aware of the difference between the automated job and dbms_stats.gather_schema_stats procedure. The first uses auto-settings (see below), which includes

1. estimate_percent of dbms_stats.auto_sample_size, which can be as high as 100% but can also be as low as near zero 0%. The values you have set are shown under the SQLT DBMS_STATS setup section. (See Figure 6-2).

2. method_opt is also set by default to for all columns size auto.

3. granulatiry is set to 'AUTO'.

4. cascade is set to dbms_stats.auto_cascade.

5. options is set to GATHER AUTO.

The second collects statistics on all objects, with any object preferences maintained.

© Stelios Charalambides 2017
S. Charalambides, *Oracle SQL Tuning with Oracle SQLTXPLAIN*, DOI 10.1007/978-1-4842-2436-6_6

You can find out if the automatic job is running or not with

```
SQL> SELECT CLIENT_NAME, STATUS FROM DBA_AUTOTASK_CLIENT WHERE CLIENT_NAME='auto optimizer
stats collection';
```

Some DBAs will disable this automatic job and collect their own statistics in their own way. This is not something to be recommended. Although it gives you complete control, the procedures tend to get complex after a while and become difficult to maintain from version to version. In my opinion the best option is to use the automation and build over this your own preferences. What kinds of statistics are there?

Statistics can be divided into four groups: Dictionary, Fixed Object, System, and User Object statistics. Each of them is important, in that bad statistics in any of these groups could cause serious problems. I'll describe each type, from the least often modified to the most often modified (on average). Your system may be different: for example, you may have a system that requires fixed object statistics to be gathered relatively often. I'll end each description with what can happen if the types of statistics are wrong (usually bad).

Dictionary Statistics

In previous versions of Oracle these were often collected when the database was newly created, which included upgrades and installations. The Dictionary statistics are about the tables and other objects that represent the information about other objects in the database (i.e., Your Tables, Indexes, and other objects). In 12c you can set the automation to collect Dictionary statistics regularly. You can do this manually with

```
SQL> exec dbms_stats.gather_system_stats();

PL/SQL procedure successfully completed.
```

Or you can set Global Preferences for the overnight procedure to collect the Dictionary statistics in the maintenance window. You would only do this if you did not want object statistics gathered.

```
SQL> exec dbms_stats.set_global_prefs('AUTOSTATS_TARGET','ORACLE');

PL/SQL procedure successfully completed.
```

Naturally SQLT collects this information and you can see it by navigating from the Top of the main report. See Figure 6-1.

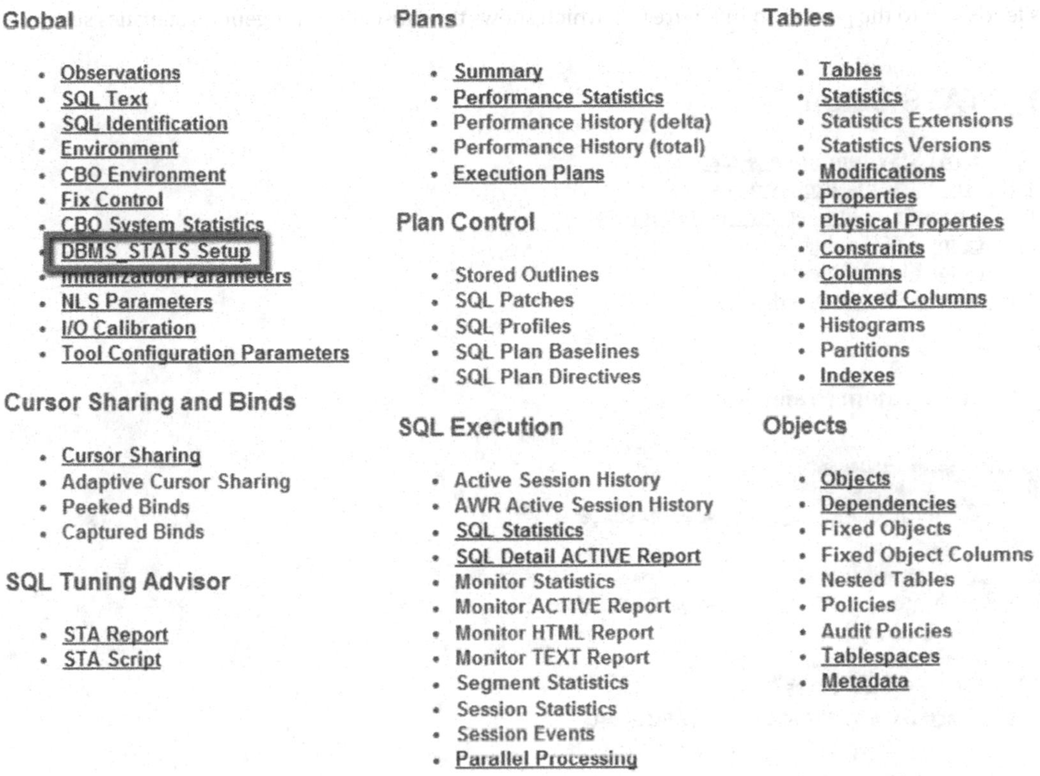

Global

- Observations
- SQL Text
- SQL Identification
- Environment
- CBO Environment
- Fix Control
- CBO System Statistics
- DBMS_STATS Setup
- Initialization Parameters
- NLS Parameters
- I/O Calibration
- Tool Configuration Parameters

Cursor Sharing and Binds

- Cursor Sharing
- Adaptive Cursor Sharing
- Peeked Binds
- Captured Binds

SQL Tuning Advisor

- STA Report
- STA Script

Plans

- Summary
- Performance Statistics
- Performance History (delta)
- Performance History (total)
- Execution Plans

Plan Control

- Stored Outlines
- SQL Patches
- SQL Profiles
- SQL Plan Baselines
- SQL Plan Directives

SQL Execution

- Active Session History
- AWR Active Session History
- SQL Statistics
- SQL Detail ACTIVE Report
- Monitor Statistics
- Monitor ACTIVE Report
- Monitor HTML Report
- Monitor TEXT Report
- Segment Statistics
- Session Statistics
- Session Events
- Parallel Processing

Tables

- Tables
- Statistics
- Statistics Extensions
- Statistics Versions
- Modifications
- Properties
- Physical Properties
- Constraints
- Columns
- Indexed Columns
- Histograms
- Partitions
- Indexes

Objects

- Objects
- Dependencies
- Fixed Objects
- Fixed Object Columns
- Nested Tables
- Policies
- Audit Policies
- Tablespaces
- Metadata

Figure 6-1. *The Dictionary Statistics set up can be seen by following this hyperlink*

This leads you to the page seen in Figure 6-2, which shows the subsections for general statistics set up.

DBMS_STATS Setup

- DBMS_STATS System Preferences
- DBMS_STATS Table Preferences
- Auto Task "auto optimizer stats collection"
- Statistics for SYS Tables
- Statistics for Fixed Objects
- DBMS_STATS Operations History

Go to Top

DBMS_STATS System Preferences

Approximate NDV:	"null"
Auto Stats Target:	ORACLE
Cascade:	DBMS_STATS.AUTO_CASCADE
Concurrent:	"null"
Degree:	NULL
Estimate Percent:	DBMS_STATS.AUTO_SAMPLE_SIZE
Granularity:	AUTO
Incremental Internal Control:	"null"
Incremental:	FALSE
Method Opt:	FOR ALL COLUMNS SIZE AUTO
No Invalidate:	DBMS_STATS.AUTO_INVALIDATE
Publish:	TRUE
Stale Percent:	10
Stats Retention:	"null"

Figure 6-2. *The DBMS_STATS section of the report lists the System Preferences*

Here we see that the "Auto Stats Target" is "ORACLE" Rather than the usual "AUTO". "ORACLE," will automatically collect Dictionary statistics in the overnight window. The value for AUTOSTATS_TARGET can also be 'ALL', which collects statistics for all objects.

If these statistics are substantially wrong then all sorts of internal operations can be slow and quite often with very little clue from the user perspective.

Fixed Objects Statistics

Fixed object statistics are for Dynamic performance tables. What is this exactly? It covers the following:

X$ Tables

V$ Tables

There are some special features about Fixed Object Statistics. First they are not automatically collected except in 12c. Because they relate to Dynamic views (which as you can guess from the name are dynamically generated when the system is active) you cannot just gather these statistics during the overnight maintenance window. You need to gather these statistics (if you are going to gather them) during the time when the Dynamic views are suitably loaded. This usually means during the time when the system is working hard. As you can imagine, not many people would volunteer to run an extra maintenance procedure during the time of peak load, so this procedure might get ignored. Failing to run this during the peak load, the next best choice is to run this after the system has been 'warmed up.' You might want to do this if your system changes in a way that substantially affects the Dynamic objects. For example, the number of objects in your system changes substantially. For example you import a new application with thousands of new tables and indexes. This might be a good occasion to regather fixed object statistics.

```
SQL> exec dbms_stats.gather_fixed_objects_stats;

PL/SQL procedure successfully completed.
```

If you do not gather Fixed Object Stats the system will use predefined values. Here is an example of a system with some objects with no statistics.

As you can see from Figure 6-3 there are 131 objects that are marked as "NO STATS." It is not unusual to have some objects with no statistics and as I mentioned in a case like this, where some Fixed Objects have no statistics, predefined values will be used.

Statistics for Fixed Objects

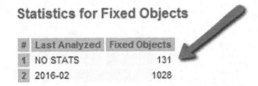

#	Last Analyzed	Fixed Objects
1	NO STATS	131
2	2016-02	1028

DBMS_STATS Operations History

List restricted up to 300 rows as per tool parameter "r_rows_table_m".
SQL [±]

#	Start Time	End Time	Operation	Target
1	2016-08-01/12:03:55.389651 -04:00	2016-08-01/12:03:55.509955 -04:00	export_table_stats	SYS.AUX_STATS$
2	2016-08-01/11:57:53.107424 -04:00	2016-08-01/11:58:13.798230 -04:00	gather_system_stats	
3	2016-07-25/15:03:01.547763 -04:00	2016-07-25/15:03:01.597070 -04:00	export_stats_for_dp	STELIOS
4	2016-07-25/14:57:19.463365 -04:00	2016-07-25/14:57:24.085330 -04:00	export_stats_for_dp	STELIOS
5	2016-07-25/14:41:57.385942 -04:00	2016-07-25/14:42:01.979829 -04:00	export_stats_for_dp	STELIOS

Go to Top

Figure 6-3. *Fixed Objects Statistics*

If Fixed Object Statistics are substantially wrong you may find that some SQLs are unexpectedly affected, especially if there are recursive SQLs being issued on your behalf (for example, checking the privilege access before parsing an object).

System Statistics

This type of Statistic is crucial to the correct cardinality estimates for the optimizer. I always feel that this is like telling the optimizer what kind of system it is on. Is it fast CPUs with slow disks, or fast CPUs with fast disks (e.g., an Exadata system) or somewhere in between. By knowing the numbers for the performance capabilities of the system it can make the best choices for when to access a disk by Full Table Scan or Index Range Scan. The numbers gathered here give a good indication of how long (wall clock time) it will take to execute a particular SQL on a system. Remember (Chapter 4) that cost is a number representing how many equivalent single-block reads we have to wait for. So a cost of 1,000 on a system with SREADTIM of 1ms will take 1 second (1000 x 1 ms = 1 second). For queries that do not do any I/O this still holds true, so for a query that has a cost of 1,000 (but no I/O component) the cost is the estimated time (which includes all components; single-block reads, multi-block reads, and CPU cycles) divided by SREADTIM. Even with I/O calibration in place these fundamental concepts are unchanged. Don't forget this is on an empty system, or at least on a system where the I/O wait time is the expected value. If your calculations for wall clock time do not tally with the cost for a plan it could be that your system statistics are wrong. You should know what reasonable values are for your type of system (you can look them up on the manufacturer's site). The numbers represented here are CPU speed, IOSEEKTIM (a component of the I/O access time), MBRC (Multi-Block Read Count), Single-block read time (SREADTIM) and Multi-Block Read Time (MREADTIM). Here is an example on a slow system (Figure 6-4).

Basis and Synthesized Values

db_block_size:	8192
db_file_multiblock_read_count:	128
_db_file_optimizer_read_count:	8
_db_file_exec_read_count:	-1
Estimated CPUSPEED:	2286
Estimated MBRC:	128
Estimated SREADTIM:	19
Estimated MREADTIM:	273
CPU Cost Scaling Factor:	2.302344e-08
CPU Cost Scaling Factor (inverse):	43434000

Figure 6-4. *System Statistics from a slow system*

The question with system statistics is how to collect them. There are two basic ways. "NOWORKLOAD" and INTERVAL mode. (START and STOP are just INTERVAL modes where you manually start and stop the clock). NOWORKLOAD will set some values up on your system without watching the workload. INTERVAL will monitor the system during a specific interval, presumably during a time when you think the workload is representative of the normal workload. For an Exadata system there is a specific value for system statistics.

```
SQL> exec dbms_stats.gather_system_stats('EXADATA');
```

If I want to collect statistics in an INTERVAL mode I would use this procedure.
First Check the old values

```
SQL> select * from sys.aux_stats$;
```

Create a new and old Statistics Table

```
SQL> exec dbms_stats.create_stat_table(ownname=>'SYS',stattab=>'oldstats');
SQL> exec dbms_stats.create_stat_table(ownname=>'SYS',stattab=>'newstats');
```

Save the old Statistics

```
SQL> exec dbms_stats.export_system_stats(stattab=>'oldstats');
```

Gather the INTERVAL statistics for 30 minutes (or whatever period makes sense on your system)

```
SQL> exec DBMS_STATS.GATHER_SYSTEM_STATS(gathering_mode=>'INTERVAL', interval=>30,
stattab=>'newstats');
```

Wait for the status of COMPLETED which you can check from

```
SQL> select c1 from sys.newstats;
```

Then import the statistics

```
SQL> exec dbms_stats.import_system_stats(stattab=>'newstats');
```

Check the new values

```
SQL> select * from sys.aux_stats$;
```

If you need to revert the statistics

```
SQL> exec dbms_stats.import_system_stats(stattab=>'oldstats');
```

If system Statistics are substantially wrong you will get wrong costs for plans and potentially wrong plans as well. It is best to have the right system statistics for your system. It stands to reason that if your system changes you also need to change you system statistics. If you migrate your database from one system to another, system statistics may no longer be applicable. If you've just moved from a slow car with bad suspension and bad brakes to a super car with amazing acceleration and superb brakes, you journey times should be shorter!

Object Statistics

This is the big one! Not because the other statistics mentioned so far are unimportant, they are. They are important and can affect your entire system. Object statistics are the big ones because this is where all the complication lies. This is where statistics most often cause problems. Consider the following complications

1. Adaptive Statistics

2. Incremental/Partitioned Statistics

3. Specific Preferences on some Tables

4. Column Groups

These are just some of the topics in this area that can cause complications. There are many others, too many to mention in one brief chapter. Detailed work on all aspects of statistics could easily be another book!)

My preferred approach to Object Statistics is to allow the automatics to do their job unless you have a good reason to suppose something is wrong. If you find something is wrong and it leads to statistics problems, then you should amend the procedures for your system. If you've applied SQL Profiles then most likely there is something wrong. Try and find out (using SQLT) what went wrong and fix the underlying statistics. If you can then remove the Profile and get as good or better performance, you have fixed the underlying problem. Let's look at adaptive statistics first.

Adaptive Statistics

If you see lines like these in your SQLT report (see Figure 6-5)

#	Plan Hash Value	SQLT Plan Hash Value[1]	SQLT Plan Hash Value2[1]	Src	Source	Plan Info		Plan Stability	Is Bind Sensitive
61	3698280055	87420	87420	AWR	DBA_HIST_SQL_PLAN	adaptive_plan	yes		
62	3752385408 [W]	34812	34812	AWR	DBA_HIST_SQL_PLAN	adaptive_plan	yes		
						dynamic_sampling	2		
63	3795467417	26909	26909	AWR	DBA_HIST_SQL_PLAN	adaptive_plan	yes		
64	3898120917	30140	30140	AWR	DBA_HIST_SQL_PLAN	adaptive_plan	yes		
						cardinality_feedback	yes		
						dynamic_sampling	2		
65	3961734325	74543	74543	AWR	DBA_HIST_SQL_PLAN	adaptive_plan	yes		
						cardinality_feedback	yes		
						dynamic_sampling	2		
66	3997239467	92330	92330	AWR	DBA_HIST_SQL_PLAN	adaptive_plan	yes		
						dynamic_sampling	2		
67	4059439692	93084	93084	AWR	DBA_HIST_SQL_PLAN	adaptive_plan	yes		
						cardinality_feedback	yes		

Figure 6-5. *Many Adaptive, plans and Dynamic Sampling*

under the execution plan list you know merely from the number of plans (67 in this case) that the optimizer is 'hunting' around for a good plan. Each time the optimizer 'realizes' the plan is non-optimal and is attempting to fix it by adapting the lines of the plan and in some cases (as in this one) is also re-parsing the SQL (Cardinality Feedback) in an attempt to get the good plan. If you see lines like these in your report, it means that the data is most likely skewed and that the object statistics have some flaws in them. This should be an indication that you should be looking at your application object statistics to determine what can be done to help the optimizer. In other words, the best course of action when you see something like this is to determine why there are Adaptive Plans and adjust your statistics. We cover adaptive statistics in more detail in Chapter 11.

Incremental/Partitioned Statistics

If you have a system with large tables that are loaded incrementally with new data on a regular basis with new partitions, incremental statistics settings can be a big improvement to your overnight maintenance procedures. For partitioned objects there are global statistics (which are collected at the table level) and partition and sub-partition level. If you set INCREMETAL=TRUE (FALSE is the default) for a Partitioned table then every time you gather statistics on a particular partition you may end up scanning the entire table. This is done to keep the global statistics up to date. Remember the purpose of INCREMENTAL statistics is to keep the statistics up to date for the entire table, just do it in a faster way. If aggregated information only is needed from other partitions then this will be used. While this may be accurate it can also be time consuming. If INCREMENTAL is set to TRUE and GRANULARITY is set to GLOBAL and PARTITION (NOT Sub-partitions) you will get Global and partition statistics without collecting statistics on the entire table, because it will be collected for you automatically if any DML has been done on other partitions, but not if no DML has been done. To see if your Global and Partitioned Statistics are being gathered in a sensible way you can click on the "YES" in the "Table Statistics" section. See Figure 6-6.

Part	Temp
NO	N
YES	N
YES	N
YES	N
YES	N

Figure 6-6. The hyperlinks "YES" show the Partition statistics dates and partition sizes

When new partitions are created one option that is useful is to seed new partitions' statistics with the statistics from old partitions. A fairly common occurrence is to create a new partition at the beginning of a period (say a new month or new year). In the initial period the row count may be small and the statistics may be inaccurate. A good option in case such as this is to copy the statistics from an old partition with representative data until the new partition has sufficient data to have good statistics collected for it.

Object Preferences

Setting object preferences is easy. Just user SET_*_PREFERENCES

1. SET_TABLE_PREFERENCES

2. SET_GLOBAL_PREFERENCES

3. SET_DATABASE_PREFERENCES

to set the preference at the appropriate level. Most often you will want to tweak a specific table, for example, to not collect a histogram on a column. For example

```
SQL> exec dbms_stats.set_table_prefs(ownname=>'STELIOS', tabname=>'TEST', pname=>'method_opt', pvalue =>'FOR COLUMNS COL1 SIZE 1');
```

This does not remove the histogram. It just sets up the preference to not collect it in future. You also have to delete the histogram if one is already there. By setting up preferences you can continue to use the automated procedures that will honor your preferences. This gets you the best of both worlds: the automation is out of the box and some preferences that are suitable to your data layout.

Automated Statistics Collection Operations

Apart from Dynamic Sampling there are some situations in which Oracle will collect statistics for you whether you asked for them or not. For example, if you create an Index in a table

```
SQL> create index i1 on t1 (owner);

Index created.

SQL> select last_analyzed from user_ind_statistics where index_name='I1';

LAST_ANAL
---------
01-AUG-16
```

   Or if you ALTER an index

```
SQL> exec dbms_stats.delete_index_stats(ownname=>'STELIOS',indname=>'I1');

PL/SQL procedure successfully completed.

SQL> select last_analyzed from user_ind_statistics where index_name='I1';

LAST_ANAL
---------

SQL> alter index i1 rebuild online;

Index altered.

SQL> select last_analyzed from user_ind_statistics where index_name='I1';

LAST_ANAL
---------
01-AUG-16
```

   The same applies to Bulk loads (but which does not collect Histograms) or to CREATE TABLE AS SELECT statements or to INSERT Statements if the table is empty.

Pending Statistics

Pending statistics are a great tool for testing changes to your statistics collection. If you collect statistics in a pending mode (by setting PUBLISH to FALSE), you can test your new statistics before unleashing them on the whole database.

```
SQL> exec dbms_stats.set_table_prefs(ownname=>'STELIOS',TABNAME=>'T1',pname=>'PUBLISH',
pvalue=>'FALSE');

PL/SQL procedure successfully completed.
```

Then when you are happy with the statistics

```
SQL> exec dbms_stats.publish_pending_stats(ownname=>'STELIOS',tabname=>'T1');
```

Volatile Tables

Some objects just by their nature have widely fluctuating counts and distribution of data: for example, Global Temporary Tables (GTTs) or Intermediate Work Tables. For these kinds of objects you should not collect statistics because at the time of the collection there will be no representative data leading to bad cardinality estimates and bad execution plans. The best option in these cases is to fill the table with representative data, collect the statistics in the normal way, then lock them with dbms_stats.lock_table_stats. In cases where empty partitions are being added to a table, which will not have good representative data for a few days (while data is being loaded), another option is to use a non-partitioned table to act as a source of good statistics for the table and then use an exchange partition to load the new partition without gathering statistics at the partition level. Here is the command for the last step.

```
SQL> alter table t1 exchange partition p1 with table t2;
```

In this case t1 is the partition table and t2 is the non-partitioned table. Think of this as a transfusion of good statistics for a new partition from a prepared non-partitioned table.

Parallel Statistics gathering

The DEGREE parameter of the dbms_stats procedures is one of the controls of parallelism for statistics gathering. An example would be

```
SQL> exec dbms_stats.gather_table_stats('SH','SALES',degree=>4);

PL/SQL procedure successfully completed.
```

Summary

Statistics gathering and maintenance is at the heart of tuning. This chapter is by no means a complete coverage of the subject. The bare bones of the subject covered here is to give you a high-level view of what can be done and should give enough of a push to go look at the published Oracle MOS notes and White Papers that cover various aspects of this subject (http://www.oracle.com/technetwork/database/bi-datawarehousing/twp-bp-for-stats-gather-12c-1967354.pdf). Do not assume that just because there are many automated options for statistics gathering that these are always appropriate for all circumstances. You should check what you are gathering and tweak it if needed with preferences on object statistics. Also please remember just because the complications lie in the Object statistics there are other statistics to be considered. Go check on them today; who knows what you might find.

## CHAPTER 7

Tracing CBO Decisions, Hints, and Query Transformations Using 10053

The Oracle query optimizer is an amazing piece of code, developed and improved over the years to generate execution plans that are both easy to generate and that run fast. The optimizer uses a number of "tricks" along the way to improve the speed of execution and implements the execution plan in a way that gives the same results as your unmodified SQL. These "tricks" (or heuristics) sometimes include query transformations.

Query transformations, as the name implies, change the SQL query from its original text into something different: but it still gives the same result. This is a little bit like saying you want to go from London to New York, and you have decided to go via Orlando, have a nice rest, visit Disneyworld, soak up the sun, and then drive up the East Coast. A query transformation would optimize your journey by using heuristics. One of the heuristics might be, "If there is a direct flight from your starting point to your destination, then avoid using stopovers in other locations." Or perhaps you could rewrite the rule and use "minimize the number of stopover points in your journey." I'm sure you can see this could get pretty complicated, even for my simple example. What if you really wanted to see Mickey Mouse? Then the plan would be more difficult to change. Sometimes even the simplest Mickey Mouse queries can cause problems when you're trying to make the journey quickly and efficiently.

What Are Query Transformations?

To explain what is meant by "query transformation," from the point of view of an SQL query, let's look at a simple example. Ask yourself a question. Is this query something that can be simplified?

```
SQL> select * from (select * from sales); -- Query 1
```

This query "obviously" simplifies to

```
SQL> select * from sales; -- Query 2
```

Or how about this

```
SQL> with t as (select * from sales) select * from t; -- Query 3
```

That's about the simplest example of a query transformation. Query 1 was transformed into query 2. There is no danger with this query transformation that the results will be different between version 1 and version 2 of the query. Query 3 is yet another way of writing the same thing with an inline view definition. This particular transformation is called "subquery unnesting." Each transformation has its name and its set of rules to follow to ensure that the end results are correct as well as optimized. Does the cost-based optimizer recognize this fact? Let's ask the optimizer to calculate a plan for a very simple query; but we'll use a hint that tells it to not use any query transformations. Here is the SQL and the execution plan.

```
SQL> select /*+ no_query_transformation */ * from (select * from sales);
Execution Plan
-------------------------------------------------------------
Plan hash value: 2635429107
```

Id	Operation	Name	Rows	Bytes	Cost (%CPU)	Time	Pstart	Pstop
0	SELECT STATEMENT		918K	76M	517 (2)	00:00:01		
1	PARTITION RANGE ALL		918K	76M	517 (2)	00:00:01	1	28
2	VIEW		918K	76M	517 (2)	00:00:01		
3	TABLE ACCESS FULL	SALES	918K	25M	517 (2)	00:00:01	1	28

We see from this example that the optimizer chose to access SALES with a full table scan. This is required because of the select * from sales inside the round brackets. Then the optimizer chose to create a view on that data and select all of the partitions to create the selected data. So the optimizer collected all the data inside the bracket and then presented the data to the next select. Now, however, let's give the optimizer a chance to show us how clever it is. Now we run the query but without our hint. Now the optimizer can use query optimizations.

```
SQL> select  * from (select * from sales);
Execution Plan
-------------------------------------------------------------
Plan hash value: 1550251865
```

Id	Operation	Name	Rows	Bytes	Cost (%CPU)	Time	Pstart	Pstop
0	SELECT STATEMENT		918K	25M	517 (2)	00:00:01		
1	PARTITION RANGE ALL		918K	25M	517 (2)	00:00:01	1	28
2	TABLE ACCESS FULL	SALES	918K	25M	517 (2)	00:00:01	1	28

Now we see that the optimizer has chosen a simpler plan. The VIEW step has been eliminated and is in fact now the same execution plan as the select statement with no subquery:

```
SQL> select * from sales;

Execution Plan
-------------------------------------------------------------
Plan hash value: 1550251865
```

Id	Operation	Name	Rows	Bytes	Cost (%CPU)	Time	Pstart	Pstop
0	SELECT STATEMENT		918K	25M	517 (2)	00:00:01		
1	PARTITION RANGE ALL		918K	25M	517 (2)	00:00:01	1	28
2	TABLE ACCESS FULL	SALES	918K	25M	517 (2)	00:00:01	1	28

Just to prove the point that query transformations are doing something, I show an example below that nests the select statements, and we see from the execution plan that the optimizer has added a view for every layer. This is because I have told the optimizer to not use any query transformations with the hint /*+ no_query_transformation */.

```
SQL> select /*+ no_query_transformation */ * from (select * from (select * from (
select * from sales)));
Execution Plan
-----------------------------------------------------------
Plan hash value: 1018107371
```

Id	Operation	Name	Rows	Bytes	Cost (%CPU)	Time	Pstart	Pstop
0	SELECT STATEMENT		918K	76M	517 (5)	00:00:01		
1	PARTITION RANGE ALL		918K	76M	517 (5)	00:00:01	1	28
2	VIEW		918K	76M	517 (5)	00:00:01		
3	VIEW		918K	76M	517 (5)	00:00:01		
4	VIEW		918K	76M	517 (5)	00:00:01		
5	TABLE ACCESS FULL	SALES	918K	25M	517 (5)	00:00:01	1	28

If we go back to the original question at the beginning of this chapter, "Can this query be simplified?," we see that in this simple case the answer is "yes." This partially answers the question: "Why do we simplify queries?" The answer to this question is that the cost-based optimizer knows some rules it can use to save the execution engine from doing some work. The example given is very simple and for illustrative purposes only, but it does explain why we need to do query transformation.

The next question you might ask is, "if the CBO knows all these rules to simplify my query, why do I need to know about it and what has this got to do with SQLT?" Let me answer the second question first.

SQLT, as a matter of routine, produces many different files that are useful. The main one is the HTML file we've looked at so far, but there are also trace files. One of the trace files is a "10053" trace file, which I'll explain in the next section. The answer to the first question is simply that when things go wrong with the CBO we sometimes need to look at the 10053 trace file to get more detailed information on what decisions the optimizer made during parsing. You can then check these steps against what you consider sensible and decide if the optimizer is making a mistake or has insufficient statistics or some other input is influencing the optimizer in some way that is producing poorly performing SQL.

The 10053 Trace File

The 10053 trace file is the result of a request to trace an SQL statement. More properly, it is a request to trace the steps the optimizer makes to produce the execution plan. The contents are verbose and cryptic but extremely useful if you want to understand what is happening with query transformation.

How Do I Get a 10053 Trace File?

SQLTXPLAIN generates the 10053 trace file automatically and places it in the main reports directory. It has 10053 in the name so it's pretty easy to spot. This is an example file name from the SQLT reports directory:

```
sqlt_s41321_10046_10053_execute.trc
```

If you want to collect 10053 manually (i.e., without using SQLTXPLAIN,) then there are few ways to do it.

Using Alter Session

```
SQL>alter session set max_dump_file_size=unlimited;
SQL> alter session set tracefile_identifier='MY_10053_TRACE';

SQL> Alter session set events 'trace[rdbms.SQL_Optimizer.*][sql:<SQL_ID_FROM_ABOVE]';
SQL> select sysdate from dual;
```

and to turn off 10053 tracing

```
SQL> alter session set events '10053 trace [rdbms.SQL_Optimizer.*] off';
SQL> exit
```

This does require the SQL statement to be executed (as shown in the example). The reason we set max_dump_file_size=unlimited, is that we need the trace file to not be truncated, just as it's getting to the interesting part.

Using Alter Session (Legacy Mode)

```
SQL>alter session set max_dump_file_size=unlimited;
SQL> alter session set tracefile_identifier='MY_10053_TRACE';
SQL> Alter session set events '10053 trace name context forever, level 1';
SQL> select sysdate from dual;
```

and to turn off 10053 tracing

```
SQL> alter session set events '10053 trace name context off';
SQL> exit
```

This also requires the SQL statement to be executed.

In my case this produces a trace file (with a file extension of trc) in the /u02/app/oracle/diag/rdbms/snc1/snc1/trace directory on my machine. The file is called snc1_ora_14738_MY_10053_TRACE.trc. The location is dependent on your operating system and system parameters. This is why it's useful to set the tracefile_identifier parameter, which allows you an easy way to spot your file among all the others. Notice how in my case the instance name (snc1) and ora are placed at the beginning of the name, then the tracefile_identifier value is used, and finally the standard extension makes the full file name.

Using Dump_Trace

The steps are as follows:

1. First we find the sql_id, by knowing the text in the SQL we can search v$sql.

2. Then we can use the dbms_sqldiag.dump_trace routine to get the 10053 trace file. This puts the trace file in the trace area, where we can review it with any text editor.

Let's see those steps in action:

```
SQL> column sql_text format a30
SQL> select sysdate from dual;
```

```
SYSDATE
---------
08-AUG-16

SQL> select sql_id from v$sql where sql_text like 'select sysdate from dual%';

SQL_ID
-------------
7h35uxf5uhmm1

SQL> execute dbms_sqldiag.dump_trace(p_sql_id=>'7h35uxf5uhmm1',
  p_child_number=>0,
  p_component=>'Compiler',p_file_id=>'DIAG');

PL/SQL procedure successfully completed.

SQL> host ls /u02/app/oracle/diag/rdbms/snc1/snc1/trace/*MY_10053*.trc

SQL> host ls -l /u02/app/oracle/diag/rdbms/snc1/snc1/trace/*MY_10053*.trc
-rw-r----- 1 oracle oinstall 127007 Aug  8 14:16
/u02/app/oracle/diag/rdbms/snc1/snc1/trace/snc1_ora_15599_MY_10053.trc
```

To edit the file we can use the text editor

```
SQL> host vi /u02/app/oracle/diag/rdbms/snc1/snc1/trace/snc1_ora_15599_MY_10053.trc
```

This method, which is part of the event infrastructure, has the added advantage that it can capture trace for an SQL statement inside a PL/SQL block. An example of this is shown below. A package specification and body are created to calculate the area of a circle. Then we identify the SQL ID inside the PL/SQL package and trace only the matching statement.

```
SQL> host type area.sql
create or replace package getcircarea as
  function getcircarea(radius number)
  return number;
end getcircarea;
/

create or replace package body getcircarea as
  function getcircarea (radius number) return number
  is area number(8,2);
  begin
    select 3.142*radius*radius into area from dual;
    return area;
  end;
  end getcircarea;
/
set serveroutput on size 100000;

declare
  area number(8,2);
```

```
  begin
    area:= getcircarea.getcircarea(10);
    dbms_output.put_line('Area is '||area);
  end;
/
```

Now let's run the SQL

```
SQL> select sql_text, sql_id from v$sqlarea where sql_text like '%3.142%';


SQL_TEXT
--------------------------------------------------------------------------------
SQL_ID
------------
SELECT 3.142*:B1 *:B1 FROM DUAL
9rjmrhbjuasav

select sql_text, sql_id from v$sqlarea where sql_text like '%3.142%'
ggux6y542z8mr
```

Now we can trace the SQL statement

```
alter session set tracefile_identifier='PLSQL';

Session altered.

alter session set events 'trace[rdbms.SQL_Optimizer.*][sql:9rjmrhbjuasav]';

Session altered.

SQL> @area

Package created.

Package body created.

Area is 314.2

PL/SQL procedure successfully completed.

SQL> host ls /u02/app/oracle/diag/rdbms/snc1/snc1/trace/*PLSQL*.trc

-rw-r----- 1 oracle oinstall 127007 Aug  8 15:16 snc1_ora_15599_PLSQL.trc
```

No more excuses about not being able to get the trace file because the SQL is inside a PL/SQL block. You can turn off tracing for that SQL ID afterwards with

```
ALTER SESSION SET EVENTS 'trace[rdbms.SQL_Optimizer.*]off';
```

What's in a 10053 Trace File?

I remember when I first looked inside a 10053 (many years ago now) thinking, *What is all this gibberish, and how can I possibly understand it?* None of this is documented, and there are many, many short codes for information that are not explained anywhere. It's not as bad as it sounds though: the 10053 trace file is, simply put, a log of what the cost-based optimizer "thought" as it parsed the query in question. It is literally a log of every step considered by the optimizer. It is not often considered a user facing file, so although it is purely text, it is pretty difficult to understand and pretty verbose. After all, the file is written to allow debugging of the optimization process and so has to include everything the optimizer does in great detail. The file was created so that support can fix problems that are discovered in the optimizer. No one to my knowledge has attempted to make the file user friendly. An example section from a 10053 trace file is shown in Figure 7-1.

```
NL Join
   Outer table: Card: 0.000000  Cost: 0.009578  Resp: 0.009578  Degree: 1  Bytes:
Access path analysis for X$KSLWT
   INDEX: 1
      Card: 1.000000
   Scan IO  Cost (Disk) =    0.000000
   Scan CPU Cost (Disk) =   3500.000000
   Total Scan IO  Cost  =    0.000000 (scan (Disk))
                      +  0.000000 (io filter eval) (= 0.000000 (per row) * 1.000000 (#rows))
                      =    0.000000
   Total Scan CPU  Cost =   3500.000000 (scan (Disk))
                      + 400.500000 (cpu filter eval) (= 400.500000 (per row) * 1.000000 (#rows))
                      =   3900.500000
   Inner table: X$KSLWT  Alias: W
   Access Path: TableScan
     NL Join: Cost: 0.009676  Resp: 0.009676  Degree: 1
       Cost_io: 0.000000  Cost_cpu: 384217
       Resp_io: 0.000000  Resp_cpu: 384217

   Best NL cost: 0.009676
          resc: 0.009676  resc_io: 0.000000  resc_cpu: 384217
          resp: 0.009676  resp_io: 0.000000  resc_cpu: 384217
    SPD: Return code in qosdDSDirSetup: NODIR, estType = JOIN
Join Card:  0.000000 = outer (0.000000) * inner (1.000000) * sel (1.000000)
Join Card - Rounded: 1 Computed: 0.000000
   Outer table: X$KSUSE  Alias: S
     resc: 0.009578  card 0.000000  bytes:    deg: 1  resp: 0.009578
   Inner table: X$KSLWT  Alias: W
     resc: 0.009822  card: 1.000000  bytes:    deg: 1  resp: 0.009822
     using dmeth: 2  #groups: 1
     SORT ressource         Sort statistics
       Sort width:          598 Area size:        827392 Max Area size:     104857600
       Degree:             1
       Blocks to Sort: 1 Row size:     39 Total Rows:            1
       Initial runs:    1 Merge passes:  0 IO Cost / pass:         0
       Total IO sort cost: 0.000000      Total CPU sort cost: 39707641
       Total Temp space used: 0
   SM join: Resc: 1.019400  Resp: 1.019400  [multiMatchCost=0.000000]
```

Figure 7-1. *A section of an example 10053 trace file*

Despite the text in a 10053 trace file being difficult to understand, we can see snippets of information that begin to make sense. For example, we've mentioned that NL is short for "nested loop" and that is a kind of join. We see that X$KSLWT is having its Access path analyzed. X$KSLWT was one of the tables involved in this query. We also see references to Cost (we've discussed those in Chapters 1 and 2), and we see a reference to an access path. For example, Table Scan – which in this case is a FIXED TABLE FULL scan. This is the approach to take with a 10053 trace file. Do not try and understand every line of it. You will not be able to because some lines cannot be decoded unless you are a developer working for Oracle. There are a number of different ways to get 10053 trace file information. The simplest way is to use SQLT XTRACT (as described in Chapter 1). This will generate a 10053 trace file and include it in the ZIP file. Sometimes, however, you do not want all the information that SQLT gives you and maybe only after the 10053 trace file, in which case you could use the DBMS_SQLDIAG package as long as you have the SQL ID of the SQL statement you are interested in.

Another advantage DBMS_SQLDIAG has is that you don't need to execute the statement. As long as you have the SQL ID you can get the 10053 trace. This feature is only available from 11g Release 2, however.

What Is a Query Transformation?

Now that we know how to get a 10053 (and SQLT makes that particularly easy), we need to look at some examples of queries (and some query transformations) that can be carried out on them. As we said earlier in the chapter, query transformation is the process the optimizer carries out to change an SQL statement to another SQL statement that is logically the same (and will give the same result).

Here is a list of common query transformations and their codes:

- Subquery Unnesting: SU

- Complex View Merging: CVM

- Join Predicate Push Down: JPPD

Luckily if you want a listing of some of the abbreviations and their meanings you can look in the 10053 trace file in the "Legend" section. Look at Figure 7-2 for an example. A section like this is shown in every 10053 trace file, and it shows all the query transformations that can be used for all SQL statements. This section is not specific to the SQL statement being examined.

```
************************************************
----- Current SQL Statement for this session (sql_id=7h35uxf5uhmm1) -----
select sysdate from dual
************************************************
Legend
The following abbreviations are used by optimizer trace.
CBQT - cost-based query transformation
JPPD - join predicate push-down
OJPPD - old-style (non-cost-based) JPPD
FPD - filter push-down
PM - predicate move-around
CVM - complex view merging
SPJ - select-project-join
SJC - set join conversion
SU - subquery unnesting
OBYE - order by elimination
OST - old style star transformation
ST - new (cbqt) star transformation
CNT - count(col) to count(*) transformation
JE - Join Elimination
JF - join factorization
CBY - connect by
SLP - select list pruning
DP - distinct placement
VT - vector transformation
qb - query block
LB - leaf blocks
DK - distinct keys
LB/K - average number of leaf blocks per key
DB/K - average number of data blocks per key
CLUF - clustering factor
NDV - number of distinct values
Resp - response cost
Card - cardinality
Resc - resource cost
NL - nested loops (join)
SM - sort merge (join)
HA - hash (join)
--------- --- - .
```

Figure 7-2. *The Legend section of the 10053 trace file*

Subquery unnesting, the first query transformation on our list, is formally defined as a query transformation that converts a subquery into a join in the outer query, which then allows subquery tables to be considered for join order, access paths, and join methods. We'll look at this example of query optimization because it is a commonly used one; examples for this are also easy to explain and to generate!

An example query that can use subquery unnesting is:

```
Select
first_name,
last_name,
hire_Date
from employees
where
hire_date IN (
select hire_date from employees where department_id = 30
);
```

The subquery part is inside the brackets, and in this subquery example we are using IN.

Let's see what happens when we trace this query with event 10053, as shown below:

```
SQL> connect hr/hr
Connected.
SQL> alter session set max_dump_file_size=unlimited;

Session altered.

SQL> alter session set events '10053 trace name context forever, level 1';

Session altered.

SQL> select /*+ hard parse */ first_name, last_name, hire_Date
  2  from employees where hire_date in
  3  (select hire_date from employees where
  4  department_id=30);

FIRST_NAME           LAST_NAME                 HIRE_DATE
-------------------- ------------------------- ---------
Den                  Raphaely                  07-DEC-02
Alexander            Khoo                      18-MAY-03
Shelli               Baida                     24-DEC-05
Sigal                Tobias                    24-JUL-05
Guy                  Himuro                    15-NOV-06
Karen                Colmenares                10-AUG-07

6 rows selected.
```

If we edit the trace file, we'll see the header shown in Figure 7-3.

```
Trace file /u02/app/oracle/diag/rdbms/snc1/snc1/trace/snc1_ora_16681.trc
Oracle Database 12c Enterprise Edition Release 12.1.0.2.0 - 64bit Production
With the Partitioning, OLAP, Advanced Analytics and Real Application Testing options
ORACLE_HOME = /u02/app/oracle/product/12.1.0.2/dbhome_1
System name:    Linux
Node name:      d12102.us.oracle.com
Release:        2.6.32-400.29.1.el5uek
Version:        #1 SMP Tue Jun 11 15:16:42 PDT 2013
Machine:        x86_64
Instance name: snc1
Redo thread mounted by this instance: 1
Oracle process number: 34
Unix process pid: 16681, image: oracle@d12102.us.oracle.com (TNS V1-V3)


*** 2016-08-08 15:17:57.879
*** SESSION ID:(56.37651) 2016-08-08 15:17:57.879
*** CLIENT ID:() 2016-08-08 15:17:57.879
*** SERVICE NAME:(SYS$USERS) 2016-08-08 15:17:57.879
*** MODULE NAME:(SQL*Plus) 2016-08-08 15:17:57.879
*** CLIENT DRIVER:(SQL*PLUS) 2016-08-08 15:17:57.879
*** ACTION NAME:() 2016-08-08 15:17:57.879

Registered qb: SEL$1 0xc1069898 (PARSER)
---------------------
QUERY BLOCK SIGNATURE
---------------------
  signature (): qb_name=SEL$1 nbfros=1 flg=0
     fro(0): flg=4 objn=92593 hint_alias="EMPLOYEES"@"SEL$1"

Registered qb: SEL$2 0xc1060e28 (PARSER)
---------------------
QUERY BLOCK SIGNATURE
---------------------
  signature (): qb_name=SEL$2 nbfros=1 flg=0
     fro(0): flg=4 objn=92593 hint_alias="EMPLOYEES"@"SEL$2"

SPM: statement not found in SMB
SPM: capture of plan baseline is OFF

****************************
Automatic degree of parallelism (AUTODOP)
****************************
Automatic degree of parallelism is disabled: Parameter.
kkopqSetForceParallelProperties: Hint:no
Query: compute:yes forced:no forceDop:0
kkopqSetDopReason: Reason why we chose this DOP is: table property.
table property forces parallelism

Global Manual DOP: 1 - Rounded?: no
PM: Considering predicate move-around in query block SEL$1 (#0)
****************************
Predicate Move-Around (PM)
****************************
OPTIMIZER INFORMATION

**************************************************
----- Current SQL Statement for this session (sql_id=3gu9t07w8zhmz) -----
select /*+ hard parse */ first_name, last_name, hire_Date
from employees where hire_date in
(select hire_date from employees where
```

Figure 7-3. *The first page of the example 10053 trace file*

We see the usual signature text, telling us about the operating system, the version of Oracle, and so on. The important part for this discussion is to check that the SQL statement we thought we were parsing is found under the "Current SQL statement for this session" section (at the bottom of Figure 7-3). In our case we put the hint /*+ hard parse */ in the original SQL, and this has appeared in the 10053 section under the "Current SQL section". So we're pretty sure it's the right SQL. So how do we know if subquery unnesting is taking place? We search the 10053 trace file for text similar to that in Figure 7-4. We would search for "subquery unnesting," but I've highlighted the section relating to subquery unnesting. Notice the "SU" at the beginning of the lines. This tells you the optimizer is looking at the query with regard to subquery unnesting.

```
*****************************
Cost-Based Subquery Unnesting
*****************************
SU: Unnesting query blocks in query block SEL$1 (#1) that are valid to unnest.
Subquery removal for query block SEL$2 (#2)
RSW: Not valid for subquery removal SEL$2 (#2)
Subquery unchanged.
Subquery Unnesting on query block SEL$1 (#1)SU: Performing unnesting that does not require
costing.
SU: Considering subquery unnest on query block SEL$1 (#1).
SU:    Checking validity of unnesting subquery SEL$2 (#2)
SU:    Passed validity checks.
SU:    Transforming ANY subquery to a join.
```

Figure 7-4. *The text in the 10053 trace file shows subquery unnesting taking place*

We can also see what the new SQL is after it has been transformed. See Figure 7-5 to see what our test query has been changed into.

```
Final query after transformations:******* UNPARSED QUERY IS *******
SELECT "EMPLOYEES"."FIRST_NAME" "FIRST_NAME","EMPLOYEES"."LAST_NAME"
"LAST_NAME","EMPLOYEES"."HIRE_DATE" "HIRE_DATE" FROM "HR"."EMPLOYEES"
"EMPLOYEES","HR"."EMPLOYEES" "EMPLOYEES" WHERE "EMPLOYEES"."HIRE_DATE"="EMPLOYEES"."HIRE_DATE"
AND "EMPLOYEES"."DEPARTMENT_ID"=30
```

Figure 7-5. *The final query after transformation*

Does this query look semantically the same as the original query to you? This was the original query:

```
Select
first_name,
last_name,
hire_Date
from employees
where
hire_date IN (
select hire_date from employees where department_id = 30
);
```

and this is the new query:

```
Select
first_name,
last_name,
hire_date
from employees A, employees B
where
A.hire_date = B.hire_date
and
A.department_id=30;
```

We see from the above example what subquery unnesting is, from a fairly simple example. The objective of subquery unnesting is to allow the optimizer to possibly use other joins or table orders to get satisfactory results more efficiently. In other words, by removing the subquery we give the optimizer more freedom to use other joins because we've moved the table name up a level into the main query. There are many variations on subquery unnesting. For example, the subquery could utilize NOT IN or NOT EXISTS. We will not cover all the variations and combinations of this technique or cover the other query transformations.

(You could easily write a whole book on just query transformations). Suffice to say the 10053 trace file will list what it has considered and show what it has done. The question you should be asking at this point is, "Why do I care, what the optimizer is doing 'under the hood' if it works properly?"

Why Would We Want to Disable Query Transformations?

There are situations in which you may want to turn off particular transformations: for example, where an optimizer bug is causing a problem. This may be because Oracle support has suggested changes or indicated that there is a problem with a query transformation. You may also see some of the hidden parameters shown below on a system that you are managing. Here are some cost-based optimizer parameters that can influence the CBO with regard to subquery unnesting:

- _complex_view_merging
- _convert_set_to_join
- _unnest_subquery
- _optimizer_cost_based_transformation
- _optimizer_extend_jppd_view_types
- _optimizer_filter_pred_pullup
- _optimizer_group_by_placement
- _optimizer_improve_selectivity
- _optimizer_join_elimination_enabled
- _optimizer_join_factorization
- _optimizer_multi_level_push_pred
- _optimizer_native_full_outer_join
- _optimizer_order_by_elimination_enabled
- _optimizer_push_pred_cost_based
- _optimizer_unnest_all_subqueries
- _optimizer_unnest_corr_set_subq
- _optimizer_squ_bottomup
- _optimizer_null_aware_antijoin
- _pred_move_around
- _push_join_predicate

These are some hints that influence this behavior:

- first_rows(n)
- no_query_transformation
- unnest
- no_unnest
- push_pred

- no_push_pred

- push_subq

- native_full_outer_join

- no_push_subq

- no_set_to_join

- qb_name

This is by no means a complete list of all the hidden parameters influencing the optimizer. These parameters can be used to turn on and off certain features. For example, "unnest_subquery" has a default value of TRUE (for versions of Oracle after 9.0) or later. In most situations you would only notice the problems if you were tuning SQL and found that some hint or some system parameter was not changing the execution plan the way you would expect. In some situations it is merely a lack of performance (or a sudden change of performance) that is the clue that something may be wrong. These parameters should only be set if Oracle support asks you to set them. They are generally only set for a short time to debug certain issues associated with these transformations and bugs associated with them, but there's no reason not to open a Service Request with Oracle and ask if you can try something. Support people at Oracle are all very helpful and accommodating (honest).

Optimizer Parameters

Luckily the 10053 trace file lists optimizer parameters and their default values so that you can tell if there have been any changes. In the section titled "PARAMETERS USED BY THE OPTIMIZER" (as shown in Figure 7-6, we see the first few entries of these parameters. Note that "Compilation Environment Dump" and "Bug Fix Control Environment" are subheadings present in both the altered values and default values section. In our case there no altered values for either of these subsections in the altered values section. In the default values section the first actual parameter shown with a default value is optimizer_mode_hinted (which is set to false). All the parameters are listed (including the hidden ones). Play with these at your peril, however. If support asks you to change one of these parameters, it is because they are helping you with some problem related to the optimizer. Also note that any non-default parameters are shown in a separate section entitled "PARAMETERS WITH ALTERED VALUES."

```
**************************************
PARAMETERS USED BY THE OPTIMIZER
**************************************
  **************************************
  PARAMETERS WITH ALTERED VALUES
  **************************************
Compilation Environment Dump
Bug Fix Control Environment


  **************************************
  PARAMETERS WITH DEFAULT VALUES
  **************************************
Compilation Environment Dump
optimizer_mode_hinted              = false
optimizer_features_hinted          = 0.0.0
parallel_execution_enabled         = true
parallel_query_forced_dop          = 0
parallel_dml_forced_dop            = 0
parallel_ddl_forced_degree         = 0
parallel_ddl_forced_instances      = 0
_query_rewrite_fudge               = 90
optimizer_features_enable          = 12.1.0.2
_optimizer_search_limit            = 5
cpu_count                          = 1
active_instance_count              = 1
parallel_threads_per_cpu           = 2
hash_area_size                     = 131072
bitmap_merge_area_size             = 1048576
sort_area_size                     = 65536
sort_area_retained_size            = 0
_sort_elimination_cost_ratio       = 0
_optimizer_block_size              = 8192
_sort_multiblock_read_count        = 2
_hash_multiblock_io_count          = 0
_db_file_optimizer_read_count      = 8
_optimizer_max_permutations        = 2000
pga_aggregate_target               = 808960 KB
_pga_max_size                      = 204800 KB
_query_rewrite_maxdisjunct         = 257
_smm_auto_min_io_size              = 56 KB
_smm_auto_max_io_size              = 248 KB
_smm_min_size                      = 808 KB
_smm_max_size_static               = 102400 KB
_smm_px_max_size_static            = 404480 KB
_cpu_to_io                         = 0
_optimizer_undo_cost_change        = 12.1.0.2
parallel_query_mode                = enabled
parallel_dml_mode                  = disabled
parallel_ddl_mode                  = enabled
optimizer_mode                     = all_rows
sqlstat_enabled                    = false
_optimizer_percent_parallel        = 101
_always_anti_join                  = choose
_always_semi_join                  = choose
_optimizer_mode_force              = true
_partition_view_enabled            = true
_always_star_transformation        = false
_query_rewrite_or_error            = false
_hash_join_enabled                 = true
cursor_sharing                     = exact
_b_tree_bitmap_plans               = true
star_transformation_enabled        = false
_optimizer_cost_model              = choose
```

Figure 7-6. *The optimizer parameter section of the 10053 trace file*

As an example, let's see what happens if we change the parameter cursor sharing from its default value of EXACT to a value of FORCE. Here we set cursor_sharing to FORCE (it was EXACT before). Then we ask for a 10053 trace and issue a query; then we look at the 10053 trace file and find the section with the parameters. Here are the commands issued:

```
SQL> show parameter cursor_sharing
NAME                                 TYPE        VALUE
------------------------------------ ----------- --------------------------
cursor_sharing                       string      EXACT

SQL> alter system set cursor_sharing=FORCE scope=memory;

System altered.

SQL> alter session set events '10053 trace name context forever, level 1';

Session altered.

SQL> explain plan for select count(*) from dba_objects;

Explained.
```

And in the figure below (Figure 7-7) we see that cursor_sharing has been changed to force.

```
******************************************
PARAMETERS USED BY THE OPTIMIZER
******************************************
  ******************************************
  PARAMETERS WITH ALTERED VALUES
  ******************************************
Compilation Environment Dump
cursor_sharing                           = force
Bug Fix Control Environment


  ******************************************
  PARAMETERS WITH DEFAULT VALUES
  ******************************************
Compilation Environment Dump
optimizer_mode_hinted                    = false
optimizer_features_hinted                = 0.0.0
parallel_execution_enabled               = true
parallel_query_forced_dop                = 0
parallel_dml_forced_dop                  = 0
parallel_ddl_forced_degree               = 0
parallel_ddl_forced_instances            = 0
_query_rewrite_fudge                     = 90
optimizer_features_enable                = 12.1.0.2
_optimizer_search_limit                  = 5
cpu_count                                = 1
active_instance_count                    = 1
parallel_threads_per_cpu                 = 2
hash_area_size                           = 131072
bitmap_merge_area_size                   = 1048576
sort_area_size                           = 65536
sort_area_retained_size                  = 0
_sort_elimination_cost_ratio             = 0
_optimizer_block_size                    = 8192
_sort_multiblock_read_count              = 2
_hash_multiblock_io_count                = 0
_db_file_optimizer_read_count            = 8
_optimizer_max_permutations              = 2000
pga_aggregate_target                     = 808960 KB
_pga_max_size                            = 204800 KB
_query_rewrite_maxdisjunct               = 257
_smm_auto_min_io_size                    = 56 KB
_smm_auto_max_io_size                    = 248 KB
_smm_min_size                            = 808 KB
_smm_max_size_static                     = 102400 KB
_smm_px_max_size_static                  = 404480 KB
_cpu_to_io                               = 0
_optimizer_undo_cost_change              = 12.1.0.2
parallel_query_mode                      = enabled
parallel_dml_mode                        = disabled
parallel_ddl_mode                        = enabled
optimizer_mode                           = all_rows
sqlstat_enabled                          = false
_optimizer_percent_parallel              = 101
_always_anti_join                        = choose
_always_semi_join                        = choose
_optimizer_mode_force                    = true
_partition_view_enabled                  = true
_always_star_transformation              = false
_query_rewrite_or_error                  = false
_hash_join_enabled                       = true
```

Figure 7-7. Here we see the parameter cursor_sharing has been changed to FORCE

We see that the 10053 trace file is useful for tracking optimizer parameters both hidden and unhidden. Now we'll look at optimizer hints.

Optimizer Hints

If you use any optimizer hints in your SQL, it is a good idea to check that these hints are being used. The optimizer will do its best to use hints given to it but will not use the hints if there is a problem with such use. The optimizer can ignore hints because the syntax is incorrect or because they are in conflict with another hint. If the hints are correct the optimizer will use them. Let's look at an example involving the query we were previously working on.

The examples we use here for hints are equally applicable to other 'directives' to the optimizer, such as SQL Profiles, Outlines, and SPM Baselines. These are all tracked and listed in a 10053 trace.

Now, armed with our knowledge of subquery unnesting, we'll write the query a different way and try a few hints. First we'll run the query with no hint and look at the execution plan. It will show a hash join. Then we'll hint a nested loop join. We'll confirm that but look at the execution plan again. Then finally we'll use conflicting hints and see that the execution plan reverts to the hash join.

```
SQL> set autotrace traceonly explain;
SQL> set lines 100
SQL> select
  a.first_name, a.last_name, a.hire_date
  from employees a, employees b
  where a.hire_date = b.hire_date
  and a.department_id=30
/

Execution Plan
----------------------------------------------------------
Plan hash value: 1407693252
```

Id	Operation	Name	Rows	Bytes	Cost (%CPU)	Time
0	SELECT STATEMENT		7	238	3 (0)	00:00:01
1	NESTED LOOPS		7	238	3 (0)	00:00:01
2	NESTED LOOPS		107	238	3 (0)	00:00:01
3	TABLE ACCESS FULL	EMPLOYEES	107	856	3 (0)	00:00:01
* 4	INDEX RANGE SCAN	EMP_DEPARTMENT_IX	1		0 (0)	00:00:01
* 5	TABLE ACCESS BY INDEX ROWID	EMPLOYEES	1	26	0 (0)	00:00:01

```
Predicate Information (identified by operation id):
----------------------------------------------------

   4 - access("A"."DEPARTMENT_ID"=30)
   5 - filter("A"."HIRE_DATE"="B"."HIRE_DATE")
SQL> select /*+ use_hash(a b) */
  a.first_name, a.last_name, a.hire_date
```

```
  from employees a, employees b
  where a.hire_date = b.hire_date
  and a.department_id=30
/
Execution Plan
-------------------------------------------------------------
Plan hash value: 2438053827


---------------------------------------------------------------------------------------------
| Id  | Operation                            |Name              | Rows| Bytes|Cost (%CPU)| Time     |
|   0 | SELECT STATEMENT                     |                  |7    | 238|   4   (0)| 00:00:01 |
|*  1 |   HASH JOIN                          |                  |7    | 238|   4   (0)| 00:00:01 |
|   2 |    TABLE ACCESS BY INDEX ROWID BATCHED| EMPLOYEES       |6    | 156|   1   (0)| 00:00:01 |
|*  3 |     INDEX RANGE SCAN                 | EMP_DEPARTMENT_IX|1   |     |   1   (0)| 00:00:01 |
|   4 |    TABLE ACCESS FULL                 | EMPLOYEES        |107 | 856|   3   (0)| 00:00:01 |
---------------------------------------------------------------------------------------------

Predicate Information (identified by operation id):
---------------------------------------------------

   1 - access("A"."HIRE_DATE"="B"."HIRE_DATE")
   3 - access("A"."DEPARTMENT_ID"=30)
SQL> select /*+ use_hash(a b) use_merge(a b) */
  a.first_name, a.last_name, a.hire_date
  from employees a, employees b
  where a.hire_date = b.hire_date
  and a.department_id=30
/


Execution Plan
-------------------------------------------------------------
Plan hash value: 1407693252


---------------------------------------------------------------------------------------------
| Id  | Operation                       | Name             | Rows | Bytes | Cost (%CPU)| Time     |
|   0 | SELECT STATEMENT                |                  |      |   7 | 238 |   3   (0)| 00:00:01 |
|   1 |   NESTED LOOPS                  |                  |      |   7 | 238 |   3   (0)| 00:00:01 |
|   2 |    NESTED LOOPS                 |                  |  107 | 238 |   3   (0)| 00:00:01 |
|   3 |     TABLE ACCESS FULL           | EMPLOYEES        |  107 | 856 |   3   (0)| 00:00:01 |
|*  4 |     INDEX RANGE SCAN            | EMP_DEPARTMENT_IX|    1 |     |   0   (0)| 00:00:01 |
|*  5 |    TABLE ACCESS BY INDEX ROWID  | EMPLOYEES        |    1 |  26 |   0   (0)| 00:00:01 |
---------------------------------------------------------------------------------------------

Predicate Information (identified by operation id):

   4 - access("A"."DEPARTMENT_ID"=30)
   5 - filter("A"."HIRE_DATE"="B"."HIRE_DATE")
```

Let's look at each step and see if we can understand what happened. In the first execution we allowed the optimizer to do its own thing. We could also confirm this by looking at the 10053 trace if we wanted to make sure there was no influence on the optimizer from hidden parameters. So in the first step the optimizer went with a Nested Loop. In the second execution, we decide (for whatever reason) we'd like to try a Hash Join instead, so we use a hint in the SQL use_hash (a b). Remember that (a b) represents the aliases of the two tables that are being joined in this hint. Gratifyingly the new execution plan uses a Hash Join. So far so good.

Now, in the third execution, we want to refine things a little further and use an additional hint; use_merge(a b). This seems somewhat contradictory, but we want to know what the optimizer will do. Will it use a hash join, will it use a sort merge join, or will it pick the best option from both of these? If we look at the resulting execution plan we see that it does neither of these things. Instead it uses a Nested Loop. So rather than guessing we now generate a 10053 trace file of the "errant" behavior. In these steps we set the dump file size to unlimited ask for a 10053 trace file run the SQL with the two hints, that we want to investigate and then run the SQL.

```
SQL> alter session set max_dump_file_size=unlimited;

Session altered.

SQL> alter session set events '10053 trace name context forever, level 1';

Session altered.

SQL> set autotrace off;
SQL> select /*+ use_hash(a b) user_merge (a b) */
  2  a.first_name, a.last_name, a.hire_date
  3  from employees a, employees b
  4  where a.hire_date=b.hire_date
  5  and a.department_id=30
  6  /
```

FIRST_NAME	LAST_NAME	HIRE_DATE
Den	Raphaely	07-DEC-02
Alexander	Khoo	18-MAY-03
Shelli	Baida	24-DEC-05
Sigal	Tobias	24-JUL-05
Guy	Himuro	15-NOV-06
Karen	Colmenares	10-AUG-07

```
6 rows selected.
```

We confirm we are looking at the right 10053 trace file by checking the text, and true enough, the hints match (see Figure 7-8).

```
----- Current SQL Statement for this session (sql_id=gc676cnx34496) -----
select /*+ use_hash(a b) use_merge(a b) */
a.first_name, a.last_name, a.hire_date
from employees a, employees b
where a.hire_date=b.hire_date
and a.department_id=:"SYS_B_0"
sql_text_length=173
sql=select /*+ use_hash(a b) use_merge(a b) */
a.first_name, a.last_name, a.hire_date
from employees a, employees b
where a.hire_date=b.hire_date
and a.department_id=:"SYS_B_0"|
```

Figure 7-8. The SQL Text section of the trace file identifies the SQL

This may seem like a superfluous step but it is easy to end up looking at the wrong trace file and that could be a big waste of time.

If we now search for the word "hint"

we'll find a section at the end of the trace file called "Dumping Hints." See Figure 7-9.

```
Dumping Hints
=============
  atom_hint=(@=0x7f0a3be523a0 err=4 resol=1 used=0 token=923 org=1 lvl=3 txt=USE_MERGE ("B") )
  atom_hint=(@=0x7f0a3be51170 err=4 resol=1 used=0 token=922 org=1 lvl=3 txt=USE_HASH  ("B") )
  atom_hint=(@=0x7f0a3be50ed8 err=4 resol=1 used=0 token=923 org=1 lvl=3 txt=USE_MERGE ("A") )
  atom_hint=(@=0x7f0a3becad10 err=4 resol=1 used=0 token=922 org=1 lvl=3 txt=USE_HASH  ("A") )
********** WARNING: SOME HINTS HAVE ERRORS
```

Figure 7-9. *The hints section of the 10053 trace file*

The important thing about this small section of the file is to note that used=0. This means the hint was not used. It was ignored completely. In fact both hints were ignored, which then allowed the optimizer to make its own decisions, which resulted in the Nested Loop being used. The execution of the SQL resulted in no error. We did not get an error message from the optimizer saying there was something wrong with the hints. This information was hidden away in a 10053 trace file (if we asked for it). So what was wrong? The err code is 4, which means that there was a conflict with another hint. In this case both hints are taking each other out. The important thing to note here is that the third execution of the SQL above did not generate an error. The optimizer recognized the hints, found they were conflicting with each other, ignored them, and developed a plan without them.

Cost Calculations

The most important job (in terms of performance) that the optimizer does is to compare costs between different execution plans. That's the overall plan, of course. The cost of the execution plan is made up of the cost of each line in the execution plan, and each line is based on calculations that depend on statistics. The different plans calculated are based on different access paths, join methods, and order of access of different parts of the query. Sounds like fun doesn't it? If you had seven different tables you could choose an order of processing in seven ways (that's seven factorial, which translates to 7x6x5x4x3x2x1)! That's 5,040 ways total, and that's before you consider the different ways of accessing the tables in the first place. The optimizer chooses a reasonable plan, picks the outer table and works down, tries a few combinations, and quickly eliminates those options that already exceed the cost of previous plans it has tried (this is highly simplified). So if, for example, the first plan the optimizer guesses is going to cost 1,000, the second plan will be abandoned if halfway through the cost calculations the plan reaches 1,500. In this case there is no need to keep calculating. It does this to save time in the overall hard parsing elapsed time. It knows you are hungry for results. Once you know that the 10053 is a story about how the optimizer derived its plan based on this approach, the trace file begins to make some sense.

After it gives some basic information about parameters and the SQL being considered and any possible query transformations that might apply, the cost-based optimizer launches into some basic information about the cost of accessing the objects involved. Below we see there is some basic information about the table

```
EMPLOYEES (twice in this case).
**************************************
BASE STATISTICAL INFORMATION
***********************
Table Stats::
  Table: EMPLOYEES  Alias:  B
```

```
  #Rows: 107 SSZ: 0  LGR: 0  #Blks:  5  AvgRowLen: 69.00  NEB: 0  ChainCnt: 0.00  SPC:
0  RFL: 0  RNF: 0  CBK: 0  CHR: 0  KQDFLG: 1
    #IMCUs: 0  IMCRowCnt: 0  IMCJournalRowCnt: 0  #IMCBlocks: 0  IMCQuotient: 0.000000
    Column (#6): HIRE_DATE(DATE)
      AvgLen: 8 NDV: 98 Nulls: 0 Density: 0.010204 Min: 2451923.000000 Max: 2454578.000000
Index Stats::
    Index: EMP_DEPARTMENT_IX  Col#: 11
    LVLS: 0  #LB: 0  #DK: 0  LB/K: 0.00  DB/K: 0.00  CLUF: 0.00  NRW: 0.00 SSZ: 0.00 LGR: 0.00
CBK: 0.00 GQL: 0.00 CHR: 0.00 KQDFLG: 1 BSZ: 1
    KKEISFLG: 1
    Index: EMP_EMAIL_UK  Col#: 4
    LVLS: 0  #LB: 0  #DK: 0  LB/K: 0.00  DB/K: 0.00  CLUF: 0.00  NRW: 0.00 SSZ: 0.00 LGR: 0.00
CBK: 0.00 GQL: 0.00 CHR: 0.00 KQDFLG: 1 BSZ: 1
    KKEISFLG: 1
    Index: EMP_EMP_ID_PK  Col#: 1
    LVLS: 0  #LB: 0  #DK: 0  LB/K: 0.00  DB/K: 0.00  CLUF: 0.00  NRW: 0.00 SSZ: 0.00 LGR: 0.00
CBK: 0.00 GQL: 0.00 CHR: 0.00 KQDFLG: 1 BSZ: 1
    KKEISFLG: 1
    Index: EMP_JOB_IX  Col#: 7
    LVLS: 0  #LB: 0  #DK: 0  LB/K: 0.00  DB/K: 0.00  CLUF: 0.00  NRW: 0.00 SSZ: 0.00 LGR: 0.00
CBK: 0.00 GQL: 0.00 CHR: 0.00 KQDFLG: 1 BSZ: 1
    KKEISFLG: 1
    Index: EMP_MANAGER_IX  Col#: 10
    LVLS: 0  #LB: 0  #DK: 0  LB/K: 0.00  DB/K: 0.00  CLUF: 0.00  NRW: 0.00 SSZ: 0.00 LGR: 0.00
CBK: 0.00 GQL: 0.00 CHR: 0.00 KQDFLG: 1 BSZ: 1
    KKEISFLG: 1
    Index: EMP_NAME_IX  Col#: 3 2
    LVLS: 0  #LB: 0  #DK: 0  LB/K: 0.00  DB/K: 0.00  CLUF: 0.00  NRW: 0.00 SSZ: 0.00 LGR: 0.00
CBK: 0.00 GQL: 0.00 CHR: 0.00 KQDFLG: 1 BSZ: 1
    KKEISFLG: 1
***********************
Table Stats::
    Table: EMPLOYEES  Alias:  A
    #Rows: 107  SSZ: 0  LGR: 0  #Blks:  5  AvgRowLen:  69.00  NEB: 0  ChainCnt: 0.00  SPC:
0  RFL: 0  RNF: 0  CBK: 0  CHR: 0  KQDFLG: 1
    #IMCUs: 0  IMCRowCnt: 0  IMCJournalRowCnt: 0  #IMCBlocks: 0  IMCQuotient: 0.000000
    Column (#6): HIRE_DATE(DATE)
      AvgLen: 8 NDV: 98 Nulls: 0 Density: 0.010204 Min: 2451923.000000 Max: 2454578.000000
Index Stats::
    Index: EMP_DEPARTMENT_IX  Col#: 11
    LVLS: 0  #LB: 0  #DK: 0  LB/K: 0.00  DB/K: 0.00  CLUF: 0.00  NRW: 0.00 SSZ: 0.00 LGR: 0.00
CBK: 0.00 GQL: 0.00 CHR: 0.00 KQDFLG: 1 BSZ: 1
    KKEISFLG: 1
    Index: EMP_EMAIL_UK  Col#: 4
    LVLS: 0  #LB: 0  #DK: 0  LB/K: 0.00  DB/K: 0.00  CLUF: 0.00  NRW: 0.00 SSZ: 0.00 LGR: 0.00
CBK: 0.00 GQL: 0.00 CHR: 0.00 KQDFLG: 1 BSZ: 1
    KKEISFLG: 1
```

A section in the 10053 showing BASE STATISTICAL INFORMATION

Once we have all this base information about the table and its indexes (note we also have the clustering factor CLUF in this basic information), we can start to determine how to get the information the cheapest way. See Figure 7-10 below. For example, the CBO will consider a single table access path and many other access paths including a `table scan` (cost 3) or IndexRange(cost 1) and then tell us which was cheapest: `Best:: AccessPath: IndexRange`. Figure 7-10 illustrates the section in the 10053 that shows this.

```
*******************************************
SINGLE TABLE ACCESS PATH
  Single Table Cardinality Estimation for EMPLOYEES[A]
  SPD: Return code in qosdDSDirSetup: NOCTX, estType = TABLE
  Column (#11):
    NewDensity:0.004717, OldDensity:0.004717 BktCnt:106.000000, PopBktCnt:103.000000,
  Column (#11): DEPARTMENT_ID(NUMBER)
    AvgLen: 3 NDV: 11 Nulls: 1 Density: 0.004717 Min: 10.000000 Max: 110.000000
    Histogram: Freq #Bkts: 11  UncompBkts: 106  EndPtVals: 11  Actualval: yes
  Table: EMPLOYEES  Alias: A
    Card: Original: 107.000000  Rounded: 6  Computed: 6.000000  Non Adjusted: 6.0000(
  Scan IO  Cost (Disk) =    3.000000
  Scan CPU Cost (Disk) =   73057.200000
  Total Scan IO  Cost  =    3.000000 (scan (Disk))
                     +    0.000000 (io filter eval) (= 0.000000 (per row) * 107.000(
                     =    3.000000
  Total Scan CPU Cost =  73057.200000 (scan (Disk))
                     + 5350.000000 (cpu filter eval) (= 50.000000 (per row) * 10/
                       78407.200000
  Access Path: TableScan
    Cost:  3.001975  Resp: 3.001975  Degree: 0
    Cost_io: 3.000000  Cost_cpu: 7840/
    Resp_io: 3.000000  Resp_cpu: 7840/
  ****** Costing Index EMP_DEPARTMENT_IX
  SPD: Return code in qosdDSDirSetup: NOCTX, estType = INDEX_SCAN
  SPD: Return code in qosdDSDirSetup: NOCTX, estType = INDEX_FILTER
  Access Path: index (AllEqRange)
    Index: EMP_DEPARTMENT_IX
    resc_io: 1.000000  resc_cpu: 200
    ix_sel: 0.056075  ix_sel_with_filters: 0.056075
    Cost: 1.000005  Resp: /000005 Degree: 1
  Best:: AccessPath: Ind/Range
  Index: EMP_DEPARTMENT_IX
         Cost: 1.000005  Degree: 1  Resp: 1.000005  Card: 6.000000  Bytes: 0.000000
```

Figure 7-10. *What the optimizer 'thought' of table EMPLOYEES*

Once this is done the optimizer considers join orders, in this case only to another version of the table EMPLOYEES.

```
Final cost for query block SEL$1 (#0) - All Rows Plan:
  Best join order: 2
  Cost: 3.002109  Degree: 1  Card: 7.000000  Bytes: 238.000000
  Resc: 3.002109  Resc_io: 3.000000  Resc_cpu: 83757
  Resp: 3.002109  Resp_io: 3.000000  Resc_cpu: 83757
```

The Optimizer makes its final decision for the cost and Join order (as seen in the text above). When we have the final Join Order only then do we show the plan and any ancillary information. See below.

```
============
Plan Table
============
-----------------------------------------------------+----------------------------------+
| Id  | Operation                      | Name            | Rows | Bytes | Cost  | Time     |
-----------------------------------------------------+----------------------------------+
|  0  | SELECT STATEMENT               |                 |      |       |   3   |          |
|  1  |  NESTED LOOPS                  |                 |    7 |   238 |   3   | 00:00:01 |
|  2  |   NESTED LOOPS                 |                 |  107 |   238 |   3   | 00:00:01 |
|  3  |    TABLE ACCESS FULL           | EMPLOYEES       |  107 |   856 |   3   | 00:00:01 |
|  4  |    INDEX RANGE SCAN            | EMP_DEPARTMENT_IX|   1 |       |   0   |          |
|  5  |   TABLE ACCESS BY INDEX ROWID  | EMPLOYEES       |    1 |    26 |   0   |          |
-----------------------------------------------------+----------------------------------+
Predicate Information:
----------------------
4 - access("A"."DEPARTMENT_ID"=:SYS_B_0)
5 - filter("A"."HIRE_DATE"="B"."HIRE_DATE")

Content of other_xml column
===========================
  db_version     : 12.1.0.2
  parse_schema   : HR
  plan_hash_full : 2833920973
  plan_hash      : 1407693252
  plan_hash_2    : 2833920973
Peeked Binds
============
  Bind variable information
    position=1
    datatype(code)=2
    datatype(string)=NUMBER
    precision=0
    scale=0
    max length=22
    value=30
  Outline Data:
  /*+
    BEGIN_OUTLINE_DATA
      IGNORE_OPTIM_EMBEDDED_HINTS
      OPTIMIZER_FEATURES_ENABLE('12.1.0.2')
      DB_VERSION('12.1.0.2')
      ALL_ROWS
      OUTLINE_LEAF(@"SEL$1")
      FULL(@"SEL$1" "B"@"SEL$1")
      INDEX(@"SEL$1" "A"@"SEL$1" ("EMPLOYEES"."DEPARTMENT_ID"))
      LEADING(@"SEL$1" "B"@"SEL$1" "A"@"SEL$1")
      USE_NL(@"SEL$1" "A"@"SEL$1")
      NLJ_BATCHING(@"SEL$1" "A"@"SEL$1")
    END_OUTLINE_DATA
  */
```

Now that we've covered some of the information that you can get from a 10053 trace file, you know how useful it is. From a careful reading of the trace file you should now be able to see why the optimizer chose to do what it did: which access paths it considered and why it rejected some of them. And if you feel that some of the access paths should not have been rejected, you should be able to work back to the root cause and determine the answer to that age-old question of all DBAs and developers: "Why did it not use my index?"

Summary

SQLTXPLAIN is a wonderful tool, and it generates the 10053 trace file by default in most cases. While it is sometimes difficult to understand, there is a mine of information that helps you tune your SQL when things are going wrong. In the next chapter we'll cover SQL*Profiles and what to when an emergency strikes and we need the right performance, fast!

CHAPTER 8

■ ■ ■

Forcing Execution Plans through Profiles

Sometimes it's best to fix a problem and figure out afterward what went wrong and determine the root cause. By this I mean that when there are production time pressures to get something done, any way that works is good enough. The idea is to get the business back up and running, then sit at your leisure and work out what went wrong, figure out how to stop it from happening again, and develop a plan to implement the permanent fix in a controlled manner during a planned outage if required. Management is not usually very tolerant of perfectionists who want to understand every detail of a problem and its solution before acting; and if they are tolerant, it's because they have another system in their pocket that's keeping the lights on and the business going.

The scenario I am about to describe is fairly common. An overnight batch job, one that is time critical (has to be finished by a certain time), suddenly starts taking much longer to run. The online day is affected, management reports are not produced on time (if at all), and the DBAs and developers are at a loss. Nothing was changed (which is never true), no releases to production, no parameter changes, no changes in statistics gathering. This is when you often hear the plaintive cry: "What's it doing?"

This is a good question to ask when you are trying to fix a problem properly; but when you need the system to behave the way it did before, there's a shortcut. This technique of fixing the problem without understanding the problem is often referred to as the "Severity 1 killer." This is because Severity 1 service requests at Oracle are the highest priority: if there is a way to fix the problem, then go for it. Understand it later.

So how do you do this? SQLT has the tools to get the job done (most of the time). As part of SQLT modus operandi, SQLT produces a script that uses an SQL profile. This SQL profile (if it is the "good" execution plan), can be applied to the troublesome SQL, which then forces the SQL to run "properly" despite whatever else is happening on the system (wrong statistics, changed parameters, etc.).

I'm sure you're saying to yourself, "this is all very well, but I can't change the code or hint anything, my code is fixed and generated by an application." Fear no more, none of the techniques I describe in this chapter involve changing code; that's why they are Severity 1 killers.

Apart from SQL Profiles, which is the main technique I describe in this chapter, I will also briefly touch on SQL Plan Baselines, which some say is a more reliable technique than Profiles and also mention the rarely used SQL Patch utility.

For now, however, let's look at what we can do with SQL profiles.

What Is an SQL Profile?

Although the title of this chapter is "Forcing Execution Plans through Profiles," SQL profiles do not exactly force an execution plan. They are more like "super hints." With hints there is always the possibility that the optimizer will find yet another way of doing the query, which is not what you want. Super hints, on the other hand, have specified so many constraints on the execution plan that the optimizer (usually) has no choices left. The word "profile" in this context is quite descriptive. The optimizer has seen this SQL statement go through many times and has determined that it behaves in a certain way: it accesses rows in a certain order and consistently uses a particular index. All this profiling information is gathered and kept for the query and can be used to "force" the statement to behave in the same way in the future if its new behavior is suboptimal.

Can SQL profiles be a bad thing? Let's examine an analogy. Everyone has their routines they stick to. Get up, brush your teeth, eat breakfast, go to work, drive home, read the newspaper, etc. The "profile" in this case is fairly simple. Make sure to brush your teeth before going to work; otherwise you might have to come back home to do it. If somebody wiped your memory (perhaps a tuning book fell off a shelf and bumped you on the head), and you forgot your routine, you might want a reminder of your previous routine until your memory returned. This routine forcing, or "profile," might be a good thing if nothing else had changed. Suppose, however, that you had also moved into a new house and now worked from home. Your profile might now be completely out of date. Driving to work would no longer make sense. Here we see that a profile might be good for a short while to get things back to normal, but every so often you need to check that the profile still makes sense.

So what does a super hint look like? Here's one:

```
/*+
    BEGIN_OUTLINE_DATA
    IGNORE_OPTIM_EMBEDDED_HINTS
    OPTIMIZER_FEATURES_ENABLE('11.2.0.4')
    DB_VERSION('12.1.0.2')
    OPT_PARAM('_b_tree_bitmap_plans' 'false')
    OPT_PARAM('_fast_full_scan_enabled' 'false')
    OPT_PARAM('_index_join_enabled' 'false')
    OPT_PARAM('_optimizer_table_expansion' 'false')
    ALL_ROWS
    OUTLINE_LEAF(@"SEL$4")
    OUTLINE_LEAF(@"SEL$A2B15E14")
    MERGE(@"SEL$B7E8C768")
...
    USE_HASH_AGGREGATION(@"SEL$7")
    NO_ACCESS(@"SEL$CF5359D5" "PERSON"@"SEL$9")
    NO_ACCESS(@"SEL$CF5359D5" "PERSON_PROJ_TIME"@"SEL$9")
    INDEX(@"SEL$CF5359D5" "PROJ"@"SEL$9" ("XX_SCAP_TIMEENTRY_PROJECTS"."PROJECT_ID"))
    LEADING(@"SEL$CF5359D5" "PERSON"@"SEL$9" "PERSON_PROJ_TIME"@"SEL$9" "PROJ"@"SEL$9")
    USE_HASH(@"SEL$CF5359D5" "PERSON_PROJ_TIME"@"SEL$9")
    USE_NL(@"SEL$CF5359D5" "PROJ"@"SEL$9")
    NLJ_BATCHING(@"SEL$CF5359D5" "PROJ"@"SEL$9")
...
FULL(@"SEL$9CDD3623" "PAA"@"SEL$42")
...
USE_MERGE_CARTESIAN(@"SEL$A2B15E14" "CP"@"SEL$5")
...
    LEADING(@"SEL$34" "FA"@"SEL$34" "GPS"@"SEL$34")
    USE_NL(@"SEL$34" "GPS"@"SEL$34")
    NO_ACCESS(@"SEL$22" "XX_SCAP_TIMEENTRY_PERIODS"@"SEL$22")
    INDEX_RS_ASC(@"SEL$23" "FA"@"SEL$23" ("XX_SCAP_TE_FND_APPLICATION"."APPLICATION_SHORT_
    NAME"))
    INDEX_RS_ASC(@"SEL$23" "GPS"@"SEL$23" ("XX_SCAP_TIMEENTRY_PRD_STATUS"."APPLICATION_ID"
    "XX_SCAP_TIMEENTRY_PRD_STATUS"."SET_OF_BOOKS_ID"
```

```
            "XX_SCAP_TIMEENTRY_PRD_STATUS"."PERIOD_NAME"))
      LEADING(@"SEL$23" "FA"@"SEL$23" "GPS"@"SEL$23")
      USE_NL(@"SEL$23" "GPS"@"SEL$23")
      END_OUTLINE_DATA
  */
```

I've shortened the hint just to highlight some sections. Notice how the hint is more verbose than the normal hint you would use to tune an SQL statement. Still, there are recognizable parts after the standard preamble (which includes BEGIN_OUTLINE_DATA, IGNORE_OPTIM_EMBEDDED_HINTS, OPTIMIZER_FEATURES_ENABLE('11.2.0.4') and DB_VERSION('12.1.0.2')). Let's list the more familiar parts:

- ALL_ROWS

- MERGE

- INDEX_RS_ASC

- FULL

- USE_NL

- NLJ_BATCHING

- USE_MERGE_CARTESIAN

You'll also notice that the references made are to obscure objects such as SEL$23 and SEL$ A2B15E14 (which are properly called "query block names"). Remember that the optimizer has transformed the SQL (through the use of query transformations as described in Chapter 7) before it gets to do more detailed cost-based tuning.(See Chapter 7 for more details on query transformations). During the transformation, the various sections of the query get these exotic names (which are unrecognizable). The profile hints then refer to these names.

So now we know what an SQL profile is and how it looks to the optimizer. We also know that keeping an unchanging profile on an SQL statement might be a bad idea. Having said all that we still know getting the production database back to an operational state might be the difference between success and failure. So with all these provisos and limitations, let's find out where SQLT gets its SQL profile.

Where Does SQLT Get Its SQL Profile?

To get the script that creates the SQL profile for you is simple. SQLT generates the required script from both the SQLT XTRACT method and from the XECUTE method. We saw in Chapter 1 how to generate an XTRACT report, and we covered XECUTE in Chapter 3. Make a note of the SQLT ID (not the SQL ID) of the report and the plan hash value that you want. See Figure 8-1 below. This shows the SQLT ID, it's the number in the title "Report: sqlt_s41321_main.html." In this case the SQLT ID is 41321.

<u>215187.1</u> SQLT XECUTE 12.1.160429 Report: sqlt_s41321_main.html

Global

- <u>Observations</u>
- <u>SQL Text</u>
- <u>SQL Identification</u>
- <u>Environment</u>
- <u>CBO Environment</u>
- <u>Fix Control</u>
- <u>CBO System Statistics</u>
- <u>DBMS_STATS Setup</u>
- <u>Initialization Parameters</u>
- <u>NLS Parameters</u>
- <u>I/O Calibration</u>
- <u>Tool Configuration Parameters</u>

Cursor Sharing and Binds

- <u>Cursor Sharing</u>
- Adaptive Cursor Sharing
- Peeked Binds
- Captured Binds

SQL Tuning Advisor

- <u>STA Report</u>
- STA Script

Plans

- <u>Summary</u>
- <u>Performance Statistics</u>
- Performance History (delta)
- Performance History (total)
- <u>Execution Plans</u>

Plan Control

- Stored Outlines
- SQL Patches
- SQL Profiles
- SQL Plan Baselines
- SQL Plan Directives

SQL Execution

- Active Session History
- AWR Active Session History
- <u>SQL Statistics</u>
- <u>SQL Detail ACTIVE Report</u>
- Monitor Statistics
- Monitor ACTIVE Report
- Monitor HTML Report
- Monitor TEXT Report
- <u>Segment Statistics</u>
- <u>Session Statistics</u>
- <u>Session Events</u>
- <u>Parallel Processing</u>

Tables

- <u>Tables</u>
- <u>Statistics</u>
- Statistics Extensions
- Statistics Versions
- Modifications
- <u>Properties</u>
- <u>Physical Properties</u>
- Constraints
- <u>Columns</u>
- Indexed Columns
- Histograms
- Partitions
- Indexes

Objects

- <u>Objects</u>
- <u>Dependencies</u>
- Fixed Objects
- Fixed Object Columns
- Nested Tables
- Policies
- Audit Policies
- <u>Tablespaces</u>
- <u>Metadata</u>

Figure 8-1. *The header page shows the SQLT ID, needed for generating the profile*

The plan hash value (PHV) can be obtained from the "Execution Plans" section of the report. See Figure 8-2 for the section showing which plan hash values are available.

Execution Plans

List ordered by phv and source.

#	Plan Hash Value	SQLT Plan Hash Value[1]	SQLT Plan Hash Value2[1]	Src	Source	Plan Info	Is Bind Sensitive	Optimizer	Optimizer Cost	Estimated Cardinality E-Rows	Rows Processed A-Rows	Plan Timestamp	Child Plans[2]	Plan ID	Task ID	Attribute
1	665279032	205	5075	STA	DBA_SQLTUNE_PLANS			HNT: ALL_ROWS	78	5557		2012-08-18/10:41:45		7405	3605	Plan from SQL tuning set
2	725901306 [B] [W]	16588	21458	MEM	GV$SQL_PLAN		N	ALL_ROWS	908	5557	1127	2012-08-18/10:38:20	1			
3	725901306 [B] [W]	16588	21458	XPL	PLAN_TABLE			ALL_ROWS	908	5557		2012-08-18/10:40:02		321		
4	725901306 [B] [W]	16588	21458	STA	DBA_SQLTUNE_PLANS			ALL_ROWS	908	5557		2012-08-18/10:41:45		7404	3605	Original
5	3005811457	7319	12189	STA	DBA_SQLTUNE_PLANS			ALL_ROWS	387	5557		2012-08-18/10:41:45		7403	3605	Using new indices

(1) SQLT PHV considers id, parent_id, operation, options, index_columns and object_name. SQLT PHV2 includes also access and filter predicates.
(2) Display of child plans is restricted up to 10 per phv as per tool parameter "r_rows_table_xs"
Go to Plan Performance Statistics
Go to Plans Summary
Go to Top

Figure 8-2. *Execution plans available and the Plan Hash Values (PHV)*

So now we have both the SQLT ID and the PHV. In the /utl directory under the SQLT installation area we can now run the script that will generate the profile, as shown in the following example. However, before you do that on a production system you should consult Oracle Support to make sure your steps are validated and your actions are supported. Just open a ticket and the friendly people at Performance will be more than happy to help you. Here is the directory listing showing the files in the utl directory. From that directory we then enable the profile creation and run the routine to generate the profile, making sure to pass in the PHV and the SQL_ID. I've shown the output from the script, and then at the end I show the new file created. It's that easy.

```
[oracle@d12102 utl]$ ls -l *.sql
-rw-r--r-- 1 oracle oinstall   130 Oct 30 2014 10053.sql
-rw-r--r-- 1 oracle oinstall 86806 Oct 30 2014 bde_chk_cbo.sql
-rw-r--r-- 1 oracle oinstall  9036 Oct 30 2014 coe_gen_sql_patch.sql
-rw-r--r-- 1 oracle oinstall  4971 Oct 30 2014 coe_gen_sql_profile.sql
-rw-r--r-- 1 oracle oinstall 10836 Oct 30 2014 coe_load_sql_baseline.sql
-rw-r--r-- 1 oracle oinstall 12860 Oct 30 2014 coe_load_sql_profile.sql
-rw-r--r-- 1 oracle oinstall 19045 Oct 30 2014 coe_xfr_sql_profile.sql
-rw-r--r-- 1 oracle oinstall  1273 Oct 30 2014 flush_cursor.sql
-rw-r--r-- 1 oracle oinstall   101 Oct 30 2014 flush.sql
-rw-r--r-- 1 oracle oinstall 79079 Oct 30 2014 mvhcdr.sql
-rw-r--r-- 1 oracle oinstall   231 Oct 30 2014 plan.sql
-rw-r--r-- 1 oracle oinstall 23690 Oct 30 2014 profiler.sql
-rw-r--r-- 1 oracle oinstall 76563 Oct 30 2014 pxhcdr.sql
-rw-r--r-- 1 oracle oinstall   435 Oct 30 2014 sel_aux.sql
-rw-r--r-- 1 oracle oinstall   475 Oct 30 2014 sel.sql
-rw-r--r-- 1 oracle oinstall  2978 Oct 30 2014 sqltcdirs.sql
-rw-r--r-- 1 oracle oinstall  4073 Oct 30 2014 sqlthistfile.sql
-rw-r--r-- 1 oracle oinstall  3197 Oct 30 2014 sqlthistpurge.sql
-rw-r--r-- 1 oracle oinstall  3146 Oct 30 2014 sqltimpdict.sql
-rw-r--r-- 1 oracle oinstall  3112 Oct 30 2014 sqltimpfo.sql
-rw-r--r-- 1 oracle oinstall  4295 Oct 30 2014 sqltimp.sql
-rw-r--r-- 1 oracle oinstall  3624 Oct 30 2014 sqltlite.sql
-rw-r--r-- 1 oracle oinstall  3982 Oct 30 2014 sqltmain.sql
-rw-r--r-- 1 oracle oinstall  3885 Oct 30 2014 sqlt_parameters.sql
-rw-r--r-- 1 oracle oinstall  5321 Oct 30 2014 sqltprofile.sql
-rw-r--r-- 1 oracle oinstall  8711 Oct 30 2014 sqltq.sql
-rw-r--r-- 1 oracle oinstall  1695 Oct 30 2014 sqltresetstatementid.sql
-rw-r--r-- 1 oracle oinstall  1358 Oct 30 2014 sqltupgdbahistash.sql
SQL> connect stelios/oracle
Connected.
SQL> exec sqltxplain.sqlt$a.set_param('custom_sql_profile','Y');

PL/SQL procedure successfully completed.

SQL> @sqltprofile 41321 1388734953
```

Please note that the sqltxplain.sqlt$a.set_param procedure is required to set this functionality. When we run sqltprofile.sql (with a valid SQLT ID and a valid plan hash value [the first and second numbers respectively]) we will see a result similar to the one shown below:

```
SQL> @sqltprofile 41321 1388734953
... please wait ...

STAID MET INSTANCE SQL_TEXT
----- --- -------- -----------------------------------------------------------
41320 XTR snc1     select sysdate from dual
41321 XEC snc1     select sysdate from dual
```

```
Parameter 1:
STATEMENT_ID (required)

PLAN_HASH_VALUE ATTRIBUTE
---------------- ----------
    1388734953 [B][W][X]

Parameter 2:
PLAN_HASH_VALUE (required)

Values passed to sqltprofile:
~~~~~~~~~~~~~~~~~~~~~~~~~~~~~
STATEMENT_ID    : "41321"
PLAN_HASH_VALUE: "1388734953"

13:14:22    0 sqlt$r: -> custom_sql_profile
13:14:22    0 sqlt$a: -> common_initialization
13:14:22    0 sqlt$a: ALTER SESSION SET NLS_NUMERIC_CHARACTERS = ".,"
13:14:22    0 sqlt$a: ALTER SESSION SET NLS_SORT = BINARY
13:14:22    0 sqlt$a: <- common_initialization
13:14:22    0 sqlt$r: <- custom_sql_profile
... getting sqlt_s41321_p1388734953_sqlprof.sql out of sqlt repository ...

sqlt_s41321_p1388734953_sqlprof.sql has been generated

SQLTPROFILE completed.
```

Now that the script has run, where do you find the script to create an SQL Profile? The SQL script can be found in the same directory where the profile script was. The directory command below shows the file in the directory, which I've indicated with a New File pointer.

```
[oracle@d12102 utl]$ ls -l *.sql
-rw-r--r-- 1 oracle oinstall    130 Oct 30  2014 10053.sql
-rw-r--r-- 1 oracle oinstall  86806 Oct 30  2014 bde_chk_cbo.sql
-rw-r--r-- 1 oracle oinstall   9036 Oct 30  2014 coe_gen_sql_patch.sql
-rw-r--r-- 1 oracle oinstall   4971 Oct 30  2014 coe_gen_sql_profile.sql
-rw-r--r-- 1 oracle oinstall  10836 Oct 30  2014 coe_load_sql_baseline.sql
-rw-r--r-- 1 oracle oinstall  12860 Oct 30  2014 coe_load_sql_profile.sql
-rw-r--r-- 1 oracle oinstall  19045 Oct 30  2014 coe_xfr_sql_profile.sql
-rw-r--r-- 1 oracle oinstall   1273 Oct 30  2014 flush_cursor.sql
-rw-r--r-- 1 oracle oinstall    101 Oct 30  2014 flush.sql
-rw-r--r-- 1 oracle oinstall  79079 Oct 30  2014 mvhcdr.sql
-rw-r--r-- 1 oracle oinstall    231 Oct 30  2014 plan.sql
-rw-r--r-- 1 oracle oinstall  23690 Oct 30  2014 profiler.sql
-rw-r--r-- 1 oracle oinstall  76563 Oct 30  2014 pxhcdr.sql
-rw-r--r-- 1 oracle oinstall    435 Oct 30  2014 sel_aux.sql
-rw-r--r-- 1 oracle oinstall    475 Oct 30  2014 sel.sql
-rw-r--r-- 1 oracle oinstall   2978 Oct 30  2014 sqltcdirs.sql
-rw-r--r-- 1 oracle oinstall   4073 Oct 30  2014 sqlthistfile.sql
-rw-r--r-- 1 oracle oinstall   3197 Oct 30  2014 sqlthistpurge.sql
-rw-r--r-- 1 oracle oinstall   3146 Oct 30  2014 sqltimpdict.sql
-rw-r--r-- 1 oracle oinstall   3112 Oct 30  2014 sqltimpfo.sql
```

```
-rw-r--r-- 1 oracle oinstall  4295 Oct 30  2014 sqltimp.sql
-rw-r--r-- 1 oracle oinstall  3624 Oct 30  2014 sqltlite.sql
-rw-r--r-- 1 oracle oinstall  3982 Oct 30  2014 sqltmain.sql
-rw-r--r-- 1 oracle oinstall  3885 Oct 30  2014 sqlt_parameters.sql
-rw-r--r-- 1 oracle oinstall  5321 Oct 30  2014 sqltprofile.sql
-rw-r--r-- 1 oracle oinstall  8711 Oct 30  2014 sqltq.sql
-rw-r--r-- 1 oracle oinstall  1695 Oct 30  2014 sqltresetstatementid.sql
-rw-r--r-- 1 oracle oinstall  3492 Aug 15 13:14 sqlt_s41321_p1388734953_sqlprof.sql <<<New File
-rw-r--r-- 1 oracle oinstall  1358 Oct 30  2014 sqltupgdbahistash.sql
```

What Can You Do with an SQL Profile?

Now that we have the `sqlt_s41321_p1388734953_sqlprof.sql` script, what can we do with it? In broad terms, we can run this script on the database where the SQL is executing and this will freeze the execution plan for that SQL ID. It can also be used to freeze an execution plan on another system. So, for example, if your development system has the right execution plan and your production system does not, you can transfer the execution plan. In a situation where the production database is in an unusable state because some vital piece of SQL is using the wrong execution plan and consequently running too slowly to fit into the execution window, this script alone is worth the price of this book. Let's look at the script.

```
SPO sqlt_s41321_p1388734953_sqlprof.log;
SET ECHO ON TERM ON LIN 2000 TRIMS ON NUMF 99999999999999999999;
REM
REM $Header: 215187.1 sqlt_s41321_p1388734953_sqlprof.sql 12.1.160429 2016/08/15 abel.macias $
REM
REM Copyright (c) 2000-2015, Oracle Corporation. All rights reserved.
REM
REM AUTHOR
REM    abel.macias@oracle.com
REM
REM SCRIPT
REM    sqlt_s41321_p1388734953_sqlprof.sql
REM
REM SOURCE
REM    Host    : d12102.us.oracle.com
REM    DB Name : SNC1
REM    Platform: Linux
REM    Product : Oracle Database 12c Enterprise Edition (64bit Production)
REM    Version : 12.1.0.2.0
REM    Language: US:AMERICAN_AMERICA.WE8MSWIN1252
REM    EBS     : NO
REM    Siebel  : NO
REM    PSFT    : NO
REM
REM DESCRIPTION
REM    This script is generated automatically by the SQLT tool.
REM    It contains the SQL*Plus commands to create a custom
REM    SQL Profile based on plan hash value 1388734953.
REM    The custom SQL Profile to be created by this script
REM    will affect plans for SQL commands with signature
```

```
REM    matching the one for SQL Text below.
REM    Review SQL Text and adjust accordingly.
REM
REM PARAMETERS
REM    None.
REM
REM EXAMPLE
REM    SQL> START sqlt_s41321_p1388734953_sqlprof.sql; <<< Note 1
REM
REM NOTES
REM    1. Should be run as SYSTEM or SYSDBA.
REM    2. User must have CREATE ANY SQL PROFILE privilege.
REM    3. SOURCE and TARGET systems can be the same or similar.
REM    4. To drop this custom SQL Profile after it has been created:
REM       EXEC SYS.DBMS_SQLTUNE.DROP_SQL_PROFILE('sqlt_s41321_p1388734953'); <<< Note 2
REM    5. Be aware that using SYS.DBMS_SQLTUNE requires a license
REM       for the Oracle Tuning Pack. <<< Note 3
REM    6. If you modified a SQL putting Hints in order to produce a desired
REM       Plan, you can remove the artifical Hints from SQL Text pieces below.
REM       By doing so you can create a custom SQL Profile for the original
REM       SQL but with the Plan captured from the modified SQL (with Hints).
REM
WHENEVER SQLERROR EXIT SQL.SQLCODE;

VAR signature NUMBER;

DECLARE
  sql_txt CLOB;
  h       SYS.SQLPROF_ATTR;
  PROCEDURE wa (p_line IN VARCHAR2) IS
  BEGIN
    SYS.DBMS_LOB.WRITEAPPEND(sql_txt, LENGTH(p_line), p_line);
  END wa;
BEGIN
  SYS.DBMS_LOB.CREATETEMPORARY(sql_txt, TRUE); <<< Note 4
  SYS.DBMS_LOB.OPEN(sql_txt, SYS.DBMS_LOB.LOB_READWRITE);
  -- SQL Text pieces below do not have to be of same length.
  -- So if you edit SQL Text (i.e. removing temporary Hints),
  -- there is no need to edit or re-align unmodified pieces.
  wa(q'[select sysdate from dual]'); <<< Note 5
  SYS.DBMS_LOB.CLOSE(sql_txt);
  h := SYS.SQLPROF_ATTR(
  q'[BEGIN_OUTLINE_DATA]',
  q'[IGNORE_OPTIM_EMBEDDED_HINTS]',
  q'[OPTIMIZER_FEATURES_ENABLE('12.1.0.2')]',
  q'[DB_VERSION('12.1.0.2')]',
  q'[ALL_ROWS]',
  q'[OUTLINE_LEAF(@"SEL$1")]',
  q'[END_OUTLINE_DATA]');

  :signature := SYS.DBMS_SQLTUNE.SQLTEXT_TO_SIGNATURE(sql_txt); <<< Note 6
```

```
SYS.DBMS_SQLTUNE.IMPORT_SQL_PROFILE ( <<< Note 7
    sql_text    => sql_txt,
    profile     => h,
    name        => 'sqlt_s41321_p1388734953',
    description => 's41321_snc1_d12102 7h35uxf5uhmm1 1388734953 '||:signature,
    category    => 'DEFAULT',
    validate    => TRUE,
    replace     => TRUE,
    force_match => FALSE /* TRUE:FORCE (match even when different literals in SQL).
FALSE:EXACT (similar to CURSOR_SHARING) */ );
    SYS.DBMS_LOB.FREETEMPORARY(sql_txt);
END;
/

WHENEVER SQLERROR CONTINUE;
SET ECHO OFF;
PRINT signature
PRO
PRO ... manual custom SQL Profile has been created
PRO
SET TERM ON ECHO OFF LIN 80 TRIMS OFF NUMF "";
SPO OFF;
PRO
PRO SQLPROFILE completed.
```

You do not need to know any of the details of how this code works; in an emergency situation you would just follow the instructions and then make your system behave as required.

1. SQL> START sqlt_s41321_p1388734953_sqlprof.sql; - This is how you run the SQL script. As it says in the notes, you should use a suitably privileged account, such as SYS.

2. SQL> EXEC DBMS_SQLTUNE.DROP_SQL_PROFILE('sqlt_s41321_p1388734953'); If for some reason you do not want to keep the profile (for example, you've found the long-term solution to your SQL performance problem) you can execute this command line, and the SQL profile will be dropped.

3. You must have the Oracle license for the tuning pack for the system on which you apply this code.

4. This is the code where a LOB is created to store your SQL text.

5. A series of calls to the procedure wa (Write Append) are used to store more and more of your SQL text until it is all stored in sql_text.

6. Create a signature for the SQL text.

7. Import the SQL profile. The procedure IMPORT_SQL_PROFILE takes the following parameters:

    a. The sql_text of the query;

    b. The hint (h) for the query;

    c. A name for the SQL profile (sqlt_s41321_p1388734953);

    d.   Some text to describe the profile, based on the SQLT ID, the SQL ID, the plan hash value and the signature;

    e.   A category, which is set to DEFAULT;

    f.   A setting to validate the SQL profile;

    g.   A setting to replace any existing profiles on the same SQL text;

    h.   A force_match flag, which is set to FALSE by default but should be set to TRUE if your SQL uses bind variables and you want all occurrences of the SQL to use the same profile.

Let's see an example run of the script. I haven't set the force_match flag in this example because I don't need it, but on a system with SQL using literals I will set the force_match flag to TRUE. In the example below I have run the profile script that was created above. This script is now a stand-alone script that generates the profile for a particular SQL ID and uses the plan for a particular PHV. It has no other purpose. Hence it takes no parameters. We know that the script has completed because we see the message "SQLPROFILE completed." Once this script has finished there is nothing more to do except find the long-term solution!

```
[oracle@d12102 utl]$ sqlplus stelios/oracle

SQL*Plus: Release 12.1.0.2.0 Production on Mon Aug 15 13:35:48 2016

Copyright (c) 1982, 2014, Oracle.  All rights reserved.

Last Successful login time: Mon Aug 15 2016 13:10:22 -04:00

Connected to:
Oracle Database 12c Enterprise Edition Release 12.1.0.2.0 - 64bit Production
With the Partitioning, OLAP, Advanced Analytics and Real Application Testing options
SQL> @sqlt_s41321_p1388734953_sqlprof.sql
SQL> REM
SQL> REM $Header: 215187.1 sqlt_s41321_p1388734953_sqlprof.sql 12.1.160429 2016/08/15 abel.
macias $
SQL> REM
SQL> REM Copyright (c) 2000-2015, Oracle Corporation. All rights reserved.
SQL> REM
SQL> REM AUTHOR
SQL> REM    abel.macias@oracle.com
SQL> REM
SQL> REM SCRIPT
SQL> REM    sqlt_s41321_p1388734953_sqlprof.sql
SQL> REM
SQL> REM SOURCE
SQL> REM    Host     : d12102.us.oracle.com
SQL> REM    DB Name  : SNC1
SQL> REM    Platform: Linux
SQL> REM    Product  : Oracle Database 12c Enterprise Edition (64bit Production)
SQL> REM    Version  : 12.1.0.2.0
SQL> REM    Language: US:AMERICAN_AMERICA.WE8MSWIN1252
SQL> REM    EBS      : NO
SQL> REM    Siebel   : NO
SQL> REM    PSFT     : NO
```

```
SQL> REM
SQL> REM DESCRIPTION
SQL> REM    This script is generated automatically by the SQLT tool.
SQL> REM    It contains the SQL*Plus commands to create a custom
SQL> REM    SQL Profile based on plan hash value 1388734953.
SQL> REM    The custom SQL Profile to be created by this script
SQL> REM    will affect plans for SQL commands with signature
SQL> REM    matching the one for SQL Text below.
SQL> REM    Review SQL Text and adjust accordingly.
SQL> REM
SQL> REM PARAMETERS
SQL> REM    None.
SQL> REM
SQL> REM EXAMPLE
SQL> REM    SQL> START sqlt_s41321_p1388734953_sqlprof.sql;
SQL> REM
SQL> REM NOTES
SQL> REM    1. Should be run as SYSTEM or SYSDBA.
SQL> REM    2. User must have CREATE ANY SQL PROFILE privilege.
SQL> REM    3. SOURCE and TARGET systems can be the same or similar.
SQL> REM    4. To drop this custom SQL Profile after it has been created:
SQL> REM           EXEC SYS.DBMS_SQLTUNE.DROP_SQL_PROFILE('sqlt_s41321_p1388734953');
SQL> REM    5. Be aware that using SYS.DBMS_SQLTUNE requires a license
SQL> REM           for the Oracle Tuning Pack.
SQL> REM    6. If you modified a SQL putting Hints in order to produce a desired
SQL> REM           Plan, you can remove the artifical Hints from SQL Text pieces below.
SQL> REM           By doing so you can create a custom SQL Profile for the original
SQL> REM           SQL but with the Plan captured from the modified SQL (with Hints).
SQL> REM
SQL> WHENEVER SQLERROR EXIT SQL.SQLCODE;
SQL>
SQL> VAR signature NUMBER;
SQL>
SQL> DECLARE
  2    sql_txt CLOB;
  3    h           SYS.SQLPROF_ATTR;
  4    PROCEDURE wa (p_line IN VARCHAR2) IS
  5    BEGIN
  6      SYS.DBMS_LOB.WRITEAPPEND(sql_txt, LENGTH(p_line), p_line);
  7    END wa;
  8  BEGIN
  9    SYS.DBMS_LOB.CREATETEMPORARY(sql_txt, TRUE);
 10    SYS.DBMS_LOB.OPEN(sql_txt, SYS.DBMS_LOB.LOB_READWRITE);
 11    -- SQL Text pieces below do not have to be of same length.
 12    -- So if you edit SQL Text (i.e. removing temporary Hints),
 13    -- there is no need to edit or re-align unmodified pieces.
 14    wa(q'[select sysdate from dual]');
 15    SYS.DBMS_LOB.CLOSE(sql_txt);
 16    h := SYS.SQLPROF_ATTR(
 17    q'[BEGIN_OUTLINE_DATA]',
 18    q'[IGNORE_OPTIM_EMBEDDED_HINTS]',
 19    q'[OPTIMIZER_FEATURES_ENABLE('12.1.0.2')]',
```

141

```
20    q'[DB_VERSION('12.1.0.2')]',
21    q'[ALL_ROWS]',
22    q'[OUTLINE_LEAF(@"SEL$1")]',
23    q'[END_OUTLINE_DATA]');
24
25    :signature := SYS.DBMS_SQLTUNE.SQLTEXT_TO_SIGNATURE(sql_txt);
26
27    SYS.DBMS_SQLTUNE.IMPORT_SQL_PROFILE (
28        sql_text    => sql_txt,
29        profile     => h,
30        name        => 'sqlt_s41321_p1388734953',
31        description => 's41321_snc1_d12102 7h35uxf5uhmm1 1388734953 '||:signature,
32        category    => 'DEFAULT',
33        validate    => TRUE,
34        replace     => TRUE,
35        force_match => FALSE /* TRUE:FORCE (match even when different literals in SQL).
          FALSE:EXACT (similar to CURSOR_SHARING) */ );
36        SYS.DBMS_LOB.FREETEMPORARY(sql_txt);
37  END;
38  /

PL/SQL procedure successfully completed.

SQL>
SQL> WHENEVER SQLERROR CONTINUE;
SQL> SET ECHO OFF;

          SIGNATURE
--------------------
  2672114946588399948

... manual custom SQL Profile has been created

SQLPROFILE completed.
```

At the end of this script the SQL profile is attached to the SQL ID and should use the same plan as shown in the outline section of the script. The three-step plan in case of emergency (emergency drop in SQL performance):

1. Break open SQLT.

2. Run sqltprofile.sql (license permitting).

3. Set the force_match flag to TRUE (if using literals) and run the script.

How Do You Confirm You Are Using an SQL Profile?

To confirm that the SQL Profile is working we need to run the SQL from the SQL prompt or re-run SQLT and look at the display showing the SQL profiles being used. Below is another example (sqlt_s89915) where I have run the SQL manually and got the execution plan.

```
SQL> @q1
1127 rows selected.

Execution Plan
----------------------------------------------------------
Plan hash value: 1574422790

---------------------------------------------------------------------------------------
| Id  |Operation                          |Name                |Rows |Cost (%CPU)|Time     |
---------------------------------------------------------------------------------------
|   0 |SELECT STATEMENT                   |                    | 5557| 7035  (1)|00:01:25|
|*  1 | HASH JOIN                         |                    | 5557| 7035  (1)|00:01:25|
|   2 |  TABLE ACCESS FULL                |PRODUCTS            |   72|    3  (0)|00:00:01|
|   3 |  NESTED LOOPS                     |                    |     |          |        |
|   4 |   NESTED LOOPS                    |                    | 5557| 7032  (1)|00:01:25|
|*  5 |    TABLE ACCESS BY INDEX ROWID    |CUSTOMERS           |   43| 2366  (1)|00:00:29|
|   6 |     BITMAP CONVERSION TO ROWIDS   |                    |     |          |        |
|   7 |      BITMAP INDEX FULL SCAN       |CUSTOMERS_GENDER_BIX|     |          |        |
|   8 |    PARTITION RANGE ALL            |                    |     |          |        |
|   9 |     BITMAP CONVERSION TO ROWIDS   |                    |     |          |        |
|* 10 |      BITMAP INDEX SINGLE VALUE    |SALES_CUST_BIX      |     |          |        |
|  11 |    TABLE ACCESS BY LOCAL INDEX ROWID|SALES             |  130| 7032  (1)|00:01:25|
---------------------------------------------------------------------------------------

Predicate Information (identified by operation id):
---------------------------------------------------

   1 - access("S"."PROD_ID"="P"."PROD_ID")
   5 - filter("C"."CUST_FIRST_NAME"='Theodorick') .
  10 - access("C"."CUST_ID"="S"."CUST_ID")
Note
-----
   - SQL profile "sqlt_s89915_p3005811457" used for this statement
Statistics
----------------------------------------------------------
          0  recursive calls
          0  db block gets
       5782  consistent gets
          0  physical reads
          0  redo size
      49680  bytes sent via SQL*Net to client
       1241  bytes received via SQL*Net from client
         77  SQL*Net roundtrips to/from client
          0  sorts (memory)
          0  sorts (disk)
       1127  rows processed
```

If you look at the execution plan, you'll see that a note is appended stating SQL profile "sqlt_s89915_p3005811457" used for this statement. If a SQLT XECUTE report was run against this system and this SQL ID you would see this list of Execution plans

See Figure 8-3, which shows this section of the report.

Execution Plans

List ordered by phv and source.

#	Plan Hash Value	SQLT Plan Hash Value[1]	SQLT Plan Hash Value2[1]	Src	Source	Plan Info	Is Bind Sensitive	Optimizer
1	665279032 [B]	205	205	AWR	DBA_HIST_SQL_PLAN			ALL_ROWS
2	665279032 [B]	205	5075	STA	DBA_SQLTUNE_PLANS	sql_profile "sqlt_s89915_p3005811457"		HINT: ALL_ROWS
3	725901306 [W]	16588	16588	AWR	DBA_HIST_SQL_PLAN			ALL_ROWS
4	725901306 [W]	16588	21458	STA	DBA_SQLTUNE_PLANS	sql_profile "sqlt_s89915_p3005811457"		HINT: ALL_ROWS
5	769355097	6207	11077	STA	DBA_SQLTUNE_PLANS	sql_profile "sqlt_s89915_p3005811457"		HINT: ALL_ROWS
6	1574422790	31964	36834	MEM	GV$SQL_PLAN	sql_profile "sqlt_s89915_p3005811457"	N	HINT: ALL_ROWS
7	1574422790	31964	36834	XPL	PLAN_TABLE	sql_profile "sqlt_s89915_p3005811457"		HINT: ALL_ROWS
8	1574422790	31964	36834	STA	DBA_SQLTUNE_PLANS	sql_profile "sqlt_s89915_p3005811457"		HINT: ALL_ROWS
9	3803650565	85134	90004	STA	DBA_SQLTUNE_PLANS	sql_profile "sqlt_s89915_p3005811457"		HINT: ALL_ROWS

(1) SQLT PHV considers id, parent_id, operation, options, index_columns and object_name. SQLT PHV2 includes also access and filter predicates.
(2) Display of child plans is restricted up to 10 per phv as per tool parameter "r_rows_table_xs".
Go to Plan Performance Statistics
Go to Plans Summary
Go to Top

Figure 8-3. *shows the Execution Plans section of the SQLT HTML report. This is the left-hand side of the page. There are more details available on the right-hand side of the page. Note the use of sql_profile in the Plan Info column*

How Do You Transfer an SQL Profile from One Database to Another?

In many cases SQLT is considered too intrusive to database operations (it isn't) or there are strict rules on a particular site that disallow the use of SQLT directly on a production database. In such cases there will often be a development or staging environment where a test SQL can be run against a representative workload (i.e., one with enough data, which is up to date). In cases like these you can often get the right execution plan in the development or staging environment, but can't in the production environment. Either because you don't have time to correct statistics or some other factor prevents you from correcting production in a timely manner. In such cases, after confirming with Oracle support, you can create an SQL profile on one system and transfer it to production. You can follow the steps described in the Oracle Support Note "How To Move SQL Profiles From One Database To Another Database [ID 457531.1]" or follow the steps described here, which are a simplified version of the note steps using SQLT.

1. Create an SQL profile script on your staging or development system (as described above). The SQL profile should be based on SQL text that matches the SQL text on the production system where you are going to transfer the SQL profile. The end result of this step is SQL text file.

2. On the Development or Staging system create a staging table with the commands

   ```
   SQL> exec dbms_sqltune.create_stgtab_sqlprof(table_name=>'STAGE', schema_
   name='STELIOS').
   ```

3. Pack the SQL profile into the staging area just created with the commands

   ```
   SQL> exec dbms_sqltune.pack_stgtab_sqlprof(staging_table_name=>'STAGE', profile_
   name=>' sqlt_s89915_p3005811457').
   ```

4. Export from the development or staging system the SQL Profile Staging table either with exp or expdp.

5. Import the dump file using imp or impdp into the production environment.

6. Unpack the staging table using the command

```
SQL> exec dbms_sqltune.unpack_stgtab_sqlprof(replace=>TRUE, staging_table_
name=>'STAGE').
```

Once you have carried out these steps your target SQL should run with the execution plan from your development or staging environment. You can check it by getting the execution plan as we did earlier on.

SQL Plan Baselines

SQL Plan Baselines are boxes of SQLs, some of which are accepted and some are not. It's an automated way of preventing SQL from regressing to worse plans. You can control the collection of new plans, the use of new plans, and the authorization or evolution of plans from collected to allowable to run. If you set up the SQL Plan Baseline so that it collects plans but does not automatically evolve them to accepted plans and only authorize the ones that you know are good, you can control which plans are accepted. This is different to Profiles where you 'force' a plan on a SQL ID. With Baselines you prevent 'bad' plans from occurring. They are different strategies for the same problem. Setting up individual policies for every SQL ID can be very cumbersome. 'Fixing' just SQLs that have gone rogue may be simpler but is more of a "wait for it to break before fixing it" approach, which will not be acceptable to everybody. You can either use SQL Plan Baselines or Profiles or both; they are not mutually exclusive.

Here is a list of differences between these two approaches.

	SQL Profiles	SQL Plan Baselines
Methodology	Tends to be reactive.	Allow good plan to evolve proactively.
When to apply	Bad plan found, so fix it.	Good plan found. Evolve it.
Method of operation	Stores hint type information about the query.	Stores different plans and if they are accepted or not.
Number of plans	No specific plan.	Many plans in a set of plans.
Suitable scenario for use	If data changes dramatically this can keep a plan stable.	If data changes dramatically this can be slow to adapt, unless you auto-accept new plans.
How many executions needed	One execution is enough to generate a profile.	More than one execution is required to generate many plans.

Now let's look at the SQL Plan Patch utility, yet another way to deal with SQLs that go off the rails.

SQL Patch Utility

From 11.2.0.3 the SQL Patch utility was introduced to control SQL statements by adding hints but without changing the SQL code. The process for setting this up is extremely simple.

```
SQL> exec sys.dbms_sqldiag_internal.i_create_patch(
  sql_text => 'select count(*), max(empno) from emp where deptno = :deptno',
    hint_text => 'BIND_AWARE',
    name =>'My_Patch');
```

The value for "hint_text" can be any valid hint.

If you want to include multiple hints, you can do so just by separating the hints with spaces. If you have a hint that require quotes such as

```
optimizer_features_enable('11.2.0.4')
```

don't forget to 'protect' the quotes by putting two quotes (see below)

```
SQL> exec sys.dbms_sqldiag_internal.i_create_patch(
  sql_text=>'select count(*) from sales',
  hint_text=>'BIND_AWARE optimizer_features_enable(''11.2.0.4'')',
  name=>'MYPATCH');
```

This results in the following plan#

```
Execution Plan
----------------------------------------------------------
Plan hash value: 3730320257

--------------------------------------------------------------------------------
| Id  | Operation                   | Name            | Rows  | Cost (%CPU)| Ps
--------------------------------------------------------------------------------
|   0 | SELECT STATEMENT            |                 |     1 |     0   (0)|
|   1 |  SORT AGGREGATE             |                 |     1 |            |
|   2 |   PARTITION RANGE ALL       |                 |  918K |            |
|   3 |    BITMAP CONVERSION COUNT  |                 |  918K |            |
|   4 |     BITMAP INDEX FAST FULL SCAN| SALES_CHANNEL_BIX |     |          |
--------------------------------------------------------------------------------

Note
-----
   -   SQL patch "MYPATCH" used for this statement
```

Notice the Note section identifies the use of the SQL Patch MYPATCH.

Summary

As you can see, SQLT is a powerful tool when used properly. Traditional tuning can seem slow and cumbersome in comparison after you have used SQLT for a while. This is the main objective of this book: to make you familiar with SQLT and then for you to use SQLT often enough to become fast and efficient at tuning SQL. When you need help fast there are many different tools that can force an execution plan. SQL Profiles, Baselines, and the Patch Utility are all useful in this area. The right use will depend on your circumstances.

In the next chapter we'll look at a feature called Adaptive Cursor Sharing. There is much confusion about how this feature works, and when it is being used and under what circumstances. SQLT has a section in the main report, which is just for Adaptive Cursor Sharing.

CHAPTER 9

███ ██ █

Adaptive Cursor Sharing

There's no doubt that Adaptive Cursor Sharing is one of the most misunderstood and confusing optimizer areas. It doesn't help that it is sometimes referred to as Intelligent Cursor Sharing or Bind Aware Peeking. Adaptive Cursor Sharing was introduced in 11g to take care of those pesky bind variables that keep changing. SQLTXTRACT has a section called "Cursor Sharing and Binds," which can be found at the top of the main report. See Figure 9-1 to remind yourself. The Adaptive Cursor Sharing section is at the bottom left of the screen.

<u>215187.1</u> **SQLT XTRACT 12.1.160429 Report: sqlt_s41322_main.html**

Global

- Observations
- SQL Text
- SQL Identification
- Environment
- CBO Environment
- Fix Control
- CBO System Statistics
- DBMS_STATS Setup
- Initialization Parameters
- NLS Parameters
- I/O Calibration
- Tool Configuration Parameters

Cursor Sharing and Binds

- Cursor Sharing
- Adaptive Cursor Sharing
- Peeked Binds
- Captured Binds

SQL Tuning Advisor

- STA Report
- STA Script

Plans

- Summary
- Performance Statistics
- Performance History (delta)
- Performance History (total)
- Execution Plans

Plan Control

- Stored Outlines
- SQL Patches
- SQL Profiles
- SQL Plan Baselines
- SQL Plan Directives

SQL Execution

- Active Session History
- AWR Active Session History
- SQL Statistics
- SQL Detail ACTIVE Report
- Monitor Statistics
- Monitor ACTIVE Report
- Monitor HTML Report
- Monitor TEXT Report
- Segment Statistics
- Session Statistics
- Session Events
- Parallel Processing

Tables

- Tables
- Statistics
- Statistics Extensions
- Statistics Versions
- Modifications
- Properties
- Physical Properties
- Constraints
- Columns
- Indexed Columns
- Histograms
- Partitions
- Indexes

Objects

- Objects
- Dependencies
- Fixed Objects
- Fixed Object Columns
- Nested Tables
- Policies
- Audit Policies
- Tablespaces
- Metadata

This report may include some content provided by the Oracle Diagnostic and/or the Oracle Tuning Packs (in particular SQL Tuning Advisor "STA", SQL Tuning Sets "STS", SQL Monitoring and/or Automatic Workload Repository "AWR"). Be aware that using this extended functionality requires a license for the corresponding pack. If you need to disable SQLT access to one of these packages, please execute one of the following commands: SQL> EXEC sqltxadmin.sqlt$a.disable_tuning_pack_access; or SQL> EXEC sqltxadmin.sqlt$a.disable_diagnostic_pack_access;

Figure 9-1. *The Adaptive Cursor Sharing section can be found in the bottom left-hand corner of the screen*

© Stelios Charalambides 2017

S. Charalambides, *Oracle SQL Tuning with Oracle SQLTXPLAIN*, DOI 10.1007/978-1-4842-2436-6_9

Understanding this area of the optimizer is not helped by the documentation either. It is not exactly crystal clear and lacks some details that are required to understand what happens when you use this feature. I will explain this feature in simple terms and show examples where it has kicked into action. If you have a system where this feature is important, you will better be able to understand what is happening and why. You will also have the option of disabling the feature completely.

Bind Variables and Why We Need Them

Before we go into Adaptive Cursor Sharing (ACS), however, we need to cover some prerequisite knowledge, which will be required for you to follow the discussion and understand the history of ACS. Bind variables are the key component of SQL, which ACS relies on. They are used by programmers in Oracle systems, because over the years Oracle has encouraged them to use bind variables. In practical terms there are pros and cons to both literals and bind variables. You really have to know your system and its design and data configuration to make an accurate judgment. In some systems you will see hundreds of thousands of cursors being generated because of literal values. Often because SQL is being created by an application that generates SQL automatically. This is an example of a bind variable in an SQL statement and a literal value of an equivalent statement:

```
variable b varchar2(5);
exec :b := 'TABLE';
select count(object_type) from dba_objects where object_type=:b;
select count(object_type) from dba_objects where object_type='TABLE';
```

Here the bind variable is b, and it is being used in the SQL statement (a select in this case) to stand in for the value TABLE. If we replaced :b with INDEX, we would have a different SQL (after the bind variable was peeked)

```
select count(object_type) from dba_objects where object_type='INDEX';
```

With the use of the new value for the bind variable we would expect different results, but the query text remains unchanged as

```
select count(object_type) from dba_objects where object_type=:b;
```

Because the query text remains unchanged the optimizer will not do a hard parse. If we used literals for the predicate of TABLE and INDEX, each example would be a hard parse. This is the reason we use bind variables.

This overhead of hard parsing is prohibitive on busy systems (more so on OLTP systems than DW systems) and each SQL cursor's details have to be kept in the shared pool, which can be a big memory overhead. Each of the statements would be exactly the same; we don't want the cost-based optimizer to look in detail at each statement each time the bind variable changed. Back in the dim and distant past (8i), bind variables were available, but were not used very often. Oracle decided that more bind variables should be used to improve performance but without necessarily having bind variables. The cursor_sharing parameter was introduced.

The CURSOR_SHARING Parameter

The solution introduced was the CURSOR_SHARING parameter, which had possible values of EXACT or FORCE. The default value was EXACT, which resulted in no change in behavior: that is, if there was a literal value in an SQL statement then it was parsed and executed. If the overhead of the parsing was too high, then you could consider setting the value to FORCE. In this case, the literal value (in the example from above this would be 'TABLE'), would be replaced by a system-defined bind variable (an example would be SYS_B_0). This resulted in an improvement in performance in some cases, but caused problems in some situations where the value of the binds made a difference to the execution plan (in other words, skewed data). A predicate with a rare value and a common value would have the same execution plan as they were using the same system-generated bind variable. This sometimes caused problems, so bind peeking was created to help. Here is an example to show the behavior:

```
SQL> alter session set cursor_sharing='FORCE';
Session altered.
SQL> @q4
  COUNT(*)
----------
         0
SQL> host type q4.sql
select count(*) from sh.products p,sh.sales s,sh.customers c where
  c.cust_id=s.cust_id and s.prod_id=p.prod_id and
  c.cust_first_name='Stelios' ;
SQL> select sql_id from v$sqlarea where sql_text like 'select count(*) from sh.products
p,sh.sales s,sh.customers c where%';
SQL_ID
-------------
44b9pnz14j4nr
SQL> select sql_text from v$sqlarea where sql_id='44b9pnz14j4nr';
SQL_TEXT
----------------------------------------------------------------
select count(*) from sh.products p,sh.sales s,sh.customers c where  c.cust_id=s.cust_id and
s.prod_id=p.prod_id and c.cust_first_name=:"SYS_B_0"

SQL> alter session set cursor_sharing='EXACT';
Session altered.
SQL> @q4
  COUNT(*)
----------
         0
SQL> select sql_id from v$sqlarea where sql_text like 'select  count(*) from sh.products
p,sh.sales s,sh.customers c where%';
SQL_ID
-------------
6hr43kgywafzy

SQL> select sql_text from v$sqlarea where sql_id=' 6hr43kgywafzy';
SQL_TEXT
----------------------------------------------------------------
select count(*) from sh.products p,sh.sales s,sh.customers c where c.cust_id=s.cust_id and
s.prod_id=p.prod_id and c.cust_first_name='Stelios'
```

In the example above I changed the default value of cursor_sharing to FORCE. My SQL then changed so that it included a system-defined bind variable called SYS_B_0. Then I set the value back to EXACT, and the current execution plan changed to show the literal. The bind value is no longer shown (although that version of the plan is still in the shared pool). This is the expected behavior.

Bind Peeking

In 9i Oracle introduced bind peeking. Bind peeking is used to look at the value being used for a bind variable, during the hard parsing process, to determine an appropriate execution plan. A new possible value of SIMILAR for CURSOR_SHARING was also introduced (SIMILAR is now long deprecated). If it was appropriate, during parsing, a new plan was generated; otherwise the plan was unchanged. The problem with this was that if the first execution plan resulted in a plan that was not good for the subsequent plans then you were stuck with a poorly executing plan.

Bind Sensitive and Bind Aware Cursors

A new hybrid system was introduced by 11g and still in use in 12c, called Adaptive Cursor Sharing (ACS), which is a little more subtle about when to introduce a new plan. The concepts of "bind sensitive" and "bind aware" were introduced. Bind sensitive is true when you have bind variables whose value *may* affect the execution plan. Bind sensitive means that the optimizer suspects that a new plan may be appropriate for some values, but it's not sure. Bind aware plans are ones where the plans actually changed.

Think of bind sensitive as the first step in becoming aware that more execution plans are needed. You have to be sensitive to the bind variables before you become aware. If you run the SQL a number of times so that the number of buffer gets significantly changed for different bind variables, eventually the cursor will be marked "bind aware." In other words, we went from bind sensitive (we have bind variables) to bind aware (these bind variables make a significant difference to the number of buffer gets). You can track the progress of the bind sensitivity and bind awareness values by looking at the SQLTXPLAIN report.

Setting Up a Bind Sensitive Cursor

To show the behavior of ACS will take a little setting up. In broad terms, here are the steps we'll carry out in the example code. We'll show the code for doing the following below:

1. Creating a test table

2. Inserting skewed data into the test table. There should be enough rows to allow the possibility of multiple execution plans.

3. Showing how skewed the data is

4. Creating indexes to allow them to be used in the execution plan

5. Gathering statistics including histograms on all columns

6. Selecting common and rare values in a number of executions until ACS is activated

7. Checking the results in SQLTXECUTE

```
-- Set up
drop table acs;
create table acs(object_id number, object_type varchar2(20));
insert into acs select object_id, object_type from dba_objects;
insert into acs select object_id, object_type from dba_objects;
select object_type, count(*) from acs group by object_type order by count(object_type);
create index i1 on acs(object_id);
create index i2 on acs(object_type);
```

```
exec dbms_stats.gather_table_stats('STELIOS','ACS', estimate_percent=>100, method_opt=>'FOR
ALL COLUMNS SIZE 254');
prompt Now we have a table, ACS with skewed data.
-- Now let's do some selecting...
variable b varchar2(20);
@@acs_query 'SYNONYM'
@@acs_query 'TABLE'
@@acs_query 'SYNONYM'
@@acs_query 'DIMENSION'
@@acs_query 'DIMENSION'
@@acs_query 'DIMENSION'
@@acs_query 'DIMENSION'
@@acs_query 'DIMENSION'
@@acs_query 'DIMENSION'
@@acs_query 'DIMENSION'
@@acs_query 'DIMENSION'
@@acs_query 'DIMENSION'
```

We've selected dba_objects yet again as a good source for pseudo-random data. In this case, we are interested in the fact that there are many more SYNONYM types in this table than there are DIMENSIONs. The script acs_query.sql contains the following:

```
exec :b := '&1'
select count(object_type) from acs where object_type=:b;
```

The output from this script looks like this:

```
SQL>@acs
Table dropped.

Table created.

101175 rows created.

101175 rows created.

OBJECT_TYPE           COUNT(*)
--------------------  ----------
EDITION                      2
RULE                         2
DESTINATION                  4
JAVA SOURCE                  4
MATERIALIZED VIEW            4
SCHEDULE                     8
SCHEDULER GROUP              8
DIMENSION                   10    <<<Count for Dimensions
INDEXTYPE                   14
UNIFIED AUDIT POLICY        16
WINDOW                      18
CLUSTER                     20
PROGRAM                     20
```

```
CONTEXT                   20
RESOURCE PLAN             22
LOB PARTITION             24
JOB CLASS                 28
EVALUATION CONTEXT        30
UNDEFINED                 34
CONSUMER GROUP            36
RULE SET                  42
DIRECTORY                 44
JOB                       46
QUEUE                     60
TABLE SUBPARTITION        64
XML SCHEMA                90
OPERATOR                 108
PROCEDURE                410
LIBRARY                  456
TYPE BODY                464
SEQUENCE                 548
JAVA DATA                620
FUNCTION                 696
TRIGGER                 1198
TABLE PARTITION         2010
LOB                     2020
JAVA RESOURCE           2028
PACKAGE BODY            2528
PACKAGE                 2650
TYPE                    5166
TABLE                   5376 <<<Count for Tables
INDEX                   9428
VIEW                   13274
INDEX PARTITION        16336
JAVA CLASS             61632
SYNONYM                74732 <<<Count for synonyms

46 rows selected.

Index created.

Index created.

PL/SQL procedure successfully completed.

Now we have a table, ACS with skewed data.

PL/SQL procedure successfully completed.

COUNT(OBJECT_TYPE)
------------------
          74732 <<<This is the count for SYNONYMS

PL/SQL procedure successfully completed.
```

```
COUNT(OBJECT_TYPE)
------------------
            5376 <<<This is the count for TABLES

PL/SQL procedure successfully completed.

COUNT(OBJECT_TYPE)
------------------
           74732<<<SYNONYMS again

PL/SQL procedure successfully completed.

COUNT(OBJECT_TYPE)
------------------
              10 <<<Count for DIMENSION

PL/SQL procedure successfully completed.

COUNT(OBJECT_TYPE)
------------------
              10

PL/SQL procedure successfully completed.

COUNT(OBJECT_TYPE)
------------------
              10

PL/SQL procedure successfully completed.

COUNT(OBJECT_TYPE)
------------------
              10

PL/SQL procedure successfully completed.

COUNT(OBJECT_TYPE)
------------------
              10

PL/SQL procedure successfully completed.

COUNT(OBJECT_TYPE)
------------------
              10

PL/SQL procedure successfully completed.

COUNT(OBJECT_TYPE)
------------------
              10
```

153

```
PL/SQL procedure successfully completed.

COUNT(OBJECT_TYPE)
------------------
                10

PL/SQL procedure successfully completed.

COUNT(OBJECT_TYPE)
------------------
                10
```

Let's summarize what happened. We created a test table, populated it with skewed data, selected a popular value, a moderately popular value, a popular value, and finally a rare value a number of times. We would expect the rare value would use an index range scan and the popular value would use a full table scan or fast full index scan.

In the example above we used only one predicate to be Bind Sensitive and Bind Aware. ACS can cope with many predicates being bind senstive and bind aware. By increasing the number of predicates we are increasing the number of dimensions in which our peeked binds can fit. If we used three dimensions it would be a box. If the value of the predicates was inside the box then we have a good use for the cursor. If it is outside we might need to take some other action.

If we generate a SQLT XTRACT report (a SQLTXECUTE report would be just as good) we can now examine what happened.

Examining ACS with a SQLTXTRACT Report

ACS information is gathered for both SQLTXTRACT and for SQLTXECUTE reports. Both of these types of SQLTXPLAIN reports collect the bind variable information (if available) and show you the information in a clear report. Our example report happens to be a SQLTXTRACT report, but the navigation and examples work for both kinds of SQLTXPLAIN reports. First we can check to see if the right SQL was picked up: see Figure 9-2, which shows the SQL with a bind variable as expected.

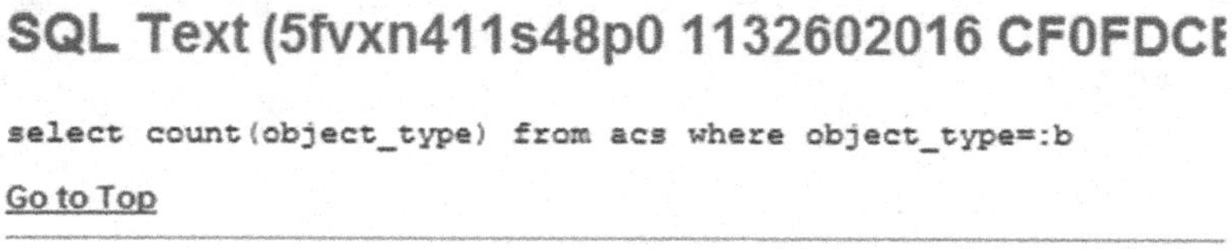

SQL Text (5fvxn411s48p0 1132602016 CF0FDCI

```
select count(object_type) from acs where object_type=:b
```

Go to Top

Figure 9-2. Shows the SQL with the bind variable

If we follow the hyperlink from the top of the main SQLTXTRACT report to the Observations section, we can see from observation that there are multiple plans for the SQL statement. See Figure 9-3, which shows this:

Observations

List of concerns identified by the health-check module. Please review. Some may require further attention.

#	Type	Name	Observation	Details
1	CBO PARAMETER	NON-DEFAULT	There is one CBO initialization parameter with a non-default value.	[+]
2	DBMS_STATS	DBA_AUTOTASK_CLIENT	Automatic gathering of CBO statistics is enabled.	[+]
3	DBMS_STATS	DBA_AUTOTASK_CLIENT_HISTORY	Automatic gathering of CBO statistics is enabled but no job was executed in the last 8 days	[+]
4	PLAN	PLAN_HASH_VALUE	2 plans were found for this SQL.	[-] Review Plans Summary.
5	PLAN CONTROL	PLAN_CONTROL	None of the plans found was created using one of these: Stored Outline, SQL Profile, SQL Patch or SQL Plan Baseline.	[+]
6	DBMS_STATS	SYSTEM STATISTICS	Single-block read time of .222 milliseconds seems too small.	[+]
7	DBMS_STATS	SYSTEM STATISTICS	Multi-block read time of .9 milliseconds seems too small.	[+]
8	ROLE	SQLT_USER_ROLE	User "STELIOS" is missing the required "SQLT_USER_ROLE" role.	[+]
9	MAT_VIEW	REWRITE_ENABLED	There is/are 2 materialized view(s) with rewrite enabled.	[+]
10	TABLE	STELIOS.ACS	Table rebuild candidate.	[+]
11	TABLE COLUMN	ACS.OBJECT_TYPE	Column is candidate for NOT NULL constraint.	[+]

Go to Top

Figure 9-3. *Shows the Observations section (notice that two plans were found for an SQL)*

If we now click on "Plan Summary" we end up at the Plan Summary section, which shows two execution plans (as expected). One plan is almost instantaneous and the other takes 0.007 seconds in elapsed time. You can guess that the faster execution time is associated with the value of the predicate when it is set to DIMENSION (the rarer value). See Figure 9-4 for the details of the execution plans.

Plans Summary

List of plans found ordered by average elapsed time.

#	Plan Hash Value[1]	Avg Elapsed Time in secs	Avg CPU Time in secs	Avg User I/O Wait Time in secs	Avg Other Wait Time in secs[2]	Avg Buffer Gets
1	2583336616 [B]	0.000	0.000	0.000	0.000	3
2	2348726875 [W]	0.007	0.004	0.000	0.000	585

(1) [B]est and [W]orst according to average elapsed time if availab

(2) Made of these wait times: application, concurrency, cluster, pla

(3) Shows accurate Plan Info when source is actually "GV$SQLAF

FOR" sources review Execution Plans section.

(4) For plans from DBA_HIST_SQLSTAT this is the time of the be

Go to Cursor Sharing

Go to Adaptive Cursor Sharing

Go to Execution Plans

Go to Top

Figure 9-4. *Two execution plans: a fast and a slow one. One relates to DIMENSION and the other relates to SYNONYM*

The figure above is the left-hand side of the section for the plan summary. As expected, we see slower execution, more CPU usage, and more buffer gets for the value Plan Hash Value 2348726875, because this is the plan associated with the predicate value SYNONYM. If we look at the right-hand side of the same section we see more corroborating evidence (see Figure 9-5).

Is Bind Sensitive	Min Opt Env	Max Opt Env	Opt Cost	Estimated Cardinality	Estimated Time in secs
Y	2580509211		3	1	0.001
Y	2580509211		158	1	0.035

Figure 9-5. *The right-hand side of the Plan Summary section shows a higher cost and higher estimated time in seconds for the second plan hash value*

To confirm this, click on the hyperlink of the plan that has value for the slower plan. This gets us to the details for this plan. See Figure 9-6.

Execution Plan phv:2348726875 [W] sqlt_phv:26100 sqlt_phv2:69857 source: 08-29/12:58:11

SQL Text: [.]

```
select count(object_type) from acs where object_type=:b
```

SQL: [+]

ID	Exec Ord	Operation	Go To	More	Peek Bind	Capt Bind	Cost[2]	Estim Card
0	3	SELECT STATEMENT					158	1
1	2	SORT AGGREGATE		[+]			158	1
2	1	INDEX FAST FULL SCAN I2	[-]	[+]	[+]	[+]	158	74732

Performance statistics are only available when parameter "statistics_level" was set to "ALL" at hard-parse time, or SQL co
(1) If estim_card * starts < output_rows then under-estimate. If estim_card * starts > output_rows then over-estimate. Color
(2) Largest contributors for cumulative-statistics columns are shown in red.
Other XML (id=1): [+]
Outline Data (id=1): [+]
Go to Tables
Go to Indexes
Go to Top

Plan Info

#	Type	Value
1	db_version	12.1.0.2
2	parse_schema	"STELIOS"
3	plan_hash	2348726875

Peeked Binds timestamp:2016-08-29/ .58:11

#	Name	Type	Value
1	:B	VARCHAR2(32)	"SYNONYM"

Captured Binds

List of captured binds is restricted up to 300 rows per Plan as tool parameter "r_rows_table_m".
SQL: [+]

#	Last Captured	Name	Type	Value
1	2016-08-29/12:58:11	:B	VARCHAR2(32)	"SYNONYM"

Go to Execution Plans
Go to Plan Performance Statistics
Go to Plans Summary
Go to Tables
Go to Indexes
Go to Top

Figure 9-6. *Here we see the execution plan, the peeked binds, and the captured binds*

As expected a slower execution resulted when the value SYNONYM was used. This was because there were 74,732 values in the table that matched "SYNONYM." A Fast Full Scan therefore seems appropriate. If we look at the execution plan for DIMENSION (which only matches 10 rows) we'd see a cost of only three and a plan based around an INDEX RANGE SCAN. See Figure 9-7, which shows this.

Execution Plan phv:2583336616 [B] sqlt_phv:74297 sqlt_phv2:18054 sourc 29/13:10:52

SQL Text: [.]

```
select count(object_type) from acs where object_type=:b
```

SQL: [±]

ID	Exec Ord	Operation	Go To	More	Peek Bind	Capt Bind	Cost²	Estim Card
0	3	SELECT STATEMENT					3	1
1	2	SORT AGGREGATE		[±]			3	1
2	1	. INDEX RANGE SCAN I2 [±]		[±]	[±]	[±]	3	10

Performance statistics are only available when parameter "statistics_level" was set to "ALL" at hard-parse time, or SQL
(1) If estim_card * starts < output_rows then under-estimate. If estim_card * starts > output_rows then over-estimate. Co₁
(2) Largest contributors for cumulative-statistics columns are shown in red.
Other XML (id=1): [±]
Outline Data (id=1): [±]
Go to Tables
Go to Indexes
Go to Top

Plan Info

#	Type	Value
1	db_version	12.1.0.2
2	parse_schema	"STELIOS"
3	plan_hash	2583336616

Peeked Binds timestamp:2016-08-29/13:10:52

#	Name	Type	Value
1	:B	VARCHAR2(32)	"DIMENSION"

Captured Binds

List of captured binds is restricted up to 300 rows per Plan as per tool parameter "r_rows_table_m".
SQL: [±]

#	Last Captured	Name	Type	Value
1	2016-08-29/13:10:52	:B	VARCHAR2(32)	"DIMENSION"

Go to Execution Plans
Go to Plan Performance Statistics
Go to Plans Summary
Go to Tables
Go to Indexes
Go to Top

Figure 9-7. *Shows the execution plan details for the plan associated with DIMENSION, a rare value*

Now let's go back to the top of the report and click on "Adaptive Cursor Sharing." This brings us to the section shown in Figure 9-8.

Adaptive Cursor Sharing

- Cursors List
- Histogram
- Selectivity
- Statistics

Go to Plans Summary
Go to Top

Cursors List

List restricted up to 300 rows as per tool parameter "r_rows_table_m".
SQL: [±]

#	Is Sharable	Inst ID	Child	Child Address	Plan Hash Value	Is Bind Sensitive	Is Bind Aware	Buffer Gets	Executions
1	Y	1	1	00000000E35AA568	2583336616 [B]	Y	Y	15	5
2	N	1	0	00000000E99E6500	2348726875 [W]	Y	N	7020	12

Histogram

List restricted up to 1000 rows as per tool parameter "r_rows_table_l".
SQL: [±]

#	Is Sharable	Inst ID	Child	Bucket ID[1]	Count
1	Y	1	1	0	5
2	Y	1	1	1	0
3	Y	1	1	2	0
4	N	1	0	0	6
5	N	1	0	1	6
6	N	1	0	2	0

(1) Rows Processed. 0:< 1K, 1:between 1K and 1M, 2:> 1M.

Selectivity

List restricted up to 1000 rows as per tool parameter "r_rows_table_l".
SQL: [±]

#	Is Sharable	Inst ID	Child	Predicate	Low	High	Range ID
1	Y	1	1	=B	0.000044	0.000054	0

Figure 9-8. *Shows the section on adaptive cursor sharing*

The section on Adaptive Cursor Sharing needs some explanation. The cursor list part of this section shows all child cursors related to the SQL text. There is a child cursor 0 and 1. The child cursor (1) relates to the DIMENSION value (as this came after the SYNONYM value). We also see under the "Is Bind Sensitive" column that both child cursors are bind sensitive, and in this case (because we ran the statement relating to DIMENSION a few times), we also have an "Is Bind Aware" value of "Y" for the Child Cursor 1. A cursor is always bind sensitive when there is a bind variable with an associated histogram. If we look at the values of IS_BIND_SENSITIVE and IS_BIND_AWARE throughout this process, we'll see the following:

```
SQL> select IS_BIND_SENSITIVE S, IS_BIND_AWARE A from v$sqlarea where sql_
id='5fvxn411s48p0';

S A
- -
Y N <<<AFTER FIRST EXECUTION (SYNONYM)

Y N <<<AFTER SECOND EXECUTION (TABLE)

Y N <<<AFTER THIRD EXECUTION (SYNONYM)

Y N <<<AFTER FOURTH EXECUTION (DIMENSION)

Y N <<<AFTER FIFTH EXECUTION (DIMENSION)

Y N <<<AFTER SIXTH EXECUTION (DIMENSION)

Y N <<<AFTER SEVENTH EXECUTION (DIMENSION)
Y Y

Y N <<<AFTER EIGHT EXECUTION (DIMENSION)
Y Y

Y N <<<AFTER NINTH EXECUTION (DIMENSION)
Y Y

Y N <<<AFTER TENTH EXECUTION (DIMENSION)
Y Y

Y N <<<AFTER ELEVENTH EXECUTION (DIMENSION)
Y Y

Y N <<<AFTER TWELFTH EXECUTION (DIMENSION)
Y Y
```

The Bind Sensitive column is always set to "yes" in this case, for all the children. But how does the second child get created and when? The algorithm is not published or documented, but the clue is in the histogram in the Adaptive Cursor Sharing section. Look at the Bucket ID column. There appear to be only three buckets: 0, 1, and 2. The annotation at the bottom mentions that a 0 bucket represents less than 1k. The 1 bucket represents greater than 1k but less than 1M, and bucket 2 represents everything that is more than 1M. So for cursor 0 (remember this was the SYNONYM and TABLE values) there were a total of twelve executions, all of them with fewer than 1M buffer gets. For child number 1 the situation is different. Every one of its twelve executions had less than 1K in buffer gets. This is why after the seventh execution a new child is created that is bind aware. Some DBAs call this "warming the bucket." The idea is there is no point in creating a new bucket (and the overhead that goes with that) if the predicate value is rarely going to be seen. We also judge if a predicate is the same as another child by this broad criteria. Once the cursor is bind aware it can be used for matching bind values that are peeked. In this simple example this would mean that two execution plans are possible and available based on the bind values.

This chapter covered what Adaptive Cursor Sharing is and how it works. The example shown is a simple one-dimensional example; there was only one column with skewed data. If you had a table with multiple columns of skewed data then you could potentially get different combinations of the columns, which would each generate their own child cursor. ACS allows for this by creating a range of selectivities for each column.

Does ACS Go Wrong?

As with all features that attempt to improve performance, there are rare cases where performance actually deteriorates. If you feel your execution plans are unstable, or the wrong plans have been chosen, you can always disable ACS by setting the following parameters (after first checking with Oracle Support):

```
SQL> alter system set "_optimizer_extended_cursor_sharing_rel"=NONE scope=both;
SQL> alter system set "_optimizer_extended_cursor_sharing"=none scope=both;
```

Now that we have disabled ACS, what is the result of running acs.sql again?

```
SQL> @acs
Table dropped.
Table created.
101177 rows created.
101177 rows created.
OBJECT_TYPE          COUNT(*)
-------------------- ----------
EDITION                     2
RULE                        2
DESTINATION                 4
JAVA SOURCE                 4
MATERIALIZED VIEW           4
SCHEDULE                    8
SCHEDULER GROUP             8
DIMENSION                  10
INDEXTYPE                  14
UNIFIED AUDIT POLICY       16
WINDOW                     18


OBJECT_TYPE          COUNT(*)
-------------------- ----------
CLUSTER                    20
PROGRAM                    20
CONTEXT                    20
RESOURCE PLAN              22
LOB PARTITION              24
JOB CLASS                  28
EVALUATION CONTEXT         30
UNDEFINED                  34
CONSUMER GROUP             36
RULE SET                   42
DIRECTORY                  44


OBJECT_TYPE          COUNT(*)
-------------------- ----------
```

```
JOB                       46
QUEUE                     60
TABLE SUBPARTITION        64
XML SCHEMA                90
OPERATOR                 108
PROCEDURE                410
LIBRARY                  456
TYPE BODY                464
SEQUENCE                 548
JAVA DATA                620
FUNCTION                 696

OBJECT_TYPE            COUNT(*)
-------------------- ----------
TRIGGER                 1198
TABLE PARTITION         2010
LOB                     2020
JAVA RESOURCE           2028
PACKAGE BODY            2528
PACKAGE                 2650
TYPE                    5170
TABLE                   5376
INDEX                   9428
VIEW                   13274
INDEX PARTITION        16336

OBJECT_TYPE            COUNT(*)
-------------------- ----------
JAVA CLASS             61632
SYNONYM                74732

46 rows selected.
```

Index created.

Index created.

PL/SQL procedure successfully completed.

Now we have a table, ACS with skewed data.

```
COUNT(OBJECT_TYPE)
------------------
            55604
S A
- -
N N
```

PL/SQL procedure successfully completed.

```
COUNT(OBJECT_TYPE)
------------------
```

```
         6194

S A
- -
N N

PL/SQL procedure successfully completed.

COUNT(OBJECT_TYPE)
------------------
           55604

S A
- -
N N

PL/SQL procedure successfully completed.

COUNT(OBJECT_TYPE)
------------------
               10

S A
- -
N N

PL/SQL procedure successfully completed.

COUNT(OBJECT_TYPE)
------------------
               10

S A
- -
N N

PL/SQL procedure successfully completed.

COUNT(OBJECT_TYPE)
------------------
               10

S A
- -
N N

PL/SQL procedure successfully completed.

COUNT(OBJECT_TYPE)
------------------
               10
```

```
S A
- -
N N

PL/SQL procedure successfully completed.

COUNT(OBJECT_TYPE)
------------------
                10

S A
- -
N N

PL/SQL procedure successfully completed.

COUNT(OBJECT_TYPE)
------------------
                10

S A
- -
N N

PL/SQL procedure successfully completed.

COUNT(OBJECT_TYPF)
------------------
                10

S A
- -
N N

PL/SQL procedure successfully completed.

COUNT(OBJECT_TYPE)
------------------
                10

S A
- -
N N

PL/SQL procedure successfully completed.

COUNT(OBJECT_TYPE)
------------------
                10
```

```
S A
- -
N N
```

Here we see that IS-BIND_SENSITIVE and IS_BIND_AWARE do not change throughout the exercise. No cursors were marked as bind sensitive or bind aware.

Summary

In this chapter, we covered the basic behavior of Adaptive Cursor Sharing. With SQLTXPLAIN we can collect information on ACS and get enough information to decide if it is going to be helpful. We also saw how it was an evolution of various features introduced over the years by Oracle. In 12c we see this type of adaptive behavior further enhanced to include Adaptive Queries and Adaptive Statistics (which are covered in the following two chapters).

■ ■ ■

## CHAPTER 10

How to Work with Adaptive Plans

Imagine you've come to conquer the planet SQL but those pesky aliens are constantly changing their bind variable values presenting skewed data all the time, and sometimes not even reporting how many rows there are. The name of the game would be Adapt and Conquer. Another adjective you could use would be Dynamic. Your space fleet's motto might well be "Victory through Adaptive and Dynamic Plans." In the world of SQL plans, Adaptive Cursor Sharing has already been introduced in the previous chapter. ACS deals with different combinations of bind variable values and adapts its plan. This allows us to change the plan based on the bind variable values. But what if our plan was so wrong that even during the execution we could see that the 'wheels were coming off the wagon'? The philosophy, up to 11g has always been to find the best plan and then stick with it. As of 12c and Adaptive Plans the plan can change while executing! This feature 'Adaptive Plans' is part of the whole new area 'Adaptive Query Optimization'. Let's review the whole area before focusing on Adaptive Plans.

Adaptive Query Optimization?

Adaptive Query Optimization is the name of the overall feature, designed to conquer all queries with Adaptive features. This feature is broken down into two main areas: those designed to deal with the actual execution and changing the plan on (possibly) the first execution. This is called Adaptive Planning and is further broken down into two other features relating to changing the way parallel slaves work with the Query coordinator (the distribution method) and the feature we are going to talk about first, called Adaptive Join Methods, where the execution plan changes during the execution. I like this feature the most because it is such a radical departure from previous behavior. See Figure 10-1 below to see the relationship of these features.

© Stelios Charalambides 2017
S. Charalambides, *Oracle SQL Tuning with Oracle SQLTXPLAIN*, DOI 10.1007/978-1-4842-2436-6_10

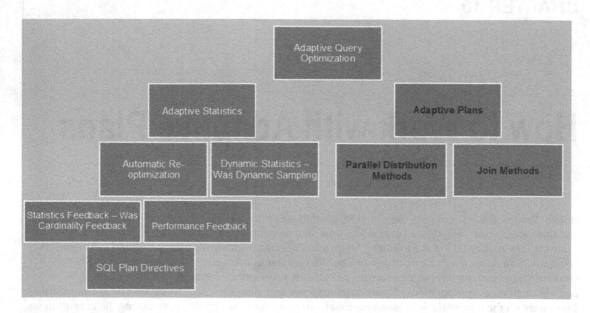

Figure 10-1. Where do Adaptive Plans fit into the Adaptive Query Optimization Features?

Adaptive Query Optimization also includes some features that have been extended from 11g and also enhanced in some interesting ways. You'll notice that this book no longer has a chapter on Cardinality Feedback, because that feature no longer exists in 12c (at least not under that name – refer to the previous edition of this book for Cardinality Feedback). Cardinality Feedback used to allow a plan to be reoptimized if the Actual Cardinality and the Expected Cardinality were different by at least a set threshold. It's worth comparing the 11g and 12c features just to get your bearings (see Figure 10-2).

Description	11g	12c
Plan Adaptation to bind values	ACS	ACS
Statistics Collection	Dynamic Statistics	Adaptive Statistics
Potential Plan change after first Execution	Cardinality Feedback	Automatic Reoptimization
Adaptive Join Methods	—	New Feature
Adaptive Parallel Distribution Methods	—	New Feature

Figure 10-2. Comparison of 11g and 12c Adaptive Features

This worked on a query level so the comparison of expected to actual was done on a whole query basis. In 12c this has been extended to work on an execution line by execution line basis of the execution plan.

For missing statistics, or inadequate statistics, Dynamic Statistics are there (previously known as Dynamic Sampling) to help the optimizer in determining the best plan. Since we now have cardinality feedback on an execution by execution plan basis, we need to keep track of what is happening for future executions. With cardinality feedback this information was attached to the SQL (as this was a whole query feedback mechanism) but now we need feedback with all the lines active in the plan. These feedback reports on the relevant execution lines of the plans are what are now know as SQL Plan Directives. We'll talk about those more in later sections of this chapter.

First let's explore the Join Methods adaptive Feature.

Adaptive Join Methods

Before we look at what Adaptive Plans look like in SQLT, we're going to go through an example of a Adaptive Plan and see the various ways we can look at the details of the adaptability. Using the sample schemas that come with Oracle we can do the following:

```
SQL> connect / as sysdba
SQL> grant select on v_$session to oe;
SQL> grant select on v_$sql_plan to oe;
SQL> grant select on v_$sql_plan_statistics_all to oe; >>>(1)
SQL> connect oe/oe
SQL> drop table order_items2;
SQL> create table order_items2 as select * from order_items;>>>(2)
SQL> set linesize 180
SQL> set pagesize 100
SQL> accept RETURN CHAR PROMPT "Explain plan shows"
SQL> explain plan for select /*+ gather_plan_statistics */ p.product_name
  from order_items2 o, product_information p
  where
    o.unit_price-15
    and o.quantity>1
    and p.product_id=o.product_id;
SQL> select * from table (dbms_xplan.display('PLAN_TABLE',null, 'ALL'));>>>(3)
```

The code is pretty straightforward, but let me explain a few things just to make things crystal clear.

1. I've granted access to these to allow OE to collect Plan statistics. This would not be appropriate on a production system.

2. I need to create a copy of the ORDER_ITEMS table but with no indexes to allow the plan to fail miserably on the first run.

3. I'm selecting the execution lines of the plan.

This is one way to see a plan with EXPLAIN PLAN. However since this does NOT execute, the Adaptive Features are not used and the plan does not adapt to a different plan. This is because the plan is not executed so the Optimizer does not know if the plan was a good one or not.

This first section of the SQL should show some output similar to the following:

```
Explain Plan shows
Explained.
PLAN_TABLE_OUTPUT
--------------------------------------------------------------------------------
Plan hash value: 983807676
```

```
-------------------------------------------------------------------------------
| Id |Operation                    | Name                 |Rows | Bytes| Cost (%CPU)| Time      |
-------------------------------------------------------------------------------
|  0|SELECT STATEMENT              |                      |   4|   128|    7   (0)| 00:00:01 |
|  1| NESTED LOOPS                 |                      |   4|   128|    7   (0)| 00:00:01 |
|  2|  NESTED LOOPS                |                      |   4|   128|    7   (0)| 00:00:01 |
|* 3|   TABLE ACCESS FULL          | ORDER_ITEMS2         |   4|    48|    3   (0)| 00:00:01 |
|* 4|   INDEX UNIQUE SCAN          | PRODUCT_INFORMATION_PK|  1|      |    0   (0)| 00:00:01 |
|  5|  TABLE ACCESS BY INDEX ROWID| PRODUCT_INFORMATION|   1|    20|    1   (0)| 00:00:01 |
-------------------------------------------------------------------------------
Query Block Name / Object Alias (identified by operation id):
-------------------------------------------------------------
   3 - SEL$1 / O@SEL$1
   4 - SEL$1 / P@SEL$1
   5 - SEL$1 / P@SEL$1
Predicate Information (identified by operation id):
---------------------------------------------------
   3 - filter("O"."UNIT_PRICE"=15 AND "O"."QUANTITY">1)
   4 - access("P"."PRODUCT_ID"="O"."PRODUCT_ID")
Column Projection Information (identified by operation id):
---------------------------------------------------------
   1 - (#keys=0) "O"."PRODUCT_ID"[NUMBER,22], "P"."PRODUCT_NAME"[VARCHAR2,50]
   2 - (#keys=0) "O"."PRODUCT_ID"[NUMBER,22], "P".ROWID[ROWID,10]
   3 - "O"."PRODUCT_ID"[NUMBER,22]
   4 - "P".ROWID[ROWID,10]
   5 - "P"."PRODUCT_NAME"[VARCHAR2,50]
Note
-----
   -   this is an adaptive plan
```

Notice that this EXPLAIN PLAN output shows a NESTED LOOP plan. The next code fragment uses the same data but uses Autotrace.

```
accept RETURN CHAR PROMPT "Autotrace shows"
set autotrace traceonly explain
select /*+ gather_plan_statistics */ p.product_name from order_items2 o, product_information p
 where
     o.unit_price=15
     and o.quantity>1
     and p.product_id=o.product_id;
set autotrace off
```

The output is almost identical.

```
Autotrace shows
Execution Plan
-------------------------------------------------------------
Plan hash value: 983807676
-------------------------------------------------------------------------------
| Id |Operation                    |Name          |Rows |Bytes | Cost (%CPU)| Time      |
-------------------------------------------------------------------------------
|  0|SELECT STATEMENT              |              |   4|   128 |    7   (0)| 00:00:01 |
```

```
|   1| NESTED LOOPS                |                        |   4| 128 |    7 (0)| 00:00:01 |
|   2|  NESTED LOOPS               |                        |   4| 128 |    7 (0)| 00:00:01 |
|*  3|   TABLE ACCESS FULL         |ORDER_ITEMS2            |   4|  48 |    3 (0)| 00:00:01 |
|*  4|   INDEX UNIQUE SCAN         |PRODUCT_INFORMATION_PK|   1|     |    0 (0)| 00:00:01 |
|   5|  TABLE ACCESS BY INDEX ROWID|PRODUCT_INFORMATION|   1|  20 |    1 (0)| 00:00:01 |
-------------------------------------------------------------------------------------------
Predicate Information (identified by operation id):
---------------------------------------------------
   3 - filter("O"."UNIT_PRICE"=15 AND "O"."QUANTITY">1)
   4 - access("P"."PRODUCT_ID"="O"."PRODUCT_ID")
Note
-----
   -   this is an adaptive plan
```

Again the plan uses NESTED LOOPS. Now finally let's actually run the SQL and see what happens to the plan. This is the SQL this time.

```
accept RETURN CHAR PROMPT "DBMS_XPLAN with ADAPTIVE show the FINAL plan"
select /*+ gather_plan_statistics */ p.product_name from order_items2 o, product_information
p
  where
    o.unit_price=15
    and o.quantity>1
    and p.product_id=o.product_id;
select * from table(dbms_xplan.display_cursor(format=>'+adaptive'));
```

Here we use the display_cursor procedure with +adaptive. This is what we get from this (I've omitted the actual query results).

```
DBMS_XPLAN with ADAPTIVE show the FINAL plan
PLAN_TABLE_OUTPUT
-------------------------------------------------------------------------------------------
--SQL_ID 6d8s5rhs7thpd, child number 0
-------------------------------------
select /*+ gather_plan_statistics */ p.product_name from order_items2
o, product_information p    where        o.unit_price=15      and
o.quantity>1       and p.product_id=o.product_id

Plan hash value: 2886494722
```

Id	Operation	Name	Rows	Bytes	Cost (%CPU)	Time
0	SELECT STATEMENT				7 (100)	
* 1	HASH JOIN		4	128	7 (0)	00:00:01
- 2	NESTED LOOPS		4	128	7 (0)	00:00:01
- 3	NESTED LOOPS		4	128	7 (0)	00:00:01
- 4	STATISTICS COLLECTOR					
* 5	TABLE ACCESS FULL	ORDER_ITEMS2	4	48	3 (0)	00:00:01
- * 6	INDEX UNIQUE SCAN	PRODUCT_INFORMATION_PK	1		0 (0)	
- 7	TABLE ACCESS BY INDEX ROWID	PRODUCT_INFORMATION	1	20	1 (0)	00:00:01
8	TABLE ACCESS FULL	PRODUCT_INFORMATION	1	20	1 (0)	00:00:01

```
Predicate Information (identified by operation id):
---------------------------------------------------

   1 - access("P"."PRODUCT_ID"="O"."PRODUCT_ID")
   5 - filter(("O"."UNIT_PRICE"=15 AND "O"."QUANTITY">1))
   6 - access("P"."PRODUCT_ID"="O"."PRODUCT_ID")

Note
-----
   -   this is an adaptive plan (rows marked '-' are inactive)
```

Now we have something different. This plan shows more lines, and some are marked with "-" indicating that these lines have been rejected. We still have NESTED LOOP lines but these have been superceded by HASH JOIN, which is shown above the NESTED LOOP Lines. This is what the 'rows marked '-' are inactive' line in the note section of plan means.

We've almost gone a whole chapter without using SQLT, what gives? Now we've seen the non-SQLT method of looking at the Adaptive plan let's look at the plan from the SQLT perspective. See Figure 10-3.

Execution Plan phv:2886494722 [B]
**[W] sqlt_phv:40196 sqlt_phv2:9561 source:GV$SQL_PLAN inst:1 child:0(00000000E1A07628) exec
09-05/15:43:12**

SQL Text: [.]

```
select /*+ gather_plan_statistics */ p.product_name from order_items2 o, product_information p
  where
    o.unit_price=15
    and o.quantity>1
    and p.product_id=o.product_id
```

SQL: [+]

ID	Exec Ord	Operation	Go To	More	Cost[2]	Estim Card	LAST Starts	LAST Output Rows	LAST Over/Under Estimate[1]	LAST CR Buffer Gets[2]
0	9	SELECT STATEMENT			7	4				
1	8	HASH JOIN		[+]	7	4	1	13	3x under	22
2	6	~~NESTED LOOPS~~		[+]	7	4	1	13	3x under	5
3	4	~~NESTED LOOPS~~		[+]	7	4	1	13	3x under	5
4	2	... ~~STATISTICS COLLECTOR~~		[+]	3		1	13		5
5	1	.... TABLE ACCESS FULL ORDER_ITEMS2	[+]	[+]	3	4	1	13	3x under	5
6	3	.. ~~INDEX UNIQUE SCAN PRODUCT_INFORMATION_PK~~	[+]	[+]	0	1	0	0		0
7	5	.. ~~TABLE ACCESS BY INDEX ROWID PRODUCT_INFORMATION~~	[+]	[+]	1	1	0	0		0
8	7	. TABLE ACCESS FULL PRODUCT_INFORMATION	[+]	[+]	1	1	1	288	** 288x under	17

Performance statistics are only available when parameter "statistics_level" was set to "ALL" at hard-parse time, or SQL contains "gather_plan_statistics" hint
*(1) If estim_card * starts < output_rows then under-estimate. If estim_card * starts > output_rows then over-estimate. Color highlights when exceeding * 10x, ***
1000x over/under-estimates.
(2) Largest contributors for cumulative-statistics columns are shown in red.
Other XML (id=1): [+]
Outline Data (id=1): [+]
Leading (id=1): [+]
Go to Tables
Go to Indexes
Go to Top

Figure 10-3. *An Adaptive Plan as shown in SQLT. Lines are crossed out*

I've pointed out the STATISTICS COLLECTEOR line in the plan, because this is the line that allows the Optimizer to determine if the plan should change to one of the subplans.

You should be asking many questions at this point. How do Adaptive Joins work? What should I do (if anything) if I see such a plan?

For a NESTED LOOP to HASH JOIN conversion the execution starts, the Optimizer 'notices' that things are not going well, and 'decides' to change the access for the outer/inner table from an INDEX ACCESS scan to a TABLE ACCESS. The rows that have been buffered up to this point are reused for the new join and execution continues. After this the plan is 'stuck' and will not change again on this execution. For other joins converting from one to the other is not simple, but at least in theory it should be possible to apply this Adaptive Methodology to other kinds of joins.

Should We Rely on Adaptive Joins?

Naturally if we find an Adaptive Join adapting we might be interested to know why it is happening, but should we try and change the behavior, figure out why it's happening, and fix it? My personal opinion is that it is like having more and more airbags in your car. Sure they could save you in an accident, and modern cars have a lot of airbags in the them, but should we regularly park our cars by crashing into the tree outside our houses? It would probably be faster to avoid all that tedious slowing down and parking. The simple answer is that Adaptive Plans should be seen as warnings that something isn't right. Just like Cardinality Feedback in 11g, it should be a message to the developer or DBA to investigate.

Can Adaptive Plans Cause Problems?

Before we attempt an answer to this question, we need to understand how Adaptive Joins are implemented. To allow subplans to happen the optimizer has to gather information on each line in an execution plan and determine if that line has performed as expected (statistics collector). If there is unexpected behavior from an execution line, a "Directive" is logged against the line. Here is an example from a plan that went wrong (see Figure 10-4).

"SUPERSEDED" Join Cardinality Misestimate Directives

Restricted up to 300 Objects and Directives as per tool parameter "r_rows_table_m".

		Internal State / Redundant[4] / Auto Drop[4] :	HAS_STATS	HAS_STATS	HAS_STATS
		Created:	2015-12-09/22:00:04	2015-12-09/22:00:04	2016-01-02/06:00:02
		Last Modified:	2015-12-13/06:00:02	2015-12-13/06:00:02	2016-01-05/22:00:03
		Last Used:	2015-12-13/06:00:02	2015-12-13/06:00:02	2016-01-05/22:00:03
#	Object in this Report[3]	(Owner.Table.Column) Object Name[2] \ Directive ID[1]	1600772214713059526	5046748721215005101	6344725655952639029
1	Yes				--F
2	Yes				
3	Yes				
4	No				
5	No				---f
6	No				--F
7	No	SYS.OBJ$	----	----	
8	No	SYS.PROFILE$	----	----	
9	No	SYS.PROFNAME$	----		
10	No	SYS.RESOURCE_MAP	----	----	

(1) "NOTES" Directive Flags under each directive is in positional order :
Letter means YES on (E)-equality_predicates_only (C)-simple_column_predicates_only (J)-index_access_by_joii filter_on_joining_object , a dash "-" means NO,
Lower case flag indicates the directive lists multiple times the same object with both YES and NO.
(2) Objects are listed in alphabetical order only one time even if directive lists it multiple times.
(3) Directives may include objects that are not collected by SQLT because they are not present in the SQL Statement but are listed here for cc
(4) Redundant is displayed only if YES and AutoDrop is displayed only if NO.

Figure 10-4. SQL Plan Directives as seen in SQLTXPLAIN

Notice that for this type of Directive (SUPERCEDED – Join Cardinality Misestimates) the objects are listed along with codes to indicate what kind of join problems there were. This is covered in detail in Chapter 12, but for now the point is that Directives are tied to the lines, not the SQL or the execution plan. So a permanent Directive will be present and may influence other SQLs that have the same execution lines.

What Are Parallel Distribution Methods?

Another thing that can go wrong with execution plans when they are run in parallel is that the Distribution method can be wrong. In Parallel execution a consumer receives work from a slave. The work from the slaves can be sent to the consumers in a number of different ways. Using the wrong method (due to poor Cardinality estimates) can result in slaves being idle or consumers waiting for Slaves.

- HASH (A Hash is calculated for the source rows and distributed to the consumers based on the hash). Think of this as a random distribution between the Producer and Consumer.

- BROADCAST (A broadcast distribution is used when there are relatively few rows to evenly distribute the rows among the Consumers. No hashing is done).

When the Distribution method chosen is suboptimal you can use the hint `pq_distribute` with values for the table and the inner and outer table method). In 12c a new Adaptive Distribution method is used called `HYBRID HASH`. Again the plan will show a Statistics Collector before the Distribution method to allow it to determine the best plan during the execution. A typical plan would look like this:

```
SELECT STATEMENT
  PX COORDINATOR
    PX SEND QC (RANDOM)
      HASH JOIN BUFFERED
        PX RECEIVE
          PX SEND HYBRID HASH >>>New Distribution method
            STATISTICS COLLECTOR >>>Needed before HYBRID HASH
              PX BLOCK ITERATOR
                TABLE ACCESS FULL
```

A Typical developer's hint might be:

```
SQL> select /*+ PQ_DISTRIBUTE (S HASH, HASH) */ a from R, S where r.c=s.c;
```

Valid combinations are (for the Inner and Outer tables):

- HASH, HASH
- Broadcast, None
- None, Broadcast
- Partition, None
- None, Partition
- None, None

With HYBRID HASH the Distribution method should adapt to something which is suitable for the actual cardinality. We'll cover working with parallel execution in Chapter 13.

How Do We Turn Off These Features?

The Adaptive features are yet another step toward allowing the Optimizer to choose the right plan even when there are poor statistics or other problems. Despite this a site may choose to disable these features.

optimizer_adaptive_features = FALSE (This turns off all the features)

optimizer_adaptive_reporting_only = TRUE (This turns off all the features but still collects information including Directives so you could see what would happen if the features were turned on).

optimizer_dynamic_sampling = Any integer from 1 to 10 (A new level 11 enabled Dynamic Sampling). Pre 12c behavior is maintained for other values.

Summary

In this chapter we learned about the new exciting Adaptive Features and how SQLT shows them and what we should do about them. We also learned how to control these features in case they are causing a problem. In the next chapter we'll look at Dynamic Statistics, which are used as part of the arsenal to determine if a plan change should be implemented.

CHAPTER 11

■ ■ ■

Dynamic Statistics

Imagine you've been given the job of sorting through some books in a house to find all the references to the word "Vienna" in the book titles. You've been told there are two or three books in the study, and that there is an index in the desk if you need it. Naturally with two or three books or even a dozen books, there's no point in using the index in the desk; you'll just look at the book titles one by one and quickly find all of the books with "Vienna" in the title. Unfortunately, what you didn't know is that since the last person looked at the books, the owner has bought the entire contents of the local public library, but you only discover this after you start. It's going to be a long day if you stick to your plan. In this analogy the table size (library) was underestimated to a few books so we used a full table scan. If we'd looked at how many books we had (dynamically sampled), we may well have changed our plan to use an index.

In this chapter we'll see how Oracle's Dynamic Statistics (formerly known as Dynamic Sampling) feature could help our poor librarian. We'll see that this feature works at the beginning of the parsing process to get the right answer fast. We'll learn that DS is not always used, and we'll learn when those occasions arise. With this knowledge fresh in our minds we'll also look at an example mystery case that we'll follow through with SQLTXPLAIN. Who will be the villain and who will be the hero this time?

Dynamic Statistics

The poor optimizer has to cope with occasionally coming across poor objects statistics (we covered that in Chapter 3) or completely missing statistics. Rather than just letting this situation occur and accepting that missing or poor statistics sometimes cause poor execution plans, Oracle developed dynamic sampling and then improved it to become Dynamic Statistics. SQLT reports when it detects that Dynamic Statistics are used (12c) or Dynamic Sampling (11g) Let's look at an example report from both 11g and 12c. Figure 11-1 shows the top of the now familiar SQLTXPLAIN main report from an older report. You can tell it is an old report because there is no mention of SQL Patches or SQL Plan Directives under the "Plan Control" section.

© Stelios Charalambides 2017

S. Charalambides, *Oracle SQL Tuning with Oracle SQLTXPLAIN*, DOI 10.1007/978-1-4842-2436-6_11

Global

- Observations
- SQL Text
- SQL Identification
- Environment
- CBO Environment
- Fix Control
- CBO System Statistics
- DBMS_STATS Setup
- Initialization Parameters
- NLS Parameters
- I/O Calibration
- Tool Configuration Parameters

Cursor Sharing and Binds

- Cursor Sharing
- Adaptive Cursor Sharing
- Peeked Binds
- Captured Binds

SQL Tuning Advisor

- STA Report
- STA Script

Plans

- Summary
- Performance Statistics
- Performance History (delta)
- Performance History (total)
- Execution Plans

Plan Control

- Stored Outlines
- SQL Profiles
- SQL Plan Baselines

SQL Execution

- Active Session History
- AWR Active Session History
- SQL Statistics
- SQL Detail ACTIVE Report
- Monitor Statistics
- Monitor ACTIVE Report
- Monitor HTML Report
- Monitor TEXT Report
- Segment Statistics
- Session Statistics
- Session Events
- Parallel Processing

Tables

- Tables
- Statistics
- Statistics Versions
- Modifications
- Properties
- Physical Properties
- Constraints
- Columns
- Indexed Columns
- Histograms
- Partitions
- Indexes

Objects

- Objects
- Dependencies
- Fixed Objects
- Fixed Object Columns
- Nested Tables
- Policies
- Audit Policies
- Tablespaces
- Metadata

Figure 11-1. *The top of the SQLTXPLAIN report from an old SQLTXPLAIN report*

From the main SQLT report page if we click on "Execution Plans" we naturally end up at the section of the report showing all the known execution plans for our current SQL (see Figure 11-2). If Dynamic Statistics were used we see a message in the report under "Plan Info." See Figure 11-3 for an example report showing Dynamic Statistics were used at level 2. This figure only shows the left-hand side of the page.

Global

- Observations
- SQL Text
- SQL Identification
- Environment
- CBO Environment
- Fix Control
- CBO System Statistics
- DBMS_STATS Setup
- Initialization Parameters
- NLS Parameters
- I/O Calibration
- Tool Configuration Parameters

Cursor Sharing and Binds

- Cursor Sharing
- Adaptive Cursor Sharing
- Peeked Binds
- Captured Binds

SQL Tuning Advisor

- STA Report
- STA Script

Plans

- Summary
- Performance Statistics
- Performance History (delta)
- Performance History (total)
- Execution Plans

Plan Control

- Stored Outlines
- SQL Patches
- SQL Profiles
- SQL Plan Baselines
- SQL Plan Directives

SQL Execution

- Active Session History
- AWR Active Session History
- SQL Statistics
- SQL Detail ACTIVE Report
- Monitor Statistics
- Monitor ACTIVE Report
- Monitor HTML Report
- Monitor TEXT Report
- Segment Statistics
- Session Statistics
- Session Events
- Parallel Processing

Tables

- Tables
- Statistics
- Statistics Extensions
- Statistics Versions
- Modifications
- Properties
- Physical Properties
- Constraints
- Columns
- Indexed Columns
- Histograms
- Partitions
- Indexes

Objects

- Objects
- Dependencies
- Fixed Objects
- Fixed Object Columns
- Nested Tables
- Policies
- Audit Policies
- Tablespaces
- Metadata

Figure 11-2. *The main report from a 12c version of SQLT is subtly different*

Execution Plans

List ordered by phv and source.

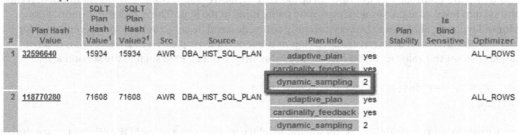

Figure 11-3. *Both execution plans used Dynamic Statistics*

What Are Dynamic Statistics?

So Dynamic Statistics were used, but what are they exactly? It is a way to improve the statistics of a query by collecting those statistics *during* the compilation process. Don't assume from this that you can ignore the collection of statistics, however. You can't. Dynamic Statistics are not a substitute for good statistics. It's a last attempt to avoid a bad execution plan. In the simplest terms, the steps the optimizer goes through are shown below:

1. The optimizer starts parsing the query.

   During the parsing process the optimizer assesses the state of the object statistics. If the optimizer finds that some statistics are missing, it may collect some more statistics. The amount, and even whether Dynamic Statistics are collected, will depend on the value of `optimizer_dynamic_sampling`. A new level 11 value has been introduced for 12c that allows the optimizer to automatically collect statistics even if base object statistics are present.

2. If no dynamic sampling is to be done, the rest of the optimization process continues, and statistics are used where available.

3. If dynamic sampling is to be done, the amount of sampling is determined from `optimizer_dynamic_sampling`, and a dynamic query is generated to gather the information.

4. If dynamic sampling was done then the statistics gathered are used to generate a better execution plan.

In Figure 11-3 we saw that Dynamic Statistics were used, along with an indication of the value used. You can also see the value of `optimizer_dynamic_sampling` in the CBO Environment part of the report. (See the section below "How to Find the Value of `optimizer_dynamic_sampling`"). Remember, this all happens *before* the query executes and during the parsing process.

How to Control Dynamic Statistics

Dynamic Statistics are controlled by the value of `optimizer_dynamic_sampling` as already mentioned. It can be set at the system level or at the session level or by using hints in the SQL. These different options allow the behavior of Dynamic Statistics to be very carefully controlled and be set to behave in different ways for different SQL (with hints) and different sessions (logon triggers, for example). Here are examples of all of these options. (I've set the value to 4. You can set any value from 0 to 11). First set it at the session level.

```
SQL> alter session set optimizer_dynamic_sampling=4 ;
Session altered.
```

You may want to set the parameter at the session level if you are testing some SQL and want to see the effect on the execution plan for a number of different values and you want to see it quickly without affecting anybody else. You can also set the value in the current instance without making the value permanent.

```
SQL> alter system set optimizer_dynamic_sampling=4 scope=memory;
System altered.
```

You might want to do this if you are testing at the system level and want to be sure it is the right choice across the system before making the change permanent. Once you've decided that setting this value at the system level is appropriate, you can set it as shown below.

```
SQL> alter system set optimizer_dynamic_sampling=4 scope=spfile;
System altered.
```

Setting the value at the system level makes changes to the spfile so that it is applied to the database the next time it starts. If you want to make changes on a more granular level, perhaps individual SQLs, you may want to use a hint. The hint version of this parameter can take two forms: a cursor level and a table level version. So, for example, to set for the cursor:

```
SQL> select /*+ dynamic_sampling (4) */ count(*) from dba_objects;
  COUNT(*)
----------
    101193
```

There is a different form of this hint that allows you to set the sampling level on a table. This is getting very specific; and you have to wonder, if you know the object statistics on this particular object are missing, why haven't you collected real statistics?

```
SQL> select /*+ dynamic_sampling (dba_objects 4) */ count(*) from dba_objects;

  COUNT(*)
----------
    101195
```

As I mentioned earlier, the amount of sampling and whether sampling is done depends on the value of the dynamic sampling parameter. Most systems will have the default value of 2.

```
[oracle@d12102 ~]$ sqlplus / as sysdba
SQL*Plus: Release 12.1.0.2.0 Production on Mon Sep 19 15:31:58 2016
Copyright (c) 1982, 2014, Oracle.  All rights reserved.
Connected to:
Oracle Database 12c Enterprise Edition Release 12.1.0.2.0 - 64bit Production
With the Partitioning, OLAP, Advanced Analytics and Real Application Testing options
SQL> show parameter optimizer_dynamic_sampling

NAME                                 TYPE        VALUE
------------------------------------ ----------- ------------------------------
optimizer_dynamic_sampling           integer     2
SQL>
```

If the default value is set and dynamic sampling is used, then the optimizer will attempt to sample 64 blocks of data, unless the query is parallelized (see section below, "Dynamic Statistics and Parallel Statements"). This is not a percentage of the table or index size, it is a fixed number of blocks. The number of rows sampled is dependent on how many rows fit into a block. Remember the objective of Dynamic Sampling is to get some very basic statistics at the last moment just before the query is executed. To minimize this overhead the sampling size is set in blocks, a clearly defined value that cannot expand or contract with the size of the table rows. Dynamic Statistics were designed this way to stop the parsing process from consuming too many resources on large tables. If the Dynamic Statistics process takes place (and we can check in the SQLTXPLAIN report), the samples collected may help to make the execution plan better than it would otherwise be. The values for the parameter (as mentioned earlier) vary from 0 to 11 and control the operation of Dynamic Statistics. If optimizer_dynamic_sampling is set to

- 0: No dynamic sampling is used under any circumstances.

- 1: If there is at least 1 unanalyzed, unindexed, nonpartitioned table and this table is bigger than 32 blocks, then 32 blocks are sampled. This means that if the table is indexed or is partitioned or is smaller than 32 blocks, no sampling will take place.

- 2: If at least one table has no statistics, whether it has been indexed or not, then 64 blocks are sampled. Partitioned and indexed tables are included in this. This will apply to all tables with no statistics unlike level 1, where some tables will be excluded.

- 3: If at least one table has no statistics and if there is a where clause with an expression, 64 blocks are sampled. This is trying to fix the problem of expressions on where clauses where it can be tricky to develop the right execution plan. This is more restrictive than level 2. This still applies to all tables just like level 2.

- 4: If at least one table has no statistics and if an OR or AND operator is used on predicates on the same table, then 64 blocks are sampled. This is attempting to deal with the problem of complex predicates. This is more restrictive that level 2. This level also applies to indexed and partitioned tables just like level 2.

For values between 5 and 8, the rules are unchanged from the value for optimizer_dynamic_sampling set to 4 but the sample sizes increase, doubling each time so that for 5 the sample size is 128 blocks and for 8 the sample size is 1024. For level 9, the sample size is 4086. For a value of 10 all blocks are sampled. As you can imagine, setting this value can be a very big overhead. For level 11 the amount of statistics are automatically determined and collected. In the case of the value being 11 statistics could be collected regardless of whether base statistics are present. The decision is based on the complexity of the query, and the execution time expected. The statistics collected in this way are available to other queries that want to access the same base tables.

If we generate the 10053 trace for a query against the sales table, we would type the following commands:

```
SQL> ALTER SESSTION SET OPTIMIZER_DYNAMIC_SAMPLING=4;
SQL> ALTER SESSION SET MAX_DUMP_FILE_SIZE = UNLIMITED;
SQL> ALTER SESSION SET TRACEFILE_IDENTIFIER = '10053_TRACE';
SQL> ALTER SESSION SET EVENTS '10053 TRACE NAME CONTEXT FOREVER, LEVEL 1';
SQL> select /*+ PARSE 5 */ count(*) from sales;
SQL> exit
```

Here I set the dump file size (the trace file) to an unlimited size and appended a string to the automatically generated file name so I can easily find the file by setting the TRACEFILE_IDENTIFIER value to 10053_TRACE. The generated name for the trace file will be made up from the sid (in this case snc1), the string "ora," a session number (4723 in this case), and then my appended string. Your file name will be different, but if you use a sensible TRACEFILE_IDENTIFIER value you should be able to find your trace file easily. If you wanted to see the overhead, you could look in the 10053 trace file for a query that was using dynamic sampling. If you search the 10053 trace file, you'll see a section similar to the one below. (I've removed some of the text for clarity).

Now if we look in /u02/app/oracle/diag/rdbms/snc1/snc1/trace, we will find a file called snc1_ora_4723_10053_TRACE.trc. If we then search this file for the string "dynamic sampling," we'll see the section below. Again, I've removed some lines for clarity.

```
*** 2016-09-19 16:14:00.446
** Performing dynamic sampling initial checks. **
** Dynamic sampling initial checks returning TRUE (level = 4).
** Dynamic sampling updated index stats.: SALES_CHANNEL_BIX, blocks=111
** Dynamic sampling updated index stats.: SALES_CUST_BIX, blocks=541
```

```
** Dynamic sampling updated index stats.: SALES_PROD_BIX, blocks=96
** Dynamic sampling updated index stats.: SALES_PROMO_BIX, blocks=86
** Dynamic sampling updated index stats.: SALES_TIME_BIX, blocks=121
** Dynamic sampling updated table stats.: blocks=1876
*** 2016-09-19 16:14:00.447
** Generated dynamic sampling query:
   query text :
SELECT /* OPT_DYN_SAMP */ /*+ ALL_ROWS IGNORE_WHERE_CLAUSE NO_PARALLEL(SAMPLESUB) opt_
param('parallel_execution_enabled', 'false') NO_PARALLEL_INDEX(SAMPLESUB) NO_SQL_TUNE */
NVL(SUM(C1),0), NVL(SUM(C2),0) FROM (SELECT /*+ NO_PARALLEL("SALES") FULL("SALES") NO_
PARALLEL_INDEX("SALES") */ 1 AS C1, 1 AS C2 FROM "SH"."SALES" SAMPLE BLOCK (1.918977 , 1)
SEED (1) "SALES") SAMPLESUB

*** 2016-09-19 16:14:00.449
** Executed dynamic sampling query:
   level : 4
   sample pct. : 1.918977 <<< Almost 2 percent of the table was sampled
   total partitions : 28
     partitions for sampling : 28 <<<There were 28 partitions in the table.
   actual sample size : 17045 <<<Sample size used
   filtered sample card. : 17045
   orig. card. : 154224
   block cnt. table stat. : 1876
   block cnt. for sampling: 1876
   max. sample block cnt. : 64
   sample block cnt. : 36
   min. sel. est. : -1.00000000
** Using dynamic sampling card. : 888234 <<< New estimated Cardinality
** Dynamic sampling updated table card.
```

Let me step through what happens in this 10053 trace file. First we see that `optimizer_dynamic_sampling` is detected at level 4. Then a dynamic sampling query is generated. The query text is shown. There are a number of interesting options used for the hints in this query.

- `/* OPT_DYN_SAMP */` - This is not a hint, it is just a comment.
- `/*+ ALL_ROWS` – The `ALL_ROWS` hint, a standard hint.
- `IGNORE_WHERE_CLAUSE` – Obviously enough it ignores any `WHERE` clauses.
- `NO_PARALLEL(SAMPLESUB)` – No parallel execution, the overhead from this dynamic query must not be allowed to take too many resources.
- `opt_param('parallel_execution_enabled','false')` – No parallel execution.
- `NO_PARALLEL_INDEX` – No parallel Index plans.
- `NO_SQL_TUNE */`

Then the dynamic sampling query is executed and from the value 4 of the parameter we were able to sample approximately 2 percent of the rows. You can see in the query that the blocks sampled are randomized (`SEED (1)` and that we are using the `SAMPLE` clause, which samples blocks from a table. So did the Dynamic Statistics query do any good? The original estimate for the cardinality was 154,224. After the Dynamic Statistics query is executed the new estimate is 888,234. This is much closer to the actual value of 918,843. The value of the controlling parameter is pretty important; so next we'll see how to find out its value.

So far I haven't mentioned which value you *should* set. If dynamic sampling is so great, why not just set the highest level and let Oracle get on with it? Obviously I don't suggest you do this. The defaults are usually fine; setting higher values than 2 will gather more data or in more cases but there is an overhead. Review the effect of the overhead versus the plan obtained before choosing to stick with a higher value of optimizer_dynamic_sampling.

How to Find the Value of optimizer_dynamic_sampling

We can see the actual value used for optimizer_dynamic_sampling by looking at the "CBO Environment" section of the SQLT report. The hyperlink is shown in Figure 11-4 below.

Global

- Observations
- SQL Text
- SQL Identification
- Environment
- CBO Environment
- Fix Control
- CBO System Statistics
- DBMS_STATS Setup
- Initialization Parameters
- NLS Parameters
- I/O Calibration
- Tool Configuration Parameters

Cursor Sharing and Binds

- Cursor Sharing
- Adaptive Cursor Sharing
- Peeked Binds
- Captured Binds

SQL Tuning Advisor

- STA Report
- STA Script

Plans

- Summary
- Performance Statistics
- Performance History (delta)
- Performance History (total)
- Execution Plans

Plan Control

- Stored Outlines
- SQL Patches
- SQL Profiles
- SQL Plan Baselines
- SQL Plan Directives

SQL Execution

- Active Session History
- AWR Active Session History
- SQL Statistics
- SQL Detail ACTIVE Report
- Monitor Statistics
- Monitor ACTIVE Report
- Monitor HTML Report
- Monitor TEXT Report
- Segment Statistics
- Session Statistics
- Session Events
- Parallel Processing

Tables

- Tables
- Statistics
- Statistics Extensions
- Statistics Versions
- Modifications
- Properties
- Physical Properties
- Constraints
- Columns
- Indexed Columns
- Histograms
- Partitions
- Indexes

Objects

- Objects
- Dependencies
- Fixed Objects
- Fixed Object Columns
- Nested Tables
- Policies
- Audit Policies
- Tablespaces
- Metadata

Figure 11-4. *The hyperlink that takes you to the non-default CBO parameters*

Once we've clicked on this we see the "CBO Environment" part of the report, which shows, among other things, the value of optimizer_dynamic_sampling. See Figure 11-5.

CBO Environment

Non-Default or Modified CBO Parameters

[.]
Non-default or modified CBO initialization parameters in effect for the session where SQLT XTRACT was executed. Includes all in:

#	Is Default[1]	Is Modified[2]	Name	Inst ID	Value	Display Value	Is Adjusted	Is Deprecated	Is Basic	Is Session Modifiable
1	FALSE	FALSE	_optimizer_extended_cursor_sharing	1	"NONE"		FALSE	FALSE	FALSE	TRUE
2	FALSE	FALSE	_optimizer_extended_cursor_sharing_rel	1	"NONE"		FALSE	FALSE	FALSE	TRUE
3	FALSE	FALSE	cursor_sharing	1	"EXACT"		FALSE	FALSE	FALSE	TRUE
4	FALSE	FALSE	statistics_level	1	"TYPICAL"		FALSE	FALSE	FALSE	TRUE
5	TRUE	SYSTEM_MOD	optimizer_dynamic_sampling	1	"5"		FALSE	FALSE	FALSE	TRUE

(1) FALSE: Parameter value was specified in the parameter file.
(2) FALSE: Parameter has not been modified after instance startup. MODIFIED: Parameter has been modified with ALTER SESSION. SYSTEM_MOD: F
modified with ALTER SYSTEM.
Go to Top

Figure 11-5. *The value of optimizer_dynamic_sampling set to the non-default value of 5*

Figure 11-5 also shows us that the value optimizer_dynamic_sampling was changed by an alter system statement. We can see this because under the "Is Modified" column we see SYSTEM_MOD. We can also find out what the value is by looking at the 10053 trace of a SQL statement (as we did above) or we can show the value:

```
SQL> show parameter optimizer_dynamic_sampling

NAME                                     TYPE        VALUE
------------------------------------     ----------  --------------
optimizer_dynamic_sampling               integer     4
```

Dynamic Statistics and Parallel Statements

The rules for deciding if Dynamic Statistics should be used for parallel execution plans are slightly different than for serially executed statements. Parallel statements are already expected to be resource intensive so the small overhead in Dynamic Statistics is worth it to ensure a good execution plan. The logic is that if the value is set to the default (optimizer_dynamic_sampling=2) then the 64-block sample size is ignored and the actual sample size is determined by looking at the table sizes and the predicate complexity. If there is a non-default value then the rules are applied as for serially executing statements.

Can Dynamic Statistics Adversely Affect Performance?

As with everything to do with the optimizer, we have to expend some resources to develop the best plan. If you expend little effort to develop a plan, there is a higher likelihood it will not be the best plan. If you expend too much effort to develop a plan, it make take too long to complete the job. The ideal amount of effort can be quite tricky to find and will vary from statement to statement.

Dynamic statistics take some resources to evaluate. Usually this is for the best, but there can be cases where the collection of dynamic statistics for a query can become the dominant feature of the elapsed time. Because dynamic statistics are not part of your query ('hidden' away in the recursive statements) you might be puzzled as to where the elapsed time is going. As always, appropriate tracing will show these statements. If the dynamic statistics statements are dominating your elapsed time, then you should consider disabling them for the SQL plan, or possibly opening a service request with Oracle to review the overall statement, in case there is a bug involved.

What Dynamic Statistics Value Should I Set?

The general rule of thumb for Dynamic Statistics is that first of all you should not rely on this feature. Remember Dynamic Statistics are there to catch potential problems in the optimization process caused by missing statistics. If your query is not performing as expected, Dynamic Statistics should not be your first port of call. You should get a SQLTXPLAIN report and look at that first. For parallel statements, especially if you have complex predicates and at least one table with missing statistics, you may well end up using Dynamic Statistics.

If you see Dynamic Statistics being used (as shown earlier in Figure 11-3) then you should check to see why it was used and what you can do to avoid using it. If you have statistics on a table and still see Dynamic Statistics, then one possibility is that you have complex predicates and have not used extended statistics (mentioned in Chapter 4).

If for some reason you want to use Dynamic Statistics but find its sampling level too low or the expected plan is not produced, you can increase the value of optimizer_dynamic_sampling, but take care to test these changes on a test system and make small changes to see that the overhead is not too great. Pick a representative SQL and see how it performs with different values. If you have done no testing on this parameter, then keep the value at its default.

If you want to disable this feature completely then set the value to 0.

There are cases where Dynamic Statistics are the only option left. For example, tables that are populated during the query will not have good statistics (as they are most likely empty during the maintenance window when statistics are gathered). Global temporary tables are a good example where Dynamic Statistics are a good idea.

If Dynamic Statistics are your last chance to get your execution plan right, then Statistics Feedback (formerly known as Cardinality Feedback) is your chance to get the execution plan right the second time around as we'll see in the next section covering a real-world example. We cover Statistics Feedback and Directives in the next chapter.

The Case of the Identical Twins

This is the kind of situation that occurs frequently in the DBA world: two apparently identical systems (11g in this case), one cloned from the other but with widely different performance in some SQL. Naturally you can suspect different DDL, statistics, or operational procedures, different resource allocation, different workloads, etc. When the hardware is identical and the databases are cloned from each other, the number of choices becomes more limited. In this case we discover by experimentation that one particular SQL is behaving well on system A (say, New York) and the cloned system B (say, London) is behaving badly. The SQL is the same, the systems are the same, the parameter settings are the same. Let me show you the steps you could follow to solve a problem like this using SQLT.

There are many ways you could solve this problem. No doubt you could do it just by collecting 10046 trace files, but we're looking at how you would do this with SQLTXPLAIN. Step by step. First, if we collect SQLT for both SQL statements, one SQL XECUTE report for New York (as it executes normally) and one SQL XTRACT report for the evil twin in London (as it takes too long to execute). From the top of SQLTXPLAIN report (see Figure 11-6) we look at the list of execution plans by clicking on "Execution Plans."

Global

- Observations
- SQL Text
- SQL Identification
- Environment
- CBO Environment
- Fix Control
- CBO System Statistics
- DBMS_STATS Setup
- Initialization Parameters
- NLS Parameters
- I/O Calibration
- Tool Configuration Parameters

Cursor Sharing and Binds

- Cursor Sharing
- Adaptive Cursor Sharing
- Peeked Binds
- Captured Binds

SQL Tuning Advisor

- STA Report
- STA Script

Plans

- Summary
- Performance Statistics
- Performance History (delta)
- Performance History (total)
- Execution Plans

Plan Control

- Stored Outlines
- SQL Profiles
- SQL Plan Baselines

SQL Execution

- Active Session History
- AWR Active Session History
- SQL Statistics
- SQL Detail ACTIVE Report
- Monitor Statistics
- Monitor ACTIVE Report
- Monitor HTML Report
- Monitor TEXT Report
- Segment Statistics
- Session Statistics
- Session Events
- Parallel Processing

Tables

- Tables
- Statistics
- Statistics Versions
- Modifications
- Properties
- Physical Properties
- Constraints
- Columns
- Indexed Columns
- Histograms
- Partitions
- Indexes

Objects

- Objects
- Dependencies
- Fixed Objects
- Fixed Object Columns
- Nested Tables
- Policies
- Audit Policies
- Tablespaces
- Metadata

Figure 11-6. The top of the SQLT report. We click on "Execution Plans"

This is for the 'evil' system. We see that cardinality feedback is in play, so something must have happened to make this feature kick in. We also see (Figure 11-7) that the estimated cardinality is very different for some of the executions (where cardinality feedback was used). We also see that the optimizer_cost is very high where cardinality feedback was used.

Execution Plans

List ordered by phv and source.

#	Plan Hash Value	SQLT Plan Hash Value[1]	SQLT Plan Hash Value2[1]	Src	Source	Plan Info	Is Bind Sensitive	Optimizer	Optimizer Cost	Estimated Cardinality E-Rows
1	204354	57413	57413	AWR	DBA_HIST_SQL_PLAN			ALL_ROWS	5143	1
2	204354	57413	9380	STA	DBA_SQLTUNE_PLANS			HINT: ALL_ROWS	6469	1
3	672102947	55717	73707	STA	DBA_SQLTUNE_PLANS			ALL_ROWS	101	1
4	1144222098	65805	33659	STA	DBA_SQLTUNE_PLANS			ALL_ROWS	8	1
5	1308298177	31045	31045	AWR	DBA_HIST_SQL_PLAN	cardinality_feedback yes		ALL_ROWS	8939018	56960
6	1308298177	31045	34078	STA	DBA_SQLTUNE_PLANS			HINT: ALL_ROWS	15608	1
7	1646136085	74542	42396	STA	DBA_SQLTUNE_PLANS			ALL_ROWS	8	1
8	2154248988	40335	8189	STA	DBA_SQLTUNE_PLANS			ALL_ROWS	8	1
9	2370439755 [B] [X]	27748	84682	MEM	GV$SQL_PLAN		N	ALL_ROWS	15514	1
10	2370439755 [B] [X]	27748	27748	AWR	DBA_HIST_SQL_PLAN			ALL_ROWS	15514	1
11	2370439755 [B] [X]	27748	84682	XPL	PLAN_TABLE			ALL_ROWS	15514	1
12	2370439755 [B] [X]	27748	84682	STA	DBA_SQLTUNE_PLANS			ALL_ROWS	15514	1
13	2518443365 [W]	66142	66142	AWR	DBA_HIST_SQL_PLAN			ALL_ROWS	5143	1
14	2518443365 [W]	66142	18109	STA	DBA_SQLTUNE_PLANS			HINT: ALL_ROWS	6469	1

Figure 11-7. The London 'evil' twin shows cardinality feedback being used and high values for estimated cardinality

Since we are comparing the good and bad systems, we should now look at the execution plans for the good system in New York. Remember these two systems are identical (same hardware, same database versions, similar volumes of data, same tables, and indexes). Here is the same part of the report for the good system (see Figure 11-8).

Execution Plans

List ordered by phv and source.

#	Plan Hash Value	SQLT Plan Hash Value[1]	SQLT Plan Hash Value2[1]	Src	Source	Plan Info	Is Bind Sensitive	Optimizer	Optimizer Cost	Estimated Cardinality E-Rows
1	1279904434	49703	78973	XPL	PLAN_TABLE	dynamic_sampling 2		ALL_ROWS	157	1
2	2221109719 [B] [W]	18842	14092	MEM	GV$SQL_PLAN	dynamic_sampling 2	N	ALL_ROWS	167	1733

Figure 11-8. *The New York good twin shows Dynamic Statistics (Dynamic Sampling) and smaller values for estimated cardinality*

We also see that there are many more different plans in London than there are in New York. We know that Dynamic Statistics are sometimes used when poor statistics are involved, so it is a reasonable route of inquiry to look at the statistics of the main objects in the query. We should be thinking throughout our investigation of the information presented by SQLT: "Why were Dynamic Statistics used and why was cardinality feedback used and why are they different?" From the top of the report we click on "Statistics." We see for the good system (Figure 11-9) that we have a "Y" under the "Temp" column. Also we have no values under "Num Rows" or "Sample Size" or "Perc." TABLE4 is of interest because as we'll see the same part of the report for the bad system is very different in this respect.

Table Statistics

#	Table Name	Owner	Part	Temp	Count[1]	Num Rows[2]	Sample Size[2]	Perc	Last Analyzed[2]	Segment Extents	Segment Blocks	Blocks[2]
1	TABLE1	SCHEMA1	NO	N	173656	173656	173656	100.0	2012-06-26/22:04:25	19	512	510
2	TABLE2	SCHEMA1	NO	N	8720	8720	8720	100.0	2011-10-24/13:39:49	1	128	48
3	TABLE3	SCHEMA1	NO	N	4583440	4583440	4583440	100.0	2012-06-29/22:02:03	221	332480	244659
4	TABLE4	SCHEMA1	NO	Y	0							

(1) SELECT COUNT(*) performed in Table as per tool parameter "count_star_threshold" with current value of 1000000.
(2) CBO Statistics.
Go to Table Statistics Versions
Go to Tables
Go to Top

Figure 11-9. *The table statistics for the 'good' system*

Before we leap to conclusions (and this is always to be avoided in investigating performance issues), we need to look at the 'bad' system and do a comparison (see Figure 11-10). Our plan is to figure out what could be different between these two systems to cause one to use dynamic sampling and the other to use cardinality feedback.

Table Statistics

#	Table Name	Owner	Part	Temp	Count[1]	Num Rows[2]	Sample Size[2]	Perc	Last Analyzed[2]	Segment Extents	Segment Blocks	Blocks[2]
1	TABLE1	SCHEMA1	NO	N	20386400	20386400	20386400	100.0	2012-09-20/20:29:40	126	56320	56201
2	TABLE2	SCHEMA1	NO	N	5127	5127	5127	100.0	2012-09-05/16:41:07	3	24	24
3	TABLE3	SCHEMA1	NO	N	37486201	37486201	37486201	100.0	2012-09-21/20:13:02	259	614528	611456
4	TABLE4	SCHEMA1	NO	Y	0	0	0		2012-09-20/20:29:12			0

(1) SELECT COUNT(*) performed in Table as per tool parameter "count_star_threshold" with current value of 1000000.
(2) CBO Statistics.
Go to Table Statistics Versions
Go to Tables
Go to Top

Figure 11-10. *The table statistics for the 'bad' system*

Now that we see both together we see something very interesting. Both databases show that TABLE4 is a temporary table and that the statistics gathering is different for these two systems for this one table. We also see that the data volume for TABLE1 is different, but TABLE4 seems much more interesting in terms of difference, at least for now because it has a count of 0 and row count of 0 also. We'll keep the TABLE1 idea as a backup. So let's check on the metadata for TABLE4 and see how it was defined. (We can get this easily enough by clicking on the "Metadata" from the top of the report). See Figure 11-11.

Global

- Observations
- SQL Text
- SQL Identification
- Environment
- CBO Environment
- Fix Control
- CBO System Statistics
- DBMS_STATS Setup
- Initialization Parameters
- NLS Parameters
- I/O Calibration
- Tool Configuration Parameters

Cursor Sharing and Binds

- Cursor Sharing
- Adaptive Cursor Sharing
- Peeked Binds
- Captured Binds

SQL Tuning Advisor

- STA Report
- STA Script

Plans

- Summary
- Performance Statistics
- Performance History (delta)
- Performance History (total)
- Execution Plans

Plan Control

- Stored Outlines
- SQL Profiles
- SQL Plan Baselines

SQL Execution

- Active Session History
- AWR Active Session History
- SQL Statistics
- SQL Detail ACTIVE Report
- Monitor Statistics
- Monitor ACTIVE Report
- Monitor HTML Report
- Monitor TEXT Report
- Segment Statistics
- Session Statistics
- Session Events
- Parallel Processing

Tables

- Tables
- Statistics
- Statistics Versions
- Modifications
- Properties
- Physical Properties
- Constraints
- Columns
- Indexed Columns
- Histograms
- Partitions
- Indexes

Objects

- Objects
- Dependencies
- Fixed Objects
- Fixed Object Columns
- Nested Tables
- Policies
- Audit Policies
- Tablespaces
- Metadata

Figure 11-11. *From the top of the SQLTXECUTE report we can navigate to the metadata for all objects for this query*

Then from the part of the report labeled "Metadata" we can select the table metadata by clicking on "Table" hyperlink, which is shown in Figure 11-12. Notice how we also have a link to index metadata if we wanted to investigate that.

Metadata

- ### Index
- ### Table

Go to Top

Figure 11-12. *The list of object types for which we have metadata, in this case tables and indexes*

The table metadata part of the SQLTXPLAIN report show links to all the tables, which are in the query for which the report was created. See Figure 11-13. In this case we have four tables. We are interested in the fourth table in this case, so we click on the "TABLE4" hyperlink.

Table - Metadata

- TABLE1
- TABLE2
- TABLE3
- TABLE4

Go to Metadata
Go to Top

Figure 11-13. *The list of table objects for which we have metadata*

This gets us to the part of the report that shows the metadata for TABLE4. We see that is is global temporary table with the clause ON COMMIT PRESERVE ROWS. This is the DDL we see:

```
CREATE GLOBAL TEMPORARY TABLE "SCHEMA1"."TABLE4"
(    "COLUMN1" NUMBER(10,0),
     "COLUMN2" NUMBER(10,0),
     "COLUMN3" NUMBER(10,0)
) ON COMMIT PRESERVE ROWS
```

There's nothing remarkable about this table. This is a default creation of a global temporary table that can be used by more than one session during SQL processing. This is often included in application designs if the developer wants to keep some temporary data in a table for processing in later steps in the application. The on commit preserve part of the DDL (metadata) ensures that data committed to the table is preserved. In this kind of table you would normally expect the table to be cleaned out at the end of processing, or sometimes at the beginning of processing. The key thing to note here is that on the 'bad' system, statistics were collected for this table (see Figure 11-10). There is a last analyzed date for TABLE4 but not on the good system. If we look at the statistics for TABLE4 where they were collected, we see that the table was empty. These statistics would then prevent Dynamic Statistics from being activated (as there are "good" statistics for TABLE4), but would not prevent cardinality feedback because data loaded during processing would make the cardinality estimates wrong. This sounds like a working theory. Somehow TABLE4 has had statistics collected on it on the "bad" system but not on the "good" system. On the "good" system the table was not analyzed. This would have allowed Dynamic Statistics to take an estimate of the statistics at runtime and determine a good execution plan. With a working theory we can now build a test case (described in Chapter 18) and attempt to get the "good" execution plan from the "bad" test case by deleting the statistics for the global temporary table.

Summary

Dynamic Statistics and Cardinality Feedback (Statistics Feedback) are useful features, for those rare occasions when statistics are missing. There is no substitute for good statistics, however. With the interplay of complex features, situations can be created that show strange behavior. Even seemingly identical systems can behave very differently if key components are changed, sometimes unwittingly. SQLTXPLAIN, because it gathers everything, is the quickest and easiest way to solve most SQL tuning mysteries. In the next chapter we'll take a closer look how Cardinality Feedback has been extended to collect Directives that benefit multiple SQLs in a system.

## CHAPTER 12

Directives and Statistics Feedback

In 11g there was a feature called Cardinality Feedback. This reoptimized (hard parsed) a query if the Cardinality Estimate of the final result was more than a certain factor out from the actual result. This was a nice simple feature that was easy to understand. If you saw this note at the end of an execution plan, you knew that Cardinality Feedback had been used.

```
SQL> select * from table(dbms_xplan.display_cursor(null,null,'ALLSTATS LAST'));
PLAN_TABLE_OUTPUT
SQL_ID  gtukt6kw8yjm6, child number 3
-------------------------------------
select /*+ gather_plan_statistics */ count(*) from test1
Plan hash value: 3896847026

-------------------------------------------------------------------------
|Id |Operation          |Name |Starts |E-Rows |A-Rows|  A-Time   |Buffers|
-------------------------------------------------------------------------
|  0|SELECT STATEMENT    |     |    1 |       |     1|00:00:00.02|   116|
|  1| SORT AGGREGATE     |     |    1 |     1 |     1|00:00:00.02|   116|
|  2|  TABLE ACCESS FULL|TEST1|    1 | 73532 | 73532|00:00:00.18|   116|
-------------------------------------------------------------------------

Note
-----
cardinality feedback used for this statement <<<
```

So how is Automatic Reoptimization better and where does the old Cardinality Feedback feature fit in?

Automatic Reoptimization

In 12c Statistics Feedback has been expanded, improved, and has changed its name. In line with the new naming convention, Cardinality Feedback has been subsumed into a greater feature called Automatic Reoptimization. Cardinality Feedback has been renamed to Statistics Feedback and the logic of keeping track of actual and estimated Cardinality has been expanded to now report on individual execution lines of a plan and keep this information in SYSAUX. These Directives are a way to influence other SQLs. Finally Performance feedback has been added to influence Parallel execution plans. Let's look at each of these features in more detail and how they can be viewed in SQLT.

© Stelios Charalambides 2017

S. Charalambides, *Oracle SQL Tuning with Oracle SQLTXPLAIN*, DOI 10.1007/978-1-4842-2436-6_12

Statistics Feedback

Statistics Feedback is a simple yet elegant way of correcting cardinality. Rather than going to endless complications to determine the right cardinality, we just wait for the result of each step in the execution plan, store it in the shared pool, and reference it on subsequent executions, in the hope that the information will give us a good idea of how well we did the last time. This simple technique naturally has its own pitfalls: how do we stop results bouncing from one estimate to another, for example? Let's look at some of the details.

How Does It Work?

Statistics Feedback could not work if information about every SQL was not stored in memory, to be accessed by latter executions of the same SQL. Let's see what information we can access. We'll run a simple query, then get the Actual and Estimated cardinalities for the execution, and then run for two queries and compare estimates and actual rows returned, with both Dynamic Statistics and Statistics Feedback disabled. Then we'll enable Statistics Feedback and repeat the experiment. In our first step we check the value of `optimizer_dynamic_sampling` and see that it is set to 0, which means this feature is disabled.

```
SQL> show parameter optimizer_dynamic_sampling
NAME                                    TYPE        VALUE
-------------------------------------- ----------- ------------
optimizer_dynamic_sampling              integer      0 <<<DS disabled
SQL> alter system set "_optimizer_use_feedback"=FALSE; <<CFB disabled
System altered.
```

■ **Note**   We could also have disabled cardinality feedback with a hint /*+ opt_param('_optimizer_use_feedback', 'false') */.

Next we create a test table that is populated from dba_objects. We use the hint /*+ gather_plan_statistics */ to ensure we have good statistics for the execution plan we want to look at.

```
SQL> create table test1 as select (object_id) from dba_objects;
Table created.
SQL> select /*+ gather_plan_statistics */ count(*) from test1;
  COUNT(*)
----------
     91601
```

Now we use the `dbms_xplan.display_cursor` to get the execution plan and the statistics associated with the execution.

```
SQL> select * from table(dbms_xplan.display_cursor(null,null,'ALLSTATS LAST'));
PLAN_TABLE_OUTPUT
SQL_ID  gtukt6kw8yjm6, child number 0
-------------------------------------
select /*+ gather_plan_statistics */ count(*) from test1
Plan hash value: 3896847026
-------------------------------------------------------------------------
|Id |Operation         |Name |Starts| E-Rows | A-Rows |   A-Time   | Buffers |
-------------------------------------------------------------------------
```

```
|  0|SELECT STATEMENT    |      |    1|         |      1 |00:00:00.01 |    144 |
|  1| SORT AGGREGATE     |      |    1|    1 |      1 |00:00:00.01 |    144 |
|  2| TABLE ACCESS FULL|TEST1|    1| 11436 |  91601 |00:00:00.01 |    144 |
--------------------------------------------------------------------------
14 rows selected.
```

We see on this line that the estimate (E-Rows) is pretty poor compared to the actual number of rows (A-Rows). This estimate count is bad enough to merit Statistics Feedback use, but in this case we have the feature turned off. So if we run the query a second time we would expect no improvement in E-Rows; and indeed this is what happens.

```
SQL> select /*+ gather_plan_statistics */  count(*) from test1;
  COUNT(*)
----------
     91601
SQL> select * from table(dbms_xplan.display_cursor(null,null,'ALLSTATS LAST'));
PLAN_TABLE_OUTPUT
SQL_ID gtukt6kw8yjm6, child number 0
-------------------------------------
select /*+ gather_plan_statistics */ count(*) from test1
Plan hash value: 3896847026

---------------------------------------------------------------------------
|Id |Operation           |Name |Starts|E-Rows |A-Rows|  A-Time   |Buffers |
---------------------------------------------------------------------------
|  0 |SELECT STATEMENT    |     |    1|         |      1 |00:00:00.09 |    116 |
|  1 | SORT AGGREGATE     |     |    1|    1 |      1 |00:00:00.09 |    116 |
|  2 | TABLE ACCESS FULL|TEST1|    1| 11436 |91601 |00:00:00.18 |    116 |
---------------------------------------------------------------------------

14 rows selected.
```

No improvement has occurred in the estimated cardinality (E-Rows) for this plan. The E-Rows value has not changed; the optimizer did not make any changes even though its estimate was so far out. The next step in our experiment is to enable cardinality feedback.

```
SQL> alter system set "_optimizer_use_feedback"=TRUE;
System altered.
```

Now we repeat the entire sequence of steps and we find that for the last step we get

```
PLAN_TABLE_OUTPUT
-------------------------------------------------------------------------------
SQL_ID  gtukt6kw8yjm6, child number 2
-------------------------------------
select /*+ gather_plan_statistics */ count(*) from test1
Plan hash value: 3896847026
-------------------------------------------------------------------------------
| Id  | Operation           | Name  | Starts | E-Rows | A-Rows |   A-Time   | Buffers |
-------------------------------------------------------------------------------
|   0 | SELECT STATEMENT    |       |    1 |         |      1 |00:00:00.01 |    144 |
|   1 |  SORT AGGREGATE     |       |    1 |    1 |      1 |00:00:00.01 |    144 |
|   2 |   TABLE ACCESS FULL| TEST1 |    1 | 91601 |  91601 |00:00:00.01 |    144 |
-------------------------------------------------------------------------------
```

```
Note
-----
statistics feedback used for this statement
```

We see that in the Note section the optimizer has left us a message indicating that Statistics Feedback was used. In our example above, we had an estimated 11,436 rows to begin with and an actual number of 91,601 rows. Without Statistics Feedback and Dynamic Statistics on the new object, our estimate is pretty poor to begin with. Because the number of estimated rows was "significantly" different, Statistics Feedback was used. It is not documented what a "significant" difference is, but approximately an eight-fold difference is enough.

There are safety features in place to stop the cardinalities bouncing back and forth between estimates, so after a small number of iterations the plan is stabilized. The fact that the actual cardinalities are stored in the SGA also explains why Statistics Feedback information is not persistent, that is, if the instance is restarted then the Statistics Feedback information will be lost, as the information held in memory is not persistent.

How Can You Tell If Statistics Feedback Is Used?

The simplest way to tell if Statistics Feedback has been used is to use the SQLTXPLAIN report. Click on "Execution Plans" (as shown in Figure 12-1) and if Statistics Feedback has been used for some of your execution plans, you will see "cardinality_feedback yes" under the "Plan Info" column. See Figure 12-1 for an example.

Execution Plans

List ordered by phv and source.

#	Plan Hash Value	SQLT Plan Hash Value[1]	SQLT Plan Hash Value2[1]	Src	Source	Plan Info	Is Bind Sensitive	Optimizer
1	204354	57413	57413	AWR	DBA_HIST_SQL_PLAN			ALL_ROWS
2	204354	57413	9380	STA	DBA_SQLTUNE_PLANS			HINT: ALL_ROWS
3	672102947	55717	73707	STA	DBA_SQLTUNE_PLANS			ALL_ROWS
4	1144222098	65805	33659	STA	DBA_SQLTUNE_PLANS			ALL_ROWS
5	1308298177	31045	31045	AWR	DBA_HIST_SQL_PLAN	cardinality_feedback yes		ALL_ROWS
6	1308298177	31045	34078	STA	DBA_SQLTUNE_PLANS			HINT: ALL_ROWS
7	1646136085	74542	42396	STA	DBA_SQLTUNE_PLANS			ALL_ROWS
8	2154248988	40335	8189	STA	DBA_SQLTUNE_PLANS			ALL_ROWS

Figure 12-1. *"Execution Plans" section shows that cardinality feedback was used for an execution plan*

To emphasize the point that Statistics Feedback is a backup mechanism, its use is also highlighted in the "Observations" section of the SQLTXPLAIN report. See the section in Figure 12-2, which you can reach by clicking on the "Observations" hyperlink from the top of the main SQLTXPLAIN report.

Observations

List of concerns identified by the health-check module. Please review. Some may require further attention

#	Type	Name	
1	TOKEN	UNIQUE_ID	SQLT XECUTE was used and SQL provided is miss
2	SYSTEM PARAMETER	MODIFIED	There are 2 system level initialization parameters w
3	CBO PARAMETER	NON-DEFAULT	There is one CBO initialization parameter with a non
4	CBO PARAMETER	MODIFIED	There are 2 CBO initialization parameters with a mo
5	DBMS_STATS	DBA_AUTOTASK_CLIENT	Automatic gathering of CBO statistics is enabled.
6	PLAN	PLAN_HASH_VALUE	9 plans were found for this SQL.
7	PLAN CONTROL	PLAN_CONTROL	None of the plans found was created using one of
8	PLAN CONTROL	CARDINALITY_FEEDBACK	One plan was created using Cardinality Feedback.
9	DBMS_STATS	SYSTEM STATISTICS	Workload CBO System Statistics are not gathered.

Figure 12-2. *Statistics Feedback usage is shown as an observation of type PLAN_CONTROL, with the name CARDINALITY_FEEDBACK*

When Is Statistics Feedback Used?

Lack of statistics or "complex" predicates that create queries with hard-to-determine cardinalities will give Statistics Feedback a chance to improve E-Rows. Here is a SQL with a "complex" predicate:

```
SQL> select product_name from order_items ord, product_information pro
  where ord.unit_price= 15 and quantity > 1
  and pro.product_id = ord.product_id;
```

Here we have a filter on unit_price (must be equal to 15 and quantity must be > 1). This situation is not very rare so Statistics feedback could be used often. However, remember that we mentioned that the statement needs to execute at least once for the optimizer to store the actual rows so that it can compare them to the estimated number of rows. If Dynamic Statistics has already been used (because it was needed and it was not disabled), then Statistics Feedback will not be used. Also because of the problems that can be introduced by bind variables (especially if you have skewed data), Statistics Feedback will not be used for parts of the statement that involve bind variables.

If you find Statistics Feedback is not useful for your site or SQL statement, you can, with the assistance of support, disable it with

```
SQL> alter system set "_optimizer_use_feedback" = FALSE;
```

If you want to disable an individual statement, then you can put this hint in the SQL

```
/*+ opt_param('_optimizer_use_feedback' 'false') */
```

A select sysdate from dual becomes

```
SQL> select /*+ opt_param('_optimizer_use_feedback' 'false') */ sysdate from dual;
```

Statistics Feedback is not persistent through instance restarts, so it is better to get your statistics from other sources, preferably from dbms_stats, but remember that Statistics Feedback is enabled by default.

One Step Further

Statistics Feedback is such a good idea that it was expanded to include individual lines of an execution plan. The idea is that after an execution is complete (just like Statistics Feedback), a record is kept of the cardinality of a particular line in the plan. If the actual cardinality and the estimated cardinality are too far apart, then a Directive is created. This Directive informs future executions of ANY SQL that has that access path that some remedial action is required for that line (usually collect statistics with Dynamic Statistics).

The first step in finding out about Directives from SQLT is to know where this is on the front page. See Figure 12-3 below.

Global

- Observations
- SQL Text
- SQL Identification
- Environment
- CBO Environment
- Fix Control
- CBO System Statistics
- DBMS_STATS Setup
- Initialization Parameters
- NLS Parameters
- I/O Calibration
- Tool Configuration Parameters

Cursor Sharing and Binds

- Cursor Sharing
- Adaptive Cursor Sharing
- Peeked Binds
- Captured Binds

SQL Tuning Advisor

- STA Report
- STA Script

Plans

- Summary
- Performance Statistics
- Performance History (delta)
- Performance History (total)
- Execution Plans

Plan Control

- Stored Outlines
- SQL Patches
- SQL Profiles
- SQL Plan Baselines
- SQL Plan Directives

SQL Execution

- Active Session History
- AWR Active Session History
- SQL Statistics
- SQL Detail ACTIVE Report
- Monitor Statistics
- Monitor ACTIVE Report
- Monitor HTML Report
- Monitor TEXT Report
- Segment Statistics
- Session Statistics
- Session Events
- Parallel Processing

Tables

- Tables
- Statistics
- Statistics Extensions
- Statistics Versions
- Modifications
- Properties
- Physical Properties
- Constraints
- Columns
- Indexed Columns
- Histograms
- Partitions
- Indexes

Objects

- Objects
- Dependencies
- Fixed Objects
- Fixed Object Columns
- Nested Tables
- Policies
- Audit Policies
- Tablespaces
- Metadata

Figure 12-3. *The SQL Plan Directives hyperlink has been added to the main page of the SQLT report for 12c*

Directives, because they relate to individual lines of an execution plan, are a little more complex than the old Cardinality Feedback. The old Cardinality Feedback was just the end result of the query compared to the expected result. No details about the reason or type of under or overestimate are kept. With Directives, however, there is more to know. What kind of situation were we in when the misestimate happened and what is the state of the misestimate Directive now, and what should we do about it? The STATE column of the dba_sql_plan_directives can have two possible values:

1. SUPERSEDED – There is a column group for this column with another directive or another SQL plan directive exists that can be used instead.

2. USABLE – The SQL Plan directive is usable.

The STATE column is telling us if the Directive is being used or not. Then we have a REASON column. This column explains why the misestimate came about. Was it a simple Table Cardinality error, or something more complex. These are the values I've come across so far.

1. Group by Cardinality Misestimate

2. Join Cardinality Misestimate

3. Single Table Cardinality Misestimate

Finally we have what do we do about the misestimate. This is the TYPE column. So far I know of only 1 possible value DYNAMIC_SAMPLING. To work with Directives, for example, to delete them or to copy them from one system to another you would work with dba_sql_plan_dir_objects and use the dbms_spd packages. Just like transporting statistics from one system to another dbms_spd has a number of packages to create staging tables, pack data, unpack data, and set preferences.

1. dbms_spd.Alter_sql_plan_directive – Can be used to change a SQL plan Directive. For example, from enabled to disabled.

2. dbms_spd.Create_stgtab_directive – Creates a staging table so that Directives can be stored, for backup purposes or for transportation from one system to another.

3. dbms_spd.Drop_sql_plan_directive – This drops an existing Directive. You need the ADMINISTER SQL MANAGEMENT OBJECT privilege to do this.

4. dbms_spd.Flush_sql_plan_directive – This flushes Directives from memory.

5. dbms_spd.Get_prefs – Can be used to get the number of weeks of retention of directives.

6. dbms_spd.Pack_stgtab_directive – Used to Pack directives into the staging table.

7. dbms_spd.set_prefs – Used to set the preferences.

8. dbms_spd.unpack_stgtab_directive – Unpack a stage table filled with Directives.

So this is all very well if you want to code things manually, but why do that when SQLT will get you all this information? If we follow the link from Figure 12-3 we some different types of directives. The first figure (12-4) shows some Usable directives for Group by Cardinality Misestimates.

SQL Plan Directives

"USABLE" Group By Cardinality Misestimate Directives

Restricted up to 300 Objects and Directives as per tool parameter "r_rows_table_m".

	Internal State / Redundant[4] / Auto Drop[4] :	MISSING_STATS
	Created:	2015-12-10/10:27:48
	Last Modified:	2015-12-10/16:13:43
	Last Used:	2015-12-10/16:13:43
# Object in this Report[3]	(Owner.Table.Column) Object Name[2] \ Directive ID[1]	3875273551967288085

Figure 12-4. *An example USABLE Directive*

This tells us that for the object listed there is a Group By Cardinality Misestimate Directive. It also tells us that the reason for the misestimate is that statistics are missing.

If some corrective action has been taken, such as running Adaptive Statistics to collect new statistics, then the status may change to HAS_STATS as seen in the next figure (Figure 12-5).

"SUPERSEDED" Group By Cardinality Misestimate Directives

Restricted up to 300 Objects and Directives as per tool parameter "r_rows_table_m".

		Internal State / Redundant[4] / Auto Drop[4] :	HAS_STATS
		Created:	2015-12-05/16:14:21
		Last Modified:	2015-12-05/06:00:12
		Last Used:	2015-12-05/06:00:12
#	Object in this Report[3]	(Owner.Table.Column) Object Name[2] \ Directive ID[1]	17833722588659491645
1	Yes	SYS.DUAL	----

*(1) *NOTES* Directive Flags under each directive is in positional order :*
Letter means YES on (E)-equality_predicates_only (C)-simple_column_predicates_only (J).
Lower case flag indicates the directive lists multiple times the same object with both YES
(2) Objects are listed in alphabetical order only one time even if directive lists it multiple times.
(3) Directives may include objects that are not collected by SQLT because they are not present in the SQL Stateme
(4) Redundant is displayed only if YES and AutoDrop is displayed only if NO.

Figure 12-5. *Some Directives may become SUPERSEDED*

In SQLT the dense information stored about Directives is show by bit fields with a '-' indicating NO and different upper- or lowercase letters indicating different things. Here's an example (see Figure 12-6).

PERMANENT	PERMANENT	NEW	PERMANENT	NEW
2015-12-05/06:00:12	2015-12-10/16:13:43	2016-01-02/06:00:02	2015-12-10/16:13:43	2015-12-13/06:00:02
2015-12-19/06:00:02	2015-12-13/06:00:02	-	2015-12-13/06:00:02	-
2016-01-02/06:00:02	2016-01-02/06:00:02	-	2015-12-13/06:00:02	-
2766079664683356979	3709877249897555075	4108009989928047025	6922289760147831760	13944108934788842003
---f	---f	---f	---f	---f
---F		---F		
	---F		---F	---F

	----			----

Figure 12-6. *The Usable directive bitmasks shown in SQLT*

The key to this field is shown in SQLT and decodes to the following possible values:

1. E – Equality Predicate (single time only)

2. e – Equality Predicate (multiple times with both YES and NO)

3. C – Column Predicate (single time only)

4. c – Column Predicate (multiple times with both YES and NO)

5. J – Index Access Join Predicate (single time only)

6. j – Index Access Join Predicate (multiple times with both YES and NO)

7. F – Filter on Join (single time only)

8. f – Filter on Join (multiple times with both YES and NO)

This information tells you what kind of Directives you have (USABLE or SUPERSEDED); which tables were involved; what the Directive was for (Group by Cardinality Misestimate, Join Cardinality Misestimate, Single Table Cardinality Misestimate); and if this was a Filter, column predicate, or Index Join access.

In addition to this information we should look at a new hyperlink in the Tables section (see Figure 12-7) below.

Table Stats Exten	Table Modif	Table Prop	Table Phys Prop	Table Cons	Table Cols	Idxed Cols	Table Hgrm	Part Key Cols	Table Part	Indexes	Single Table SQL Plan Directives	Table Meta
		Prop	Phys		1							Meta
	Modif	Prop	Phys	14	20	5	5	PKey	23	5		Meta
1	Modif	Prop	Phys	10	11	8	4	PKey	23	8	1	Meta
	Modif	Prop	Phys	9	6	3		PKey	23	2		Meta
	Modif	Prop	Phys	12	11	5	3	PKey	23	3		Meta

Figure 12-7. The hyperlink to table-related Directives

This hyperlink takes you straight to the Directives that relate to this table. See Figure 12-8.

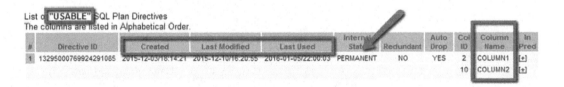

Figure 12-8. The Table Directive view

This table gives us vital information to understand why the Directive is there. It tells us when the Directive was created, when it was modified, and when it was last used. For example, if a Directive was created long ago and the data has changed since then, do you think the Directive is still applicable? It might not be. We also see that the Internal State is PERMANENT, which says that this Misestimate is not going away. Most important, the columns involved are highlighted. With this information you decide if you need to take action to collect better statistics or delete the Directives. If the Directives are causing a problem you can move them (stage, pack, export, copy, import, unpack) or you can drop them using the dbms_spd packages.

Performance Feedback

The final feature in the Automatic reoptimization suite is relatively simple in comparison to the Directives feature. When Automatic Degree Of Parallelism is enabled it will evaluate, in the same way as Statistics Feedback, at the end of an execution of a parallel statement, based on CPU, if the degree chosen was optimal or not. If it wasn't then the DOP may change. If Performance Feedback was used again, we will have a note at the execution plan.

```
Note
----
  - performance feedback used for this statement
```

This feature is controlled by the parameter `parallel_degree_policy` that can take the value AUTO MANUAL or ADAPTIVE.

1. MANUAL – AUTO is disabled and DOP is calculated manually.

2. AUTO – DOP is calculated for you when the query is parsed.

3. ADAPTIVE – DOP is calculated for you when the query is parsed and will be reevaluated at the end of the execution for a possible change.

Summary

In this chapter we covered some new 12c features that have made the Oracle optimizer more adaptive and automatic. Many features that were in 11g have been enhanced and expanded. The most interesting new feature, Directives, which have the potential to affect multiple queries on the system and bring a new level of adaptability to the system, and complicate the analysis and debugging of poorly executing queries, although this should happen less often. Luckily SQLT is there to collect all the required information. In the next chapter we look at Parallel Execution in general and look at some of the new reports that SQLT collects for this.

CHAPTER 13

■ ■ ■

Parallel Execution

What Is Parallel Execution?

In general terms, parallel execution is pretty easy to understand. 'Many hands make light work' or so the saying goes, but have you also heard 'too many cooks spoil the broth'? Therein lies the problem. We can throw resources at a problem, in this case execution of some SQL, but the parallel execution has to be managed for the best results. For a simple case such as taking an inventory in a department store, we could allocate one person to a floor and let them get on with it. Their results then would be collated by their supervisor. In our analogy the parallelism is equivalent to the people involved and the supervisor is the query coordinator (PX COORDINATOR in an execution plan – see below for a description of the elements of an execution plan). Sounds simple, doesn't it? More parallel execution slaves means faster response, right? Wrong! Just recall the Marx brothers scene in "A Night at the Opera." Could the activities being orchestrated by Groucho Marx be done by more people crowding into their tiny stateroom? I have seen many cases of problems with parallel execution where the response to slower-than-expected response has been more slaves (and three more hard boiled eggs).

Counting socks (`select count(socks) from department_Store;`) is one thing, but for more complex parallel tasks there is often a collector of information and a receiver of information and then a coordinator. In such cases (which is most of them), the number of parallel slaves is twice the degree of parallelism (DOP). As the tasks get more complex so does the plan; again for small tasks, Oracle will not parallelize (or cannot).

Let's also not forget the very important redistribution phase; this is the phase of the operation where an operation's data is collected and collated, sorted, grouped, or aggregated in some way. All of these steps are shown in the execution plan. We'll go through some execution plans so you can see what is shown in the following sections.

What Can Be Parallelized?

Many different kinds of operation can be parallelized: data loading, queries, DML, RMAN operations, and statistics collection; there may be others. This last one is particularly interesting to me because I often come across cases where a serial execution can cause a recursive SQL to be executed in parallel. For example, this happens with when Dynamic Statistics are needed for an execution. These recursive parallel queries are sometimes not obvious and are often only noticed when tracing is enabled. In this chapter we'll cover query execution parallelization, but for the sake of completeness I'll list the methods for parallelization in each of the options I listed above.

1. Data loading (Includes INSERT and EXTERNAL Tables). External data files can speed loading by separating data into different files. In this case the limit of parallelism is governed by the number of files. Oracle can also automatically divide work up into granules for parallel processing in some cases. The ACCESS parameters of the data loading cartridge keywords can specify PARALLEL to use parallelism.

© Stelios Charalambides 2017
S. Charalambides, *Oracle SQL Tuning with Oracle SQLTXPLAIN*, DOI 10.1007/978-1-4842-2436-6_13

2. Queries – This is covered in this chapter.

3. DML – By default DML will not run in parallel. Create Table As Select (CTAS) – This generally uses a higher degree of parallelism for the operations rather than the CREATE statement, for example:

    ```
    CREATE TABLE PARALLEL_LOAD PARALLEL 8 As SELECT /*+ Parallel (64) */ * from
    EXTERNAL_TABLE;
    ```

4. RMAN Operations – RMAN parallel operations are governed by RMAN keywords such as PARALLELISM, here's an example:

    ```
    CONFIGURE DEVICE TYPE DISK PARALLELISM 2;
    ```

5. Statistics collection. To ensure that parallel operations are not automatically downgraded to serial, you may need to set parallel_adaptive_multi_user to false.

    ```
    alter session set parallel_adaptive_multi_user=false;
    ```

    and set DEGREE appropriately in the DBMS_STATS procedure.

What Are Distribution Methods?

We briefly mentioned that the number of slaves in an execution for some operations is twice the degree of parallelism. This is because when producers have to pass on their work to the consumers they could do this on a one-to-one basis or in some other way. If we have asked for a green sock count in our department store, we might find a high level of skewness from the different floors of our department store. In this case a way of distributing the work between the producers and the consumers might speed up execution. If we did this on a one-to-one basis, one consumer and one producer might end up doing all the work while the other consumers were idle. Here is a list of the distribution methods and what they mean.

1. HASH – This hashes the key and then decides where to send the data based on the hash. The hash distribution method is very helpful for achieving an equal distribution of work. Useful if there is skew in the data.

2. BROADCAST: Useful when the data set from one slave or set of slaves is much smaller than the others. The smaller data set is sent to all Slaves.

3. HYBRID HASH: New in 12c, switches from HASH To BROADCAST if the data requires it. A new line is inserted before this distribution method called STATISTICS COLLECTOR, which checks the results as they are generated to make a decision about which distribution method to use.

4. RANGE: This is useful for sorting operations where the expected results should be in order.

5. KEY: This ensures that particular key values are worked on together. This would happen typically when the operation involves partition-wise joins.

6. Partition-wise Joins: At least one of the tables in the join has to be partitioned on the join key. A full partition-wise join may be used if two tables are partitioned and equi-partitioned on the same join key. The advantage is that the query slaves can complete the entire join for their own partitions.

In-Memory Parallel Execution

I mention in-parallel execution as it is strictly a parallel technique. It can dramatically increase performance by using memory access instead of disk access. The access method is different in that it is columnar, that is, the data is organized by column and not by row. In-memory is designed for large volumes of data. The columnar compressed format allow for rapid joins. The only controls you have as a DBA is the size of the in-memory area. For OLTP operations in-memory operations are limited to 80% of the buffer cache. ABTC (automatic Big Table Caching). If you have the memory this could be a useful technique.

Why Do We Want Parallel Execution?

Parallel execution reduces the elapsed time for the execution of the operation involved. If you have the memory, the CPU capacity, and the I/O bandwidth you should try and improve the elapsed time of your queries with parallel execution.

How Much Parallelism Do You Need?

Once you've decided that parallelism can help, you need to review the situation and consider the resources available. There's no point in setting parallelism to 64 if you only have one CPU. All that will happen is that you will have contention for the run queue. If the joins are going to use a lot of CPU or other resources, you need to count your CPUs and have a rough idea how many sessions will be created from your parallel query. Remember the number is going to be twice the DOP. If the expected elapsed time of the execution is too short, then most likely it's not worth the effort of setting up the query coordinator and the associated slaves and the overhead of the redistribution of the data to get the result. Finally the number of granules of work (the minimum chunk size of work) should be bigger than the chosen degree of parallelism. In the case of partition-wise joins, consider the partition count as the granule count. So, for example, if you have a table with 10 partitions and 4 CPUs, parallelism should be set to a low number like to maybe even 4. Also make sure that you do not increase the parallelism so much that you take all the resources on the system. If you do you will end up with CPU queues and overall slower execution.

What Do Parallel Execution Plans Look Like?

It's important to recognize when you are looking at an execution plan when it is parallel. See an example from SQLT below (Figure 13-1).

```
SELECT /*+ PARALLEL(4) */ customers.cust_first_name, customers.cust_last_name,
   MAX(QUANTITY_SOLD), AVG(QUANTITY_SOLD)
FROM sales, customers
WHERE sales.cust_id=customers.cust_id
GROUP BY customers.cust_first_name, customers.cust_last_name
```

SQL: [+]

ID	Exec Ord	Operation	Go To	More	Cost²	Estim Card	LAST Starts	LAST Output Rows
0	19	SELECT STATEMENT			268		9	3776
1	18	PX COORDINATOR		[+]	268		1	3776
2	17	. PX SEND QC (RANDOM) :TQ10003		[+]	268	7059	4	3776
3	16	.. HASH GROUP BY		[+]	268	7059	4	3776
4	15	... PX RECEIVE		[+]	268	7059	4	4076
5	14	.... PX SEND HASH :TQ10002		[+]	268	7059	4	4076
6	13	....+ HASH GROUP BY		[+]	268	7059	4	4076
7	12	....+. HASH JOIN		[+]	267	7059	4	7059
8	9	....+. PX RECEIVE		[+]	149	7059	4	28236
9	8	....+. PX SEND BROADCAST :TQ10001		[+]	149	7059	4	28236
10	7	....+.... VIEW VW_GBC_5		[+]	149	7059	4	7059
11	6	....+....+ HASH GROUP BY		[+]	149	7059	4	7059
12	5	....+....+. PX RECEIVE		[+]	149	7059	4	24204
13	4	....+....+. PX SEND HASH :TQ10000		[+]	149	7059	4	24204
14	3	....+....+... HASH GROUP BY		[+]	149	7059	4	24204
15	2	....+....+... PX BLOCK ITERATOR		[+]	143	918843	4	918843
16	1	....+....+....+ TABLE ACCESS FULL SALES	[+]	[+]	143	918843	46	918843
17	11	....+.. PX BLOCK ITERATOR		[+]	117	55500	4	55500
18	10	....+... TABLE ACCESS FULL CUSTOMERS	[+]	[+]	117	55500	51	55500

Performance statistics are only available when parameter "statistics_level" was set to "ALL" at hard-parse time, or SQL contains "gather_pl.
(1) If estim_card * starts < output_rows then under-estimate. If estim_card * starts > output_rows then over-estimate. Color highlights when e
(2) Largest contributors for cumulative-statistics columns are shown in red.

Other XML (id=1): [+]

Figure 13-1. *An example parallel execution plan as shown in SQLT*

In the example plan I've highlighted some components that I've mentioned so far. In this case the optimizer has chosen to scan the table CUSTOMERS on a block basis, so each slave will work on a block granule before moving onto the next one. This is PX BLOCK ITERATOR. I've also mentioned the slave sets PX SEND and PX RECEIVE, in this examples, cases for both HASH and BROADCAST.

Parallel Execution Components

From the operating system point of view the parallel slaves are all individual processes. They can be recognized by names 'ora_p000_snc1' from the command 'ps -efl'. The above process is the first slave of a parallel execution slave on the instance snc1.

When you look at the execution plan for a parallel execution, it looks very 'busy'. There are more elements in the plan. This is because there is more happening. There are slaves, there are senders and receivers, statistics collectors and aggregators. I'll list the elements in a plan below, and then we'll look at some example plans and talk through what's happening.

Here are the names and meanings of parallel execution line components:

1. PX COORDINATOR – This is the top process; it starts the slaves and it organizes the work from all the slave sets and presents the results to the top level.

2. PX BLOCK ITERATOR (Based on the granule size). When a parallel statement is parsed there is the possibility that a table can be divided into blocks and different slaves work on different blocks down to a minimum granule size. This operation breaks down the table into blocks and hands them out for slaves to execute.

3. PX SEND HASH – This is a distribution method and achieves an equal distribution of work for the receivers.

4. PX SEND BROADCAST – This is a distribution method. This should happen when the data set size distribution is uneven, so one is much smaller than the other. If we used an even distribution one RECEIVER would be busy while another was idle. It can also be seen as a BROADCAST LOCAL in a RAC environment to indicate that it is not using the interconnect.

5. PX SEND RANGE – This is a distribution method. This is useful when a sort is involved so particular ranges can be used.

6. PX SEND QC (ORDER) – An ordered send to the query coordinator PX COORDINATOR.

7. PX SEND KEY – Used for Partition-wise joins.

8. PX SEND HYBRID HASH – The decision on the distribution method is delayed until execution when the distribution method is determined by the size of the data sets. Introduced in 12c. Needs the new plan step STATISTICS COLLECTOR (Once a preset limit is reached it will do HASH distribution), otherwise it will use BROADCAST.

9. PX RECEIVE – This is the receiving end of the distribution.

10. PX SEND QC – This sends to the query coordinator.

11. PX PARTITION HASH ALL – Partition-wise HASH.

12. PX PARTITION RANGE ALL – Partition-wise all partitions. See some details below.

13. PX PARTITION RANGE ITERATOR – Partition-wise join composite.

14. PX PARTITION HASH JOIN_FILTER – Indicates a join on a Bloom filter.

Example Parallel Plan

In Figure 13-2, we see the same example of a parallel execution in the SQL Monitor format.

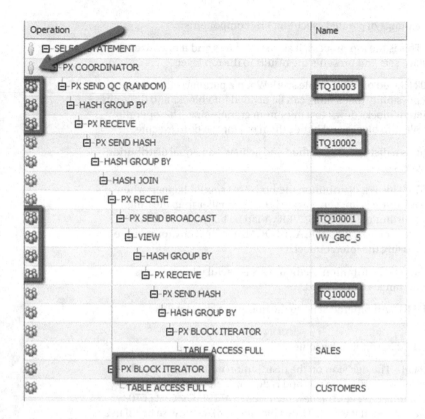

Figure 13-2. *An example parallel execution plan*

In the example we see that some slaves are shown in blue, and some slaves are shown in red, and some are processes are shown in green. The green sessions are the top-level processes. They will coordinate the work from the slaves and present it to the top layer.

For example, the top blue slaves in the figure are doing PX RECEIVE, HASH GROUP BY, and PX SEND QC (RANDOM). The red slaves below them are doing PX RECEIVE, HASH JOIN, HASH GROUP BY, and PX SEND HASH(to the previous blue group I mentioned). Each of these actions requires temporary areas to keep the work organized. These are called TQ10003, TQ10002, TQ10001, and TQ10000 in this case. Also notice the PX BLOCK ITERATOR I mentioned earlier.

Partition-Based Joins

Partition-based joins are useful because by selecting partitions to join we can avoid unneeded data interconnect traffic on RAC, and by limiting the joins to partitions we make the joins smaller and faster.

1. Full Partition-Wise Joins: Single-Level – Single-Level – To do this type of join the join key must be the partition key. The number of parallel slave pairs is equal to the number of partitions.

2. Full Partition-Wise Joins: Composite – Single-Level – In this kind of join one table (usually the bigger one) is divided into partitions and the smaller table is joined via a different sub-partition key. This limits the join work to the required sub-partitions.

3. Full Partition-Wise Joins: Composite- composite – In this kind of join the partition and sub-partition can be joined to other join keys in a variety of combinations from the partition or sub-partition.

4. Partial Partition-Wise Joins – In this join only one table needs to be partitioned.

5. Partial Partition-Wise Joins: Single-Level Partitioning.

6. Partial Partition-Wise Joins: Composite.

Example in an Execution Plan

The "Note" section of a parallel execution plan will show the reason for the degree of parallelism chosen.

Example Is SQL MONITOR

SQL Monitor is particularly useful for parallel execution. You can get this of course with SQLT. I find it useful because we see the slave work distribution for each slave set. This is where you can find out if the slave distributions are appropriate (Figure 13-3).

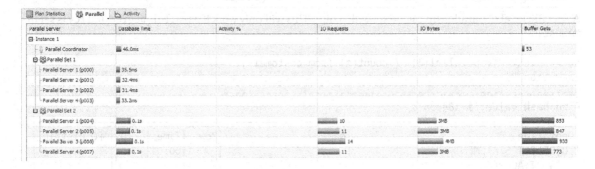

Figure 13-3. *The Parallel section of the SQL Monitor report*

Notice how the Parallel section of the SQL Monitor report shows 4 slaves (blue and red) and shows how much work each is doing. You can see that for parallel slave set 2 that each slave set is doing roughly the same amount of work. This is good.

What Can Go Wrong?

Swamping

One problem you can encounter with parallelism is setting the slave count too high. In such a case you could overwhelm the server very quickly. Data sets are so huge these days that even a powerful Exadata server may find it cannot cope with the settings. In such cases you need only reduce parallel_max_servers.

Over Parallelizing

Even on a server that is not overloaded with too many parallel slaves the distribution method might be wrong or the slave count forced could result in some slaves working hard while others are idle, which essentially serializes the query and results in nowhere near the performance improvements expected.

Wrong Distribution Method

Sometimes in 11g the optimizer may not choose the best distribution method between the senders and the receivers. The HYBRID HASH distribution method makes the choice for the distribution method at the time of the collection so it can avoid this problem.

How to Influence Parallelism

There are two main modes of controlling parallelism. You can either set `parallel_degree_policy` to AUTO, in which case the decisions are made automatically (see the section below), or you can take varying degrees of manual control. If the estimated elapsed time is going to be less than `parallel_min_time_threshold` then parallel execution is not considered. Then based on the CPU and I/O resources available the DOP is calculated. To limit the DOP, so that it does not get too large the DOP will always have a value less than `parallel_degree_limit`. The default DOP is calculated from the formula

```
parallel_threads_per_Cpu * sum(cpu_count)
```

How to Influence It at the Query Level (Hints)

A specific level of parallelism can be set with a hint. This will only work if `parallel_degree_policy` is set to MANUAL.

```
SQL> select /*+ parallel(4) */ count(*) from customers;
Execution Plan
-----------------------------------------------------------
Plan hash value: 1718497476
```

							Id
Operation	Name	Rows	Time	TQ	PQ Distrib
0	SELECT STATEMENT		1	00:01			
1	SORT AGGREGATE		1				
2	PX COORDINATOR						
3	PX SEND QC (RANDOM)	:TQ10000	1		Q1,00	QC(RAND)	
4	SORT AGGREGATE		1		Q1,00		
5	PX BLOCK ITERATOR		55500	00:01	Q1,00		
6	BITMAP CONVERSION COUNT		55500	00:01	Q1,00		
7	BITMAP INDEX FAST FULL SCAN	CUSTOMERS_GENDER_BIX			Q1,00		

```
Note
-----
   -    Degree of Parallelism is 4 because of hint

Parallel index hint
```

You can set the default level of parallelism by specifying /*+ parallel(default) */.

How to Influence Parallelism at the Session Level

By default Oracle has parallel SQL enabled, but you can also enable parallel DML with the following statement.

```
SQL> alter session enable parallel dml;
```

The above statement sets the default degree of parallelism. To set a non-default value use a value in the statement

```
SQL> alter session force parallel query parallel 8;
```

How to Influence Parallelism at the DDL Level

```
SQL> alter table customers parallel default
SQL> select degree, instances from dba_tables where table_name='CUSTOMERS' and owner='SH';
```

A fixed degree of parallelism can be set like this:

```
SQL> alter table customers parallel 8;
SQL> alter table sales parallel 8;
```

How Do You Control Parallelism at the System Level?

Controlling the amount of parallelism at the system level is easy if you set the required parameters. If you set parallel_degree_policy to AUTO, you have to do almost nothing. When set to AUTO the parallelism is controlled for you and the maximum and minimum number of slaves are controlled with

1. parallel_degree_policy – Can be "AUTO", "LIMITED", "ADAPTIVE" or "MANUAL". When set to MANUAL AUTO is disabled and you set the parallelism. When set to AUTO the parallelism is automatically calculated. The following parameters can be adjusted to change the behavior.

2. db_big_table_cache_percent_target – The threshold that controls the point at which 'big' tables are to automatically use the in-memory option.

3. parallel_min_time_threshold - Default value is "AUTO." Controls the point at which Oracle will automatically parallelize an SQL statement. The default for this parameter is 10 seconds. If this estimated elapsed time for the statement, based on parsing is over this threshold parallel execution will be chosen.

4. parallel_degree_limit – Default value is "CPU," which means the DOP is limited by the DOP of the system, which is calculated by (parallel_threads_per_cpu x SUM (CPU_COUNT). The upper limit for parallel execution is DOP. This can also be set to a specific value.

5. parallel_threads_per_cpu – This should be set to 1 for Exadata systems.

6. parallel_automatic_tuning – With a value of TRUE the DOP is calculated for you.

7. `parallel_adaptive_multi_user` – If set to true, this setting will, in a multiuser environment reduce the level of parallelism to reduce load on the system if the system is overloaded at the time of the start of the query.

8. `paralle_degree_level` – Defaults to 100. Can be used to control the level of parallelism by reducing it by half (50) or doubling it (200).

9. `parallel_degree_limit` - The maximum degree of parallelism used when Auto DOP is enabled. If you are using Auto DOP, ensure that the setting of this parameter does not limit the requested degree of parallelism. For example, if this parameter is set to a value of 16, no operation running under Auto DOP will be capable of allocating more parallel execution servers, irrespective of the size of the operation.

10. `parallel_execution_message_size` - The message buffer size used for communication between parallel execution servers. This parameter should be set to 16K. A larger message size will reduce the overhead of message packing and exchange. This is the default beginning with Oracle Database 11g Release 2.

11. `parallel_force_local` – Forces execution of all slaves to be local. Also see parallel_instance_group.

12. `parallel_instance_group` – Controls which nodes in a RAC system can be used for spawning parallel slaves.

13. `parallel_io_cap_enabled` – Defaults to `false`. When set to true it controls the degree of parallelism to a level that the I/O system can deliver. You must use `dbms_resource_manager.calibrate_io` for this to work.

14. `parallel_max_servers` - Controls the maximum number of parallel execution servers that are provided by an instance; this number will never be exceeded. Note that in a Real Application Clusters environment, the total number of available processes in the cluster is the sum of all parallel_max_servers settings. Leave this parameter as it is set by default by the Oracle database.

15. `parallel_min_percent`. – This controls whether you receive an error message or not when you request a certain degree of parallelism and you do not at least receive this percentage of it. For example if you set this parameter to 10 (10%) and you run a query with a requested parallelism of 128 and the system can only deliver 8 then you will receive an error. If you could receive a DOP of 16 you will not get an error.

16. `parallel_min_servers` - Controls the minimal number of parallel execution servers that are spawned at instance startup and made available all the time. Note that in a Real Application Clusters environment, the total number of processes in the cluster that are spawned at startup time is the sum of all parallel_min_servers settings. To ensure the startup of a single parallel load can occur without a delay for process allocation, you should set this value to a minimum of 2* `CPU_COUNT`.

17. `parallel_server_limit` - When using Auto DOP, the maximum number of parallel execution servers that can be used before statement queuing kicks in. When Auto DOP is used exclusively, then this parameter should be set close to PARALLEL_MAX_SERVERS, for example 90%+ of its value.

Calculating Auto DOP

If your SQL serial estimated elapsed time is greater than parallel_min_time_threshold (default 10 seconds) then a parallel plan will be considered by calculating the degree of parallelism. Once parallel processing is considered the optimizer has to work out how fast the system can process the data. In 12c this is based on the v$optimizer_processing_rate view (in 11g the processing rate was based only on I/O processing speed – which you can get from DBA_RSRC_IO_CALIBRATE. In 11g if you have not done I/O calibration this table will not be populated and you will not use Auto DOP and you will see a message on your execution plan notes like this:

```
automatic DOP: skipped because of IO calibrate statistics are missing
```

Unless you manually set the values in resource_io_calibrate$ with a statement like this:

```
SQL> delete from resource_io_calibrate$;
SQL> insert into resource_io_calibrate$ values (trunc(sysdate), trunc(sysdate), 0,0,
200,0,0);
```

The number 200 is a reasonable value for a fast system. If statistics are not missing then Auto DOP will be calculated. The degree of parallelism will then be calculated based on the largest table scanned in the execution plan.

In 12c the need to collect I/O calibration statistics has been removed. Now if those statistics are missing, default values will be used for processing rates and the CPU will also be taken into account. This additional information is kept in v$optimizer_processing_rate, which has values for IO_BYTES_PER_SEC, CPU_BYTES_PER_SEC and CPU_ROWS_PER_SEC.

The default values for these settings are

```
IO_BYTES_PER_SEC=200
CPU_BYTES_PER_SEC=1000
CPU_ROWS_PER_SEC=1000000
```

Because the method to calculate the DOP uses more variables and considers each line of the plan (rather than the line with the scan in it – like 11g) the DOP for 12c will tend to be higher than 11g.

Summary

Parallel execution is not suitable for every environment or for every data set. Oracle has built-in rules to take care of these various cases, but the control levers for parallel execution can be somewhat confusing. Hopefully the choices are somewhat clearer now. We briefly touched on SQL Monitor reports in this chapter and how useful they are; in the next chapter we dig a little more into the SQL Monitor report and what it is useful for.

CHAPTER 14

■ ■ ■

SQL Monitor Active Reports

Why is SQL Monitor so great?

In days long past the best tool for tuning SQL was the humble 10046 trace, and it's still useful today, but other tools have been developed over the years, to give us the high level picture with some deep dives when needed. Not least of which is SQLTXPLAIN. SQL Monitor has been around for a while but in 12c it has been improved and is now especially useful for parallel execution.

10046 is useful because it tells us what has actually happened. Not what we think is going to happen. The same applies to SQL Monitor. If we have an execution plan with hundreds of lines or even thousands of lines we cannot be expected to debug the performance quickly if we don't have some method of triage which helps us zoom in to the problem lines.

The key lines that affect performance are easily identifiable in a SQL monitor report. In figure 14-1 , which line do you think is worth investigating?

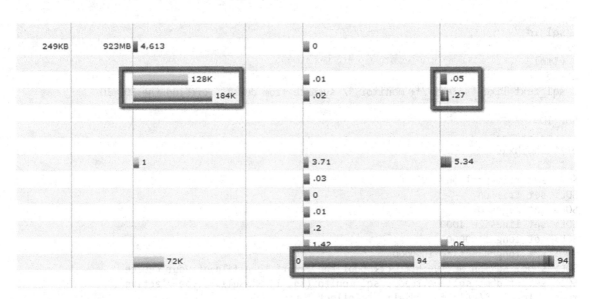

Figure 14-1. *Where to start looking on a SQL Monitor active report*

I've only show a small part of the report, because I want to emphasize how you start an analysis. We could for example be convinced that there is some kind of I/O problem and be concentrating on the lines in the area highlighted in the top left hand corner of the diagram. This column is called "IO Requests". Although

© Stelios Charalambides 2017
S. Charalambides, *Oracle SQL Tuning with Oracle SQLTXPLAIN*, DOI 10.1007/978-1-4842-2436-6_14

these lines are doing the bulk of the I/O if we look at the highlighted area on the top right of the diagram we see that these activities are only .05 and 0.27 % of the wait time. The right most column is Wait Activity and the next column to the left is CPU activity. Now we know that whatver is happening to this SQL, it is spending time on the bottom line in this report. This does not mean the problem is with this line, you have to look at what this line is doing and determine if what it is doing is based on good statistics based on what you understand about the query. Think of SQL monitor active reports as the SQL tuning equivalent of AWR. Just like AWR tells you where to look for performance generally; SQL or system, memory or I/O, CPU, so SQL monitor tells you where to look in the SQL so that you don't waste time tuning SQL in ways which make no difference to the real world experience. So now lets look at how we get these reports.

How can you get SQL Monitor?

The first thing to realize is that a SQL monitor report can be collected as long as the SQL statement has executed at least once. It can be collected during the run of the statement or after the run of the statement. As we saw in figure 14-1 above, the report makes it very easy to identify which lines in the plan need investigation. Writing (and maintaining) scripts to query v$ views to gather information is not needed. Nor do we need to enable tracing to do this.

There are essentially three ways you can get these reports. The first and easiest is to use the direct method

```
SQL> select /*+ monitor */ sysdate from dual; <<< monitor hint added to the SQL
SYSDATE
---------
15-NOV-16

SQL> select
  sql_id
from
  v$sql
where
  sql_text like 'select /*+ monitor */ sysdate from dual%'; <<<Find the SQL ID


SQL_ID
-------------
9f7ttbh69hxxu


SQL> set trimspool on
SQL> set trim on
SQL> set pages 0
SQL> set linesize 1000
SQL> set long 1000000
SQL> set longchunksize 1000000
SQL> spool sqlmon_active.html <<<Spool the report to a file of your choice
SQL> select dbms_sqltune.report_sql_monitor(sql_id=>'&sqlid',type=>'active',
report_level=>'ALL') from dual; <<<Collect the report
SQL> spool off
```

This is the first, and my favored way of getting the SQL monitor active report. The second is to use the Oracle Enterprise Manager to select the SQL while it is running and request that a report be generated. This is done in the obvious way from the Performance tab (see figure 14-2 below).

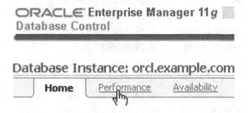

Figure 14-2. *Go to the OEM Performance tab*

Then select "SQL Monitoring" from the "Additional Monitoring Links" section

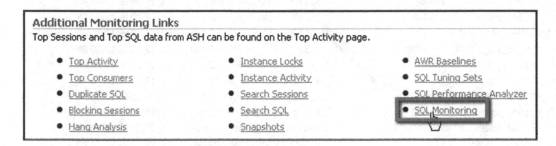

Figure 14-3. *Choose SQL Monitoring*

In the SQL Monitoring section you will see the SQLs you can monitor and the details shows the SQL Active monitoring for them.

The third method and the best is to collet a SQLT report. SQLT collects the monitor report for you.

query1.sql	3 KB	SQL File	6/19/2016 11:45 AM
sqlt_s81546_10046_10053_execute.trc	45,515 KB	TRC File	6/19/2016 12:34 PM
sqlt_s81546_10046_execute.trc	45,519 KB	TRC File	6/19/2016 12:35 PM
sqlt_s81546_10053_execute.trc	2 KB	TRC File	6/19/2016 12:35 PM
sqlt_s81546_10053_explain.trc	140 KB	TRC File	6/19/2016 12:30 PM
sqlt_s81546_addmrpt_0007.zip	29 KB	Compressed (zippe…	6/19/2016 12:31 PM
sqlt_s81546_ashrpt_0009.zip	24 KB	Compressed (zippe…	6/19/2016 12:31 PM
sqlt_s81546_awrrpt_0007.zip	567 KB	Compressed (zippe…	6/19/2016 12:31 PM
sqlt_s81546_cell_state.zip	1 KB	Compressed (zippe…	6/19/2016 12:35 PM
sqlt_s81546_driver.zip	15 KB	Compressed (zippe…	6/19/2016 12:35 PM
sqlt_s81546_lite.html	485 KB	Chrome HTML Docu…	6/19/2016 12:30 PM
sqlt_s81546_log.zip	1,793 KB	Compressed (zippe…	6/19/2016 12:35 PM
sqlt_s81546_main.html	7,726 KB	Chrome HTML Docu…	6/19/2016 12:30 PM
sqlt_s81546_opatch.zip	563 KB	Compressed (zippe…	6/19/2016 12:35 PM
sqlt_s81546_px_trca_35156.html	4,461 KB	Chrome HTML Docu…	6/19/2016 12:35 PM
sqlt_s81546_px_trca_35156.log	320 KB	Text Document	6/19/2016 12:35 PM
sqlt_s81546_px_trca_35156.txt	2,268 KB	Text Document	6/19/2016 12:35 PM
sqlt_s81546_readme.html	19 KB	Chrome HTML Docu…	6/19/2016 12:30 PM
sqlt_s81546_sql_detail_active.html	1,648 KB	Chrome HTML Docu…	6/19/2016 12:30 PM
sqlt_s81546_sql_monitor.html	2,192 KB	Chrome HTML Docu…	6/19/2016 12:30 PM
sqlt_s81546_sql_monitor.txt	924 KB	Text Document	6/19/2016 12:30 PM
sqlt_s81546_sql_monitor_active.html	1,420 KB	Chrome HTML Docu…	6/19/2016 12:30 PM
sqlt_s81546_sqldx.zip	2,828 KB	Compressed (zippe…	6/19/2016 12:37 PM
sqlt_s81546_tc.zip	3,045 KB	Compressed (zippe…	6/19/2016 12:35 PM
sqlt_s81546_tcb.zip	6 KB	Compressed (zippe…	6/19/2016 12:31 PM
sqlt_s81546_tcx.zip	132 KB	Compressed (zippe…	6/19/2016 12:35 PM
sqlt_s81546_tkprof_nosort.txt	153 KB	Text Document	6/19/2016 12:35 PM
sqlt_s81546_tkprof_sort.txt	153 KB	Text Document	6/19/2016 12:35 PM
sqlt_s81546_trc.zip	20,585 KB	Compressed (zippe…	6/19/2016 12:35 PM
sqlt_s81546_trca_e35157.html	958 KB	Chrome HTML Docu…	6/19/2016 12:35 PM
sqlt_s81546_trca_e35157.log	22 KB	Text Document	6/19/2016 12:35 PM
sqlt_s81546_trca_e35157.txt	480 KB	Text Document	6/19/2016 12:35 PM
sqlt_s81546_xecute.zip	36,283 KB	Compressed (zippe…	6/19/2016 2:51 PM
sqlt_s81546_xpand.sql	3 KB	SQL File	6/19/2016 12:31 PM

Figure 14-4. The SQL monitor report is collected for you by SQLT

You can look at the report directly as an HTML report or you can click on the "Monitor ACTIVE report" on the main SQLT page. See Figure 14-5 below.

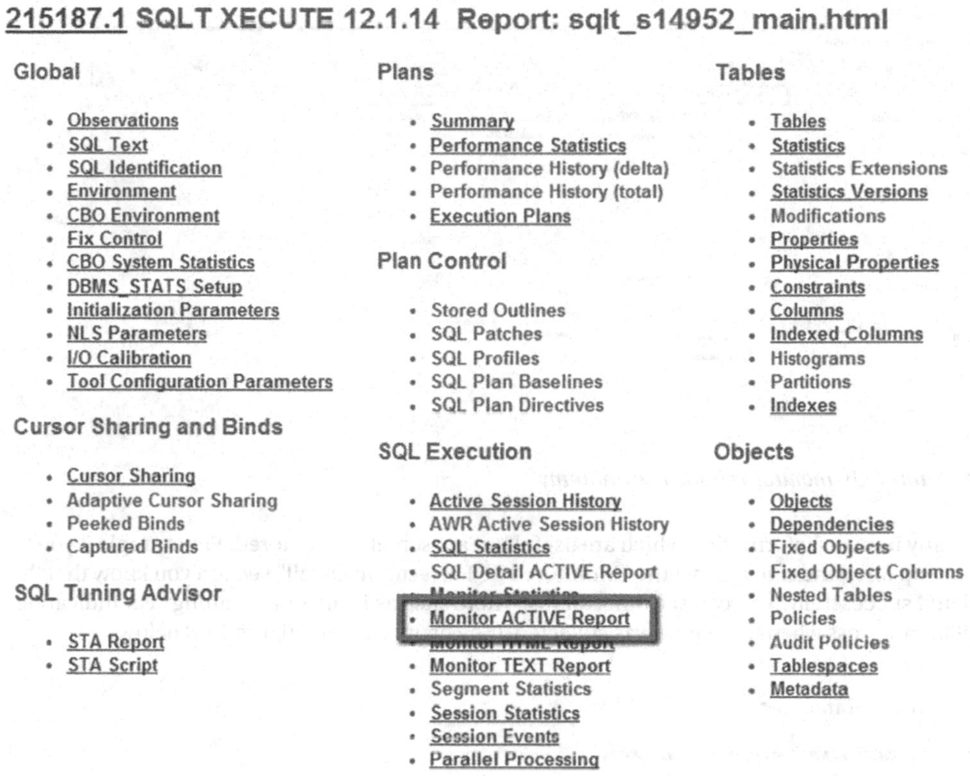

215187.1 SQLT XECUTE 12.1.14 Report: sqlt_s14952_main.html

Global

- Observations
- SQL Text
- SQL Identification
- Environment
- CBO Environment
- Fix Control
- CBO System Statistics
- DBMS_STATS Setup
- Initialization Parameters
- NLS Parameters
- I/O Calibration
- Tool Configuration Parameters

Cursor Sharing and Binds

- Cursor Sharing
- Adaptive Cursor Sharing
- Peeked Binds
- Captured Binds

SQL Tuning Advisor

- STA Report
- STA Script

Plans

- Summary
- Performance Statistics
- Performance History (delta)
- Performance History (total)
- Execution Plans

Plan Control

- Stored Outlines
- SQL Patches
- SQL Profiles
- SQL Plan Baselines
- SQL Plan Directives

SQL Execution

- Active Session History
- AWR Active Session History
- SQL Statistics
- SQL Detail ACTIVE Report
- Monitor Statistics
- Monitor ACTIVE Report
- Monitor HTML Report
- Monitor TEXT Report
- Segment Statistics
- Session Statistics
- Session Events
- Parallel Processing

Tables

- Tables
- Statistics
- Statistics Extensions
- Statistics Versions
- Modifications
- Properties
- Physical Properties
- Constraints
- Columns
- Indexed Columns
- Histograms
- Partitions
- Indexes

Objects

- Objects
- Dependencies
- Fixed Objects
- Fixed Object Columns
- Nested Tables
- Policies
- Audit Policies
- Tablespaces
- Metadata

Figure 14-5. *SQLT knows about SQL Monitor*

So once you have your report wha do they look like? They can look very busy and confusing, but there really are some very simple things to look for. Lets see.

What do reports look like?

From the example above "select sysdate from dual" we got this very simple report (see figure 14-6). This is a simple SQL and so the report is also simple, but I show it here because I want to explain the anatomy of the report.

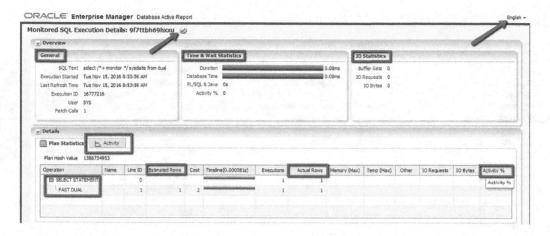

Figure 14-6. *A simple SQL monitor report. The anatomy*

There are many items of information which are useful but are sometimes ignored. For example if you see the tick in the top left hand side against the "Monitored SQL Execution Detail" section you know that the SQL has completed successfully. You can see other statuses here such as Error, or a spinning gear indicating the SQL was still in progress when the report was collected. (See figure 14-7 and figure 14-8 below).

Figure 14-7. *This SQL failed before completion*

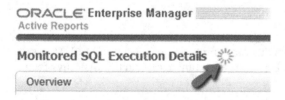

Figure 14-8. *This SQL is still running*

As an added bonus you can select the language of the report (see top right of figure 14-6).

Then we have the "General" section which covers the SQL text and some broad statistics about the SQL such the Start time and the user who executed the SQL. Then in the Time & Wait Statistics we see the overall statistics for the execution such as the Duration of the SQL (in this case only 0.08 seconds). This is a very simple SQL statement so there is not much activity on the database. When we get to more complex SQLs we'll see that this section breask down the activity into the different classes. The main tabs in this case are Plan Statistics, which shows the plan steps and Activity which shows the activity in a timeline fashion so that you can see which resources were used as the plan was executed.

The plan statistics also has all the usual information needed for tuning, such as Estimated Rows, Actual Rows, and percentage activity. Let's look at a slightly more complex example now. See Figure 14-9. In this next example we only have a DOP of 8, but a much longer SQL statement.

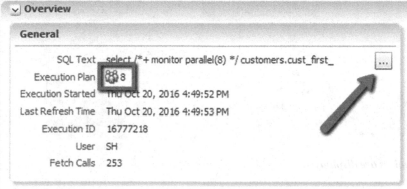

Figure 14-9. Parallel execution DOP shown and more details can be seen

In the example we see that a parallel execution was used and that it was set at 8. We also see that there is a button we can press to get more details about the SQL. In Figure 14-10 we can see what happens when we click on the details button.

SQL Text

```
LENGTH(REPLACE(:7 ,'>','')) + 1            )
and              SH.SERVREQ_EVENT_TYPE_ID IN   (          SELECT
TRIM(      SUBSTR(       txt1,           INSTR(txt1, '>', 1, LEVEL) + 1,
INSTR(txt1, '>', 1, LEVEL + 1) - INSTR(txt1, '>', 1, LEVEL) - 1      )      )
as token1            FROM    (     SELECT      '>'||:8 ||'>' txt1
FROM     DUAL    )     connect by LEVEL <= LENGTH(:9 ) -
LENGTH(REPLACE(:10 ,'>','')) + 1          )
AND              ROWNUM <= :11 + 1                 ORDER
BY SH.SERVREQ_TRANSACTION_TS DESC
```

Show SQL Binds   Save   OK

Figure 14-10. The details page gives us a number of options

This gives us the option to look at the value of the bind variables and optionally save them with the "Save" button. See the next figure (14-11).

SQL Binds

Position ▲	Name	Value	Type
1	:1	78720C0F010101	TIMESTAMP as HEXDUMP
2	:2	7873060F183C3C3B8B87C0	TIMESTAMP as HEXDUMP
3	:3	ES7903	VARCHAR2(128)
4	:4	22	NUMBER
6	:6	3>10	VARCHAR2(128)
7	:7	3>10	VARCHAR2(128)

Save   OK

Figure 14-11. *The bind variables are displpayed*

If you click the save button either on this detail screen or on the previous screen you can save the SQL with the bind variables embeded. See the following figure (Figure 14-12).

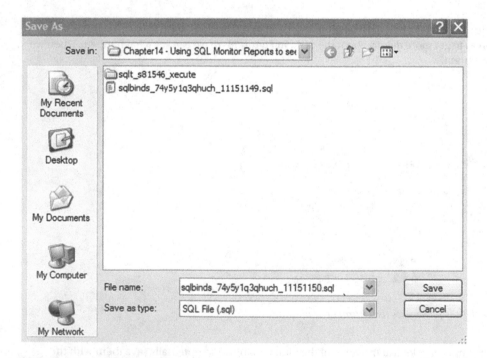

Figure 14-12. *The save button for the SQL bind variables*

The file sqlbinds_74y5y1q3qhuch_11151149.sql contains the following.

```
-- ============================================================================ --
-- This file is generated by EM Database
   Express.                                        --
-- The SQL bind variables, if any, will be declared
   below.                                          --
-- ============================================================================ --
-- Note: If bind names were invalid SQL identifiers, then the bind variables may have been
   renamed below. --
declare
    74y5y1q3qhuch_bind1     TIMESTAMP              := 78720C0F010101;  -- HEXDUMP
    74y5y1q3qhuch_bind2     TIMESTAMP              := 7873060F183C3C3B8B87C0;  -- HEXDUMP
    74y5y1q3qhuch_bind3     VARCHAR2(128)          := '99999';
    74y5y1q3qhuch_bind4     NUMBER                 := 22;
    74y5y1q3qhuch_bind6     VARCHAR2(128)          := '30';
    74y5y1q3qhuch_bind7     VARCHAR2(128)          := '310';
    74y5y1q3qhuch_bind9     VARCHAR2(128)          := '18';
    74y5y1q3qhuch_bind10    VARCHAR2(128)          := '18';
    74y5y1q3qhuch_bind11    NUMBER                 := 50;
begin
    --
    SELECT
```

I have not shown the rest of the SQL text because the important part is the bind variables which have been captured. Apart from the SQL text we also have the time and wait statistics and I/O metrics. In figure 14-13, we see the total duration and the different parts of the database time spent on the query.

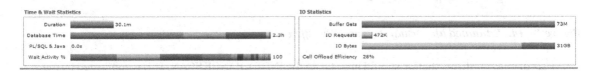

Figure 14-13. *Database, wait and I/O statistics*

These sections give you an overall idea of where time was spent in the query. In this case the duration was 30.1 minutes (with database time of 2.3 hours, due to the parallel execution) where most of the time was spent on the left most section of the stacked bar, which "cluster" waits. We also see I/O statistics and if on Exadata some cell offload efficiency. In this case 28%.

There is also the Details section of the report which shows the execution lines and various metrics for each of the lines in the plan. In figure 14-14, I've only shown the left side and compressed come of the columns for clarity. We see that one line shows Estimated Rows and Actual Rows to be widely different.

Operation	N...	Line ID	Estimated Rows	Cost	Timelin...	E...	Actual Rows
⊟ SELECT STATEMENT		0				1	0
⊟ SORT ORDER BY		1	1	14		1	0
⊟ COUNT STOPKEY		2				1	0
⊟ FILTER		3				1	0
⊟ HASH JOIN		4	1	13		1	0
⊟ NESTED LOOPS OUTER		5	1	11		1	0
⊟ HASH JOIN		6	1	10		1	0
⊟ MERGE JOIN CARTESIAN		7	1	9		1	0
⊟ MERGE JOIN CARTESIAN		8	1	6		1	1
⊟ VIEW	VW_N	9	1	3		1	1
⊟ HASH UNIQUE		10	1	3		1	1
⊟ CONNECT BY WITHOUT FILTERING (UNIQUE)		11				1	6
FAST DUAL		12	1	2		1	1
⊟ BUFFER SORT		13	1	6		1	1
⊟ VIEW	VW_N	14	1	3		1	2
⊟ HASH UNIQUE		15	1	3		1	2
⊟ CONNECT BY WITHOUT FILTERING (UNIQUE)		16				1	2
FAST DUAL		17	1	2		1	1
⊟ BUFFER SORT		18	1	6		1	0
⊟ SORT UNIQUE		19	1	3		1	0
⊟ PARTITION RANGE ITERATOR		20	1	3		1	0
⊟ TABLE ACCESS BY LOCAL INDEX ROWID BATC...	SERVF	21	1	3		2	0
INDEX RANGE SCAN	PK_SE	22	5	2		2	11M
⊟ PARTITION RANGE ITERATOR		23	1	1		0	0
⊟ TABLE ACCESS BY LOCAL INDEX ROWID BATCHED	SERVF	24	1	1		0	0

Figure 14-14. *Estimated and Actual rows are very different*

This display confirms that we should investigate the INDEX RANGE SCAN. This is confirmed by the right hand side of the report (see Figure 14-15) which shows that most of the time was spent on this line and the preceding line.

⊟ SORT UNIQUE		19	1	3		1	0		
⊟ PARTITION RANGE ITERATOR		20	1	3		1	0		
⊟ TABLE ACCESS BY LOCAL INDEX ROWID BATC...	SERVF	21	1	3		2	0	1.. 9...	26
INDEX RANGE SCAN	PK_SE	22	5	2		2	11M	6.. 4...	24

Figure 14-15. *The INDEX RANGE SCAN line is indeed where most of the time was spent*

Once we have this kind of high level information we can go and investigate these lines, with SQLT and look at the statistics on these lines and see why the estimates were so far out. If you have large complex plans it is sometimes useful to expand and collapse parts of the plan by clicking on the "-" and "+" lines of the Operation field. If your plan is over 300 lines long by default you will not get all the plan lines unless you set "_sqlmon_max_planlines" to a higher number. Here is one with many of the lines collapsed.

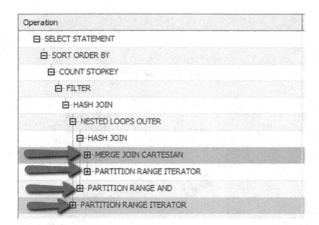

Figure 14-16. *Expandable plans*

In the "Details" section there are sometimes different tabs, depending on the query, which allow access to more details

1. Plan Statistics – This section shows the plan and associated details.

2. This shows the plan in either tabular or graphical form and also shows predicate details.

3. Parallel – Shows parallel details including slave activity and work distribution

4. Activity – Shows the work of the query in a time line and its use of resources along that time line.

5. Metrics – Shows the work usage by the query along the time line.

Below in figures 14-17 to 14-21, I show each of these screens. For general information.

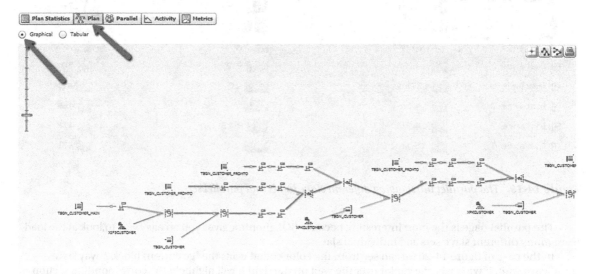

Figure 14-17. *Plan screen in graphical form*

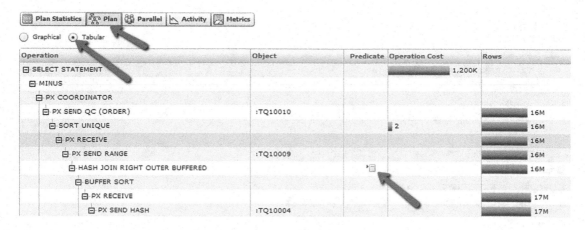

Figure 14-18. *Plan information in tabular form showing predicate links*

If you hover over the Predicate information link you will see details relating to the predicate for that line in the plan. If a filter is also used this will also be shown.

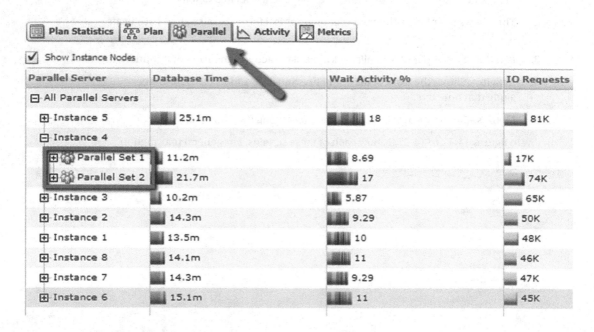

Figure 14-19. *The parallel tab showing different slave loads and parallel sets*

The parallel page is the most interesting because SQL monitor gives you an easy way to look at the load from many different slave sets and individual slaves.

In the case of figure 14-20 we can see from the color coded waits the "gc current block 2-way" is a significant wait. If we hover the cursor over the wait on the right it will highlight the corresponding section of the chart on the right. We can also see on the metrics tab shown in figure 14-21 the system resources used over time.

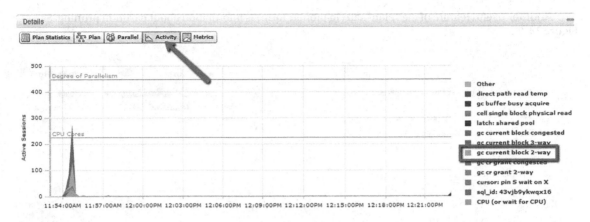

Figure 14-20. *The activity tab shows the wait type detail*

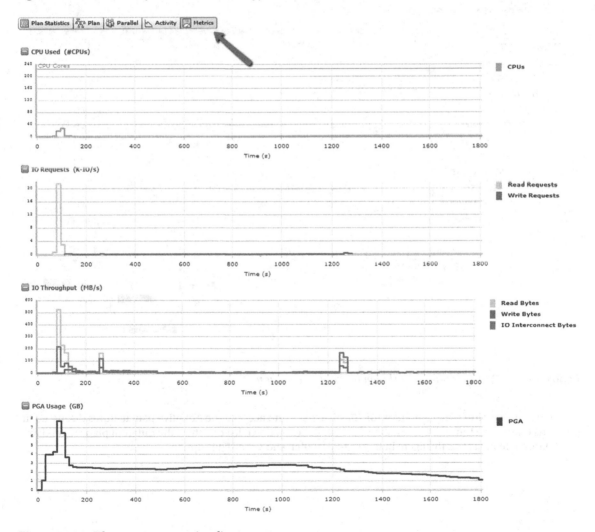

Figure 14-21. *The resource usage time line*

Another useful feature of the "Plan" tab (in tabular form) is information about partition pruning. See Figure 14-22.

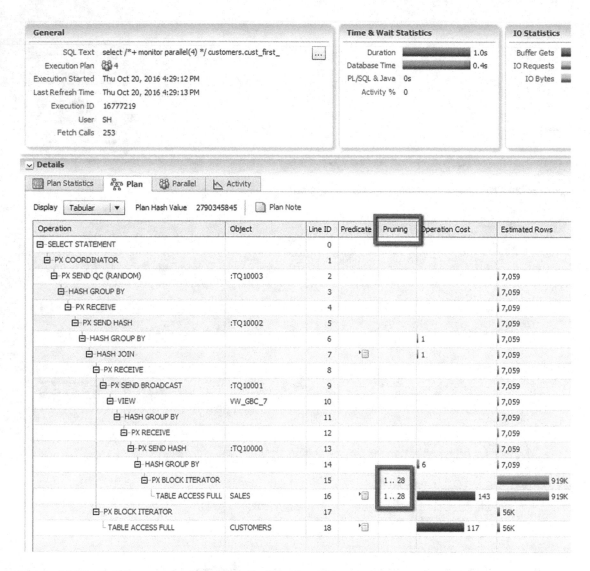

Figure 14-22. Partition pruning is shown in the "Plan" section

This new version of SQL Monitor for 12c also takes into account the Adaptive plan features discussed in previous chapters. Under the "Plan Statistics" tab the drop down list can show the different plans related to the Adaptive feature. See the figure below (14-23) which show the "Full" option.

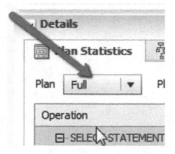

Figure 14-23. *Adaptive options for the plan display*

The different options are:

1. FINAL – This is the plan finally chosen without the failed adaptive lines shown, which are shown as crossed out in SQLT.

2. FULL – This is the full plan with the failed lines shown as greyed out.

Now that we know what SQL monitor can show us we can look at some specific parallel features and how we can spot these with SQL Monitor.

SQL Monitor and Parallel execution

In the previous chapter we dealt with parallel execution and how it could be influenced, and what it was, and some aspects of how it can go wrong. In this chapter because SQL Monitor is by far the best tool to analyze parallel execution we'll also cover some of the ways in which SQL Monitor can help with other aspects of problems with parallel execution. In this next figure (Figure 14-24) we see that the number of parallel slaves was downgraded from the original expected number. This can be dealt with by reviewing your parallel settings at the parallel slave level (see the previous chapter for the server parameters that influence this).

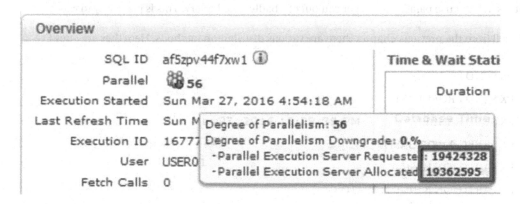

Figure 14-24. *The red down arrow shows that the DOP was downgraded*

If we hover the cursor over the downgraded icon we see the true numbers for the parallel servers. The reason for the downgrade is shown under "Other Statistics" on the plan page (see figure 14-25).

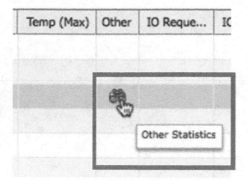

Figure 14-25. *Other statistics can show the downgrade reason*

Here are the possible values

- 351 – DOP downgrade due to adaptive DOP.
- 352 – DOP downgrade due to resource manager max DOP
- 353 – DROP downgrade due to insufficient number of processes
- 354 – DOP downgrade because slaves failed to join

You can also get this information from this query

```
SQL> select qksxareasons , indx from x$qksxa_reason where qksxareasons like
'%DOP downgrade%';
```

Based on these values you can investigate why the action was taken. For example 354 will prompt you to determine why the slaves failed to join.

Apart from the usual tuning problems (cardinality estimates, statistics, etc) parallel execution can also go wrong in the distribution methods. Remember to tune the query first as if it was serial then tune the parallel aspects. Do not use parallelism to get you out of a badly tuned query. This is just a way to waste resources.

If you recall from the previous chapter there are various distribution methods. Here they are ones I've found so far.

1. PX SEND HASH

2. PX SEND BROADCAST

3. PX SEND RANGE

4. PX SEND HYBRID HASH

5. PX PARTITION HASH ALL

6. PX PARTITION RANGE ITERATOR

7. PX PARTITON HASH JOIN_FILTER

We'll talk only about the first two as those have well known problems which we can mention.

Uneven work distribution

Uneven work distribution is the first sign that something about the parallel operation is not as good as it could be. If all the slaves are working efficiently together and all finish their work at about the same time you are more likely to have a good plan. If one slave is working while all the other slaves have finished long ago, the final result will be delayed. So look at the "Parallel" tab and look for a single slave or possibly a number of slaves (a few compared to the total) which are working for much longer than the other slaves. Based on the step in the plan look at what the slave is doing and understand what data is being accessed.

Bad cardinality

HASH DISTRIBUTION – If you see uneven workload distribution and a HASH distribution method, it could be because the optimizer thinks the table is bigger than it actually is. In this case Estimated rows is higher than Actual rows and the HASH method becomes inefficient, with one slave doing too much work while other slaves are waiting. The solution to this is to fix the statistics on those tables.

BROADCAST DISTRIBUTION – If you see uneven workload distribution and a BROADCAST method you most likely have the opposite situation for the same reason, i.e. a low estimated number of rows but a higher Actual number of rows leading to uneven workload distribution method. The solution is the same as above.

Skewness

If estimated and actual cardinalities are now widely different and you are are still seeing uneven work distribution then the reason is most likely to be skewed data. In such cases because of the filter or join one slave is doing more work than the others. The best solution for this is to use the new 12c distribution method HYBRID HASH. Skewness can be found on both the source side and the distribution side. The source side is the data being used for the query. The distribution is the data distribution after the data is broadcase to the parallel consumers. In 12c (12.1.0.1) this is handled by Skew handling on both the input and the output side of the parallel slaves.

Summary

In this chapter we covered the use of SQL Monitor and how to read it. It is so useful that SQLT will collect SQLT active reports by default if it can and put the link for it right there on the main report. Parallel execution can be daunting to fix when it goes wrong, but if you can look at the big picture and focus on those aspects which are wrong, parallel tuning is just as easy as any other tuning. SQL monitor is especially useful because it tells you what really happened, just like 10046 trace, but is much easier to navigate and interpret. In the next chapter we look at Dataguard and its special circumstances.

CHAPTER 15

∎∎∎

Using SQLTXPLAIN with an Active Data Guard Environment

SQLTXPLAIN is a great tool designed to help with SQL tuning problems, but its effectiveness is limited when the database is a read-only Data Guard physical standby database. Read only databases like Data Guard physical standby databases cannot be written to utilities such as SQLTXPLAIN. In this chapter we explore the special tools created just to deal with Data Guard.

Data Guard Physical Standby Database

Data Guard is a piece of technology, developed by Oracle in response to a "what if" scenario. What if my data center is completely wiped out by flooding? What if a fire destroys the building my database is housed in? Traditionally this has been answered by timely backups, shipped offsite, and stored in a secure location that can then be accessed within an agreed time scale and restored to backup hardware made available at another site (presumably a site not in the disaster zone). This strategy had many difficulties: taking the backup, shipping the backup to a safe location, getting the right backup from the secure location, re-creating your systems with the use of the backup and your restore procedures, and finally getting access to those systems for the staff required to use them. Finally and most important, you need to test these procedures on a regular basis; otherwise come the day of the disaster you may have all the data and equipment, but you'll have no idea how to put it all together to make a working system. Of course, this restore procedure can take a considerable amount of time. You have tested your recovery procedure, haven't you? One site I worked with took this so seriously that on the day of the test, they would go around and put red stickers on people and equipment and tell the people they were not available for this test (presumably they had been abducted by the aliens in the "Aliens abduct your data center" scenario). It was hard to test these scenarios; and not surprisingly, many sites did not do adequate testing and crossed their IT fingers and hoped for the best.

Data Guard makes preserving your data site much simpler. All of the aforementioned complications can potentially be eliminated. The technology that makes Data Guard physical standby work is in concept very simple. The archive logs (or redo logs) that track every change in your database are transferred by special processes on your source system to special processes on the standby system, where the changes are applied, block by block, to a copy of your source database. This process called propagation can apply data on the standby database. The data can be applied in lock step with the primary database or it can lag behind the primary database by a preset amount. You can even have multiple standby databases all collecting changes from the primary database. One of the more interesting features to me is the new 12c Far Sync instance feature that allows you to have a standby database, in maximum protection mode, over any distance. With Data Guard active standby, you can even allow the failover (the process whereby the primary fails and the standby has to take over) to happen with the minimum of fuss.

© Stelios Charalambides 2017
S. Charalambides, *Oracle SQL Tuning with Oracle SQLTXPLAIN*, DOI 10.1007/978-1-4842-2436-6_15

Data Guard is a huge leap forward in disaster-recovery technology. Complete coverage goes well beyond the scope of this book; but a basic, high-level understanding of the tool is useful.

■ **Note** I could not hope to cover any more than the briefest details of Data Guard here. It is a book-length topic by itself. The latest book is entitled *Oracle Data Guard 11g Handbook* by Larry Carpenter et. al. (Oracle Press, 2009).

Suffice it to say that Oracle Data Guard Physical Standby allows the data center to be online all of the time. There is no downtime. Naturally you still need backups for those pesky systematic errors (you deleted the wrong data). Data Guard makes your testing scenario much simpler. Now you need only carry out a switchover (a controlled switch of the computer roles as opposed to the failover), and once the switchover is complete you can start your testing immediately.

Since 11g release 1, Oracle's Active Data Guard's read-only mode (which requires an additional license) allowed reports to run on the standby database. Many sites found that this was a massive boon to their operations. Now they could move their expensive reporting operations (in terms of resource usage) to the standby database and free up the primary for On-Line Transaction Processing (OLTP).

SQLTXTRSBY

Once reporting operations moved to the physical standby (and logical standby) we could once more have poorly performing SQL. Performance problems that are on a read/write database are the sort of thing that SQLT can help us with. The only problem being that SQLTXTRACT and SQLTXECUTE need read/write access to the database (to store data in the SQLT repository and to install packages and procedures). How is it possible for SQLT to help us if we can't even store data about the performance on the database with the performance problem? This is where SQLTXTRSBY comes into play.

It provides some special procedures that deal with these special circumstances. As Data Guard (and other read-only databases) became more popular, more of the performance problems mentioned above appeared on Data Guard instances. To deal with these problems SQLTXTRACT was adapted to work without any local storage. This was done by making special routines that ran from a read/write database and reached out across a database link to the read-only database, collected the required information, and collated it and presented it on the read-write database. Let's take a more detailed look at some of SQLTXTRACT's limitations and then discuss using SQLTXTRSBY.

SQLTXTRACT Limitations

I always think of SQLTXTRACT (alias XTRACT) and SQLTXTRSBY (alias XTRSBY) as a superhero and his (or her) sidekick. XTRACT the superhero can seemingly do it all, but every superhero has their Achilles heel; in this case it is the inability to work on a read-only database. XTRSBY has those special skills that the main hero does not have. In this case XTRSBY can go into a read-only Data Guard system and get out with the information, where XTRACT cannot. Physical standbys do not allow writes. Data Guard is a one-way replication process, not a two-way replication process. This is why the physical standby database is open in read-only mode. If you do happen to wander onto a read-only database and try and insert some data, you'll get an error message like this:

```
SQL> insert into test1 values (1);
insert into test1 values (1)
            *
ERROR at line 1:
```

```
ORA-00604: error occurred at recursive SQL level 1
ORA-16000: database or pluggable database open for read-only access
```

What we see in the above example is that inserting data into a read-only database is not possible. The error message is even somewhat descriptive of what happened. XTRSBY solves this problem by pulling the required data across a database link to a read/write database and stores it locally rather than on the read-only database.

Another thing that XTRACT needs to do is to run anonymous blocks during installation and running of procedures.

XTRACT also relies on creating a user so that it can store its objects safely. XTRACT cannot do that on a read-only database.

So if we can't create the SQLTXPLAIN schema, or any procedures, how do we use XTRACT against this database? XTRSBY solves this problem by using local users (on a read-only database) and creating procedures that use database links to the read-only database.

How Do We Use XTRSBY?

We've just seen all the things that cannot happen on a Data Guard Physical standby database. This is when XTRSBY can step forward and do most of what XTRACT can do. I say "most" because XTRSBY is not exactly the same as XTRACT in terms of the results (we'll see the differences in the "What does an XTRSBY report look like?"). There's enough in the report, however, to help tune queries on the Data Guard instance. So how do we get XTRSBY to work on a Data Guard database? The brief steps in getting XTRSBY to work on a Data Guard standby database are as follows:

1. Install SQLTXPLAIN on the primary (we already covered this in Chapter 1 of this book).

2. Allow the DDL to be propagated to the standby database.

3. Create a database link accessible to the SQLTXPLAIN schema linking to the standby database. I'll give an example below.

4. Run XTRSBY from the primary specifying the SQL ID of the SQL on the standby and the database link.

5. The report is produced on the primary.

Step 1 above is covered in Chapter 1. Step 2 is a matter of waiting for the schema to be propagated (or copied as part of the normal Data Guard operations) to the standby. Step 3 is merely creating a public database link (or link available from SQLTXPLAIN): these are the commands I typed on my read-write database to create a publicly available database link that connects to the read-only database.

```
SQL> show user
USER is "SYS"
SQL> create public database link TO_STANDBY.us.oracle.com connect to sqltxplain identified
by oracle using '(DESCRIPTION=(ADDRESS=(PROTOCOL=TCP)(HOST=localhost)(Port=1521))(connect_
data=(SID=SNC2)))';

Database link created.

SQL> select sysdate from dual@to_standby.us.oracle.com;

SYSDATE
---------
22-NOV-14
```

Here I have simulated the standby database with a read-only database, hence in my connect string for the public database link I have used `localhost`. In a real-world example you would use the hostname of the standby database. Also in my example I have used a `PUBLIC` database link, but you may have standards on your site for creating database links, which require you to create a private link or a two-part link where the link information and the password are specified separately. As long as SQLTXPLAIN has access to the link to find the standby database the routine `xtrsby.sql` should work. Once these prerequisites are in place we can use XTRSBY to collect information about a standby SQL, by running `sqlxtrsby` on the primary.

First let's run some SQL on the standby. This would be equivalent to the reports that are run on the standby database.

```
SQL> select count(1) from dba_objects where object_type ='DIMENSION';

  COUNT(1)
----------
         5

SQL> select sql_id from v$sql where sql_text like 'select count(1) from dba_objects where
object_type =''DIMENSION''';

SQL_ID
-------------
gaz0dgkpffqrr

SQL>
```

In the steps above we ran some arbitrary SQL and got the SQL ID for that SQL. Remember we ran the SQL on the standby database (where our reports might have run). We can't store any data on the Data Guard Physical Standby database, so now we have to capture information about the SQL from across the database link from the primary database that consists of the following command:

```
SQL> @sqltxtrsby gaz0dgkpffqrr to_standby
```

This produces the zip file in the directory where the SQLTXPLAIN routine was run. This produces fewer reports than SQLTXPLAIN; this is because the read-only status of the standby restricts what can be done. Production of the XTRSBY report, as you can see, is only a little more complicated to produce. The additional steps already described are that one additional link is required, and the link name needs to be passed in the call to the routine. These are all that is required to get XTRSBY working.

What Does an XTRSBY Report Look Like?

Now that you have a report, what can we do with it? Let's look at the top of another example report. See Figure 15-1.

215187.1 SQLT XTRSBY 11.4.4.6 Report: sqlt_s75291_main.html

Global

- Observations
- SQL Text
- SQL Identification
- Environment
- CBO Environment
- Fix Control
- CBO System Statistics
- DBMS_STATS Setup
- Initialization Parameters
- NLS Parameters
- I/O Calibration
- Tool Configuration Parameters

Cursor Sharing and Binds

- Cursor Sharing
- Adaptive Cursor Sharing
- Peeked Binds
- Captured Binds

SQL Tuning Advisor

- STA Report
- STA Script

Plans

- Summary
- Performance Statistics
- Performance History (delta)
- Performance History (total)
- Execution Plans

Plan Control

- Stored Outlines
- SQL Profiles
- SQL Plan Baselines

SQL Execution

- Active Session History
- AWR Active Session History
- SQL Statistics
- SQL Detail ACTIVE Report
- Monitor Statistics
- Monitor ACTIVE Report
- Monitor HTML Report
- Monitor TEXT Report
- Segment Statistics
- Session Statistics
- Session Events
- Parallel Processing

Tables

- Tables
- Statistics
- Statistics Versions
- Modifications
- Properties
- Physical Properties
- Constraints
- Columns
- Indexed Columns
- Histograms
- Partitions
- Indexes

Objects

- Objects
- Dependencies
- Fixed Objects
- Fixed Object Columns
- Nested Tables
- Policies
- Audit Policies
- Tablespaces
- Metadata

Figure 15-1. The top of a SQLT XTRSBY report. Some features are not available

Some features are not available. For example, in Figure 15-1 I've highlighted two sections that do not have links, as they are not available in XTRSBY. This is because routines on the standby cannot be run (we saw earlier in the chapter what happens). What about the execution plans? They are visible as usual. You'll see in Figure 15-2 that there is no real difference in the information collected.

Execution Plan phv:55841097 sqlt_phv:99244 sqlt_phv2:13233 source:GV$SQL_PLAN inst:1 child:3(43D99120) executio

SQL Text: [..]

```
select /* xtract */ v.*, (orders_total - credit_limit) over_limit
from customer_v v
where orders_total > credit_limit
and customer_type = :b1
order by over_limit desc
```

SQL: [±]

ID	Exec Ord	Operation	Go To	More	Capt Bind	Cost²	Estim Card	LAST Starts	LAST Output Rows	LAST Over/Under Estimate¹
0	15	SELECT STATEMENT				1095	108			
1	14	SORT ORDER BY		[+]		1095	108	1	22	5x over
2	13	. HASH JOIN		[+]		1087	108	1	22	5x over
3	1	.. TABLE ACCESS FULL CUSTOMER@TO_STANDBY	[+]	[+]	[+]	15	2150	1	2715	1x
4	12	.. VIEW		[+]		1070	8351	1	2402	3x over
5	11	... SORT GROUP BY		[+]		1070	8351	1	2402	3x over
6	10	.... NESTED LOOPS		[+]		973	13521	1	2743	5x over
7	8	....+ HASH JOIN		[+]		973	13521	1	2743	5x over
8	2	....+. TABLE ACCESS FULL SALES_ORDER@TO_STANDBY	[+]	[+]		25	13521	1	2747	5x over
9	7	....+. VIEW		[+]		935	33860	1	33860	1x
10	6	....+.. SORT GROUP BY		[+]		935	33860	1	33860	1x
11	5	....+... HASH JOIN		[+]		210	237311	1	237311	1x
12	3	....+.... TABLE ACCESS FULL PART@TO_STANDBY	[+]	[+]		26	21396	1	21396	1x
13	4	....+.... TABLE ACCESS FULL ORDER_LINE@TO_STANDBY	[+]	[+]		134	237311	1	237311	1x
14	9	....+ INDEX UNIQUE SCAN CUSTOMER_PK@TO_STANDBY	[+]	[+]			1	2743	2743	1x

Performance statistics is only available when parameter "statistics_level" was set to "ALL" at hard-parse time, or SQL contains "gather_plan_statistics" hint.
(1) If estim_card * starts < output_rows then under-estimate. If estim_card * starts > output_rows then over-estimate. Color highlights when exceeding * 10x, ** 100x and *** 1000x over/under-est
(2) Largest contributors for cumulative-statistics columns are shown in red.
Go to Tables
Go to Indexes
Go to Top

Figure 15-2. *An execution plan collected by XTRSBY shows the links used*

In Figure 15-2 we see that all the usual features described in previous chapters are present and can be interpreted in the same way. In this new example (created on a different machine) the link name, still called TO_STANDBY, is shown in the execution plan. We also see that under the "Environment" heading (which we can reach by clicking on "Environment" from the top of the report), we see that the standby database link is shown. See Figure 15-3.

Environment

Host Name:	host01.example.com
CPUs:	2
Exadata:	"null"
RAC:	FALSE
NLS Characterset (database_properties):	WE8MSWIN1252
DB Time Zone (database_properties):	-04:00
DB Block Size (db_block_size):	8192
Optim Peek User Binds (_optim_peek_user_binds):	TRUE
DB Size in Terabytes (dba_data_files):	0.004 TB
Platform:	Linux
Product Version:	Oracle Database 11g Enterprise Edition (Production)
RDBMS Version:	11.2.0.3.0
Standby Database Link:	@TO_STANDBY
Language:	US:AMERICAN_AMERICA.WE8MSWIN1252

Figure 15-3. *The standby database link is shown in the Environment section*

Apart from those few minor differences the SQLTXPLAIN report is the same. Even though XTRSBY is very useful in its limited way, we still need to collect some information on the standby system itself. In earlier versions of SQLT (11.4.4.6 and before) the read-only tool `roxtract.sql` would be used. This tool is now replaced with SQLHC and SQLHCXEC both covered in Chapter 20). The read-only (ro) tool is still useful, and if you have an older version of SQLT you may want to use this tool anyway. The tool is named with an RO prefix to indicate it is a read-only tool and does most of what the main XTRACT tool does. It is however not available from version 11.4.5.1 of SQLT onward.

The roxtract Tool

The `utl` area of the SQLT directory has many useful utilities in it. One of these, in older versions of SQLT, is roxtract.sql. This read-only routine is specially designed for running in a read-only database and so is ideal for a Data Guard Physical Standby Database open in read-only mode. I'm sure you're already asking how this routine is different from the xtrsby.sql routine we've just been looking at. The simple answer is that running remotely (like xtrsby.sql) across a database link doesn't get us everything. Some things are better done locally, and we'll see shortly what roxtract.sql produces. This routine runs directly on the read-only Data Guard standby database (with a suitably privileged account) and produces the reports locally unlike xtrsby.sql, which produces its reports on the read-write database. To get at this extra information we have to use the routines provided in the utl directory.

How Do We Use roxtract?

roxtract.sql can be found in the utl directory of the SQLT unzipped area in older versions of SQLT. You still need this procedure to be present on the target system, but you do not need the SQLTXPLAIN schema; in fact in the case of roxtract.sql you run the script as SYS. This is the target SQL in this case from an older Windows system:

```
SQL>

select /*+ GATHER_PLAN_STATISTICS MONITOR*/
  cust_first_name,
  amount_sold
from
  customers C,
  sales S
where
  c.cust_id=s.cust_id
  and amount_sold > 1750
```

Now we get the SQL ID:

```
SQL> select sql_id from v$sqlarea where sql_text like 'select /*+ GATHER_PLAN_STATISTICS%';
SQL_ID
-------------
dck1xz983xa8c
```

Now that we have the SQL ID we can run the roxtract script from the SYS account. Notice that we have to enter the SQL ID at the licensing level and if we want to select 10053 information. Notice there is no prompt for the SQLTXPLAIN schema password, because we do not use it.

```
SQL>@roxtract
Parameter 1:
Oracle Pack License (Tuning, Diagnostics or None) [T|D|N] (required)
Enter value for 1: T <<<You must enter a value here
PL/SQL procedure successfully completed.

Parameter 2:
SQL_ID of the SQL to be analyzed (required)

Enter value for 2: dck1xz983xa8c <<<This is the SQL ID we are investigating

Parameter 3:
EVENT 10053 Trace (on 11.2 and higher) [Y|N]

Enter value for 3: Y <<<We want a 10053 trace file.

PL/SQL procedure successfully completed.

Values passed:
~~~~~~~~~~~~~
License: "T"
SQL_ID : " dck1xz983xa8c"
Trace  : "Y"

PL/SQL procedure successfully completed.

SQL>
SQL>DEF script = 'roxtract';
SQL>DEF method = 'ROXTRACT';
SQL>
SQL>--
SQL>-- begin common
SQL>--
SQL>
SQL>DEF mos_doc = '215187.1';
SQL>DEF doc_ver = '11.4.4.6';
SQL>DEF doc_date = '2012/06/02';
SQL>DEF doc_link = 'https://support.oracle.com/CSP/main/article?cmd=show&type=NOT&id=';
SQL>DEF bug_link = 'https://support.oracle.com/CSP/main/article?cmd=show&type=BUG&id=';
SQL>
SQL>-- tracing script in case it takes long to execute so we can diagnose it
SQL>ALTER SESSION SET TRACEFILE_IDENTIFIER = "^^script._^^unique_id.";

Session altered.

Elapsed: 00:00:00.00
SQL>ALTER SESSION SET STATISTICS_LEVEL = 'ALL';
```

I've excluded most of this output, because it is very long. The output finishes with this:

```
Ignore CP or COPY error below
'cp' is not recognized as an internal or external command,
operable program or batch file.
f:\app\stelios\diag\rdbms\snc2\snc2\trace\snc2_ora_5768_DBMS_SQLDIAG_10053_20121103_111817.trc
        1 file(s) copied.
  adding: roxtract_SNC2_locutus_11.2.0.1.0_dck1xz983xa8c_20121103_111855_10053_trace_from_
  cursor.trc (164 bytes security) (deflated 80%)
test of roxtract_SNC2_locutus_11.2.0.1.0_dck1xz983xa8c_20121103_111855.zip OK

ROXTRACT files have been created:
roxtract_SNC2_locutus_11.2.0.1.0_dck1xz983xa8c_20121103_111855_main.html.
roxtract_SNC2_locutus_11.2.0.1.0_dck1xz983xa8c_20121103_111855_monitor.html.
```

We can see from the above that a zip file has been created. If we extract the contents of this zip file into a directory we will see a number of files.

```
11/03/2012  11:22 AM    <DIR>          .
11/03/2012  11:22 AM    <DIR>          ..
11/03/2012  11:18 AM            17,035 roxtract.log
11/03/2012  11:19 AM           133,666 roxtract_SNC2_locutus_11.2.0.1.0_
                                       dck1xz983xa8c_20121103_111855_10053_trace_from_cursor.trc
11/03/2012  11:19 AM           122,477 roxtract_SNC2_locutus_11.2.0.1.0_
                                       dck1xz983xa8c_20121103_111855_main.html
11/03/2012  11:19 AM            10,113 roxtract_SNC2_locutus_11.2.0.1.0_
                                       dck1xz983xa8c_20121103_111855_monitor.html
               4 File(s)        283,291 bytes
               2 Dir(s)   7,103,459,328 bytes free
```

We see four files, one of which is the log of the roxtract.sql procedure. The remaining three files represent some of the missing output from XTRSBY. The first is the 10053 trace file, which we specifically requested. The other two are HTML files, the "main" HTML file and the "monitor" HTML file. Let's look at what information roxtract.sql provides.

What Do roxtract Reports Look Like?

The first report roxtract_SNC2_locutus_11.2.0.1.0_dck1xz983xa8c_20121103_111855_main.html (in this example) is the roxtract main report. It is a trimmed-down version of the SQLTXTRACT report, but nonetheless an amazingly useful HTML file. Let's look at the top of this HTML file, as shown in Figure 15-4.

<u>215187.1</u> ROXTRACT 11.4.4.6 Report: roxtract_SNC2_|

```
License    : T
SQL_ID     : dck1xz983xa8c
SIGNATURE  : 8361790997504183086
SIGNATUREF : 17787687049564729689
RDBMS      : 11.2.0.1.0
Platform   : 32-BIT WINDOWS
Instance   : 1
CPU Count  : 2
Block Size : 8192
OFE        : 11.2.0.1
DYN_SAMP   : 2
EBS        : ""
SIEBEL     : ""
PSFT       : ""
Date       : 2012-11-03/11:18:55
```

- <u>SQL Text</u>
- <u>Tables Summary</u>
- <u>Indexes Summary</u>
- <u>Current SQL Statistics (GV$SQL)</u>
- <u>Historical SQL Statistics (DBA_HIST_SQLSTAT)</u>
- <u>Current Execution Plans (last execution)</u>
- <u>Current Execution Plans (all executions)</u>
- <u>Historical Execution Plans</u>
- <u>Tables</u>
- <u>Table Columns</u>
- <u>Indexes</u>
- <u>Index Columns</u>
- <u>System Parameters with Non-Default or Modified Values</u>
- <u>Instance Parameters</u>

SQL Text

```
select /*+ GATHER_PLAN_STATISTICS MONITOR*/
cust_first_name,
amount_sold
from
customers C,
sales S
where
c.cust_id=s.cust_id
and amount_sold > 1750
```

Figure 15-4. *The top of the HTML ROXTRACT report*

As you can see, roxtract is weaker than the powerful XTRACT report. The number of sections it covers is reduced, but you still have the execution plans, table information, and many other sections.

The other file supplied by roxtract is `roxtract_SNC2_locutus_11.2.0.1.0_` `dck1xz983xa8c_20121103_111855_monitor.html`. The HTML defaults to the Plan Statistics tab as shown in Figure 15-5.

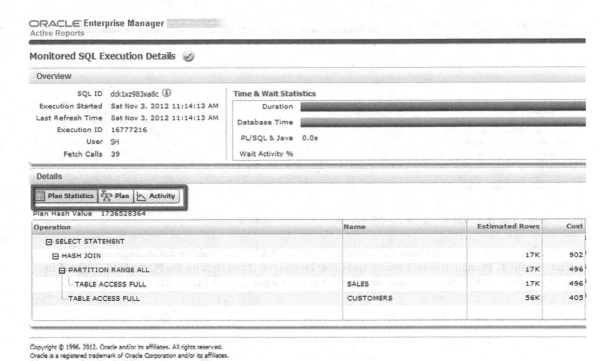

Figure 15-5. *The left-hand side of the page of the Monitored Execution Details page*

The figure above shows only the left-hand side of the report. We see the expected execution steps and the estimated number of rows and the associated cost. We also have access to the menu, which allows us to choose between different displays. The right hand of the report shows us more information about the actual rows returned I/O requests and any wait activity. For this SQL there is nothing much to say, but you need to know those entries are there. See Figure 15-6.

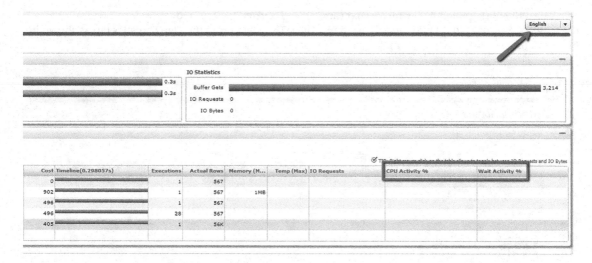

Cost	Timeline(0.298057s)	Executions	Actual Rows	Memory (M...	Temp (Max)	IO Requests	CPU Activity %	Wait Activity %
0		1	567					
902		1	567	1MB				
496		1	567					
496		28	567					
405		1	56K					

Figure 15-6. The right-hand side of the Monitored Execution Details page

There's even a button to change the language of the report. The drop-down list includes English, German, Spanish, French, Italian, Korean, and other languages. If you click on the Plan tab, highlighted in Figure 15-5, you can also get a flow diagram version of the execution plan (as seen in Figure 15-7).

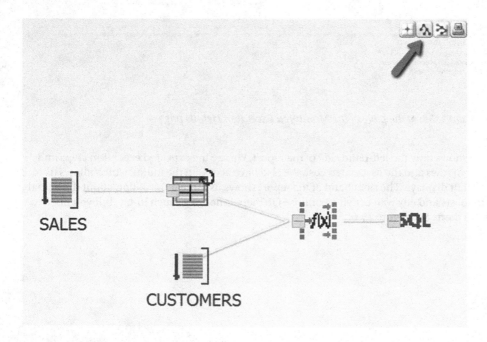

Figure 15-7. Shows the flow chart representation of the execution plan

Some developers prefer this representation of the execution plan. They even get a choice of the flow going left to right or bottom to top.

Summary

In this chapter we covered the special case of Data Guard tuning and the utilities that SQLTXPLAIN gives us to deal with this situation. You should not view Data Guard as a black box where no tuning can be done if it is open in read-only mode. Many companies do this, and you should be able to investigate performance if you need to. Now you can with XTRSBY. In the next chapter we will deal with building a test case. This is a very powerful first step in exploring an execution plans and what has happened to make it non-optimal, even though nothing changed.

CHAPTER 16

■ ■ ■

Building Good Test Cases

Occasionally there are tuning problems where the solution is not obvious from the examination of the SQLTXTRACT or SQLTXECUTE report. All the usual suspects have been eliminated and a more thorough investigation may be required. In cases like these it is useful to build a test case to allow experimentation away from the main environment. Say, for example, if this statement

```
select
  country_name, sum(AMOUNT_SOLD)
from sales s, customers c, countries co
where
  s.cust_id=c.cust_id
  and co.country_id=c.country_id
  and country_name in (
    'Ireland','Denmark','Poland','United Kingdom',
    'Germany','France','Spain','The Netherlands','Italy')
  group by country_name order by sum(AMOUNT_SOLD);
```

was suddenly performing less well than it used to. If you are investigating a problematic SQL in a test environment, normally you would try and make the environment the same as the environment you are attempting to replicate. This is often very difficult to do because there are many factors affecting an environment that need to be copied. Here are some of them.

- Hardware

- Software

- CBO Parameters

- Object Statistics

- Dictionary Statistics

- Data

- Table Clustering Factors

- Indexes

- Sequences

- Tables

There are many other factors; some factors may be crucial to your problem, but others may not be. You can try and build a test case the old-fashioned way, by exporting the data and associated statistics to a test environment, but this is an error-prone manual process, unless you've built a script to do this. Luckily SQLT

© Stelios Charalambides 2017
S. Charalambides, *Oracle SQL Tuning with Oracle SQLTXPLAIN*, DOI 10.1007/978-1-4842-2436-6_16

does everything needed to build a test case in a few very simple steps. It's platform independent, so you can run a Solaris test case on Windows for example: it's easy to use and automated. The only thing it does not replicate is the data (because that would usually make the test case too big). However, data can always be added later to a test case if it is needed.

■ **Warning**   Only run test case setup scripts in environments that you can easily replace. Some of the scripts involved in setting up the test environment will change the operational environment. There is a good reason you need access to SYS to carry out these operations. They will change system setup. Typically, you would create a stand-alone database for a test case and work with only that test case in your environment. When you are finished with the test case you would drop the entire database. Reusing such a database would be a dangerous course of action. Any number of CBO parameters may have been changed. Only set up test cases in scrap databases. You have been warned.

What Can You Do with Test Cases?

In some situations, tuning can be a tricky job. Before you can start to investigate the problem, you have to understand what all the parts of the execution plan are doing. Sometimes this understanding comes from tinkering with a copy of the SQL and its environment. You can add indexes, change hints, change optimizer parameters, drop histogram statistics — the list is endless. These kinds of things are done not at random but based on some understanding (or at least as much as you have at the time) of the problem at hand.

All this kind of tinkering cannot be done on a production environment, and it is often difficult to do on a development environment because the risk is too high that some aspect of your case will affect someone else: for example, public synonyms or sequences. On the other hand if you can set up a little private database with a good test case, you can change all sorts of parameters without affecting anyone directly. As long as the versions of the database are the same and your statistics are the same, you will get mostly the same behavior. I say "mostly" because in some cases (such as Exadata) there are specific issues that need an environment closer to the one you are replicating. Hybrid columnar compression, for example, needs either special hardware or an Exadata environment. DBAs and developers have been creating scripts to create test cases for their environment ever since Oracle was released, but as the complexity of environments increased, setting up good robust cases has taken longer and longer. These handcrafted test cases are useful but too time consuming to create. SQLT does all of the hard work for you by automatically collecting all the required metadata and statistical information.

Building a Test Case

To get a test case requires no additional effort above running an SQLT report. Running SQLTXTRACT alone creates enough information for a test case. Here is an example directory showing the files from the main SQLT zip file.

```
-rw-r--r-- 1 oracle oinstall  270025 Nov 29 13:49 sqlt_s30922_10053_explain.trc
-rw-r--r-- 1 oracle oinstall  208833 Nov 29 13:49 sqlt_s30922_10053_i1_c0_extract.trc
-rw-r--r-- 1 oracle oinstall    3768 Nov 29 13:49 sqlt_s30922_ashrpt_0001.zip
-rw-r--r-- 1 oracle oinstall     656 Nov 29 13:49 sqlt_s30922_cell_state.zip
-rw-r--r-- 1 oracle oinstall    7579 Nov 29 13:49 sqlt_s30922_driver.zip
-rw-r--r-- 1 oracle oinstall   25143 Nov 29 13:49 sqlt_s30922_lite.html
-rw-r--r-- 1 oracle oinstall  846015 Nov 29 13:49 sqlt_s30922_log.zip
```

```
-rw-r--r-- 1 oracle oinstall 2861876 Nov 29 13:49 sqlt_s30922_main.html
-rw-r--r-- 1 oracle oinstall   97976 Nov 29 13:49 sqlt_s30922_opatch.zip
-rw-r--r-- 1 oracle oinstall  372472 Nov 29 13:49 sqlt_s30922_perfhub_0001__.html
-rw-r--r-- 1 oracle oinstall   17422 Nov 29 13:49 sqlt_s30922_readme.html
-rw-r--r-- 1 oracle oinstall    3050 Nov 29 13:49 sqlt_s30922_sql_detail_active.html
-rw-r--r-- 1 oracle oinstall   65720 Nov 29 13:49 sqlt_s30922_sqldx.zip
-rw-r--r-- 1 oracle oinstall   13414 Nov 29 13:49 sqlt_s30922_sta_report_mem.txt
-rw-r--r-- 1 oracle oinstall    1466 Nov 29 13:49 sqlt_s30922_sta_script_mem.sql
-rw-r--r-- 1 oracle oinstall  163430 Nov 29 13:49 sqlt_s30922_tcb.zip
-rw-r--r-- 1 oracle oinstall     431 Nov 29 13:49 sqlt_s30922_tc_script.sql
-rw-r--r-- 1 oracle oinstall     326 Nov 29 13:49 sqlt_s30922_tc_sql.sql
-rw-r--r-- 1 oracle oinstall  111970 Nov 29 13:49 sqlt_s30922_tcx.zip<<<Express Case File
-rw-r--r-- 1 oracle oinstall  574547 Nov 29 13:49 sqlt_s30922_tc.zip<<<Test Case File
-rw-r--r-- 1 oracle oinstall  223794 Nov 29 13:49 sqlt_s30922_trc.zip
-rw-r--r-- 1 oracle oinstall     601 Nov 29 13:49 sqlt_s30922_xpand.sql
-rw-r--r-- 1 oracle oinstall 2736150 Nov 29 13:49 sqlt_s30922_xtract_9x00p9wc9kux7.zip
```

I've highlighted two of the files from this directory listing. The first one sqlt_s30922_tc.zip is the standard test case file. We'll deal with what you can do with this file in the next section. The second file sqlt_s30922_tcx.zip is an express file. We'll discuss that in the section on test case express.

A Test Case Step by Step

The first step in creating your test case is to create a subdirectory of the main SQLT area. Then copy the sqlt_s30922_tc.zip file into this area and unzip the file. A number of files are created and we'll describe each of them. Here is a sample listing.

```
-rw-r--r-- 1 oracle oinstall     187 Nov 29 13:49 10053.sql
-rw-r--r-- 1 oracle oinstall     101 Nov 29 13:49 flush.sql
-rw-r--r-- 1 oracle oinstall     273 Nov 29 13:49 plan.sql
-rw-r--r-- 1 oracle oinstall     431 Nov 29 13:49 q.sql
-rw-r--r-- 1 oracle oinstall      37 Nov 29 13:49 readme.txt
-rw-r--r-- 1 oracle oinstall     370 Nov 29 13:49 sel_aux.sql
-rw-r--r-- 1 oracle oinstall     412 Nov 29 13:49 sel.sql
-rw-r--r-- 1 oracle oinstall     438 Nov 29 13:49 setup.sql
-rw-r--r-- 1 oracle oinstall     261 Nov 29 13:49 sqlt_s30922_del_hgrm.sql
-rw-r--r-- 1 oracle oinstall 3194880 Nov 29 13:49 sqlt_s30922_exp.dmp
-rwxrwxrwx 1 oracle oinstall     674 Nov 29 13:49 sqlt_s30922_import.sh
-rw-r--r-- 1 oracle oinstall   29977 Nov 29 13:49 sqlt_s30922_metadata.sql
-rw-r--r-- 1 oracle oinstall   97976 Nov 29 13:49 sqlt_s30922_opatch.zip
-rw-r--r-- 1 oracle oinstall     238 Nov 29 13:49 sqlt_s30922_purge.sql
-rw-r--r-- 1 oracle oinstall   15040 Nov 29 13:49 sqlt_s30922_readme.txt
-rw-r--r-- 1 oracle oinstall     747 Nov 29 13:49 sqlt_s30922_restore.sql
-rw-r--r-- 1 oracle oinstall  184329 Nov 29 13:49 sqlt_s30922_set_cbo_env.sql
-rw-r--r-- 1 oracle oinstall    1261 Nov 29 13:49 sqlt_s30922_system_stats.sql
-rw-r--r-- 1 oracle oinstall  574547 Nov 29 13:49 sqlt_s30922_tc.zip
-rw-r--r-- 1 oracle oinstall     935 Nov 29 13:49 tc_pkg.sql
-rw-r--r-- 1 oracle oinstall     137 Nov 29 13:49 tc.sql
-rwxrwxrwx 1 oracle oinstall     114 Nov 29 13:49 xpress.sh
-rw-r--r-- 1 oracle oinstall    1049 Nov 29 13:49 xpress.sql
```

The files in this directory are all that is needed (along with SQLT to create a test case on your database). In the next section we'll look at these files in detail.

The Test Case Files

The scripts and other files in this directory are designed to work together to produce a test case simply and quickly. I list below each of the files and what they are for. Later we'll see how these files work together to produce a realistic test environment

- `10053.sql` – Sets 10053 tracing at level 1.

- `flush.sql` – Flushes the shared pool.

- `plan.sql` – Displays the execution plan for the most recently executed SQL and spools the output to `plan.log`. It uses the `dbms_xplan.display_cursor` procedure.

- `q.sql` – The SQL being investigated.

- `readme.txt` – The instructions. They are very brief: for example, "connect as sys and execute setup.sql."

- `sel.sql` – Computes predicate selectivity. This little script relies on `sel_aux.sql` (see below) and prompts for a table name and predicate and then gives you the predicted cardinality and selectivity. There is an example of the use of `sel.sql` below.

- `sel_aux.sql` – Produces expected cardinality and selectivity with `sel.sql`, based on different predicates.

- `setup.sql` – Sets up system statistics, creates the test user and metadata, imports the object statistics and the optimizer environment, executes the test query, and displays the execution plan.

- `sqlt_snnnnn_del_hgrm.sql` – Deletes histograms for the TC schema.

- `sqlt_snnnn_exp.dmp` – Dump file containing the statistics.

- `sqlt_snnnnn_import.sh` – Unix version of the import script for the SQLT objects.

- `sqlt_snnnnn_metadat.sql` – Script called from `setup.sql`; creates the test case user and user objects.

- `sqlt_snnnnn_purge.sql` – Removes the reference to the test case SQL from the SQLT repository.

- `sqlt_snnnnn_readme.txt` – Documentation for the specific test case, containing brief instructions on exporting and importing the SQLT repository, restoring CBO statistics, and implementing a test case in both express mode and custom mode.

- `sqlt_snnnnn_restore.sql` – Imports the CBO statistics into the test case.

- `sqlt_snnnn_set_cbo_env.sql` – Sets the CBO environment for the test case.

- `sqlt_snnnnn_system_stats.sql` – Sets the system statistics on the test system.

- `tc.sql` – Runs the test sql and displays the execution plan.

- `tc_pkg.sql` – Creates a `tc.zip` file for a small test case file.

- `xpress.sh` – The unix version of the script that runs `xpress.sql`. Builds the entire test case.

- `xpress.sql` – The SQL script that builds the entire test case in express mode.

As you can see there are quite a few files in the TC directory once you've unzipped it. Most of them are called from xpress.sql and setup.sql so we will not go into great detail on each of them, but some have some interesting stand-alone functions that we'll look at after we've built the test case.

The SQL Statement

Remember that SQLT is about tuning one SQL statement at a time. In our example case, we will be using this SQL:

```
select
  country_name, sum(AMOUNT_SOLD)
from sales s, customers c, countries co
where
  s.cust_id=c.cust_id
  and co.country_id=c.country_id
  and country_name in (
    'Ireland','Denmark','Poland','United Kingdom',
     'Germany','France','Spain','The Netherlands','Italy')
group by country_name order by sum(AMOUNT_SOLD);
```

This example SQL totals the spending from each European country. This is the result of running this query:

```
COUNTRY_NAME                                  SUM(AMOUNT_SOLD)
-------------------------------------------   ----------------
Poland                                                8447.14
Denmark                                            1977764.79
Spain                                              2090863.44
France                                             3776270.13
Italy                                              4854505.28
United Kingdom                                     6393762.94
Germany                                            9210129.22

7 rows selected.
```

What it does is not important for this example. We only need the SQL ID (9x00p9wc9kux7) and an SQLT XTRACT report. The intention here is to build a test case in another schema and then adjust the environment so that we can test different theories in isolation. In the normal way (as discussed in Chapters 1 and 3) we collect a SQLT XTRACT report and then place the zip file in a convenient place. In this case it is in the /run directory.

How to Build a Test Case Fast (xpress.sql)

First we create a directory to put the SQLTXTRACT report files in. In this directory I created a TC directory and put the test case zip file in the TC directory. Now that we have a test case directory and we've unzipped the test case files, the quickest and simplest thing to do is to set up the test case user. Remember you need to be logged into SYS to do this operation. This is because some of the steps in xpress will change the database environment. This environment cannot be shared with anyone else. So with all the warnings out of the way let's proceed to create a test case.

First we'll run `xpress.sql`. This will pause in various sections to give you a chance to review the steps and to check for any errors. If there are none, then normally you would press return to go to the next section. The steps in the script are each highlighted by a heading such as this:

```
1/7 Press ENTER to create TC user and schema objects for statement_id 30922.
```

The following list provides a high-level view of the script's steps. Next, we'll look at each of the several steps in more detail:

1. Create the test case user, the user objects (including tables and indexes), and the name of the user is of the form TCnnnn. In step 1 you are prompted for a suffix for the name of the test case user. You can just hit Return at this point, or enter a suffix such as DEV. At the end of this section you should check to see if there are any invalid objects. Valid objects are also listed.

2. The SQL repository is purged of any previous incarnation of the SQL statement.

3. The SQL statement is imported into the SQL repository, and the system environment is restored using the import utility. You will be prompted to enter the password for the SQLTXPLAIN user. This step is one of the reasons why you should not run xpress on a system you cannot afford to lose.

4. The test user schema object statistics are restored.

5. The system statistics are restored.

6. You are connected to the test schema and the CBO environment is set up.

7. The test schema environment is set up, the SQL is executed, and the execution plan is displayed.

Once you reach this stage, assuming there are no errors along the way, you are free to make changes to the test case environment (remember that this is a system that can be junked after this testing). You can change whatever you need to change to improve the performance of your test case, or sometimes you may want to change something about the test case to more fully understand what is happening and why the execution plan is the way it is. Next, we'll look at each of the seven steps above in much more detail. We'll see example output and explain what is happening. We'll go through all the steps to set up a test case that you can work.

1. In step 1 you are asked to confirm that you want to create a test case user in my case TC30922 and the schema objects.

   ```
   1/7 Press ENTER to create TC user and schema objects for statement_id 30922.
   ```

   If you press Enter you complete step 1. In this step the script `sqlt_snnnnn_metadata.sql` is run. You are prompted for a test case user suffix. A typical value might be "_1", but you can press RETURN to accept the default, which is no suffix. This then creates the metadata objects, such as tables and indexes as well as any constraints, functions, packages, views, or any other metadata. At the end of this step you are shown the status of these objects. They should all be valid. Here is the screen from my example.

   ```
   SQL>
   SQL>
   SQL> /****************************************************************/
   SQL>
   ```

```
SQL> REM PACKAGE
SQL>
SQL>
SQL> /*********************************************************************/
SQL> REM VIEW
SQL>
SQL>
SQL> /*********************************************************************/
SQL>
SQL> REM FUNCTION, PROCEDURE, LIBRARY and PACKAGE BODY
SQL>
SQL>
SQL> /*********************************************************************/
SQL>
SQL> REM OTHERS
SQL>
SQL>
SQL>
SQL> /*********************************************************************/
SQL>
SQL> SET ECHO OFF VER OFF PAGES 1000 LIN 80 LONG 8000000 LONGC 800000;

PL/SQL procedure successfully completed.

:VALID_OBJECTS
--------------------------------------------------------------------------------
VALID TABLE TC64661 COUNTRIES
VALID TABLE TC64661 CUSTOMERS
VALID TABLE TC64661 SALES
VALID INDEX TC64661 COUNTRIES_PK
VALID INDEX TC64661 CUSTOMERS_GENDER_BIX
VALID INDEX TC64661 CUSTOMERS_MARITAL_BIX
VALID INDEX TC64661 CUSTOMERS_PK
VALID INDEX TC64661 CUSTOMERS_YOB_BIX
VALID INDEX TC64661 SALES_CHANNEL_BIX
VALID INDEX TC64661 SALES_CUST_BIX
VALID INDEX TC64661 SALES_PROD_BIX
VALID INDEX TC64661 SALES_PROMO_BIX
VALID INDEX TC64661 SALES_TIME_BIX

:INVALID_OBJECTS
--------------------------------------------------------------------------------

SQL> REM In case of INVALID OBJECTS: review log, fix errors and execute again.
SQL> SPO OFF;
SQL> SET ECHO OFF;

2/7 Press ENTER to purge statement_id 30922 from SQLT repository.
```

In my example all my metadata objects are valid, and I have no packages, views, functions, or procedures. Since there are no invalid objects, I press Return to proceed with step 2.

2. In step 2 sqlt_snnnnn_purge.sql is run. This purges the SQLT repository of any data related to the SQL statement that is being analyzed. It is common to reload a test case when needed. The script output looks like this.

```
SQL> @@sqlt_s30922_purge.sql
SQL> REM Purges statement_id 30922 from local SQLT repository. Just execute
"@sqlt_s30922_purge.sql" from sqlplus
SQL> SPO sqlt_s30922_purge.log;
SQL> SET SERVEROUT ON;
SQL> EXEC sqltxplain.sqlt$a.purge_repository(30922, 30922);
14:00:45    0 sqlt$a: purging statement_id = "30922"
14:00:46    1 sqlt$a:        0 rows deleted from SQLI$_DBA_HIST_PARAMETER
14:00:46    0 sqlt$a:        0 rows deleted from SQLI$_DB_LINK
14:00:46    0 sqlt$a:       49 rows deleted from SQLI$_FILE
14:00:46    0 sqlt$a:        0 rows deleted from SQLI$_STGTAB_SQLPROF

... Output truncated for clarify

14:00:50    0 sqlt$a:       11 rows deleted from SQLT$_STGTAB_SQLSET
14:00:50    0 sqlt$a:        0 rows deleted from SQLI$_STGTAB_SQLPROF
14:00:50    0 sqlt$a:       11 rows deleted from SQLI$_STGTAB_SQLSET
14:00:50    0 sqlt$a: 131 tables were purged for statement_id = "30922"

PL/SQL procedure successfully completed.

SQL> SET SERVEROUT OFF;
SQL> SPO OFF;
SQL> SET ECHO OFF;

3/7 Press ENTER to import SQLT repository for statement_id 30922.
```

3. Step 3 imports the data collected from the target system into the SQLT repository. Here is the prompt that you see.

```
SQL> HOS imp SQLTXPLAIN FILE=sqlt_s30922_exp.dmp LOG=sqlt_s30922_imp.log
TABLES=sqlt% IGNORE=Y

Import: Release 12.1.0.2.0 - Production on Tue Nov 29 14:04:16 2016

Copyright (c) 1982, 2014, Oracle and/or its affiliates.  All rights reserved.

Password:

Connected to: Oracle Database 12c Enterprise Edition Release 12.1.0.2.0 - 64bit
Production
With the Partitioning, OLAP, Advanced Analytics and Real Application Testing
options

Export file created by EXPORT:V12.01.00 via conventional path
import done in US7ASCII character set and AL16UTF16 NCHAR character set
import server uses WE8MSWIN1252 character set (possible charset conversion)
```

```
. importing SQLTXPLAIN's objects into SQLTXPLAIN
. importing SQLTXPLAIN's objects into SQLTXPLAIN
. . importing table        "SQLT$_SQL_STATEMENT"           1 rows imported
. . importing table          "SQLT$_AUX_STATS$"           13 rows imported
. . importing table    "SQLT$_DBA_AUTOTASK_CLIENT"         1 rows imported
. . importing table "SQLT$_DBA_COL_STATS_VERSIONS"       439 rows imported
. . importing table        "SQLT$_DBA_COL_USAGE$"         13 rows imported
. . importing table       "SQLT$_DBA_CONSTRAINTS"         39 rows imported
. . importing table    "SQLT$_DBA_HIST_PARAMETER_M"       21 rows imported
. . importing table     "SQLT$_DBA_HIST_SNAPSHOT"         10 rows imported
. . importing table "SQLT$_DBA_HISTGRM_STATS_VERSN"     2606 rows imported
. . importing table       "SQLT$_DBA_IND_COLUMNS"         10 rows imported
. . importing table     "SQLT$_DBA_IND_PARTITIONS"       140 rows imported
. . importing table     "SQLT$_DBA_IND_STATISTICS"       150 rows imported
. . importing table "SQLT$_DBA_IND_STATS_VERSIONS"       145 rows imported
. . importing table          "SQLT$_DBA_INDEXES"         10 rows imported
. . importing table          "SQLT$_DBA_OBJECTS"        181 rows imported
. . importing table "SQLT$_DBA_OPTSTAT_OPERATIONS"       885 rows imported
. . importing table "SQLT$_DBA_PART_COL_STATISTICS"      196 rows imported
. . importing table    "SQLT$_DBA_PART_HISTOGRAMS"      3702 rows imported
. . importing table   "SQLT$_DBA_PART_KEY_COLUMNS"         6 rows imported
. . importing table         "SQLT$_DBA_SEGMENTS"        103 rows imported
. . importing table         "SQLT$_DBA_TAB_COLS"         40 rows imported
. . importing table    "SQLT$_DBA_TAB_HISTOGRAMS"        816 rows imported
. . importing table    "SQLT$_DBA_TAB_PARTITIONS"         28 rows imported
. . importing table    "SQLT$_DBA_TAB_STATISTICS"         31 rows imported
. . importing table "SQLT$_DBA_TAB_STATS_VERSIONS"        60 rows imported
. . importing table           "SQLT$_DBA_TABLES"          3 rows imported
. . importing table      "SQLT$_DBA_TABLESPACES"          6 rows imported
. . importing table          "SQLT$_DBMS_XPLAN"         148 rows imported
. . importing table "SQLT$_GV$ACTIVE_SESSION_HISTOR"       2 rows imported
. . importing table     "SQLT$_GV$NLS_PARAMETERS"         19 rows imported
. . importing table   "SQLT$_GV$OBJECT_DEPENDENCY"         11 rows imported
. . importing table         "SQLT$_GV$PARAMETER2"        383 rows imported
. . importing table      "SQLT$_GV$PARAMETER_CBO"        429 rows imported
. . importing table           "SQLT$_GV$PQ_SLAVE"         16 rows imported
. . importing table         "SQLT$_GV$PQ_SYSSTAT"         20 rows imported
. . importing table         "SQLT$_GV$PX_PROCESS"         16 rows imported
. . importing table "SQLT$_GV$PX_PROCESS_SYSSTAT"         15 rows imported
. . importing table              "SQLT$_GV$SQL"           1 rows imported
. . importing table         "SQLT$_GV$SQL_PLAN"          11 rows imported
. . importing table "SQLT$_GV$SQL_SHARED_CURSOR"          1 rows imported
. . importing table     "SQLT$_GV$SQL_WORKAREA"           3 rows imported
. . importing table          "SQLT$_GV$SQLAREA"           1 rows imported
. . importing table "SQLT$_GV$SQLAREA_PLAN_HASH"          1 rows imported
. . importing table         "SQLT$_GV$SQLSTATS"           1 rows imported
. . importing table "SQLT$_GV$SQLSTATS_PLAN_HASH"          1 rows imported
. . importing table "SQLT$_GV$SQLTEXT_WITH_NEWLINES"        6 rows imported
. . importing table   "SQLT$_GV$SYSTEM_PARAMETER"        381 rows imported
. . importing table                "SQLT$_LOG"         1814 rows imported
. . importing table           "SQLT$_METADATA"          111 rows imported
```

```
. . importing table "SQLT$_NLS_DATABASE_PARAMETERS"        20 rows imported
. . importing table          "SQLT$_OUTLINE_DATA"          56 rows imported
. . importing table        "SQLT$_PLAN_EXTENSION"          22 rows imported
. . importing table             "SQLT$_PLAN_INFO"          12 rows imported
. . importing table         "SQLT$_SQL_PLAN_TABLE"         11 rows imported
. . importing table              "SQLT$_STATTAB"         4682 rows imported
. . importing table         "SQLT$_STGTAB_SQLSET"          11 rows imported
. . importing table   "SQLT$_V$SESSION_FIX_CONTROL"      1070 rows imported
. . importing table        "SQLT$_WRI$_ADV_TASKS"           1 rows imported
Import terminated successfully without warnings.

SQL> SET ECHO OFF;

4/7 Press ENTER to restore schema object stats for TC30922.
```

As you can see from the list of objects imported, step 3 has imported information captured by SQLT during the SQLTXTRACT and is now storing it in the SQLT repository. Then you are prompted to proceed to step 4, which will restore the statistics for the test case objects.

4. Press Enter to proceed to step 4. In step 4 we replace the data dictionary information for the test case from the SQLT repository. This is why the system you are doing this on has to be one that you can re-create. Here is what you see for step 4.

```
SQL> @@sqlt_s30922_restore.sql
SQL> REM Restores schema object stats for statement_id 30922 from local SQLT
repository into data dictionary. Just execute "@sqlt_s30922_restore.sql" from
sqlplus.
SQL> SPO sqlt_s30922_restore.log;
SQL> SET SERVEROUT ON;
SQL> TRUNCATE TABLE SQLTXPLAIN.SQLI$_STATTAB_TEMP;

Table truncated.

SQL> ALTER SESSION SET optimizer_dynamic_sampling = 0;

Session altered.

SQL> ALTER SESSION SET EVENTS '10046 TRACE NAME CONTEXT FOREVER, LEVEL 12';

Session altered.

SQL> -- if you need to upload stats history so you can use SQLT XHUME you need to
pass p_load_hist as Y
SQL> EXEC SQLTXADMIN.sqlt$a.import_cbo_stats(p_statement_id => 's30922', p_
schema_owner => '&&tc_user.', p_include_bk => 'N', p_make_bk => 'N', p_load_hist
=> 'N');
remapping stats into user TC30922(143)
obtain statistics staging table version for this system
statistics version for this system: 7
+-----+
```

```
upgrade/downgrade of sqli$_stattab_temp to version 7 as per this system
restoring cbo stats for table TC30922.COUNTRIES
restoring cbo stats for table TC30922.CUSTOMERS
restoring cbo stats for table TC30922.SALES
+
|
|    Stats from id "s30922_snc1_d12102"
|    have been restored into data dict
|
|            METRIC   IN STATTAB  RESTORED  OK
|    -------------    ----------  --------  --
|       STATS ROWS:         4682      4682  OK
|           TABLES:            3         3  OK
|       TABLE PART:           28        28  OK
|    TABLE SUBPART:            0         0  OK
|          INDEXES:           10        10  OK
|       INDEX PART:          140       140  OK
|    INDEX SUBPART:            0         0  OK
|          COLUMNS:          791       791  OK
|      COLUMN PART:         3710      3710  OK
|   COLUMN SUBPART:            0         0  OK
|       EXTENSIONS:            0         0  OK
|     AVG AGE DAYS:         56.7      56.7  OK
|
+

PL/SQL procedure successfully completed.

SQL> ALTER SESSION SET SQL_TRACE = FALSE;

Session altered.

SQL> ALTER SESSION SET optimizer_dynamic_sampling = 2;

Session altered.

SQL> SET SERVEROUT OFF;
SQL> SPO OFF;
SQL> SET ECHO OFF;

5/7 Press ENTER to restore system statistics.
```

We just imported object statistics into TC30922 (from the repository) into the system so that they are the statistics for the test schema. At the end of this process we see that each object's statistics were imported successfully, and then we are prompted to proceed to step 5.

5. Now in step 5 we delete the existing system statistics (did I mention that you do this only on a system you can replace with no production data and no other users?). Then the new values are set for the system statistics. Then you are prompted to proceed to step 6.

```
SQL> EXEC SYS.DBMS_STATS.DELETE_SYSTEM_STATS;

PL/SQL procedure successfully completed.

SQL> EXEC SYS.DBMS_STATS.SET_SYSTEM_STATS('CPUSPEEDNW', 3308.97009966777);

PL/SQL procedure successfully completed.

SQL> EXEC SYS.DBMS_STATS.SET_SYSTEM_STATS('IOSEEKTIM', 10);

PL/SQL procedure successfully completed.

SQL> EXEC SYS.DBMS_STATS.SET_SYSTEM_STATS('IOTFRSPEED', 4096);

PL/SQL procedure successfully completed.

SQL>
SQL> SPO OFF;
SQL> SET ECHO OFF;

6/7 Press ENTER to connect as TC30922 and set CBO env.
```

6. In step 6 we connect as the test user. You see this line in the output.

```
SQL> CONN &&tc_user./&&tc_user.
Connected.
SQL> @@sqlt_s30992_set_cbo_env.sql
```

The script sqlt_s30922_set_cbo_env.sql will set the CBO environment. It is important and you will be prompted before you run it.

```
ALTER SESSION SET optimizer_features_enable = '12.1.0.2';

SET ECHO OFF;
```

When you press Enter at this point, *all* of the CBO environment settings are set to those from the system where the SQL came from.

During this script we are changing parameters like optimizer_dynamic_ sampling. Apart from non-default system parameters we also set the session parameters. Here is a section from the log file where we set a number of hidden session parameters:

```
SQL>
SQL> -- compute join cardinality using non-rounded input values
SQL> ALTER SESSION SET "_optimizer_new_join_card_computation" = TRUE;

Session altered.

SQL>
SQL> -- null-aware antijoin parameter
SQL> ALTER SESSION SET "_optimizer_null_aware_antijoin" = TRUE;
```

```
Session altered.

SQL> -- Use subheap for optimizer or-expansion
SQL> ALTER SESSION SET "_optimizer_or_expansion_subheap" = TRUE;

Session altered.

SQL>
SQL> -- Eliminates order bys from views before query transformation
SQL> ALTER SESSION SET "_optimizer_order_by_elimination_enabled" = TRUE;

Session altered.
```

Notice how in the preceding example, hidden parameters are included. We even set the fix_control parameters, in the next example. The fix_control parameters control whether certain bug fixes (included with the database) are enabled or disabled. Here is a section from the fix control part of the log file (we'll talk more about fix control in the next chapter).

```
SQL>
SQL> -- high memory usage with table expansion (ofe 8.0.0) (event 0)
SQL> ALTER SESSION SET "_fix_control" = '18959892:1';

Session altered.

SQL>
SQL> -- Skip the expensive plan check for AUTO DOP for IMC affintization (event
0)
SQL> ALTER SESSION SET "_fix_control" = '18960760:0';

Session altered.

SQL>
SQL> /**************************************************************************
**********/
SQL>
SQL> SPO OFF;
SQL> SET ECHO OFF;
```

7/7 Press ENTER to execute test case. At the end of step 6 we are prompted to execute the test case.

7. In step 7 we finally get to execute the SQL from our test case. Executing the test case as the test case user will output the result of the query and then the execution plan for the query. The result in our example will look something like this.

```
SQL> @@tc.sql
SQL> REM Executes SQL on TC then produces execution plan. Just execute "@tc.sql"
from sqlplus.
SQL> SET APPI OFF SERVEROUT OFF;
SQL> @@q.sql
```

```
SQL> REM $Header: 215187.1 sqlt_s30922_tc_script.sql 12.1.160429 2016/11/29 abel.macias $
SQL>
SQL> select
  2    /* ^^unique_id */  country_name, sum(AMOUNT_SOLD)
  3   from sh.sales s, sh.customers c, sh.countries co
  4   where
  5     s.cust_id=c.cust_id
  6     and co.country_id=c.country_id
  7     and country_name in (
  8        'Ireland','Denmark','Poland','United Kingdom',
  9         'Germany','France','Spain','The Netherlands','Italy')
 10     group by country_name order by sum(AMOUNT_SOLD);

no rows selected

SQL> @@plan.sql
SQL> REM Displays plan for most recently executed SQL. Just execute "@plan.sql" from
sqlplus.
SQL> SET PAGES 2000 LIN 180;
SQL> SPO plan.log;
SQL> SPO plan.log;
SQL> --SELECT * FROM TABLE(DBMS_XPLAN.DISPLAY_CURSOR);
SQL> SELECT * FROM TABLE(DBMS_XPLAN.DISPLAY_CURSOR(NULL,NULL,'BASIC ROWS COST PREDICATE'));

PLAN_TABLE_OUTPUT
-------------------------------------------------------------------------------------------
EXPLAINED SQL STATEMENT:
-----------------------
select  /* ^^unique_id */  country_name, sum(AMOUNT_SOLD) from sales s,
customers c, countries co where    s.cust_id=c.cust_id    and
co.country_id=c.country_id    and country_name in (
'Ireland','Denmark','Poland','United Kingdom',
'Germany','France','Spain','The Netherlands','Italy')    group by
country_name order by sum(AMOUNT_SOLD)


Plan hash value: 3035550245
```

```
---------------------------------------------------------------------------
| Id  | Operation                       | Name         | Rows  | Cost (%CPU)|
---------------------------------------------------------------------------
|   0 | SELECT STATEMENT                |              |       | 576  (100)|
|   1 |  SORT ORDER BY                  |              |    9  | 576   (11)|
|   2 |   HASH GROUP BY                 |              |    9  | 576   (11)|
|*  3 |    HASH JOIN                    |              | 435K  | 555    (8)|
|*  4 |     TABLE ACCESS FULL           | COUNTRIES    |    9  |   3    (0)|
|   5 |     NESTED LOOPS                |              | 918K  | 550    (8)|
|   6 |      NESTED LOOPS               |              | 918K  | 550    (8)|
|   7 |       PARTITION RANGE ALL       |              | 918K  | 517    (2)|
|   8 |        TABLE ACCESS FULL        | SALES        | 918K  | 517    (2)|
|*  9 |        INDEX UNIQUE SCAN        | CUSTOMERS_PK |    1  |   0    (0)|
|  10 |       TABLE ACCESS BY INDEX ROWID| CUSTOMERS   |    1  |   0    (0)|
---------------------------------------------------------------------------
```

```
Predicate Information (identified by operation id):
---------------------------------------------------

   3 - access("CO"."COUNTRY_ID"="C"."COUNTRY_ID")
   4 - filter(("COUNTRY_NAME"='Denmark' OR "COUNTRY_NAME"='France' OR
              "COUNTRY_NAME"='Germany' OR "COUNTRY_NAME"='Ireland' OR
              "COUNTRY_NAME"='Italy' OR "COUNTRY_NAME"='Poland' OR
              "COUNTRY_NAME"='Spain' OR "COUNTRY_NAME"='The Netherlands' OR
              "COUNTRY_NAME"='United Kingdom'))
   9 - access("S"."CUST_ID"="C"."CUST_ID")

38 rows selected.
```

Notice how in my case there are no results from the query because I did not retain the schema name in the SQL; the test case can work, with the same execution plan and with no data. The CBO only works based on what the statistics say about the tables, and we replaced that statistical data during the import steps. Since normally there is no data in your test case system you will get an output such as this (here I have replaced sh.sales, sh.countries, and sh.customers with sales, countries, and customers, as these tables now exist in the test case schema (but with no data in them).

```
SQL> @tc
SQL> REM Executes SQL on TC then produces execution plan. Just execute "@tc.sql" from
sqlplus.
SQL> SET APPI OFF SERVEROUT OFF;
SQL> @@q.sql
SQL> REM $Header: 215187.1 sqlt_s30922_tc_script.sql 12.1.160429 2016/11/29 abel.macias $
SQL>
SQL>
SQL> select
  2    /* ^^unique_id */  country_name, sum(AMOUNT_SOLD)
  3    from sales s, customers c, countries co
  4    where
  5      s.cust_id=c.cust_id
  6      and co.country_id=c.country_id
  7      and country_name in (
  8        'Ireland','Denmark','Poland','United Kingdom',
  9        'Germany','France','Spain','The Netherlands','Italy')
 10    group by country_name order by sum(AMOUNT_SOLD);

no rows selected
SQL> @@plan.sql
SQL> REM Displays plan for most recently executed SQL. Just execute "@plan.sql" from
sqlplus.
SQL> SET PAGES 2000 LIN 180;
SQL> SPO plan.log;
SQL> --SELECT * FROM TABLE(DBMS_XPLAN.DISPLAY_CURSOR);
SQL> SELECT * FROM TABLE(DBMS_XPLAN.DISPLAY_CURSOR(NULL,NULL,'BASIC ROWS COST PREDICATE'));

PLAN_TABLE_OUTPUT
--------------------------------------------------------------------------------------
--------------------------------------------------------------------------------------
EXPLAINED SQL STATEMENT:
```

```
---------------------------------
select  /* ^^unique_id */  country_name, sum(AMOUNT_SOLD) from sales s,
customers c, countries co where   s.cust_id=c.cust_id    and
co.country_id=c.country_id   and country_name in (
'Ireland','Denmark','Poland','United Kingdom',
'Germany','France','Spain','The Netherlands','Italy')   group by
country_name order by sum(AMOUNT_SOLD)

Plan hash value: 3035550245
```

```
----------------------------------------------------------------------------
| Id | Operation                      | Name         | Rows | Cost (%CPU)|
----------------------------------------------------------------------------
|  0 | SELECT STATEMENT               |              |      | 576 (100)|
|  1 |  SORT ORDER BY                 |              |   9  | 576  (11)|
|  2 |   HASH GROUP BY                |              |   9  | 576  (11)|
|* 3 |    HASH JOIN                   |              | 435K | 555   (8)|
|* 4 |     TABLE ACCESS FULL          | COUNTRIES    |   9  |   3   (0)|
|  5 |     NESTED LOOPS               |              | 918K | 550   (8)|
|  6 |      NESTED LOOPS              |              | 918K | 550   (8)|
|  7 |       PARTITION RANGE ALL      |              | 918K | 517   (2)|
|  8 |        TABLE ACCESS FULL       | SALES        | 918K | 517   (2)|
|* 9 |        INDEX UNIQUE SCAN       | CUSTOMERS_PK |   1  |   0   (0)|
| 10 |       TABLE ACCESS BY INDEX ROWID| CUSTOMERS  |   1  |   0   (0)|
----------------------------------------------------------------------------
```

```
Predicate Information (identified by operation id):
---------------------------------------------------

   3 - access("CO"."COUNTRY_ID"="C"."COUNTRY_ID")
   4 - filter(("COUNTRY_NAME"='Denmark' OR "COUNTRY_NAME"='France' OR
             "COUNTRY_NAME"='Germany' OR "COUNTRY_NAME"='Ireland' OR
             "COUNTRY_NAME"='Italy' OR "COUNTRY_NAME"='Poland' OR
             "COUNTRY_NAME"='Spain' OR "COUNTRY_NAME"='The Netherlands' OR
             "COUNTRY_NAME"='United Kingdom'))
   9 - access("S"."CUST_ID"="C"."CUST_ID")
```

Now we have reached that point in the test case where we can do some work on exploring the setup of the environment and changing things to see what we can achieve or to see how the SQL, under the microscope, can be influenced to do what we want.

Exploring the Execution Plan

Now that we have a test case, we can explore the execution plan by changing all those things that can affect the execution plan. I've listed some of them below:

- Optimizer Parameters

- SQL Hints

- Optimizer Versions

- Structure of the SQL

- Adding or Removing Indexes
- System Statistics
- Object Statistics

Of these environmental factors, the last two require the setting of object statistics through routines. Normally you would not change object statistics (as you are likely investigating a regression and the object statistics in your test case are the ones set by SQLT from the source system). I give a short example of setting object statistics at the end of this section. System statistics can also be set and tested; but again, this is not generally a test that is carried out because it implies you are planning for a different machine. (I give a short example of this at the end of the section). The things most commonly explored using the test case are optimizer parameters and the structure of the SQL.

While this kind of testing can be done in other ways (set autotrace, EXPLAIN PLAN, etc.), setting up the environment can be time consuming and tricky. Even if you do set up an environment to be a duplicate of another environment, how will you know you've got everything right? The optimizer works the same way and produces an execution plan when you test. With an SQLT test case everything is brought in, and nothing is missing. You get the environment right every time. If you copy the data you will also have a very similar copy of the source environment. An additional advantage of this method of working is that the system environment can also be changed.

Optimizer Parameters

If a developer comes to you and says my SQL would work fine if optimizer_index_cost_adj was set to 10, you can now test the suggestion with a test case in your own test environment. Of course, good (or bad) suggestions for tuning can come from any source; the point here is that you can take a suggestion, put it through the optimizer via the test case you built, and see what the cost and execution plan will be. Below we see such an example. Notice that I am setting the optimizer parameter at the session level, but this would normally be a precursor to setting the parameter at the system level. By the way I would not suggest you make changes like this on a real system without extensive testing; there is too much scope for other SQL to be affected by changes like this. This is an exploration of what the optimizer might be able to do for us if the environment were different. So here's the result.

Plan hash value: 698535804

```
---------------------------------------------------------------------------------------
| Id  | Operation                                    | Name           | Rows  | Cost (%CPU)|
---------------------------------------------------------------------------------------
|   0 | SELECT STATEMENT                             |                |       |   343 (100)|
|   1 |  SORT ORDER BY                               |                |     9 |   343  (11)|
|   2 |   HASH GROUP BY                              |                |     9 |   343  (11)|
|   3 |    NESTED LOOPS                              |                |  435K |   323   (6)|
|   4 |     NESTED LOOPS                             |                |  918K |   323   (6)|
|   5 |      NESTED LOOPS                            |                |  918K |   318   (5)|
|   6 |       PARTITION RANGE ALL                    |                |  918K |   314   (4)|
|   7 |        TABLE ACCESS BY LOCAL INDEX ROWID BATCHED| SALES       |  918K |   314   (4)|
|   8 |         BITMAP CONVERSION TO ROWIDS          |                |       |            |
|   9 |          BITMAP INDEX FULL SCAN              | SALES_PROMO_BIX|       |            |
|  10 |       TABLE ACCESS BY INDEX ROWID            | CUSTOMERS      |     1 |     1   (0)|
|* 11 |        INDEX UNIQUE SCAN                     | CUSTOMERS_PK   |     1 |     1   (0)|
|* 12 |      INDEX UNIQUE SCAN                       | COUNTRIES_PK   |     1 |     1   (0)|
|* 13 |     TABLE ACCESS BY INDEX ROWID             | COUNTRIES      |     1 |     1   (0)|
---------------------------------------------------------------------------------------
```

```
Predicate Information (identified by operation id):
---------------------------------------------------

  11 - access("S"."CUST_ID"="C"."CUST_ID")
  12 - access("CO"."COUNTRY_ID"="C"."COUNTRY_ID")
  13 - filter(("COUNTRY_NAME"='Denmark' OR "COUNTRY_NAME"='France' OR
              "COUNTRY_NAME"='Germany' OR "COUNTRY_NAME"='Ireland' OR "COUNTRY_NAME"='Italy' OR
              "COUNTRY_NAME"='Poland' OR "COUNTRY_NAME"='Spain' OR "COUNTRY_NAME"='The
              Netherlands'
              OR "COUNTRY_NAME"='United Kingdom'))
```

In this example, I've removed some of the execution plan columns for clarity. We can see that the cost has gone down from 576 to 343. Let me emphasize this next point, as it is very important. This does not mean that changing optimizer_index_cost_adj is a good idea: rather, this means that if the optimizer environment were set correctly the optimizer could choose a better plan. The next step in this scenario would be to investigate why the optimizer is choosing a suboptimal plan. The important fact to remember here is that the test case allows you to confirm that there is a better plan.

Adding and Removing Hints

In my previous example we saw that setting session parameters can change the execution plan and that on our test system we can see those changes without having all the data. We saw that setting optimizer_index_cost_adj made a difference and that maybe we need an index hint to help. So setting optimizer_index_cost_adj back to the default value of 100, and then at random I selected the index SALES_CUST_BIX (which we'll see wasn't a good choice). I modify the SQL to include the hint /*+ INDEX(S SALES_CUST_BIX) */ and run tc.sql. The result in my case is:

```
Plan hash value: 386847891

--------------------------------------------------------------------------------------------
| Id  | Operation                                    | Name           | Rows  | Cost (%CPU)|
--------------------------------------------------------------------------------------------
|   0 | SELECT STATEMENT                             |                |       | 3531 (100)|
|   1 |  SORT ORDER BY                               |                |     9 | 3531   (2)|
|   2 |   HASH GROUP BY                              |                |     9 | 3531   (2)|
|*  3 |    HASH JOIN                                 |                |  435K | 3510   (2)|
|*  4 |     TABLE ACCESS FULL                        | COUNTRIES      |     9 |    3   (0)|
|   5 |     NESTED LOOPS                             |                |  918K | 3505   (2)|
|   6 |      NESTED LOOPS                            |                |  918K | 3505   (2)|
|   7 |       PARTITION RANGE ALL                    |                |  918K | 3471   (1)|
|   8 |        TABLE ACCESS BY LOCAL INDEX ROWID BATCHED| SALES       |  918K | 3471   (1)|
|   9 |         BITMAP CONVERSION TO ROWIDS          |                |       |           |
|  10 |          BITMAP INDEX FULL SCAN              | SALES_CUST_BIX |       |           |
|* 11 |       INDEX UNIQUE SCAN                      | CUSTOMERS_PK   |     1 |    0   (0)|
|  12 |       TABLE ACCESS BY INDEX ROWID            | CUSTOMERS      |     1 |    0   (0)|
--------------------------------------------------------------------------------------------

Predicate Information (identified by operation id):
---------------------------------------------------

   3 - access("CO"."COUNTRY_ID"="C"."COUNTRY_ID")
```

```
    4 - filter((("COUNTRY_NAME"='Denmark' OR "COUNTRY_NAME"='France' OR
            "COUNTRY_NAME"='Germany' OR "COUNTRY_NAME"='Ireland' OR "COUNTRY_NAME"='Italy' OR
            "COUNTRY_NAME"='Poland' OR "COUNTRY_NAME"='Spain' OR "COUNTRY_NAME"='The
            Netherlands'
            OR "COUNTRY_NAME"='United Kingdom'))
   11 - access("S"."CUST_ID"="C"."CUST_ID")
```

Again, I've removed some columns from the execution plan display to emphasize the important columns. We see in this example that the cost has increased, and so we decide that this hint is not helpful to us. The steps to check the effect of this hint are to modify q.sql (add the hint) and run tc.sql. Nothing more is needed.

Versions of the Optimizer

Suppose we upgraded or transferred SQL from version 11g to version 12c. We think that maybe the execution plan changed between these two versions. We can test this idea by changing optimizer_features_enable to '11.2.0.4'. Then we can do that easily and simply by setting the parameter at the session level and retesting.

The steps to carry out this test are:

```
SQL> alter session set optimizer_features_enable='11.2.0.4';
SQL> @tc
```

In this case we see that the execution plan is unchanged, but in other cases we may see some changes, usually the better execution plan is from 12c although not always. Remember that optimizer_features_ enable is like a super-switch that sets a number of features in the database on or off. Setting this parameter to a value that was there before the feature was introduced can turn off any new features. For example, you could disable SQL Plan management by setting this parameter to 10.2.0.5, a version of the database that existed when this feature was not present. This is not a recommended solution to any particular problem, but will help in giving the developer or DBA a clue, if it improves a particular SQL, that the solution may lie in investigating one of the new features introduced in the later version. As the optimizer_features_enable parameter made no difference we set it back to 12.1.0.2

Structure of the SQL

The test case once built allows you to investigate the target SQL in many ways, including changing the SQL itself, as long as your SQL does not include any new tables (which were not captured by XTRACT), you could test the SQL in the same way. In this example I changed the SQL from

```
select /*+ INDEX(S SALES_CUST_BIX) */
  country_name, sum(AMOUNT_SOLD)
from sales s, customers c, countries co
where
  s.cust_id=c.cust_id
  and co.country_id=c.country_id
  and country_name in ('Ireland','Denmark','Poland',
  'United Kingdom','Germany','France','Spain','The Netherlands','Italy')
  group by country_name order by sum(AMOUNT_SOLD);
```

to

```
select /*+ INDEX(S SALES_CUST_BIX) */
  country_name, sum(AMOUNT_SOLD)
from sales s, customers c, countries co
where
  s.cust_id=c.cust_id
  and co.country_id=c.country_id
  and country_name in ( select country_name from sh.countries where
  country_name in ('Ireland','Denmark','Poland',
  'United Kingdom','Germany','France','Spain','The Netherlands','Italy'))
group by country_name order by sum(AMOUNT_SOLD);
```

In this case there was a change to the execution plan. In this case the cost is about the same. So we can remove this change and try some changes to the indexes.

Indexes

We currently are using an index due to this hint /*+ INDEX(S SALES_CUST_BIX) */

We see that the execution plan looks like this:

```
Plan hash value: 386847891
```

```
---------------------------------------------------------------------------------------
| Id  | Operation                                    | Name          | Rows  | Cost (%CPU)|
---------------------------------------------------------------------------------------
|   0 | SELECT STATEMENT                             |               |       | 3531 (100)|
|   1 |  SORT ORDER BY                               |               |     9 | 3531   (2)|
|   2 |   HASH GROUP BY                              |               |     9 | 3531   (2)|
|*  3 |    HASH JOIN                                 |               |  435K | 3510   (2)|
|*  4 |     TABLE ACCESS FULL                        | COUNTRIES     |     9 |    3   (0)|
|   5 |     NESTED LOOPS                             |               |  918K | 3505   (2)|
|   6 |      NESTED LOOPS                            |               |  918K | 3505   (2)|
|   7 |       PARTITION RANGE ALL                    |               |  918K | 3471   (1)|
|   8 |        TABLE ACCESS BY LOCAL INDEX ROWID BATCHED| SALES      |  918K | 3471   (1)|
|   9 |         BITMAP CONVERSION TO ROWIDS          |               |       |           |
|  10 |          BITMAP INDEX FULL SCAN              | SALES_CUST_BIX|       |           |
|* 11 |        INDEX UNIQUE SCAN                     | CUSTOMERS_PK  |     1 |    0   (0)|
|  12 |         TABLE ACCESS BY INDEX ROWID          | CUSTOMERS     |     1 |    0   (0)|
---------------------------------------------------------------------------------------
```

```
Predicate Information (identified by operation id):
---------------------------------------------------

   3 - access("CO"."COUNTRY_ID"="C"."COUNTRY_ID")
   4 - filter(("COUNTRY_NAME"='Denmark' OR "COUNTRY_NAME"='France' OR
             "COUNTRY_NAME"='Germany' OR "COUNTRY_NAME"='Ireland' OR "COUNTRY_NAME"='Italy' OR
             "COUNTRY_NAME"='Poland' OR "COUNTRY_NAME"='Spain' OR "COUNTRY_NAME"='The
             Netherlands'
             OR "COUNTRY_NAME"='United Kingdom'))
  11 - access("S"."CUST_ID"="C"."CUST_ID")
```

But we suspect that the index use was a bad idea, so we want to disable it without changing the code.

```
SQL> alter index sales_cust_bix invisible;
SQL> @tc
Plan hash value: 3035550245
```

```
-------------------------------------------------------------------------------
| Id  | Operation                      | Name         | Rows  | Cost (%CPU)|
-------------------------------------------------------------------------------
|   0 | SELECT STATEMENT               |              |       | 576 (100)|
|   1 |  SORT ORDER BY                 |              |    9  | 576  (11)|
|   2 |   HASH GROUP BY                |              |    9  | 576  (11)|
|*  3 |    HASH JOIN                   |              | 435K  | 555   (8)|
|*  4 |     TABLE ACCESS FULL          | COUNTRIES    |    9  |   3   (0)|
|   5 |     NESTED LOOPS               |              | 918K  | 550   (8)|
|   6 |      NESTED LOOPS              |              | 918K  | 550   (8)|
|   7 |       PARTITION RANGE ALL      |              | 918K  | 517   (2)|
|   8 |        TABLE ACCESS FULL       | SALES        | 918K  | 517   (2)|
|*  9 |       INDEX UNIQUE SCAN        | CUSTOMERS_PK |    1  |   0   (0)|
|  10 |      TABLE ACCESS BY INDEX ROWID| CUSTOMERS   |    1  |   0   (0)|
-------------------------------------------------------------------------------
```

```
Predicate Information (identified by operation id):
---------------------------------------------------

   3 - access("CO"."COUNTRY_ID"="C"."COUNTRY_ID")
   4 - filter(("COUNTRY_NAME"='Denmark' OR "COUNTRY_NAME"='France' OR
              "COUNTRY_NAME"='Germany' OR "COUNTRY_NAME"='Ireland' OR
              "COUNTRY_NAME"='Italy' OR "COUNTRY_NAME"='Poland' OR
              "COUNTRY_NAME"='Spain' OR "COUNTRY_NAME"='The Netherlands' OR
              "COUNTRY_NAME"='United Kingdom'))
   9 - access("S"."CUST_ID"="C"."CUST_ID")
```

As expected the index sales_cust_bix is no longer being used. We now see a different execution plan, which looks slightly better

Setting Object Statistics

Here's a short example of setting object statistics. You might want to do this if you were thinking that the plan changed because of data volumes, or maybe you reached a tipping point in the volume that caused a catastrophic change in plan. We will look at dbms_stats.set_table_stats (the procedure for set_index_stats and set_column_stats is exactly the same). From the source table find out the basic statistics you are considering changing.

```
SQL> select num_rows, blocks, avg_row_len from user_Tables where table_name='SH';
```

```
NUM_ROWS         BLOCKS  AVG_ROW_LEN
---------------- ------- -------------
40000            1000             40
```

These values are then inserted into the call to SET_TABLE_STATS.

```
SQL> EXEC DBMS_STATS.SET_TABLE_STATS(ownname=>'SH', tabname=>'CUSTOMER', partname=>null,
stattab=>null, statid=>null, numrows=>40000, numblks=>1000, avrglen=>40);
```

For testing the change in volume you might reduce these numbers by 20% (but obviously not avrglen, as this remains unchanged). Do not make these changes on live tables; always use your test case on a dummy table to check the application of the stats before proceeding.

Setting System Statistics

As an example of the power of setting system statistics, I'll carry out the steps to do this to my test rig. If you wanted to do something similar to your throwaway test environment to make it similar to another environment, you could get the system statistics and set them manually as I am going to do in this example. From the example above our best cost so far was 576. We also know that our source machine had a CPU speed of 3308 MHz and I/O seek time of 10ms and an I/O transfer speed of 4096. In this example I'll set the CPU speed to 10 times the current value:

```
SQL> EXEC DBMS_STATS.SET_SYSTEM_STATS('CPUSPEEDNW', 33080.00);
```

Then when we next run the test case (after flushing the shared Pool) we get this execution plan:

```
-----------------------------------------------------------------------------
| Id  | Operation                      | Name         | Rows  | Cost (%CPU)|
-----------------------------------------------------------------------------
|   0 | SELECT STATEMENT               |              |       | 521  (100)|
|   1 |  SORT ORDER BY                 |              |    9  | 521    (2)|
|   2 |   HASH GROUP BY                |              |    9  | 521    (2)|
|*  3 |    HASH JOIN                   |              | 435K  | 517    (1)|
|*  4 |     TABLE ACCESS FULL          | COUNTRIES    |    9  |   3    (0)|
|   5 |     NESTED LOOPS               |              | 918K  | 514    (1)|
|   6 |      NESTED LOOPS              |              | 918K  | 514    (1)|
|   7 |       PARTITION RANGE ALL      |              | 918K  | 511    (1)|
|   8 |        TABLE ACCESS FULL       | SALES        | 918K  | 511    (1)|
|*  9 |        INDEX UNIQUE SCAN       | CUSTOMERS_PK |    1  |   0    (0)|
|  10 |       TABLE ACCESS BY INDEX ROWID| CUSTOMERS  |    1  |   0    (0)|
-----------------------------------------------------------------------------
```

Please note that in this case the plan has not changed; however, what we do see is that the cost has been slightly reduced slightly from 576 seconds to 521. Most of the cost of the query is in the I/O, and the CPU is not crucial to the execution time. We could conclude from this that if we wanted a bigger better machine, that a much more important parameter to pay attention to would be the transfer speed of the disks rather the speed of the CPU (as far as this query is concerned, of course). Playing around in your test environment with settings like this can allow you to discover how to improve performance in your environment and how to save time so you can concentrate on what is important and ignore what is less important.

Object Statistics

You can set object statistics for all the objects in the query also, but this is a tricky operation and not recommended for this kind of exploration. You are better off looking at the 10053 trace file to see why your costs are the way they are than by changing the costs to see what happens.

Debugging the Optimizer

Creating and using a test case is mostly something that you should expect Oracle support to do on your behalf. They will take the test case files that you supply and explore them sufficiently to be able to solve your problem. You can also use the test case files (as I've described above) to do some testing in a free-standing test environment that nobody else is using. The test case routines are mostly used to explore the behavior of the optimizer. Everything in the test case files is designed to make the optimizer think it is on the original source system. If there is a bug that causes the optimizer to change its execution plan in an inappropriate way, then a test case is what Oracle support will use possibly in conjunction with your data to determine if there is a true bug or some unexpected behavior that is not a bug. Sometimes in rare cases some particular execution plan can cause a bug to be exposed, and in these cases you can sometimes avoid the bug by setting some optimizer environmental factor.

Other Test Case Utilities

As if the ability to explore your SQL in a stand-alone test environment isn't enough, SQLT provides further utilities for understanding what's happening in any particular SQL. Sometimes you want to do more than just change environmental settings and retry your query. Just like a dependable Swiss Army knife of tuning, SQLT has a tool for nearly every job.

What Does sel.sql Do?

Sel is a nice little utility that you would probably write if it wasn't already written for you. Here is the code for sel.sql:

```
REM Computes predicate selectivity using CBO. Requires sel_aux.sql.
SPO sel.log;
SET ECHO OFF FEED OFF SHOW OFF VER OFF;
PRO
COL table_rows NEW_V table_rows FOR 999999999999;
COL selectivity FOR 0.000000000000 HEA "Selectivity";
COL e_rows NEW_V e_rows FOR 999999999999 NOPRI;
ACC table PROMPT 'Table Name: ';
SELECT num_rows table_rows FROM user_tables WHERE table_name = UPPER(TRIM('&&table.'));
@@sel_aux.sql
```

This routine prompts for the table to be accessed after setting up the column formats and then calls sel_aux.sql:

```
REM Computes predicate selectivity using CBO. Requires sel.sql.
PRO
ACC predicate PROMPT 'Predicate for &&table.: ';
DELETE plan_table;
```

```
EXPLAIN PLAN FOR SELECT /*+ FULL(t) */ COUNT(*) FROM &&table. t WHERE &&predicate.;
SELECT MAX(cardinality) e_rows FROM plan_table;
SELECT &&e_rows. "Comp Card", ROUND(&&e_rows./&&table_rows., 12) selectivity FROM DUAL;
@@sel_aux.sql
```

sel_aux.sql uses explain plan to determine the cardinality and selectivity by selecting this information from the plan_table populated by explain plan. It displays the computed cardinality and selectivity for any particular predicate and table in the test case. At the end of the routine sel_aux is called again to give a chance to select a different value for a predicate or a different predicate entirely. So if you were looking at problems regarding a particular value you might want to test cardinality by using sel.sql. In the example below I choose the SALES table to investigate, and I'm interested in the cardinality of a query against SALES where the CUST_ID is 100 and 200.

```
SQL> @sel

Table Name: sales

   TABLE_ROWS
-------------
       918843

Predicate for sales: cust_id=100

 Comp Card     Selectivity
---------- ---------------
       130  0.000141482277

Predicate for sales: cust_id=200

 Comp Card     Selectivity
---------- ---------------
       130  0.000141482277

Predicate for sales: cust_id between 100 and 300

 Comp Card     Selectivity
---------- ---------------
      2080  0.002263716435

Predicate for sales:
```

I can see that the statistics estimate that the cardinality for SALES for CUST_ID is 130. The same value is seen for cust_id=200. Since I also have the data on this system, I can see what the actual values are.

```
SQL> select count(*) From sh.sales where cust_id=100;

  COUNT(*)
----------
        30

SQL> select count(*) From sh.sales where cust_id=200;
```

```
   COUNT(*)
----------
        68

SQL> select count(*) From sh.sales where cust_id between 100 and 300;

   COUNT(*)
----------
     18091
```

Notice that each of the estimates is wrong. The estimates are so far off that using the BETWEEN clause gives me an estimate of 2,080, whereas the actual value is 18,091. We can see from this that the statistics on the objects need to be improved. Perhaps a histogram on the CUST_ID column would help here.

What Does sqlt_snnnnn_del_hgrm.sql Do?

Often histograms can cause a problem, if they are not properly sampled or are inappropriately used. In such cases, with the test case utility you can try deleting the histograms to see what the effect on the execution plan is. In this example we delete all the histograms registered against the test schema.

```
SQL> @sqlt_s30922_del_hgrm.sql
Enter value for tc_user: TC309224

delete_column_hgrm: TC30922.CBO_STAT_TAB_4TC.<partname>.C1
delete_column_hgrm: TC30922.CBO_STAT_TAB_4TC.<partname>.C2
delete_column_hgrm: TC30922.CBO_STAT_TAB_4TC.<partname>.C3
delete_column_hgrm: TC30922.CBO_STAT_TAB_4TC.<partname>.C4
delete_column_hgrm: TC30922.CBO_STAT_TAB_4TC.<partname>.C5

...Removed some entries for clartity
PL/SQL procedure successfully completed.
```

In this case there was no difference in the execution plan, so we know that deleting the histograms make no difference for this query, but it could still be that we need better histograms. We cannot of course go back to the target system and delete the histograms because there could be other SQL that relies on those histograms to execute effectively.

What Does sqlt_snnnnn_tcx.zip Do?

In the latest version of SQLT you can create test cases that have no dependence on SQLT on the target platform. In other words, once you have run SQLTXECUTE or SQLTXTRACT you can take the test case (as described in the sections above) and use the sqlt_snnnnn_tcx.zip file to create a test case on the target platform and not be reliant on SQLT being installed on that database. In this section I'll use the same SQL as before to create a test case on a new database that has no SQLT installed on it. As usual I have put the files from this zip file into a subdirectory. Now on my new standard database I'll install the test case with the install.sql script provided in the list of files. Here is the list of files in the sqlt_s11996_tcx directory I created.

```
-rw-r--r-- 1 oracle oinstall     187 Nov 29 13:49 10053.sql
-rw-r--r-- 1 oracle oinstall     101 Nov 29 13:49 flush.sql
-rwxrwxrwx 1 oracle oinstall     115 Nov 29 13:49 install.sh
-rw-r--r-- 1 oracle oinstall     925 Nov 29 13:49 install.sql<<<
```

```
-rw-r--r-- 1 oracle oinstall   2872 Nov 29 13:49 pack_tcx.sql
-rw-r--r-- 1 oracle oinstall    273 Nov 29 13:49 plan.sql
-rw-r--r-- 1 oracle oinstall    431 Nov 29 13:49 q.sql
-rw-r--r-- 1 oracle oinstall    370 Nov 29 13:49 sel_aux.sql
-rw-r--r-- 1 oracle oinstall    412 Nov 29 13:49 sel.sql
-rw-r--r-- 1 oracle oinstall 794624 Nov 29 13:49 sqlt_s30922_exp2.dmp
-rw-r--r-- 1 oracle oinstall  28946 Nov 29 13:49 sqlt_s30922_metadata1.sql
-rw-r--r-- 1 oracle oinstall   3987 Nov 29 13:49 sqlt_s30922_metadata2.sql
-rw-r--r-- 1 oracle oinstall   2177 Nov 29 13:49 sqlt_s30922_schema_stats.sql
-rw-r--r-- 1 oracle oinstall 184329 Nov 29 13:49 sqlt_s30922_set_cbo_env.sql
-rw-r--r-- 1 oracle oinstall   1261 Nov 29 13:49 sqlt_s30922_system_stats.sql
-rw-r--r-- 1 oracle oinstall 111970 Nov 29 13:49 sqlt_s30922_tcx.zip
-rw-r--r-- 1 oracle oinstall    137 Nov 29 13:49 tc.sql
```

All of these files are recognizable from the TC files we saw earlier. The new interesting file for us is install.sql, which installs the test case in our new database. If we run this script we see the final page as shown below, where the test case user (in this case TC30922) has been created and the test SQL run.

```
Plan hash value: 3035550245


--------------------------------------------------------------------------
| Id | Operation                    | Name         | Rows  | Cost (%CPU)|
--------------------------------------------------------------------------
|  0 | SELECT STATEMENT             |              |       |  576 (100)|
|  1 |  SORT ORDER BY               |              |    9  |  576  (11)|
|  2 |   HASH GROUP BY              |              |    9  |  576  (11)|
|* 3 |    HASH JOIN                 |              |  435K |  555   (8)|
|* 4 |     TABLE ACCESS FULL        | COUNTRIES    |    9  |    3   (0)|
|  5 |     NESTED LOOPS             |              |  918K |  550   (8)|
|  6 |      NESTED LOOPS            |              |  918K |  550   (8)|
|  7 |       PARTITION RANGE ALL    |              |  918K |  517   (2)|
|  8 |        TABLE ACCESS FULL     | SALES        |  918K |  517   (2)|
|* 9 |       INDEX UNIQUE SCAN      | CUSTOMERS_PK |    1  |    0   (0)|
| 10 |      TABLE ACCESS BY INDEX ROWID| CUSTOMERS |    1  |    0   (0)|
--------------------------------------------------------------------------

Predicate Information (identified by operation id):
---------------------------------------------------

   3 - access("CO"."COUNTRY_ID"="C"."COUNTRY_ID")
   4 - filter(("COUNTRY_NAME"='Denmark' OR "COUNTRY_NAME"='France' OR
              "COUNTRY_NAME"='Germany' OR "COUNTRY_NAME"='Ireland' OR
              "COUNTRY_NAME"='Italy' OR "COUNTRY_NAME"='Poland' OR
              "COUNTRY_NAME"='Spain' OR "COUNTRY_NAME"='The Netherlands' OR
              "COUNTRY_NAME"='United Kingdom'))
   9 - access("S"."CUST_ID"="C"."CUST_ID")

SQL> show user
USER is "TC30922"
```

This database is completely fresh. There is no SH schema (I dropped the schema after creation of the database) or SQLT schema (I never installed SQLT on this database). All the schemas are the standard account, and yet if I log in as TC30922 I can execute my test case and do all the things to try and improve the execution plan as I would normally be able to do with SQLT. There is one additional wrinkle to TCX that is sometimes useful. There is a file called pack_tcx.sql that allows you to pack the test case even more tightly. If you run this file, a new zip file is produced called tcx.zip, which contains the files shown below (some of these file names will be different in your case).

```
-rw-r--r-- 1 oracle oinstall    187 Nov 29 13:49 10053.sql
-rw-r--r-- 1 oracle oinstall    101 Nov 29 13:49 flush.sql
-rw-r--r-- 1 oracle oinstall    273 Nov 29 13:49 plan.sql
-rw-r--r-- 1 oracle oinstall    431 Nov 29 13:49 q.sql
-rwxrwxrwx 1 oracle oinstall     72 Nov 29 15:19 readme.txt
-rw-r--r-- 1 oracle oinstall   1445 Nov 29 15:19 setup.sql
-rw-r--r-- 1 oracle oinstall   3987 Nov 29 13:49 sqlt_s30922_metadata2.sql
-rw-r--r-- 1 oracle oinstall 184329 Nov 29 13:49 sqlt_s30922_set_cbo_env.sql
-rw-r--r-- 1 oracle oinstall   1261 Nov 29 13:49 sqlt_s30922_system_stats.sql
-rw-r--r-- 1 oracle oinstall 778240 Nov 29 15:19 TC30922_expdat.dmp
```

After unzipping tcx.zip we run just setup.sql as sys and the test case user is created. While these extra options to create test cases may seem a little redundant when you have SQLT already installed (and I encourage you to do this), these increasingly smaller test cases that show your problem SQL and execution plan are extremely helpful when trying to convince someone (for example, Oracle support) that you have a problem. The fewer extraneous details included in your test case (as long as it still shows the problem), the better it is for trying to solve the problem.

Including Test Case Data

SQLT test cases do not by default include application data. This is because the problem (1) has nothing to do with the application data, (2) there is too much data, or (3) the data is privileged in some way and cannot be shown to anyone else. In some rare cases data may be required to show the problem. Luckily SQLT has an option to allow this as long as the other hurdles can be overcome. In the later versions of SQLT you can do it like this:

```
SQL> EXEC SQLTXADMIN.sqlt$a.set_param('tcb_export_data', 'TRUE');

PL/SQL procedure successfully completed.
```

In the older versions of SQLT, find this section of code in the sqcpkgi.pkb file in the install directory and change the FALSE to TRUE. This is what the code fragment looks like before it is changed:

```
EXECUTE IMMEDIATE
  'BEGIN DBMS_SQLDIAG.EXPORT_SQL_TESTCASE ( '||
  'directory     => :directory, '||
  'sql_id        => :sql_id, '||
  'exportData    => FALSE , '||  <<<Change this to TRUE
  'timeLimit     => :timeLimit, '||
  'testcase_name => :testcase_name, '||
  'testcase      => :testcase ); END;'
```

Then rebuild this package
```
SQL> @sqcpkgi.pkb
```

Package body created.

No errors.

Once you've selected this option you can run `sqltxecute.sql` (or `sqltxtract.sql`) and collect a test case that contains application data. All the setup steps are exactly the same after this; you run `xpress.sql` and follow the steps outlined in previous sections.

Summary

I hope you've enjoyed looking at the features of the test case utility with me. They are powerful and flexible. They are also the beginning of a new world of tuning. Once you have a test case you can change (on a stand-alone system), you can endlessly explore the CBO environment looking for the best performance. As your knowledge of SQL and tuning concepts increases you will be able to try more and more methods to improve the execution plan. Your bedrock in all these endeavors will be SQLTXPLAIN's test case utility. In the next chapter we'll look at a way you can use the test case to find a solution to a problem. With the XPLORE method you'll use a sledgehammer to crack a nut.

■ ■ ■

## CHAPTER 17

Using XPLORE to Investigate Unexpected Plan Changes

I'm sure by now you're thinking that SQLTXPLAIN is a pretty cool tool to be familiar with, if you want to tune Oracle SQL. In Chapter 16 we discussed the test case utility and how that could build an entire environment for testing SQL, system parameter, optimizer settings, objects statistics, and enough of the settings in fact to make the optimizer behave as if it was on the source system.

Once you achieve that state you have a superb environment to go exploring the optimizer's choices. This intelligent, directed approach is extremely fruitful when you have a rough idea what the problem might be and you suspect that you are only a few changes away from the solution. In those kinds of situations you can create the test case, try your changes, and test the result.

This is a good way to solve tuning problems, but what if you had no idea what had caused a regression to some SQL after an upgrade or patch to Oracle or if an SQL plan changed unexpectedly. Then what could you do? There are hundreds of parameter changes you could try, but it would take far too long to go through them all. On the other hand, computers are pretty good at churning through hundreds of choices to find the best one, and this is exactly what XPLORE does.

When Should You Use XPLORE?

The XPLORE method was designed with one purpose in mind: to do a brute force attack on an SQL statement by trying every choice of parameter and then presenting you with the answers. Even though XPLORE can explore many changes to the optimizer environment, it was designed with one specific goal: to find bugs caused by upgrades and patches to the Oracle engine. It is not designed to tune SQL directly, as there are adequate features in other parts of SQLT to deal with that scenario. Nonetheless, it can still be used in a non-upgrade situation if you've run out of ideas and need a hint or if you've hit a bug on a new SQL and you think a fix control change may help. It is designed to deal with situations where an upgrade has occurred and the system works just fine, except for one or two SQLs that for some unspecified reason have regressed. In this scenario it is possible that some feature upgrade of the Oracle engine has caused a specific SQL to no longer be optimal. Generally speaking, SQL performance improves from version to version, but with every version upgrade if 1000s of SQL statements improve maybe one or two will be worse off. If those one or two SQL happen to be crucial to your operation, you'll need XPLORE to find the reason. Can you use XPLORE to tune statements that just need some tuning? It's possible that if you ran XPLORE, and it came up with some parameter changes that might be beneficial, those changes might give you some ideas for improvements. But it's generally not the best use of XPLORE.

© Stelios Charalambides 2017

S. Charalambides, *Oracle SQL Tuning with Oracle SQLTXPLAIN*, DOI 10.1007/978-1-4842-2436-6_17

How Does XPLORE Work?

XPLORE relies on a working test case (as described in Chapter 16). You must have used XECUTE or XTRACT to create a zip file that contains a test case file. Once you have been through the steps to create your test case you will have a test case that XPLORE can work from. Once this test case is in place, XPLORE goes to work. It generates a script with every possible value for every optimizer parameter available, including the hidden ones as well as the fix control settings (we'll discuss those shortly). This script then runs the test case for each possible value for all the parameters and generates an HTML file with the results. The results of all these tests are summarized and hyperlinked in the HTML file to the execution plan and the setting that was changed. It's a real workout for the cost-based optimizer, but remember there's no data (usually).

There are four basic steps to using XPLORE.

1. Get access to the test case.

2. Set the baseline environment for the test case.

3. Create a script that can run your test case.

4. Create a superscript that will run all possible values with your test case.

Let's talk about each of these steps in more detail.

Step 1 is described in detail in Chapter 16 so there's no need to go through that process again except to emphasize that it must be a working test case. You must be able to run q.sql without an error and be able to generate the execution plan. Both of these are requirements, because if the SQL does not run you cannot generate an execution plan, and if you cannot generate an execution plan you cannot generate costs. Without costs you cannot go exploring.

The second step allows you to set some special characteristic of the test case that applies to all the variants tested. Whatever you select here (it could be an optimizer parameter or a fix control or some other environmental setting) it will be done before each iteration of the XPLORE process. You might choose to do this if you were sure that the problem you were investigating had some characteristic you did not want to deviate from. Then you let the brute force method take over.

The third step is to generate a generic script based on your settings, which is used as a framework for the superscript.

The final step is to use this framework script to iterate over all the possible values of the choices you have selected (optimizer parameter, fix control, and Exadata parameters) to create a very big script that does all the work. This big script (the superscript) collects all the information from all the executions and puts all the information into one HTML document. This is the HTML document you then look at manually and apply your intelligence to.

What Can XPLORE Change?

As we mentioned earlier, XPLORE can look at the effect of changes to the optimizer parameters, the fix control settings, and the special Exadata parameters. It cannot be used to test for bad statistics, skewed data, index changes, or similar structural changes to the database objects. If you choose CBO parameters you will only get a report covering the standard CBO parameters (including the hidden ones). This is a much shorter report than including the fix control settings. If you suspect that some optimizer feature related to a bug is the cause of the problem, then you may choose to use the fix control settings and ignore the optimizer parameters. If you suspect an Exadata specific problem then you can choose to select only those parameters related to Exadata. There are not many (18) Exadata specific parameters, so I think it would be useful to list them here. You can get this list from sqlt$_v$parameter_exadata. You can get a similar list for the "normal" non-Exadata parameters, but the list is too long to put here (I list these in Appendix B).

```
SQL> select name, description from sqlt$_v$parameter_exadata;

NAME                                       DESCRIPTION
------------------------------------------ -------------------------------------------------
_kcfis_cell_passthru_enabled               Do not perform smart IO filtering on the cell
_kcfis_dump_corrupt_block                  Dump any corrupt blocks found during smart IO
_kcfis_kept_in_cellfc_enabled              Enable usage of cellsrv flash cache for kept
objects
_kcfis_rdbms_blockio_enabled               Use block IO instead of smart IO in the smart IO
module on RDBMS
_kcfis_storageidx_disabled                 Don't use storage index optimization on the storage
cell
_kcfis_control1                            Kcfis control1
_kcfis_control2                            Kcfis control2
_cell_storidx_mode                         Cell Storage Index mode
cell_offload_processing                    enable SQL processing offload to cells
_slave_mapping_enabled                     enable slave mapping when TRUE
_projection_pushdown                       projection pushdown
_bloom_filter_enabled                      enables or disables bloom filter
_bloom_predicate_enabled                   enables or disables bloom filter predicate pushdown
_bloom_folding_enabled                     Enable folding of bloom filter
_bloom_pushing_max                         bloom filter pushing size upper bound (in KB)
_bloom_minmax_enabled                      enable or disable bloom min max filtering
_bloom_pruning_enabled                     Enable partition pruning using bloom filtering
parallel_force_local                       force single instance execution

18 rows selected.
```

Optimizer parameters, the fix control settings, and the special Exadata parameters are the only things that you can explore with this method, but remember you can still change the baseline environment and rerun your explore each time. Each XPLORE iteration takes a considerable amount of time, so if you do make changes like these you need to be sure you're on the right track before committing to an XPLORE run.

What XPLORE Cannot Change

XPLORE cannot change the structure of your SQL or suggest an index to remove on a table. It is purely designed to find the changes that occur when CBO parameters are changed or when fix control changes are made. Even though XPLORE cannot change these things for you, you're free to change the query in q.sql and rerun XPLORE. For example you might decide that you need to run or change an index type or remove an index. This is again somewhat beyond the scope of XPLORE and can be done in better ways.

What Is Fix Control?

Oracle is an extremely flexible product, with many features and bug fixes, some of which are turned off by default and some of which are turned on by default. Fix Control then is the facility within Oracle that allows bug fixes to be changed from 0 (FALSE or OFF) to 1 (TRUE or ON) or vice versa. As you can imagine, enabling or disabling bug fixes in this way should only be done on a throwaway database as it can severely damage your database (open a support call before making any changes like this to a production database). Let's look at one of these settings from the many that are used in xplore_script_1.sql, the main script of the whole XPLORE process. We'll look at the 6897034 fix control parameter as an example. There are many

275

other fix control parameters like this that we will not describe, but they are all controlled in a similar way. This particular fix control parameter controls the bug fix that takes into account NULL rows in estimating cardinality. When "_fix_control" is true (or 1 or ON) the optimizer takes NULLS into account. Here we set it to FALSE (or 0 or OFF), which is not likely to be something you would want to do in a real-life situation.

```
ALTER SESSION SET "_fix_control" = '6897034:0';
```

   or

```
ALTER SESSION SET "fix_control" ='6897034:FALSE'
```

   or

```
ALTER SESSION SET "fix_control" ='6897034:OFF'
```

You can always check the status of these settings in GV$SESSION_FIX_CONTROL or the equivalent V$ views (or in GV$SYSTEM_FIX_CONTROL or the equivalent V$ views).

The script, xplore_script_1.sql, which is the main driving script for the XPLORE process will, in one of the iterations of XPLORE, change this fix control setting from its default to its non-default value. In this case it will be changed from 1 to 0. When it is set to 1 this fix control setting is on. When it is set to 0 this fix control feature is off. We can find out what the feature is that this fix control setting represents by querying v$system_fix_control. Below I show a query where I interrogate my local database for the meaning of this particular fix control setting:

```
SQL> select
  BUGNO,
  VALUE,
  DESCRIPTION,
  OPTIMIZER_FEATURE_ENABLE,
  IS_DEFAULT
from
  v$system_fix_control
where
  bugno=6897034;
```

BUGNO	VALUE	DESCRIPTION	OPTIMIZER_FEATURE_ENABLE	IS_DEFAULT
6897034	1	index cardinality estimates not taking into account NULL rows	10.2.0.5	1

In this particular case bug number 6897034 has to do with index cardinality estimates and those estimates in relation to NULLs in rows. That could be a pretty serious problem, so by default this has been set to 1 (TRUE). The script I am running will set it to 0 to see if that makes a difference to the execution plan. The oldest version of Oracle in which this value was set to 1 was 10.2.0.5. In the previous version, 10.2.0.4 the value was 0 (or this bug fix was not introduced).

Remember I said that optimizer_features_enable was like a super switch. Well, we can test that now by setting optimizer_features_enable to 10.2.0.4 and seeing what happens to this particular fix control. First I show the current value of optimizer_features_enable, and then I show the current value of the fix control. Then I change the super parameter to 10.2.0.4, (first at the session level then at the system level). The value I have to set is the value just before 10.2.0.5, which is the value of the OPTIMIZER_FEATURE_ENABLE column for the fix control. (Yes the column is OPTIMIZER_FEATURE_ENABLE, and the parameter is optimizer_features_ enable). After setting the super parameter at the system level I re-query the value of the fix control and I see that the super parameter has done its job and set the fix control as it would have been in that version.

```
SQL> show parameter optimizer_features_enable;

NAME                                 TYPE         VALUE
------------------------------------ ----------- -------------------------------
optimizer_features_enable            string       12.1.0.2

SQL> select
  BUGNO,
  VALUE,
  DESCRIPTION,
  OPTIMIZER_FEATURE_ENABLE,
  IS_DEFAULT
from
  v$system_fix_control
where
  bugno=6897034;

    BUGNO      VALUE DESCRIPTION             OPTIMIZER_FEATURE_ENABLE  IS_DEFAULT
---------- ---------- -------------------- ------------------------- ----------
   6897034          1 index cardinality est 10.2.0.5                          1
                      imates not taking int
                      o account NULL rows

SQL> alter session set optimizer_features_enable='10.2.0.4';

Session altered.

SQL> select
  BUGNO,
  VALUE,
  DESCRIPTION,
  OPTIMIZER_FEATURE_ENABLE,
  IS_DEFAULT
from
  v$system_fix_control
where
  bugno=6897034;

    BUGNO      VALUE DESCRIPTION             OPTIMIZER_FEATURE_ENABLE  IS_DEFAULT
---------- ---------- -------------------- ------------------------- ----------
   6897034          1 index cardinality est 10.2.0.5                          1
                      imates not taking int
                      o account NULL rows

SQL> alter system set optimizer_features_enable='10.2.0.4' scope=memory;

System altered.
```

```
SQL> select
  BUGNO,
  VALUE,
  DESCRIPTION,
  OPTIMIZER_FEATURE_ENABLE,
  IS_DEFAULT
from
  v$system_fix_control
where
  bugno=6897034;

     BUGNO      VALUE DESCRIPTION               OPTIMIZER_FEATURE_ENABLE  IS_DEFAULT
---------- ---------- ------------------------- ------------------------- ----------
   6897034          0 index cardinality est 10.2.0.5                               1
                      imates not taking int
                      o account NULL rows
```

If we run the super script it will do this step so that this parameter is set. The result will be that during that step of the XPLORE script we have a non-default setup for the session. It seems unlikely that this parameter is going to improve your query, but it's not impossible. Imagine a case where some SQL is reliant on a faulty calculation for cardinality, which is then "fixed" by applying the fix for bug 6897034. Then the SQL could regress (perform less well), and it could then appear that the SQL was broken by an upgrade to 10.2.0.5. However, the XPLORE method is only applying a brute force approach; it just powers through every single option and lets you supply the intelligence to determine what is important and what is not. Now we know how XPLORE works, when to use it, and how to use it. We also know XPLORE is not the panacea for tuning problems but just one more tool on the Swiss Army knife of tuning.

An Example XPLORE Session

In this XPLORE session we will go through every single step, including looking at the results and explaining what they tell us about the SQL in relation to the parameters that were changed. In this example test case, I am using an XTRACT test case with no data; it is case S30923. This is the SQL being explored:

```
select country_name, sum(AMOUNT_SOLD)
from sales s, customers c, countries co
where
  s.cust_id=c.cust_id
  and co.country_id=c.country_id
  and country_name in (
    'Ireland','Denmark','Poland','United Kingdom',
    'Germany','France','Spain','The Netherlands','Italy')
group by country_name order by sum(AMOUNT_SOLD);
```

It is being run on 12.1.0.2, and the SQL ID is 8phvh8qxxubvq. I'm curious to know if this SQL ran better in previous versions of Oracle. I also want to know if I can set up my throwaway database to run this more quickly. I could also be interested in running XPLORE for this SQL because I recently wrote it, it's not performing as I expected, and I think this may be because of a bug. It's a long shot, but I'm willing to give XPLORE a shot.

Getting Your Test Case Built

As I mentioned earlier there is no way to run XPLORE without first building a test case. By this I mean that we have already run xpress for test case TC30923. By navigating to the xplore directory under utl I am able to easily run XPLORE's install script.

```
$ pwd
/home/oracle/sqlt/utl/xplore
$ sqlplus / as sysdba
SQL*Plus: Release 12.1.0.2.0 Production on Mon Dec 5 23:17:18 2016
Copyright (c) 1982, 2014, Oracle.  All rights reserved.
Connected to:
Oracle Database 12c Enterprise Edition Release 12.1.0.2.0 - 64bit Production
With the Partitioning, OLAP, Advanced Analytics and Real Application Testing options

SQL>
SQL> @install
Test Case User: TC30923
Password: TC30923
```

This install script grants the test case user enough privileges (DBA) to run the scripts that are to follow. Remember this can only be run on a stand-alone system that can be replaced easily. The script finishes with

```
Package created.
No errors.
Package body created.
No errors.
Installation completed.
You are now connected as TC30923.
1. Set CBO env if needed
2. Execute @create_xplore_script.sql
```

The first step "Set CBO env if needed" is reminding you that if your test case needs to set any environmental settings that you want to be constant for all the runs of your test case, then you must set it here. This is then applied to the baseline and is executed before each execution of the scripts for each test. By giving the install script the test case user you have changed the user into a DBA of the system and allowed it to change all system parameters and fix control settings. The test case user also knows the script that needs to be run and will then proceed to build the template script and then the superscript.

Building the First Script

This first script does nothing more than collect your settings for your XPLORE session and then calls xplore. create_xplore_script with those parameters. Here is the line from the script:

```
EXEC xplore.create_xplore_script(
    '&&xplore_method.',        <<<This can take a value of XECUTE or XPLAIN
    '&&include_cbo_parameters.',<<<Include CBO parameters or not
    '&&include_exadata_parameters.',<<<Include Exadata specific parameters or not
    '&&include_fix_control.',   <<<Include Fix control or not
    '&&generate_sql_monitor_reports.'); <<<Generate SQL monitor reports or not.
```

These lines all make a difference to the final report that is created. The xplore_method controls XPLORE to allow it to run in XPLAIN mode or in XECUTE mode. In XPLAIN mode there is no execution of the SQL. XPLAIN mode is generally fast enough for most cases. XECUTE executes the SQL, and if there is also data present then this can take a very long time to complete. To clarify, the XECUTE option here is not related to the XECUTE method: this is an option of XPLORE utility we are talking about here. If the SQL can be executed relatively quickly, or if you have enough time to wait for the result, then XECUTE will give you more information.

The next two parameters control the groups of parameters that you wish to explore. You can choose to explore all of them; in other words try all values for all CBO parameters, and all Exadata-specific parameters. If your test case is from an Exadata machine then you may be interested in choosing this option also. If your test case is not from Exadata, then there is no point in choosing this option because these tests will only have an effect on an Exadata machine. Then you can choose to set fix control parameters (we mentioned these in a previous section of this chapter). You may be interested in checking these parameters if you suspect you are suffering from an optimizer bug. When you run this script and enter the required parameters, a new bigger script will be generated.

Building the Superscript

Now we come to the last step before running the XPLORE session. The first thing we need to do is copy the test SQL script to the utl\xplore directory. This is to allow the XPLORE session to access the script. In my case this is the command I issued:

```
$cp
$ pwd
/home/oracle/sqlt/utl/xplore
$ cp ../../run/sqlt_s30923_xtract_8phvh8qxxubvq/sqlt_s30923_tc/q.sql .
```

We run the create_xplore_script.sql, which will prompt for the parameters described in the previous section. Here we see a run of the script where we have chosen XECUTE mode and chosen to explore CBO parameters, Exadata parameters, and fix control parameters and to produce SQL monitor reports.

```
SQL> @create_xplore_script.sql
Parameter 1:
XPLORE Method: XECUTE (default) or XPLAIN
"XECUTE" requires /* ^^unique_id */ token in SQL
"XPLAIN" uses "EXPLAIN PLAN FOR" command
Enter "XPLORE Method" [XECUTE]: XECUTE
Parameter 2:
Include CBO Parameters: Y (default) or N
Enter "CBO Parameters" [Y]: Y
Parameter 3:
Include Exadata Parameters: Y (default) or N
Enter "EXADATA Parameters" [Y]: Y
Parameter 4:
Include Fix Control: Y (default) or N
Enter "Fix Control" [Y]: Y
Parameter 5:
Generate SQL Monitor Reports: N (default) or Y
Only applicable when XPLORE Method is XECUTE
Enter "SQL Monitor" [N]: Y
Review and execute @xplore_script_1.sql
```

The script created now is extremely long. We can get a general feeling for what's in this script by looking at a few entries near the top of the file.

```
1. SET DEF ON ECHO OFF TERM ON APPI OFF SERVEROUT ON SIZE 1000000 NUMF "" SQLP SQL>;
2. SET SERVEROUT ON SIZE UNL;
3. SET ESC ON SQLBL ON;
4. SPO xplore_script_1.log;
5. COL connected_user NEW_V connected_user FOR A30;
6. SELECT user connected_user FROM DUAL;
7. PRO
8. PRO Parameter 1:
9. PRO Name of SCRIPT file that contains SQL to be xplored (required)
10. PRO Note: SCRIPT must contain comment /* ^^unique_id */
11. PRO
12. SET DEF ^ ECHO OFF;
13. DEF script_with_sql = '^1';
14. PRO
15. PRO Parameter 2:
16. PRO Password for ^^connected_user. (required)
17. PRO
18. DEF user_password = '^2';
19. PRO
20. PRO Value passed to xplore_script.sql:
21. PRO ~~~~~~~~~~~~~~~~~~~~~~~~~~~~~~~~~~22. PRO SCRIPT_WITH_SQL: ^^script_with_sql
23. PRO
24. PRO -- begin common
25. PRO DEF _SQLPLUS_RELEASE
26. PRO SELECT USER FROM DUAL;
27. PRO SELECT TO_CHAR(SYSDATE, 'YYYY-MM-DD HH24:MI:SS') current_time FROM DUAL;
28. PRO SELECT * FROM v$version;
29. PRO SELECT * FROM v$instance;
30. PRO SELECT name, value FROM v$parameter2 WHERE name LIKE '%dump_dest';
31. PRO SELECT directory_name||' '||directory_path directories FROM dba_directories WHERE
directory_name LIKE 'SQLT$%' OR directory_name LIKE 'TRCA$%' ORDER BY 1;
32. PRO -- end common
33. PRO
34. SET VER ON HEA ON LIN 2000 PAGES 1000 TRIMS ON TI OFF TIMI OFF;
```

I've numbered the lines in the code, as it is worth explaining what's happening in detail here for some of these lines. Some lines are just PROMPT, which is just a blank line.

1. **SET DEF ON ECHO OFF TERM ON APPI OFF SERVEROUT ON SIZE 1000000 NUMF "" SQLP SQL>;** - Sets up the default format for output as the script relies on the format to produce a workable HTML file as it runs the script

2. **SET SERVEROUT ON SIZE UNL;** - Makes sure the size of output is unlimited

3. **SET ESC ON SQLBL ON;** - Sets ESCAPE Mode on and blank line mode

4. **SPO xplore_script_1.log;** - The script we are spooling to

5. **COL connected_user NEW_V connected_user FOR A30;** - Sets the format for the connected_user column

6. **SELECT user connected_user FROM DUAL;** - Gets the connected user

8. **PRO Parameter 1:** - Gets the script name

9. **PRO Name of SCRIPT file that contains SQL to be explored (required)** – Prompts for information

12. **SET DEF ^ ECHO OFF;** - Sets up more environmental settings

13. **DEF script_with_sql = '^1';** - Sets up the interaction count (script_with_sql) to ^1

16. **PRO Password for ^^connected_user. (required)** – Gets the password for the test case user

18. **DEF user_password = '^2';** - Sets the password for the test case user to the variable user_password

22. **PRO SCRIPT_WITH_SQL: ^^script_with_sql** – Gets the script file name and sets the variable script_with_sql

26. **PRO SELECT USER FROM DUAL;** - Selects the current connected user

27. **PRO SELECT TO_CHAR(SYSDATE, 'YYYY-MM-DD HH24:MI:SS') current_time FROM DUAL;** - Selects the date and time

28. **PRO SELECT * FROM v$version;** - Selects the current version

29. **PRO SELECT * FROM v$instance;** - Selects the instance information

30. **PRO SELECT name, value FROM v$parameter2 WHERE name LIKE '%dump_dest';** - Shows the dump destinations

31. **PRO SELECT directory_name||' '||directory_path directories FROM dba_directories WHERE directory_name LIKE 'SQLT$%' OR directory_name LIKE 'TRCA$%' ORDER BY 1;** - Checks the Oracle Directories are set up

34. **SET VER ON HEA ON LIN 2000 PAGES 1000 TRIMS ON TI OFF TIMI OFF;** - At the end of the common section, sets the required format environment

This is the end of the common code. Now we have code that is generated in a loop. I show the first section of this script that modifies the test case to set "_cursor_plan_unparse_enabled" to FALSE

```
--
1. SET ECHO ON;
2. --in case of disconnects, suspect 6356566 and un-comment workaround in line below if needed
3. --ALTER SESSION SET "_cursor_plan_unparse_enabled" = FALSE;
4. WHENEVER SQLERROR EXIT SQL.SQLCODE;
5. --
6. COL run_id NEW_V run_id FOR A4;
7. SELECT LPAD((NVL(MAX(run_id), 0) + 1), 4, '0') run_id FROM xplore_test;
8. --
9. DELETE plan_table_all WHERE statement_id LIKE 'xplore_{001}_[^^run_id.]_(%)';
10. EXEC xplore.set_baseline(1);
11. --
12. ALTER SESSION SET STATISTICS_LEVEL = ALL;
13. DEF unique_id = "xplore_{001}_[^^run_id.]_(00000)"
14. @^^script_with_sql.
15. EXEC xplore.snapshot_plan('xplore_{001}_[^^run_id.]_(00000)', 'XECUTE', 'Y');
16. WHENEVER SQLERROR CONTINUE;
```

```
17. --
18. CONN ^^connected_user./^^user_password.
19. EXEC xplore.set_baseline(1);
20. ALTER SESSION SET "_adaptive_window_consolidator_enabled" = FALSE;
21. ALTER SESSION SET STATISTICS_LEVEL = ALL;
22. DEF unique_id = "xplore_{001}_[^^run_id.]_(00001)"
23. @^^script_with_sql.
24. WHENEVER SQLERROR CONTINUE;
```

The above 15 lines are the core of XPLORE. I'll explain what is happening here.

Lines 1–4. Ensures that echo is on so that we get some output and ensure that an error stops the SQL

Lines 5–8. Sets the format for the column run_id, and selects the current run_id from the table xplore_test

Line 9. Deletes the entries in the PLAN_TABLE where there are any matching statements to the about to be executed statement.

Line 10. Sets the baseline that we decided as users to set before the execution of every iteration of the XPLORE

Lines 11–14. Sets the statistics level to ALL, defines the unique_id value and executes the script.

Line 15. Executes the combination script name. Once you've reviewed this script and are happy that it will produce the right results, then you can run the xplore_script_1.sql. I know I've gone into more detail here than is needed to use the script, but these few lines are the very core of the XPLORE method. We could go into more detail and look at the procedure snapshot_plan in xplore.pkb, but that is beyond the scope of this book.

Running the Script

Running the script is just a matter of executing xplore_script_1.sql. I show below the first run-through of the script, with the collection of the parameters:

```
SQL>@xplore_script_1.sql
TC30923

Parameter 1:
Name of SCRIPT file that contains SQL to be xplored (required)
Note: SCRIPT must contain comment /* ^^unique_id */
Enter value for 1: q.sql
Parameter 2:
Password for TC30923 (required)
Enter value for 2: TC30923
Value passed to xplore_script.sql:
~~~~~~~~~~~~~~~~~~~~~~~~~~~~~~~~~~
SCRIPT_WITH_SQL: q.sql
-- begin common
DEF _SQLPLUS_RELEASE
SELECT USER FROM DUAL
```

```
SELECT TO_CHAR(SYSDATE, 'YYYY-MM-DD HH24:MI:SS') current_time FROM DUAL
SELECT * FROM v$version
SELECT * FROM v$instance
SELECT name, value FROM v$parameter2 WHERE name LIKE '%dump_dest'
SELECT directory_name||' '||directory_path directories FROM dba_directories WHERE directory_
name LIKE 'SQLT$%' OR directory_name like 'TRCA$%' ORDER BY 1
-- end common
SQL>--in case of disconnects, suspect 6356566 and un-comment workaround in line below if
needed
SQL>--ALTER SESSION SET "_cursor_plan_unparse_enabled" = FALSE;
SQL>WHENEVER SQLERROR EXIT SQL.SQLCODE;
SQL>--
SQL>COL run_id NEW_V run_id FOR A4;
SQL>SELECT LPAD((NVL(MAX(run_id), 0) + 1), 4, '0') run_id FROM xplore_test;
RUN_
----
0001
SQL>--
SQL>DELETE plan_table_all WHERE statement_id LIKE 'xplore_{001}_[^^run_id.]_(%)';
old   1: DELETE plan_table_all WHERE statement_id LIKE 'xplore_{001}_[^^run_id.]_(%)'
new   1: DELETE plan_table_all WHERE statement_id LIKE 'xplore_{001}_[0001]_(%)'
```

We've set the environment now and have to set any baseline set up before running the script we are investigating.

```
SQL>EXEC xplore.set_baseline(1);
--
-- begin set_baseline
--
--
-- end set_baseline
--
SQL>--
SQL>ALTER SESSION SET STATISTICS_LEVEL = ALL;
SQL>DEF unique_id = "xplore_{001}_[^^run_id.]_(00000)"
SQL>@^^script_with_sql.
SQL>REM $Header: 215187.1 sqlt_s30923_tc_script.sql 12.1.160429 2016/12/05 abel.maacias $
SQL>
SQL>-- These are the non-default or modified CBO parameters on source system.
SQL>-- ALTER SYSTEM commands can be un-commented out on a test environment.
SQL>
SQL>select /* ^^unique_id */  country_name, sum(AMOUNT_SOLD)
  2     2 from sh.sales s, sh.customers c, sh.countries co
  3  where
  4    s.cust_id=c.cust_id
  5    and co.country_id=c.country_id
  6    and country_name in (
  7      'Ireland','Denmark','Poland','United Kingdom',
  8       'Germany','France','Spain','The Netherlands','Italy')
  9    group by country_name order by sum(AMOUNT_SOLD);
old   2:  /* ^^unique_id */  country_name, sum(AMOUNT_SOLD)
new   2:  /* xplore_{001}_[0001]_(00000) */  country_name, sum(AMOUNT_SOLD)
```

```
SQL>EXEC xplore.snapshot_plan('xplore_{001}_[^^run_id.]_(00000)', 'XECUTE', 'Y');
SQL>WHENEVER SQLERROR CONTINUE;
SQL>--
```

The data from this run will be collected, along with all the other runs into the SQLT repository ready to produce the report at the end of the run.

Reviewing the Results

When the script finally finishes (it can take hours if you have data), you will see a message indicating that the HTML files are being compressed and the main report is being created. The XPLORE Completed message is a big clue that we are now ready to read the report. Here is the output at the end of the XPLORE run.

```
test of xplore_sql_monitor_report_1.zip OK

   adding: xplore_sql_monitor_report_1.zip (stored 0%)
   adding: xplore_report_1.html (deflated 97%)
   adding: xplore_script_1.log (deflated 98%)
   adding: xplore_script_1.sql (deflated 95%)
test of xplore_1.zip OK

XPLORE Completed.
Disconnected from Oracle Database 12c Enterprise Edition Release 12.1.0.2.0 - 64bit
Production
With the Partitioning, OLAP, Advanced Analytics and Real Application Testing options
```

A new file has been created called xplore_1.zip, which is in the directory where we ran the XPLORE superscript.

```
ls -l xplore_1.zip
-rw-r--r-- 1 oracle oinstall 234957 Dec  6 00:08 xplore_1.zip
```

To use this report it is best to create a subdirectory and unzip the files in xplore_1.zip. In the zip file is an HTML file (the main report), a log file of the run, and the xplore script that was run. The only file of interest to us now is the HTML file. If we open this file with a browser we see it is much less fussy than a normal XECUTE or XTRACT report. It starts with a simple title "XPLORE Report for baseline:1 runid:1", and we are straight into endless numbers. This "Plan Summary" part of the report shows all the discovered plans for our one SQL. Let's look at Figure 17-1, which shows this part of the report. This is the jumping-off point to all the other parts of the report.

XPLORE Report for baseline:1 runid:1

Plans Summary

Plans for each test have been captured into TC30923.SQL_PLAN_STATISTICS_ALL or TC30923.PLAN_TABLE_ALL.

#	Plan Hash Value	Total Tests	Max Cost	Min Cost	Max Buffer Gets	Min Buffer Gets	Max CPU (secs)	Min CPU (secs)	Max Disk Reads	Min Disk Reads	Max ET[1] (secs)	Min ET[1] (secs)	Max Actual Rows	Min Actual Rows	Max Estim Rows	Min Estim Rows
1	283749337	8	3845	963	3	3	.004	.002	0	0	.004	.003	0	0	9	9
2	922729823	1	5046	5046	1	1	0	0	0	0	.004	.004	0	0	9	9
3	1531112568	2	11441	11441	3	3	.004	.004	0	0	.004	.004	0	0	9	9
4	2881491907	14	816519	766343	3	3	.004	.002	0	0	.004	.003	0	0	8	8
5	2938593747	1483	3886	629	911	1	.094	0	3	0	.422	.002	0	0	9	9
6	3622901094	21	1321	651	6	3	.006	0	0	0	.006	.004	0	0	9	9
7	4206637151	2	589	94	3	3	.004	.004	0	0	.005	.004	0	0	9	9

(1) If tables are empty, then Elapsed Time is close to Parse Time.

Figure 17-1. *The top part of the XPLORE report*

There were only seven different plans in this case (it was a very simple piece of SQL). For example, PHV 922729823 only had one test so it is not surprising that the maximum and minimum cost was the same at 5046. The original plan had a cost of 966, so this option clearly is not a good one. If we look at what that test was we'll be able to see why it didn't turn out so well. Scroll to the section show in Figure 17-1, which shows the "Discovered Plans," just below the "Plans Summary." Here I want to know why my original cost of 966 increased to 5,046. The arrow is pointing to the hyperlink that takes me to a different section of the same report, which details what happened on this test. See Figure 17-2, which shows the "Discovered Plans" section of the report.

Discovered Plans

Plans for each test have been captured into TC30923.SQL_PLAN_STATISTICS_ALL or

#	Plan Hash Value	SQLT Plan Hash Value[1]	SQLT Plan Hash Value2[1]	Total Tests	Plan Cost	Tests	Max Buffer Gets	Min Buffer Gets	Max CPU (secs)	Min CPU (secs)
1	283749337	74249	77790	8	963	4	3	3	.004	.002
					965	2				
					3845	2				
2	922729823	30551	25462	1	5046	1	1	1	0	0
3	1531112568	56627	84870	2	11441	2	3	3	.004	.004
4	2881491907	53527	57068	14	766343	2	3	3	.004	.002
					810705	2				
					816519	10				
5	2938593747	52453	55994	1478	629	1	911	1	.094	0
					651	1				
					696	1				
					786	1				
					962	3				
					964	1				
					965	1455				
					966	11				
					1321	1				
					1880	1				
					2710	1				
					3886	1				
6	2938593747	52453	56830	2	965	2	3	3	.003	.003
7	2938593747	52453	68165	1	965	1	3	3	.003	.003
8	2938593747	55800	59341	2	965	2	3	3	.005	.002
9	3622901094	56929	85172	21	651	1	6	3	.006	0
					696	1				
					786	1				
					965	17				
					1321	1				
10	4206637151	5496	9037	2	94	1	3	3	.004	.004
					589	1				

(1) SQLT PHV considers id, parent_id, operation, options, index_columns and object_name. SQLT PH

(2) If tables are empty, then Elapsed Time is close to Parse Time.

(3) B: Includes BASELINE.

(4) F: Includes at least one *_fix_control*.

Figure 17-2. *You can get to the test details by clicking on the hyperlink under the "Total Tests" column*

Once we click on this hyperlink we are taken to the section of the report showing what was done and what happened. Figure 17-3 shows the details for this particular plan hash value.

Completed Tests for Plan 922729823 30551 25462

#	Test Id	Test	Baseline Value	Plan Cost	Buffer Gets	CPU (secs)	Disk Reads	ET (secs)	Actual Rows	Estim Rows
1	00055	ALTER SESSION SE "_hash_join_enabled" = FALSE;	TRUE	5046	1	0	0	.004	0	9

Figure 17-3. The details for the PHV 922729823

We can see that the test for this PHV was to set "_hash_join_enabled"=FALSE if we look at the original execution plan from the XTRACT report for this SQL (see Figure 17-4).

SQL: [±]

ID	Exec Ord	Operation	Go To	More	Cost²	Estim Card	PStart	PStop
0	9	SELECT STATEMENT			966	9		
1	8	SORT ORDER BY		[+]	966	9		
2	7	. HASH GROUP BY		[+]	966	9		
3	6	.. HASH JOIN		[+]	946	435241		
4	3	... HASH JOIN		[+]	426	26289		
5	1	.... TABLE ACCESS FULL COUNTRIES	[+]	[+]	3	9		
6	2	.... TABLE ACCESS FULL CUSTOMERS	[+]	[+]	423	55500		
7	5	... PARTITION RANGE ALL		[+]	517	918843	1	28
8	4	.... TABLE ACCESS FULL SALES	[+]	[+]	517	918843	1	28

Performance statistics are only available when parameter "statistics_level" was set to "ALL" at hard-parse time, or SQL c
*(1) If estim_card * starts < output_rows then under-estimate. If estim_card * starts > output_rows then over-estimate. Col*
*100x and *** 1000x over/under-estimates.*
(2) Largest contributors for cumulative-statistics columns are shown in red.
Other XML (id=1): [±]
Outline Data (id=1): [±]
Leading (id=1): [±]
Go to Tables
Go to Indexes
Go to Top

Figure 17-4. The original execution plan as shown in the XTRACT report for the SQL

The original plan was to use "TABLE ACCESS FULL" for COUNTRIES and CUSTOMERS and the use a hash join, followed by another hash join of that with the result of the "TABLE ACCESS FULL" of SALES. The main thrust of this plan is to use hash join. Now our XPLORE has disabled this option by setting the hidden parameter, which is not too surprising because the plan has become more costly. If we click on the number under the "Test Id" column (as shown in Figure 17-3) we will see which plan was actually chosen. This is the plan we see.

```
-----------------------------------------------------------------------------------
| Id  |Operation                         |Name         | Cost (%CPU)|   A-Time   | Buffers |
-----------------------------------------------------------------------------------
|   0 |SELECT STATEMENT                  |             | 5046 (100)|00:00:00.01 |    1 |
|   1 | SORT ORDER BY                    |             | 5046  (2)|00:00:00.01 |    1 |
|   2 |  HASH GROUP BY                   |             | 5046  (2)|00:00:00.01 |    1 |
|   3 |   MERGE JOIN                     |             | 5025  (1)|00:00:00.01 |    1 |
|   4 |    SORT JOIN                     |             |  840  (1)|00:00:00.01 |    1 |
|   5 |     MERGE JOIN                   |             |  648  (1)|00:00:00.01 |    1 |
|*  6 |      TABLE ACCESS BY INDEX ROWID|COUNTRIES     |    2  (0)|00:00:00.01 |    1 |
|   7 |       INDEX FULL SCAN            |COUNTRIES_PK  |    1  (0)|00:00:00.01 |    1 |
|*  8 |      SORT JOIN                   |             |  646  (1)|00:00:00.01 |    0 |
|   9 |       TABLE ACCESS FULL          |CUSTOMERS     |  423  (1)|00:00:00.01 |    0 |
|* 10 |    SORT JOIN                     |             | 4185  (1)|00:00:00.01 |    0 |
|  11 |     PARTITION RANGE ALL          |             |  517  (2)|00:00:00.01 |    0 |
|  12 |      TABLE ACCESS FULL           |SALES         |  517  (2)|00:00:00.01 |    0 |
-----------------------------------------------------------------------------------
```

No sign of a hash join, as expected. The optimizer has honored our requirement and avoided this, but it has been detrimental to our plan, so we know not to force the optimizer to not use a hash join. This is where the intelligence part comes in. We know that a hash join is a good idea here, but the brute force approach of XPLORE does not.

Finding the Best Execution Plan

So enough of how the plan can be made worse. Let's go back to the plan summaries (see Figure 17-1) and now look to see if there have been any improvements. We see that there was a big improvement for PHV 420667151. Here we see a plan that shows a minimum cost of 123 (much less than our original plan cost of 966. If we then look at the "Discovered Plans" section (Figure 17-5),

Discovered Plans

Plans for each test have been captured into TC30923.SQL_PLAN_STATISTICS_ALL or

#	Plan Hash Value	SQLT Plan Hash Value[1]	SQLT Plan Hash Value2[1]	Total Tests	Plan Cost	Tests	Max Buffer Gets	Min Buffer Gets	Max CPU (secs)	Min CPU (secs)	
1	283749337	74249	77790	8	963	4	3	3	.004	.002	
					965	2					
					3845	2					
2	922729823	30551	25462	1	5046	1	1	1	0	0	
3	1531112568	56627	84870	2	11441	2	3	3	.004	.004	
4	2881491907	53527	57068	14	766343	2	3	3	.004	.002	
					810705	2					
					816519	10					
5	2938593747	52453	55994	1478	629	1	911	1	.094	0	
					651	1					
					696	1					
					786	1					
					962	3					
					964	1					
					965	1455					
					966	11					
					1321	1					
					1880	1					
					2710	1					
					3886	1					
6	2938593747	52453	56830	2	965	2	3	3	.003	.003	
7	2938593747	52453	68165	1	965	1	3	3	.003	.003	
8	2938593747	55800	59341	2	965	2	3	3	.005	.002	
9	3622901094	5692	85172	21	651	1	6	3	.006	0	
					696	1					
					786	1					
					965	17					
					1321	1					
10	4206637151	5496	9037	2	94	1	3	3	.004	.004	
					589	1					

Figure 17-5. *Looking for the lowest cost plan*

we see that there were two tests done. If we now click on the hyperlinked "2" we see the completed tests for this PHV (see Figure 17-6).

Completed Tests for Plan 4206637151 5496 9037

#	Test Id	Test	Baseline Value	Plan Cost	Buffer Gets	CPU (secs)	Disk Reads	ET (secs)	Actual Rows	Estim Rows
1	00450	ALTER SESSION SET optimizer_index_cost_adj = 1;	100	94	3	.004	0	.005	0	9
2	00451	ALTER SESSION SET optimizer_index_cost_adj = 10;	100	589	3	.004	0	.004	0	9

Figure 17-6. *The test details for PHV4206637151*

We see in this already that the reason the cost was so low in this case was that we set `optimizer_index_cost_adj` to 1. In other words, we forced indexes to be used. We can see the plan used for the test 450 by clicking on the hyperlinked 450. This is the plan we see (I've removed some columns for clarity).

```
Plan hash value: 4206637151
--------------------------------------------------------------------------------------
|Id |Operation                                |Name                | E-Rows | Cost (%CPU)|
--------------------------------------------------------------------------------------
|  0|SELECT STATEMENT                         |                    |        |  589 (100)|
|  1| SORT ORDER BY                           |                    |      9 |  589   (6)|
|  2|  HASH GROUP BY                          |                    |      9 |  589   (6)|
|* 3|   HASH JOIN                             |                    |   435K |  568   (3)|
|* 4|    HASH JOIN                            |                    |  26289 |  252   (1)|
|* 5|     TABLE ACCESS FULL                   |COUNTRIES           |      9 |    3   (0)|
|  6|     TABLE ACCESS BY INDEX ROWID BATCHED |CUSTOMERS           |  55500 |  249   (1)|
|  7|      BITMAP CONVERSION TO ROWIDS        |                    |        |           |
|  8|       BITMAP INDEX FULL SCAN            |CUSTOMERS_GENDER_BIX|        |           |
|  9|    PARTITION RANGE ALL                  |                    |   918K |  314   (4)|
| 10|     TABLE ACCESS BY LOCAL INDEX ROWID BATCHED|SALES          |   918K |  314   (4)|
| 11|      BITMAP CONVERSION TO ROWIDS        |                    |        |           |
| 12|       BITMAP INDEX FULL SCAN            |SALES_PROMO_BIX     |        |           |
--------------------------------------------------------------------------------------
```

It looks like using the bitmap indexes is useful in this case, as the cost is so low. We have to ask why the optimizer did not choose the index in the first place, and for this we would need to look at the statistics in the original XTRACT report. We see from the system observations that `optimizer_dynamic_sampling` is set to 1 (so in this case no dynamic sampling would have been done).

As we have a value of 1 for dynamic sampling we know that dynamic sampling could take place but in this case did not because the tables involved are not unindexed (see Chapter 8 for details on cardinality feedback and dynamic sampling). Still not using dynamic sampling is not an excuse for getting the plan wrong, but it could explain why the plan was not saved by dynamic sampling if statistics are missing.

Reviewing the Original Test Case

If we look at the observations in the original report we see that the many of the partition statistics are missing and are out of date (which doesn't matter in my case as the data is static). However as it looks like the statistics are the cause of the wrong plan being selected, I'll update them and retry the SQL.

The SQL I used to collect the new up-to-date statistics was this:

```
SQL> exec dbms_stats.gather_Table_stats(ownname=>'TC64661',
  tabname=>'SALES', estimate_percent=>dbms_stats.auto_sample_size,cascade=>TRUE)

PL/SQL procedure successfully completed.

SQL> exec dbms_stats.gather_Table_stats(ownname=>'TC64661',
  tabname=>'COUNTRIES', estimate_percent=>dbms_stats.auto_sample_size,cascade=>TRUE);

PL/SQL procedure successfully completed.
```

```
SQL> exec dbms_stats.gather_Table_stats(ownname=>'TC64661',
  tabname=>'CUSTOMERS', estimate_percent=>dbms_stats.auto_sample_size,cascade=>TRUE);

PL/SQL procedure successfully completed.
```

Remember, in this case I also used data from the source tables (which is not always the case). If I collect fresh statistics on all of the relevant tables (as shown above) and rerun my test case, I get this execution plan:

```
SQL> @tc

COUNTRY_NAME                             SUM(AMOUNT_SOLD)
---------------------------------------- ----------------
Poland                                          8447.14
Denmark                                      1977764.79
Spain                                        2090863.44
France                                       3776270.13
Italy                                        4854505.28
United Kingdom                               6393762.94
Germany                                      9210129.22

7 rows selected.

PLAN_TABLE_OUTPUT
--------------------------------------------------------------------------------------------
---------------------------------------
SQL_ID  f43bszax8xh07, child number 0
---------------------------------------
select  /* ^^unique_id */  country_name, sum(AMOUNT_SOLD) from sales s,
customers c, countries co where   s.cust_id=c.cust_id   and
co.country_id=c.country_id   and country_name in (
'Ireland','Denmark','Poland','United Kingdom',
'Germany','France','Spain','The Netherlands','Italy')   group by
country_name order by sum(AMOUNT_SOLD)

Plan hash value: 1235134607
```

Id	Operation	Name	Rows	Bytes	Cost (%CPU)	Time
0	SELECT STATEMENT				4 (100)	
1	SORT ORDER BY		1	87	4 (50)	00:00:01
2	HASH GROUP BY		1	87	4 (50)	00:00:01
3	NESTED LOOPS		1	87	2 (0)	00:00:01
4	NESTED LOOPS		1	52	2 (0)	00:00:01
5	PARTITION RANGE ALL		1	26	2 (0)	00:00:01
6	TABLE ACCESS FULL	SALES	1	26	2 (0)	00:00:01
7	TABLE ACCESS BY INDEX ROWID	CUSTOMERS	1	26	0 (0)	
* 8	INDEX UNIQUE SCAN	CUSTOMERS_PK	1		0 (0)	
* 9	TABLE ACCESS BY INDEX ROWID	COUNTRIES	1	35	0 (0)	
* 10	INDEX UNIQUE SCAN	COUNTRIES_PK	1		0 (0)	

```
Predicate Information (identified by operation id):
---------------------------------------------------

   8 - access("S"."CUST_ID"="C"."CUST_ID")
   9 - filter(("COUNTRY_NAME"='Denmark' OR "COUNTRY_NAME"='France' OR "COUNTRY_
NAME"='Germany' OR
              "COUNTRY_NAME"='Ireland' OR "COUNTRY_NAME"='Italy' OR "COUNTRY_NAME"='Poland'
OR "COUNTRY_NAME"='Spain'
              OR "COUNTRY_NAME"='The Netherlands' OR "COUNTRY_NAME"='United Kingdom'))
  10 - access("CO"."COUNTRY_ID"="C"."COUNTRY_ID")

36 rows selected.
```

This plan is even better than the one found by XPLORE. It has a cost of 4. We found this plan because we used XPLORE to give us a hint. The hint was that using indexes would be a good idea for everything except sales. We need to do a TABLE ACCESS FULL on sales as we are summing sales for a big group of countries. However, using TABLE ACCESS FULL on the other tables didn't make sense. It's not surprising that example came out this way (I planned it that way), but real-life examples are exactly like this. The steps in the discovery usually go like this:

1. Something unexpected happens to some SQL (slows down invariably).

2. Get the XTRACT test case.

3. Discover what is wrong with the SQL or its environment by studying the report.

4. If the previous step fails, run an XPLORE, which sometimes finds an interesting change to consider (such as the optimizer_index_cost_adj in our example above).

5. We compare the "good" plan from the XPLORE with the "bad" plan from the XTRACT and figure out what the difference is in terms of optimizer steps. In our case it was lack of index use.

6. Review the XTRACT report again to see if you can determine why the action that should have taken place did not (in our case it was "why were the indexes not used").

7. Amend the original test environment to make the optimizer action take place and compare the execution plan costs again.

8. If step 7 has the desired effect, do more testing, and if everything goes as expected, implement the improvement.

These steps are an example of the standard tuning methodology: test, make single changes, and test again. The test case allows you to do this quickly and efficiently. As you get more proficient with XTRACT you will find that using XPLORE is not needed. It's a bit like weather forecasting: "The accuracy of a weather forecast is in direct proportion to the number of gray hairs of the forecaster." The lesson to remember from this chapter is that although we found that setting optimizer_index_cost_adj to 1 made our execution plan much better, that was not the solution. That only prompted us to find the real solution, which was to fix the statistics.

In other words, we found a problem that was not related to an upgrade (i.e., the statistics were wrong), but XPLORE hinted at the solution. This is the surprising thing about XPLORE. Again, it is primarily used to determine what changes (due to upgrades) were made to the optimizer and may have regressed execution plans. However, if we use XPLORE *in extremis*, we may find in one of the execution plans a kernel of an idea that suggests a solution to our tuning problem, even though the original problem may not be related to changes in the optimizer behavior.

Other Information in XPLORE

In our example XPLORE we focused directly on finding the best plan and didn't stop to look at all the other information presented by XPLORE. Here we'll briefly look at some other sections that need to be mentioned. The first one is the "Baseline" section, which shows the settings for each of the tests. See Figure 17-7, which shows the top part of the baseline section of the XPLORE report.

#	is Default	is Modified	Name	Value	is Session Modifiable	is System Modifiable	Type
432	TRUE		_fix_control	10004943:1			2
433	TRUE		_fix_control	10013899:1			2
434	TRUE		_fix_control	10015652:1			2
435	TRUE		_fix_control	10026972:1			2
436	TRUE		_fix_control	10038373:1			2
437	TRUE		_fix_control	10038517:1			2
438	TRUE		_fix_control	10041074:1			2
439	TRUE		_fix_control	10043801:1			2
440	TRUE		_fix_control	10046368:1			2
441	TRUE		_fix_control	10068316:1			2
442	TRUE		_fix_control	10080014:1			2
443	TRUE		_fix_control	10101489:1			2
444	TRUE		_fix_control	10106423:1			2
445	TRUE		_fix_control	10117760:1			2
446	TRUE		_fix_control	10134677:1			2
447	TRUE		_fix_control	10145667:1			2
448	TRUE		_fix_control	10148457:1			2
449	TRUE		_fix_control	10158107:1			2
450	TRUE		_fix_control	10162430:1			2

Figure 17-7. *The top part of the baselines report in XPLORE*

This part of the report shows the starting position of the tests. It starts by listing all the fix control settings as they are on the test database before we start and then goes on to list all the optimizer parameters (including the hidden ones). The table shows the default value for the setting, the modified status (true or false), the name of the control, the current value, and if it is session or system modifiable.

As you can see there are many fix controls on a normally installed database. This is not a cause for concern or a problem. The Oracle code ships that way to allow the flexibility I describe here.

Along with all this information in the main report there is also a zip file created in the XPLORE zip file (yes, a zip file inside a zip file). This zip file called xplore_sql_monitor_report_1.zip contains the SQL monitor html output for every single execution of the script. This is a vast amount of information. You would never look at every single one of these execution reports, but if you have data and you have finally settled on a plan that you like, then you can investigate the SQL monitor report for this one test more closely. As usual you should create a directory and put the zip file in there. Then unzip the file. In this directory you will end up with 732 HTML reports: one for each test and one SQL file that shows how the scripts were created. Remember you will only get realistic reports if you included the data from the original test case. Let's look at one of these monitor reports. Look at Figure 17-8, which shows the left-hand side of the monitor report.

Details

Plan Statistics | Plan | Activity | Metrics

Plan Hash Value 2917593948

Operation	Name	Estimated Ro...	Cost	Timeline(18s)	Executions	Actual Rows
⊟ SELECT STATEMENT					1	7
⊟ SORT ORDER BY		9	123		1	7
⊟ HASH GROUP BY		9	123		1	7
⊟ HASH JOIN		435K	84		1	250K
⊟ HASH JOIN		26K	31		1	30K
— TABLE ACCESS FULL	COUNTRIES	9	3		1	9
⊟ TABLE ACCESS BY INDEX ROWID	CUSTOMERS	56K	27		1	56K
⊟ BITMAP CONVERSION TO RO...					1	56K
— BITMAP INDEX FULL SCAN	CUSTOMERS_GENDER_				1	5
⊟ PARTITION RANGE ALL		919K	49		1	919K
⊟ TABLE ACCESS BY LOCAL INDEX...	SALES	919K	49		28	919K
⊟ BITMAP CONVERSION TO RO...					28	919K
— BITMAP INDEX FULL SCAN	SALES_PROMO_BIX				28	54

Copyright © 1996, 2012, Oracle and/or its affiliates. All rights reserved.
Oracle is a registered trademark of Oracle Corporation and/or its affiliates.
Other names may be trademarks of their respective owners.

Figure 17-8. *The left-hand side of the SQL Monitor report*

We can see the execution plan and the cost for each step, but we can also see the amount of time spent on each step of the plan. We can see that much of the time was spent on BITMAP INDEX FULL SCAN of SALES_PROMO_BIX. In fact if we hover the mouse over the duration bar for this bitmap index we will see the duration in seconds for that step. Let's look at the right-hand side of the same report (as shown in Figure 17-9).

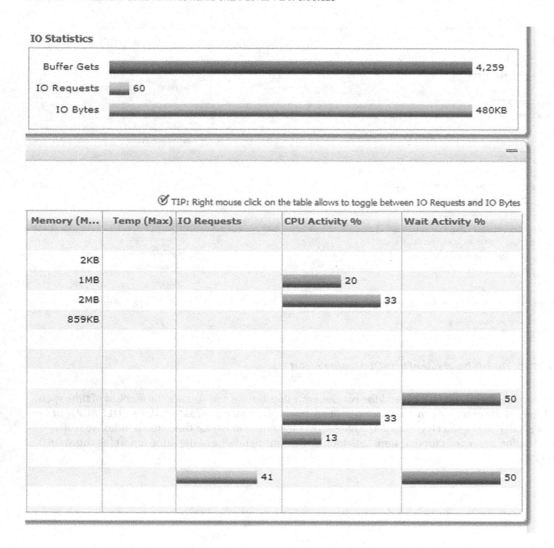

Figure 17-9. *The right-hand side of the SQL Monitor report*

This shows that 50 percent of the wait activity was for BITMAP INDEX FULL SCAN on CUSTOMERS and the other 50 percent was for a BITMAP INDEX FULL SCAN on SALES. Because this plan was obtained by setting optimizer_index_cost_adj to 1, we can see that indexes were used inappropriately and the change has resulted in a better plan than the original bad plan. With this information we know that working on these two indexes is the way to improve the execution time because they are the biggest contributors to the wait time.

Summary

I hope you are impressed with what XPLORE can do for you, especially in conjunction with XTRACT and XECUTE and of course with your knowledge of how the optimizer works. Although the example in this chapter was a nice simple piece of SQL, this same methodology can work with very complex SQL and execution plans. Large pieces of SQL can be broken down into smaller steps and attacked in order of importance, the importance being governed by the cost of each step. XPLORE can investigate all the changes that are likely to have affected the optimizer's calculations, and this is most often the case when the optimizer changes when the versions of the database change. Use XPLORE wisely and you will capture more of those pesky SQLs that go awry.

I must emphasize that all of the XPLORE activity must be run on a disposable database. It bears repeating that setting environmental variables and system parameters and statistics that XPLORE does could cause havoc for any system that you might be sharing with somebody else.

For all its power and flexibility, XPLORE is not the ideal tool for general tuning but is extremely useful in those cases where something has changed unexpectedly. In the next chapter we'll look at the more advanced methods available in SQLT.

CHAPTER 18

▪ ▪ ▪

Trace Files, TRCANLZR, and Modifying SQLT Behavior

Even with SQLT helping you, sometimes you need to look at 10046 trace files and analyze these to determine what's happening. How you analyze and interpret 10046 files is outside the scope of this book. The standard guide for this is Cary Millsap's book *Optimizing Oracle Performance* (O'Reilly, 2003). (This book is a little dated now, but still contains useful information on 10046 trace files). How to more easily collect these trace files, however, and format them so they are easier to interpret is not beyond the scope of this book, as SQLT provides a number of methods for collecting this information more quickly and more easily.

The 10046 trace files are log files of the Oracle engine's activity as it executes SQL. These files are difficult to interpret, full of obscure codes, and also very long. The 10053 trace files (as I mentioned in Chapter 7) are equally obscure, difficult to understand, and also very long. When SQL statements are executed in parallel and 10046 tracing is enabled, each slave process that is helping with the execution creates its own trace file. This makes the interpretation and understanding of what is happening with parallel execution even more difficult. You can have hundreds of trace files all relating to the same SQL all working in parallel and communicating with each other to achieve a common goal. When things go wrong with these complex cases, it can be hard enough just collecting the right trace files, let alone analyzing those trace files and getting a coherent picture from potentially hundreds of trace files.

In this chapter I'll describe the following methods, building from the simplest to the more complex. I'll try building on the simpler cases to explain the more complex cases.

- 10046 trace: The raw trace file or files of information.

- TKPROF: Provides a high-level view of the 10046 trace file. The input to this is the 10046 trace file; the output is the TKPROF report.

- TRCASPLIT: Takes the raw 10046 and 10053 trace file or files and splits off the 10046 trace file information. This data can then be fed into TKPROF or any other utility that needs 10046 trace.

- 10053 trace: Is the raw trace file of the optimizer's choices during parsing.

- TRCANLZR: Takes the raw 10046 and produces a graphical report that makes understanding the data easier.

- TRCAXTR: Takes the raw 10046 trace and produces an SQLTXTRACT report.

Each of the above tools takes 10046 or 10046 and 10053 mixed together and produces some simpler version of the information.

© Stelios Charalambides 2017
S. Charalambides, *Oracle SQL Tuning with Oracle SQLTXPLAIN*, DOI 10.1007/978-1-4842-2436-6_18

We'll start with methods to collect 10046 trace, then look at the oldest tool available, TKPROF (which has been around since Oracle 7, and not part of SQLT), then we'll look at TRCASPLIT, which is used to separate 10046 and (usually) 10053 trace information. Consider this method the simplest of the advanced tools. Then we'll look at collecting 10053 trace. TRCANLZR is the next step, and it works from a single or multiple files to produce an extended version of TKPROF. TRCANLZR is part of SQLT, unlike TKPROF.

Finally we'll talk about TRCAXTR, which combines TRCANLZR and XTRACT to produce a report on multiple SQLs. Each of these sections will be explained with the aid of an example SQL.

10046 Trace

10046 is essentially a low-level logging facility of the activity of the Oracle engine while it is processing your SQL statement. It produces a file called a "trace" file, which is a text file, with details of the low-level step of the execution. This trace can be configured (depending on the trace level selected) to collect wait events, bind variables, and bind values (see below for the different levels that can be selected). There is an overhead in collecting this information, and it can consume a considerable amount of disk space and take resources away from the executing statement in producing the trace file.

Why Collect 10046 Trace?

Collecting 10046 trace is not an activity to take lightly. As mentioned above, it can take considerable resources (especially disk space). Considering the overhead in collecting 10046 trace you would not lightly choose to collect this information. It would not normally be collected unless there was a good reason. To investigate tuning problems that are not solvable by looking at the high-level aggregated information, 10046 trace is specifically collected. In these more difficult cases, some low-level piece of information (which is lost in the aggregation) is needed as a vital clue in the puzzle we are solving. This is because it contains very detailed information of what is happening during the SQL execution.

The 10046 trace can also be produced by enabling trace in other ways, such as at a system level or by tracing another session instead of your own. The information collected is the same and the decode is the same; only the method of initiating the trace will change. In each case the trace file is a stand-alone file found in the default trace area. You can find this location by doing the following:

```
SQL> select value from v$diag_info where name='Default Trace File';
```

```
VALUE
--------------------------------------------------------------------------------
/u02/app/oracle/diag/rdbms/snc1/snc1/trace/snc1_ora_3670.trc
```

You can also get other useful locations from this table.

```
NAME
-----------------------------------------------------------------
Diag Enabled
ADR Base
ADR Home
Diag Trace
Diag Alert
Diag Incident
Diag Cdump
Health Monitor
```

```
Default Trace File
Active Problem Count
Active Incident Count
```

10046 Decode

Some people will read 10046 directly; this can be useful, as it contains low-level information that is sometimes not included in an aggregation (this is the nature of aggregation). This is a typical snippet of a SQL 10046 trace file.

```
EXEC #1:c=0,e=162,p=0,cr=0,cu=0,mis=0,r=0,dep=0,og=1,plh=2938593747,tim=6801557607
WAIT #1: nam='SQL*Net message to client' ela= 6 driver id=1111838976 #bytes=1 p3=0 obj#=-1
tim=6801557680
WAIT #1: nam='Disk file operations I/O' ela= 821 FileOperation=2 fileno=5 filetype=2 obj#=-1
tim=6801559064
*** 2012-12-26 09:59:43.625
WAIT #1: nam='asynch descriptor resize' ela= 4 outstanding #aio=0 current aio
limit=4294967295 new aio limit=257 obj#=-1 tim=6802577972
WAIT #1: nam='asynch descriptor resize' ela= 2 outstanding #aio=0 current aio
limit=4294967295 new aio limit=257 obj#=-1 tim=6802578401
FETCH #1:c=0,e=1020838,p=0,cr=3180,cu=0,mis=0,r=1,dep=0,og=1,plh=2938593747,tim=6802578585
WAIT #1: nam='SQL*Net message from client' ela= 302 driver id=1111838976 #bytes=1 p3=0
obj#=-1 tim=6802578974
WAIT #1: nam='SQL*Net message to client' ela= 3 driver id=1111838976 #bytes=1 p3=0 obj#=-1
tim=6802579032
FETCH #1:c=0,e=45,p=0,cr=0,cu=0,mis=0,r=6,dep=0,og=1,plh=2938593747,tim=6802579064
STAT #1 id=1 cnt=7 pid=0 pos=1 obj=0 op='SORT ORDER BY (cr=3180 pr=0 pw=0 time=0 us cost=947
size=315 card=9)'
STAT #1 id=2 cnt=7 pid=1 pos=1 obj=0 op='HASH GROUP BY (cr=3180 pr=0 pw=0 time=18 us
cost=947 size=315 card=9)'
STAT #1 id=3 cnt=250069 pid=2 pos=1 obj=0 op='HASH JOIN  (cr=3180 pr=0 pw=0 time=1261090 us
cost=909 size=15233435 card=435241)'
```

Easy to understand, right? In the subsections below I have produced a 10046 trace file we can use to see the sort of sections that appear in a trace file and do at least a partial decode. Here is the SQL example:

```
SQL> alter session set events '10046 trace name context forever, level 64';

Session altered.

SQL> select count(*) from sh.sales;

  COUNT(*)
----------
    918843

SQL> exit
```

I've broken the decode of a 10046 trace file into three main sections: the header, the main section record format, and the decode of the details on each line.

The Header

Although the header itself is not part of the SQL execution it is important that you look at the header. Here is an example header of the SQL I have executed as an example.

```
Trace file /u02/app/oracle/diag/rdbms/snc1/snc1/trace/snc1_ora_4110.trc
Oracle Database 12c Enterprise Edition Release 12.1.0.2.0 - 64bit Production
With the Partitioning, OLAP, Advanced Analytics and Real Application Testing options
ORACLE_HOME = /u02/app/oracle/product/12.1.0.2/dbhome_1
System name:    Linux
Node name:      d12102.us.oracle.com
Release:        2.6.32-400.29.1.el5uek
Version:        #1 SMP Tue Jun 11 15:16:42 PDT 2013
Machine:        x86_64
Instance name: snc1
Redo thread mounted by this instance: 1
Oracle process number: 7
Unix process pid: 4110, image: oracle@d12102.us.oracle.com (TNS V1-V3)

*** 2016-12-12 09:17:05.831
*** SESSION ID:(357.19017) 2016-12-12 09:17:05.831
*** CLIENT ID:() 2016-12-12 09:17:05.831
*** SERVICE NAME:(SYS$USERS) 2016-12-12 09:17:05.831
*** MODULE NAME:(sqlplus@d12102.us.oracle.com (TNS V1-V3)) 2016-12-12 09:17:05.831
*** CLIENT DRIVER:(SQL*PLUS) 2016-12-12 09:17:05.831
*** ACTION NAME:() 2016-12-12 09:17:05.83 1
```

The header section sets the stage for the information to follow. This should be checked to make sure you are looking at the correct trace file. For example, the right instance, and the right time. The 10046 trace starts immediately after this section.

The Main 10046 Tracing Section

Once we get into the main 10046 trace section we see a single line for each piece of information bounded by a divider. Here is an example below. I've truncated the lines on the right because we are concentrating on the text at the beginning of the line and emphasizing that the trace file has a logical structure. We see at the beginning of each line the code words:

```
===============
PARSING IN CURSOR - Gives you the cursor number
select  - This is statement being issued on your behalf
END OF STMT - The end of the SQL statement is marked
PARSE - Now we parse the statement
EXEC - Now we execute the statement
FETCH - Now we fetch rows for the statement
STAT - Status information
WAIT - Wait for something
STAT - Status information
CLOSE - Close the cursor we are finished with this statement.
===============
```

Here is what it looks like in the raw form.

```
CLOSE #140702095348992:c=0,e=1,dep=0,type=1,tim=2040957035
=====================
PARSING IN CURSOR #140702095357736 len=29 dep=0 uid=0 oct=3 lid=0 tim=2041669241
hv=3864810328 ad='b3572168' sqlid='dqg0t4gm5snus'
select count(*) from sh.sales
END OF STMT
PARSE #140702095357736:c=1000,e=711966,p=0,cr=0,cu=0,mis=1,r=0,dep=0,og=1,plh=1123225294,t
im=2041669239
EXEC #140702095357736:c=0,e=55,p=0,cr=0,cu=0,mis=0,r=0,dep=0,og=1,plh=1123225294,t
im=2041669394
FETCH #140702095357736:c=1000,e=758,p=0,cr=92,cu=0,mis=0,r=1,dep=0,og=1,plh=1123225294,t
im=2041670198
STAT #140702095357736 id=1 cnt=1 pid=0 pos=1 obj=0 op='SORT AGGREGATE (cr=92 pr=0 pw=0
time=768 us)'
STAT #140702095357736 id=2 cnt=54 pid=1 pos=1 obj=0 op='PARTITION RANGE ALL PARTITION: 1 28
(cr=92 pr=0 pw=0 time=993 us cost=27 size=0 card=918843)'
STAT #140702095357736 id=3 cnt=54 pid=2 pos=1 obj=0 op='BITMAP CONVERSION COUNT (cr=92 pr=0
pw=0 time=721 us cost=27 size=0 card=918843)'
STAT #140702095357736 id=4 cnt=54 pid=3 pos=1 obj=92921 op='BITMAP INDEX FAST FULL SCAN
SALES_PROMO_BIX PARTITION: 1 28 (cr=92 pr=0 pw=0 time=258 us)'
FETCH #140702095357736:c=0,e=2,p=0,cr=0,cu=0,mis=0,r=0,dep=0,og=0,plh=1123225294,t
im=2041680518

*** 2016-12-12 09:17:14.710
XCTEND rlbk=0, rd_only=1, tim=2049835775
CLOSE #140702095357736:c=0,e=10,dep=0,type=0,tim=2049835849
CLOSE #140702096517360:c=0,e=10,dep=0,type=0,tim=2049835879
CLOSE #140702095281376:c=0,e=7,dep=0,type=0,tim=2049835899
CLOSE #140702100958888:c=0,e=4,dep=0,type=0,tim=2049835914
```

Although the raw 10046 trace can look intimidating, it has the huge advantage that it is logical in its layout. This makes it relatively easy to decode with utilities. For example TKPROF (which we'll mention later) can read this raw file and produce an aggregated file. The downside of such facilities is that the interpretation of the file may leave out details you need or the decode can be wrong, causing you to see the wrong information and possibly come to the wrong conclusion.

Decoding Records and Keywords

The main 10046 tracing section consists of record keywords (at the beginning of a line) and keywords within the record (detail keywords), which give detailed information about what is happening. Table 18-1 provides the decodes for the record keywords.

Table 18-1. *The 10046 Record Keywords*

Record Keyword	Description
APPNAME	Application name setting
PARSING IN CURSOR #n	The cursor number that is currently being parsed
PARSE ERROR	Seen if there is a parsing error
ERROR	Seen if there is an error
END OF STMT	The end of the SQL statement is marked
PARSE #n	Timing and CPU information for parsing activities on the cursor #n
BINDS #n	Shows the binds information if selected
EXEC #n	The cursor number being executed
FETCH #n	The cursor number for which we are fetching rows
RPC	Remote procedure call
SORT UNMAP	Closing operating System temporary files
STAT #n	Status information for the cursor number
UNMAP	Closing of a temporary segment
CLOSE #n	Close the cursor, we are finished with this statement
WAIT #n	Information relating to the cursor we are dealing with, including timing and event information
XCTEND	Transaction end

The detail keywords occur within the record itself and are preceded by record keywords. The table below covers the majority of the keywords used; however, there may be others.

Detail Keyword	Description
act	Action
ad	Address of SQL
c	The number of CPU seconds used
card	Estimated cardinality
cnt	Number of rows
cost	Optimizer cost
cr	The number of consistent read gets (blocks)
cu	Current mode consistent reads
dep	The depth of the cursor. 0 represents a top-level statement. dep=1 and 2 indicate trigger involvement and dep=3 represents a trigger called from a trigger.
dty	Data Type
e	Elapsed time in microseconds
err	Standard Error code
flg	Flag indicating bind status
hv	Hash value

(*continued*)

Detail Keyword	Description
len	The character count of the string representing the SQL statement
lid	Privilege user ID
mis	Number of shard pool misses
mod	Module name
mxl	Maximum length of bind variables
oct	The Oracle command type (2=insert, 3=select, 6=update, 7=delete, 26=lock table, 35=alter database, 42=alter session, 44=commit, 47=anonymous block, 45=rollback.
nam	Name of the wait
oacflg	Bind options
obj	Object ID
og	Optimizer goal. 1=ALL_ROWS, 2=FIRST_ROWS, 3=RULE, 4=CHOOSE
op	The operation being done. Examples are PARTITION RANGE ALL, SORT AGGREGATE, etc.
p	Physical blocks read from disk
p1, p2, p3	Parameter for a given wait
pr	Physical reads
pre	Precision
pid	Parent ID of the row source
pw	Physical writes
r	Number of rows returned
rd_only	No data changed in the database on commit
rlbk	Rollback. 0=Commit, 1=Rollback
size	Estimated size in bytes
sqlid	The SQL ID inside single quotes
tim	The timestamp. Measured in 1 millionths of a second.
time	Elapsed time in microseconds
uid	The user Id of the schema doing the parsing
value	The value of a bind variable

So, for example, given this line in the raw 10046 trace file:

```
PARSE #140702095357736:c=1000,e=711966,p=0,cr=0,cu=0,mis=1,r=0,dep=0,og=1,plh=1123225294,
tim=2041669239
```

We could translate this into:

"We are parsing in cursor number140702095357736, which was issued either directly from the application or from a trigger or from recursive SQL. The elapsed time was 711966 milliseconds (0.711966 seconds) and no physical reads were done, nor any consistent reads or current mode consistent reads. No rows were returned, the depth of the cursor was top level, and the optimizer goal was ALL_ROWS for the plan hash value 1123225294, the time stamp was 2041669239." Here's another line from a FETCH.

```
FETCH #140702095357736:c=1000,e=758,p=0,cr=92,cu=0,mis=0,r=1,dep=0,og=1,plh=1123225294,t
im=2041670198
```

Interpreting the "tim" field: The "tim" field is in millionths of a second. The time through the file can be calculated by subtracting the initial tim value and dividing by 1,000,000.

Cursor number 140702095357736 using 1000 CPU milliseconds, elapsed time was 758, physical reads was 0, consistent reads was 92, current reads were 0, shared pool misses were 0, 1 row was returned, from a top-level cursor (dep=0), using ALL_ROWS with Plan Hash Value of 1123225294.

The meaning of depth (dep). If dep=0 the cursor originates from the application. Other values such dep=1 (trigger or optimizer or space management), dep=2 (called from a trigger), dep=3 (called from a trigger inside a trigger).

As you can see, this dense tracing information has a lot of information in it. A number of tools have grown up around interpreting this and managing the information. But why and how do we get this trace file in the first place?

How Do We Collect 10046 Trace?

There are different ways 10046 can be collected and at different levels. If you have the luxury of being able to execute the SQL statement directly, then you can enable and disable the collection of trace with:

```
SQL> alter session set sql_trace=true
```

To turn this off:

```
SQL> alter session set sql_trace=false
```

Or if you want to adjust the level of trace (discussed below):

```
SQL> alter session set events '10046 trace name context forever, level n'
```

Or collect it with:

```
SQL> exec dbms_monitor.session_trace_enable;
```

or

```
SQL> exec dbms_monitor.session_trace_enable(waits=>TRUE, binds=>TRUE);
```

To turn this off:

```
SQL> alter session set events '10046 trace name context off'
```

or

```
SQL> exec dbms_monitor.session_trace_disable;
```

You can also enable trace for another session (with pid n) with and or a debug command.

```
SQL> oradebug setorapid n
SQL> oradebug event 10046 trace name contect forever, level m;
```

This issues the trace for the pid n to 10046 trace level m. You can even trace a session with a logon trigger, that is a trigger, which is fired when a session logs into the database. Before the user session begins some commands are carried out that enable tracing for that session. The "triggering" code usually begins with something like this:

```
Create or replace trigger Start_10046_trace after logon on database
  begin
  execute immediate 'alter session set timed_statistics=true';
  execute immediate 'alter session set events "10046 trace name context forever level 4" '
end;
```

The above trigger will trace every session that logs into the database, but you may want to restrict the collection of trace information by checking on the user or some other user context to limit the amount of trace collected. You may also want to identify each trace file and set the file size to unlimited. In these cases you should add code such as this before the 10046 trace command:

```
execute immediate 'alter session set max_dump_file_size=unlimited';
execute immediate 'alter session set tracefile_identifier="My_trace"';
```

If for some reason you want to trace SQLTXPLAIN itself, you can set keep_trace_10046_open to TRUE. Changing these SQLT parameters is described below in "Modifying SQLT behavior." A full description of this parameter (and many other parameters) is shown in Appendix C.

Different Levels of Trace

Different types of information are collected for different investigations. Here are the levels and what they do as of 12c. The default collects the least information, thus protecting you from excessive size of trace files. With option 4 you also collect information on bind variables

> 1 – Default4 – Standard plus binds

With this level of parsing we see a BINDS section. Here is an example.

```
BINDS #1:
 Bind#0
  oacdty=02 mxl=22(22) mxlc=00 mal=00 scl=00 pre=00
  oacflg=03 fl2=1000000 frm=00 csi=00 siz=24 off=0
  kxsbbbfp=0e90cbb8  bln=22  avl=02  flg=05
  value=100
```

> 8 – standard plus waits

With this level of tracing we see the waits indicating where we spend the time in the statement.

> 12 – standard plus waits and binds

With this level we collect not only the binds but also the waits

> 16 – Generate STAT line dumps for each execution

> 32 – Never dump execution statistics

> 64 – Adaptive dump of STAT lines (11.2.0.2+)

A typical example of generating this trace would be as follows:

1. Find the location of trace file from v$diag_info.

2. Set the file size to unlimited if possible.

3. Set the `statistics_level` to all.

4. Select the tracing level based on the values above.

Here is an example set of steps, beginning with setting the identifier for the trace file name, which will allow you to easily find the trace file.

1. Set the identifier:

   ```
   SQL> alter session set tracefile_identifier='10046_STELIOS';
   Session altered.
   ```

2. Now I want to make sure I don't lose information if the trace file is too long, so I set the size to `unlimited`.

   ```
   SQL> alter session set max_dump_file_size=unlimited;
   Session altered.
   ```

3. Set the `statistics_level` parameter to all to collect as much information as possible.

   ```
   SQL> alter session set statistics_level=all;
   Session altered.
   ```

4. Now set the 10046 trace event to collect tracing information at `level 12` (which includes binds and waits).

   ```
   SQL> alter session set events '10046 trace name context forever, level 12';
   Session altered.
   ```

5. Now I execute my SQL

   ```
   SQL> @q3

   COUNTRY_NAME                              SUM(AMOUNT_SOLD)
   ---------------------------------------- ----------------
   Poland                                            8447.14
   Denmark                                        1977764.79
   Spain                                          2090863.44
   France                                         3776270.13
   Italy                                          4854505.28
   United Kingdom                                 6393762.94
   Germany                                        9210129.22

   7 rows selected.
   ```

6. Then turn off the tracing

```
SQL> alter session set events '10046 trace name context off';
```

This is the SQL that ran:

```
select
  country_name, sum(AMOUNT_SOLD)
from sh.sales s, sh.customers c, sh.countries co
where
  s.cust_id=c.cust_id
  and co.country_id=c.country_id
  and country_name in (
    'Ireland','Denmark','Poland','United Kingdom',
    'Germany','France','Spain','The Netherlands','Italy')
  group by country_name order by sum(AMOUNT_SOLD);
```

■ **Note** If you want to follow along with these examples and collect your own trace files and view them yourself, you can easily do so by using all the code in these examples. All of the data and examples used rely on the standard example schemas shipped with every database installation. If you do not have the schemas SH and HR, you can either select to install the example schemas at installation time or manually add them afterward with the instructions here: https://docs.oracle.com/database/121/COMSC/installation.htm#COMSC001.

7. Finally I want to find the file so I query v$diag_info

```
SQL> select value from v$diag_info where name='Diag Trace';
```

```
VALUE
--------------------------------------------------------------------------------
/u02/app/oracle/diag/rdbms/snc1/snc1/trace
```

This is all very well if you want to look at raw 10046 trace files, but what if you wanted to interpret what was going on more quickly? First we'll look at one of the oldest utilities around for processing 10046 trace, TKPROF, which is still used today to get a good overview of what has been happening. TKPROF is not part of SQLT; but as it is commonly used, we'll give it a brief mention.

TKPROF

No doubt some people can read 10046 trace files in the raw (and it wouldn't be too difficult to do once you gather the translation of the short codes), but this is a pretty inefficient way of going about things. It would be like listing the position, velocity, and direction of every atom in a football, when in fact you could aggregate the information to describe the ball's trajectory with just a few parameters. TKPROF aggregates information and presents a summary of the high-level view of what's going on. TKPROF is not part of SQLT and has been in existence since early versions of Oracle. TKPROF is best explained through the use of an example: we'll take a trace file produced as described above and generate the TKPROF output. To use TKPROF just run the TKPROF command with the input of the trace file:

```
tkprof snc1_ora_4857_10046_STELIOS.trc snc1_ora_4857_10046_STELIOS.txt
TKPROF: Release 12.1.0.2.0 - Development on Mon Dec 12 09:59:10 2016

Copyright (c) 1982, 2014, Oracle and/or its affiliates.  All rights reserved.
```

309

If we look at the TKPROF output file and find our SQL, we then see this kind of information:

```
****************************************************************************

select
  country_name, sum(AMOUNT_SOLD)
from sh.sales s, sh.customers c, sh.countries co
where
  s.cust_id=c.cust_id
  and co.country_id=c.country_id
  and country_name in (
    'Ireland','Denmark','Poland','United Kingdom',
    'Germany','France','Spain','The Netherlands','Italy')
  group by country_name order by sum(AMOUNT_SOLD)
```

call	count	cpu	elapsed	disk	query	current	rows
Parse	1	0.00	0.00	0	0	0	0
Execute	1	0.00	0.00	0	0	0	0
Fetch	2	7.37	7.45	0	3145	0	7
total	4	7.37	7.46	0	3145	0	7

```
Misses in library cache during parse: 1
Optimizer mode: ALL_ROWS
Parsing user id: 105


Number of plan statistics captured: 1


Rows (1st) Rows (avg) Rows (max)  Row Source Operation
---------- ---------- ----------  -------------------------------------------------
7      7      7  SORT ORDER BY (cr=3145 pr=0 pw=0 time=7459718 us cost=965 size=315 card=9)
7      7      7   HASH GROUP BY (cr=3145 pr=0 pw=0 time=7459664 us cost=965 size=315 card=9)
250069 250069 250069 HASH JOIN(cr=3145 pr=0 pw=0 time=7104150 us cost=945 size=15233435
card=435241)
30473  30473  30473  NESTED LOOPS(cr=1525 pr=0 pw=0 time=261791 us cost=945 size=15233435
card=435241)
30473  30473  30473   NESTED LOOPS(cr=1525 pr=0 pw=0 time=193565 us)
30473  30473  30473    STATISTICS COLLECTOR  (cr=1525 pr=0 pw=0 time=125476 us)
30473  30473  30473    HASH JOIN(cr=1525 pr=0 pw=0 time=56524 us cost=426 size=657225
card=26289)
9      9      9     TABLE ACCESS FULL COUNTRIES(cr=3 pr=0 pw=0 time=52 us cost=3 size=135
card=9)
55500  55500  55500 TABLE ACCESS FULL CUSTOMERS (cr=1522 pr=0 pw=0 time=7935 us cost=423
size=555000 card=55500)
0      0      0   PARTITION RANGE ALL PARTITION: 1 28 (cr=0 pr=0 pw=0 time=0 us)
0      0      0    BITMAP CONVERSION TO ROWIDS (cr=0 pr=0 pw=0 time=0 us)
0      0      0     BITMAP INDEX SINGLE VALUE SALES_CUST_BIX PARTITION: 1 28 (cr=0 pr=0 pw=0
time=0 us)(object id 92834)
0      0      0    TABLE ACCESS BY LOCAL INDEX ROWID SALES PARTITION: 1 1 (cr=0 pr=0 pw=0
time=0 us cost=517 size=170 card=17)
```

```
918843 918843 918843 PARTITION RANGE ALL PARTITION: 1 28 (cr=1620 pr=0 pw=0 time=3228830 us
cost=517 size=9188430 card=918843)
918843 918843 918843 TABLE ACCESS FULL SALES PARTITION: 1 28 (cr=1620 pr=0 pw=0 time=1151831
us cost=517 size=9188430 card=918843)

Elapsed times include waiting on following events:
  Event waited on                             Times   Max. Wait  Total Waited
  ----------------------------------------    Waited  ---------  ------------
  SQL*Net message to client                       2       0.00          0.00
  SQL*Net message from client                     2      10.23         10.24
********************************************************************************
```

In the TKPROF of the SQL we see the SQL statement, a summary section that describes the execution times for "Parse," "Execute," and "Fetch," as well as an execution plan and a brief description of the wait times. Compare this kind of information with the sections on 10046 trace file interpretation. Which do you think would be faster? I know which one I prefer to look at. That kind of aggregation of information makes interpretation of what is happening much simpler and faster. Now that we've briefly mentioned 10046 tracing (and we mentioned 10053 tracing in Chapter 7), we look at what TRCASPLIT can do for us.

TRCASPLIT

TRCASPLIT, the first of the trace utilities available in SQLT, simply separates a 10046 trace from other traces. While this may be a simple task, in theory it would be very difficult and error prone to do manually. TRCASPLIT does the job in no time and presents you with the results in a zip file. First let me show you what we are going to collect, then we will collect it. Then we will split using TRCASPLIT.

In this example we are going to collect both 10046 and 10053 trace file information. In other words we are turning on debugging information for both running the SQL and for parsing it. As before we will also ensure that the dump file is not truncated by setting the dump file size to unlimited, and we'll also set the statistics collection level to the highest possible level of all.

```
SQL> alter session set tracefile_identifier='10046_10053';
Session altered.
SQL> alter session set max_dump_file_size=unlimited;
Session altered.
SQL> alter session set statistics_level=all;
Session altered.
SQL> alter session set events '10046 trace name context forever, level 12';
Session altered.
SQL> alter session set events '10053 trace name context forever, level 1';
Session altered.
SQL> alter system flush shared_pool;
System altered.
SQL> @q3
```

I'm sure we don't need to see the results of this query again. What we do need to look at is the trace file created. In the trace file we see sections that are clearly 10046 type lines such as:

```
EXEC #139954356296656:c=1000,e=5520,p=0,cr=0,cu=0,mis=1,r=0,dep=1,og=4,plh=1457651150,t
im=5372073238
FETCH #139954356296656:c=0,e=62,p=0,cr=2,cu=0,mis=0,r=1,dep=1,og=4,plh=1457651150,t
im=5372073328
```

```
STAT #139954356296656 id=1 cnt=1 pid=0 pos=1 obj=22 op='TABLE ACCESS BY INDEX ROWID USER$
(cr=2 pr=0 pw=0 time=64 us cost=1 size=170 card=1)'
```

These are related to 10046 tracing, but we also see:

```
****************************************
PARAMETERS USED BY THE OPTIMIZER
*****************************
  ****************************************
  PARAMETERS WITH ALTERED VALUES
  *****************************
Compilation Environment Dump
sqlstat_enabled                     = true
statistics_level                    =
```

all these lines are recognizable as 10053 tracing. We don't see any of the logical 10046 tracing information related to the execution lines of code and waits. There are no codes at the beginning of lines related to what is happening. Any program designed to decode 10046 would have to stop and ask for help at this point, but TRACSPLIT helps us by sifting the two out of information. To split these we need only run `sqltrcasplit.sql`. In this example I've copied the trace file produced in the trace directory to the local directory. There is only one parameter to pass to `sqltrcasplit.sql`, the name of the trace file that needs to be split.

```
sqlplus / as sysdba @sqltrcasplit.sql snc1_ora_5201_10046_10053.trc
SQL*Plus: Release 12.1.0.2.0 Production on Mon Dec 12 10:21:56 2016

Copyright (c) 1982, 2014, Oracle.  All rights reserved.
Connected to:
Oracle Database 12c Enterprise Edition Release 12.1.0.2.0 - 64bit Production
With the Partitioning, OLAP, Advanced Analytics and Real Application Testing options
PL/SQL procedure successfully completed.
Parameter 1:
Trace Filename (required)
Value passed to sqltrcasplit.sql:
TRACE_FILENAME: snc1_ora_5201_10046_10053.trc
PL/SQL procedure successfully completed.
Splitting snc1_ora_5201_10046_10053.trc
***
*** NOTE:
*** If you get error below it means SQLTXPLAIN is not installed:
***    PLS-00201: identifier 'SQLTXADMIN.SQLT$A' must be declared.
*** In such case look for errors in NN_*.log files created during install.
***

***
*** NOTE:
*** If running as SYS in 12c make sure to review sqlt_instructions.html first
***


SQLT_VERSION
----------------------------------------
SQLT version number: 12.1.160429
SQLT version date  : 2016-04-29
```

```
Installation date  : 2016-11-29/13:18:54

... please wait ...  adding: alert_snc1.log (deflated 88%)
To monitor progress, login into another session and execute:
SQL> SELECT * FROM SQLTXADMIN.trca$_log_v;

... splitting trace(s) ...

Execution ID: 65243 started at 2016-12-12 10:22:00
In case of premature termination, read trcanlzr_error.log located in SQL*Plus default
directory
/****************************************************************************/
10:22:00 => trcanlzr
10:22:00 file_name:"snc1_ora_5201_10046_10053.trc"
10:22:00 analyze:"NO"
10:22:00 split:"YES"
10:22:00 tool_execution_id:"65243"
10:22:00 directory_alias_in:"SQLT$STAGE"
10:22:00 file_name_log:""
10:22:00 file_name_html:""
10:22:00 file_name_txt:""
10:22:00 file_name_10046:""
10:22:00 file_name_10053:""
10:22:00 out_file_identifier:""
10:22:00 calling trca$p.parse_main
10:22:00 => parse_main
10:22:00 analyzing input file snc1_ora_5201_10046_10053.trc in /u02/app/oracle/diag/rdbms/
snc1/snc1/trace (SQLT$STAGE)
10:22:00 -> parse_file
10:22:00 parsing file snc1_ora_5201_10046_10053.trc in /u02/app/oracle/diag/rdbms/snc1/snc1/
trace
10:22:00 parsed snc1_ora_5201_10046_10053.trc (input 1378431 bytes, parsed as 1378431 bytes)
10:22:00 <- parse_file
10:22:00 parsed 1 file(s) (input 1378431 bytes)
10:22:00 first trace: /u02/app/oracle/diag/rdbms/snc1/snc1/trace/snc1_ora_5201_10046_10053.
trc
10:22:00 <= parse_main
10:22:00 <= trcanlzr
/****************************************************************************/
Trace Analyzer executed successfully.
There are no fatal errors in this log file.
Execution ID: 65243 completed at 2016-12-12 10:22:00

Trace Split completed.
Review first sqltrcasplit_error.log file for possible fatal errors.
Review next trca_e65243.log for parsing messages and totals.Copying now generated files into
local directory

  adding: trca_e65243_10046.trc (deflated 92%)
  adding: trca_e65243.log (deflated 65%)
  adding: trca_e65243_not_10046.trc (deflated 84%)
  adding: sqltrcasplit_error.log (deflated 80%)
```

```
deleting: sqltrcasplit_error.log

File trca_e65243.zip has been created.
#####
The SQLT has collected information and place it in a repository in the database, exported it
and zip it.
The collected info can be purged from the database using the following file :
Enter value for filename: 10046_10053.txt
... getting 10046_10053.txt out of sqlt repository ...

SQLTRCASPLIT completed.
```

Once the script has finished, I have a zip file in the local directory called trca_e665243.zip (in my example) containing the results of the split. If I create a directory and put the files from the zip file in this directory I see that there are two files. One is named trca_e65243_10046.trc and one is named trca_e65243_not_10046.trc. Now we can look at the 10046 trace file without the 10053 trace information making the interpretation simpler.

TRCANLZR

TRCANLZR is used to analyze multiple trace files and generate one aggregated form of information. In the example below I have added a parallel hint to force parallel execution and multiple trace files. This is the SQL I used with the hint in place.

```
select /*+ parallel (s, 2) */
  country_name, sum(AMOUNT_SOLD)
from sh.sales s, sh.customers c, sh.countries co
where
  s.cust_id=c.cust_id
  and co.country_id=c.country_id
  and country_name in (
    'Ireland','Denmark','Poland','United Kingdom',
    'Germany','France','Spain','The Netherlands','Italy')
  group by country_name order by sum(AMOUNT_SOLD);
```

Once I have enabled tracing for 10046 (see the earlier section "How Do We Collect 10046 Trace"), I have a number of trace files in the trace directory. To allow TRCANLZR to know which files to analyze, I created a text file called control.txt that lists the file names in the trace directory that relate to the execution of the SQL. This is what control.txt contains.

```
snc1_p003_3714_STELIOS3.trc
snc1_p002_3682_STELIOS3.trc
snc1_p001_3678_STELIOS3.trc
snc1_p000_3674_STELIOS3.trc
snc1_ora_5722_STELIOS3.trc
```

When I run sqltracnlzr.sql I am prompted for a control file name or a trace file to analyze. In my case I have a number of trace files so I entered control.txt. This file is located in the same directory as the trace files. The execution of sqltrcanlzr finishes with the following screen.

```
  adding: trca_e65244.html (deflated 92%)
  adding: trca_e65244.log (deflated 87%)
  adding: trca_e65244_nosort.tkprof (deflated 78%)
  adding: trca_e65244_sort.tkprof (deflated 78%)
  adding: trca_e65244.txt (deflated 89%)
  adding: sqltrcanlzr_error.log (deflated 84%)
deleting: sqltrcanlzr_error.log

File trca_e65244.zip has been created.
#####
The SQLT has collected information and place it in a repository in the database, exported it
and zip it.
The collected info can be purged from the database using the following file :
Enter value for filename: stelios3.html
... getting stelios3.html out of sqlt repository ...

SQLTRCANLZR completed.
```

In the run directory of SQLT I now have a zip file, which as usual I create a directory for and unzip the files into that directory. The HTML file in this directory is the Trace Analyzer file. It starts with the list of trace files it analyzed. See Figure 18-1.

224270.1 TRCA Trace Analyzer 12.1.160429 Report: trca_e65244.html

```
snc1_p003_3714_STELIOS3.trc (5550 bytes)
snc1_p002_3682_STELIOS3.trc (5839 bytes)
snc1_p001_3678_STELIOS3.trc (10743 bytes)
snc1_p000_3674_STELIOS3.trc (10357 bytes)
snc1_ora_5722_STELIOS3.trc (1087337 bytes)
```

Figure 18-1. *The top of the TRCANLZR report*

This list at the top of the file ensures that we have the right TRCANLZR output. Below this is a summary of the sections of the report that can be reached. See Figure 18-2.

- Glossary of Terms Used
- Response Time Summary
- Overall Time and Totals
- Non-Recursive Time and Totals
- Recursive Time and Totals
- Top SQL
- Non-Recursive SQL
- SQL Genealogy
- Individual SQL
- Overall Segment I/O Wait Summary
- Hot I/O Blocks
- Gaps in Trace
- ORA errors in Trace
- Transactions Summary
- Non-default Initialization Params
- Trace Header
- Tool Data Dictionary
- Tool Execution Environment
- Tool Configuration Parameters

Figure 18-2. *The header section includes the links to other parts of the report*

Look at Figure 18-2. There are many sections here all with useful information. The first is the "Glossary of Terms Used." You might be tempted to go straight to the "Response Time Summary" as the "Glossary of Terms Used" sounds boring. If you did go to the "Glossary of Terms Used," on first glance it looks like there is not much there. See Figure 18-3. Understanding exactly what each of the terms used is crucial to your understanding of the report and so the "Glossary of Terms Used" should be examined. You just need to click on the plus under the heading to get the details. See Figure 18-3, which shows the screen after I expand the section.

Glossary of Terms Used

[.]
DB Call
Database kernel operation, such as "Parse", "Execute", "Fetch", "Unmap" and "Sort Unmap".

" + "CPU Time
Amount of CPU time consumed by one db call, or a set of calls.

Wait Event" + "
Sequence of kernel instructions that consume wall-clock time.

Non-Idle Wait Event
Wait event that originates within a db call, for example " + ""db file sequential read".

Idle Wait Event
Wait event that originates between db calls, for example "SQL*Net message from client".

" + "Non-Idle Wait Time
Wall-clock time or duration of a non-idle wait event.

Idle Wait Time
Wall-clock time or duration of an idle wait event." + "

Unaccounted-for Time
Under-counted (+) or over-counted (-) time difference between wall-clock time and that recorded in a trace file." + "
There are several valid reasons for this unaccounted-for time. Refer to literature for further explanation.
Ignore this time slice if it accounts for less than a small threshold " + "(like 10% of total wall-clock time).

Elapsed Time
Wall-clock time of a db call or a set of calls. It includes CPU and non-idle wait times.
Elapsed Time = " + ""CPU" + "Non Idle Wait" + "Elapsed Unaccounted-for" times.

Response Time" + "
Wall-clock time for a traced process. It is also refered as user time.
Response time has been measured using timestamps of first and last db calls found in trace." + "
It includes elapsed time and idle wait times. It can be analyzed slicing it into its components in several ways.
Response Time = "End of last db Call" - "Start of fisrt db Call" + "".
Response Time = "Elapsed" + "Idle Wait" + "Response Unaccounted-for" times.
Response Time = "CPU" + "Non-Idle Wait" + " + ""Elapsed Unaccounted-for" + "Idle Wait" + "Response Unaccounted-for" times.
Response Time = "CPU" + "Non-Idle Wait" + "Idle Wait" + " + ""Unaccounted-for" times.
Response Time = "CPU" + "Wait" + "Unaccounted-for" times.

Response Time Accounted-for" + "
Response Time Accounted-for = "Elapsed" + "Idle Wait" times.

Buffer Gets in Consistent Read Mode" + "
Oracle buffers reads from the buffer cache, usually associated with queries.

Buffer Gets in Current Mode" + "
Oracle buffers reads from the buffer cache, usually associated with updates.

Logical IO
Buffer gets from buffer cache in either mode " + "(consistent or current). LIOs are CPU intensive.
PIOs counts are included in LIOs counts.

Operating System Buffer Gets" + "
Oracle blocks obtained from the OS. They are also referred as Physical IOs. PIOs are Non-Idle Wait intensive.

Figure 18-3. *The glossary of terms used is not normally displayed*

The reason I mention the glossary of terms is because TRCANLZR needs to be interpreted correctly. There are many measures of time, and each one needs to be understood for you to get the right picture of what is happening. For example the "response time" is the measure of time that the user perceives if they were sitting at a terminal running the SQL. That time is made up of actual work (Elapsed) and non-idle wait times. Idle wait times can be ignored as they are due the end user not responding (normally shown as `SQL*Net message from client`. Non-idle wait times are usually made up of activities that happen during steps in the SQL, for example, fetching data from a disk. Once we have these definitions clear we can look at the "Response Time Summary." Look at Figure 18-4, which shows an example response time summary for the SQL (this is for a simple SQL with no complications).

Response Time Summary

Response Time Component	Time (in secs)	pct of total resp time	Time (in secs)	pct of total resp time	Time (in secs)	pct of total resp time
CPU Time:	194.768	99.6%				
Non-idle Wait Time:	0.029	0.0%				
ET Unaccounted-for Time:	0.613	0.3%				
Total Elapsed Time[1]:			195.411	99.9%		
Idle Wait Time:			0.084	0.0%		
RT Unaccounted-for Time:			0.100	0.1%		
Total Response Time[2]:					195.595	100.0%

(1) Total Elapsed Time = "CPU Time" + "Non-Idle Wait Time" + "ET Unaccounted-for Time".
(2) Total Response Time = "Total Elapsed Time" + "Idle Wait Time" + "RT Unaccounted-for Time".
Total Accounted-for Time = "CPU Time" + "Non-Idle Wait Time" + "Idle Wait Time" = 195.495 secs.
Total Unccounted-for Time = "ET Unaccounted-for Time" + "RT Unaccounted-for Time" = 0.714 secs.
Go to Top

Figure 18-4. *The response time summary shown*

This response time summary shows the following:

- The CPU time was 194.768 seconds.

- Non-idle wait time was 0.029 seconds.

- Unaccounted for elapsed time was 0.613 seconds.

- The percentage of each of the above times.

- The total elapsed time, which is a sum of the CPU Time, Non-Idle Wait time, and The unaccounted for Time in this example 195.411.

- Idle wait time was 0084 seconds.

- Unaccounted for time was 0.1 seconds.

- The total time for everything was 195.595 seconds.

This is an aggregation of all the information from all trace files. This gives you an idea of where your time is going and which item in the list above is worth attacking. In this case 99.6% of all time is spent on the CPU so if there is any improvement that is where it will be made. This kind of report also lists all the related SQL (if it is recursive, for example), so you will see a "Top SQL" section of this report (see Figure 18-5).

Top SQL

[-]

There is only one SQL statement with "Response Time Accounted-for" larger than threshold of 10.0% of the "Total Response Time Accounted-for".

Rank	Trace RT Pct[1]	Self Response Time[2]	Elapsed Time	CPU Time	Non-Idle Wait Time	Idle Wait Time	Recursive Response Time[3]	Exec Count	User	Depth	SQL Text
1:	87.6%	82.572	51.280	9.969	0.195	31.292	7.129	5	95	0	select /*+ parallel (s, 2) */ country_name, st

(1) Percent of "Total Response Time Accounted-for", which is 94.275 secs.
(2) "Self Response Time Accounted-for" in secs (caused by this SQL statement).
(3) "Recursive Response Time Accounted-for" in secs (caused by recursive SQL invoked by this statement).
Go to Top

Figure 18-5. The "Top SQL" section of the TRCANLZR report

TRCAXTR

TRCAXTR is a combination report, which takes the same parameters as TRCANLZR (as described in the section above) but then determines the top SQL from the report and runs that through XTRACT. In the case above the top SQL would be the one under the heading "SQL Text" in Figure 18-5. You run `sqltrcaxtr.sql` by entering the following on the command line:

```
SQL> @sqltrcaxtr.sql
```

You will be prompted for the same parameters as for TRCANLZR but after that ends you will be prompted for the parameters to run XTRACT.

Here are the parameters that you will be prompted for:

- The file containing the trace file or control file containing the trace files (as was mentioned earlier `control.txt` is the 'control' file and can contain multiple trace file names)

- The SQLT explain password

The process is very long (because it goes through all the trace files generating XTRACTs for each SQL. The top-level zip file is called `sqlt_snnnnn_set.zip`. This files contains all the XTRACTs for each of the SQLs in the trace file. This simple routine, with very few parameters, can produce many files to analyze. It can be a quick way to collect information for a whole session, but be warned that the zip files produced can be very big.

Modifying SQLT Behavior

SQLT has many aspects to it and many tools that can be used. Despite this there are still situations where SQLT could do better or be modified to help with some situation. Luckily this is covered by the parameters that can be set to change SQLT's behavior. If we look at the now familiar first page of the main report (see Figure 18-6), we see the "Tool Configuration Parameters" link.

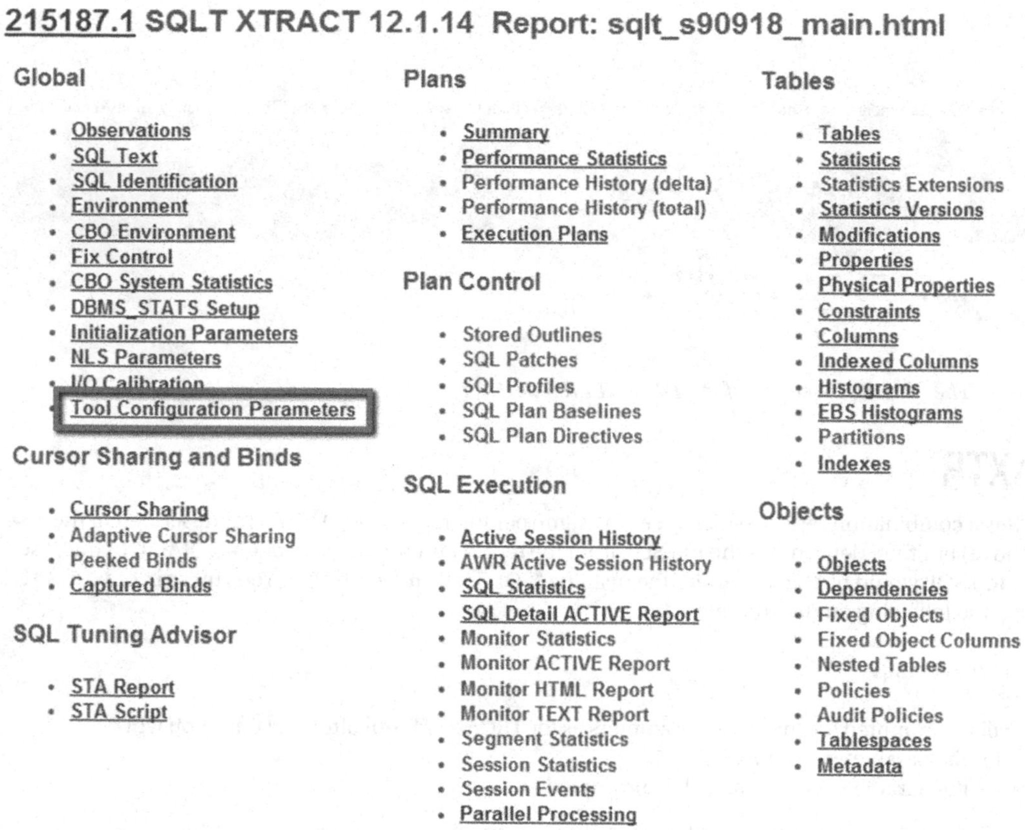

215187.1 SQLT XTRACT 12.1.14 Report: sqlt_s90918_main.html

Global

- Observations
- SQL Text
- SQL Identification
- Environment
- CBO Environment
- Fix Control
- CBO System Statistics
- DBMS_STATS Setup
- Initialization Parameters
- NLS Parameters
- I/O Calibration
- Tool Configuration Parameters

Cursor Sharing and Binds

- Cursor Sharing
- Adaptive Cursor Sharing
- Peeked Binds
- Captured Binds

SQL Tuning Advisor

- STA Report
- STA Script

Plans

- Summary
- Performance Statistics
- Performance History (delta)
- Performance History (total)
- Execution Plans

Plan Control

- Stored Outlines
- SQL Patches
- SQL Profiles
- SQL Plan Baselines
- SQL Plan Directives

SQL Execution

- Active Session History
- AWR Active Session History
- SQL Statistics
- SQL Detail ACTIVE Report
- Monitor Statistics
- Monitor ACTIVE Report
- Monitor HTML Report
- Monitor TEXT Report
- Segment Statistics
- Session Statistics
- Session Events
- Parallel Processing

Tables

- Tables
- Statistics
- Statistics Extensions
- Statistics Versions
- Modifications
- Properties
- Physical Properties
- Constraints
- Columns
- Indexed Columns
- Histograms
- EBS Histograms
- Partitions
- Indexes

Objects

- Objects
- Dependencies
- Fixed Objects
- Fixed Object Columns
- Nested Tables
- Policies
- Audit Policies
- Tablespaces
- Metadata

Figure 18-6. *The Tool configuration option is under the Global section*

If we click on this link we see the list of parameters that can be set within SQLT to change behavior or options (see Figure 18-7 below). Many of the options here turn on features or turn off features, such as `automatic_workload_repository`. The "Domain" column lists the possible values, in this case "Y" or "N."

Tool Configuration Parameters

#	Is Default	Name	System Value[1]	Session Value[2]	Default Value	Domain
1	TRUE	addm_reports	6	6	6	0-9999
2	TRUE	ash_reports	6	6	6	0-9999
3	TRUE	ash_reports_source	BOTH	BOTH	BOTH	BOTH, MEM, AWR, NONE
4	TRUE	automatic_workload_repository	Y	Y	Y	Y, N
5	TRUE	awr_reports	6	6	6	0-9999
6	TRUE	bde_chk_cbo	Y	Y	Y	Y, N
7	TRUE	c_ash_hist_days	31	31	31	0-999
8	TRUE	c_awr_hist_days	31	31	31	0-999
9	TRUE	c_cbo_stats_vers_days	31	31	31	0-999
10	TRUE	c_dba_hist_parameter	Y	Y	Y	Y, N
11	TRUE	c_gran_cols	SUBPARTITION	SUBPARTITION	SUBPARTITION	SUBPARTITION, PARTITION, GLOBAL
12	TRUE	c_gran_hgrm	SUBPARTITION	SUBPARTITION	SUBPARTITION	SUBPARTITION, PARTITION, GLOBAL
13	TRUE	c_gran_segm	SUBPARTITION	SUBPARTITION	SUBPARTITION	SUBPARTITION, PARTITION, GLOBAL
14	TRUE	c_inmemory	Y	Y	Y	Y, N
15	TRUE	c_sesstat_xtract	N	N	N	Y, N
16	TRUE	colgroup_seed_secs	0	0	0	0-3600
17	TRUE	collect_perf_stats	Y	Y	Y	Y, N
18	TRUE	connect_identifier				Null, or @connect_identifier
19	TRUE	count_star_threshold	10000	10000	10000	0-1000000000
20	TRUE	custom_sql_profile	N	N	N	N, Y
21	TRUE	distributed_queries	Y	Y	Y	Y, N
22	TRUE	domain_index_metadata	Y	Y	Y	Y, N, E
23	TRUE	event_10046_level	12	12	12	12, 8, 4, 1, 0
24	TRUE	event_10053_level	1	1	1	1, 0
25	TRUE	event_10507_level	1023	1023	1023	0-1023
26	TRUE	event_others	N	N	N	N, Y
27	TRUE	export_dict_stats	N	N	N	Y, N
28	TRUE	export_repository	Y	Y	Y	Y, N
29	TRUE	export_utility	EXP	EXP	EXP	EXP, EXPDP
30	TRUE	generate_10053_xtract	Y	Y	Y	N, Y, E

Figure 18-7. The first page of configuration parameters

If you are in doubt of the meaning of these parameters then you can just hover your mouse over the parameter and the descriptive comment will be shown. You can see that in Figure 18-8. (For your convenience, Appendix C includes a full list of these parameters and their descriptions.)

Tool Configuration Parameters

#	Is Default	Name	System Value[1]	Session Value
1	TRUE	addm_reports	6	6
2	TRUE	ash_reports	6	6
3	TRUE	ash_reports_source	BOTH	BOTH
4	TRUE	automatic_workload_repository	Y	Y
5	TRUE	awr_reports	6	6
6	TRUE	bde_chk_cbo	Y	Y
7	TRUE	c_ash_hist_days	31	31
8	TRUE	c_awr_hist_days	31	31
9	TRUE	c_cbo_stats vers days	31	31
10	TRUE	c_dba_his		
11	TRUE	c_gran_co		
12	TRUE	c_gran_hc		
13	TRUE	c_gran_se		
14	TRUE	c_inmemc		
15	TRUE	c_sesstat		

> **c_cbo_stats_vers_days**
> Days of CBO statistics versions to be collected. If set to 0 no statistics versions are collected. If set to a value larger than actual stored days, then SQLT collects the whole history. A value of 7 means collect the past 7 days of CBO statistics versions for the schema objects related to given SQL. It includes tables, indexes, partitions, columns and histograms.

Figure 18-8. Hover the mouse over the parameter names to get detailed descriptions

These parameters make the SQLT utility even more flexible and useful than it would otherwise be. At the end of the second page (see Figure 18-9) we see that the way to set these parameters is described:

#	Is Default	Name	System Value[1]	Session Value[2]	Default Value	Domain
31	TRUE	healthcheck_blevel	Y	Y	Y	Y, N
32	TRUE	healthcheck_endpoints	Y	Y	Y	Y, N
33	TRUE	healthcheck_ndv	Y	Y	Y	Y, N
34	TRUE	healthcheck_num_rows	Y	Y	Y	Y, N
35	TRUE	keep_trace_10046_open	Y	Y	Y	Y, N
36	TRUE	keyword_font_color	crimson	crimson	crimson	crimson, red, orange, green, none
37	TRUE	mask_for_values	CLEAR	CLEAR	CLEAR	CLEAR, SECURE, COMPLETE
38	TRUE	plan_stats	BOTH	BOTH	BOTH	BOTH, LAST, ALL
39	TRUE	predicates_in_plan	Y	Y	Y	N, Y, E
40	TRUE	r_gran_cols	PARTITION	PARTITION	PARTITION	PARTITION, GLOBAL
41	TRUE	r_gran_hgrm	PARTITION	PARTITION	PARTITION	PARTITION, GLOBAL
42	TRUE	r_gran_segm	PARTITION	PARTITION	PARTITION	PARTITION, GLOBAL
43	TRUE	r_gran_vers	COLUMN	COLUMN	COLUMN	COLUMN, SEGMENT, HISTOGRAM
44	TRUE	r_rows_table_l	1000	1000	1000	100-10000
45	TRUE	r_rows_table_m	300	300	300	30-3000
46	TRUE	r_rows_table_s	100	100	100	10-1000
47	TRUE	r_rows_table_xs	10	10	10	1-100
48	TRUE	refresh_directories	Y	Y	Y	Y, N
49	TRUE	search_sql_by_sqltext	Y	Y	Y	Y, N
50	TRUE	show_binds_in_predicates	Y	Y	Y	Y, N
51	TRUE	skip_metadata_for_object				Null, or full/partial object name
52	TRUE	sql_monitor_reports	12	12	12	1-9999
53	TRUE	sql_monitoring	Y	Y	Y	Y, N
54	TRUE	sql_tuning_advisor	Y	Y	Y	Y, N
55	TRUE	sql_tuning_set	Y	Y	Y	Y, N
56	TRUE	sqldx_reports_format	CSV	CSV	BOTH	HTML, CSV, BOTH, NONE
57	TRUE	sqlt_max_file_size_mb	200	200	200	1-1024
58	TRUE	sta_time_limit_secs	1800	1800	1800	30-86400
59	TRUE	tcb_export_data	FALSE	FALSE	FALSE	FALSE, TRUE
60	TRUE	tcb_export_pkg_body	FALSE	FALSE	FALSE	FALSE, TRUE
#	Is Default	Name	System Value[1]	Session Value[2]	Default Value	Domain
61	TRUE	tcb_sampling_percent	100	100	100	0-100
62	TRUE	tcb_time_limit_secs	1800	1800	1800	30-86400
63	TRUE	test_case_builder	Y	Y	Y	Y, N
64	TRUE	trace_analyzer	Y	Y	Y	Y, N
65	TRUE	traces_directory_path				Null, valid directory path on server
66	TRUE	upload_trace_size_mb	100	100	100	1-1024
67	TRUE	validate_user	Y	Y	Y	Y, N
68	TRUE	xecute_script_output	KEEP	KEEP	KEEP	KEEP, ZIP, DELETE
69	TRUE	xpand_sql	Y	Y	Y	Y, N

(1) To permanently set a tool parameter issue: SQL> EXEC sqltxadmin.sqlt$a.set_param('Name', 'Value');
(2) To temporarily set a tool parameter for a session issue: SQL> EXEC sqltxadmin.sqlt$a.set_sess_param('Name', 'Value');
Go to Top

Figure 18-9. *The second page of configuration parameters*

To set the value for the tool for all sessions:

```
SQL> EXEC SQLTXADMIN.sqlt$a.set_param('Name', 'Value');
```

And to set the value for one session only:

```
SQL> EXEC SQLTXADMIN.sqlt$a.set_sess_param('Name', 'Value');
```

With these options available we can make smaller test cases, or limit the number of AWR records reviewed or exclude the test case builder.

Summary

In this chapter we covered the use of the tools to analyze trace files that are available in SQLT. These are special tools over and above what TKPROF can offer and are useful in cases where you have 10046 trace files to analyze. SQLT XTRACT is still the best tool for helping with tuning in most cases, but sometimes you have a busy system that does not show a specific SQL to investigate. In cases such as these TRCANLZR can help to find the SQL that is the problem. If you use TRCAXTR as well, then you can combine the best of both worlds. In the next chapter we'll look at how to quickly do a comparison of two SQL execution plans using SQLT.

CHAPTER 19

■ ■ ■

Comparing Execution Plans

Comparing execution plans is one of the most useful diagnostic tests you can do. If you're lucky enough to have a good execution plan, you can use that plan to correct the bad execution plan. In Chapter 8 we talked about using SQL Profiles to apply a plan onto another database's SQL, in order to have an emergency option. Suppose, however, you have more time to consider the difference and try to fix it properly, rather than using the SQL Profile sticking plaster. SQLTCOMPARE is the tool for the job. It will compare two target systems for the same SQL and produce a report that describes the differences. You can even import the SQLTXPLAIN repositories from the two target systems and do the comparison there. This chapter is a pure SQLTXPLAIN chapter: we will be using SQLTXPLAIN's method SQLTCOMPARE and showing how our tuning knowledge from previous chapters can be used to diagnose a problem.

How Do You Use SQLTCOMPARE?

We will go through the steps for using SQLTCOMPARE in more detail with a practical example, but in broad terms the steps to use SQLTCOMPARE are as follows:

1. Get the SQL ID of the SQL you are investigating on both target databases. They don't have to be the same (for example, you could have hints to help you identify the different statements).

2. Then run a main method on this SQL on BOTH target systems.

3. Make a note of the statement ID from both runs of the main method.

4. Create a directory to keep the files from your main method zip files.

5. Unzip both main methods into their respective directories.

6. Create another directory inside the main method directory to keep just the test case file (which is from a zip file inside the main method files: yes a zip file within a zip file).

7. Unzip the test case files into the test case dedicated area.

8. Then import one of the repositories of the statement ID to the other database or import both repositories to a third database (this is the method we will use).

9. Finally, run SQLTCOMPARE.

SQLTCOMPARE relies on the information in the SQLT repository to do its comparison and must have the information that's collected from one of the main methods. The main methods are these:

- XTRACT (We covered this in Chapter 1)

- XECUTE (Also covered in Chapter 1)

- XTRXEC

- XPLAIN

- XTRSBY (We covered this in Chapter 15)

Because SQLTCOMPARE can be used with any of the main methods, it can also be used to compare SQL statements from two different systems, or from a primary and a standby database (if you use XTRSBY). It can even be used to compare execution on two different platforms: for example, a Linux and Windows and from a different version of the database as well. For example, 10g on Linux could be compared with 11g from Solaris.

A Practical Example

In this example we will compare the executions of the following statement against two target databases, but the steps apply to any SQL:

```
SQL> host ls chapter19_01.sql
select /*+ a good plan */
  s.amount_sold,
  c.cust_id,
  p.prod_name
from
  sh.products p,
  sh.sales s,
  sh.customers c
where
  c.cust_id=s.cust_id
  and s.prod_id=p.prod_id
  and c.cust_first_name='Theodorick';
```

Usually you would notice a difference in performance of a particular SQL if your batch times were different or if your OLTP performance was markedly different and you were investigating the databases looking for differences. You could also be doing an evaluation of the relative performance of two different platforms before migration. For the purposes of this example, we have noticed that our target SQL has a different plan on system 1 than on system 2. We created the tables on system 2 from system 1, and the databases are on the same platform and hardware, but we see some differences in the execution plan. On the first database we see this execution plan:

```
SQL> show user
USER is "SH"
SQL> set autotrace traceonly explain
SQL> set lines 300
SQL> @chapter19_01.sql
Execution Plan
----------------------------------------------------------
Plan hash value: 3066457883
```

Id	Operation	Name	Rows	Bytes	Cost(%CPU)	Time	Pstart	Pstop
0	SELECT STATEMENT		5557	303K	942 (2)	00:00:01		
1	NESTED LOOPS		5557	303K	942 (2)	00:00:01		
2	NESTED LOOPS		5557	303K	942 (2)	00:00:01		

```
|* 3|    HASH JOIN           |            |  5557 |  141K|  941  (1)|00:00:01|      |     |
|* 4|     TABLE ACCESS FULL   |CUSTOMERS  |   43  |  516 |  423  (1)|00:00:01|      |     |
|  5|     PARTITION RANGE ALL |            |  918K |  12M |  517  (2)|00:00:01|   1  |  28 |
|  6|      TABLE ACCESS FULL   |SALES      |  918K |  12M |  517  (2)|00:00:01|   1  |  28 |
|* 7|    INDEX UNIQUE SCAN    |PRODUCTS_PK|   1   |      |    0  (0)|00:00:01|      |     |
|  8| TABLE ACCESS BY INDEX ROWID|PRODUCTS|   1   |  30  |    0  (0)|00:00:01|      |     |
---------------------------------------------------------------------------------------------
Predicate Information (identified by operation id):
---------------------------------------------------

   3 - access("C"."CUST_ID"="S"."CUST_ID")
   4 - filter("C"."CUST_FIRST_NAME"='Theodorick')
   7 - access("S"."PROD_ID"="P"."PROD_ID")
Note
-----
this is an adaptive plan
```

On the second system we see the execution plan is different:
```
SQL> set autotrace traceonly explain
SQL> set lines 200
SQL> /
```

```
Execution Plan
----------------------------------------------------------
Plan hash value: 725901306

-----------------------------------------------------------------------------------------
|Id |Operation              |Name      |Rows |Bytes|Cost(%CPU)|Time     |Pstart|Pstop |
-----------------------------------------------------------------------------------------
|  0|SELECT STATEMENT        |          | 5557| 303K|  945  (2)|00:00:01|      |      |
|* 1| HASH JOIN              |          | 5557| 303K|  945  (2)|00:00:01|      |      |
|  2|  TABLE ACCESS FULL     |PRODUCTS  |   72|2160 |    3  (0)|00:00:01|      |      |
|* 3|  HASH JOIN             |          | 5557| 141K|  941  (1)|00:00:01|      |      |
|* 4|   TABLE ACCESS FULL    |CUSTOMERS |   43| 516 |  423  (1)|00:00:01|      |      |
|  5|    PARTITION RANGE ALL |          | 918K| 12M |  517  (2)|00:00:01|   1  |  28  |
|  6|     TABLE ACCESS FULL  |SALES     | 918K| 12M |  517  (2)|00:00:01|   1  |  28  |
-----------------------------------------------------------------------------------------

Predicate Information (identified by operation id):
---------------------------------------------------

   1 - access("S"."PROD_ID"="P"."PROD_ID")
   3 - access("C"."CUST_ID"="S"."CUST_ID")
   4 - filter("C"."CUST_FIRST_NAME"='Theodorick')
```

The cost is different, the join order is different, there could also be other differences, but that's not the point here. What can SQLTCOMPARE tell us about the difference between these two identical pieces of SQL that behave differently? In the non-SQLTXPLAIN world, we would now be searching for differences between the systems, looking at all the likely suspects one by one, with all their special tools, which would be a long-winded and error-prone process. With SQLTCOMPARE, however, we collect all the information and do a comparison of everything in one go. Then we decide what's important.

Collecting the Main Method Repository Data

The steps in collecting the SQLTXPLAIN data are just the standard methods we have already used. In this example we'll use SQLTXECUTE. To recap, the steps are to identify the SQL ID, create a file with the SQL statement in it (including any bind variables), and then run SQLTXECUTE on both systems.

We already mentioned the SQL statement above, and we can check on both systems what the SQL ID is.

For each main method we use we are collecting information about the SQL statement and we need to take note of the statement ID (not the SQL IDs). That's the statement number that SQLTXPLAIN assigns to the run of the SQLT method. So on the first system we run SQLTXECUTE like this:

```
SQL> @sqltxecute chapter19_01.sql
```

The file chapter16_01.sql contains the SQL mentioned above. When the SQLTXECUTE method completes we see this output.

```
#####
The SQLT has collected information and place it in a repository in the database, exported it
and zip it.
The collected info can be purged from the database using the following file :
... getting sqlt_s30931_purge.sql out of sqlt repository ...

SQLTXECUTE completed.
```

Here we take a note of the statement ID, in this case it is 30931. Similarly on the second system we run the same SQL (remember we checked the SQL ID) and use the same file to run SQLTXECUTE again. The output from the second system is this:

```
#####
The SQLT has collected information and place it in a repository in the database, exported it
and zip it.
The collected info can be purged from the database using the following file :
... getting sqlt_s30932_purge.sql out of sqlt repository ...

SQLTXECUTE completed.
```

Preparing the Main Method Repository Data

The execution of sqltxecute creates zip files that contain important information. The information in this zip file contains instructions on how to import the data into another SQLT repository, but first you must unzip the main zip file. From the execution of the two main methods on the target systems we see that the statement IDs are 30931 (low CBO cost) and 430932 (higher CBO cost). In this case I created two directories, sqlt_s30931and sqlt_s430932, each with the corresponding zip file in it, which I then unzipped. Each directory contains many files as we've learned, but in this case we are interested in the readme file, called sql_snnnnn_readme.html. This is your go to file in case of doubt (and this book of course). In this file the exact steps are described to carry out many functions including SQLTCOMPARE actions. This is the top of the readme file for the SQLTXECUTE report we ran on the first target system (see Figure 19-1).

215187.1 SQLT XECUTE 12.1.160429 Report: sqlt_s30931_readme.html

Instructions to perform the following:

- **Export SQLT repository**
- **Import SQLT repository**
- **Using SQLT COMPARE**
- **Restore CBO schema statistics**
- **Restore CBO system statistics**
- **Implement SQLT Test Case (TC)**
- **Create TC with no SQLT dependencies**
- **Restore SQL Set**
- **Create SQL Plan Baseline from SQL Set**
- **Gather CBO statistics without Histograms (using SYS.DBMS_STATS)**
- **Gather CBO statistics with Histograms (using SYS.DBMS_STATS)**
- **List generated files**

Figure 19-1. *The top of the readme file*

If we click on the "Using SQLT COMPARE" hyperlink in this part of the report, we are taken to the steps describing the actions we need to take to import the data into a new database (or in fact the same database) to do the comparison. See Figure 19-2 for the readme section for s30931.

Using SQLT COMPARE

You need to have a set of SQLT files (sqlt_sNNNNN_method.zip) from two executions of the SQLT tool. They can be from any method (XTRACT, XECUTE or XPLAIN) and they can be from the same or different systems. They do not have to be from same release or platform. For example, a SQLT from 10g on Linux and a SQLT from 11g on Unix can be compared.

To use the COMPARE method you need 3 systems: SOURCE1, SOURCE2 and COMPARE. The 3 could all be different, or all the same. For example, SOURCE1 could be PROD, SOURCE2 DEV and COMPARE DEV. In other words, you could do the COMPARE in one of the sources. Or the COMPARE could be done on a 3rd and remote system.

Basically you need to restore the SQLT repository from both SOURCES into the COMPARE system. In most cases it means "restoring" the SQLT repository from at least one SOURCE into the COMPARE. Once you have both SQLT repositories into the COMPARE system, then you can execute this method.

Steps:

1. Unzip `sqlt_s30931_tc.zip` from this SOURCE in order to get `sqlt_s30931_expdp.dmp`.
2. Copy `sqlt_s30931_exp.dmp` to the server (BINARY).
3. Execute import on server:

```
imp sqltxplain FILE=sqlt_s30931_exp.dmp TABLES=sqlt% IGNORE=Y
```

4. Perform the equivalent steps for the 2nd SOURCE if needed. You may want to follow its readme file.
5. Execute the COMPARE method connecting into SQL*Plus as SYS. You will be asked to enter which 2 statements you want to compare.

```
START sqlt/run/sqltcompare.sql
```

Figure 19-2. *The instructions for SQLTCOMPARE show the import*

Notice that we have to unzip the `sqlt_s30931_tc.zip` file, which is found inside the main SQLT zip file. This is the test case file we dealt with in Chapter 16. For the moment, however, we need only concern ourselves with the dump file found inside the test case zip file. I've unzipped this file into a directory called "TC" inside the unzipped area. Now make sure that your SID is set up appropriately(in my case I am importing into a third database), we execute the instructions to import the data into our third database.

Importing the Respository Data

Importing the repository data is the last step before we can actually run SQLTCOMPARE. As long as we've kept track of the various zip files along the way, it should only be a matter of importing the files.

```
imp sqltxplain file=sqlt_s30931_exp.dmp tables=sqlt% ignore=y

Import: Release 12.1.0.2.0 - Production on Mon Nov 28 14:48:24 2016

Copyright (c) 1982, 2014, Oracle and/or its affiliates.  All rights reserved.

Password:

Connected to: Oracle Database 12c Enterprise Edition Release 12.1.0.2.0 - 64bit Production
With the Partitioning, OLAP, Advanced Analytics and Real Application Testing options
Export file created by EXPORT:V12.01.00 via conventional path
import done in US7ASCII character set and AL16UTF16 NCHAR character set
import server uses WE8MSWIN1252 character set (possible charset conversion)
. importing SQLTXPLAIN's objects into SQLTXPLAIN
. importing SQLTXPLAIN's objects into SQLTXPLAIN
. . importing table          "SQLT$_SQL_STATEMENT"            1 rows imported
. . importing table            "SQLT$_AUX_STATS$"           13 rows imported
. . importing table     "SQLT$_DBA_AUTOTASK_CLIENT"          1 rows imported
. . importing table "SQLT$_DBA_COL_STATS_VERSIONS"         248 rows imported
. . importing table         "SQLT$_DBA_COL_USAGE$"          13 rows imported

---Output removed for clarity

. . importing table                "SQLT$_STATTAB"        3445 rows imported
. . importing table            "SQLT$_STGTAB_SQLSET"        10 rows imported
. . importing table  "SQLT$_V$SESSION_FIX_CONTROL"        1070 rows imported
. . importing table          "SQLT$_WRI$_ADV_TASKS"          2 rows imported
Import terminated successfully without warnings.
```

This has imported the required information from the first database (the good execution plan) into the SQLTXPLAIN schema on the third database. Now we repeat the entire process for the second database.

```
imp sqltxplain file=sqlt_s43994_exp.dmp tables=sqlt% ignore=y

Import: Release 12.1.0.2.0 - Production on Mon Nov 28 15:02:14 2016

Copyright (c) 1982, 2014, Oracle and/or its affiliates.  All rights reserved.

Password:

Connected to: Oracle Database 12c Enterprise Edition Release 12.1.0.2.0 - 64bit Production
With the Partitioning, OLAP, Advanced Analytics and Real Application Testing options

Export file created by EXPORT:V12.01.00 via conventional path
import done in US7ASCII character set and AL16UTF16 NCHAR character set
import server uses WE8MSWIN1252 character set (possible charset conversion)
. importing SQLTXPLAIN's objects into SQLTXPLAIN
```

```
. importing SQLTXPLAIN's objects into SQLTXPLAIN
. . importing table          "SQLT$_SQL_STATEMENT"            1 rows imported
. . importing table              "SQLT$_AUX_STATS$"          13 rows imported
. . importing table     "SQLT$_DBA_AUTOTASK_CLIENT"           1 rows imported
. . importing table "SQLT$_DBA_COL_STATS_VERSIONS"          248 rows imported
---Output removed for clarity


. . importing table       "SQLT$_SQL_SHARED_CURSOR_D"         1 rows imported
. . importing table                 "SQLT$_STATTAB"        3445 rows imported
. . importing table            "SQLT$_STGTAB_SQLSET"          14 rows imported
. . importing table    "SQLT$_V$SESSION_FIX_CONTROL"       1070 rows imported
. . importing table           "SQLT$_WRI$_ADV_TASKS"           2 rows imported
Import terminated successfully without warnings.
```

Now all that remains to be done is to run the SQLTCOMPARE method. The script for this is in the "run" area. Logged in as SQLTXPLAIN we run SQLTCOMPARE.

Running SQLTCOMPARE

Once we have imported the data we can run SQLTCOMPARE. We can run it with or without the parameters on the command line. In this case I'll omit the parameters so that we can see what the prompts are:

```
SQL> @sqltcompare

---Output removed for clarity
STAID MET INSTANCE SQL_TEXT
----- --- -------- ------------------------------------------------------------
30931 XEC snc1     select /*+ A good plan */ s.amount_sold,  c.cust_id,   p.p
90110 XEC snc1     select /*+ Bad USE_HASH(P C S)   s.amount_sold,   c.cust_id,

Parameter 1:
STATEMENT_ID1 (required)

Enter value for 1: 30931

Parameter 2:
STATEMENT_ID2 (required)

Enter value for 2:30932
```

We see that the SQLTCOMPARE method immediately identifies the statements that we could compare and shows them to us (because we did not specify the statement Ids on the command line). Our good execution plan was run on snc1 (statement ID 30931), and our not-so-good execution plan was also run on snc1. I always like to compare good to bad, so for the first statement ID I'll enter 30931 and for the second I'll enter the only remaining statement ID 30932. (When you do your own comparisons you can compare the SQLs anyway you like, but I like the good vs. bad convention to keep me focused on finding the differences the right way around).

Now we are presented with the plan hash value history for each of the statements on each instance so we can choose which plan hash values to compare. In this case I'll compare the best plan on both systems.

```
PLAN_HASH_VALUE  SQLT_PLAN_HASH_VALUE  STATEMENT_ID ATTRIBUTE
---------------  --------------------  ------------ ---------
     3066457883                 85018        30931 [B][W][X]


Parameter 3:
PLAN_HASH_VALUE1 (required if more than one)

Enter value for 3: 3066457883


PLAN_HASH_VALUE  SQLT_PLAN_HASH_VALUE  STATEMENT_ID ATTRIBUTE
---------------  --------------------  ------------ ---------
      725901306                 16588        30932 [B][W][X]


Parameter 4:
PLAN_HASH_VALUE2 (required if more than one)

Enter value for 4: 725901306
Values passed to sqltcompare:
STATEMENT_ID1    : "30931"
STATEMENT_ID2    : "30932"
PLAN_HASH_VALUE1: "3066457883"
PLAN_HASH_VALUE2: "725901306"... please wait ...

14:17:04  365 sqlt$c: => compare_report
14:17:04    0 sqlt$a: -> common_initialization
14:17:04    0 sqlt$a: ALTER SESSION SET NLS_NUMERIC_CHARACTERS = ".,"
14:17:04    0 sqlt$a: ALTER SESSION SET NLS_SORT = BINARY
14:17:04    0 sqlt$a: <- common_initialization
14:17:04    0 sqlt$c: -> header
14:17:04    0 sqlt$c: Getting s_file_rec.file_text
14:17:04    0 sqlt$c: Got s_file_rec.file_text
14:17:04    0 sqlt$c: -> sql_text
14:17:04    0 sqlt$c: -> sql_identification
14:17:04    0 sqlt$c: -> environment
14:17:04    0 sqlt$c: -> nls_parameters
14:17:04    0 sqlt$c: -> io_calibration
14:17:04    0 sqlt$c: -> cbo_environment
14:17:04    0 sqlt$c: -> fix_control
14:17:04    0 sqlt$c: -> cbo_system_statistics
14:17:04    0 sqlt$c: -> execution_plan
14:17:04    0 sqlt$c: plan 30931 "GV$SQL_PLAN" "3066457883" "-1" "1" "0" "00000000AC5EF990"
14:17:04    0 sqlt$c: plan 30932 "GV$SQL_PLAN" "725901306" "-1" "1" "1" "00000000B562D5A0"
14:17:05    1 sqlt$c: -> tables
14:17:05    0 sqlt$c: -> table_partitions
14:17:05    0 sqlt$c: -> indexes
14:17:05    0 sqlt$c: -> index_partitions
14:17:05    0 sqlt$c: -> columns
14:17:05    0 sqlt$c: -> footer_and_closure
14:17:05    0 sqlt$c: <= compare_report
sqlt_s30931_s30932_compare.html has been generated
#####
```

The SQLT has collected information and place it in a repository in the database, exported it and zip it.
The collected info can be purged from the database using the following file :

SQLTCOMPARE completed.
Now we have a file called sqlt_s30931_s30932_compare.html

SQL>host ls sqlt_s3093*_compare.html
sqlt_s30931_s30932_compare.html

Reading the SQLTCOMPARE Report

The HTML file produced by running SQLTCOMPARE contains information that compares the plan hash value from each of the two target databases. In this case the first system was slightly faster than the second system. There could be many reasons for this, but the key element here is to see which sections are there for investigation. We already know the execution plan is slightly different. Here is the top of the SQLTCOMPARE report for our example (see Figure 19-3).

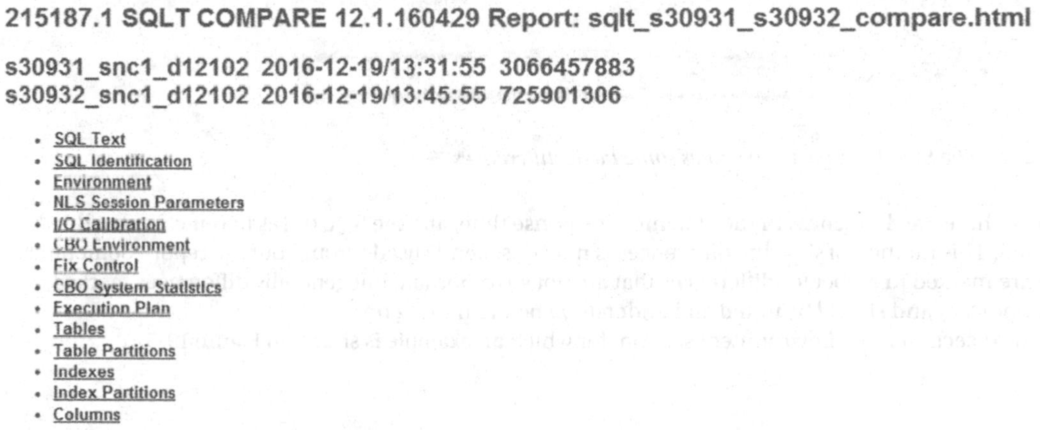

215187.1 SQLT COMPARE 12.1.160429 Report: sqlt_s30931_s30932_compare.html

s30931_snc1_d12102 2016-12-19/13:31:55 3066457883
s30932_snc1_d12102 2016-12-19/13:45:55 725901306

- SQL Text
- SQL Identification
- Environment
- NLS Session Parameters
- I/O Calibration
- CBO Environment
- Fix Control
- CBO System Statistics
- Execution Plan
- Tables
- Table Partitions
- Indexes
- Index Partitions
- Columns

Figure 19-3. *The top of the SQLTCOMPARE report*

If we click on the SQL Identification hyperlink from the top of the report, we'll see differences (if there are any) as shown in Figure 19-4.

SQL Identification

	s30931_snc1_d12102	s30932_snc1_d12102
SQL ID	0fpfqq7um12un	3zkx2scfbh9bj
Hash Value	4113599316	481830257
Plan Hash Value	3066457883	725901306
SQLT Plan Hash Value	85018	16588
SQLT Plan Hash Value2	1952	21458
Signature for Stored Outlines	B8DFF321DCD10A3A5A31A9C62B86964D	9CA62F4CE6DD25348668EF349AF7F8B9
Signature for SQL Profiles (force match FALSE)	15041647971269667972	14713161447544257454
Signature for SQL Profiles (force match TRUE)	10636863870283202904	10914563331874178739
"EXPLAIN PLAN FOR" SQL ID for stripped sql_text	4vpspwz295rvq	4fua544rkng91
Signature for Stored Outlines for unstripped sql_text	B8DFF321DCD10A3A5A31A9C62B86964D	9CA62F4CE6DD25348668EF349AF7F8B9
Signature for SQL Profiles for unstripped sql_text (force match FALSE)	15041647971269667972	14713161447544257454
Signature for SQL Profiles for unstripped sql_text (force match TRUE)	10636863870283202904	10914563331874178739
Statement Response Time	+00 00:00:06.520437	+00 00:00:01.320242

Go to Top

Figure 19-4. *The SQL Identification shows some basic differences*

Notice there are differences in the Statement response time, and the SQL ID (as in our case we added some hints). This method of showing differences is not consistently used throughout the report. Sometimes sections are marked in amber for differences that are not so important, but generally differences marked in red are important and should be noted and understood before moving on.

The next section is the Environment section, for which an example is shown in Figure 19-5.

Environment

	s30931_snc1_d12102	s30932_snc1_d12102
Host Name	d12102.us.oracle.com	d12102.us.oracle.com
CPU_Count	4	4
Num CPUs	4	4
Num Cores	4	4
Num Sockets	1	1
Exadata	NO	NO
RAC	FALSE	FALSE
NLS Characterset (database_properties)	WE8MSWIN1252	WE8MSWIN1252
DB Time Zone (database_properties)	00:00	00:00
DB Block Size (db_block_size)	8192	8192
Optim Peek User Binds (_optim_peek_user_binds)	TRUE	TRUE
DB Size in Terabytes (dba_data_files)	0.003 TB	0.004 TB
TC Data Size in Gigabytes (dba_segments)	0.830 GB	0.830 GB
Platform	Linux	Linux
Product Version	Oracle Database 12c Enterprise Edition (64bit Production)	Oracle Database 12c Enterprise Edition (64bit Production)
RDBMS Version	12.1.0.2.0	12.1.0.2.0
Language	US:AMERICAN_AMERICA.WE8MSWIN1252	US:AMERICAN_AMERICA.WE8MSWIN1252
Database Name and ID	SNC1(1478727753)	SNC1(1478727753)
Instance Name and ID	snc1(1)	snc1(1)
EBS	NO	NO
Siebel	NO	NO
PSFT	NO	NO
User Name and ID	SH (105)	SH (105)
Input Filename	chapter19_01.sql	q2.sql

Go to Top

Figure 19-5. The Environment section of the SQLTCOMPARE report

Here the things that are the same are just as important as the things that are different. In my case there will be no differences because I used the same platform for both tests. In your case you may find differences that are significant. SQLT handily marks these as red if they are different.

In the main HTML Compare report (as shown in Figure 19-3) we can scan from top to bottom. This is not a long complicated report like the main SQLTXTRACT or SQLTXECUTE report. There are also sections on the following:

- SQL Text
- SQL Identification
- Environment
- NLS session parameters
- I/O calibration
- CBO parameters
- Fix control
- CBO System statistics
- Execution plans

335

- Table information
- Table partition information
- Index information
- Index partition information
- Column information
- Peeked binds
- Captured binds

And of course there are the execution plans (as shown in Figure 19-6). Much of this information is exactly the same as you would see in a SQLTXRACT report, so we won't dwell on it too much here. The important thing to note is that it gives you an easy side-by-side comparison for many features including the execution plan (see Figure 19-6). This is a great way to quickly spot differences, especially if you have hundreds of lines in your execution plan and only one line is different (yes, it does happen and yes, it can make a vast difference in the execution time). Notice that in our case one plan was adaptive and one was not.

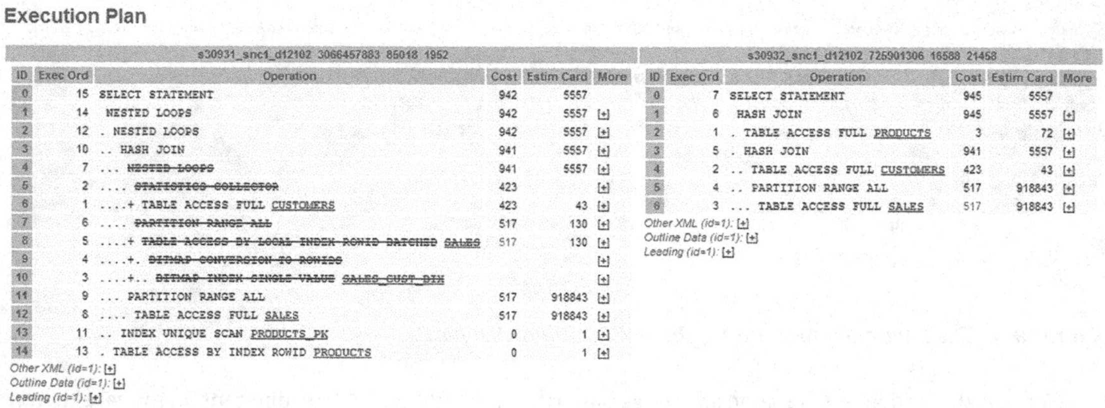

Execution Plan

s30931_snc1_d12102 3066457883 85018 1952

ID	Exec Ord	Operation	Cost	Estim Card	More
0	15	SELECT STATEMENT	942	5557	
1	14	NESTED LOOPS	942	5557	[+]
2	12	. NESTED LOOPS	942	5557	[+]
3	10	.. HASH JOIN	941	5557	[+]
4	7	... ~~NESTED LOOPS~~	941	5557	[+]
5	2	.... ~~STATISTICS COLLECTOR~~	423		[+]
6	1	....+ TABLE ACCESS FULL CUSTOMERS	423	43	[+]
7	6	.... ~~PARTITION RANGE ALL~~	517	130	[+]
8	5	....+ ~~TABLE ACCESS BY LOCAL INDEX ROWID BATCHED SALES~~	517	130	[+]
9	4	....+. ~~BITMAP CONVERSION TO ROWIDS~~			[+]
10	3	....+.. ~~BITMAP INDEX SINGLE VALUE SALES_CUST_BIX~~			[+]
11	9	... PARTITION RANGE ALL	517	918843	[+]
12	8	.... TABLE ACCESS FULL SALES	517	918843	[+]
13	11	.. INDEX UNIQUE SCAN PRODUCTS_PK	0	1	[+]
14	13	. TABLE ACCESS BY INDEX ROWID PRODUCTS	0	1	[+]

Other XML (id=1): [+]
Outline Data (id=1): [+]
Leading (id=1): [+]

s30932_snc1_d12102 725901306 16588 21458

ID	Exec Ord	Operation	Cost	Estim Card	More
0	7	SELECT STATEMENT	945	5557	
1	6	HASH JOIN	945	5557	[+]
2	1	. TABLE ACCESS FULL PRODUCTS	3	72	[+]
3	5	. HASH JOIN	941	5557	[+]
4	2	.. TABLE ACCESS FULL CUSTOMERS	423	43	[+]
5	4	.. PARTITION RANGE ALL	517	918843	[+]
6	3	... TABLE ACCESS FULL SALES	517	918843	[+]

Other XML (id=1): [+]
Outline Data (id=1): [+]
Leading (id=1): [+]

Figure 19-6. *The Execution plans side by side*

The most important sections are the Optimizer Environment and the Plan Summary. This shows the optimizer settings and also the average elapsed time and CPU time for both compared SQL statements. We see an example of this in Figure 19-7.

Optimizer Environment

s30931_snc1_d12102 3066457883 85018 1952			s30932_snc1_d12102 725901306 16588 21458		
#	Name	Value	#	Name	Value
1	solstat_enabled	true	1	solstat_enabled	true
2	statistics_level	all	2	statistics_level	all

Plan Summary

Name	s30931_snc1_d12102	s30932_snc1_d12102
Plan Hash Value	3066457883	725901306
SQLT PHV	85018	16588
SQLT PHV2	1952	21458
Avg Elapsed Time in secs	6.459	0.996
Avg CPU Time in secs	6.397	0.954
Avg User I/O Wait Time in secs	0.000	0.000
Avg Buffer Gets	4424	3221
Avg Disk Reads	0	0
Avg Direct Writes	0	0
Avg Rows Processed	1127	1127
Total Executions	1	1
Total Fetches	77	77
Total Version Count	1	2
Total Loads	1	2
Total Invalidations	0	0
Is Bind Sensitive	N	N
Min Optimizer Env	3355847575	3355847575
Max Optimizer Env	3355847575	4077259249
Optimizer Cost	942	945
Estimated Cardinality	5557	5557
Estimated Time in secs	11.304	11.340
Plan Timestamp	2016-12-19/13:31:57	2016-12-19/13:41:48
First Load Time	2016-12-19/13:31:57	2016-12-19/13:41:48
Last Load Time	2016-12-19/13:31:57	2016-12-19/13:45:58
Src	MEM	MEM
Source	GV$SQLAREA_PLAN_HASH	GV$SQLAREA_PLAN_HASH

Go to Top

Figure 19-7. The Plan Summary section of the report

The optimizer environment can make a huge difference. So this section can be crucial. We also see how the two statements compare in terms of elapsed time (which might be misleading if the load on the two systems is different), but we also see the CPU time in seconds and the average number of buffer gets, which is usually a good measure of how good an execution plan is compared to a different run of the same SQL. I've highlighted the buffer gets with an arrow.

- Naturally every line of the plan summary is telling us something. I've listed below the items I consider important:

- Avg. Elapsed Time in secs: clearly important if the load on the systems is comparable as it is an indication of the performance of the SQL.

- Avg. CPU Time in secs: the CPU time in comparison to the total elapsed time can tell you if the SQL is CPU bound or not.

- Avg. User I/O Wait Time in secs: a measure of how much time is spent on I/O could tell you if you are I/O bound.

- Avg. Buffer Gets: can be a good comparison between individual runs of the same SQL on busy systems with much activity where relative performance from one run to another is hard to gauge.

- Avg. Disk Reads: shows how many of your reads are going to disk.

- Avg. Direct Writes: indicates how much of your I/O is a direct write.

- Avg. Rows Processed: in comparisons you would expect these to be the same if the data was the same.

- Total Executions: this gives you an idea of how many times the SQL was run on each system.

- Total Fetches: a measure of the data returned in all executions.

- Total Version Count: a count of the number of versions of the cursor found on the system.

- Total Loads: the number of times the SQL was loaded.

- Total Invalidations: shows how many times the SQL was made invalid.

- Is Bind Sensitive: discussed in Chapter 9.

- Min Optimizer Environment: shows the minimum optimizer environment hash value.

- Max Optimizer Environment: shows the maximum optimizer environment hash value (this and the previous value are useful for comparing environment values).

- Optimizer Cost: useful to compare overall cost.

- Estimated Cardinality: useful to see what the optimizer estimated.

- Estimated Time in Seconds: another measure of the optimizer calculations.

- Plan Time Stamp: shows when the execution plan was calculated.

- First Load Time: when the plan was first loaded into memory.

- Last Load Time: when the plan was loaded into memory last.

- Src: shows where the information was derived from.

- Source: shows which source was used in this case GV$SQLAREA_PLAN_HASH.

We see a lot of sections that are different from one another, but Compare is not intelligent enough to tell us what is important in all cases. In this case we can confirm that the elapsed time was higher on the first run compared to the second run. In this case the amber color used in the report indicates that the comparisons are not so different as to cause a problem but should probably be investigated if there aren't any other more pressing problems. In percentage terms "Avg CPU Time in secs" is very different (as one of the values is less than a second and the other is over 6 seconds), so this is highlighted in red. Other differences are not so important (such as plan timestamp), but these are shown in red anyway. Remember these are only guidelines, so you must decide what's important in terms of a difference because you know your environment and circumstances. SQLTCOMPARE is there to show you the differences so as to allow you to make a good decision quickly.

Summary

Comparison of two SQL statement IDs and plan hash values is an invaluable method for highlighting differences, which sometimes do not stand out on individual inspection. SQLTCOMPARE is also invaluable in confirming the differences detected by users or developers and thereby eliminating other sources as the cause of differences. Different environments can often be challenging to compare because there are so many differences that can affect the execution plan. SQLTCOMPARE grabs all the information available and shows it side by side in a simple-to-read report. It's yet another case of SQLTXPLAIN making a complex job fast and easy. In the next chapter we look at one of SQLTXPLAIN's simple health check reports.

CHAPTER 20

■ ■ ■

Running a Health Check

The SQL health check script is not SQLT. It is a completely separate utility downloaded from a different Metalink note and used in a different way. Why is it even mentioned in this book? SQLHC is considered a backup option when SQLT cannot be installed. This does not happen very often, but when it does it is usually because of site restrictions. There are many reasons for this:

- Not allowed to install anything on production (security reasons)

- Not allowed to install anything on production (fear of affecting production)

- Installation and testing procedures take too long and you have a problem on production

- Don't trust SQLT

- SQLT is too complicated

- Not enough space to install SQLT

Let me start by saying that SQLT has a small footprint and has been tried and tested on many different systems. Business reasons may preclude the installation of new packages in a timely manner: for example, if you have to test on development and QA before you can get to production. If you have those rules in place you should honor those business rules or local IT standards and consider using the health check script instead. However, I hope I've shown that SQLT is a trustworthy tool with many benefits for the user. If you come across a situation in which the use of SQLT is prohibited, then you can still choose the second best option, which is to run an SQL health check script against the target SQL.

What Is SQL Health Check?

The SQL health check (SQLHC) script is available as a free download from Oracle Metalink note 1366133.1. It is a zip file containing three simple SQL scripts (`sqldx.sql`, `sqlhc.sql`, and `sqlhcxec.sql`) that you run as sys on the target system. Until recently `sqlhc.sql` was the only script, so we'll talk about that script mostly and cover the other scripts later in this chapter. With all of these scripts nothing is installed: they are just SQL scripts and are very simple to use. These scripts were developed in response to the requirements on some sites that precluded the installation of SQLT (which has a schema, schema objects, tables and indexes, packages and functions). Because a script such as `sqlhc.sql` is just a simple script, more sites will accept it so more sites can take advantage of the recommendations that come from SQLHC. SQLHC was developed from SQLT (it provides a subset of SQLT's functionality) and so discussions of what SQLHC can do cover many of the topics already covered in this book.

© Stelios Charalambides 2017
S. Charalambides, *Oracle SQL Tuning with Oracle SQLTXPLAIN*, DOI 10.1007/978-1-4842-2436-6_20

Here are some of the sections that are covered in an SQL health check report:

- An observation report, similar to SQLT but limited because of the limited access to the database

- The SQLT text

- A summary of the table information including the number of rows and statistical sampling size

- The number of columns and histograms for each table

- A summary of all the index information for each table

- A description of SQL plan baselines and profiles that are used for the SQL

- The status of cursor sharing and the reasons for sharing

- A history of the SQL plans with associated statistics

- A history of the execution plans

- Active session history information

- Column statistics and histogram types

- System parameters and their values and default or non-default nature

- A detailed description of all the execution plans

- An SQL monitor report of the SQL

The above functionality is produced by the main script of SQLHC, which is `sqlhc.sql`: in fact, the previous versions of SQLHC consisted of only this script. Later versions also included `sqldx.sql` and `sqlhcxec.sql`. The sqldx routine is a superb utility that produces a test case with no dependence on SQLT. We'll talk more about that in the section "The sqldx.sql Script." We'll also cover sqhcxec. For now let's look at the main script `sqlhc.sql`. The first step in any tuning exercise should be to look for the obvious wrong things. This is called a checklist: why go into a long tuning exercise when you're missing an obvious index?

The list of things that can be done incorrectly on a database or on any particular SQL is very long. The health check script and SQLT have these error checks built in. SQLHC has approximately a hundred checks that it carries out (SQLT has two to three times that many). With these built-in checks you can find and fix those problems before you start any tuning exercise. In SQLT these errors are pointed out in the "Observations" section of the main report (see Chapter 1). In SQLHC there is also an observations section of the report in the first page of the SQLHC HTML file. If only a few of your SQLs are caught before they go to production with some "obvious" mistakes, it will be well worth your time to download and use the SQL health check scripts.

The sqlhc.sql Script

The `sqlhc.sql` script is a single SQL script that produces one zip file, which contains four HTML files, and three zip files. If you do nothing else but run `sqlhc.sql` on each new SQL you introduce to your system, the health check script will have been worth the effort. The HTML files are reports in their own right and are well worth a careful read. The `sqlhc.sql` script is easy to use and takes only two parameters (we'll look at an example run later in this chapter in the section "Running the SQLHC Script."

Remember that these files can be reviewed in any order, and one does not depend on another. If you have a particular area you want to check, you can look at the appropriate file directly without looking at files in between. However, if you want to be thorough and check everything, the main HTML files are numbered for your convenience. Example file names are shown below:

- `sqlhc_20161220_095807_8nsdvk4u6wcvk_1_health_check.html`

- `sqlhc_20161220_095807_8nsdvk4u6wcvk_2_diagnostics.html`

- `sqlhc_20161220_095807_8nsdvk4u6wcvk_3_execution_plans.html`

- `sqlhc_20161220_095807_8nsdvk4u6wcvk_4_sql_detail.html`

We'll look at all the files produced by `sqlhc.sql` in the next section.

What sqlhc.sql Produces

This section describes the main report files. The first four files mentioned are the HTML pages created by `sqlhc.sql`. They all contain the SQL text so you can make sure you're looking at the right file and view these in order from one to four.

- The first HTML report, the main health check script, gives you a good overview of observations and the general checks on the SQL. It covers observations and table and index summaries. The observations should be carefully reviewed for any problems.

- The second HTML report is more detailed and covers many miscellaneous areas, but most importantly it covers the current statistics (in the Current SQL Statistics section) and instance and system parameters. It also covers cursor sharing information and execution plan summaries. Historical information is also included, on tables, columns, indexes, instance, and system parameters. This report also covers SQL Plan baselines and profiles, as well as SQL_Patches.

- Report three is useful if you think there is some issue with the execution plan or the execution plan has changed unexpectedly. Both current and historical execution plans are shown.

- The fourth report will give you some timings and shows you where you should concentrate your tuning effort.

Other files include the following:

- A zip file with the SQL Monitor execution details for each of the execution plans.

- A zip file containing the log of the run and some ancillary SQL.

- Lastly, an SQLDX zip file that contains all of the discovered information in a CSV format. This will allow further post-processing using spreadsheets.

There are many useful files here, but the most useful parts of this output are the four HTML files and the SQL Monitor output. I'll show some examples of these after running an example script. You can see that although we have not run SQLT, we still have a lot of information to work with.

Running the SQLHC Script

Before I start the example, I have already logged in to Metalink (or My Oracle Support) and downloaded the one zip file that constitutes the SQLHC script files. The file is called `sqlhc.zip`. It contains `sqldx.sql`, `sqlhc.sql`, and `sqlhcxec.sql`. This one simple zip file is all that is required to get the information listed in the example below. When considering the endless HTML reports and historical information-gathering execution plans reports, why would you not want to run this script as a check for each deployed SQL?

If you consider how much information you get from the SQL health check script and how little effort you have to put in to get this information, it's a wonder that this script is free to supported customers. In the example below, I will log in as sys, run my q3.sql test script, and get the SQL ID. Here is the q3.sql script we are using.

```
SQL> select country_name, sum(amount_sold)
from sh.sales s, sh.customers c, sh.countries t
where t.country_id = c.country_id
and c.cust_id = s.cust_id
group by country_name;
```

We'll follow through all the required steps and show the example output.

```
>sqlplus / as sysdba
SQL*Plus: Release 11.2.0.1.0 Production on Thu Dec 27 09:29:45 2012
Copyright (c) 1982, 2010, Oracle.  All rights reserved.
Connected to:
Oracle Database 11g Enterprise Edition Release 11.2.0.1.0 - Production
With the Partitioning, OLAP, Data Mining and Real Application Testing options

SQL> @q3

COUNTRY_NAME                             SUM(AMOUNT_SOLD)
---------------------------------------- ----------------
Poland                                         8447.14
Denmark                                     1977764.79
Spain                                       2090863.44
France                                      3776270.13
Italy                                       4854505.28
United Kingdom                              6393762.94
Germany                                     9210129.22

7 rows selected.

SQL> select sql_id, sql_text from v$sqlarea where sql_text like 'select%parallel%Poland%';

SQL_ID
-------------
SQL_TEXT
--------------------------------------------------------------------------------
8nsdvk4u6wcvk

select /*+ parallel (s, 2) */
  country_name,
  sum(AMOUNT_SOLD)
from
  sh.sales s,
  sh.customers c,
  sh.countries co
where
  s.cust_id=c.cust_id
  and co.country_id= c.country_id
```

```
and country_name in (      'Ireland','Denmark','Poland',
'United Kingdom',
'Germany','France','Spain','The Netherlands','Italy')
group by country_name order by sum(AMOUNT_SOLD);
```

Now that we have the SQL ID of the SQL we want to investigate, we need only run the `sqlhc.sql` script. We will be prompted for the license level of the database (I enter "T" in my case) and the SQL ID. That's all there is to it. This is much simpler than SQLT.

```
SQL> @sqlhc.sql
Parameter 1:
Oracle Pack License (Tuning, Diagnostics or None) [T|D|N] (required)

Enter value for 1: T
PL/SQL procedure successfully completed.
Parameter 2:
SQL_ID of the SQL to be analyzed (required)
Enter value for 2: 8nsdvk4u6wcvk
```

Then the SQL script runs and produces an output file. The final page of the output looks like this:

```
SQLDX files have been added to sqlhc_20161220_095807_8nsdvk4u6wcvk.zip

Archive:  sqlhc_20161220_095807_8nsdvk4u6wcvk.zip
  Length      Date    Time     Name
 --------     ----    ----     ----
    15696   12-20-16  09:58    sqlhc_20161220_095807_8nsdvk4u6wcvk_1_health_check.html
   160971   12-20-16  09:59    sqlhc_20161220_095807_8nsdvk4u6wcvk_2_diagnostics.html
     3793   12-20-16  09:59    sqlhc_20161220_095807_8nsdvk4u6wcvk_3_execution_plans.html
    10910   12-20-16  09:59    sqlhc_20161220_095807_8nsdvk4u6wcvk_4_sql_detail.html
    24096   12-20-16  09:59    sqlhc_20161220_095807_8nsdvk4u6wcvk_9_log.zip
    14019   12-20-16  09:59    sqlhc_20161220_095807_8nsdvk4u6wcvk_5_sql_monitor.zip
    67873   12-20-16  09:59    sqlhc_20161220_095807_8nsdvk4u6wcvk_8_sqldx.zip
 --------                     -------
   297358                     7 files
```

A directory listing of the local directory shows a zip file that is produced.

```
sqlhc_20161220_095807_8nsdvk4u6wcvk.zip
```

Now I put the zip file in a separate directory I created and unzip it.

```
>mkdir sqlhc_20161220_095807_8nsdvk4u6wcvk
>mv sqlhc_20161220_095807_8nsdvk4u6wcvk.zip sqlhc_20161220_095807_8nsdvk4u6wcvk/
> cd sqlhc_20161220_095807_8nsdvk4u6wcvk
> unzip sqlhc_20161220_095807_8nsdvk4u6wcvk.zip
Archive:  sqlhc_20161220_095807_8nsdvk4u6wcvk.zip
  inflating: sqlhc_20161220_095807_8nsdvk4u6wcvk_1_health_check.html
  inflating: sqlhc_20161220_095807_8nsdvk4u6wcvk_2_diagnostics.html
  inflating: sqlhc_20161220_095807_8nsdvk4u6wcvk_3_execution_plans.html
```

```
 inflating:  sqlhc_20161220_095807_8nsdvk4u6wcvk_4_sql_detail.html
extracting:  sqlhc_20161220_095807_8nsdvk4u6wcvk_9_log.zip
extracting:  sqlhc_20161220_095807_8nsdvk4u6wcvk_5_sql_monitor.zip
```

extracting: sqlhc_20161220_095807_8nsdvk4u6wcvk_8_sqldx.zip. And that's all there is in the running of the health check script. Now we need only look at each of the individual files.

The Main Health Check Report

The first HTML file contains the main report, which covers the observations, the SQL text (so we can make sure we are looking at the right page), and the table and index summary information. Figure 20-1 shows the top part of page 1.

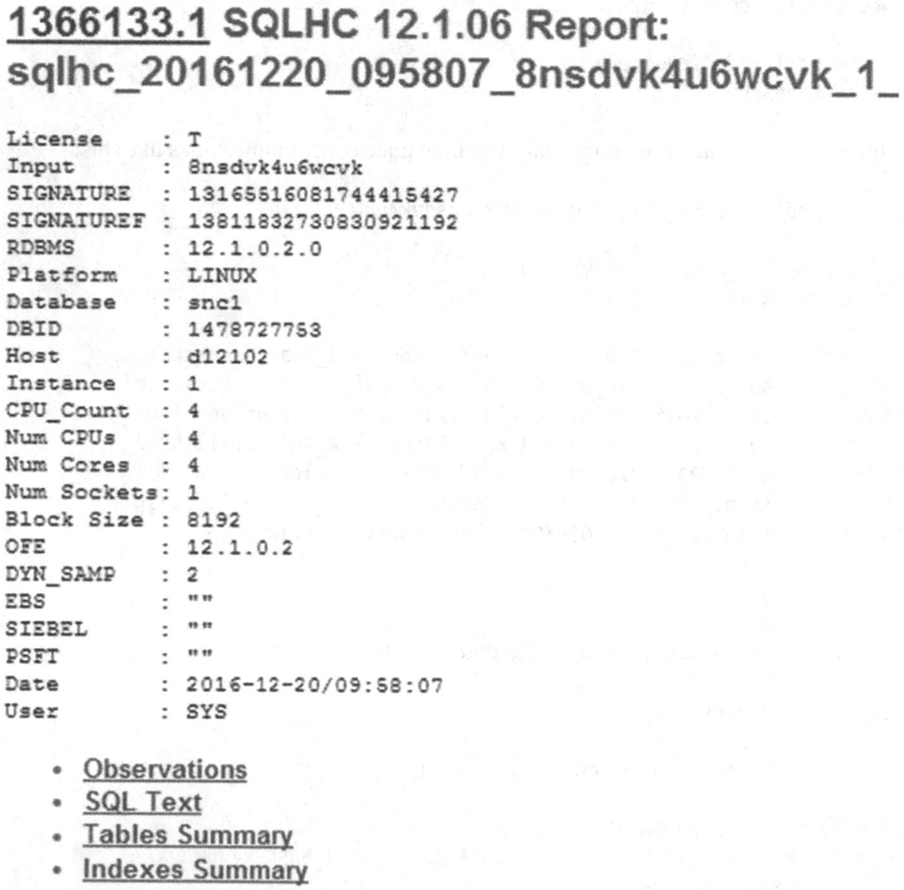

<u>1366133.1</u> SQLHC 12.1.06 Report:
sqlhc_20161220_095807_8nsdvk4u6wcvk_1_

```
License     : T
Input       : 8nsdvk4u6wcvk
SIGNATURE   : 13165516081744415427
SIGNATUREF  : 13811832730830921192
RDBMS       : 12.1.0.2.0
Platform    : LINUX
Database    : snc1
DBID        : 1478727753
Host        : d12102
Instance    : 1
CPU_Count   : 4
Num CPUs    : 4
Num Cores   : 4
Num Sockets : 1
Block Size  : 8192
OFE         : 12.1.0.2
DYN_SAMP    : 2
EBS         : ""
SIEBEL      : ""
PSFT        : ""
Date        : 2016-12-20/09:58:07
User        : SYS
```

- <u>Observations</u>
- <u>SQL Text</u>
- <u>Tables Summary</u>
- <u>Indexes Summary</u>

Figure 20-1. The top of the first SQLHC HTML file

Each of the sections in the HTML report can be reached by use of the hyperlinks in the section shown above in the figure. I'll look at three of the four sections of this report in the following sections, omitting the SQL Text section, which is self-explanatory.

The Observations Section

The most interesting one is the "Observations" section, which lists what it considers observations of interest. Usually these are complaints about nonstandard settings or architectural items that do not conform to best practices. Let's look at an example "Observations" section as shown in Figure 20-2.

Observations below are the outcome of several heath-checks on the schema objects accessed by your SQL and its environment. Review them ca

#	Type	Name	Observation
1	CBO PARAMETER	PARALLEL_DEGREE	CBO initialization parameter "parallel_degree" with a non-default value of "2" as per V$SQL_OPTIMIZER_ENV
2	CBO PARAMETER	PARALLEL_QUERY_DEFAULT_DOP	CBO initialization parameter "parallel_query_default_dop" with a non-default value of "8" as per V$SQL_OPTI
3	DBMS_STATS	DBA_AUTOTASK_CLIENT	Automatic gathering of CBO statistics is enabled.
4	DBMS_STATS	DBA_AUTOTASK_CLIENT	Automatic gathering of CBO statistics is enabled but no job was executed in the last 8 days
5	DBMS_STATS	SYSTEM STATISTICS	Workload CBO System Statistics are not gathered. CBO is using default values.
6	MAT_VIEW	REWRITE_ENABLED	There are 2 materialized views with rewrite enabled.
7	TABLE	SH.COUNTRIES	Table contains 1 column(s) where the number of buckets is 1 for a "FREQUENCY" histogram.
8	TABLE	SH.CUSTOMERS	Table contains 1 column(s) where the number of buckets is 1 for a "FREQUENCY" histogram.
9	TABLE	SH.SALES	Table CBO statistics are 21 days old: 2016-11-29/09:34:53.
10	TABLE PARTITION	SH.SALES	12 out of 28 partition(s) with number of rows equal to zero according to partition's CBO statistics.
11	INDEX PARTITION	SH.SALES_CHANNEL_BIX	12 out of 28 partition(s) with number of rows equal to zero according to partition's CBO statistics.
12	INDEX PARTITION	SH.SALES_CUST_BIX	12 out of 28 partition(s) with number of rows equal to zero according to partition's CBO statistics.
13	INDEX PARTITION	SH.SALES_PROD_BIX	12 out of 28 partition(s) with number of rows equal to zero according to partition's CBO statistics.
14	INDEX PARTITION	SH.SALES_PROMO_BIX	12 out of 28 partition(s) with number of rows equal to zero according to partition's CBO statistics.
15	INDEX PARTITION	SH.SALES_TIME_BIX	12 out of 28 partition(s) with number of rows equal to zero according to partition's CBO statistics.
#	Type	Name	Observation

Figure 20-2. *The Observations section of the health check*

The Observations section has many interesting suggestions for ways to improve your SQL. I have only shown the left side of the screen. In Figure 20-3 I show the corresponding right side of the screen, which tells us what needs to be done to remedy or investigate the observations. I have highlighted three observations in Figure 20-2, which could be useful to investigate. The first one is related to the degree of parallelism. The second one is related to a histogram that has only one bucket and the third relates to old object statistics on SH.SALES. Let's look at the right-hand side of the display (Figure 20-3) to see the column labeled "Details."

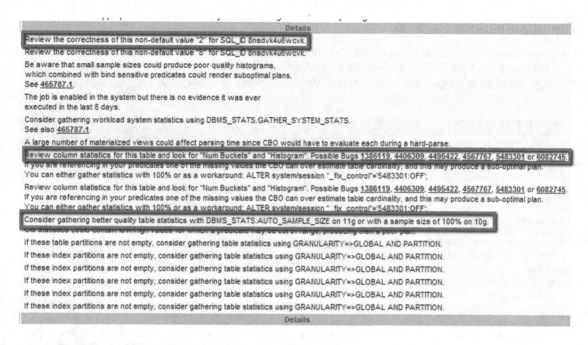

Figure 20-3. *The right-hand side of the observations section*

The "Details" column should really be called the "suggestion" column. For example, in the case of the non-default `parallel_degree` parameter the suggestion is "Review the correctness of this non-default value "2" for SQL_ID 8nsdvk4u6wcvk." This means that the value 2 was found, and it was "suggested" that we should think long and hard before sticking to the current value of 2 (4 might be better). If this were an SQL going into production, there would have to be a discussion between DBAs and developers about why the value was set to 2 and whether 4 would be better.

In the case of the histogram for SH.COUNTRIES, the suggestion is this:

"Review column statistics for this table and look for "Num Buckets" and "Histogram". Possible Bugs **1386119**, **4406309**, **4495422**,**4567767**, **5483301** or **6082745**. If you are referencing in your predicates one of the missing values the CBO can over estimate table cardinality, and this may produce a sub-optimal plan. You can either gather statistics with 100% or as a workaround: ALTER system/session "_fix_control"='5483301:OFF';

This suggestion is saying that the histogram on this column is not useful and should be dropped. It will only waste time. You even get a list of possible bugs that might be related to this behavior. Again, if this appeared in a preproduction test there would have to be some discussion about this histogram and whether it was useful or not.

In the third case we have old statistics. Statistics are crucial to the optimizer so we should check to see that these statistics are appropriate.

I've only mentioned three of the observations as examples. There are many suggestions (even for my simple SQL), and there are many other observation possibilities that do not appear because I did not violate the rules that cause them to appear. When you see the suggestions for your SQL you should carefully review them. Sometimes they are important (for example, the three mentioned above would be considered important), and in such cases you should either change your system (after careful testing) or have a good reason why those suggestions can be ignored. In most cases, observations are not generated when you run SQLHC because you did not trigger the rule by doing (or not doing) whatever it was that triggers the observation. This means that if you have a short list of observations you are doing well. If you have a long list of observations you may be doing badly.

In the case of this example I would consider "Automatic gathering of CBO statistics is enabled" as a relatively unimportant observation (in this case), since I am aware I am gathering statistics in that way and I know that if needed I will collect specific statistics to cover certain objects if needed. The warning is about small sample sizes in some cases causing non-optimal plans. It is not always easy to distinguish important observations from unimportant ones. How important an observation is will depend to some extent on your circumstances. Remember SQLHC is only following rules: it doesn't "know" your environment. You have to judge if an observation is important or not. With practice and a good knowledge of your environment you can develop the skill to quickly separate the wheat from the chaff. Each of the four HTML lists the SQL text, but there's nothing to say about the SQL text; it's just the text of your SQL. If you've run the SQL many times with many parameters or hints, it may be worth giving it a quick glance to make sure you're looking at the right report.

The Tables Summary Section

The "Tables Summary" section is the usual collection of information that you should be familiar with from an SQLT XTRACT or XECUTE report. See Figure 20-4.

Tables Summary

Values below have two purposes:
1. Provide a quick view of the state of Table level CBO statistics, as well as their indexes and columns.
2. More easily allow the comparison of two systems that are believed to be similar.

#	Table Name	Owner	Num Rows	Table Sample Size	Last Analyzed	Indexes	Avg Index Sample Size	Table Columns	Columns with Histogram	Avg Column Sample Size
1	COUNTRIES	SH	23	23	05-DEC-16 22:02:39	1	23	10	3	23
2	CUSTOMERS	SH	55500	55500	05-DEC-16 22:02:41	4	13900	23	4	49914
3	SALES	SH	918843	918843	29-NOV-16 09:34:53	5	7090	7	2	700340
#	Table Name	Owner	Num Rows	Table Sample Size	Last Analyzed	Indexes	Avg Index Sample Size	Table Columns	Columns with Histogram	Avg Column Sample Size

Figure 20-4. The "Tables Summary" section of the first page of the SQLHC report

In this report we see the tables involved in the query and the time of the statistics gathering. We also see some information about the number of indexes and columns, but notice no hyperlinks are present to guide us quickly through the report.

The Indexes Summary Section

The indexes are shown in Figure 20-5 and can be reached by clicking on "Indexes Summary" at the top of the page. There are no sophisticated links from the Tables section like there are in SQLT reports. This is because the SQLHC script is much simpler and cannot link in this way so easily.

Indexes Summary

Values below have two purposes:
1. Provide a quick view of the state of Index level CBO statistics, as well as their columns.
2. Ease a compare between two systems that are believed to be similar.
This section includes data captured by AWR. If this is a stand-by read-only database then the AWR

#	Table Name	Table Owner	Index Name	Index Owner	In MEM Plan	In AWR Plan	Num Rows	Index Sample Size
1	COUNTRIES	SH	COUNTRIES_PK	SH			23	23
2	CUSTOMERS	SH	CUSTOMERS_GENDER_BIX	SH			5	5
3	CUSTOMERS	SH	CUSTOMERS_MARITAL_BIX	SH			18	18
4	CUSTOMERS	SH	CUSTOMERS_PK	SH			55500	55500
5	CUSTOMERS	SH	CUSTOMERS_YOB_BIX	SH			75	75
6	SALES	SH	SALES_CHANNEL_BIX	SH			92	92
7	SALES	SH	SALES_CUST_BIX	SH			35808	35808
8	SALES	SH	SALES_PROD_BIX	SH			1074	1074
9	SALES	SH	SALES_PROMO_BIX	SH			54	54
10	SALES	SH	SALES_TIME_BIX	SH			1460	1460
#	Table Name	Table Owner	Index Name	Index Owner	In MEM Plan	In AWR Plan	Num Rows	Index Sample Size

Figure 20-5. *The index report from SQLHC*

A similar page is made available for the indexes involved in the query. So the first HTML report from SQLHC is a fairly simple collection of data on the SQL tables and indexes and any observations related to these. The next SQLHC HTML report has more sections in it, including some historical information.

The Diagnostics Report

The second page of the SQLHC report can potentially show many pieces of information: for example, instance parameters. Some sections may contain no information: for example, in my case there are no profiles in use. In fact, if you go to that section in the report you will see the text:

Available in 10g or higher. If this section is empty that means there are no profiles for this SQL.

(We covered profiles in more detail in Chapter 6). Figure 20-6 shows the header part of the HTML report.

- SQL Text
- SQL Plan Baselines (DBA_SQL_PLAN_BASELINES)
- SQL Profiles (DBA_SQL_PROFILES)
- SQL Patches (DBA_SQL_PATCHES)
- Cursor Sharing and Reason
- Cursor Sharing List
- Current Plans Summary (GV$SQL)
- Current SQL Statistics (GV$SQL)
- Historical Plans Summary (DBA_HIST_SQLSTAT)
- Historical SQL Statistics - Delta (DBA_HIST_SQLSTAT)
- Historical SQL Statistics - Total (DBA_HIST_SQLSTAT)
- Active Session History by Plan (GV$ACTIVE_SESSION_HISTORY)
- Active Session History by Plan Line (GV$ACTIVE_SESSION_HISTORY)
- AWR Active Session History by Plan (DBA_HIST_ACTIVE_SESS_HISTORY)
- AWR Active Session History by Plan Line (DBA_HIST_ACTIVE_SESS_HISTORY)
- DBMS_STATS System Preferences
- Tables
- DBMS_STATS Table Preferences
- Table Columns
- Table Partitions
- Table Constraints
- Tables Statistics Versions
- Indexes
- Index Columns
- Index Partitions
- Indexes Statistics Versions
- System Parameters with Non-Default or Modified Values
- Instance Parameters
- Metadata

Figure 20-6. *We see here the header section of page 2 of the SQLHC report*

From the header you can link to all the sections mentioned through hyperlinks. There is much more detailed statistical information in this report. For example, we have all the system parameters (not just the default ones) along with the description of the parameter. This section should be scanned by the DBA to ensure that the understanding of the system matches with what you see in this section. For example, I see that sga_max_size is set to 1520M (see Figure 20-7).

341	sga_max_size	1	TRUE	FALSE	1593835520		1520M	max total SG,
342	sga_target	1	FALSE	FALSE	1593835520		1520M	Target size o
343	shadow_core_dump	1	TRUE	FALSE	partial			Core Size for
344	shared_memory_address	1	TRUE	FALSE	0			SGA starting
345	shared_pool_reserved_size	1	TRUE	FALSE	16777216		16M	size in bytes
346	shared_pool_size	1	TRUE	FALSE	0			size in bytes

Figure 20-7. *A snippet from the Instance Parameter section of the report*

Is this what I expected? In my case, yes. This is to check your instance settings against what you are expecting for the instance. Another example might be that `optimizer_mode` is set to `ALL_ROWS`. Luckily I know this is the default, and this is the value I expect. For every parameter on the system you should have a good understanding of why it is set that way. In Figure 20-8 we see the non-default parameters. You should pay even more attention to these because SQLHC is telling you that these are out of the ordinary.

System Parameters with Non-Default or Modified Values

Collected from GV$SYSTEM_PARAMETER2 where isdefault = 'FALSE' OR ismodified != 'FALSE'. "Is Def

#	Name	Inst	Ord	Is Default	Is Modified	Value
1	audit_file_dest	1	1	FALSE	FALSE	/u02/app/oracle/admin/snc1/adump
2	audit_trail	1	1	FALSE	FALSE	DB
3	compatible	1	1	FALSE	FALSE	12.1.0.2.0
4	control_files	1	1	FALSE	FALSE	/u03/app/oracle/oradata/snc1/control01.ctl
5	control_files	1	2	FALSE	FALSE	/u02/app/oracle/fast_recovery_area/snc1/control02.ctl
6	db_block_size	1	1	FALSE	FALSE	8192
7	db_domain	1	1	FALSE	FALSE	us.oracle.com
8	db_name	1	1	FALSE	FALSE	snc1
9	db_recovery_file_dest	1	1	FALSE	FALSE	/u02/app/oracle/fast_recovery_area
10	db_recovery_file_dest_size	1	1	FALSE	FALSE	4781506560
11	diagnostic_dest	1	1	FALSE	FALSE	/u02/app/oracle

Figure 20-8. Part of the Non-default System Parameter section of the report

We see in the figure that the default values of parameters are highlighted and if their current value is manually set. If we look at this page (see Figure 20-9) we see the descriptions of the parameters.

Name	Inst	Ord	Is Default	Is Modified	Value	Display Value	Description
audit_file_dest	1	1	FALSE	FALSE	/u02/app/oracle/admin/snc1/adump		Directory in which auditing files are to reside
audit_trail	1	1	FALSE	FALSE	DB		enable system auditing
compatible	1	1	FALSE	FALSE	12.1.0.2.0		Database will be completely compatible with this software version
control_files	1	1	FALSE	FALSE	/u03/app/oracle/oradata/snc1/control01.ctl		control file names list
control_files	1	2	FALSE	FALSE	/u02/app/oracle/fast_recovery_area/snc1/control02.ctl		control file names list
db_block_size	1	1	FALSE	FALSE	8192		Size of database block in bytes
db_domain	1	1	FALSE	FALSE	us.oracle.com		directory part of global database name stored with CREATE DATABASE
db_name	1	1	FALSE	FALSE	snc1		database name specified in CREATE DATABASE
db_recovery_file_dest	1	1	FALSE	FALSE	/u02/app/oracle/fast_recovery_area		default database recovery file location
db_recovery_file_dest_size	1	1	FALSE	FALSE	4781506560	4560M	database recovery files size limit
diagnostic_dest	1	1	FALSE	FALSE	/u02/app/oracle		diagnostic base directory
dispatchers	1	1	FALSE	FALSE	(PROTOCOL=TCP) (SERVICE=snc1XDB)		specifications of dispatchers
local_listener	1	1	FALSE	FALSE	LISTENER_SNC1		local listener
open_cursors	1	1	FALSE	FALSE	300		max # cursors per session

Figure 20-9. The descriptions of the intialization parameters

Finally we can look at the historical information that SQHC can provide (Figure 20-10). All the usual information is there: disk reads, buffer gets, etc. Just as in SQLT we can use this information to relate the history to any change in the execution plan.

Inst ID	Plan HV	Vers Cnt	Execs	Fetch	Loads	Inval	Parse Calls	Buffer Gets	Disk Reads
1	3572724195	1	1	2	0	0	5	7016	1630
1	3572724195	1	1	2	0	0	5	7016	1643
Inst ID	Plan HV	Vers Cnt	Execs	Fetch	Loads	Inval	Parse Calls	Buffer Gets	Disk Reads

Figure 20-10. The historical information from our example SQL. (Only the left-hand side of the report is shown)

As you can see, the second report from the SQLHC report is useful because it shows the metrics related to the statistics execution, as well as reports on non-default parameters and a historical view of the execution of your SQL. The historical information in conjunction with the plan hash value (the unique identifier for a specific execution plan [PHV for short]), and the system initialization parameters can be very useful in working out what is happening with your SQL.

The Execution Plan Report

The next report shows the execution plan for all the SQLs captured. See Figure 20-11, which shows the execution plan for the latest execution.

Current Execution Plans (last execution)

Captured while still in memory. Metrics below are for the last execution of each child cursor.
If STATISTICS_LEVEL was set to ALL at the time of the hard-parse then A-Rows column is populated.

Inst: 1   Child: 0   Plan hash value: 3572724195

```
| Id  | Operation                    | Name      | E-Rows |E-Bytes| Cost (%CPU)|
-------------------------------------------------------------------------------
|   0 | SELECT STATEMENT             |           |        |       | 708 (100)|
|   1 |  PX COORDINATOR              |           |        |       |          |
|   2 |   PX SEND QC (ORDER)         | :TQ10003  |     9  | 315   | 708   (5)|
|   3 |    SORT ORDER BY             |           |     9  | 315   | 708   (5)|
|   4 |     PX RECEIVE               |           |     9  | 315   | 708   (5)|
|   5 |      PX SEND RANGE           | :TQ10002  |     9  | 315   | 708   (5)|
|   6 |       HASH GROUP BY          |           |     9  | 315   | 708   (5)|
|   7 |        PX RECEIVE            |           |     9  | 315   | 708   (5)|
|   8 |         PX SEND HASH         | :TQ10001  |     9  | 315   | 708   (5)|
|   9 |          HASH GROUP BY       |           |     9  | 315   | 708   (5)|
|* 10 |           HASH JOIN          |           |  435K  |  14M  | 686   (2)|
|  11 |            BUFFER SORT       |           |        |       |          |
|  12 |             PX RECEIVE       |           | 26289  | 641K  | 409   (1)|
|  13 |              PX SEND BROADCAST| :TQ10000 | 26289  | 641K  | 409   (1)|
|* 14 |               HASH JOIN      |           | 26289  | 641K  | 409   (1)|
|* 15 |                TABLE ACCESS FULL| COUNTRIES|    9  | 135   |   3   (0)|
|  16 |                TABLE ACCESS FULL| CUSTOMERS| 55500 | 541K  | 406   (1)|
|  17 |            PX BLOCK ITERATOR |           |  918K  | 8973K | 274   (3)|
|* 18 |             TABLE ACCESS FULL| SALES     |  918K  | 8973K | 274   (3)|
-------------------------------------------------------------------------------
```

Figure 20-11. The left-hand side of the report showing the execution plan of the last execution

I've shown only the left-hand side of the report, but all the usual columns are present for the execution plan. This execution plan shows a parallelized execution with a hash join between SALES and the hash join of COUNTRIES and CUSTOMERS. As you would for an XTRACT report, look at the steps and determine if they are appropriate. Later in this chapter we'll also see an SQL monitor report (we covered SQL Monitor active reports in Chapter 14) that shows where time was spent during the execution. Look at the expected rows, and look at the cost of each line and see if they meet your expectations. Additionally you can see the historical execution plans for the same SQL. Remember all this information is available from a system where you have NOT installed SQLT.

The Monitor Reports

There are two types of monitor reports. The first one is the previously mentioned HTML file that provides a summary of the activity of all the SQL being monitored. The second type of monitor report consists of the details of execution plans. A zip file includes a separate report with the details for each execution plan.

The SQL Monitor Summary Report

The purpose of the first report is to put the SQL under investigation into some sort of context. After all, if you are tuning an SQL statement, you want to make sure it's having a significant effect on the system. In other words, there's no point in tuning an SQL statement so that it takes half the time (if it's only run once), and it uses only 1 percent of the system resources when there's another statement that takes 50 percent of the system resources.

This summary view has three panes: "General," "Time & Wait statistics," "IO Statistics," and "Details." You can expand and minimize these sections by clicking the minimize icons on the left-hand side of the pane. The "Detail" pane has four icons, which cover "Plan Statistics," "Parallel," "Activity," and "Metrics."

- Activity: This shows the active sessions in a graphic form and shows what the active sessions were doing. For example, in Figure 20-12 we see the "Activity" button in the "Details" section, which shows a spike in "direct path read" and "db file sequential read" near the end of the sampling interval.

- Time & Wait Statistics: Shows overall plan statistics. See Figure 20-13.

- Plan Statistics: Shows the execution plan in graphic form. An example of this is shown in Figure 20-14, showing the plan in left-to-right style.

- Parallel: Shows the details of the activities of the parallel slaves.

- Parallel: Shows the duration, users, serial/parallel status, and other statistics related to the SQL ID. An example of this is shown in Figure 20-15.

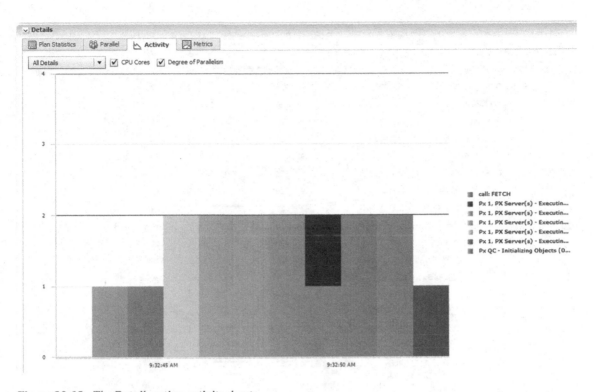

Figure 20-12. *The Detail section activity chart*

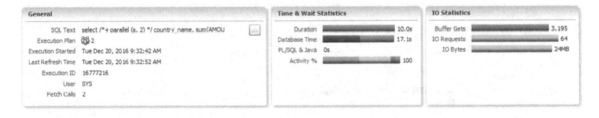

Figure 20-13. *Showing an example statistics page from the General section of the report*

Operation	Name	L...	Estima...	C...	Timeline(10s)	Ex...	Actu...	Mem...	Tem...	O.	IO R...
⊟ SELECT STATEMENT		0			■	5	7				
⊟ PX COORDINATOR		1			▬▬▬▬▬	5	7				▬ 16
⊟ PX SEND QC (ORDER)	:TQ10003	2	9	726	■	2	7				
⊟ SORT ORDER BY		3	9	726	■	2	7	4KB			
⊟ PX RECEIVE		4	9	726	■	2	7				
⊟ PX SEND RANGE	:TQ10002	5	9	726	■	2	7				
⊟ HASH GROUP BY		6	9	726	■	2	7	1MB			
⊟ PX RECEIVE		7	9	726	■	2	14				
⊟ PX SEND HASH	:TQ10001	8	9	726	■	2	14			⧓	
⊟ HASH GROUP...		9	9	726	▬▬▬▬	2	14	2MB			
⊟ HASH JOIN		10	435K	714	▬▬▬▬	2	250K	4MB		⧓	
⊟ PX RECEI...		11	26K	426	■	2	61K				
⊟ PX SEN...	:TQ10000	12	26K	426	■	2	61K				
⊟ PX S...		13			■	2	30K				
⊟ HA...		14	26K	426	■	2	30K	1MB		⧓	
T...	COUNTRIES	15	9	3	■	2	9				⎪2
T...	CUSTOMERS	16	56K	423	▬▬▬▬	1	56K				▬ 29
⊟ PX BLOC...		17	919K	287	▬▬▬	2	919K				
TABLE A...	SALES	18	919K	287	▬▬▬▬	17	919K				▬ 17

Figure 20-14. *Shows the plan section of the Detail tab*

Plan Statistics	👬 **Parallel**	⑂ Activity	🔲 Metrics				

Parallel Server	Database Time	Activity %	IO Requests	IO Bytes	Buffer Gets
⊟ Instance 1					
Parallel Coordinator	■ 1.2s	▬ 12	▬▬ 16	⎪ 128KB	⎪ 48
⊞ 👬 Parallel Set 1	▬▬▬▬▬▬ 13.9s	▬▬▬▬▬▬ 82	▬▬ 17	▬▬▬▬▬ 12MB	▬▬ 1,622
⊞ 👬 Parallel Set 2	■ 1.9s	▬ 5.88	▬▬▬▬ 31	▬▬▬▬▬ 12MB	▬▬ 1,525

Figure 20-15. *The Parallel tab on the Details page*

This report shows that for the current SQL text, almost 50% of the database activity was on the CPU. We see in the bottom half of the report that my SQL took 10 seconds to run and that it ran in parallel. The result of this was that it used almost 17.1 seconds of CPU time. For more details on the SQL Monitor Detailed report, refer to Chapter 14.

The sqldx.sql Script

Sqldx was written to collect detailed information about one SQL statement. It does not need SQLT and produces many CSV formatted files (comma-separated values) to take away for further analysis. It also produces over 20 HTML formatted files.

In the example below I've used the same sql, q3.sql, which I have used throughout this chapter. To generate a report from sqldx.sql, we need only run the script on the system where the SQL has run. The SQL_ID in this case is 8nsdvk4u6wcvk. When we run sqldx.sql we get a prompt to confirm our license level. Select the appropriate license level. In my case this is T.

```
SQL> @sqldx
Parameter 1:
Oracle Pack License (Tuning or Diagnostics) [T|D] (required)
Enter value for 1: T
PL/SQL procedure successfully completed.
```

Now I need to enter the format of the report. H stands for HTML and C stands for a CSV report and B stands for both. I'm going to choose B in this case to create the maximum number of files. Generally speaking the HTML files are the most useful. The CSVs are a nice to have. They contain information I have not used thus far.

```
Parameter 2:
Output Type (HTML or CSV or Both) [H|C|B] (required)
Enter value for 2: B
PL/SQL procedure successfully completed.
Parameter 3:
SQL_ID of the SQL to be analyzed (required)
Enter value for 3: 8nsdvk4u6wcvk
```

Before the main execution starts, we see the values passed as a confirmation that we are doing what we wanted.

```
Values passed:
~~~~~~~~~~~~~~
License: "T"
Output : "B"
SQL_ID : " 8nsdvk4u6wcvk"
```

The execution proceeds – it takes just a few minutes usually – but may take longer if there is more data in your database to analyze. After a couple of pages of output we see the final result.

```
SQLDX files have been created.
```

```
Archive:  sqldx_20161220_113703.zip
  Length     Date   Time     Name
 --------    ----    ----     ----
   25585   12-20-16 11:37    sqldx_20161220_113703_8nsdvk4u6wcvk_csv.zip
   43387   12-20-16 11:37    sqldx_20161220_113703_8nsdvk4u6wcvk_html.zip
   13428   12-20-16 11:37    sqldx_20161220_113703_13811832730830921192_force_csv.zip
   24713   12-20-16 11:37    sqldx_20161220_113703_13811832730830921192_force_html.zip
   26921   12-20-16 11:37    sqldx_20161220_113703_global_csv.zip
   17991   12-20-16 11:37    sqldx_20161220_113703_global_html.zip
    7539   12-20-16 11:37    sqldx_20161220_113703_8nsdvk4u6wcvk_log.zip
 --------                    -------
  159564                     7 files
```

The zip file produced contains seven more zip files. Yes, that's what I said: zip files within zip files. If you want to keep track of which file came from which, create a directory for each zip file and unpack the zip file into that directory. If that zip file contains other zip files then create a subdirectory to keep those and so on.

The sqlhcxec.sql Script

By now of course you're an SQLT pro and can probably take a good guess at what this routine does. This routine takes as parameter the license level and the name of a file containing the SQL you want to analyze. Remember this is all working without SQLT being installed on the database. The output files consist of two main files: a result file, showing the result of the query; and a zip file containing all the reports.

The zip file for sqlhcxec contains eight files:

- A health check HTML file that is identical to the sqlhc.sql output (mentioned above).

- A diagnostics HTML file, which is also the same as the sqlhc.sql output mentioned above as the Diagnostics and profiles page.

- An execution plan HTML file that shows the current execution plan and the historical execution plans (which sqlhc.sql did not). See Figure 20-16 below.

- An SQL detail HTML file just like the one produced by sqlhc.sql.

- SQL Monitor HTML files inside a zip file for each of the known historical executions of the SQL.

- An sqldx zip file, containing all of the same reports as the results of sqldx.sql.

- A zipped-up log file.

1366133.1 SQLHCXEC 12.1.06 Report: sqlhcxec_20161220_115814_8nsdvk4u6wcvk_3_execution_

```
License     : T
Input       : q3.sql
SIGNATURE   : 13165516081744415427
SIGNATUREF  : 13811832730830921192
RDBMS       : 12.1.0.2.0
Platform    : LINUX
Database    : snc1
DBID        : 1478727753
Host        : d12102
Instance    : 1
CPU_Count   : 4
Num CPUs    : 4
Num Cores   : 4
Num Sockets: 1
Block Size : 8192
OFE         : 12.1.0.2
DYN_SAMP    : 2
EBS         : ""
SIEBEL      : ""
PSFT        : ""
Date        : 2016-12-20/11:58:14
User        : SYS
```

- SQL Text
- Current Execution Plans (last execution)
- Current Execution Plans (all executions)
- Historical Execution Plans

SQL Text

```
select /*+ parallel (s, 2) */
country_name,
sum(AMOUNT_SOLD)
from
sh.sales s,
sh.customers c,
sh.countries co
where
s.cust_id=c.cust_id
and co.country_id= c.country_id
and country_name in (       'Ireland','Denmark','Poland',
'United Kingdom',
'Germany','France','Spain','The Netherlands','Italy')
group by country_name order by sum(AMOUNT_SOLD)
```

Figure 20-16. *The sqlhcxec execution plans report, showing historical execution plans*

Summary

The SQL health check utility, although it not directly linked to SQLT and does not rely on it, has many of the same elements in it as SQLT. It was created so that sites that do not want to or cannot install SQLT can get some benefit from using sqlhc.sql and its associated scripts instead. SQLHC is not as interlinked as SQLT nor does it have as many potential observations (SQLHC has about 100 possible observations, while SQLT has 200 to 300 observations). SQLHC is sufficiently useful that it should be considered a minimum requirement for SQLHC to be run against a new production SQL to check against observations and expected execution plans. We've reached the end of our journey with SQLT, and so in the next chapter I'll summarize what we've learned.

CHAPTER 21

■ ■ ■

The Final Word

The key to successful tuning with SQLT is to use SQLT regularly and for real-life problems. If you've reached the final chapter, you should now consider yourself a card-carrying member of the SQLT supporters club. You've learned a lot about what SQLT can do, and along the way you've probably learned some things about the cost-based optimizer and the Oracle engine.

In my day-to-day interactions with DBAs and developers around the world, I regularly come across interesting and sometimes puzzling problems. Whether these are strange partition behaviors, unexpected use of Directives in plans, or faulty statistics, the problem methodology I describe and the SQLT tool I use regularly are always central to my strategy.

Let me remind you of some of the features we came across on our journey:

- The effect of statistics on execution plans

- The effect of skewness on execution plans

- How the optimizer transforms SQL during parsing

- How profiles can help you temporarily freeze an execution plan

- How adaptive cursor sharing works

- How adaptive plans work

- How adaptive statistics work

- How reoptimization works

- How to investigate problems with parallel execution

- How to use active SQL Monitor to find out what's happening

- How you can use SQLT with Data Guard

- How test cases can be built with SQLT to allow exploration of the execution plans

- How to use the brute force of XPLORE to look for unexpected effects on the CBO from upgrades and other changes

- How to use the Health check script

Last but not least we talked about the SQLTCOMPARE, which allowed comparison of SQLs from different platforms and versions. In this chapter I'll try and give you a quick overview of a methodology I use to approach a tuning problem. Naturally all methodologies have exceptions, but it's better to have a default plan than having to determine a new one for every occasion. I'll also give my opinion as to why SQLT is the best tool available for tuning (apart from being free). Then I'll discuss some platform issues and assure you that SQLT and the examples we've covered do not just work on one platform. Finally I'll mention a few resources you should be aware of as you continue your greater journey into the world of tuning.

© Stelios Charalambides 2017
S. Charalambides, *Oracle SQL Tuning with Oracle SQLTXPLAIN*, DOI 10.1007/978-1-4842-2436-6_21

Tuning Methodology

Tuning methodology is not this book's main theme, but I feel I need to say something about it because SQLT can be a central element to a good strategy. The lack of a central methodology to attack SQL tuning problems has always, in my opinion, been the main problem for DBAs especially but also for developers who have to create efficient code. When you have a tuning problem, where do you start? Usually it all depends on what kind of problem you have. To help you, here's my five-step method.

1. Get an AWR report for the problem time. If there is a "significant" problem in the "Top 5 waits" section of the report, deal with that first. If there is nothing obvious there then check the "SQL Report" section of the AWR report. If there is an SQL using more resources than other SQLs, then get an appropriate SQLT report. Always be led by the evidence presented in the AWR report and not by your own hunches or guesswork, or a developer who tells you what the problem is.

2. If it's an individual SQL problem, start with SQLT XTRACT or XEXCUTE (depending on whether you can reliably run the SQL) and then use the information to go from there. If you can't use SQLT, then use SQLHC.

3. Evaluate the information collected and scrutinize any information that looks out of the ordinary (this is where the constant practice helps, because you begin to recognize out-of-the-ordinary behavior on your system).

4. Investigate any anomalies and make sure you understand them. They may be benign. If the anomalies cannot be explained, then try and assess if they could be the cause of your problems.

5. If you do end up investigating an individual SQL that has changed performance, remember there are many SQL tools that can be deployed to get more information. Build a test case and use COMPARE or SQL monitor, if possible, or use XPLORE in desperation (if you have the time).

This high-level methodology has a few key elements. The first is to recognize things that are out of the ordinary. To do this you must first understand what is normal, just like our alien visitor back in Chapter 3. The second element is the knowledge of how things work in the optimizer. This takes practice and some reading (hopefully this book helped).

It's important to recognize that SQLT is not the first step in this methodology. Although SQLT is useful for many tuning problems, the first step should be to assess the overall system performance, which can be best done from an AWR report against the appropriate database. If the problem is related to the operating system, you may find your solution there and need never look at an SQLT report or indeed any SQL. If your problem is with the database then the AWR report is a good starting point for memory requirements, unexpected waits (seen in the top ten events). See Figure 21-1, which shows the section of the AWR report with the top ten waits on the system.

Top 10 Foreground Events by Total Wait Time

Event	Waits	Total Wait Time (sec)	Wait Avg(ms)	% DB time	Wait Class
DB CPU		36.1K		64.6	
library cache lock	2,807	9366.7	3337	16.8	Concurrency
cursor: pin S wait on X	3,943	9315.7	2363	16.7	Concurrency
direct path read temp	53,403	380.1	7	.7	User I/O
gc current block 2-way	1,461,058	132.4	0	.2	Cluster
PX Deq: reap credit	6,093,147	69.5	0	.1	Other
direct path write temp	11,584	60.4	5	.1	User I/O
DFS lock handle	84	39.9	475	.1	Other
cell single block physical read	93,731	33.1	0	.1	User I/O
gc cr multi block request	23,542	23.4	1	.0	Cluster

Figure 21-1. The top 10 waits in AWR

If your system is heavily loaded, you should see waits in this section of the report that may require investigation. Depending on what these waits are, you may be led to the SQL section of the report, which then may suggest an investigation of a particular SQL or perhaps one or two. Then SQLT can be used to good effect (as long as the SQL is not some internal Oracle code). See below in Figure 21-2 for the top SQL sorted by buffer gets.

SQL ordered by Gets

- Resources reported for PL/SQL code includes the resources used by all SQL statements called by the
- %Total - Buffer Gets as a percentage of Total Buffer Gets
- %CPU - CPU Time as a percentage of Elapsed Time
- %IO - User I/O Time as a percentage of Elapsed Time
- Total Buffer Gets: 2,602,423,190
- Captured SQL account for 98.3% of Total

Buffer Gets	Executions	Gets per Exec	%Total	Elapsed Time (s)	%CPU	%IO	SQL Id
372,490,519	0		14.31	3,602.97	99.1	.1	f2vdtn646dwdh
372,466,247	0		14.31	3,602.98	99.1	.1	fc4qzpukdhm0f
256,148,970	0		9.84	3,603.99	99.4	0	891nvpr7pjkcw
244,485,097	0		9.39	3,602.99	99.4	0	30pbs24s0mp2t

Figure 21-2. The SQL ordered by gets, part of the AWR report

In the atypical report above we see that one SQL is taking 14 percent of all the gets; that's pretty unusual on a production system, and you should probably investigate this (unless you know what it is and why it's using that much of the system). Sometimes if many SQLs have regressed you can use SQLT to look at one SQL in detail: this is to assess the problem afflicting that SQL in the hope that whatever has affected that SQL will be the same solution for all the SQLs. Refer to Chapter 2, where we dealt with AWR in more detail.

Why SQLT Is, Hands Down, the Best Tuning Utility

Now that we've put SQLT in its proper place in the strategy of tuning a system, we should acknowledge that for tuning individual SQLs, SQLT is hands down the best starting tool for the job. It's true that there are many tuning utilities out there: some of them on the Oracle MOS site and some of them paid-for products. For example, TRCANLZR is available as a stand-alone utility, TKPROF comes with Oracle as a utility, 10046 and 10053 tracing can be collected from a standard Oracle installation. All of them, however, are focusing on one particular aspect or are going into great detail on a problem without giving a bigger picture. SQLT is the main tool for focusing on one SQL and gives you the big picture in an easily digestible form. SQLT does require you to do some work of course, and analysis of the reports and building the overall picture of the SQL takes some time and some expertise. Sometimes you will need more information than a particular run of SQLT has supplied (for example, the shared pool was flushed, or the system was rebooted, so much information was lost). Depending on what you learn by looking at the SQL history and statistics, you could look at the COMPARE method, for example (if you have a good run of the SQL). If you need to experiment you can use the test case on a stand-alone system to try out a few things, and if you know changes have come about because of optimizer version changes, you can use XPLORE. SQLT is like a helpful assistant at a shopping mall:

"I think you need the statistics department today, sir. Try floor two, just two doors along."

A Word about Platforms

A platform, in IT jargon, is the hardware and operating system on which other applications reside. In the case of the Oracle product itself, it can be loaded onto many different platforms: Unix, Linux, OpenVMS, Solaris, Windows, and others. As far as SQL commands are concerned, the platform makes very little difference. A "select" is still a "select." SQLT can be used on Unix (including Linux) and Windows. Other platforms will not allow the full functionality of SQLT. SQLHC, the health check script, will run on as many platforms as Oracle runs on, as it relies only on Oracle.

In this book almost all my examples are based on a Linux platform, but on a day-to-day basis I use SQLT on both Linux and Windows, and I have noticed no difference in behavior. I also regularly use SQLT on an Exadata platform and again everything works as you would expect. Every example shown in the book for Windows can just as easily work on Linux and vice versa. The interaction of SQLT with the operating system is usually only during the end phases of reports where files are being collected and being zipped up. In these phases commands such as cp (copy on Windows) and ls (DIR on windows) will generate messages indicating that those commands do not exist on the current platform. This is not a serious error, and the alternative command will have been issued for the appropriate platform.

Other Resources

This may be the final word in this book, but there are many other good resources available on SQLT. There are many Metalink notes: I haven't counted them but there are many more than the ones listed here. Luckily many of these notes are linked to each other so these are good starting points:

- 215187.1 – The main SQLT note where you can download SQLT
- 1454160.1 – FAQ about SQLT
- 1465741.1 – How to create test cases using SQLT with test data
- 1455583.1 – Gives you access to an SQLHC video
- 1366133.1 – SQL Health Check Script

There are even webcasts (look at Note 740964.1), which lead to the Oracle Webcast Program. Select "Oracle Database" and then browse the archived recordings. For SQLT here are some interesting topics for 2012:. For example, "Understanding SQLTXPLAIN Main Report by Navigating Through Some Samples."

Summary

The SQLTXPLAIN utility, one of the most useful free utilities available to Oracle customers, has evolved over many versions and many generations of the Oracle product. The latest version 12.1.160429 (April 16, 2016) has come a long way, and there are many new features. It is still evolving and no doubt will continue to evolve for many years. SQLT is a deceptively complex utility with many features hidden away in innocuous-looking scripts. I hope I've cast some light on those features, so that maybe you'll be inspired to look at other scripts I have not mentioned. Get the latest SQLT version from the MOS site: `http://support.oracle.com`.

I hope you've enjoyed the journey, and I sincerely hope you use SQLT to learn more about your system and the SQL running on it. Remember, the key is to use SQLT regularly and investigate anything you don't understand using reliable sources; soon, you will be tuning with the best of them.

APPENDIX A

■ ■ ■

Installing SQLTXPLAIN

You may ask, why show the installation log for a utility that installs in five minutes and only has at most five parameters as inputs? The plain fact of the matter is that despite the simplicity of the inputs and that most installs can be quick and easy, there are situations where the installation can fail: either because the inputs were wrong or because the installation steps were not done from suitably privileged accounts. You occasionally get questions about an installation that may have worked, but the user is not clear. This is another reason to show what a "normal" installation looks like. I also look at alternative ways in which SQLT can be installed, including a "silent" mode and a remote install mode. There are also ways to change the setup of SQLT after it has installed, and I mention some of the options available there. Finally I also mention how to de-install SQLT, in case you want to install a later version, for example. By showing these options and describing the installation, I hope to convince you that the installation is simple and robust and should be considered an asset to any system rather than a liability.

A Standard SQLT Installation

As assistance to anyone installing SQLT I have supplied a partial install log of the SQLT utility, which can be downloaded from MOS note 215187.1 I have highlighted and documented those areas of the installation that are of interest and note. Newcomers to SQLT may find this useful, but regular users will find the section on other ways to install SQLT more interesting. In the example SQLT installation below I have bolded my responses to make it clear where I am entering data, and I have removed blank lines for brevity. In this example the SQLT zip file has been downloaded to a local directory and unzipped. Inside the zip file we find the sqlt directory and the install directory (as we saw in Chapter 1). Now we connect as SYS into SQL*Plus and start the main installation script sqcreate.sql. (Or if you prefer you can use @install, which calls sqcreate.sql).

```
SQL> @sqcreate
  adding: 161222084915_00_sqdrop.log (deflated 90%)

zip error: Nothing to do! (SQLT_installation_logs_archive.zip)
Ignore errors from here until @@@@@ marker as this is to test for NATIVE PLSQL Code Type
@@@@ marker . You may ignore prior errors about NATIVE PLSQL Code Type
old   1: ALTER SESSION SET PLSQL_CODE_TYPE = &&plsql_code_type
new   1: ALTER SESSION SET PLSQL_CODE_TYPE = NATIVE
```

So far the installation has initialized. The next steps are to gather information so that the installation can be properly targeted. For most circumstances installing into the local database is the easiest and simplest option. You only need a tablespace in which SQLT will store its information, packages, functions, and the data repository. The size of this is generally very small (in my small installation this was about 2 Mbytes). If you specify a remote connection here the data will be stored elsewhere, such as on a remote database.

© Stelios Charalambides 2017

S. Charalambides, *Oracle SQL Tuning with Oracle SQLTXPLAIN*, DOI 10.1007/978-1-4842-2436-6

```
Specify optional Connect Identifier (as per Oracle Net)
Include "@" symbol, ie. @PROD
If not applicable, enter nothing and hit the "Enter" key.
You *MUST* provide a connect identifier when installing
SQLT in a Pluggable Database in 12c
This connect identifier is only used while exporting SQLT
repository everytime you execute one of the main methods.

Optional Connect Identifier (ie: @PROD):
```

The optional Connect Identifier is not often used, as you are normally installing SQLT locally. We cover the case of a remote install later, in the section "A Remote SQLT Installation." In this case, however, we just press Return (remember this is for a local installation).

```
PL/SQL procedure successfully completed.

PL/SQL procedure successfully completed.

Define SQLTXPLAIN password (hidden and case sensitive).

Password for user SQLTXPLAIN:oracle
Re-enter password:oracle
PL/SQL procedure successfully completed.
```

Now we collect information about the tablespaces on the system. On some systems there can be many tablespaces, so we allow the option of skipping collection of information on tablespaces in case you know where you want to install SQLT.

```
...
The Tablespace name is case sensitive.

Do you want to see the free space of each tablespace [YES]
or is it ok just to show the list of tablespace [NO]?

Type YES or NO [Default NO]:

please wait
TABLESPACE                       FREE_SPACE_MB
------------------------------ --------------
EXAMPLE
USERS
Specify PERMANENT tablespace to be used by SQLTXPLAIN.
Tablespace name is case sensitive.
Default tablespace [UNKNOWN]:USERS
PL/SQL procedure successfully completed.
... please wait
TABLESPACE
------------------------------
TEMP
Specify TEMPORARY tablespace to be used by SQLTXPLAIN.
Tablespace name is case sensitive.
```

```
Temporary tablespace [UNKNOWN]:TEMP
PL/SQL procedure successfully completed.
```

The next section is the part of the installation that most often causes confusion. The "main application user of SQLT" is the schema name of the user that actually executes the SQL to be analyzed. This is not SQLTXPLAIN. Throughout most of this book my example schema is called STELIOS, so I enter **STELIOS** here. If for some reason you want to change this or add another schema you only need to grant the SQLT_USER_ROLE role to the user in question. This would be done with grant SQLT_USER_ROLE to <username>;. Normally this username should be connectable from the SQL*Plus prompt so that you can run the SQLT methods.

■ **Note**   In some systems SQL is executed via a remote connection from another system (for example, through JDBC connections), and the account used for these connections cannot be locally connected through SQL*Plus due to security restrictions. In these cases the next best next option is to create a schema or use another schema that can execute the SQL and has access to the same data and objects as the target schema. Be wary in this case that you are not creating a different environment that does not show your problem.

```
The main application user of SQLT is the schema
owner that issued the SQL to be analyzed.
For example, on an EBS application you would
enter APPS.
You will not be asked to enter its password.
To add more SQLT users after this installation
is completed simply grant them the SQLT_USER_ROLE
role.
Main application user of SQLT:STELIOS<<<An invalid user at this point will cause an error
PL/SQL procedure successfully completed.
SQLT can make extensive use of licensed features
provided by the Oracle Diagnostic and the Oracle
Tuning Packs, including SQL Tuning Advisor (STA),
SQL Monitoring and Automatic Workload Repository
(AWR).
To enable or disable access to these features
from the SQLT tool enter one of the following
values when asked:
```

The following is another section of the installation where there is much confusion because quite often the installer of SQLT is not aware of the license level for the database in question. There is no shortcut to this, unfortunately.

```
"T" if you have license for Diagnostic and Tuning
"D" if you have license only for Oracle Diagnostic
"N" if you do not have these two licenses
Oracle Pack license [T]:
```

The main installation of SQLT starts here; and as it mentions in the prompts, there are some errors generated during a fresh installation of SQLT. These are normal Oracle errors generated during attempts to drop objects in the SQLT schemas that do not yet exist.

No more errors should be seen from the installation until we get to the section on privileges being revoked. These errors are normal and should be ignored.

Finally we get to the end of the installation.

```
VALID    PACKAGE BODY 11.4.5.0       TRCA$R
VALID    PACKAGE BODY 12.1.160429    TRCA$T
VALID    PACKAGE BODY 11.4.5.0       TRCA$X

Deleting CBO statistics for SQLTXPLAIN objects ...

09:37:01    0 sqlt$a: -> delete_sqltxplain_stats
09:37:05    4 sqlt$a: <- delete_sqltxplain_stats

PL/SQL procedure successfully completed.

SQCPKG completed.
  adding: 161222093638_08_sqcpkg.log (deflated 79%)

TAUTLTEST completed.
  adding: 161222093705_09_tautltest.log (deflated 59%)

SQUTLTEST completed.
  adding: 161222093705_10_squtltest.log (deflated 59%)

SQLT users must be granted SQLT_USER_ROLE before using this tool.

SQCREATE completed. Installation completed successfully.
```

This last message SQCREATE completed is a good sign that all has gone well. Before the installation will work you must carry out one more task manually.

```
SQL> GRANT INHERIT PRIVILEGES ON USER SYS TO SQLTXADMIN
```

Although the amount of work that SQLT does for you during the installation may seem daunting, the installation itself usually takes no more than five minutes. Even if you get something wrong during the installation it takes a very short time to correct the error by simply removing SQLT and reinstalling it with the correct settings, or if you prefer you can change the setting after the installation. For example, if you get the license level wrong during installation, you can correct it with one of the following four routines:

```
disable_tuning_pack_access;

enable_tuning_pack_access;

disable_diagnostic_pack_access;

enable_diagnostic_pack_access;
```

I've given more details on the use of these routines in the section "How to Change the Licensing Level after a SQLT Installation" below

How to Change the Licensing Level after a SQLT Installation

The default settings for a SQLT installation work for most situations, yet sometimes you may want to change them. For example, after installing SQLT you buy a diagnostic pack or tuning pack license. The tuning pack and diagnostic pack can be bought separately or as a bundle from Oracle. If you have neither of these packs you should use disable_tuning_pack_access and disable_diagnostic_pack_access if you installed with option "T" in a normal installation. Here are the example steps

```
SQL> exec sqltxadmin.sqlt$a.disable_tuning_pack_access;
PL/SQL procedure successfully completed.
SQL> exec sqltxadmin.sqlt$a.disable_diagnostic_pack_access;
PL/SQL procedure successfully completed.
```

No parameters are needed for these routines; just execute these from the SQLT account on the databases where SQLT is installed. You could change the license level by just reinstalling SQLT, but this would not be a good idea if you had many records in the SQLT repository that you wanted to keep. The list of configurable settings can be found under the Global section of the main SQLTXECUTE or SQLTXTRACT report. See Figure A-1.

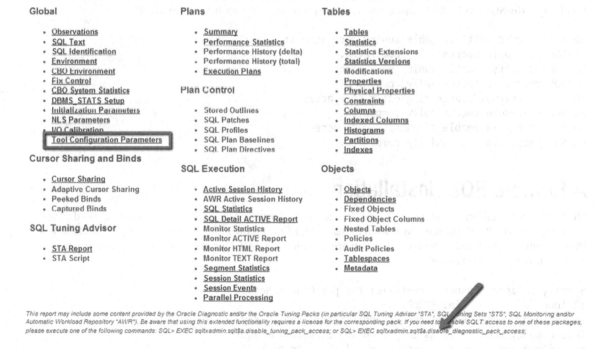

Figure A-1. *The top of a SQLTXECUTE report highlighting the configuration section*

The license levels are more important and there are special routines for these. If we installed the product with the wrong license level then we can change this with the sqltxadmin.sqlt$a packages, which has the previously mentioned four procedures related to the licensing levels:

```
disable_tuning_pack_access;

enable_tuning_pack_access;

disable_diagnostic_pack_access;

enable_diagnostic_pack_access;
```

These four procedures disable and enable the tuning pack and diagnostic pack functionality in SQLT. The arrow in Figure A-1 points to the prompt at the top of the SQLT main report that shows the example code. Below I've disabled and enabled the tuning pack and then disabled and enabled the diagnostic pack to end up with the same license level I started with.

```
SQL> exec sqltxadmin.sqlt$a.disable_tuning_pack_access;
PL/SQL procedure successfully completed.
SQL> exec sqltxadmin.sqlt$a.enable_tuning_pack_access;
PL/SQL procedure successfully completed.
SQL> exec sqltxadmin.sqlt$a.disable_diagnostic_pack_access;
PL/SQL procedure successfully completed.
SQL> exec sqltxadmin.sqlt$a.enable_diagnostic_pack_access;
PL/SQL procedure successfully completed.
```

Please note that in earlier versions of SQLT (before 11.4.4.6 and older) the routines to change the license level are in the SQLTXPLAIN schema, and so the command to change the license level is

```
SQL> SQL> exec sqlt$a.disable_tuning_pack_access;
PL/SQL procedure successfully completed.
SQL> exec sqlt$a.enable_tuning_pack_access;
PL/SQL procedure successfully completed.
SQL> exec sqlt$a.disable_diagnostic_pack_access;
PL/SQL procedure successfully completed.
SQL> exec sqlt$a.enable_diagnostic_pack_access;
PL/SQL procedure successfully completed.
```

A Remote SQLT Installation

During the installation you will see the optional connect identifier prompt. Normally this is ignored as you are installing locally. If, however, you want to install SQLT in remote mode you can specify a remote link. In these examples the local system is where you are connected to SQL Plus and the remote system is where the SQLT repository can be found.

```
Specify optional Connect Identifier (as per Oracle Net)
Include "@" symbol, ie. @PROD
If not applicable, enter nothing and hit the "Enter" key.
This connect identifier is only used while exporting SQLT
repository everytime you execute one of the main methods.
Optional Connect Identifier (ie: @PROD):@REMOTE
```

This appends **@REMOTE** to all SQL operations so that if you run @sqltxtract on the local database it will reach over to the remote database to store SQLT information.

In a remote installation the sequence of steps to run a report are slightly different than running everything locally.

1. Install SQL on the remote node from the local node.

2. Run the SQL on the remote node.

3. Run the SQLTXTRACT or SQLTXECUTE report on the local node but that runs on the remote node.

4. The reports are produced on the local node, but the repository data is stored on the remote node.

Other Ways to Install SQLT

If you want to deploy SQLT to many systems (and who wouldn't?) you might want to do a noninteractive installation. In this case you can populate a number of variables and then run `sqcsilent.sql`. An example variable definition file is provided in the installation directory of SQLT called `sqdefparams.sql`.

This is what it contains. These are all the values we've supplied in the interactive installation.

```
DEF connect_identifier      = '';
DEF enter_tool_password     = 'sqltxplain';
DEF re_enter_password       = 'sqltxplain';
DEF default_tablespace      = 'USERS';
DEF temporary_tablespace    = 'TEMP';
DEF main_application_schema = '';
DEF pack_license            = 'T';
```

These variables should be changed to suit your environment: for example, the password should be changed, and the tablespace and main application user could be different. When you have your own values in the file you can run `sqcsilent.sql`, which will then execute in "silent" mode with no prompts for parameters.

```
SQL> @sqcsilent.sql
```

You can also run the installation with all the parameters on the line as in the example below.

```
SQL> @sqcsilent2.sql '' sqltxplain USERS TEMP '' T
```

This will also execute a normal installation with no prompts for information. This could be a quick way to do a standard install on a number of different systems.

How to Remove SQLT

If for some reason you wish to de-install SQLT (perhaps a new version has become available), you can use the routine in the /install directory called `sqdrop.sql`. There are no parameters to this routine.

```
SQL> @sqdrop
uninstalling SQLT, please wait
TADOBJ completed.

SQDOLD completed. Ignore errors from this script

SQDOBJ completed. Ignore errors from this script
SQL>
```

```
SQL> DECLARE
  2    my_count INTEGER;
  3
  4  BEGIN
  5    SELECT COUNT(*)
  6      INTO my_count
  7      FROM sys.dba_users
  8     WHERE username = 'TRCADMIN';
  9
 10    IF my_count = 0 THEN
 11      BEGIN
 12        EXECUTE IMMEDIATE 'DROP PROCEDURE sys.sqlt$_trca$_dir_set';
 13      EXCEPTION
 14        WHEN OTHERS THEN
 15          DBMS_OUTPUT.PUT_LINE('Cannot drop procedure sys.sqlt$_trca$_dir_set.
              '||SQLERRM);
 16      END;
 17
 18      FOR i IN (SELECT directory_name
 19                  FROM sys.dba_directories
 20                 WHERE directory_name IN ('SQLT$UDUMP', 'SQLT$BDUMP', 'SQLT$STAGE',
                      'TRCA$INPUT1', 'TRCA$INPUT2', 'TRCA$STAGE'))
 21      LOOP
 22        BEGIN
 23          EXECUTE IMMEDIATE 'DROP DIRECTORY '||i.directory_name;
 24          DBMS_OUTPUT.PUT_LINE('Dropped directory '||i.directory_name||'.');
 25        EXCEPTION
 26          WHEN OTHERS THEN
 27            DBMS_OUTPUT.PUT_LINE('Cannot drop directory '||i.directory_name||'.
                '||SQLERRM);
 28        END;
 29      END LOOP;
 30    END IF;
 31  END;
 32  /
Dropped directory SQLT$STAGE.
Dropped directory TRCA$STAGE.
Dropped directory SQLT$UDUMP.
Dropped directory SQLT$BDUMP.
Dropped directory TRCA$INPUT1.
Dropped directory TRCA$INPUT2.

PL/SQL procedure successfully completed.

SQL>
SQL> WHENEVER SQLERROR CONTINUE;
SQL>
SQL> PAU About to DROP users &&tool_repository_schema. and &&tool_administer_schema.. Press
RETURN to continue.
```

At this point you are prompted to confirm that you want to do a drop user SQLTXADMIN cascade; and a drop user SQLTXPLAIN cascade;:

```
About to DROP users SQLTXPLAIN and SQLTXADMIN. Press RETURN to continue.

SQL>
SQL> DROP USER &&tool_administer_schema. CASCADE;
old   1: DROP USER &&tool_administer_schema. CASCADE
new   1: DROP USER SQLTXADMIN CASCADE

User dropped.

SQL> DROP USER &&tool_repository_schema. CASCADE;
old   1: DROP USER &&tool_repository_schema. CASCADE
new   1: DROP USER SQLTXPLAIN CASCADE

User dropped.

SQL> DROP ROLE &&role_name.;
old   1: DROP ROLE &&role_name.
new   1: DROP ROLE SQLT_USER_ROLE

Role dropped.

SQL>
SQL> SET ECHO OFF;

SQDUSR completed.

SQDROP completed.
```

And that's it. Now the schemas are dropped along with all related objects.

If you do have any problems with installation there is a useful note in MOS "FAQ: Common SQLT (SQLTXPLAIN) Runtime/Installation Errors (Doc 1670677.1)"

Installation and Runtime Errors

In those rare cases where an installation fails, you should be able to fix the installation problem by checking a few simple things. It is usually pretty easy to fix a faulty installation if you follow a few simple steps.

12c Privilege Missing

Most commonly in 12c a change in security has resulted in the need to enter the final step.

```
SQL> grant inherit privileges on user sys to sqltxadmin;
```

Not doing this results in the SQLT not working as expected, despite the fact that no errors are reported during the installation. If the installation seems to have worked but SQLTXTRACT does not work, then please try this step first!

Where to Find the Log Files

If the privilege check is OK, the next step is to locate the log file of the installation. This can be found in the 'install' directory and will be called SQLT_installations_archive.zip. Inside this zip file you will find the main installation log (<time-stamp>_01_sqcreate.log). This log file contains all the steps from the main installation. If you log an SR with Oracle for the failed installation of SQLT then this will be the file that support will want to look at.

One or Both of the SQLT Users Not Created

Sometimes the main SQLT users (SQLTXPLAIN and SQLTXADMIN) are not created. This can be because of a password policy violation, when the supplied SQLTXPLAIN password does not conform, or it can be due to other reasons. In any case the log of the creation of the user can be found in the log file <time-stamp>_02_sqcuser.log. If the problem was a password policy violation you will see an error message like this

```
ORA-28003: password verification for the specified password failed
```

in the log file.

Installation Hanging

In the section after SQUTLTEST you may see no screen activity for some time. This is not a cause for concern. If you want to see what the installation is doing:

```
SQL> select sid, state, event, blocking_session, sql_id
  from v$session
  where username = 'SYS'
  and status = 'ACTIVE';
```

You will most likely see something like this:

```
    SID STATE           EVENT                 BLOCKING_SESSION SQL_ID
    135 WAITING         library cache lock    135              8bhmvqtvy6zq2
```

This indicates that the session is waiting for a library cache lock and is probably compiling packages. Further investigation of the active SQL with

```
SQL> select sql_text from v$sql where sql_id = '8bhmvqtvy6zq2';
```

will show SQL like the two examples below:

```
/*SQL Analyze(135,0)*/ SELECT /*+ NOPARALLEL */ * FROM "SQLTXPLAIN"."TRCA_CONTROL"
```

```
/*SQL Analyze(135,0)*/ SELECT /*+ NOPARALLEL */ * FROM "SQLTXPLAIN"."TRCA_IND_COLUMNS"
```

If the SQL is unchanging after several minutes then installation may be hanging.

SQLT_USER_ROLE Not Granted

If you see the error

```
ORA-01924: role 'SQLT_USER_ROLE' not granted or does not exist
```

Then simply grant the user executing the SQLT function the SQLT_USER_ROLE role.

```
SQL> grant sqlt_user_role to <application-user>;
```

■ ■ ■

The CBO Parameters (12.1.02)

SQLT has within it the entire list of parameters that affect your query performance. It uses this list for the XPLORE method. Some parameters are hidden (only sporadically documented in various places), and some are non-hidden (documented in Oracle's online documentation: database reference manual https://docs.oracle.com/database/121/REFRN/GUID-FD266F6F-D047-4EBB-8D96-B51B1DCA2D61.htm#REFRN-GUID-FD266F6F-D047-4EBB-8D96-B51B1DCA2D61). You can get this list by issuing the following query from SQLTXPLAIN:

```
SQL> select name, description from sqlt$_v$parameter_cbo order by name;
```

In SQLT 12c there are in fact two users created for the SQLTXPLAIN utility. The users are SQLTXPLAIN and SQLTXADMIN. The second of these is locked by default and does not use the same password as SQLTXPLAIN and should not be used for day-to-day work. This is for security reasons. The SQLTXADMIN account should not be unlocked.

The parameter list included in the "Full List of Parameters" section later in this chapter is from a version 12.1.0.2 database. It is here to act as a partial reference and to point out that you can get the latest set from SQLT queries. You should not, however, consider this a list of parameters that you think might improve your SQL; the default parameter settings are there for a reason: they give the best overall results. But if your XPLORE report highlights some parameter that might make a difference, this list can give you a clue, along with the description as to what is happening in your query. Remember that just knowing the name of the hidden parameter is useful, as it gives you the chance to search My Oracle Support for even more clues.

Dealing with hidden parameters (they are hidden for a reason) can be a tricky business. The purpose of the list in this appendix is to inform, not to give a template for experimentation. I'll give some guidelines, caveats, and more detailed descriptions of certain important hidden parameters, but the general rule is this: talk to support. The names and effects of these parameters can change with any release. Oracle support will have the latest set of parameters and their effects.

General Approach to Dealing with Hidden Parameters

In the general scheme of things, hidden parameters are needed only rarely or under special environments. For example, Exadata installations are recommended to use a small number of hidden parameters. Apart from these special circumstances you will sometimes be requested to set some hidden parameters by Oracle support. Hidden parameters, when suggested by support, will be attempts to confirm some bug that has affected performance (wrong execution plan) or has resulted in wrong results or has even caused errors to be generated (ORA-00600's or ORA-07445's). The setting of these parameters usually follows the following steps:

© Stelios Charalambides 2017
S. Charalambides, *Oracle SQL Tuning with Oracle SQLTXPLAIN*, DOI 10.1007/978-1-4842-2436-6

1. A specific error occurs (wrong result, bad plan, ORA-00600, ORA-07445).

2. The characteristics of the wrong result, bad plan steps, or trace file of the ORA-00600 or trace file of the ORA-07445 suggest a course of action.

3. Often the suggested bug will have a workaround that consists of setting some parameter, sometimes a hidden parameter, to either mitigate the problem (avoid the error), change the execution plan back to the correct one, or to ensure the retrieval of correct data.

4. If the suggested changes have the desired effect and the bug is confirmed, using this technique and other techniques, you then have the options of setting the hidden parameter or parameters at the system level or at the session level if possible, as a short-term workaround or tolerating the error while a bug fix is produced. This will depend on many factors including your special circumstances and the effect of the parameters on your system generally.

This is why I specify with all of these parameters that you should be working with Oracle support. Changing hidden parameters without knowing the full implications can be disastrous (corrupted database springs to mind). The following descriptions and list give you the understanding to allow you to work more knowledgeably with Oracle support. If you have a database that is expendable, then you can do some experimentation with these parameters; but they should never be applied to production, development, QA, or testing databases without checking with Oracle support. I think that's enough of a warning.

More Detailed Descriptions of Some Hidden Parameters

For general information I have listed below some of the hidden parameters that may be used to alleviate problems under certain circumstances. None of this information should be used without the assistance of Oracle support. There are sometimes unforeseen effects of setting these parameters. If Oracle support suggests some of these parameters for exploratory investigation, you will usually be asked to do this at the session level to determine the effect and also to determine if you are being affected by a particular bug or to assess the efficacy of a bug fix. The defaults are as of 12.1, and these may change in future versions of Oracle, or indeed may be removed completely.

_and_pruning_enabled

With composite partitioned tables you may be affected by some bugs, which if they involve "AND" partition pruning, can be fixed by setting this parameter to FALSE. The default is TRUE.

_bloom_filter_enabled

Bloom filters are a memory-efficient way of determining the membership of a set for a particular value. This can be very effective with Oracle queries and large data sets. If your execution plan shows a bloom filter (BF) in the plan and you get wrong results or ORA-00600's, you may want to open a Service Request with Oracle support and discuss setting this parameter to FALSE. The default is TRUE.

_complex_view_merging

Under some circumstances the process of merging complex views can cause problems. By default this parameter is set to TRUE (as of 8i of Oracle) to allow the view query transformation to take place. If you have wrong results or ORA-00600s you may want to consult with Oracle support to check if setting this to FALSE might help. The default is TRUE.

_disable_function_based_index

A function-based index contains a function (obviously). An example would be

```sql
sql> create index fbi_1 on t (upper(col1));
```

Here the function is upper. In some rare cases you may get wrong results, which can be temporarily fixed (until you get a bug fix applied) by setting this value to the non-default value of FALSE.

_hash_join_enabled

There are a number of bugs that can be worked around by setting this hidden parameter to FALSE. The default value is TRUE. Just because you see a hash join in a statement and your statement crashes doesn't mean setting this parameter to false is the solution. Open a service request and give support the information. There may be other factors at work. Setting this value to FALSE will disable hash joins.

_optimizer_extended_cursor_sharing_rel

We already discussed disabling adaptive cursor sharing in Chapter 9, where we disabled ACS with

```sql
SQL> alter system set "_optimizer_extended_cursor_sharing_rel"=NONE scope=both;
SQL> alter system set "_optimizer_extended_cursor_sharing"=none scope=both;
```

Both parameters are needed to disable ACS. The default values are "SIMPLE" for _optimizer_extended_cursor_sharing_rel and "UDO" for _optimizer_extended_cursor_sharing.

_optimizer_cartesian_enabled

Disable the Cartesian join if set to FALSE. This may be a useful way of debugging a failing statement, in conjunction with Oracle supports help (also see "_optimizer_mjc_enabled"). The default value is TRUE.

_optimizer_cost_model

This changed the basis for costing of activity by the CBO. It can be set to cpu, io, or choose. The name is a little misleading; by setting cpu we do not optimize for reducing CPU usage, we optimize for reducing cost as before but are now taking CPU into account for I/O operations. The value choose allows the optimizer to make a choice based on statistics available in sys.aux_stats$. The default value is choose.

_optimizer_ignore_hints

This hidden parameter allows the optimizer to ignore embedded hints. The default value is FALSE. You might want to try this if you felt the hints were not producing the best plan and wanted to disable these at the session level with

```sql
SQL> alter session set "_optimizer_ignore_hints"=TRUE;
```

_optimizer_max_permutations

If you feel somehow that the optimizer is not working hard enough, there is always the option to set _optimizer_max_permutations to something other than the default value of 2,000. The parameter controls the number of different permutations that the optimizer will try per query block when joining a number of tables. There may be circumstances where this value can be as high as 80,000. The value is overridden by _optimizer_search_limit, where _optimizer_search_limit is the number factorial of join permutations.

_optimizer_use_feedback

Controls the cardinality feedback feature as discussed in Chapter 10. The default is TRUE. Set to FALSE to disable this feature.

_optimizer_search_limit

The default value for this parameter is 5. This is the factorial number of maximum Cartesian joins that will be considered. 5! (read as "five factorial") is equivalent to 5x4x3x2x1, which equals 120.

Full List of Parameters

Why include a full list of parameters that we should not as DBAs change unless directed to by Oracle support? There are two possible answers.

- Oracle support may suggest some parameter for some investigation, and it is useful to be able to have at least a brief description of what the parameter does. You should ask Oracle support for this description before applying to any database anyway. This list is your backup for this information.

- Read and research each of these parameters carefully or try things out on a disposable database to give you insight as to how the optimizer works and what it is doing for us. This greater understanding becomes a story that cements clear knowledge about some aspect of the optimizer. An example of this is _optimizer_max_permutations. Before I came across the parameter, I happily assumed that the optimizer tried *all* permutations of joins. A moment's thought would have disabused me of that opinion. But now I know there is a limit to the number of join choices and how to control it.

The following list of CBO parameters (version 12.1.0.2.0) is a sample output of the SQLT query discussed at the beginning of this appendix:

```
SQL> select name, description from sqlt$_v$parameter_cbo order by name;
NAME                                    DESCRIPTION
_adaptive_window_consolidator_enabled   enable/disable adaptive window consolidator PX plan
_add_stale_mv_to_dependency_list        add stale mv to dependency list
_aggregation_optimization_settings      settings for aggregation optimizations
_allow_level_without_connect_by         allow level without connect by
_always_anti_join                       always use this method for anti-join when possible
_always_semi_join                       always use this method for semi-join when possible
_always_star_transformation             always favor use of star transformation
_always_vector_transformation           always favor use of vector transformation
_and_pruning_enabled                    allow partition pruning based on multiple mechanisms
```

_approx_cnt_distinct_gby_pushdown	perform group-by pushdown for approximate distinct count query
_approx_cnt_distinct_optimization	settings for approx_count_distinct optimizations
_arch_comp_dbg_scan	archive compression scan debug
_array_cdb_view_enabled	array mode enabled for CDB views
_b_tree_bitmap_plans	enable the use of bitmap plans for tables w. only B-tree indexes
_bloom_filter_enabled	enables or disables bloom filter
_bloom_filter_size	bloom filter vector size (in KB)
_bloom_folding_enabled	Enable folding of bloom filter
_bloom_minmax_enabled	enable or disable bloom min max filtering
_bloom_predicate_enabled	enables or disables bloom filter predicate pushdown
_bloom_predicate_offload	enables or disables bloom filter predicate offload to cells
_bloom_pruning_enabled	Enable partition pruning using bloom filtering
_bloom_pushing_max	bloom filter pushing size upper bound (in KB)
_bloom_rm_filter	remove bloom predicate in favor of zonemap join pruning predicate
_bloom_serial_filter	enable serial bloom filter on exadata
_bloom_sm_enabled	enable bloom filter optimization using slave mapping
_bt_mmv_query_rewrite_enabled	allow rewrites with multiple MVs and base tables
_cdb_cross_container	Debug flag for cross container operations
_cdb_view_parallel_degree	Parallel degree for a CDB view query
_cell_materialize_all_expressions	Force materialization of all offloadable expressions on the cells
_cell_materialize_virtual_columns	enable offload of expressions underlying virtual columns to cells
_cell_offload_complex_processing	enable complex SQL processing offload to cells
_cell_offload_expressions	enable offload of expressions to cells
_cell_offload_sys_context	enable offload of SYS_CONTEXT evaluation to cells
_common_data_view_enabled	common objects returned through dictionary views
_complex_view_merging	enable complex view merging
_connect_by_use_union_all	use union all for connect by
_convert_set_to_join	enables conversion of set operator to join
_cost_equality_semi_join	enables costing of equality semi-join
_cpu_to_io	divisor for converting CPU cost to I/O cost
_db_file_optimizer_read_count	multiblock read count for regular clients
_dbg_scan	generic scan debug
_default_non_equality_sel_check	sanity check on default selectivity for like/range predicate
_deferred_constant_folding_mode	Deferred constant folding mode
_dimension_skip_null	control dimension skip when null feature
_direct_path_insert_features	disable direct path insert features
_disable_datalayer_sampling	disable datalayer sampling
_disable_function_based_index	disable function-based index matching
_disable_parallel_conventional_load	Disable parallel conventional loads
_distinct_agg_optimization_gsets	Use Distinct Aggregate Optimization for Grouping Sets
_distinct_view_unnesting	enables unnesting of in subquery into distinct view
_dm_max_shared_pool_pct	max percentage of the shared pool to use for a mining model
_dml_frequency_tracking	Control DML frequency tracking

_dml_monitoring_enabled	enable modification monitoring
_eliminate_common_subexpr	enables elimination of common sub-expressions
_enable_dml_lock_escalation	enable dml lock escalation against partitioned tables if TRUE
_enable_query_rewrite_on_remote_objs	mv rewrite on remote table/view
_enable_row_shipping	use the row shipping optimization for wide table selects
_enable_type_dep_selectivity	enable type dependent selectivity estimates
_extended_pruning_enabled	do runtime pruning in iterator if set to TRUE
_external_table_smart_scan	External Table Smart Scan
_fast_full_scan_enabled	enable/disable index fast full scan
_fast_index_maintenance	fast global index maintenance during PMOPs
_fic_area_size	size of Frequent Itemset Counting work area
_first_k_rows_dynamic_proration	enable the use of dynamic proration of join cardinalities
_force_datefold_trunc	force use of trunc for datefolding rewrite
_force_rewrite_enable	control new query rewrite features
_force_slave_mapping_intra_part_loads	Force slave mapping for intra partition loads
_force_temptables_for_gsets	executes concatenation of rollups using temp tables
_force_tmp_segment_loads	Force tmp segment loads
_full_pwise_join_enabled	enable full partition-wise join when TRUE
_gby_hash_aggregation_enabled	enable group-by and aggregation using hash scheme
_gby_vector_aggregation_enabled	enable group-by and aggregation using vector scheme
_generalized_pruning_enabled	controls extensions to partition pruning for general predicates
_globalindex_pnum_filter_enabled	enables filter for global index with partition extended syntax
_gs_anti_semi_join_allowed	enable anti/semi join for the GS query
_hash_join_enabled	enable/disable hash join
_hash_multiblock_io_count	number of blocks hash join will read/write at once
_hashops_prefetch_size	maximum no of rows whose relevant memory locations are prefetched
_improved_outerjoin_card	improved outer-join cardinality calculation
_improved_row_length_enabled	enable the improvements for computing the average row length
_index_join_enabled	enable the use of index joins
_indexable_con_id	indexing of CON_ID column enabled for X$ tables
_inmemory_dbg_scan	In-memory scan debugging
_inmemory_pruning	In-memory pruning
_inmemory_query_fetch_by_rowid	In-memory fetch-by-rowid enabled
_inmemory_query_scan	In-memory scan enabled
_kdt_buffering	control kdt buffering for conventional inserts
_key_vector_caching	Enables vector key vector caching
_key_vector_max_size	maximum key vector size (in KB)
_key_vector_offload	controls key vector offload to cells
_key_vector_predicate_enabled	enables or disables key vector filter predicate pushdown
_key_vector_predicate_threshold	selectivity pct for key vector filter predicate pushdown
_left_nested_loops_random	enable random distribution method for left of nestedloops

_like_with_bind_as_equality	treat LIKE predicate with bind as an equality predicate
_local_communication_costing_enabled	enable local communication costing when TRUE
_local_communication_ratio	set the ratio between global and local communication (0..100)
_max_rwgs_groupings	maximum no of groupings on materialized views
_minimal_stats_aggregation	prohibit stats aggregation at compile/partition maintenance time
_mmv_query_rewrite_enabled	allow rewrites with multiple MVs and/or base tables
_mv_generalized_oj_refresh_opt	enable/disable new algorithm for MJV with generalized outer joins
_nested_loop_fudge	nested loop fudge
_new_initial_join_orders	enable initial join orders based on new ordering heuristics
_new_sort_cost_estimate	enables the use of new cost estimate for sort
_nlj_batching_enabled	enable batching of the RHS IO in NLJ
_no_or_expansion	OR expansion during optimization disabled
_object_link_fixed_enabled	object linked views evaluated using fixed table
_oltp_comp_dbg_scan	oltp compression scan debug
_oneside_colstat_for_equijoins	sanity check on default selectivity for like/range predicate
_optim_adjust_for_part_skews	adjust stats for skews across partitions
_optim_enhance_nnull_detection	TRUE to enable index [fast] full scan more often
_optim_new_default_join_sel	improves the way default equijoin selectivity are computed
_optim_peek_user_binds	enable peeking of user binds
_optimizer_adaptive_cursor_sharing	optimizer adaptive cursor sharing
_optimizer_adaptive_plan_control	internal controls for adaptive plans
_optimizer_adaptive_plans	enable adaptive plans
_optimizer_adaptive_random_seed	random seed for adaptive plans
_optimizer_adjust_for_nulls	adjust selectivity for null values
_optimizer_ads_max_table_count	maximum number of tables in a join under ADS
_optimizer_ads_time_limit	maximum time limit (seconds) under ADS
_optimizer_ads_use_partial_results	Use partial results of ADS queries
_optimizer_ads_use_result_cache	use result cache for ADS queries
_optimizer_aggr_groupby_elim	group-by and aggregation elimination
_optimizer_ansi_join_lateral_enhance	optimization of left/full ansi-joins and lateral views
_optimizer_ansi_rearchitecture	re-architecture of ANSI left, right, and full outer joins
_optimizer_aw_join_push_enabled	Enables AW Join Push optimization
_optimizer_aw_stats_enabled	Enables statistcs on AW olap_table table function
_optimizer_batch_table_access_by_rowid	enable table access by ROWID IO batching
_optimizer_better_inlist_costing	enable improved costing of index access using in-list(s)
_optimizer_block_size	standard block size used by optimizer
_optimizer_cache_stats	cost with cache statistics
_optimizer_cartesian_enabled	optimizer cartesian join enabled
_optimizer_cbqt_factor	cost factor for cost-based query transformation
_optimizer_cbqt_no_size_restriction	disable cost based transformation query size restriction
_optimizer_cluster_by_rowid	enable/disable the cluster by rowid feature

_optimizer_cluster_by_rowid_batched	enable/disable the cluster by rowid batching feature
_optimizer_cluster_by_rowid_control	internal control for cluster by rowid feature mode
_optimizer_coalesce_subqueries	consider coalescing of subqueries optimization
_optimizer_complex_pred_selectivity	enable selectivity estimation for builtin functions
_optimizer_compute_index_stats	force index stats collection on index creation/rebuild
_optimizer_connect_by_cb_whr_only	use cost-based transformation for whr clause in connect by
_optimizer_connect_by_combine_sw	combine no filtering connect by and start with
_optimizer_connect_by_cost_based	use cost-based transformation for connect by
_optimizer_connect_by_elim_dups	allow connect by to eliminate duplicates from input
_optimizer_correct_sq_selectivity	force correct computation of subquery selectivity
_optimizer_cost_based_transformation	enables cost-based query transformation
_optimizer_cost_filter_pred	enables costing of filter predicates in IO cost model
_optimizer_cost_hjsmj_multimatch	add cost of generating result set when #rows per key > 1
_optimizer_cost_model	optimizer cost model
_optimizer_cube_join_enabled	enable cube join
_optimizer_degree	force the optimizer to use the same degree of parallelism
_optimizer_dim_subq_join_sel	use join selectivity in choosing star transformation dimensions
_optimizer_disable_strans_sanity_checks	disable star transformation sanity checks
_optimizer_distinct_agg_transform	Transforms Distinct Aggregates to non-distinct aggregates
_optimizer_distinct_elimination	Eliminates redundant SELECT DISTNCT's
_optimizer_distinct_placement	consider distinct placement optimization
_optimizer_dsdir_usage_control	controls optimizer usage of dynamic sampling directives
_optimizer_eliminate_filtering_join	optimizer filtering join elimination enabled
_optimizer_enable_density_improvements	use improved density computation for selectivity estimation
_optimizer_enable_extended_stats	use extended statistics for selectivity estimation
_optimizer_enable_table_lookup_by_nl	consider table lookup by nl transformation
_optimizer_enhanced_filter_push query transformation	push filters before trying cost-based
_optimizer_extend_jppd_view_types	join pred pushdown on group-by, distinct, semi-/anti-joined view
_optimizer_extended_cursor_sharing	optimizer extended cursor sharing
_optimizer_extended_cursor_sharing_rel	optimizer extended cursor sharing for relational operators
_optimizer_extended_stats_usage_control	controls the optimizer usage of extended stats
_optimizer_false_filter_pred_pullup	optimizer false predicate pull up transformation
_optimizer_fast_access_pred_analysis	use fast algorithm to traverse predicates for physical optimizer
_optimizer_fast_pred_transitivity	use fast algorithm to generate transitive predicates
_optimizer_filter_pred_pullup	use cost-based flter predicate pull up transformation
_optimizer_filter_pushdown	enable/disable filter predicate pushdown
_optimizer_fkr_index_cost_bias	Optimizer index bias over FTS/IFFS under first K rows mode

_optimizer_free_transformation_heap	free transformation subheap after each transformation
_optimizer_full_outer_join_to_outer	enable/disable full outer to left outer join conversion
_optimizer_gather_feedback	optimizer gather feedback
_optimizer_gather_stats_on_load	enable/disable online statistics gathering
_optimizer_generate_transitive_pred	optimizer generate transitive predicates
_optimizer_group_by_placement	consider group-by placement optimization
_optimizer_hll_entry	number of entries in hll hash table
_optimizer_hybrid_fpwj_enabled	enable hybrid full partition-wise join when TRUE
_optimizer_ignore_hints	enables the embedded hints to be ignored
_optimizer_improve_selectivity	improve table and partial overlap join selectivity computation
_optimizer_inmemory_access_path	optimizer access path costing for in-memory
_optimizer_inmemory_autodop	optimizer autoDOP costing for in-memory
_optimizer_inmemory_bloom_filter	controls serial bloom filter for in-memory tables
_optimizer_inmemory_cluster_aware_dop	Affinitize DOP for inmemory objects
_optimizer_inmemory_gen_pushable_preds	optimizer generate pushable predicates for in-memory
_optimizer_inmemory_minmax_pruning	controls use of min/max pruning for costing in-memory tables
_optimizer_inmemory_table_expansion	optimizer in-memory awareness for table expansion
_optimizer_instance_count	force the optimizer to use the specified number of instances
_optimizer_interleave_jppd	interleave join predicate pushdown during CBQT
_optimizer_join_elimination_enabled	optimizer join elimination enabled
_optimizer_join_factorization	use join factorization transformation
_optimizer_join_order_control	controls the optimizer join order search algorithm
_optimizer_join_sel_sanity_check	enable/disable sanity check for multi-column join selectivity
_optimizer_key_vector_aggr_factor	the required aggregation between IJK and DGK
_optimizer_max_permutations	optimizer maximum join permutations per query block
_optimizer_min_cache_blocks	set minimum cached blocks
_optimizer_mjc_enabled	enable merge join cartesian
_optimizer_mode_force	force setting of optimizer mode for user recursive SQL also
_optimizer_multi_level_push_pred	consider join-predicate pushdown that requires multi-level pushdown to base table
_optimizer_multi_table_outerjoin	allows multiple tables on the left of outerjoin
_optimizer_native_full_outer_join	execute full outer join using native implementaion
_optimizer_nested_rollup_for_gset	number of groups above which we use nested rollup exec for gset
_optimizer_new_join_card_computation	compute join cardinality using non-rounded input values
_optimizer_nlj_hj_adaptive_join	allow adaptive NL Hash joins
_optimizer_null_accepting_semijoin	enables null-accepting semijoin
_optimizer_null_aware_antijoin	null-aware antijoin parameter
_optimizer_or_expansion	control or expansion approach used
_optimizer_or_expansion_subheap	Use subheap for optimizer or-expansion
_optimizer_order_by_elimination_enabled	Eliminates order bys from views before query transformation
_optimizer_outer_join_to_inner	enable/disable outer to inner join conversion
_optimizer_outer_to_anti_enabled	Enable transformation of outer-join to anti-join

	if possible
_optimizer_partial_join_eval	partial join evaluation parameter
_optimizer_percent_parallel	optimizer percent parallel
_optimizer_performance_feedback	controls the performance feedback
_optimizer_proc_rate_level	control the level of processing rates
_optimizer_proc_rate_source	control the source of processing rates
_optimizer_push_down_distinct	push down distinct from query block to table
_optimizer_push_pred_cost_based	use cost-based query transformation for push pred optimization
_optimizer_random_plan	optimizer seed value for random plans
_optimizer_reduce_groupby_key	group-by key reduction
_optimizer_reuse_cost_annotations	reuse cost annotations during cost-based query transformation
_optimizer_rownum_bind_default	Default value to use for rownum bind
_optimizer_rownum_pred_based_fkr	enable the use of first K rows due to rownum predicate
_optimizer_search_limit	optimizer search limit
_optimizer_self_induced_cache_cost	account for self-induced caching
_optimizer_skip_scan_enabled	enable/disable index skip scan
_optimizer_skip_scan_guess	consider index skip scan for predicates with guessed selectivity
_optimizer_sortmerge_join_enabled	enable/disable sort-merge join method
_optimizer_sortmerge_join_inequality	enable/disable sort-merge join using inequality predicates
_optimizer_squ_bottomup	enables unnesting of subquery in a bottom-up manner
_optimizer_star_tran_in_with_clause	enable/disable star transformation in with clause queries
_optimizer_star_trans_min_cost	optimizer star transformation minimum cost
_optimizer_star_trans_min_ratio	optimizer star transformation minimum ratio
_optimizer_starplan_enabled	optimizer star plan enabled
_optimizer_strans_adaptive_pruning	allow adaptive pruning of star transformation bitmap trees
_optimizer_system_stats_usage	system statistics usage
_optimizer_table_expansion	consider table expansion transformation
_optimizer_transitivity_retain	retain equi-join pred upon transitive equality pred generation
_optimizer_try_st_before_jppd	try Star Transformation before Join Predicate Push Down
_optimizer_undo_changes	undo changes to query optimizer
_optimizer_undo_cost_change	optimizer undo cost change
_optimizer_unnest_all_subqueries	enables unnesting of every type of subquery
_optimizer_unnest_corr_set_subq	Unnesting of correlated set subqueries (TRUE/FALSE)
_optimizer_unnest_disjunctive_subq	Unnesting of disjunctive subqueries (TRUE/FALSE)
_optimizer_unnest_scalar_sq	enables unnesting of of scalar subquery
_optimizer_use_cbqt_star_transformation	use rewritten star transformation using cbqt framework
_optimizer_use_feedback	optimizer use feedback
_optimizer_use_gtt_session_stats	use GTT session private statistics
_optimizer_use_histograms	enable/disable the usage of histograms by the optimizer
_optimizer_use_subheap	Enables physical optimizer subheap
_optimizer_vector_cost_adj	cost adjustment for vector aggregation processing estimates

_optimizer_vector_fact_dim_ratio	cost based vector transform dimension to fact ratio
_optimizer_vector_min_fact_rows	min number of rows required for vector aggregation transform
_optimizer_vector_transformation	perform vector transform
_or_expand_nvl_predicate	enable OR expanded plan for NVL/DECODE predicate
_ordered_nested_loop	enable ordered nested loop costing
_parallel_broadcast_enabled	enable broadcasting of small inputs to hash and sort merge joins
_parallel_cluster_cache_policy	policy used for parallel execution on cluster(ADAPTIVE/CACHED)
_parallel_ctas_enabled	enable/disable parallel CTAS operation
_parallel_fault_tolerance_enabled	enables or disables fault-tolerance for parallel statement
_parallel_fault_tolerance_threshold	total number of faults fault-tolerance will handle
_parallel_inmemory_min_time_threshold	threshold above which a plan is a candidate for parallelization for in-memory tables (in seconds)
_parallel_inmemory_time_unit	unit of work used to derive the degree of parallelism for in-memory tables (in seconds)
_parallel_scalability	Parallel scalability criterion for parallel execution
_parallel_syspls_obey_force	TRUE to obey force parallel query/dml/ddl under System PL/SQL
_parallel_time_unit	unit of work used to derive the degree of parallelism (in seconds)
_partial_pwise_join_enabled	enable partial partition-wise join when TRUE
_partition_advisor_srs_active	enables sampling based partitioning validation
_partition_cdb_view_enabled	partitioned cdb view evaluation enabled
_partition_view_enabled	enable/disable partitioned views
_pga_max_size	Maximum size of the PGA memory for one process
_pivot_implementation_method	pivot implementation method
_pre_rewrite_push_pred	push predicates into views before rewrite
_pred_move_around	enables predicate move-around
_pred_push_cdb_view_enabled	predicate pushdown enabled for CDB views
_predicate_elimination_enabled	allow predicate elimination if set to TRUE
_project_view_columns	enable projecting out unreferenced columns of a view
_push_join_predicate	enable pushing join predicate inside a view
_push_join_union_view	enable pushing join predicate inside a union all view
_push_join_union_view2	enable pushing join predicate inside a union view
_px_adaptive_dist_method	determines the behavior of adaptive distribution methods
_px_adaptive_dist_method_threshold	Buffering / decision threshold for adaptive distribution methods
_px_autodop_pq_overhead	adjust auto dop calculation using pq overhead
_px_back_to_parallel	allow going back to parallel after a serial operation
_px_broadcast_fudge_factor	set the tq broadcasting fudge factor percentage
_px_cdb_view_enabled	parallel cdb view evaluation enabled
_px_cdb_view_join_enabled	disable parallelism cap on CDB view
_px_concurrent	enables pq with concurrent execution of serial inputs

389

_px_cpu_autodop_enabled	enables or disables auto dop cpu computation
_px_cpu_process_bandwidth	CPU process bandwidth in MB/sec for DOP computation
_px_external_table_default_stats	the external table default stats collection enable/disable
_px_filter_parallelized	enables or disables correlated filter parallelization
_px_filter_skew_handling	enable correlated filter parallelization to handle skew
_px_groupby_pushdown	perform group-by pushdown for parallel query
_px_hybrid_TSM_HWMB_load	Enable Hybrid Temp Segment Merge/High Water Mark Brokered load method
_px_join_skew_handling	enables skew handling for parallel joins
_px_join_skew_minfreq	sets minimum frequency(%) for skewed value for parallel joins
_px_join_skew_ratio	sets skew ratio for parallel joins
_px_load_monitor_threshold	threshold for pushing information to load slave workload monitor
_px_loc_msg_cost	CPU cost to send a PX message via shared memory
_px_minus_intersect	enables pq for minus/interect operators
_px_monitor_load	enable consumer load slave workload monitoring
_px_net_msg_cost	CPU cost to send a PX message over the internconnect
_px_numa_support_enabled	enable/disable PQ NUMA support
_px_object_sampling_enabled	use base object sampling when possible for range distribution
_px_parallelize_expression	enables or disables expression evaluation parallelization
_px_partial_rollup_pushdown	perform partial rollup pushdown for parallel execution
_px_partition_scan_enabled	enables or disables parallel partition-based scan
_px_partition_scan_threshold	least number of partitions per slave to start partition-based scan
_px_pwg_enabled	parallel partition wise group by enabled
_px_pwmr_enabled	parallel partition wise match recognize enabled
_px_replication_enabled	enables or disables replication of small table scans
_px_scalable_invdist	enable/disable px scalable plan for inverse distribution functions
_px_single_server_enabled	allow single-slave dfo in parallel query
_px_tq_rowhvs	turn on intra-row hash valueing sharing in TQ
_px_ual_serial_input	enables new pq for UNION operators
_px_wif_dfo_declumping	NDV-aware DFO clumping of multiple window sorts
_px_wif_extend_distribution_keys	extend TQ data redistribution keys for window functions
_query_cost_rewrite	perform the cost based rewrite with materialized views
_query_execution_time_limit	Query execution time limit in seconds
_query_mmvrewrite_maxcmaps	query mmv rewrite maximum number of cmaps per dmap in query disjunct
_query_mmvrewrite_maxdmaps	query mmv rewrite maximum number of dmaps per query disjunct
_query_mmvrewrite_maxinlists	query mmv rewrite maximum number of in-lists per disjunct
_query_mmvrewrite_maxintervals	query mmv rewrite maximum number of intervals

	per disjunct
_query_mmvrewrite_maxpreds	query mmv rewrite maximum number of predicates
	per disjunct
_query_mmvrewrite_maxqryinlistvals	query mmv rewrite maximum number of query in-list
	values
_query_mmvrewrite_maxregperm	query mmv rewrite maximum number of region
	permutations
_query_rewrite_1	perform query rewrite before&after or only before
	view merging
_query_rewrite_2	perform query rewrite before&after or only after
	view merging
_query_rewrite_drj	mv rewrite and drop redundant joins
_query_rewrite_expression	rewrite with cannonical form for expressions
_query_rewrite_fpc	mv rewrite fresh partition containment
_query_rewrite_fudge	cost based query rewrite with MVs fudge factor
_query_rewrite_jgmigrate	mv rewrite with jg migration
_query_rewrite_maxdisjunct	query rewrite max disjuncts
_query_rewrite_or_error	allow query rewrite, if referenced tables are
	not dataless
_query_rewrite_setopgrw_enable	perform general rewrite using set operator summaries
_query_rewrite_vop_cleanup	prune frocol chain before rewrite after view-merging
_rc_sys_obj_enabled	result cache enabled for Sys Objects
_rdbms_internal_fplib_enabled	enable CELL FPLIB filtering within rdbms
_remove_aggr_subquery	enables removal of subsumed aggregated subquery
_replace_virtual_columns	replace expressions with virtual columns
_result_cache_auto_size_threshold	result cache auto max size allowed
_result_cache_auto_time_threshold	result cache auto time threshold
_right_outer_hash_enable	Right Outer/Semi/Anti Hash Enabled
_row_shipping_explain	enable row shipping explain plan support
_row_shipping_threshold	row shipping column selection threshold
_rowsets_cdb_view_enabled	rowsets enabled for CDB views
_rowsets_enabled	enable/disable rowsets
_rowsets_max_rows	maximum number of rows in a rowset
_rowsets_target_maxsize	target size in bytes for space reserved in the frame
	for a rowset
_rowsrc_trace_level	Row source tree tracing level
_selfjoin_mv_duplicates	control rewrite self-join algorithm
_simple_view_merging	control simple view merging performed by the
	optimizer
_slave_mapping_enabled	enable slave mapping when TRUE
_smm_auto_cost_enabled	if TRUE, use the AUTO size policy cost functions
_smm_auto_max_io_size	Maximum IO size (in KB) used by sort/hash-join in
	auto mode
_smm_auto_min_io_size	Minimum IO size (in KB) used by sort/hash-join in
	auto mode
_smm_max_size_static	static maximum work area size in auto mode (serial)
_smm_min_size	minimum work area size in auto mode
_smm_px_max_size_static	static maximum work area size in auto mode (global)
_sort_elimination_cost_ratio	cost ratio for sort eimination under first_rows mode
_sort_multiblock_read_count	multi-block read count for sort
_spr_push_pred_refspr	push predicates through reference spreadsheet
_sql_compatibility	sql compatability bit vector

_sql_hvshare_threshold	threshold to control hash value sharing across operators
_sql_model_unfold_forloops	specifies compile-time unfolding of sql model forloops
_stat_aggs_one_pass_algorithm	enable one pass algorithm for variance-related functions
_subquery_pruning_enabled	enable the use of subquery predicates to perform pruning
_subquery_pruning_mv_enabled	enable the use of subquery predicates with MVs to perform pruning
_system_index_caching	optimizer percent system index caching
_table_scan_cost_plus_one	bump estimated full table scan and index ffs cost by one
_trace_virtual_columns	trace virtual columns exprs
_union_rewrite_for_gs	expand queries with GSets into UNIONs for rewrite
_unnest_subquery	enables unnesting of complex subqueries
_upddel_dba_hash_mask_bits	controls masking of lower order bits in DBA
_use_column_stats_for_function	enable the use of column statistics for DDP functions
_use_hidden_partitions	use hidden partitions
_vector_operations_control	control different uses/algorithms related to vector transform
_vector_serialize_temp_threshold	threshold for serializing vector transform temp table writes
_virtual_column_overload_allowed	overload virtual columns expression
_with_subquery	WITH subquery transformation
_zonemap_control	control different uses/algorithms related to zonemaps
_zonemap_use_enabled	enable the use of zonemaps for IO pruning
active_instance_count	number of active instances in the cluster database
bitmap_merge_area_size	maximum memory allow for BITMAP MERGE
cell_offload_compaction	Cell packet compaction strategy
cell_offload_plan_display	Cell offload explain plan display
cell_offload_processing	enable SQL processing offload to cells
cpu_count	number of CPUs for this instance
cursor_sharing	cursor sharing mode
db_file_multiblock_read_count	db block to be read each IO
deferred_segment_creation	defer segment creation to first insert
dst_upgrade_insert_conv	Enables/Disables internal conversions during DST upgrade
hash_area_size	size of in-memory hash work area
inmemory_force	Force tables to be in-memory or not
inmemory_query	Specifies whether in-memory queries are allowed
inmemory_size	size in bytes of in-memory area
optimizer_adaptive_features	controls adaptive features
optimizer_adaptive_reporting_only	use reporting-only mode for adaptive optimizations
optimizer_capture_sql_plan_baselines	automatic capture of SQL plan baselines for repeatable statements
optimizer_dynamic_sampling	optimizer dynamic sampling
optimizer_features_enable	optimizer plan compatibility parameter
optimizer_index_caching	optimizer percent index caching
optimizer_index_cost_adj	optimizer index cost adjustment

optimizer_inmemory_aware	optimizer in-memory columnar awareness
optimizer_mode	optimizer mode
optimizer_secure_view_merging	optimizer secure view merging and predicate pushdown/movearound
optimizer_use_invisible_indexes	Usage of invisible indexes (TRUE/FALSE)
optimizer_use_pending_statistics	Control whether to use optimizer pending statistics
optimizer_use_sql_plan_baselines	use of SQL plan baselines for captured sql statements
parallel_degree_level	adjust the computed degree in percentage
parallel_degree_limit	limit placed on degree of parallelism
parallel_degree_policy	policy used to compute the degree of parallelism (MANUAL/LIMITED/AUTO/ADAPTIVE)
parallel_execution_message_size	message buffer size for parallel execution
parallel_force_local	force single instance execution
parallel_min_time_threshold	threshold above which a plan is a candidate for parallelization (in seconds)
parallel_threads_per_cpu	number of parallel execution threads per CPU
pga_aggregate_target	Target size for the aggregate PGA memory consumed by the instance
query_rewrite_enabled	allow rewrite of queries using materialized views if enabled
query_rewrite_integrity	perform rewrite using materialized views with desired integrity
result_cache_mode	result cache operator usage mode
skip_unusable_indexes	skip unusable indexes if set to TRUE
sort_area_retained_size	size of in-memory sort work area retained between fetch calls
sort_area_size	size of in-memory sort work area
star_transformation_enabled	enable the use of star transformation
statistics_level	statistics level
workarea_size_policy	policy used to size SQL working areas (MANUAL/AUTO)

APPENDIX C

■ ■ ■

Tool Configuration Parameters and the Express Methods

From the main SQL page you can click on the "Tool Configuration Parameters" link. See Figure C-1 below.

215187.1 SQLT XECUTE 12.1.160429 Report: sqlt_s30932_main.html

Global

- Observations
- SQL Text
- SQL Identification
- Environment
- CBO Environment
- Fix Control
- CBO System Statistics
- DBMS_STATS Setup
- Initialization Parameters
- NLS Parameters
- I/O Calibration
- Tool Configuration Parameters

Cursor Sharing and Binds

- Cursor Sharing
- Adaptive Cursor Sharing
- Peeked Binds
- Captured Binds

SQL Tuning Advisor

- STA Report
- STA Script

Plans

- Summary
- Performance Statistics
- Performance History (delta)
- Performance History (total)
- Execution Plans

Plan Control

- Stored Outlines
- SQL Patches
- SQL Profiles
- SQL Plan Baselines
- SQL Plan Directives

SQL Execution

- Active Session History
- AWR Active Session History
- SQL Statistics
- SQL Detail ACTIVE Report
- Monitor Statistics
- Monitor ACTIVE Report
- Monitor HTML Report
- Monitor TEXT Report
- Segment Statistics
- Session Statistics
- Session Events
- Parallel Processing

Tables

- Tables
- Statistics
- Statistics Extensions
- Statistics Versions
- Modifications
- Properties
- Physical Properties
- Constraints
- Columns
- Indexed Columns
- Histograms
- Partitions
- Indexes

Objects

- Objects
- Dependencies
- Fixed Objects
- Fixed Object Columns
- Nested Tables
- Policies
- Audit Policies
- Tablespaces
- Metadata

Figure C-1. The Tool Configuration hyperlink is on the main page

© Stelios Charalambides 2017
S. Charalambides, *Oracle SQL Tuning with Oracle SQLTXPLAIN*, DOI 10.1007/978-1-4842-2436-6

The table below lists the parameters that are adjustable to control the behavior of SQLT from the appropriately privileged account.

For example, to limit the number of ADDM reports to 1.

```
SQL> exec sqltxadmin.sqlt$a.set_param('addm_reports',1);
```

The Express reports XPREXT and XPREXC change the default values of various parameters in SQLT to achieve a much smaller report, which is faster to produce.

This is done to achieve this:

```
EXEC sqlt$a.set_sess_param('addm_reports', '0');
EXEC sqlt$a.set_sess_param('ash_reports_source', 'NONE');
EXEC sqlt$a.set_sess_param('ash_reports', '0');
EXEC sqlt$a.set_sess_param('awr_reports', '0');
EXEC sqlt$a.set_sess_param('bde_chk_cbo', 'N');
EXEC sqlt$a.set_sess_param('c_dba_hist_parameter', 'N');
EXEC sqlt$a.set_sess_param('c_gran_cols', 'GLOBAL');
EXEC sqlt$a.set_sess_param('c_gran_hgrm', 'GLOBAL');
EXEC sqlt$a.set_sess_param('c_gran_segm', 'GLOBAL');
EXEC sqlt$a.set_sess_param('distributed_queries', 'N');
EXEC sqlt$a.set_sess_param('domain_index_metadata', 'N');
EXEC sqlt$a.set_sess_param('r_gran_cols', 'GLOBAL');
EXEC sqlt$a.set_sess_param('r_gran_hgrm', 'GLOBAL');
EXEC sqlt$a.set_sess_param('r_gran_segm', 'GLOBAL');
EXEC sqlt$a.set_sess_param('search_sql_by_sqltext', 'N');
EXEC sqlt$a.set_sess_param('sql_monitor_reports', '1');
EXEC sqlt$a.set_sess_param('sql_monitoring', 'N');
EXEC sqlt$a.set_sess_param('sql_tuning_advisor', 'N');
EXEC sqlt$a.set_sess_param('sql_tuning_set', 'N');
EXEC sqlt$a.set_sess_param('sqldx_reports_format', 'NONE');
EXEC sqlt$a.set_sess_param('test_case_builder', 'N');
```

This table includes all the tool configuration parameters and their descriptions.

Parameter	Description
addm_reports	Maximum number of ADDM reports to generate. Default value is 6. Can be as high as 9999. Default value is 6.
ash_reports	Maximum number of ASH reports to generate. Default value is 6. Can be as high as 9999.
ash_reports_source	Generate ASH reports from memory (MEM) and/or from active workload repository (AWR). The default is BOTH.
automatic_workload_repository	Access to the Automatic Workload Repository (AWR) requires a license for the Oracle Diagnostic Pack. If you don't have it you can set this parameter to N.
awr_reports	Maximum number of AWR reports to generate. Default is 31.
bde_chk_cbo	On EBS applications SQLT automatically executes bde_chk_cbo.sql from Note:174605.1.

(continued)

Parameter	Description
c_ash_hist_days	Days of ASH history to be collected. If set to 0 no ASH history is collected. If set to a value larger than actual stored days, then SQLT collects the whole history. A value of 7 means collect the past 7 days of ASH history. Default is 31 days.
c_awr_hist_days	Days of AWR history to be collected. If set to 0 no AWR history is collected. If set to a value larger than actual stored days, then SQLT collects the whole history. A value of 7 means collect the past 7 days of AWR history.
c_cbo_stats_vers_days	Days of CBO statistics versions to be collected. If set to 0 no statistics versions are collected. If set to a value larger than actual stored days, then SQLT collects the whole history. A value of 7 means collect the past 7 days of CBO statistics versions for the schema objects related to given SQL. It includes tables, indexes, partitions, columns, and histograms.
c_dba_hist_parameter	Collects relevant entries out of DBA_HIST_PARAMETER. If automatic_ workload_repository and c_dba_hist_parameter are both set to Y then SQLT collects relevant rows out of view DBA_HIST_PARAMETER.
c_gran_cols	Collection Granularity for Columns. Default value of "SUBPARTITION" allows SQLT to collect into its repository CBO statistics for columns at all levels: table, partitions, and subpartitions. All related to the one SQL being analyzed.
c_gran_hgrm	Collection Granularity for Histograms. Default value of "SUBPARTITION" allows SQLT to collect into its repository CBO statistics for histograms at all levels: table, partitions, and subpartitions. All related to the one SQL being analyzed.
c_gran_segm	Collection Granularity for Segments (Tables and Indexes). Default value of "SUBPARTITION" allows SQLT to collect into its repository CBO statistics for tables, indexes, partitions, and subpartitions. All related to the one SQL being analyzed.
c_inmemory	Collects information about In-Memory Option. Default value is N.
c_sessstat_xtract	Collects GV$SESSTAT information during XTRACT execution looking for other sessions running the same SQL ID.
colgroup_seed_secs	Controls if SQLT will enable DBMS_STATS.SEED_COL_USAGE for the specified number of seconds during 10053 trace capture, requires param event_10053_level enabled. Default is null.
collect_exadata_stats	Collects Exadata-Specific performance statistics on XECUTE method. Default is null.
collect_perf_stats	Collects performance statistics on XECUTE method.
connect_identifier	Optional Connect Identifier (as per Oracle Net). This is used during export of SQLT repository. Include "@" symbol, that is, @PROD. You can also set this parameter to NULL.(You have to use this if you are SQL locally on a machine and connecting to a remote machine).
count_star_threshold	Limits the number or rows to count while doing a SELECT COUNT(*) in set of tables accessed by SQLs passed. If you want to disable this functionality set this parameter to 0.

(continued)

Parameter	Description
custom_sql_profile	Controls if a script with a Custom SQL Profile is generated with every execution of SQLT main methods.
distributed_queries	SQLT can use DB links referenced by the SQL being analyzed. It connects to those remote systems to get 10053 and 10046 traces for the SQL being distributed.
domain_index_metadata	This parameter controls if domain index metadata is included in main report and metadata script. If you get an ORA-07445, and the alert. log shows the error is caused by CTXSYS.CTX_REPORT.CREATE_ INDEX_SCRIPT, then you want to set this parameter to N.
event_10046_level	SQLT XECUTE turns event 10046 level 12 on by default. You can set a different level or turn this event 10046 off using this parameter. It only affects the execution of the script passed to SQLT XECUTE. Level 0 means no trace, level 1 is standard SQL Trace, level 4 includes bind variable values, level 8 includes waits, and level 12 includes both binds and waits.
event_10053_level	SQLT XECUTE, XTRACT, and XPLAIN turn event 10053 level 1 on by default. You can turn this event 10053 off using this parameter. It only affects the SQL passed to SQLT. Level 0 means no trace, level 1 traces the CBO.
event_10507_level	SQLT XECUTE uses this event on 11g to trace Cardinality Feedback CFB. You can turn this event 10507 off using this parameter. It only affects the SQL passed to SQLT. Level 0 means no trace; for meaning of other levels see MOS Doc ID 740052.1.
event_others	This parameter controls the use of events 10241, 10032, 10033, 10104, 10730, 46049, but only if 10046 is turned on (any level but 0). It only affects the execution of the script passed to SQLT XECUTE.
export_dict_stats	SQLT export dictionary stats into the repository. Default is N.
export_repository	Methods XTRACT, XECUTE, and XPLAIN automatically perform an export of corresponding entries in the SQLT repository. This parameter controls this automatic repository export.
export_utility	SQLT repository can be exported automatically using one of two available utilities: traditional export "exp" or data pump "expdp." With this parameter you can specify which of the two should be used by SQLT.
generate_10053_xtract	Generation of 10053 using DBMS_SQLDIAG.DUMP_TRACE on XTRACT can be eliminated as a workaround to a disconnect ORA-07445 on SYS.DBMS_SQLTUNE_INTERNAL. SQLT detects an ORA-07445 and disables the call to DBMS_SQLDIAG.DUMP_TRACE (and SYS.DBMS_SQLTUNE_INTERNAL) in next execution. If this parameter has a value of E or N, then you may have a low-impact bug in your system.
healthcheck_blevel	Compute index/partition/subpartition by level and check if they change more than 10 percent from one statistics gathering to the next.
healthcheck_endpoints	Compute histogram endpoints count and check if they change more than 10 percent from one statistics gathering to the next.

(continued)

Parameter	Description
healthcheck_ndv	Review if number of distinct values for columns changes more than 10 percent from one statistics gathering to the next.
healthcheck_num_rows	Review table/partition/subpartition number of rows and check if they change more than 10 percent from one statistics gathering to the next.
keep_trace_10046_open	If you need to trace an execution of SQLT XECUTE, XTRACT, or XPLAIN, this parameter allows you to keep trace 10046 active even after a custom SCRIPT completes. It is used by XECUTE, XTRACT, and XPLAIN. When set to its default value of N, event 10046 is turned off right after the execution of the custom SCRIPT or when 10053 is turned off.
keyword_font_color	Sets font color for following keywords in SQL text: SELECT, INSERT, UPDATE, DELETE, MERGE, FROM, WHERE. Default is crimson.
mask_for_values	Endpoint values for table columns are part of the CBO statistics. They include column low/high values as well as histograms. If for privacy reasons these endpoints must be removed from SQLT reports, you can set this parameter to SECURE or COMPLETE. SECURE displays only the year for dates, and one character for strings and numbers. COMPLETE blocks completely the display of endpoints, and it also disables the automatic export of the SQLT repository. The default is CLEAR, which shows the values of endpoints. If considering changing to a non-default value, bear in mind that selectivity and cardinality verification requires some knowledge of the values of these column endpoints. Be also aware that 10053 traces also contain some low/high values that are not affected by this parameter.
perfhub_reports	Maximum number of PerfHub reports to generate. Default is 1.
plan_stats	Execution plans from GV$SQL_PLAN may contain statistics for the last execution of a cursor and for all executions of it (if parameter statistics_level was set to ALL when the cursor was hard-parsed). This parameter controls the display of the statistics of both (last execution as well as all executions).
predicates_in_plan	Predicates in plan can be eliminated as a workaround to bug 6356566. SQLT detects an ORA-07445 and disables predicates in next execution. If this parameter has a value of E or N, then you may have bug 6356566 in your system. You may want to apply a fix for bug 6356566, then reset this parameter to its default value.
r_gran_cols	Report Granularity for Columns. Default value of "PARTITION" reports table partition columns. All related to the one SQL being analyzed.
r_gran_hgrm	Report Granularity for Table Histograms. Default value of "PARTITION" reports table and partition histograms. All related to the one SQL being analyzed.
r_gran_segm	Report Granularity for Segments (Tables and Indexes). Default value of "PARTITION" reports tables, indexes, and partitions. All related to the one SQL being analyzed.
r_gran_vers	Report CBO Statistics Version Granularity for Tables. Default value of "COLUMN" reports statistics versions for segments and their columns. All related to the one SQL being analyzed.

(continued)

Parameter	Description
r_rows_table_l	Restricts number of elements for large HTML tables or lists.
r_rows_table_m	Restricts number of elements for medium HTML tables or lists.
r_rows_table_s	Restricts number of elements for small HTML tables or lists.
r_rows_table_xs	Restricts number of elements for extra-small HTML tables or lists.
refresh_directories	Controls if SQLT and TRCA directories for UDUMP/BDUMP should be reviewed and refreshed every time SQLT is executed.
search_sql_by_sqltext	XPLAIN method uses the SQL text to search in memory and AWR for known executions of SQL being analyzed. If prior executions of this SQL text are found, corresponding plans are extracted and reported.
skip_metadata_for_object	This case-sensitive parameter allows you to specify an object name to be skipped from metadata extraction. It is used in cases where DBMS_METADATA errors with ORA-7445. You can specify a full or a partial object name to be skipped (examples: "CUSTOMERS" or "CUSTOMER%" or "CUST%" or "%"). To find the object name where metadata errored out you can use: SELECT * FROM sqlt$_log WHERE statement_id = 99999 ORDER BY line_id; You have to replace 99999 with the correct statement_id. To actually fix an error behind ORA-7445, you can use alert.log and the trace referenced by it.
sql_monitor_reports	Maximum number of SQL Monitor Active reports to generate. Default is 12.
sql_monitoring	Be aware that using SQL Monitoring (V$SQL_MONITOR and V$SQL_PLAN_MONITOR) requires a license for the Oracle Tuning Pack. If you don't have it you can set this parameter to N.
sql_tuning_advisor	Be aware that using SQL Tuning Advisor (STA) DBMS_SQLTUNE requires a license for the Oracle Tuning Pack. If you don't have it you can set this parameter to N.
sql_tuning_set	Generates an SQL Tuning Set for each plan when using XTRACT.
sqldx_reports_format	SQL dynamix eXtract (SQLDX) report format. Default is BOTH.
sqlt_max_file_size_mb	Maximum size of individual SQLT files in megabytes.
sta_time_limit_secs	STA time limit in seconds. See sql_tuning_advisor. Be aware that using SQL Tuning Advisor (STA) DBMS_SQLTUNE requires a license for the Oracle Tuning Pack. The default is 1800.
tcb_export_data	Value for parameter exportData on API DBMS_SQLDIAG.EXPORT_SQL_TESTCASE. If value TRUE is passed then TCB creates the Test Case with application data (of the objects referenced in the SQL should be exported). Default is FALSE.
tcb_export_pkg_body	Value for parameter exportPkgbody on API DBMS_SQLDIAG.export_SQL_TESTCASE. If value TRUE is passed then TCB creates the Test Case with package bodies (of the packages referenced in the SQL area exported). Default is FALSE.

(continued)

Parameter	Description
tcb_sampling_percent	Value of the parameter samplingPercent on API DBMS_SQLDIAG. EXPORT_SQL_TESTCASE. The value is used to determine the percentage of application data TCB creates the Test Case with (of the objects referenced in the SQL should be exported). Default is 100.
tcb_time_limit_secs	TCB (test case builder) time limit in seconds. See test_case_builder.
test_case_builder	11g offers the capability to build a test case for a SQL. TCB is implemented using the API DBMS_SQLDIAG.EXPORT_SQL_TESTCASE. SQLT invokes this API whenever possible. When TCB is invoked by SQLT, the parameter exportData gets passed a value of FALSE, thus no application data is exported into the test case created by TCB.
trace_analyzer	SQLT XECUTE invokes Trace Analyzer - TRCA (Note:224270.1). TRCA analyzes the 10046_10053 trace created by SQLT. It also splits the trace into two stand-alone files: 10046 and 10053.
trace_directory_path	This case-sensitive parameter allows you to specify the directory path for trace files, other than the one specified by initialization parameter user_dump_dest. You can specify any valid directory path and SQLT will use this as a source to TKPROF commands executed automatically within SQLT. For example: /u01/app/oracle/diag/rdbms/v1123/v1123/trace/ Default is null.
upload_trace_size_mb	SQLT uploads to its repository traces generated by events 10046 and 10053. This parameter controls the maximum amount of megabytes to upload per trace.
validate_user	Validates that user of main methods has been granted the SQLT_USER_ROLE or DBA roles; or that user is SQLTXPLAIN or SYS.
xecute_script_output	SQLT XECUTE generates a spool file with the output of the SQL being analyzed (passed within input script). This file can be kept in the local directory, or included in the zip file, or simply removed.
xpand_sql	SQLT will expand the views SQL text. Default is Y.

Index

■ T, U, V

Get the eBook for only $5!

Why limit yourself?

With most of our titles available in both PDF and ePUB format, you can access your content wherever and however you wish—on your PC, phone, tablet, or reader.

Since you've purchased this print book, we are happy to offer you the eBook for just $5.

To learn more, go to http://www.apress.com/companion or contact support@apress.com.

Apress®

All Apress eBooks are subject to copyright. All rights are reserved by the Publisher, whether the whole or part of the material is concerned, specifically the rights of translation, reprinting, reuse of illustrations, recitation, broadcasting, reproduction on microfilms or in any other physical way, and transmission or information storage and retrieval, electronic adaptation, computer software, or by similar or dissimilar methodology now known or hereafter developed. Exempted from this legal reservation are brief excerpts in connection with reviews or scholarly analysis or material supplied specifically for the purpose of being entered and executed on a computer system, for exclusive use by the purchaser of the work. Duplication of this publication or parts thereof is permitted only under the provisions of the Copyright Law of the Publisher's location, in its current version, and permission for use must always be obtained from Springer. Permissions for use may be obtained through RightsLink at the Copyright Clearance Center. Violations are liable to prosecution under the respective Copyright Law.

 **⟨IOUG⟩** independent oracle users group *For the Complete Technology & Database Professional*

IOUG represents the **voice of Oracle technology and database professionals** - empowering you to be **more productive in your business** and career by **delivering education,** sharing **best practices** and providing technology direction and **networking opportunities.**

Context, Not Just Content

IOUG is dedicated to helping our members become an #IOUGenius by staying on the cutting-edge of Oracle technologies and industry issues through practical content, user-focused education, and invaluable networking and leadership opportunities:

- *SELECT Journal* is our quarterly publication that provides in-depth, peer-reviewed articles on industry news and best practices in Oracle technology

- Our #IOUGenius blog highlights a featured weekly topic and provides content driven by Oracle professionals and the IOUG community

- Special Interest Groups provide you the chance to collaborate with peers on the specific issues that matter to you and even take on leadership roles outside of your organization

- COLLABORATE is our once-a-year opportunity to connect with the members of not one, but three, Oracle users groups (IOUG, OAUG and Quest) as well as with the top names and faces in the Oracle community.

Who we are...

... **more than 20,000** database professionals, developers, application and infrastructure architects, business intelligence specialists and IT managers

... **a community of users** that share experiences and knowledge on issues and technologies that matter to you and your organization

Interested? Join IOUG's community of Oracle technology and database professionals at www.ioug.org/Join.

Independent Oracle Users Group | phone: (312) 245-1579 | email: membership@ioug.org
330 N. Wabash Ave., Suite 2000, Chicago, IL 60611

Printed in the United States
By Bookmasters